Moodle 4 Administration

An administrator's guide to configuring, securing, customizing, and extending Moodle

Alex Büchner

BIRMINGHAM—MUMBAI

Moodle 4 Administration

Group Product Manager: Pavan Ramchandani
Publishing Product Manager: Bhavya Rao
Senior Editor: Aamir Ahmed
Senior Content Development Editor: Rakhi Patel
Technical Editor: Saurabh Kadave
Copy Editor: Safis Editing
Project Coordinator: Manthan Patel
Proofreader: Safis Editing
Indexer: Hemangini Bari
Production Designer: Prashant Ghare
Marketing Coordinators: Anamika Singh and Marylou De Mello

First Edition: September 2008
Second Edition: October 2011
Third Edition: February 2016
Fourth Edition: October 2022

Production reference: 1211022

Published by Packt Publishing Ltd.
Livery Place
35 Livery Street
Birmingham
B3 2PB, UK.

ISBN 978-1-80181-672-4
www.packt.com

To Ursel. R.I.P.

–Alex Büchner

Contributors

About the author

Alex Büchner is the co-founder of the Premium Moodle and Platinum Totara partner Synergy Learning. He has implemented Moodle-based projects in the corporate, public, and third sectors for over two decades. He has been configuring learning management systems of all shapes and sizes since their advent in the educational landscape.

Alex holds a Ph.D. in computer science and an M.Sc in software engineering. He has authored over 50 international publications, including six books, and is a frequent speaker on Moodle, Moodle Workplace, and open source technologies. He can be contacted at openumlaut.com.

I want to thank my family for their support and patience while I have been occupying the kitchen table writing this book.

About the reviewers

E. Adolfo Suarez is an educator with a strong background in computer science, having over 20 years of experience in the field. He holds a B.Ed., specializing in mathematics, and for many years, he alternated between teaching math and computer science.

Adolfo holds a virtual teacher specialization from UC Irvine Extension, obtained through the Coursera MOOC project. He is passionate about online learning and has over 10 years of experience as a Moodle administrator, dealing with student information systems, exams remote proctoring, e-books, plagiarism detection tools, and more.

Adolfo has been blessed with four grandchildren, and his best times are spent playing with them.

Dr. Laurie E. Korte is an e-learning professional you can count on, with expertise in motivational instructional design, user experience, and accessibility. The organizations she works with are able to focus on learning program objectives and not worry about the complex demands of site growth and engaging design. Laurie's education and experience extend beyond her Ph.D. in educational technology. She has presented at many local, national, and international conferences, and she has authored books on collaborative and creative thinking skill development, Moodle, and open source. Dr. Korte is also an elected Moodle Users Association Committee Member.

Sarah Ashley, as a solution architect with Moodle US, uses her 15 years of experience in Moodle, instructional design, and instructional technology to provide learning design consultation, crafting creative solutions for new and existing implementation projects, as well as offering technical and functional support for Moodle and Moodle Workplace. She has presented at mini-Moots, iMoots, and many in-person and online Moodle Moots, sharing creative uses of database activity reports and other configurable reports for learning analytics and producing innovative workflows. Sarah has an M.Ed in instructional technology and an M.Sc. and a B.Sc. in computer science. She loves to sing, play drums and piano, and solve all kinds of puzzles – jigsaws, logic, word, Rubik's cubes, and more!

Big thanks to my husband, Rev. Samuel Kofi Ashley, and son, Sammy, for your support during the review of this book. Thank you to my sister, Dr. Jeanette Paintsil, and brother, Abdel-Azim Brown, for your endless encouragement throughout my life's journeys. Thanks to my parents, Mr. and Mrs. Brown, in Ghana, for making sure I got a quality education. Thanks, Dr. Martin Dougiamas, for creating Moodle, giving me the daily opportunity to empower others with education.

Table of Contents

3

Exploring Courses, Users, and Roles   53

4

Managing Courses and Enrolments   67

5

Managing Users, Cohorts, and Authentication   117

6

Managing Permissions, Roles, and Capabilities   171

7

Enhancing Moodle's Look and Feel   203

8

Understanding Moodle Plugins 251

9

Configuring Educational Features 273

10

Configuring Technical Features   319

11

Enabling Mobile Learning   353

12

Gaining Insights through Moodle Reporting and Analytics   377

15

16

Appendix

Preface

Since its launch in 2002, Moodle has become the benchmark that every learning management system is measured against. It has won a wide range of international accolades and established itself as an ecosystem for educational tools and services.

There are two versions of Moodle: **Moodle LMS** and **Moodle Workplace**.

Moodle LMS is the original version of Moodle, targeted at educational institutions such as schools, colleges, universities, and training providers. Moodle Workplace is designed for corporate and organizational training, resulting in a powerful and flexible platform for workplace learning.

While this book covers the administration of Moodle LMS, it can also be used with Moodle Workplace, since the latter is an extension of the former. References to Moodle Workplace and samples will be provided throughout.

A fun way to demonstrate the various Moodle subjects is in the form of a tube/subway/metro/underground map, where any icon(ic) stations represent Moodle Workplace-only features (you can download higher-quality versions in multiple languages and up-to-date features from www.openumlaut.com):

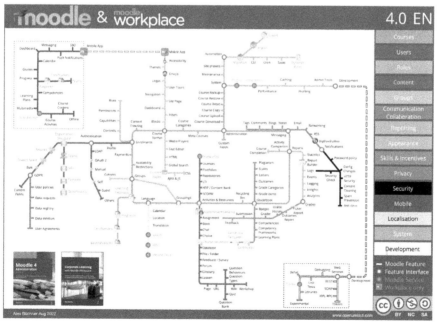

Figure P.1 – Moodle and Moodle Workplace map

Moodle 4 Administration is a complete, practical guide to administering Moodle sites. It covers setting up Moodle, configuration, day-to-day administrative tasks, and advanced options to customize and extend Moodle.

The author, who has been at the cutting edge of Moodle since its advent, has adopted a problem-solution approach to bring the content in line with your day-to-day operations. The practical examples will help you set up Moodle for large organizations and small entities alike.

This is a one-stop reference for tasks you will encounter when administering a Moodle site of any shape or size. It not only covers core Moodle functionality but also some third-party tools and add-ons that will increase your flexibility and efficiency even further when dealing with administrative duties.

The fourth edition of this title has been written from scratch to align with Moodle's latest version. It has been further augmented with over 120 diagrams, checklists, and workflows. I hope you find its content useful when administering your Moodle system. Happy Moodling!

Who is this book for

This book is written for technicians and systems administrators as well as academic staff – that is, basically anyone who has to administer a Moodle system. Whether you are dealing with a small-scale local Moodle system or a large-scale multi-site **Learning Management System** (**LMS**), this book will assist you with any administrative tasks.

Some basic Moodle knowledge would be helpful but is not essential.

LMS job functions

A Moodle administrator is an LMS administrator who manages a Moodle system. A quick search through recruitment agencies specializing in the educational sector reveals a growing number of dedicated job titles closely related to LMS administration. A few examples are as follows:

- LMS administrator (or VLE administrator or MLE administrator)
- LMS support officer
- LMS architect
- LMS engineer
- LMS coordinator

The list does not include functions that regularly act in an administrative capacity, such as IT support. It also does not include roles in the pedagogical field that often take on the work of an LMS administrator, such as learning technologists or e-learning coordinators.

An LMS administrator usually works closely with the staff responsible for IT systems, databases, and networks. It has been proven beneficial to have some basic skills in these areas. Additionally, links with other departments are more likely in larger organizations where content management systems, student information management systems, and other related infrastructure are present.

Given this growing number of LMS administration-related roles, let's look at some key obligations of the job functions and what skills are essential and desirable.

Obligations and skill sets of an LMS administrator

The responsibilities of an LMS administrator differ from organization to organization. However, some obligations are common across installations and setups:

- User management (learners, teachers, and others)
- Course management (prospectus mapping)
- Module management (functionality provided to users)
- Look and feel of the LMS (often carried out by a web designer)
- Year-end maintenance (if applicable)
- Beginning-of-year setup (if applicable)
- Support teaching staff and learners

In addition to these generic LMS-specific features, you must ensure that your system is secure, stable, and performs well. Backups have to be in place, monitoring has to be set up, usage reports have to be produced, and regular system maintenance has to be carried out.

If you host your own system, you will be responsible for all of the listed tasks and many more. If your LMS is hosted in a managed environment, the hosting provider will carry out some tasks closer to the system level, so it is essential that they have a good understanding of Moodle. Either way, you will be the first person to be contacted by staff and learners if anything goes wrong, if they require new functionality, or if some administrative task has to be carried out.

With great power comes great responsibility!

What this book covers

The book is organized in five parts, as shown in the following diagram:

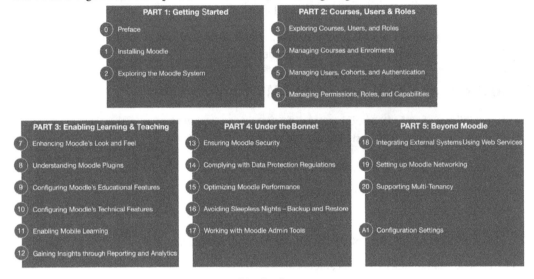

Figure P.2 – Book structure

Part 1: Getting Started

These two initial chapters will get you off the ground. You will learn different techniques on how to install Moodle and how to keep it up to date. You will further familiarize yourself with the Moodle system and its user interface. This part comprises the following chapters.

Chapter 1, *Installing Moodle*, tells you about the most suitable Moodle setup for your organization, including software and hardware requirements. You will learn how to install Moodle in a LAMP environment before Moodle update options are covered in detail. Throughout the chapter, you will learn how to perform the described operations using the Moodle **Command-Line Interface (CLI)**, Git, and the third-party Moodle Shell (Moosh).

Chapter 2, *Exploring the Moodle System*, covers the building blocks of the learning platform. First, we present the Moodle architecture – that is, the main Moodle components – and where its data and code are stored. You will then acquire the skills to find your way around Moodle via its intuitive user and administration interface and where to find help if required. Finally, you will learn how Moodle's file management works and how to configure the recycle bin.

Part 2: Courses, Users, and Roles

Courses, users, and roles form the backbone of Moodle. You will learn how to manage courses and categories and different options to enrol users in courses. We will then deal with the management of users and cohorts and how to set up different authentication methods. Finally, you will learn how to manage permissions by applying roles and capabilities in different contexts. This part comprises the following chapters.

Chapter 3, Exploring Courses, Users, and Roles, gives you an overview of Moodle courses, users, and roles. It covers the basics of the key concepts and demonstrates how the three core elements are inherently intertwined.

Chapter 4, Managing Courses and Enrolments, shows you how to set up new courses (manually and in bulk) and organize them in categories. You will learn how to add custom course fields and deal with course requests. The remainder of the chapter deals with an array of enrolment options, covering Moodle's internal enrolment (manual, self, and guest), cohort enrolment and synchronization, and database-driven enrolments – for instance, via LDAP, meta courses, and payment-driven enrolments.

Chapter 5, Managing Users, Cohorts, and Authentication, explains how to manage users on your system. We first cover what user profiles look like and how they can be extended before presenting (manual and bulk) standard user actions. We then explain how to add users to Moodle manually – that is, one by one and via batch upload – before dealing with cohorts. Then, we will learn about a plethora of authentication mechanisms that Moodle equips us with. Finally, we will discuss the best practices of user-naming schemes.

Chapter 6, Managing Permissions, Roles, and Capabilities, guides you through permission management. This applies roles and capabilities to users in different contexts. We will cover the assignment of roles, modification of existing roles, and the creation of new roles before we deal with any administrative role- and context-related settings, including context freezing.

Part 3: Enabling Learning and Teaching

This part is about how you, as an administrator, ensure the best possible environment for your learners and teachers. You will learn different enhancement options for Moodle's look and feel and how to manage Moodle plugins, covering educational and technical features. This part comprises the following chapters.

Chapter 7, Enhancing Moodle's Look and Feel, tells you how to adapt your Moodle system to align with your organization's corporate branding. We will cover the customization of the appearance of your system, where you will learn how to change the layout of key pages before we deal with different login workflows and how to adjust the header. We will further deal with some appearance tools that impact the look and feel throughout the site: the block drawer, the Atto HTML editor, video and audio, and finally, user tours. We will briefly cover theme customization before you learn how to support users with accessibility requirements.

Chapter 8, Understanding Moodle Plugins, explains in detail what plugins are and how to extend your Moodle system via third-party add-ons. We will cover how to manage Moodle plugins, which includes their installation, configuration, and removal. Finally, you will be able to distinguish between good add-ons and not-so-good add-ons before we cover some popular extensions.

Chapter 9, Configuring Educational Features, deals with the educational configuration of your Moodle system. Pedagogical topics that are covered are collaboration tools (blogs, comments, and tags), content creation features (the content bank and H5P, LTI platforms and tools, filters, plagiarism prevention, and licenses), grades and assessments, and the management of skills and incentives (competencies, learning plans, badges, and certificates).

Chapter 10, Configuring Technical Features, deals with the technical configuration of your Moodle system. Technical subjects that are dealt with include synchronous and asynchronous communication (chats and BigBlueButton, messages, notifications, and RSS feeds), localization (languages, calendars, and time zones), repositories, and portfolios.

Chapter 11, Enabling Mobile Learning, teaches you how to prepare, configure, and customize the Moodle app. We will cover the different subscriptions Moodle offers, including the branded mobile app, before dealing with the preparatory steps you must take before your learners can use the app. The app configuration covers mobile features, notifications, the app policy, and the app's look and feel.

Chapter 12, Gaining Insights through Reporting and Analytics, equips you with the tools required to interpret and analyze the vast amount of usage data that Moodle collects. We will first focus on Moodle's custom report builder, covering data sources, report building, report audiences, and schedules. After a detailed overview of the underlying Moodle logging framework with its components, events, and log stores, you will then learn how to interact with Moodle logs. Finally, we will deal with two more reporting techniques that use logs as their basis: Moodle statistics and Moodle analytics.

Part 4: Under the Bonnet

This part covers all topics that are mostly invisible to learners and teachers but are critical to guarantee the smooth operation of your Moodle system. You will learn how to ensure security, comply with data protection regulations, optimize Moodle's performance, implement a solid backup and restore strategy, and work with helpful admin tools. This part comprises the following chapters.

Chapter 13, Ensuring Moodle Security, focuses on ensuring that the data in your Moodle system is protected from any misuse. You will learn about security notifications, user security, content security, and system security.

Chapter 14, Complying with Data Protection Regulations, deals with data privacy and the protection of personal data. You will learn about Moodle's implementation of the General Data Protection Regulation, covering designating a privacy officer, managing policies, configuring the data registry, and handling subject access requests.

Chapter 15, Optimizing Moodle Performance, ensures your Moodle system runs to its full potential. We will cover configuring, monitoring, and fine-tuning your learning management system for maximum speed. You will learn how to optimize Moodle feature performance and discuss the trade-off between improved speed and potentially reduced functionality. We will then cover the powerful **Moodle Universal Cache** (**MUC**), including cache types, stores, and definitions. Finally, you will learn how to configure various system-related performance settings, namely session handling, cron management, scheduled tasks, global search, and system paths.

Chapter 16, Avoiding Sleepless Nights – Moodle Backup and Restore, focuses on ensuring that your data would not be lost in the event of a disaster. We will cover course backups, site backups, system backups, and restoring data from the taken data archives. You will learn about two procedures that use backup and restore facilities: planning year-end procedures and implementing course templates.

Chapter 17, Working with Moodle Admin Tools, covers Moodle tools that assist you with specific administrative tasks. These include site admin presets, database tools, as well as CLI scripts. We will also look at some add-ons, especially the powerful Moodle Shell, Moosh.

Part 5 – Beyond Moodle

No Moodle is an island. While many Moodle systems are operated in isolation, there are scenarios where your LMS must cooperate with external entities, whether exchanging data with other systems via web services, connecting disparate Moodle instances, or supporting multiple tenants. This part deals with setting up such topologies and comprises the following chapters.

Chapter 18, Integrating External Systems Using Web Services, looks at ways to integrate Moodle with other systems via web services. We will provide information about the basic concepts of Moodle web services before you learn how to set up external systems and users controlling Moodle.

Chapter 19, Setting Up Moodle Networking, tells you how to connect disparate Moodle systems in a peer-to-peer setup or via a Moodle hub. You will further learn how to enable MoodleNet, a platform to find, share and curate open educational resources.

Chapter 20, Supporting Multi-Tenancy, discusses different approaches and models to design and implement a multi-tenancy in Moodle. We distinguish between different multi-tenancy setups: multi-tenancy by categories, multi-tenancy by isolated systems, and multi-tenancy in Moodle Workplace.

Appendix, Configuration Settings, provides you with a list of parameters that can be modified in Moodle's configuration file and the impact each of these values will have. The areas covered are administration settings and system settings.

To get the most out of this book

For Moodle, you must have the following components up and running on your server (at the time of writing for version 4.0):

- **Database**: MySQL (version 5.7 or later utilizing the ACID-compliant InnoDB storage engine), PostgreSQL 10+, MariaDB 10.2.29+, Aurora MySQL (on Amazon Web Services), Microsoft SQL Server 2017+, and Oracle 11.2+.

- **Web server**: Apache is the preferred web server option, but Moodle works well with any other web server that supports PHP, such as Microsoft IIS.

- **PHP** 7.3.0 is the minimum PHP version to run Moodle 4; PHP 7.4.0 is the minimum version from Moodle 4.1 onwards. PHP 8 is also supported.

- **PHP extensions**: Moodle makes use of a number of PHP extensions, most of which are compiled in PHP by default: `curl`, `ctype`, `dom`, `fileinfo`, `gd`, `hash`, `iconv`, `intl`, `json`, `mbstring`, `openssl`, `pcre`, `simplexml`, `spl`, `xml`, `xmlreader`, `zip`, and `zlib`.

Depending on your specific setup, additional software might be required.

If you don't have access to the preceding components, ensure that you have full administrator access to a Moodle system. You won't be able to carry out any system-level operations but will be able to administer Moodle via its web interface fully.

Download the color images

We also provide a PDF file that has color images of the screenshots and diagrams used in this book. You can download it here: `https://packt.link/PnRUP`

Conventions used

There are a number of text conventions used throughout this book.

`Code in text`: Indicates code words in text, database table names, folder names, filenames, file extensions, pathnames, dummy URLs, user input, and Twitter handles. Here is an example: "To prevent `dataroot` from being accessible, move the directory outside the web directory and modify `config.php` accordingly by changing the `$CFG->dataroot` entry."

A block of code is set as follows:

```
/* Change toolbar background color to orange */
.toolbar-background
{
   background: orange;
}
```

Bold: Indicates a new term, an important word, or words you see on screen. For example, words in menus or dialog boxes appear in the text like this. An example is "Go to **General | Advanced features** and tick the **Enable web services for mobile devices** option."

> **Tips or Important Notes**
> Appear like this.

Get in touch

Feedback from our readers is always welcome.

General feedback: If you have questions about any aspect of this book, email us at customercare@ packtpub.com and mention the book title in the subject of your message.

Errata: Although we have taken every care to ensure the accuracy of our content, mistakes do happen. If you have found a mistake in this book, we would be grateful if you would report this to us. Please visit www.packtpub.com/support/errata and fill in the form.

Piracy: If you come across any illegal copies of our works in any form on the internet, we would be grateful if you would provide us with the location address or website name. Please contact us at copyright@packt.com with a link to the material.

If you are interested in becoming an author: If there is a topic that you have expertise in and you are interested in either writing or contributing to a book, please visit authors.packtpub.com.

Share Your Thoughts

Once you've read *Moodle 4 Administration*, we'd love to hear your thoughts! Scan the QR code below to go straight to the Amazon review page for this book and share your feedback.

https://packt.link/r/1801816727

Your review is important to us and the tech community and will help us make sure we're delivering excellent quality content.

Download a Free PDF copy of this book

Thanks for purchasing this book!

Do you like to read on the go but are unable to carry your print books everywhere? Is your eBook purchase not compatible with the device of your choice?

Don't worry, now with every Packt book you get a DRM-free PDF version of that book at no cost.

Read anywhere, any place, on any device. Search, copy, and paste code from your favorite technical books directly into your application.

The perks don't stop there, you can get exclusive access to discounts, newsletters, and great free content in your inbox daily

Follow these simple steps to get the benefits:

1. Scan the QR code or visit the link below

https://packt.link/free-ebook/9781801816724

2. Submit your proof of purchase
3. That's it! We'll send your free PDF and other benefits to your email directly

1

Installing Moodle

In this first chapter, we'll start by installing Moodle.

After providing an overview describing the most suitable setup, we will outline the necessary software and hardware requirements before covering the following installations:

- Installing Moodle in a LAMP environment
- Installing Moodle via the **command-line interface (CLI)**
- Upgrading Moodle manually and via the CLI and Git

We won't be covering the installation on operating systems other than Linux, but we will provide some pointers to resources for Windows and macOS.

Moodle can be scaled from a single instructor to an entire institution. We will only cover *basic* installations and present solutions to some common problems. We will also assume you are familiar with basic Linux system administration.

In this chapter, we will be covering the following topics:

- Preparing your Moodle installation
- Installation in a LAMP environment
- Installation via the command-line interface
- Updating Moodle

Preparing your Moodle installation

Before you start installing Moodle, you have to decide which setup is right for your organization. Once you have decided, there are several hardware and software prerequisites you have to fulfill before you can get started.

Choosing your best setup

There are many different environments in which you can set up Moodle. The three main criteria that will help you determine the correct setup are as follows:

- **Flexibility**: If you want to have complete control over your system, install plugins, be able to tweak system settings, and make frequent changes to the setup, you should host your own server. However, if your preferred choice is to only administer Moodle while somebody else is looking after the operating system, the web server, and backups, it is better to opt for a professionally-hosted setup, particularly the offerings provided by authorized Moodle Partners.

- **Scalability**: This is entirely driven by the number of active learners and educators logged in to Moodle simultaneously. Moodle on a small server will not be able to cope with hundreds of concurrently logged-in users. On the other hand, a load-balanced cluster would be overkill for a small institution with a few dozen learners. The following table provides some indicative setups for different types of educational organizations:

Max. number of concurrent users	Recommended setup
1 (to experiment locally)	Desktop, laptop, memory stick
100 (small school / company)	Shared server
250 (large school / company)	Dedicated server
500 (medium-to-large college)	Separate app and database servers
+500 (university/corporate)	Load-balanced cluster

Figure 1.1 – Moodle setups depending on user numbers

Please bear in mind that these are only indicative numbers that are not written in stone and also depend on the other factors mentioned here.

Each Moodle instance must be installed on a dedicated or shared server, either hosted in-house or externally. If you decide to go down the hosted route, avoiding a cheap hosting package is highly recommended as those systems are not optimized for Moodle usage; their one-size-fits-all approach will significantly impact the system's performance, especially with an increasing number of concurrent users.

Moodle HQ offers hosting on moodlecloud.com; however, these packages come with some limitations (the numbers depend on the chosen plan): user limits, storage limits, no way to install plugins or custom themes, and the inability to modify some hard-coded admin settings. If these restrictions are acceptable, hosting on moodlecloud.com might be suitable for your organization.

- **Cost**: Budgetary constraints will undoubtedly play an important role. Unless you already have the appropriate infrastructure in place, it will likely be more cost effective to host your Moodle system externally as it saves you from purchasing servers and renting a 24/7 data connection that caters to your users' needs. The licensing cost will be significantly higher if you use commercial operating systems, web servers, and database systems instead of an open source solution. Either way, Moodle is designed to support a wide range of possible infrastructures suitable to your organization's IT policy.

In addition to these three criteria, which influence the decision about the underlying infrastructure, other factors, such as **in-house expertise**, **compatibility with other systems**, **IT policies**, **personal preference**, and **existing resources**, will impact your decision.

We will be covering the most popular operating system for hosting Moodle – Linux. For other operating systems or setups, such as in virtualized environments or on multi-server clusters, please consult your local Moodle Partner (moodle.com/solutions/certified-service-providers). Some hosting companies offer quick one-click installations; while the resulting Moodle system is sufficient for experimental sites, it is certainly unsuitable for production environments.

Fulfilling Moodle prerequisites

Several hardware and software requirements must be satisfied before we can start installing Moodle.

Hardware requirements

These requirements apply if you host Moodle yourself or if it is hosted on an external server (shared, virtual, dedicated, or clustered). On cheaper hosting packages, the hardware configuration is often insufficient to run Moodle efficiently:

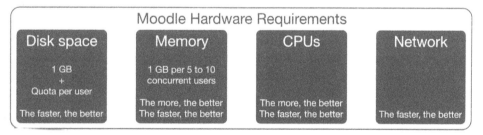

Figure 1.2 – Moodle hardware

Let's take a look at these requirements in more detail:

- **Disk space:** Moodle itself takes up approximately 1 GB of disk space. However, this only provides you with a naked system and does not consider the space you require for any learning resources. The faster the disks, the better. RAIDed disks are recommended but are not essential on smaller installations.

- **Memory**: A good rule of thumb is to have 1 GB of RAM for every 5 to 10 **concurrent** users. You have to double this calculation on Windows-based systems due to the higher overhead of the operating system. Of all the hardware components, RAM will impact Moodle's performance the most.

> **Important note**
> The more RAM, the better; the faster the RAM, the better.

- **CPUs**: Processor type and speed are essential too, but not as important as RAM. As always, the faster the CPU, the better, and the more cores a CPU has, the more powerful it will be.

- **Network**: While Moodle can run on a standalone machine, its full potential is in a networked environment. Fast network cards are essential, as is good upload and download speed if the LMS is accessed over the internet.

Now, let's look at the software requirements.

Software requirements

While it is recommended to have the latest version installed, for Moodle 4, you must have the following components up and running on your server (release-specific notes can be found at `moodledev. io/general/releases`):

- **Database**: Moodle officially supports the following database systems: MySQL (version 5.7 or later utilizing the ACID-compliant InnoDB storage engine), PostgreSQL 10+, MariaDB 10.2.29+, Aurora MySQL (on Amazon Web Services), Microsoft SQL Server 2017+, and Oracle 11.2+.

- **Web server**: Apache is the preferred web server option, but Moodle works well with any other web server that supports PHP, such as Microsoft IIS.

- **PHP**: PHP 7.3.0 is the minimum PHP version for running Moodle 4; PHP 7.4.0 is the minimum version from Moodle 4.1 onwards. PHP 8 is also supported. You might have to change some PHP settings in the `php.ini` or `.htaccess` file (for more details, see `docs.moodle. org/en/Installing_Moodle`).

- **PHP extensions**: Moodle **makes** use of several extensions, most of which are compiled into PHP by default. They are as follows:

  - **Compulsory extensions**: `curl`, `ctype`, `dom`, `fileinfo`, `gd`, `hash`, `iconv`, `intl`, `json`, `mbstring`, `openssl`, `pcre`, `simplexml`, `spl`, `xml`, `xmlreader`, `zip`, and `zlib`

  - **Recommended extensions**: `exif`, `soap`, `sodium`, `tokenizer`, and `xmlrpc`

  - **Conditional extensions**: `mysql`, `odbc`, and `pgsql` (depending on the database) and `ldap`, `ntlm`, and others (depending on the authentication mechanism used)

Depending on your specific setup, additional software might be required. It is assumed that the database, web server, PHP, and extensions have been installed correctly, as this is not an LMS administrator task. Once this is the case, we are ready to go.

> **Important note**
>
> To access Moodle, a modern web browser (the latest version of Firefox, Google Chrome, Edge, or Safari) is required.

Before we start the installation process, it is worth familiarizing yourself with Moodle's releases and versions.

Understanding Moodle versions

Moodle versions follow a strict calendar that is published and updated regularly on `moodledev.io/general/releases`. If a planned feature is not ready for the imminent release, it will be moved to the next version; that is, a release date will never be changed, but the time when features will be introduced might be.

The release frequency for **major versions** (4.0, 4.1, and so on) is twice a year (the second Monday of May and November).

Moodle releases **minor versions** (4.1.1, 4.1.2, and so on) on the second Monday of March, May, July, September, and November. The same applies to unscheduled releases in the case of a severe security issue or serious regression being fixed.

Moodle distinguishes between two types of releases:

- **Standard support release**: Bugs will be fixed for 12 months, and security issues will be provided for 18 months
- **Long-term support release**: Bugs will be fixed for 12 months, and security issues will be provided for 36 months

The simplified release calendar is shown in the following timeline; you can find a more detailed version at `moodledev.io/general/releases`:

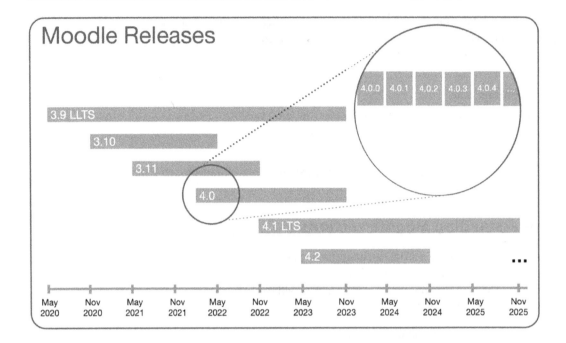

Figure 1.3 – Moodle releases

When Moodle 4.0 was released in April 2022, versions 3.9 to 3.11 were still supported. By the time Moodle 4.1 is released, only version 3.9 will be supported since its lifetime has been extended (hence the long-long-term support label) to give admins more time to upgrade to the version 4 branch.

If you wish to stay up-to-date with future releases, check Moodle's roadmap at `moodledev.io/general/community/roadmap`, where you will find the current plans for the future technical development of all Moodle's products and services.

OK, enough of version numbers and release dates. Let's learn how to install (the latest version of) Moodle.

Installation in a LAMP environment

Moodle is developed in Linux using Apache, MySQL, and PHP (known as the **LAMP stack**). If you have a choice, this is the preferred environment to use. There is an ongoing debate about whether PostgreSQL is the more suitable database option, but we will stick with MySQL/MariaDB as this is the system most administrators are familiar with. Also, some organizations are bound to Microsoft SQL or Oracle. If this is the case, please refer to the respective installation guide, as this is beyond the scope of this book.

The high-level installation process is shown in the following process diagram:

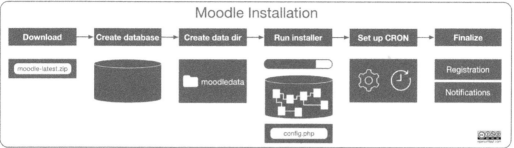

Figure 1.4 – Moodle installation process

We will go through each phase in the remaining subsections, covering each installation step in a Linux environment. The process is the same for other operating systems, which we won't cover; here are some pointers that should get you started:

- For Windows servers with a small number of users, the **XAMPP**-based Moodle distribution is suitable. XAMPP is a free Apache distribution that contains MySQL and PHP (as well as Perl) and exists for several operating systems. The Moodle distribution for Windows makes full use of XAMPP and is located at `download.moodle.org/windows`. The installation works on all the latest Windows PCs and server variants.

- For larger **Windows** installations, you have to install Moodle manually, which involves installing a database server (MS SQL or any other supported system), a web server (Microsoft IIS or Apache), and PHP separately. You can find details about this process at `docs.moodle.org/en/Windows_installation`.

- **MAMP** is a free distribution that contains Apache (and Nginx), MySQL, and PHP for macOS. Like its Windows counterpart, the Moodle distributions for macOS are only intended for local installations and not for production environments. Moodle4Mac is available as universal binaries via MAMP, located at `download.moodle.org/macosx`.

Now, let's go through the installation process, starting with downloading Moodle.

Downloading Moodle

Go to `download.moodle.org` and select the latest release:

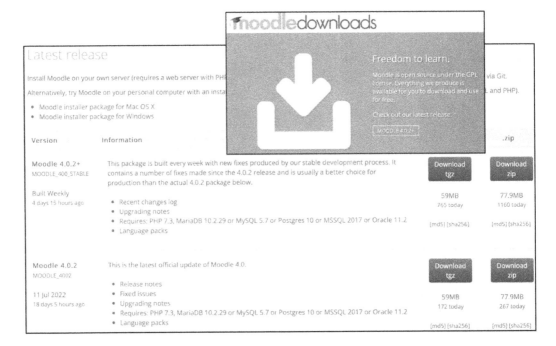

Figure 1.5 – Moodle downloads

A newer version is likely to be available by the time you read this. If you wish to go with the 4.0.x version this book has been written for, select **Other supported releases**; otherwise, feel free to go with the latest stable build; most content in this book will still be applicable.

There are five types of builds available on Moodle's download site:

- **Latest release**: There are two releases for the current version of Moodle: the latest stable build and the latest official release. The latest stable version is created weekly (every Wednesday) and is the best choice for a new server. The latest official release contains the stable build and new fixes, but the version will not have gone through the weekly code review and might contain unresolved issues.

- **Other supported releases**: The Moodle development team maintains older versions than the current ones, as outlined in the release schedule earlier.

- **Security-only-supported releases**: Critical fixes impacting security or data loss will be provided for one further release, but no other bug fixes will be back-ported. See the information on Moodle versions provided earlier.

- **Legacy releases**: For older versions, the last build is made available. However, these are not maintained any further.

- **Development releases**: Moodle also gives you the option to download beta releases of the software (if available) and the latest development release. These should only be downloaded for testing or development purposes, never in production environments!

Each version is made available in two compressed formats: TGZ (use the `tar` command to uncompress) and ZIP (use the `unzip` command to extract it). You can download them by clicking on the respective link or, if you have (secure) shell access, retrieving the file directly by using the `wget` command:

```
wget http://download.moodle.org/moodle/moodle-latest.zip
```

> **Important note**
> The location where you install Moodle is referred to as **dirroot**.

If you make use of **Moodle Shell** (**MOOSH**), which is described in more detail in *Chapter 17, Working with Moodle Admin Tools*, you can use the following command to download the latest stable branch of Moodle:

```
moosh download-moodle
```

Once you have moved the file to the location where you want to install it on your web server (`dirroot`), extract the file using the `unzip` command or `tar` if you downloaded the TGZ version:

```
unzip moodle-latest.zip
tar xvfz moodle-latest.tgz
```

If you place the entire folder in your web server documents directory, the site will be located at www. yourwebserver.com/moodle. To access your site from www.yourwebserver.com, copy the contents directly into the main web server's documents directory.

> **Important note**
> The URL via which Moodle is accessed is referred to as **wwwroot**.

Once the download step has been completed, you must create the database that Moodle uses to store its data.

Creating the Moodle database

Moodle requires a database where it can store its information. While sharing an existing database is possible, creating a separate database for Moodle is highly recommended. Adding a new database can either be done via a web interface, as provided for hosted servers, or via the command line.

Using a hosted server

Most hosting providers provide a dedicated web interface to carry out basic database operations. Alternatively, you can use **phpMyAdmin**, open source software that allows you to manage MySQL databases over the web. phpMyAdmin is part of most Linux distributions and many control panels, but it is often configured not to allow new databases to be created. If this is the case, you must create the database from the database manager in your control panel.

phpMyAdmin allows you to perform both steps – creating a database and adding a new user – in a single action, as shown in the following screenshot. We will create a user, `packt`, and also check the **Create database with same name and grant all privileges** option:

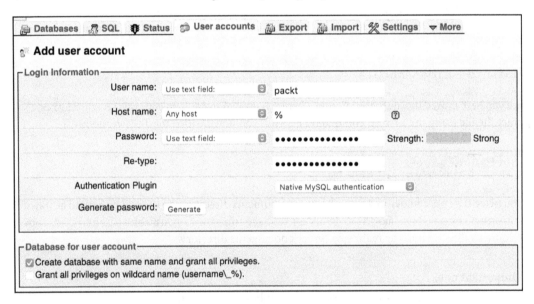

Figure 1.6 – Creating a Moodle database and user in phpMyAdmin

While you can use an existing database user account, creating a dedicated user for the Moodle database is good practice.

> **Important note**
> Do not use the MySQL root account for your Moodle database!

You don't need to create any tables; Moodle will populate the database during installation.

Creating the Moodle database via a web interface is simple, but most technical administrators prefer to work via the command line.

Using the command line

If you don't have access to a web interface to create MySQL databases and user accounts, or if you prefer to use a Linux shell, you can perform these steps via the command line:

1. Start the database command-line tool by entering `mysql -root -p` and enter the password at the prompt.

2. Create a database (called `packt`) by entering `CREATE DATABASE packt;` (all MySQL commands must be terminated with a semicolon).

3. Set the default character and collation order to UTF8 by entering `ALTER DATABASE packt DEFAULT CHARACTER SET utf8 COLLATE utf8_unicode_ ci;`.

4. Create a user and password (here, packt@localhost and password, respectively) and grant database access permissions by entering `GRANT SELECT, INSERT, UPDATE, DELETE, CREATE, CREATE TEMPORARY TABLES, DROP, INDEX, ALTER ON packt.* TO packt@localhost IDENTIFIED BY 'password';`.

5. Exit the MySQL command tool by entering `QUIT`.

It is necessary to reload the grant tables using the following command line:

```
mysqladmin -u root -p reload
```

With that, you have set up the database. All you have to do now is create Moodle's data directory. Then, you can start installing Moodle itself.

Creating the Moodle data directory

Moodle stores most of its information in the database you have just created. However, uploaded files such as assignments, course images, or user pictures are stored in a separate directory. This data directory in Moodle is usually referred to as **moodledata**.

> **Important note**
> The location that holds your Moodle data files is referred to as `dataroot`.

Later, the Moodle installer will attempt to create this directory, but in some setups, this operation will fail due to security restrictions. To be on the safe side, it is better to create `moodledata` manually or via a web-based file manager, as provided by some systems.

> **Important note**
>
> It is crucial to create `moodledata` on your server where it cannot be accessed publicly – that is, outside your web directory.

`moodledata` is where all the uploaded files by course authors and learners will be stored, so ensure this is adequately dimensioned. You may also consider creating `moodledata` in a separate partition.

Any `moodledata` permissions should be `rwxrwx---` (`chmod -R 0770 moodledata`). If you use `0777`, everybody on the server will have access to the files.

Change the user and group of the directory to that of your web server (usually, this will be `apache` or `www-data` and `nobody` or `www-data`) by entering `chown -R apache:nobody moodledata`.

If you don't have permission to create the data directory in a secure location, create the `.htaccess` file in your home directory and ensure it contains the following two lines:

```
order deny,allow
deny from all
```

These two settings prevent files from being accessed without users having permission to do so.

We have completed the first three steps – downloading Moodle, creating the database, and preparing `moodledata` – which are the prerequisites for running the installer script.

Running the installer script

The installer script performs two main actions – populating the database and creating the configuration file, `config.php`. The Moodle installer is initiated by entering the URL of `wwwroot` (the location where you copied Moodle) into your web browser; Moodle will recognize that it hasn't been installed yet and start the process automatically.

The Moodle installer has to set a session cookie. If your browser has been configured to trigger a warning, make sure you accept that cookie.

The first screen lets you choose the language to be used during installation – this is not the locale used for Moodle, only the language for the installation:

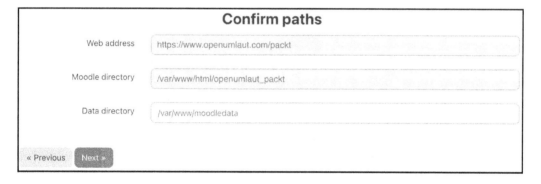

Figure 1.7 – Moodle installation – Choose a language

The following screenshot displays the expected values for the **Web address** entry of the site (wwwroot), the **Moodle directory** (dirroot) entry, and the **Data directory** (dataroot) entry; you might have to modify the **Data directory** entry if the location of your moodledata differs:

Figure 1.8 – Moodle installation – Confirm paths

If dataroot cannot be located or does not have the correct permissions, an error message containing details will be displayed. The same applies if dataroot is accessible directly via the web and is not secure.

You must select which database you wish to use on the following screen. Only the drivers for MySQL, MariaDB, Aurora MySQL, and PostgresSQL are installed on my system. The respective PHP extension must be installed first if you wish to use other database systems such as Oracle or MS SQL Server:

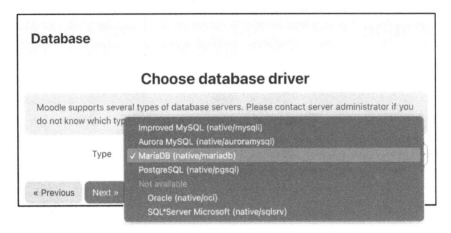

Figure 1.9 – Moodle installation – Choose database driver

This interface uses the configuration details previously established. The following screenshot shows the required fields but will look slightly different if you have chosen a database driver other than MySQL:

Database

Database settings

Improved MySQL (native/mysqli)

The database is where most of the Moodle settings and data are stored and must be configured here.

The database name, username, and password are required fields; table prefix is optional.

The database name may contain only alphanumeric characters, dollar ($) and underscore (_).

If the database currently does not exist, and the user you specify has permission, Moodle will attempt to create a new database with the correct permissions and settings.

Database host	localhost
Database name	packt
Database user	packt
Database password	password
Tables prefix	mdl_
Database port	
Unix socket	

« Previous   Next »

Figure 1.10 – Moodle installation – Database settings

The **Database host** entry's default is `localhost` (`127.0.0.1`), which is correct if the database is located on the same server as the web server. If it is located on a separate server, specify the IP address (preferably unresolved to improve performance).

All the tables the Moodle installer will create will be prefixed with `mdl_`. The **Tables prefix** entry should only be changed if you run multiple Moodle installations using the same database.

Next, the Moodle installer checks whether certain components have been installed. Not all the modules are compulsory – see the *Moodle prerequisites* section of this chapter and the notice on-screen. The installer also verifies the critical PHP settings. If any of the tests have not passed, you must go back to the *Software requirements* section to resolve any problems and restart the installation process after the issues have been fixed. Otherwise, some features may not work, or the installer will not continue, depending on the importance of the module:

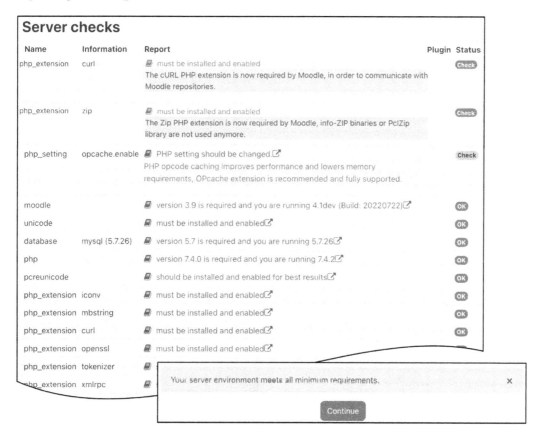

Figure 1.11 – Moodle installation – Server checks

When you have confirmed the server check screen, the installer will display Moodle's copyright notice, which you must confirm. The appearance of this screen also means that the Moodle configuration file, `config.php`, has been successfully created. The installer will display the config file's content if the creation fails (usually because of incorrect permissions). You will have to copy the text from the screen and paste it manually into `config.php` in your `dirroot`.

Once you have accepted the agreement (you can find the full text of the GPL license at `docs.moodle.org/dev/License`), all the database tables will be created. This process might take a few minutes.

Once the table has been created and populated, you will see the screen where you can set up the administrator account. The default **Username** is admin, which should be changed for security reasons. You must fill in the following self-explanatory fields: **New password**, **First name**, **Surname**, and **Email address**. In *Chapter 5, Managing Users, Cohorts, and Authentication*, all other fields will be explained in great detail:

Installation

On this page you should configure your main administrator account which will have complete control over the site. Make sure you give it a secure username and password as well as a valid email address. You can create more admin accounts later on.

Expand all

⌄ General

Username	❷	admin
Choose an authentication method	❷	Manual accounts

The password must have at least 8 characters, at least 1 digit(s), at least 1 lower case letter(s), at least 1 upper case letter(s), at least 1 special character(s) such as as *, -, or #

New password	❶ ❷	··········· ✎ 👁
		☐ Force password change ❷
First name	❶	Alex
Surname	❶	Büchner
Email address	❶	packt@openumlaut.com

Figure 1.12 – Moodle installation – setting up the admin account

The last screen of the installation script asks you to enter some home page settings; namely, **Full site name**, **Short name for site**, and **Site home summary**. These home page settings can be modified later (see *Chapter 7, Enhancing Moodle's Look and Feel*).

Change the **Default timezone** entry to the location of your server, not your location. The installer allows you to turn on **Self registration**. Leave this disabled for now until you have read *Chapter 5, Managing Users, Cohorts, and Authentication*. You must also provide a **Support email** (for your user queries) and a **No-reply address** (to avoid email issues).

Once this information has been entered and the screen has been confirmed, you are ready to start using Moodle. However, first, you must set up the execution of Moodle's maintenance script.

Setting up the cron process

Moodle has to perform plenty of background tasks regularly.

> **Important note**
> The **cron script**, executed by the **cron process**, performs Moodle's background tasks.

An entire page has been dedicated to cron in the Moodle documentation; you can find it at `docs.moodle.org/en/Cron`. You must set up the cron process; otherwise, any timed Moodle features, such as scheduled backups, sending forum notifications, statistics processing, and so on, will not work.

The script, `cron.php`, is located in the admin directory and can be triggered manually through a web browser (if allowed in the security settings). Once executed, the output from the script (`<yoursite>/admin/cron.php`) is shown on-screen, and you have to navigate back to your Moodle system manually.

There are several ways to call the cron script. The most popular option is via the `wget` command:

```
wget -q -O /dev/null http://<yoursite>/admin/cron.php
```

However, if this does not suit your setup, check out `docs.moodle.org/en/Cron` for alternatives.

Most control panels allow you to set up scheduled tasks via a cron job management tool. Bear in mind that this is not part of Moodle but part of your hosting package. Alternatively, you can create a crontab entry, a file located in the `/etc` directory that contains all the system-wide cron entries. This file can also be edited manually using `crontab -e`, but ensure you get the syntax right!

To run the CLI cron script every minute, add the following line, replacing `<yourpath>` with the directory where your Moodle system is located (`dirroot`):

```
* * * * * /usr/bin/php <yourpath>/cron.php >/dev/null
```

> **Important note**
> It is highly recommended to run the cron process every minute!

That's it. Moodle is now ready to go. Two optional steps you should quickly run through are covered in the next section.

Finalizing the installation

To make sure that Moodle is running without problems, go to **Notifications** in the **Site administration** menu of the **General** tab:

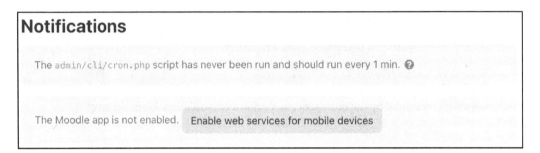

Figure 1.13 – Moodle installation – checking system notifications

In the case of my installation, there are two issues – the cron script has not been configured and the mobile app is not enabled. I need to fix the former issue; the latter can wait until *Chapter 11, Enabling Mobile Learning*. Other messages might appear in the **Notifications** area, and you should resolve them promptly.

Moodle provides some statistics about its usage on `moodle.net/stats`, and to be included in these figures, you have to register your Moodle site via **Site administration** | **General** | **Registration**. Registration with Moodle is optional and free, and you decide what information will be made public.

> **Important note**
> Even if you opt out of providing any usage patterns for your site, it is still highly recommended to register to receive information on new Moodle releases, security alerts, and other important news.

The following is the registration form, alongside a screenshot from the public statistics:

Registration information

Name	❓	Packt
Site listing	❓	Do not list my site
Description	❓	Moodle 4 Administration by Packt Publishing
Language	❓	English
Country	❓❓	Germany
Admin email address	❓❓	packt@openumlaut.com
Notifications of new Moodle releases, security alerts and other important news	❓	☑ Yes, notify me of new Moodle releases ☐ Use different email
Moodle newsletter	❓	☑ Yes, I would like to receive the Mood ☐ Use different email
Privacy notice and data processing agreement		☑ I agree to the Privacy notice and da

› More information

Register your site

Statistics

Sites	Courses
174,000	41,000,000
Users	Enrolments
326,000,000	1,892,000,000
Forum posts	Resources
718,000,000	357,000,000
Quiz questions	Countries
6,862,000,000	244

Figure 1.14 – Moodle registration and statistics

This concludes the installation process for Moodle in a LAMP environment. If you have encountered any issues that have not been covered in these instructions or if your setup differs from the one described, go to `docs.moodle.org/en/Installing_Moodle`, where more installation details are provided, and exceptions are covered in great detail.

An alternative to installing Moodle via the web interface is via the **command-line interface** (**CLI**), which is the topic of the following section.

Installation via the command-line interface

Moodle provides a CLI that lets you perform several administrative tasks from the Unix shell prompt. There is no CLI for Windows-based systems. CLI-based installations are useful if you need to automate setups, for example, in an environment where you host multiple Moodle instances.

The CLI is not for the faint-hearted, so be careful when using it. You must execute the installation script as the web server user, usually `www-data` or `apache`. You can run the installation script, `install.php`, in interactive mode (you will have to enter any parameters by hand) or in non-interactive mode, where the script will run silently.

From your `dirroot`, you can initiate the interactive script as follows:

```
sudo -u www-data /usr/bin/php admin/cli/install.php
```

Something more interesting is the CLI's non-interactive mode, as this can be used for scripting and automation purposes. A list of all the available parameters can be displayed using the `--help` command:

```
sudo -u www-data /usr/bin/php admin/cli/install.php --help
```

The output of the executed command is shown in the following screenshot:

```
Options:
--chmod=OCTAL-MODE     Permissions of new directories created within dataroot.
                       Default is 2777. You may want to change it to 2770
                       or 2750 or 750. See chmod man page for details.
--lang=CODE            Installation and default site language.
--wwwroot=URL          Web address for the Moodle site,
                       required in non-interactive mode.
--dataroot=DIR         Location of the moodle data folder,
                       must not be web accessible. Default is moodledata
                       in the parent directory.
--dbtype=TYPE          Database type. Default is mysqli
--dbhost=HOST          Database host. Default is localhost
--dbname=NAME          Database name. Default is moodle
--dbuser=USERNAME      Database user. Default is root
--dbpass=PASSWORD      Database password. Default is blank
--dbport=NUMBER        Use database port.
--dbsocket=PATH        Use database socket, 1 means default. Available for some databases only.
--prefix=STRING        Table prefix for above database tables. Default is mdl_
--fullname=STRING      The fullname of the site
--shortname=STRING     The shortname of the site
--summary=STRING       The summary to be displayed on the front page
--adminuser=USERNAME   Username for the moodle admin account. Default is admin
--adminpass=PASSWORD   Password for the moodle admin account,
                       required in non-interactive mode.
--adminemail=STRING    Email address for the moodle admin account.
--sitepreset=STRING    Admin site preset to be applied during the installation process.
--supportemail=STRING  Email address for support and help.
--upgradekey=STRING    The upgrade key to be set in the config.php, leave empty to not set it.
--non-interactive      No interactive questions, installation fails if any
                       problem encountered.
--agree-license        Indicates agreement with software license,
                       required in non-interactive mode.
--allow-unstable       Install even if the version is not marked as stable yet,
                       required in non-interactive mode.
--skip-database        Stop the installation before installing the database.
-h, --help             Print out this help

Example:
\$sudo -u www-data /usr/bin/php admin/cli/install.php --lang=cs
```

Figure 1.15 – Moodle installation via the CLI

An example command line would look similar to the following, where you will have to adjust the parameters to your local setup:

```
sudo -u www-data /usr/bin/php admin/cli/install.php
--wwwroot=http://123.54.67.89/moodle --dataroot=/var/
moodledata/ --dbtype=mysqli --dbhost=localhost --dbname=moodle
--dbuser=moodle --dbpass=password --fullname=moodle4
--shortname=moodle4 --adminpass=Password123! --non-interactive
--agree-license
```

More Moodle tasks can be administered via the CLI, for example, resetting passwords or putting Moodle in maintenance mode. We will show the relevant syntax at the appropriate places throughout this book and have also dedicated a section to the CLI in *Chapter 17, Working with Moodle Admin Tools*.

Once your Moodle system is up and running, you need to ensure that it is kept up to date. Updating Moodle manually and via the command line is covered in the following section.

Updating Moodle

We provided an overview of Moodle's release calendar earlier in this chapter. There is usually no need to install every single minor point release; however, there are several scenarios when you should upgrade your Moodle system:

- Security patches have been issued
- New features have been added
- Bugs have been fixed that affect your setup
- A major version is released
- The support cycle of your setup comes to an end

There are principally two ways Moodle systems can be updated: you can run updates manually (using the web interface or the CLI) or stay up to date using Git commands. Both procedures will be described in this section.

Either way, before you start, ensure you put Moodle in maintenance mode to ensure that no other user is logged in during the update. Go to **Site administration | Server | Maintenance mode**, choose **Enable** for **Maintenance mode**, and enter a maintenance message:

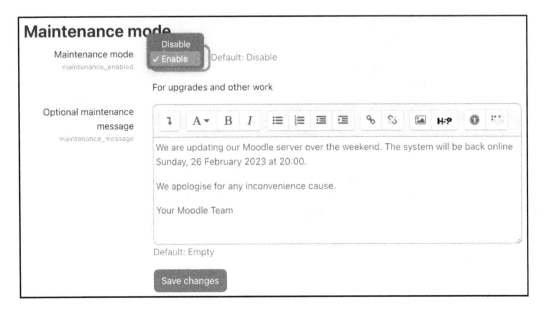

Figure 1.16 – Enabling maintenance mode

You can also put Moodle in maintenance mode using its CLI, as follows:

```
sudo -u www-data /usr/bin/php admin/cli/maintenance.php
--enable
```

Using the --enablelater=MINUTES flag, you can specify the period before entering CLI maintenance mode, which is useful when you run an automatic update.

To change back to normal mode, use the --disable parameter instead of --enable, as follows:

```
sudo -u www-data /usr/bin/php admin/cli/maintenance.php -
disable
```

Once Moodle has been put in maintenance mode, you are ready to update your Moodle system.

Updating Moodle manually

The high-level process for updating Moodle manually is as follows:

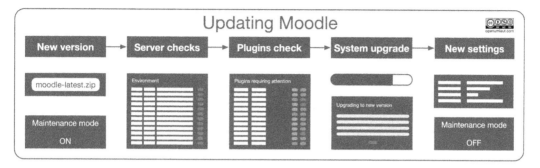

Figure 1.17 – Updating Moodle

If you update from a previous version of Moodle, the process is the same. However, double-check the upgrading document at docs.moodle.org/en/Upgrading for any version-specific issues.

> **Important note**
>
> You have to be at least on version 3.6 to update directly to Moodle 4. If you're upgrading from earlier versions, you must upgrade to 3.6 as a first step.

Before you install a new update, it is highly recommended that you run a **backup** of your Moodle system. While most updates will run smoothly, a backup will be required if you have to revert the system to the pre-updated version. Backups will be covered in detail in *Chapter 16, Avoiding Sleepless Nights – Moodle Backup and Restore*. Ensure that you run a system backup that includes the database, moodledata, and dirroot (in particular, config.php).

Now, let's go through the update workflow step by step:

1. **New version**

   Once you have created a backup, it is time to replace the old version of dirroot with the latest code. Simply copy the new files over the existing ones; existing files will be overridden, except config.php, which is not part of the download bundle.

   Alternatively, you can rename the old dirroot folder and create a new directory. However, you must copy the following files and directories from your old directory to your new dirroot:

   - config.php
   - .htaccess (if present)

- Any theme folders that have been created

- Any modified language packs

- The content of the local directory

- Any third-party modules and custom code not located in `local`

Once you go to the location of your Moodle site and log in as an administrator, the system will recognize that a new version is available and kick off the installer automatically.

The first screen displays the build of the new version (here, 4.0.2) and asks you to confirm that you wish to go ahead with the upgrade:

Upgrading Moodle database from version 4.0.1 (Build: 20220509) (2022041901.00) to 4.0.2 (Build: 20220711) (2022041902.00)

Confirm

Your Moodle files have been changed, and you are about to automatically upgrade your server to this version:

4.0.2 (Build: 20220711) (2022041902.00)

Once you do this you can not go back again. Please note that this process can take a long time.

Are you sure you want to upgrade this server to this version?

 Continue   Cancel

Figure 1.18 – Updating Moodle – New version

2. **Server checks**

    Next, a screen is displayed that links the release notes and performs the same server check as the one described during installation.

3. **Plugins check**

    Moodle plugins, whether core (**Standard**) or third-party (**Additional**), sometimes cause problems when upgrading Moodle. The **Source/Status** column highlights any actions required or problems found, and you should resolve any issues. Refer to *Chapter 8, Understanding Moodle Plugins*, for more details:

Figure 1.19 – Updating Moodle – Plugins check

4. **System upgrade**

    Once this screen has been confirmed, the actual system upgrade starts, during which new database fields are created, and data is modified if and when necessary.

5. **New settings**

    Any new system settings added to Moodle are shown and can be changed straight away. For example, in the following screenshot, a new **Number of participants per page** parameter has been added:

Packt

The settings shown below were added during your last Moodle upgrade. Make any changes necessary to the defaults and then click the 'Save changes' button at the bottom of this page.

New settings - Course default settings

Number of participants per page

moodlecourse | participantsperpage

20   Default: 20

The number of users shown per page on the participants page in each course.

Save changes

Figure 1.20 – Updating Moodle – New settings

Once the upgrade process has been completed, check the **Notifications** page. Also, don't forget to turn off **Maintenance mode**!

An alternative to manually updating Moodle is to utilize the CLI, which we will cover in the following subsection.

Updating Moodle via the CLI

As expected, Moodle updates can also be run using the already-discussed CLI. Once you have backed up your data and updated to the latest version, all you need to do is run the following script:

```
sudo -u www-data /usr/bin/php admin/cli/upgrade.php --non-
interactive
```

Updating Moodle via the CLI is even more powerful when combined with the Git checkout of the Moodle source code. That is what we'll look at next.

An alternative approach exists to keep a current version up to date, which uses the open source versioning system **Git**. All checked-in Moodle code is made available via this method, which only allows you to update the modules that have changed.

Setting up Git is a cumbersome process, which is beyond the scope of this book. You can find details at docs.moodle.org/en/Git_for_Administrators. However, once set up, Git is a very streamlined system, particularly in conjunction with the CLI mentioned earlier. The following is a sample script that gets the latest version of the source code, puts Moodle in maintenance mode, merges the old code with the new, runs the upgrade script, and disables maintenance mode:

```
git fetch
sudo -u www-data /usr/bin/php admin/cli/maintenance.php
--enable
git merge origin/cvshead
sudo -u www-data /usr/bin/php admin/cli/upgrade.php
sudo -u www-data /usr/bin/php admin/cli/maintenance.php
--disable
```

The execution of the `git fetch` command can be seen in the following screenshot:

```
$ git fetch
remote: Enumerating objects: 56741, done.
remote: Counting objects: 100% (23499/23499), done.
remote: Compressing objects: 100% (7762/7762), done.
remote: Total 17338 (delta 12590), reused 13084 (delta 8941), pack-reused 0
Receiving objects: 100% (17338/17338), 6.42 MiB | 8.57 MiB/s, done.
Resolving deltas: 100% (12590/12590), completed with 2846 local objects.
From https://github.com/moodle/moodle
   0d0f09bc7f..24f97edd91  master      -> origin/master
 * [new tag]               v4.0.0      -> v4.0.0
 * [new tag]               v4.0.0-rc1 -> v4.0.0-rc1
 * [new tag]               v4.0.0-rc2 -> v4.0.0-rc2
 * [new tag]               v4.0.0-rc3 -> v4.0.0-rc3
 * [new tag]               v4.0.0-rc4 -> v4.0.0-rc4
$
```

Figure 1.21 – Fetching the new Moodle version

If you have changed any core code, potential conflicts might arise and must be resolved (Git will prompt you to do so).

Most commercial Moodle providers use Git to keep their Moodle instances up to date. If you feel comfortable using shell scripts, this should be your preferred method since it streamlines the update workflow and reduces the number of issues that can arise.

There is one last issue we haven't covered yet: when do you know that updates are available? That's what update notifications are there for.

Update notifications

Moodle can notify you about a newly available version via email or message. To support this feature, the **Automatically check for available updates** setting under **Site administration | Server | Update notifications** has to remain enabled, as follows:

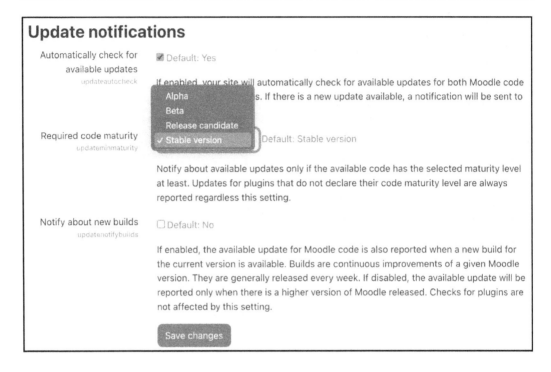

Figure 1.22 – Update notifications

On your production site, the **Required code maturity** option should be set to **Stable version**; other maturity levels should only be considered on test instances. The same holds for the **Notify about new builds** parameter.

Alternatively, you can check for updates (core and plugins) by going to **Site administration** | **General** | **Notifications**. This information is updated every 24 hours via the cron process you set up earlier and takes into account the update notification settings. You can also initiate the request via the **Check for available updates** button:

Figure 1.23 – Update notifications

This concludes this section on updating your Moodle site, both manually and via the command line.

Summary

This chapter taught you how to install and update Moodle.

After providing an overview describing the most suitable setup, we outlined the necessary software and hardware requirements and described Moodle's versioning strategy and release calendar.

Then, we covered Moodle's installation via the web and its powerful CLI. We did the same for Moodle upgrades, where we briefly introduced Git.

The fact that Moodle uses a portable software architecture and facilitates standard open source components allows it to be installed on multiple platforms. However, this also means that different peculiarities and quirks must be considered in different environments.

Now that your system is up and running, in the next chapter, we'll look at the components of Moodle, which will give you a better understanding of the system and how to administer it.

2
Exploring the Moodle System

Now that your Moodle system is up and running, we will look at the components that make up the learning platform. Think of these as the foundation on which Moodle is built.

In this chapter, you will learn about the architecture of Moodle, what the main components of Moodle are, and where its data is stored. Moodle has a modern and intuitive user interface that takes a little bit of time to get used to. You will learn about its main navigation and where to find help if required. Dealing with files in web-based applications is not always straightforward. Therefore, you will learn how Moodle's file management works and how to configure the recycle bin.

In this chapter, we will cover the following topics:

- Understanding the Moodle architecture
- Navigating Moodle as an administrator
- File management in Moodle
- Recycle bin

By the end of this chapter, you will know more about how Moodle is structured internally, how to work with it as an admin, and how files are managed.

Understanding the Moodle architecture

First, we will look at the overall architecture on which Moodle is based before we cover the internal components of the LMS's application layer.

We will take a top-down approach and look at the overall architecture first before zooming into how Moodle Core is structured. We will conclude at the lowest level, where we will be dealing with files and the management thereof.

The LAMP architecture

Moodle has been developed on the open-source LAMP framework, which consists of Linux (operating system), Apache (web server), MySQL (database), and PHP (programming language). Due to the portability of these components and the modularity of Moodle itself (that's what the "M" stands for), a wide range of operating systems, database systems, and web servers are supported. However, while Moodle runs on other technology stacks, we will focus on LAMP since it has proven the most popular setup among Moodle administrators.

The following diagram shows a simple overview of the overall architecture:

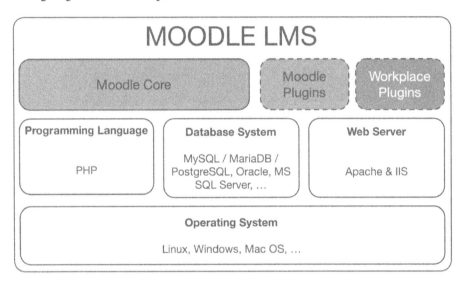

Figure 2.1 – Moodle's overall architecture

Let's have a closer look at the components of Moodle's overall architecture:

- **Moodle Core** is what is often referred to when people talk about Moodle. This is also what we installed in the previous chapter and will be covered in this book.

- **Moodle plugins**: While Moodle Core is a powerful and comprehensive LMS, few sites solely rely on the base system. Instead, add-on modules supplement the feature set of standard Moodle to customize the platform to individual requirements. These add-ons are called Moodle plugins and are mostly community-contributed additions to standard Moodle, extending its functionality for a specific use case. At the time of writing, there are almost 2,000 (!) entries in the official Moodle plugins database at `moodle.org/plugins`.

> **Important note**
>
> **Moodle LMS** is effectively standard Moodle plus – optionally – one or many Moodle plugins.

An exciting set of plugins has been made available by Moodle HQ. **Moodle Workplace** is a commercial offering designed for corporate and organizational training, resulting in a powerful and flexible platform for workplace learning. More information on Moodle Workplace can be found at `moodle.com/workplace` or in the title *Corporate Learning with Moodle Workplace*, by Packt Publishing.

- **PHP** is the programming language in which Moodle is written (accompanied by HTML, JavaScript, and CSS files). It is the only component that cannot be replaced with any other counterpart. Specific PHP libraries must be installed – see *Chapter 1, Installing Moodle*.

- **MySQL** is the database of choice for most opensource applications, but other systems, such as Microsoft SQL Server, Oracle, and PostgreSQL, are fully supported. MariaDB, a MySQL fork, has become very popular among Moodle administrators after Oracle acquired MySQL.

- **Apache** has become the de facto standard for large-scale web applications, closely followed by Microsoft IIS. Both web servers are supported like any other that supports PHP, such as nginx. This book will focus on Apache, the most popular option for Moodle setups.

- **Operating system**: The lowest level is the operating system. While **Linux** is the preferred platform – since this is where all code is developed and tested –other operating systems are also supported, such as Windows, Mac OS X, and various Unix derivatives.

The following diagram shows the interaction among the elements in the Moodle architecture:

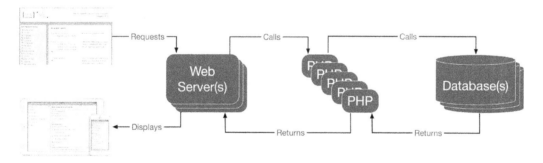

Figure 2.2 – Moodle's interaction among underlying components

The user makes requests via the web browser interface or a mobile Moodle application. The web browser passes the request to the web server(s), which calls the PHP module responsible for the call. The PHP module calls the database(s) with an action (a query, update, insert, or delete operation) that returns the requested data. Based on this information, the PHP module returns data (usually in HTML or JavaScript) to the web server(s), which passes the information to be displayed back to the user's browser or application.

The component of most interest to us is Moodle Core, which we will dive into in more detail next.

Moodle Core

Now, let's look at the Moodle Core layer in more detail. Moodle's main building blocks are shown in the following diagram:

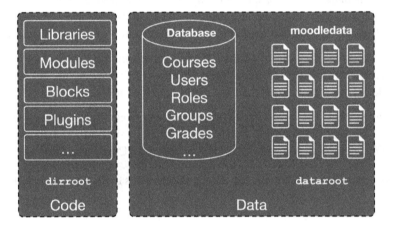

Figure 2.3 – Moodle's building blocks

Moodle distinguishes between code (primarily written in PHP, HTML, and CSS) and data (mostly values and files added via the Moodle interface).

Moodle libraries, modules (such as resources and activities), blocks, plugins, admin tools, and other entities are represented in code. It is always stored in the filesystem in a Moodle directory referred to as `dirroot`, which was specified during the installation process in the previous chapter. The code includes all the elements that deal with the backend (server) and frontend (user interface) operations.

Moodle courses, users, roles, groups, competencies, learning plans, grades, and other data, such as learning resources added by educators, forum posts added by learners, and system settings added by the administrator, are mostly stored in the Moodle database. However, files such as user pictures or uploaded assignments are stored in another Moodle directory, known as `moodledata`, located in a directory called `dataroot`. Information about files (metadata such as the name, location, last modification, license, and size) is stored in the database, referencing the respective files.

> **Important note**
>
> Moodle manages its files internally, and it is important to stress that interfering with any files in `moodledata` will break the application.

Even copying a file from one folder to another or adding a file manually will break the consistency of your system, which means that further behavior cannot be predicted. Internally, Moodle uses a mechanism called SHA1 hashing. Moodle fully supports Unicode filenames and avoids redundant storage when the same file is used twice (even by different users). Again, you must not modify any Moodle files at the system level!

Now, let's have a closer look at how the Moodle files area – the directory structure – is organized.

Code and data locations

Though Moodle takes care of organizing its code and data, it is usually good to know where a file is located in your learning system, for example, when installing add-ons or manually applying patches.

System files – files required to run Moodle – are located in several directories under `dirroot` (the root directory of your Moodle installation). The following table shows the folder name, a brief description, and the chapter in which the topic is covered in this book:

Folder	Description	Chapter
admin	Moodle admin tools and scripts	All
adminpresets	Management of admin presets	17
analytics	Learning analytics	12
auth	User authentication plugins	5
availability	Management of availability restrictions	9
backup	Backup and restore operations	16
badges	Management of badges	10
blocks	Blocks placed various pages	7
blog	Internal and external blogging functionality	10
cache	Cache stores and performance scripts	15
calendar	Calendar and event management	11
cohort	Handling of site-wide groups (cohorts)	4
comment	Comments used in courses	10
competency	Competencies and learning plans	10
completion	Course completion criteria and aggregation	4
contentbank	H5P content bank	9
course	Courses, categories, and course formats	4
customfield	Custom field types	4+5
dataformat	Data export formats	12
enrol	User enrolment plugins	4
error	Error handling; mostly used by developers	—
favourites	Handling of starred courses	7
files	File management	2
filter	Filters applied to text authored in the editor	9
grade	Grades, grade book, and grade reports	9
group	Groups and groupings handling	5
h5p	H5P integration	9
install	Moodle installation and update scripts	1
iplookup	Look up IP addresses	12
lang	Localization strings (one folder per lang)	11
lib	Libraries of core Moodle code	2
local	Local customizations	8
login	Login handling and account creation	5
message	Messaging tool (one folder per channel)	11
mnet	Peer-to-peer and hub networking	19
mod	Core Moodle course modules	8
my	Users' personal dashboards (myMoodle)	7
notes	Handling of notes in user profiles	—
payment	Payment subsystem and gateways	4
pix	Generic site graphics	—
plagiarism	Plagiarism detection plugins	9
portfolio	Portfolio plugins to export data	10
privacy	Privacy and policies / GDPR	14
question	Question bank and question types	9
rating	Handling of user ratings	9
report	Report plugins and events list	12
reportbuilder	Custom report builder	12
repository	Repository plugins to export data	10
rss	RSS feeds	10
search	Global search	15
tag	Tagging	9
theme	Themes to change branding of site	7
user	User management	5
userpix	Display thumbnails of user profile pictures	5
webservice	Web services functionality	18

Figure 2.4 – Code and data locations

The `moodledata` directory (`dataroot`) is organized as follows:

```
📁 antivirus_quarantine   Storing of quarantined antivirus files
📁 cache . . . . . . . . . . . . . .   Caching data
📁 filedir . . . . . . . . . . .   The actual user content—files that have been uploaded
📁 filter . . . . . . . . . . . .   Caching of filtered data
📁 lang . . . . . . . . . . . . . .   Locally used language packs and customizations
📁 localcache . . . . . . . .   Caching data of plugins
📁 lock . . . . . . . . . . . . . .   Locked files
📁 models . . . . . . . . . . . .   Cache of analytics models
📁 muc . . . . . . . . . . . . . . .   Moodle Universal Cache files
📁 repository . . . . . . . .   External location accessible from within Moodle
📁 sessions . . . . . . . . . .   Session information
📁 temp . . . . . . . . . . . . . .   Temporary files
📁 trashdir . . . . . . . . . .   Deleted files
```

Figure 2.5 – moodledata directories

If problems occur before carrying out an update, it is sometimes necessary to delete caching data and any temporary information Moodle has created. This data is located in the respective directories in the structure shown in the preceding table. In other words, once everybody has logged out, you can safely delete any files in the directories named `cache`, `filter`, `localcache`, `lock`, `models`, `muc`, `sessions`, `temp`, and `trashdir`. Purging can either be done manually or, better, via **Site administration** | **Development** | **Purge caches** | **Purge all caches** in the Moodle interface.

This concludes this section on the Moodle architecture, which dealt with the LAMP framework and Moodle's main components before we drilled down to Moodle Core and the location of code and data files.

Navigating Moodle as an administrator

In this section, you will learn how to work with Moodle, which covers the horizontal navigation of the site administration section and handy tools such as admin search, bookmarks, and access to various help and support sites and channels.

The essential navigational items for administrators are as follows:

- **Site menu**: The main menu across all pages; the **Site administration** item opens up the admin menu.

- **Admin menu**: Access to all admin sections and subsections. As an administrator, you will be performing most tasks from here. We will cover all aspects of these menus and sub-menus throughout the remainder of this book.

- **User menu**: Access to personal settings, such as the user profile, preferences, or the selected language.

- **Admin search**: Search facility, which we will cover later.

- **Edit mode toggle**: Switch between editing mode and non-editing mode.

- **Block drawer**: Moodle blocks are placed here; edit mode must be activated to make changes to the block drawer.

These navigation elements have been highlighted in the following screenshot:

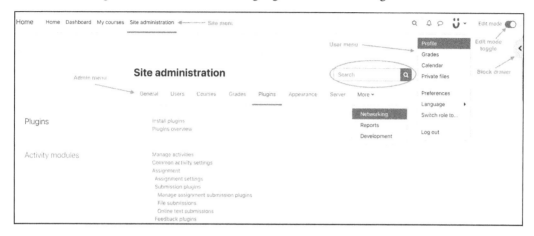

Figure 2.6 – Moodle navigation

The items displayed in the preceding screenshot might be different on your system. Depending on which features have been activated, the theme used, and your screen size, some admin menu items might move to the **More** dropdown, or the **Language** setting might appear in the user menu.

Moodle's user interface has been built from the ground up in version 4 – gone is the breadcrumb trail, and previously omnipresent blocks have been downgraded to the block drawer. This redevelopment also impacts the navigational admin facilities, which we will cover next.

Administrator search facility

A search facility is provided to help you identify any setting in the administration section, which is located above the **Site administration** menu (encircled in the previous screenshot).

Moodle displays the results in an expanded form when searching for any term that allows you to change settings immediately. For example, when searching for "calendar," numerous sections appear as a result, which can be changed in each section straight away, rather than having to navigate to each separate section to make changes.

The search facility is also highly beneficial when upgrading from older versions of Moodle, where configuration settings have been reorganized, and their location is sometimes difficult to trace.

Next up are admin bookmarks, which can potentially reduce the usage of the admin search facility.

Admin bookmarks

Bookmarks are shown in the **Admin bookmarks** block, which can be added by turning on **Edit mode**, opening the block drawer, and selecting the block from the **Add a block** list. They allow you to bookmark any admin menu to access regularly required pages easily. Select **Bookmark this page** to add a bookmark and **Unbookmark this page** to delete it. Moodle automatically displays the latter option when you are on a bookmarked page:

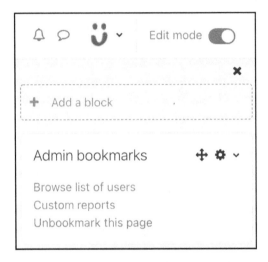

Figure 2.7 – Admin bookmarks

In the preceding screenshot, two pages have already been bookmarked (**Browse list of users** and **Custom reports**), and the mentioned link is provided to unbookmark the current marker.

Admin search and bookmarks are useful when you know what you are looking for. Next up is Moodle Docs, which assists you when you are stuck with a feature or require further support.

Moodle Docs and help

The entire Moodle documentation is online at `docs.moodle.org`. If you wish to provide your own documentation, modify the **Moodle Docs document root** setting by going to **Site administration | Appearance | Moodle Docs**. You can also select the **Language for docs used** option in links for the documentation pages and enable the **Open in new window** option on this screen.

At the bottom of each page, you will see a **Support icon**. Once selected, it will display the following help-related links:

- **Help and documentation**: Reference to the relevant page in Moodle Docs.

- **Services and support**: Link to `moodle.com/help`, where professional services from Moodle Certified Service Providers are offered.

- **Contact site support**: The standard email client will be opened, and the recipient of the support contact will be filled in. You can change the support email address by going to **Site administration | Server | Support contact**. This feature is more relevant to your users rather than to you as an administrator.

In addition to the online documentation, some features provide inline help, indicated by a question mark symbol. When clicked, a help window will appear to provide assistance that's relevant to the respective topic or setting:

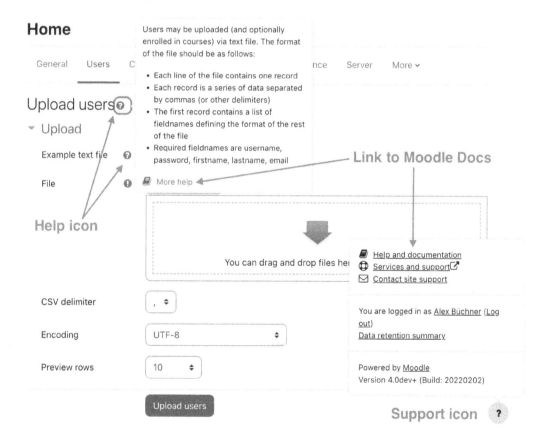

Figure 2.8 – Moodle help

For instance, when clicking on the **Help and documentation** link in the **Upload users** section, the following article will be opened: `docs.moodle.org/400/en/Upload_users`. For each version of Moodle, separate Moodle Docs are published. The preceding link is from version 4.0, where documentation for most pages exists in different languages.

When you access certain pages for the first time, Moodle will display a so-called user tour. For example, when you navigate to **My courses**, the following popup will be displayed:

Figure 2.9 – User tour

We will cover user tours in detail in *Chapter 7, Enhancing Moodle's Look and Feel*.

The Moodle community is growing continuously and, at the time of writing, has well over 1 million registered users (yes, that's 1 million!), of which over 5% are active. If you cannot find a solution to your Moodle problems in Moodle Docs, use the **Search** functionality at the top of the screen at `moodle.org`. In order of priority, the search brings forth the already mentioned Moodle Docs, the most active user forums, and the Moodle Tracker, which keeps track of all issues and feature requests (`tracker.moodle.org`). A search in Moodle forums can often result in a large number of links. Use the **Advanced search** area in the **Search forums** block to narrow the search space. If you still cannot find the solution to your problem, which is relatively rare, post a question on the relevant forum; somebody is likely to assist you further.

A popular site that might also be of interest is Moodle Academy (`moodle.academy`), which includes an administrator learning pathway covering short, self-paced courses on basic Moodle administration.

This concludes this section on navigating Moodle, which introduced you to the site administration menu and various helpful tools such as admin search, admin bookmarks, and Moodle Docs.

File management in Moodle

This section is all about files: how to access them, how they are organized in folders, how to upload them, how to configure private files, the difference between copying and linking, file types, increasing the upload file limit, and how to deal with deleted files via the recycle bin. This is a lot to take in, so let's get started.

Dealing with files in web-based applications is not always straightforward. While Moodle provides a user interface to perform this task, it is sometimes necessary that, as the administrator, you will have to bypass this mechanism and use other means. First, let's look at the built-in file handling that students and teachers also use.

Moodle file management interface

Moodle offers a basic file management interface that lets you upload, move, delete, and rename files and directories. It is also possible to copy or link to files from third-party services such as Dropbox; on the same note, Moodle isn't a content management system.

We have already talked about how Moodle stores files at the system level—the ones we shouldn't touch! At the application level, it arranges files according to Moodle's structure:

> **Important note**
> In Moodle, a file is always connected to the particular bit of Moodle that uses it.

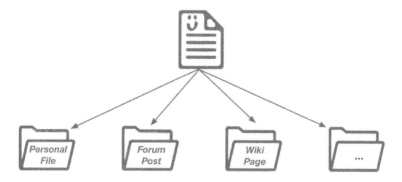

Figure 2.10 – Moodle files

Files are organized in a tree-like structure, which has three types of main branches:

- Categories/Courses/Activities and Resources
- Users (private files and personal backups)
- Site home (Moodle's front page)

We will be dealing with all those concepts at later stages, so, for now, let's just take them for granted. Courses are arranged in categories (and subcategories) and consist of activities and resources, and there are usually further subdirectories inside activities and resources.

There are multiple users on your system, each with a dedicated file area that can be accessed from anywhere in Moodle, but there is only a single Site Home. Remember, a file is always connected to the particular bit of Moodle content that uses it, reflected by the directory-like structure:

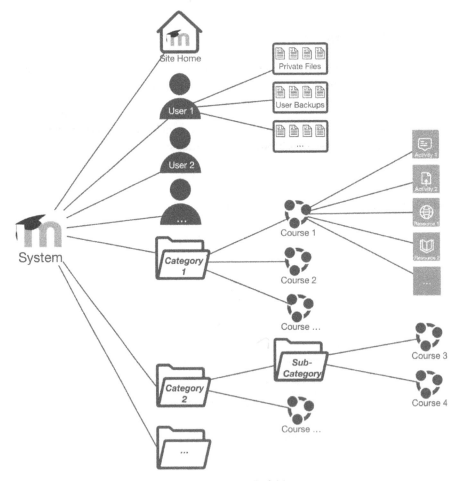

Figure 2.11 – Moodle folders

Now that we know how files and folders are organized, let's look at how to upload data and create directories.

Uploading files

Uploading files usually takes place via drag and drop. While this feature is vital for learners and trainers, as an administrator, you will also have to upload files from time to time, for instance, uploading users in batch mode via a CSV file.

Adding single or multiple files is straightforward: simply select the files in your Explorer (Windows) or Finder (Mac) and drag them onto the provided area inside the dotted lines shown in the following screenshot:

Figure 2.12 – Moodle files and folders

When you click on a file once it has been uploaded, you have the option to **Download** or **Delete** the file. If the selected file is a compressed archive, you have the option to **Unzip** it. Additionally, meta-information about the file (name, author, license, path, icon, last modified, created, and size) is displayed at the bottom of the window, as shown in the following screenshot:

Figure 2.13 – Moodle file details

For some file operations, it is necessary to use the **File picker**, a tool utilized whenever files have to be added to a particular object in Moodle. A user can choose from multiple file sources, known as repositories. The File picker can be accessed using the **Add…** button at the top left of the files area. We will be dealing with repositories in *Chapter 10, Configuring Technical Features*.

Closely related to uploading files is configuring the upload limit.

Upload limit

Your site has a file upload limit set to 2 MB by default. If you need to support files larger than the 2 MB threshold, you will have to increase the limit.

In your `php.ini` file (find its location using the `php -i` command and locate the `Loaded Configuration File` entry), modify the following two lines; `<value>` represents the maximum limit (multiple input formats are supported, for example, 20M or 20971520):

- `upload_max_filesize = <value>`
- `post_max_size = <value>`

If you don't have access to the `php.ini` file, create a `.htaccess` file in your main Moodle directory and add the following two lines:

- `php_value upload_max_filesize = <value>`
- `php_value post_max_size = <value>`

You will also have to increase the `LimitRequestBody` parameter on some systems, usually found in the Apache `httpd.conf` configuration file. You may also need to modify your database configuration, such as the `max_allowed_packet` size:

Figure 2.14 – Moodle upload limit

Once these changes have been applied, ensure the **Maximum upload file size** parameter under **Site administration** | **Security** | **Site security settings** has been set to **Site upload limit**. You can also change the user quota for private files via the **Private file space** parameter. When changing these two values, bear in mind that they will potentially impact the bandwidth and disk space, respectively.

For very large files such as high-quality learning resources, it would be helpful to be able to upload the content via (secure) FTP and then use the built-in unzip functionality in the File picker. However, it is not possible to upload files directly via FTP. Instead, you have to make use of the filesystem repository, which will be discussed in detail in *Chapter 10, Configuring Technical Features*.

Now that you are familiar with uploading files, let's deal with personal files that belong to individual users.

Private files

Every user has an area where personal files can be stored and managed. These are only visible to the user to whom the private files belong. Any item stored in this protected area can be used throughout the site. Private files can be accessed via the File picker, the **Private files** block, or directly via the **Private files** link in the user menu:

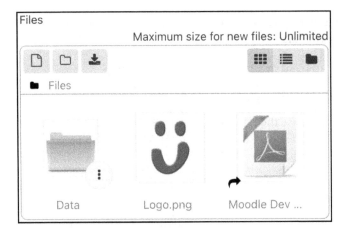

Figure 2.15 – Moodle File picker

Handling files and directories is identical to handling other files. However, you might have spotted the **Link** icon in the PDF file in the preceding screenshot, which leads us nicely to the following subsection.

To link or to copy?

By default, files in Moodle are copied. When you add a file from a source (for instance, your computer or your private files), it will be copied, which means that the source and the resulting file will be logically separated. For example, if you have stored an image in your private files and you use this in three different courses, there are three logical copies. The three images will not be affected if you change the source in your private files.

Moodle also supports linking files, also known as file aliases. Let's stick to the same example, but this time round, the three images are linked. If the source is changed, the three files in the courses will also have changed. Beware that there are some access restrictions with linked files; for example, instructor A might not be able to link to instructor B's file.

When you select a file from a source (repository) that supports linking, an option is provided to **Link to the file**:

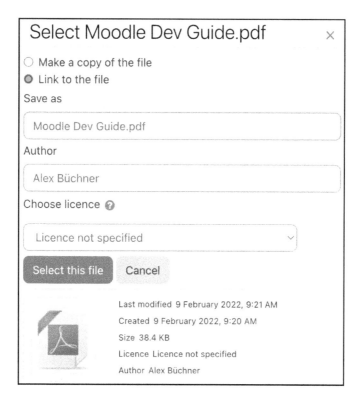

Figure 2.16 – Moodle files – copy and link

Moodle keeps track of linked files and guarantees that inconsistencies cannot occur:

- When deleting a linked file, copies of the file will be created for each link

- When a linked file is overwritten, all links are updated

- When a file overwrites a link, the files are "separated"

Linking and copying are about how files are being dealt with internally; next up are file types, which dictate how they are dealt with when users download them.

File types

Moodle does not restrict which types of files users can upload, for instance, an assignment in a course. Moodle comes with predefined values for the most popular file types in terms of the icon displayed and the program that will be opened, for example, PDF files or PowerPoint documents. However, as depicted in the following screenshot, you can add new file types and view, modify, and delete existing file types by going to **Site administration | Server | File types**:

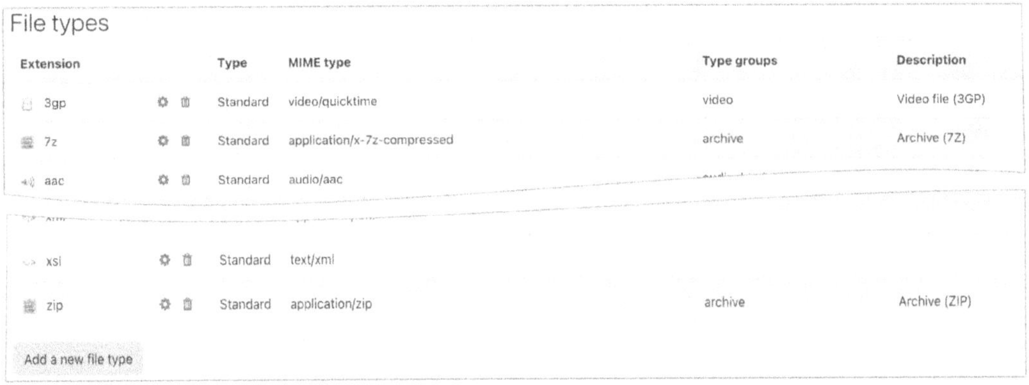

File types						
Extension			Type	MIME type	Type groups	Description
3gp	⚙	🗑	Standard	video/quicktime	video	Video file (3GP)
7z	⚙	🗑	Standard	application/x-7z-compressed	archive	Archive (7Z)
aac	⚙	🗑	Standard	audio/aac		
xsl	⚙	🗑	Standard	text/xml		
zip	⚙	🗑	Standard	application/zip	archive	Archive (ZIP)
Add a new file type						

Figure 2.17 – Moodle file types

When you add a new file type via the button at the bottom of the screen, you must provide the file's **Extension** and its **MIME type**. Furthermore, you have the option to select **File icon**, **Type groups** (such as image or document), **Description type**, **Custom description** (if **Description type** is **Custom description specified in this form**), **Alternative language string** (if selected in **Description type**) and **Default icon for MIME type**.

So far, we have covered how files are stored, organized, and added to Moodle. Now, let's look at what happens when files are deleted (by accident).

Recycle bin

As an administrator, we have all been there: a user has deleted a file, an assignment with all its submissions, or even an entire course – all by accident, of course, and usually very close to an urgent deadline. Recovering the lost data is, as always, the highest priority, and you will spend the next hour or so trawling through last night's backup to help out your panicking colleague.

To avoid scenarios like the ones described, Moodle provides a recycle bin, allowing users to retrieve course elements and courses that were mistakenly deleted. The feature is turned on by default, but you have a range of options to configure the tool's behavior as an administrator.

To access the **Recycle bin** configuration, navigate to **Site administration** | **Plugins** | **Admin tools** | **Recycle bin**, where you will see three groups of settings:

Figure 2.18 – Moodle's Recycle bin settings

The **Recycle bin** options are as follows:

- The **Enable course recycle bin** option collects any deleted resources and activities inside a course. The items will be kept for the period set in the **Item lifetime** parameter.

- The **Enable category recycle bin** option collects any deleted courses inside a category. The courses will be kept for the period set in the **Course lifetime** parameter.

- When the **Auto hide** checkbox is selected, the corresponding menu item will only be shown if the user's bin contains any elements; otherwise, it will be hidden from the **More** menu in the course or category.

Items and courses will be purged permanently from the recycle bin when the respective lifetime expiry dates have passed. The life cycle of a deleted course item or a course category is depicted in the following diagram:

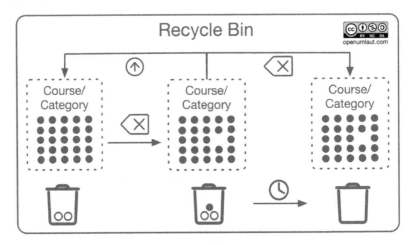

Figure 2.19 – Moodle Recycle bin

Initially, the recycle bin is empty or may already contain removed items or courses (in our example, two). When an element is deleted, it is moved to the user's recycle bin, which can either be restored or purged permanently. Suppose, in the meantime, the specified lifetime of the element has expired. In that case, the file or course will be deleted permanently, alongside any other elements where the expiry date has also been reached.

As mentioned previously, the recycle bin works out of the box; if yours doesn't function as expected, double-check the following three configurations:

- Most processes of the recycle bin are kicked off by the cron process, for example, the regular purging mechanism we just mentioned. Therefore, it is crucial that the cron process is set up correctly and runs every minute (see the dedicated *Setting up the cron process* section in *Chapter 1, Installing Moodle*).

- Internally, the recycle bin uses Moodle's backup and restore functionality. In particular, the following two settings have to be enabled on the **Automated backup setup** page: **Include activities and resources** (`backup_auto_activities`) and **Automated backup setup** (`backup_auto_users`). Additionally, **General restore defaults** (`restore_general_users`) must be ticked on the **General restore** defaults page. You can find more detailed information on these settings in *Chapter 16, Avoiding Sleepless Nights – Moodle Backup and Restore*.

- If your users experience difficulties working with the recycle bin, ensure none of the required capabilities have been revoked from their roles. These are **tool/recyclebin:viewitems**, **tool/recyclebin:restoreitems**, and **tool/recyclebin:deleteitems**. More on roles and capabilities will be provided in *Chapter 6, Managing Permissions, Roles, and Capabilities.*

Learning how to use the recycle bin concludes this section on files and the management thereof.

Summary

In this chapter, we learned what the building blocks of Moodle Core look like and where they are located. Furthermore, we looked at the new intuitive user interface in an administrator's context. Lastly, we dealt with files, folders, and the recycle bin.

As we learned in the previous chapter, Moodle can be installed on multiple operating systems, supports a wide range of databases, and can be used with different web servers. Due to the openness of Moodle, all its components can be accessed without any restrictions. Similarly, any type of file can be handled in Moodle, regardless of its type or size. An intuitive and modern user interface accompanies this setup for learners, educators, and administrators.

Now that your system is up and running and you know what its insides look like, it's time to deal with courses, users, and roles in the next chapter.

3

Exploring Courses, Users, and Roles

The objective of this chapter is to give you a quick rundown of the underlying foundation of Moodle: courses, users, and roles.

The three concepts are inherently intertwined, and any one of these cannot be used without the other two. We will deal with the basics of the three core elements and show how they work together.

Moodle courses are central to Moodle, as this is where learning takes place. Teachers upload their learning resources, create activities, assist in learning, grade work, monitor progress, and so on. Students, on the other hand, read, listen to, or watch learning resources, participate in activities, submit work, collaborate with others, and so on. You will be introduced to courses and how they are organized in categories. You will also learn about the key components of courses, namely activities and resources.

Moodle users are individuals accessing our Moodle system. Typical users are students and teachers/trainers, but there are others such as teaching assistants, managers, parents, assessors, examiners, or guests. Oh, and the administrator, of course! We will cover the basic concepts of authentication – how to get access to Moodle – and enrolment – how to get access to a course – before briefly dealing with two different types of user collections: cohorts and groups.

Moodle roles are, effectively, permissions that specify which features users can access, and where and when (in Moodle) they can access them. You will become familiar with the concepts of roles, contexts, and capabilities, which are essential for controlling permissions in Moodle.

Bear in mind that this chapter only covers the basic concepts of these three core elements. The dedicated chapters – *Chapter 4, Managing Courses and Enrolments, Chapter 5, Managing Users, Cohorts, and Authentication*, and *Chapter 6, Managing Permissions, Roles, and Capabilities* – will deal with the three concepts in greater detail.

In this chapter, we will be covering the following:

- A high-level overview of core Moodle concepts
- Exploring Moodle courses
- Exploring Moodle users
- Exploring Moodle roles

By the end of the chapter, you will have a good understanding of Moodle's three core concepts: courses, users, and roles.

A high-level overview of core Moodle concepts

Let's look at the following diagram to give you an overview of courses, users, and roles. It shows how central the three concepts are and how other features are related to them. Again, all their intricacies will be dealt with in due course, so for now, just start getting familiar with some Moodle terminology.

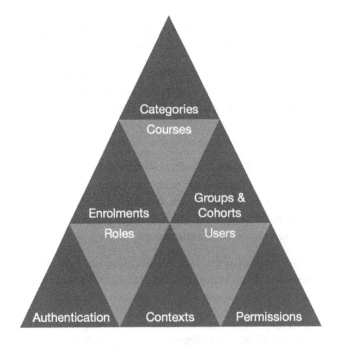

Figure 3.1 – Core Moodle concepts

Let's start at the bottom left and cycle through the pyramid in a roughly clockwise fashion. Users have to go through an **Authentication** process to get access to Moodle. They then have to go through the **Enrolments** step to participate in **Courses**, which themselves are organized into **Categories**. **Groups & Cohorts** are different ways to group users at course level or site-wide, respectively. **Users** are granted **Roles**, in particular, **Contexts**, which are ring-fenced Moodle areas; the scope of the role is specified by configuring **Permissions**.

The diagram also demonstrates a chicken-and-egg situation. If we start with users, we have no courses to enrol them on; if we start with courses, we have no users who can participate in them. Not to worry, though – Moodle lets us go back and forth between administrative areas and often perform multiple tasks simultaneously.

A short note on the **enrol vs enroll** lingua dispute that appears to be as old as Moodle itself. While this book has to be written in US English, we decided to use the British English spelling for the term for two main reasons: first, in Moodle internally, *enrolment* is used throughout – for example, as a parameter in batch files – and second, Moodle Docs use *enrol* (Moodle is Australian after all). So, *enrol* and *enrolment* it is! Switch to the **en_us** language pack if this drives you mad. Or crazy. Or both.

Now that you have been given a high-level overview, let's start with the top corner of our triangle, dealing with courses.

Exploring Moodle courses

Courses are central to Moodle, as this is where content is presented to learners and most of the learning and collaboration takes place.

In the following sections, first, we will cover the two most essential learning elements of courses: resources and activities. Then, we will look at categories that organize courses hierarchically. Finally, you are going to create your first course.

> **Important note**
> Moodle is a course-centric system.

Resources and activities

Moodle manages activities and stores resources in courses, and this is where the vast majority of learning takes place:

- **Resources** are learning elements where the learner is passive – for instance, a PDF document can be read, a URL can be navigated to, a podcast can be listened to, or a video can be watched

- **Activities** are learning elements where the learner is active and more engaged – for example, posting to a discussion forum, responding to a feedback questionnaire, collaborating with others to author FAQs, or answering questions in a SCORM-based quiz

Resources and activities can be arranged in any order, and dependencies can be specified via a combination of access restrictions and activity completion criteria. To illustrate the workings of the sequencing versus non-sequencing of content, let's look at a sample blended learning course. In our example, this comprises three phases (called topics in Moodle), but any other structure would be possible: *preparation* (pre-seminar), *webinar* (face-to-face), and *follow-up* (post-seminar):

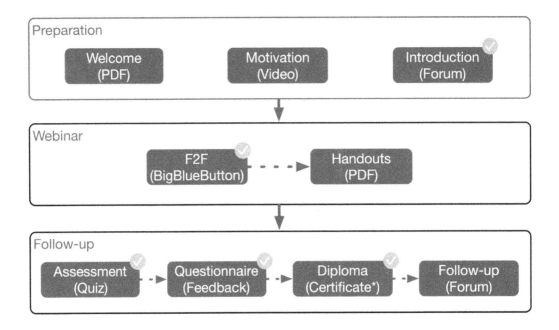

Figure 3.2 – Sample course content

During the preparation section, participants are welcome to read the provided PDF document and watch a motivational video. They are also asked to introduce themselves in a forum, so attendees can start networking before the event. While the first two activities are optional, the introduction is compulsory and a prerequisite for attending the seminar. The trainer must mark the webinar activity off before access to the handouts is granted. The follow-up comprises four activities: a certain percentage has to be achieved in the quiz to complete the assessment, and the feedback questionnaire has to be submitted before the diploma (via a third-party plugin) is issued. Access to the alumni forum will only be granted when all three activities have been completed.

Course categories

Categories act as containers for courses, and they can have subcategories, sub-subcategories, and so on. The hierarchical arrangement is similar to that of files and folders on your computer, where categories are like folders and courses are like files:

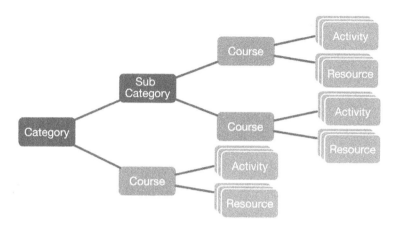

Figure 3.3 – Categories, courses, activities, and resources

Moodle comes with a default category called **Category 1**, which is sufficient to show the basics of courses. We will deal with categories in more detail in *Chapter 4, Managing Courses and Enrolments*.

> **Important note**
>
> A course always belongs to a category. It cannot belong to multiple categories and cannot be without a category.

Creating a Moodle course

The quickest way to create a new course is via **Site administration | Courses | Add a new course**. For now, let's focus on the two compulsory fields, namely **Course full name** and **Course short name**:

1. Enter a course full name (here, we used `Algorithms & Data Structures I`), which is displayed at various places in Moodle.

2. Enter a course short name (here, we used ALGDS1), which is used by default to identify the course.

Figure 3.4 – Creating a Moodle course

You can also see the already mentioned default course category, **Category 1**. To change its name or add other categories and subcategories, you need to select the respective option in the menu at the top.

For now, we will leave all the other fields empty or at their default values and save the course by clicking on the **Save and display** button at the bottom. The displayed screen shows the skeleton of the course without any content, except an announcement forum.

When you select the **Participants** tab, you will see that your account has already been added. Moodle does this automatically. However, we cannot add any further learners to the course yet, since we haven't added any users to our system. Let's rectify this situation by adding some users before returning to this screen.

Exploring Moodle users

Each user in Moodle is represented as a **user account**, which contains information about the person's profile. In the following subsections, we will briefly explain the difference between user authentication and enrolment before creating your first user account(s) and enroling these users in a course.

Authentication and enrolment

Before we start, it is vital to understand the difference between authentication and enrolment. Users must be authenticated to log in to Moodle, and **authentication** grants your users access to the system through a login where a username and password must be given. Moodle supports a significant number of authentication mechanisms, such as MS-AD, LDAP, and SAML. For now, let's work with so-called manual authentication to simplify overall user management.

Enrolment happens at a course level. However, a user must be authenticated on the system before enrolment on a course can take place. The house and key analogy might help: you need a key (authentication) to the house (Moodle), and you then need a separate key (enrolment) for each room (course).

So, a typical workflow is as follows (there are exceptions as always, but this will do for now):

1. Create your courses (and categories)
2. Create user accounts
3. Associate users with courses and assign roles

Again, this sequence demonstrates nicely how intertwined courses, users, and roles are in Moodle. Another way of looking at the difference between authentication and enrolment is how a user will get access to a course. Please bear in mind that this is a very simplistic view that ignores supported features such as external authentication, guest access, and self-enrolment:

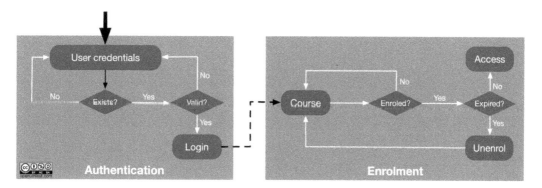

Figure 3.5 – Authentication and enrolment

During the authentication phase, a user enters their credentials (username and password), or they are entered automatically via single sign-on. The user is granted access if the account exists locally – that is, within Moodle – and the password is valid. The check will be carried out remotely if the account is held externally – for instance, in an active directory.

Once this is successful, the next phase is enrolment. If the user is enroled and the enrolment hasn't expired, access is granted to the course where resources and activities can be worked through. As mentioned before, this graphic only shows the very basics, but for now, it hopefully demonstrates the difference between authentication and enrolment. You will come across a more detailed version of these graphics in *Chapter 4, Managing Courses and Enrolments*, when we deal with various enrolment methods.

Adding a user account

To add a user account manually, go to **Site administration | Users | Add a new user**. As with courses, we will only focus on the mandatory fields, which should be self-explanatory:

1. Provide a *unique* username.

2. Set a new password. If a password policy has been set, certain rules might apply.

3. Enter the user's first name and surname.

4. Provide the user's email address. It must be unique, although there are ways around this restriction.

5. Ensure you save the account information by selecting **Create user** at the bottom of the page:

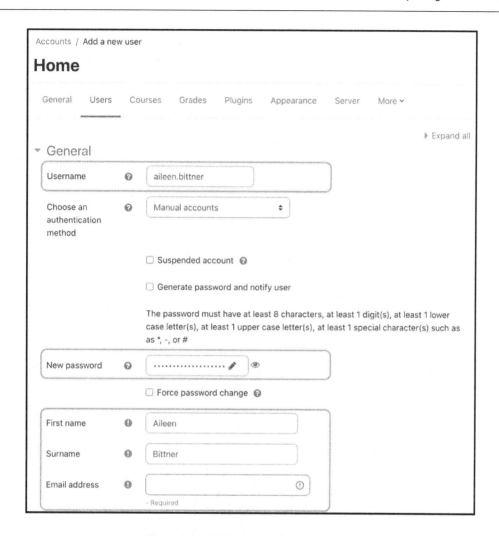

Figure 3.6 – Adding a Moodle user account

Here, a few more accounts were created via batch upload, which will be dealt with in *Chapter 5, Managing Users, Cohorts, and Authentication*. To see who has access to your Moodle system, select **Users | Browse list of users** from the **Site administration** menu, where you will see all users:

First name / Surname	Email address	City/town	Country	Last access	Edit		
Adam Stevenson	adam.stevenson@openumlaut.com	Heidelberg	Germany	Never	🗑	👁	⚙
Aileen Bittner	aileen.bittner@openumlaut.com	Paris	France	Never	🗑	👁	⚙
Alex Büchner	packt@openumlaut.com	Heidelberg	Germany	8 secs	⚙		
Alex Newton	alex.newton@openumlaut.com	Heidelberg·	Germany	Never	🗑	👁	⚙
Amanda Binnington	amanda.binnington@openumlaut.com	Heidelberg	Germany	Never	🗑	👁	⚙
Amanda hutchingson	amanda.hutchinson@openumlaut.com	Heidelberg	Germany	Never	🗑	👁	⚙
Andrew Craig	andrew.craig@openumlaut.com	Heidelberg	Germany	Never	🗑	👁	⚙
Andrew Elleray	andrew.elleray@openumlaut.com	Heidelberg	Germany	Never	🗑	👁	⚙
Andrew Greenhouse	andrew.greenhouse@openumlaut.com	Heidelberg	Germany	Never	🗑	👁	⚙
Andrew Simpson	andrew.simpson@openumlaut.com	Heidelberg	Germany	Never	🗑	👁	⚙
Andrew Wright	andrew.w.wright@openumlaut.com	Heidelberg	Germany	Never	🗑	👁	⚙
Andy Hodnett	andy.hodnett@openumlaut.com	Heidelberg	Germany	Never	🗑	👁	⚙
Andy Lowes	andy.lowles@openumlaut.com	Heidelberg	Germany	Never	🗑	👁	⚙
Anthony Bennett	antony.bennett@openumlaut.com	Heidelberg	Germany	Never	🗑	👁	⚙
Barrie Saxby	barrie.saxby@openumlaut.com	Heidelberg	Germany	Never	🗑	👁	⚙
Barry Pullin	barry.pullin@openumlaut.com	Heidelberg	Germany	Never	🗑	👁	⚙

Figure 3.7 – Moodle user accounts

Now that we have a few users on our system, let's go back to the course we created earlier and manually enrol new participants.

Enroling users

To achieve this, go to **My courses** on the **Site** menu. Why does the course appear in the list of my courses? Remember that when we created the course earlier on, Moodle automatically added our account to the course. Click on a course, select the **Participants** tab again, and click on the **Enrol users** button to add more users. A pop-up window will appear, where you select one or many users via the **Search** field:

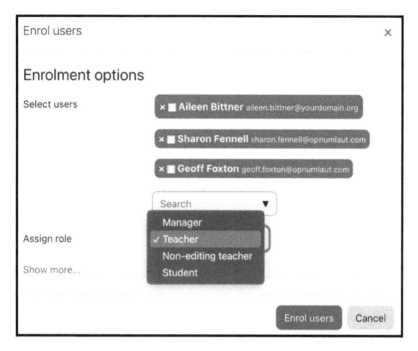

Figure 3.8 – Enroling users

You have probably spotted the **Assign role** dropdown below the list of selected user accounts. This is where you select what role the selected user(s) will be granted, which leads us to the third vertex of our triangle: *roles*.

Exploring Moodle roles

Roles define what users can or cannot see and do in your Moodle system. Moodle comes with several predefined roles – we already saw **Student** and **Teacher** – but it also allows us to create our own roles – for instance, guardians or external assessors.

Putting roles into context

Each role has a specific scope (called its **context**), defined by a set of permissions (expressed as **capabilities**). For example, a teacher is allowed to grade an assignment, whereas a student isn't. Alternatively, a student is allowed to submit an assignment, whereas a teacher isn't.

> **Important note**
>
> A role is assigned to a user in a context.

Okay, so what is a context? A context is a ring-fenced area in Moodle where roles can be assigned to users. A user can be assigned different roles in different contexts. The context can be a course, a category, an activity module, another user, a block, the home page, or Moodle itself. For instance, you are assigned the **Administrator** role for the entire system, but additionally, you might be assigned the **Teacher** role in any courses you are responsible for; or a learner will be given the **Student** role in a course, but might have been granted the **Teacher** role in a forum to act as a (temporary) moderator.

Defining roles

To give you a feel of how a role is defined, let's go to **Site administration** | **Users** | **Permissions** | **Define roles**. Click on the **Teacher** role, and after some general settings, you will see a (very) long list of capabilities:

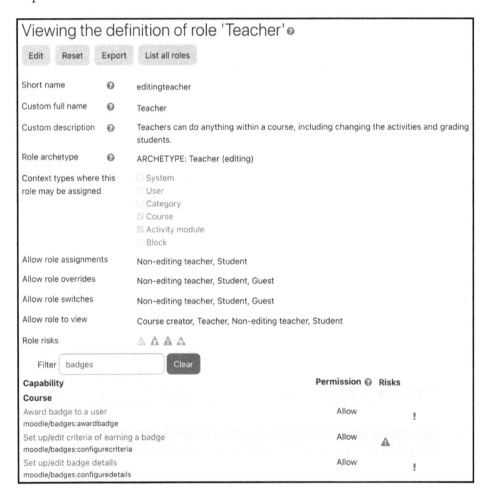

Figure 3.9 – Roles, permissions, and capabilities

We will deal with all this in greater detail in *Chapter 6, Managing Permissions, Roles, and Capabilities*, so there's no need to panic!

For now, we only want to stick with the example we used throughout the chapter. Now that we know what roles are, we can slightly rephrase what we have done. Instead of saying, "We have enroled the user `aileen.bittner` in the course `ALGDS1` as a student," we would say, "We have assigned the student role to the user `aileen.bittner` in the context of the course `ALGDS1`."

Roles are critical when granting and denying permissions to users. However, try sticking with the preconfigured roles in Moodle when you get started, since they have proven to be sufficient in most setups. You can always adjust roles at a later stage, if or when required.

This concludes the section on permissions, completing the triangle of courses, users, and roles. Being equipped with this knowledge, you are now ready to take on the three core concepts in more detail.

Summary

This chapter briefly introduced the concepts of Moodle courses, users, and roles. We also saw how central they are to Moodle and how they are inherently intertwined. Any one of these concepts simply cannot exist without the other two, which is something you should remember throughout.

Just to recap, the three key takeaways from this chapter are as follows:

- Courses comprise activities and resources, and this is where your students' learning takes place. Courses are organized hierarchically into categories.

- Users are represented by an account; access is granted to the system by authentication and courses by enrolment.

- Roles grant permissions for certain features to certain users in certain contexts, such as courses.

If you haven't fully understood any of the three areas, don't worry. The intention was to provide you with a high-level overview of the three core components and touch upon the basics.

There are chapters dedicated to each concept, hopefully clarifying any outstanding issues and going significantly into them in more detail. In the next chapter, we will tackle courses and the management thereof.

4

Managing Courses and Enrolments

Moodle stores learning resources and activities in courses, which is the topic of this chapter, which has been divided into two main parts: **course management** and **course enrolments**.

In the first part of this chapter, you will learn about the following aspects of managing courses and course categories:

- Organizing courses into categories and subcategories
- Creating and managing courses
- Adding custom course fields
- Dealing with course requests
- Managing courses in bulk

In the second part of the chapter, we will cover different ways of enrolling users in courses. The enrolment mechanisms that will be covered are the following:

- Internal enrolment (manual, self, and guest)
- Cohort enrolment and synchronization
- Database-driven enrolment (LDAP, external databases, flat files, and IMS Enterprise files)
- Meta courses
- Payment-driven enrolment (payment accounts and gateways, such as PayPal)

The following diagram shows a high-level overview of how the mentioned topics (courses, categories, and enrolment methods) are connected:

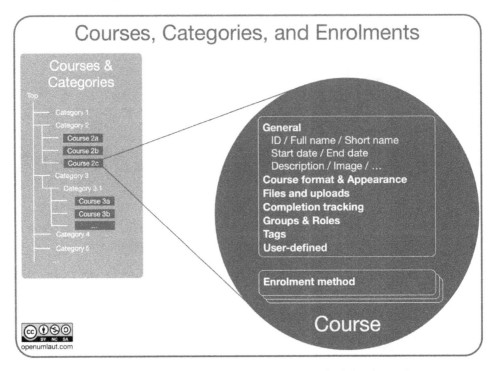

Figure 4.1 – Courses, categories, and enrolments – a high-level overview

By the end of this chapter, you will know everything about the management of courses and categories. Furthermore, you will be able to select and configure the correct enrolment method(s) for the Moodle system in your organization.

Let's get going with course management in general and course categories in particular.

Organizing courses into categories

The role of the Moodle administrator is to manage categories and courses. This section provides an overview of course categories and introduces a running example before introducing all aspects of category management: **creation**, **arrangement**, and **removal**.

Providing an overview of course categories

In the previous chapter, we briefly introduced the concept of categories, which act as containers for courses. They can have subcategories, which can further have sub-subcategories, and so on.

There are different ways of organizing course and category hierarchies – for instance, by department, subject area, or semester. The following figure shows two different category hierarchies representing the same organization:

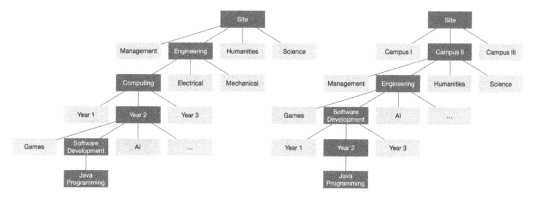

Figure 4.2 – Example category hierarchies

As you can see, each hierarchy represents the same information but in different forms. There is no right or wrong way to organize your categories and courses. The structure depends on the following parameters:

- The size of your organization
- The number of courses you offer
- The type of courses you run
- The frequency of course commencement (once a term, once a year, roll-on/roll-off, etc.)

It is highly advisable to get the structure right the first time around, as changing it is time-consuming and potentially confusing for the users. Also, try to plan ahead, thinking about whether the structure will work in the future – for example, when changing from one academic year to another (see also *Chapter 16, Avoiding Sleepless Nights – Moodle Backup and Restore*, where we look at end-of-year procedures).

As mentioned before, different organizations apply different categorization approaches. Some examples of the category levels are as follows:

- **Campus | Department/School | Year | Subject**
- **Year of entry | Topic | Subject**
- **Customer | Subject | Proficiency level**
- **Trainer | Module**
- **Course repository | Topic**

Sometimes, deep levels of categories can be off-putting, as their management is cumbersome. However, remember that only you, as the administrator, will see the entire category structure. The students and teachers will usually only see the courses that they are enrolled in or to which they are assigned unless they browse the full course index.

> **Important note**
>
> Developing a suitable naming convention for courses and categories is highly recommended – it simplifies maintenance and reduces unnecessary complexity.

If you require a complete separation of organizational divisions, for instance, customers or self-contained business entities in an enterprise, course categories are usually not a suitable tool. Instead, you might want to consider Moodle Workplace, which supports multi-tenancy, including entirely isolated entities with their own look and feel, structure, users, and learning spaces (see *Chapter 20, Supporting Multi-Tenancy*, for details). More information on Moodle Workplace can be found at `moodle.com/solutions/workplace` or in the title *Corporate Learning with Moodle Workplace* by Packt Publishing.

Now that we have shown the flexibility and versatility of category hierarchies, creating and managing your course categories is the next step.

Managing course categories

Once you have planned your category hierarchy structure, it is time to represent the organization in Moodle. Categories are administered in **Site administration** | **Courses** | **Manage courses and categories**, as shown in the following screenshot:

Figure 4.3 – Course categories

Initially, Moodle contains a single category called **Category 1**. The preceding screenshot shows that the default category has been renamed to **Computing** and three subcategories for years one to three have already been created.

In addition to the **Course categories** part of the screen, there are up to two more parts: one shows the list of **Courses** of the selected category, and one displays **Course details** once a course has been selected. This arrangement is depicted in the following diagram:

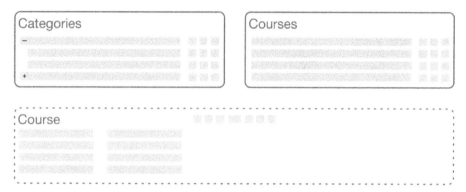

Figure 4.4 – Managing courses and categories

All three parts will be shown underneath each other on very narrow screens (tablets or smartphones). You can switch between the three views via the **Viewing** dropdown and show **Course categories and courses** (default), only **Course categories**, or only **Courses**:

Figure 4.5 – Managing courses and categories

Now that you are familiar with the category management interface, let's add our first course category to your Moodle site.

Adding course categories

Click on the **Create new category** button or go directly to **Site administration** | **Courses** | **Add a category** and enter a new name in the **Category name** field to add a new category. The **Parent category** drop-down menu indicates the course's location in the hierarchy. We will leave this set to **Top** and come back to it shortly. It is good practice to provide the optional **Category ID number** and **Description** information; the former is used when automating certain tasks, such as user uploads, while the latter is, for example, shown in the course index:

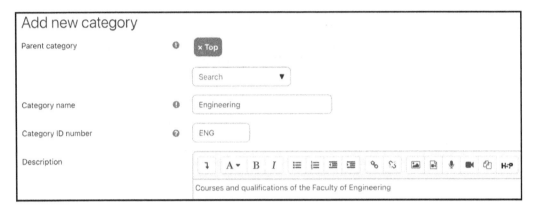

Figure 4.6 – Adding a course category

Next up is the creation of course subcategories to create a category hierarchy.

Creating course subcategories

As mentioned earlier, to improve the organization of courses, Moodle allows the creation of subcategories. You can create a subcategory by choosing an existing category and then selecting **Create new subcategory** from the drop-down menu in the options or adding a new category (as shown in the preceding screenshot) and moving it into a parent category using the drop-down menus on the **Course categories** page. For example, create the **Computing Year 1**, **Computing Year 2**, and **Computing Year 3** subcategories in **Computing**, and then move them into **Computing** using the drop-down menu. Alternatively, you can select the correct parent category when creating the subcategory.

So far, we have created categories and subcategories. Now, let's look at how to rearrange categories in case you need to modify your hierarchy.

Organizing courses and categories

The logical arrangement of categories has three main purposes:

- The category hierarchy or the order of categories is displayed on various pages in Moodle – for example, when you need to specify the category to which a course has to be restored.

- Access permissions can be granted to a category and all its subcategories – for instance, all users from the Math department have access to the Math category.

- Easier maintenance of the category structure. This only applies to the site admins and category administrators.

There are two operations to (re-)organize categories: **sorting** and **moving**.

Let's start with **moving** categories around. The easiest way to change the position of categories is by using the standard up and down arrows. A more flexible way is to select one or many categories and then select a new location from the **Move selected categories to** drop-down before pressing the **Move** button. When you move a parent category, all the child categories will move with it:

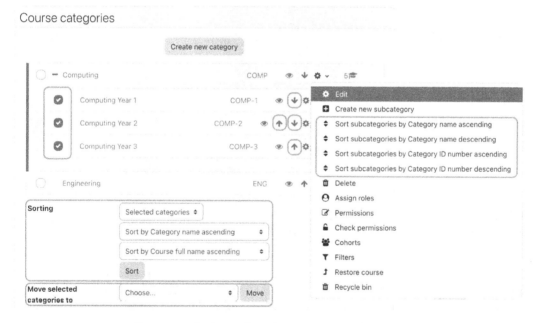

Figure 4.7 – Sorting and moving categories and courses

You have various options to sort categories. From the **Sorting** menu, you can choose to order by **All categories**, by **Selected category**, or by **This category** (which represents the current one). Categories can be sorted by their **name** or **ID number** in ascending or descending order, and they can also be unsorted (that is, you can put them in the original order when they were created). Once you have selected your option, press the **Sort** button.

Alternatively, you can expedite this process by selecting a sorting option from the pull-down menu for each parent category. From the options menu, several actions can be triggered, and they are as follows in the table:

Option	Description	Chapter
Edit	Modify category details	
Create new subcategory	It does exactly what it says on the tin	
Sort ...	(Re-)ordering of categories	
Delete	Remove category after choosing some options	
Assign roles	Assign category roles	6
Permissions	Manage permissions in category	6
Check permissions	Check permissions in category	6
Cohorts	Manage category cohorts	5
Filters	Link to course filters	9
Restore course	Restore a course in this category	16
Recycle bin	Retrieve deleted categories and courses	2

Figure 4.8 – Category options

You can also hide categories using the eye icon (such as **COMP-3** in our case), which is usually done when courses within a category are undergoing development or if you want to create an experimental area (or sandpit) that is not to be seen by anybody without permission to see hidden courses. Hidden categories are only visible to site administrators or those with the `moodle/course:viewhiddencourses` capability.

Once you select a category, it shows all its courses in the course area, and depending on your device and screen size, this can be to its right or underneath the categories area.

While you can use the up and down arrows to reorganize courses, you can use the crossbar at the left and drag each course to its new location – a very handy feature, indeed. Courses can be sorted in ascending and descending order by their **full name**, **short name**, **ID number**, and **time created** information, and you also have an option to modify the number of courses shown per page. Hiding and moving selected courses works in the same way as it does for categories:

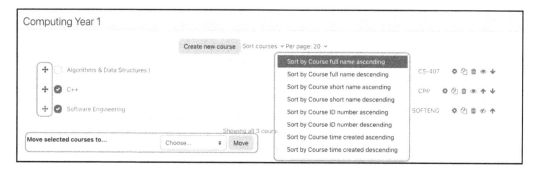

Figure 4.9 – Moving and sorting courses

To sort courses across categories, you must choose the **All categories** option from the **Sorting** menu in the **Course categories** section. The ordering options are the same as in the context menu shown in the previous screenshot.

Now that we have dealt with creating, modifying, and rearranging course categories, only one operation is missing: removing.

Deleting course categories

When deleting a course category using the respective option in the drop-down menu, you must decide **What to do** with courses and subcategories if any exist:

- **Move contents to another category**: You will need to select one from the **Move into** option.

- **Delete all – cannot be undone**: This step cannot be undone!

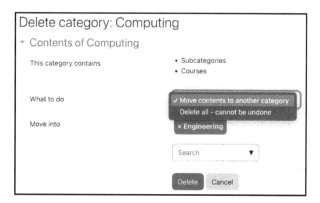

Figure 4.10 – Deleting a course category

This concludes the section on managing course categories. The next step is to move down a level from categories to courses and how to create them, which we will deal with in the next section.

Creating courses

Courses are fundamental in Moodle. Learners and trainers spend most of their time in courses since this is where teaching, learning, and collaboration take place.

> **Important note**
>
> We have mentioned it before, but because it is critical to administering Moodle, here it goes again: Moodle is a course-centric system!

Before we start creating our first course, let's briefly look at a typical course creation workflow.

Course creation workflows

Different types of organizations offer different types of courses. Courses in a school are usually linked to a syllabus, whereas courses a commercial online provider offers are driven by a catalog or provided on an ad hoc basis. However, several steps are common in most course creation workflows, shown in the following diagram, where the top row shows the tasks to be carried out and the bottom row the role that is usually responsible:

Figure 4.11 – A typical course creation workflow

The steps are as follows:

1. **Course request**: Somebody requests a new course, which is often driven by a syllabus or can be an ad hoc requirement by a teacher.

2. **Create course**: The course skeleton can be created manually or automatically; both options will be dealt with after introducing this course creation workflow.

3. **Notify teacher**: Letting the requester know that the course has been added. Again, this can either be done manually or automatically.

4. **Adjust settings**: The new course owner responsible for the course will add any missing information – for example, the course description.

5. **Populate course**: The course requester is handed over an empty course or a skeleton based on a course template. It is up to the teacher to populate the course with learning content, activities, and interdependencies.

6. **Enrol users**: There are various options for adding users to a course. This can either be an automated process driven by the admin, done manually by the teacher, or, depending on your setup, by the learners themselves. We have dedicated the entire second part of this chapter to course enrolments, so hang in there for now.

7. **Start course**: At some stage, the course will be let loose into the wild, either from a specific start date (for instance, the beginning of the semester) or flexibly with a more dynamic setup (for example, self-paced online courses).

This process is not written in stone and might look different in your organization. Additional steps might have been added, or the order of specific tasks might be different, such as when enrolment occurs. However, the steps outlined are usually present in most course creation workflows. OK, enough processes and procedures; let's add the first course to your Moodle system.

Creating a new course

Once the **Create new course** button has been pressed, Moodle directs you to the settings page where course details must be entered. When we created our first course, we already came across this screen in *Chapter 3, Exploring Courses, Users, and Roles*.

The following settings are available in the **General** and **Description** sections:

Setting	Description
Course full name*	The course's full name is displayed at the top of the screen and in the list of courses, for example, on the dashboard.
Course short name*	Many organizations have a short form for referring to a course. The field is used in several places where the full name is inappropriate, such as in the navigation, when uploading users in batch files, or as a subject line in email communication.
Course category*	The category to which the course belongs. See previous section for details.
Course visibility	If set to **Hide**, the course won't appear in course listings, and students cannot access it. Other than the course teacher(s) and administrators (and anyone with permission to view hidden courses), no one will be able to view it in any course listings.
Enable download course content	If enabled, the course content can be downloaded by users with the capability `moodle/course:downloadcoursecontent` (by default, students and teachers). The feature has to be activated in **Site administration | Courses | Download course content**, where a maximum size per file can also be specified.
Course start/end date	See the following details on date fields.
Relative dates mode	See the following details on date fields.
Course ID number	The course code (often used in conjunction with external systems).
Course summary	Writing a concise paragraph explaining what the course is about is recommended. The summary is displayed when a user clicks on the information icon, and when the course appears in a list.
Course image	You have the option to upload an image, which will be shown in the course listing. This is highly recommended to make the course catalogue more attractive.

* Compulsory field

Figure 4.12 – Course settings

By default, the **Course full name**, **Course short name**, **Course category**, **Course ID number**, and **Course summary** fields can be modified by a teacher. You can disallow this by changing the appropriate permissions for the **Teacher** role by navigating to **Site administration | Users | Permissions | Define roles** (search for capabilities starting with moodle/course:change using the **Filter** box). *Chapter 6, Managing Permissions, Roles, and Capabilities*, will deal with this in more detail.

Course formats

The following section in the course settings lets you choose a **Course format** option. A course format dictates how course content will be presented to the learner. Moodle ships with four formats, but more can be installed (see the *Installing third-party add-ons* section in *Chapter 8, Understanding Moodle Plugins*). Once you have selected a course format, the screen refreshes to load the respective course format settings:

- **Single-activity format**: This only shows the selected activity in a course – for instance, a SCORM package, assignment, forum, quiz, and so on
- **Social format**: This is one main (social) forum, which is listed on the main course page – for example, a notice board
- **Topics format**: This is similar to the weekly format, except that each week is called a topic, and no time restriction applies
- **Weekly format**: In this format, a course is organized week-by-week, with a start and a finish date

You can specify the default course format for new courses by going to **Site administration | Courses | Course default settings**.

Course dates

While most course fields are (almost) self-explanatory, the date-related settings probably need more explanation, especially when used in conjunction with the **Weekly format** option just mentioned:

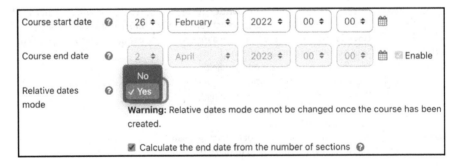

Figure 4.13 – Course date settings

Somewhat surprisingly, Moodle course dates don't allow or restrict course access; instead, **Course start date** and **Course end date** affect whether course logs are displayed, the heading of each topic when run in **Weekly format**, and the status of a user's course (in progress, future, or past).

By default, course dates are absolute; the start and end dates are the same for each user. Moodle also supports relative course dates, where each user is given an individual start and end date: the relative start date is equal to the user's enrolment date unless the enrolment took place before the course begins, in which case, the individual start date is the one that has been specified manually, that is, the course start date.

> **Important note**
> **Relative dates mode** cannot be changed once the course has been created.

The following table summarizes the discussed date-related settings in a course:

	Start date	End date
Absolute dates	Manual	Manual / Open
Relative dates	Enrolment date Start date	Dynamic

Figure 4.14 – Course date settings

The individual **course status** is calculated as follows, taking into account the dates and modes we have discussed:

- **In progress**: start date ≤ today [≤ end date]
- **Past**: today > end date
- **Future**: today < start date

The **Calculate the end date from the number of sections** option only appears when you run the course in **Weekly format**. If enabled, the course end date is calculated automatically based on the course start date (relative or absolute) and the number of sections or weeks. If course sections or weeks are added or removed, the course end date is adjusted automatically. If this checkbox is ticked, the course end date cannot be set manually.

Note that at the time of writing, **Relative dates mode** is an experimental setting, as it has not yet been implemented in all activities (such as Quiz) or features (for instance, restrict access). It must be enabled via the **Enable course relative dates** setting in **Site administration | Development | Experimental | Experimental settings**.

Other course fields

The remaining options in the **Appearance**, **Files and uploads**, **Completion tracking**, and **Groups** sections are as follows:

Setting	Description
Force theme	The theme to be applied for this course is forced through this option. This requires course themes to be enabled in **Site administration	Appearance	Themes	Theme Settings** (see *Chapter 7, Enhancing Moodle's Look & Feel*).
Force language	If set, the selected language is used throughout the course and cannot be changed.
Number of announcements	Determines how many recent items appear on your course home page in the news section (if any). Set this to 0 if the default news forum shown in a course should not be re-created automatically once deleted!
Show gradebook to students	Determines whether students are shown the **Grades** link. You can set this to **No** and still grade your activities.
Show activity reports	Determines whether students can see their own activity reports (see *Chapter 12, Gaining Insights Through Moodle Reporting and Analytics*) via their profile page.
Show activity dates	Determines whether activity dates are shown below each activity in addition to being displayed on the activity page.
Maximum upload size	Limits the size of a file a user can upload into this course.
Enable completion tracking	Once completion tracking is enabled sitewide (**Advanced features**), it has to be activated at the course level.
Show activity completion conditions	Determines whether activity completion conditions are shown below each activity in addition to being displayed on the activity page. **Enable completion tracking** must be enabled.
Group mode	This sets the group mode of the course to: • **No groups**: There are no subgroups. Everyone is part of one big community or class • **Separate groups**: Users can only see their own group, while other groups are invisible • **Visible groups**: Users work in their own group but can also see other groups
Force group mode	If set, the selected group mode is used for every activity, and group settings in individual activities are ignored. Forcing group mode is useful when the same course is run multiple times with separate batches of students. Also, if group mode is forced and set to **No groups**, the **Groups** link is hidden in the course administration menu.
Default grouping	If grouping is enabled and used within the course, the grouping to be used as default can be selected.

Figure 4.15 – Course settings

Once a course has been created, you can assign users to various roles in the course (such as enrolling students and assigning teachers); we have briefly covered this in *Chapter 3*, *Exploring Courses, Users, and Roles*, and have dedicated the entire *Roles management* section in *Chapter 6*, *Managing Permissions, Roles, and Capabilities*, to roles, and will therefore be ignoring the **Role renaming** part for now. The same holds for an optional **Tags** section, which is dealt with in *Chapter 9*, *Configuring Educational Features*.

Internally, each course is given an ID. As mentioned before, a course always belongs to a single category and cannot belong to multiple categories or be without a category. However, the home page (`course id = 1`) is one exception to this rule. Internally, the home page is treated as a course that neither belongs to a category nor can be deleted.

You can specify the course default settings for most parameters when creating new courses; you can find these in **Site administration | Courses | Course default settings**. The fields and values are identical to those described in the preceding screenshots.

All course settings you have come across so far are part of Core Moodle. Custom course fields can be added to extend the list of options covered in the next section.

Custom course fields

Course fields in Moodle are organized into course categories such as **General**, **Course format**, or **Appearance**. Additional categories can be created, and user-defined fields can then be placed within these new categories, which teachers can configure. You find this feature by navigating to **Site administration | Courses | Course custom fields**:

Figure 4.16 – Custom course fields

In our demo system, we have already created a category called **Curriculum** with four course fields: **Notional learning hours**, **Course type**, **Link to syllabus**, and **Curriculum update**. To create a new category, click the **Add a new category** button and rename the default name (**Other fields**) using the standard **Edit** icon. Once a category has been created, five types of profile fields can be added via the **Add a new custom field** dropdown menu:

- **Checkbox**: The values are true or false
- **Date and time**: Contains the date and an optional time field

- **Dropdown menu**: Selection of a single value from a predefined list
- **Short text**: A single line of text or a number
- **Text area**: Multiline formatted text

At **Site administration | Plugins | Custom fields | Manage custom field types,** you can hide or uninstall custom field types. The latter is only recommended for field types that have been installed; for those, you might also find settings that do not exist for the five described core types.

Once you have chosen your field type, you are taken to a settings screen for that field, which contains three sections:

- **General** settings apply to all custom fields
- **Field settings** contain parameters that apply only to the chosen field type
- **Common course custom field settings** deal with permissions and visibility

Let's look at these three sections in a little more detail.

The **General** section contains the following fields: the **Name** field is the label displayed in the course settings and the **Short name** field is a unique field identifier. An optional **Description** field can be given, which is displayed underneath the field in the course settings. If the field is obligatory, the **Required** option must be set to **Yes**. If the value entered needs to be unique, the **Unique data** field must be changed accordingly:

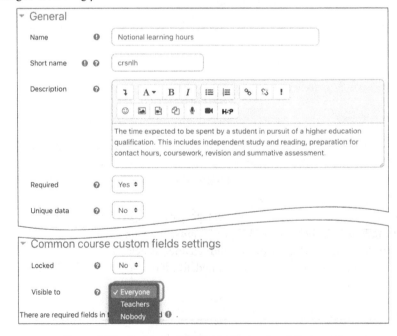

Figure 4.17 – Custom course fields (General and Common)

In addition to the general field settings, specific settings have to be provided for each profile field type:

- **Checkbox**: This type has only a single setting. It specifies whether the checkbox will be **Checked by default** in new user profiles or not.

- **Date and time**: The **Minimum value** (the start date – by default, today) and **Maximum value** (end date – by default, also today) settings can be enabled and specified. An optional time field can be included by checking the **Include time** option.

- **Dropdown menu**: For this type, a list of **Menu options (one per line)** and an optional **Default value** must be provided. The list consists of a single item per line. If you wish to allow empty values, leave the first entry empty. In the following screenshot, three options (**Syllabus**, **Extra-curricular**, and **None**) have been entered, with **Syllabus** being the default:

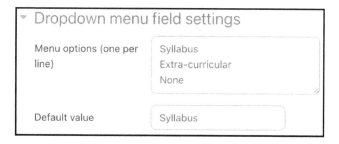

Figure 4.18 – Custom course fields in the dropdown settings

- **Short text**: For this type, the **Default value**, **Form input size** (as in, the textbox width), and **Maximum number of characters** details must be provided. Additionally, you must specify whether the field is a **Password field** type, which will lead to masking being turned on if enabled. The **Link** field lets you create dynamic links, where $$ represents the parameter that will be replaced with the entered text. In the following screenshot, we have specified `https://yourorganization/syllabus/$$`. The transformed link will be shown in the list of available courses or all courses. **Link target** specifies where this link will be opened once it's selected:

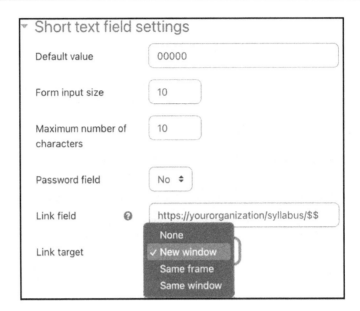

Figure 4.19 – Custom course field in the short text field settings

- **Text area**: This type allows users to define an optional **Default value** in a free-form textbox.

There are only two settings in the **Common course custom field** settings. The field can be **Locked**; that is, the teacher is prevented from modifying it. This option is useful when you have a central system for course management containing data such as internal course codes, which nobody should change. Locking is often used in conjunction with one of the following three **Visible to** options:

- **Everyone** (default): This is used for course information that teachers and students can see, and potentially users outside the course

- **Teacher**: Fields containing sensitive information students should not see, which can be as trivial as the teacher's course resources for preparation

- **Nobody**: This is typically set by an administrator who wants to hold data on the courses, such as the aforementioned internal course code

Once all the required fields have been added, the order in which they will be displayed in the user profile can be changed using the up and down arrows.

The management of custom course fields has been described in great detail here. The same mechanism is available for other custom parameters, such as the user profile or appointment custom fields (Moodle Workplace only).

So far, we have created courses manually, a potentially time-consuming and error-prone process. To tackle these shortcomings, you have two options – course requests and bulk upload – which we will cover in the subsequent two subsections. Let's start by partly delegating the task to teachers using course requests.

Course requests – enabling teachers to ask for new courses

Only administrators or course creators (or any other role with course creation rights) have permission to create new courses. Moodle offers a course requesting facility to streamline the procedure for requesting courses, especially in larger organizations. This feature has to be enabled by going to **Site administration** | **Courses** | **Course request**.

You must specify the **Default category for course requests** setting, which controls where the courses created upon request will be placed. You can also disable **Prevent category selection** if your users are familiar with the course category structure. As the courses have to be approved, you can specify the **Course request notification** recipient(s):

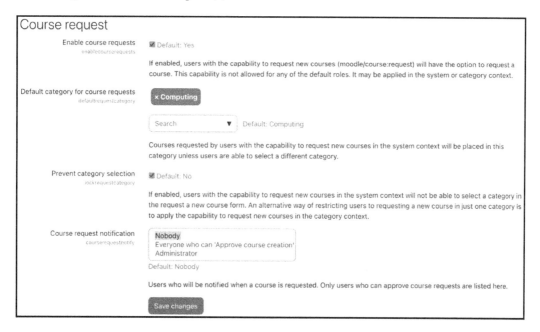

Figure 4.20 – Course requests

Once the feature is enabled, each teacher can request new courses (via the **Request a course** option on the **My courses** screen). The information that has to be provided by the requestee is as follows:

- **Course full name**
- **Course short name**

- **Course category** (if selected above)
- **Summary**
- **Reasons for course request**

A new item, **Courses | Pending requests**, appears in the **Site administration** section. On selection, the list of requested courses is shown, which you can then **Approve** or **Reject** by selecting the appropriate button:

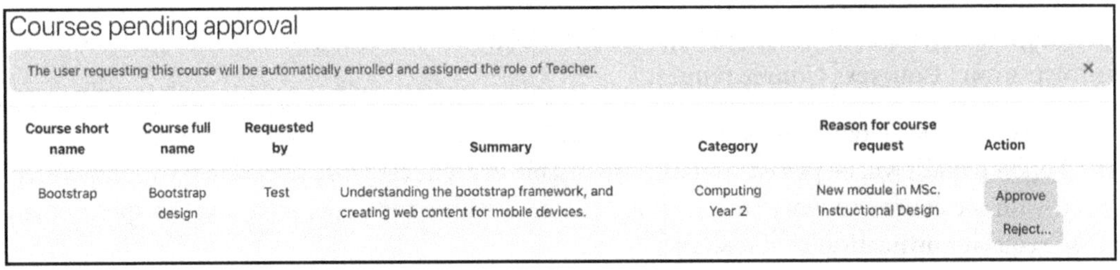

Courses pending approval

The user requesting this course will be automatically enrolled and assigned the role of Teacher.

Course short name	Course full name	Requested by	Summary	Category	Reason for course request	Action
Bootstrap	Bootstrap design	Test	Understanding the bootstrap framework, and creating web content for mobile devices.	Computing Year 2	New module in MSc. Instructional Design	Approve Reject...

Figure 4.21 – Course approval

When you approve a course, the familiar course settings screen appears. This screen already contains the provided course values specified in the system settings. Furthermore, users who have requested the course will be automatically enrolled, and, by default, they will be assigned the teacher role. If you reject a course, a reason must be given, which is emailed to the requester.

Course requests only semi-automate the course creation process because you still have to approve or reject them manually. Uploading courses in bulk introduces a versatile way to create, modify, and remove courses without further intervention.

Managing courses in bulk

So far, all the operations in this chapter have been carried out manually. However, this process should be automated in an organization with many courses and categories. In **Site administration | Courses | Upload courses**, Moodle provides us with a powerful tool to manage courses in bulk. This not only lets us create new courses but it also works for updating and deleting courses, importing courses, and restoring courses from backups and course templates.

To create courses in batch mode, you will need to create a CSV file, which contains the following fields (the complete list can be found at `docs.moodle.org/en/Upload_courses`):

- **Course information fields**: These are identical to the fields on the course settings page – for example, short name, full name, and ID number. The content of each course information field has to conform to its type; for example, a date field has to be provided with a date value. Custom course fields are fully supported and must be labeled with `customfield_<shortname>` – for instance, `customfield_duration`.

To specify the category in which the course has to be placed, you have three options (in order of precedence): `category` (internal ID), `category_idnumber` (ID number), and `category_path`, where a forward slash surrounded by spaces must separate subdirectories (`[category]<space>/<space>[subcategory]`...).

The following is a sample file demonstrating all three options:

```
shortname,fullname,category,category_idnumber,category_
path
course1,Course One,4,,
course2,Course Two,,COMP-1,
course3,Course Three,,,Computing / Computing - Year 1
```

> **Important note**
>
> Categories cannot be created in batch mode; they must exist! Alternatively, use MOOSH, a Moodle Shell, explained in more detail in *Chapter 17, Working with Moodle Admin Tools*.

- **Enrolment fields**: These let you enable and configure enrolment plugins. We will be dealing with enrolments further down in this section, so here is a sample to configure self-enrolment:

```
shortname,fullname,category,enrolment_1,enrolment_1_
startdate
course1,Course One,4,self,06/10/14
course2,Course Two,4,manual,06/10/14
course3,Course Three,4,manual,06/10/14
```

At the time of writing, only the manual, self, guest, and cohort enrolment methods are supported by course uploads. To monitor progress on this missing subfeature, monitor `MDL-73838` in the bug tracker database.

- **Role renaming**: This provides a means to rename standard roles. We will deal with roles in *Chapter 5, Managing Users, Cohorts, and Authentication*.

In addition to these three field types, so-called course action fields can be specified to perform an action other than creating courses:

- **delete**: "1" to delete a course.

- **rename**: Add a new course short name.

- **backupfile**: The absolute path of a backup file (.mbz), used as a source. This can potentially lead to performance problems (check out $CFG-> keeptempdirectoriesonbackup in *Appendix*, *Configuration Settings*).

- **templatecourse**: The shortname of an existing course used as a source.

- **reset**: "1" to reset the course and remove any user data.

Once a file has been uploaded, you will have to change the **CSV delimiter** and **Encoding** file format settings if they are incorrect. You can further specify the number of **Preview rows**. Then, the following import options can be configured (depending on the upload mode selected, some settings will be shown or hidden):

Option	Description
Upload mode	There are four self-explanatory options whether courses will be created or updated: • Create new courses only, skip existing ones • Create all, increment if needed (see templates further down) • Create new courses, or update the existing ones • Only update the existing ones If any of the latter two options are selected, the following settings will become available.
Update mode	The mode specifies what data source will be used for updating fields: • No changes • Update with CSV data only • Update with CSV data only and defaults • Fill in missing items from CSV and defaults
Allow deletes	Determines whether the delete field will be accepted or not
Allow renames	Determines whether the rename field will be accepted or not
Allow resets	Determines whether the reset field will be accepted or not

Figure 4.22 – Uploading courses

The counterpart on the screen looks as follows:

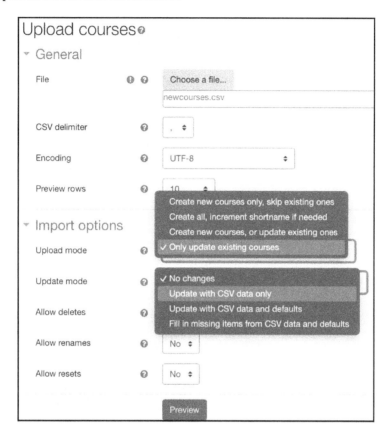

Figure 4.23 – Uploading courses

When in preview mode, you will see these import options again and the **Course process** settings, **Default course values**, and, if custom course fields have been added, **Default values** for each custom course category. The latter two are the values used if not provided in the CSV file and an update mode is chosen that supports defaults. The course process supports two types of templates, which require some explanation:

- **Course name templates**: If the CSV file does not contain a shortname column, you can use template syntax to set the name, depending on either idnumber (%i) or fullname (%f). For instance, the given **Template to generate a shortname** is Packt %i with **Upload mode** set to **Create all, increment shortname if needed** would result in the three courses, Packt_1, Packt_2, and Packt_3, with our previously used input file.

- **Course content templates**: You can either specify the absolute path of a Moodle backup file or the short name of an existing course as a content template for the newly-created course. We will be dealing with backup in *Chapter 16, Avoiding Sleepless Nights – Moodle Backup and Restore*, so for now, let's assume that they have a suffix, `.mbz`. Suppose either option is chosen and you have opted to update existing courses. In that case, you should select the **Allow resets** and **Reset course after upload** options to remove any user data that has been added in the source course:

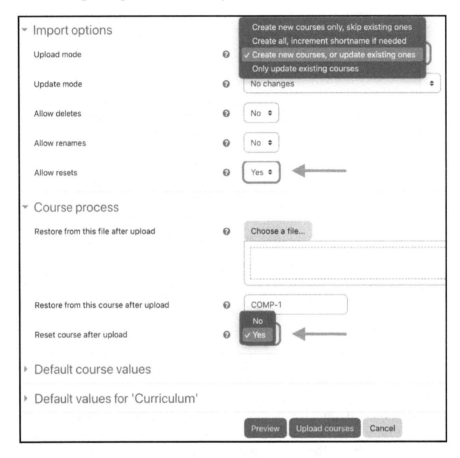

Figure 4.24 – Uploading courses

After selecting the **Preview** button, the sneak-peak list at the top of the screen will be updated based on the values chosen, which is an excellent way to trial and error your way through your CSV file before uploading it. Once courses have been uploaded, you will see the summary of results:

```
shortname,fullname,category,category_idnumber,category_path,
enrolment_1,enrolment_1_startdate,delete
packt1,Course One,1,,,self,26/02/22,0
packt2,Course Two,,1,,self,26/02/22,0
packt3,Course Three,,|,1,self,26/02/22,0
packt4,Course Four,1,,,,,
COMP-3,,,,,,,1
```

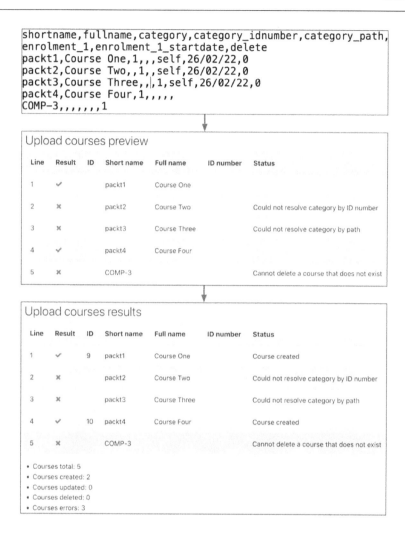

Upload courses preview

Line	Result	ID	Short name	Full name	ID number	Status
1	✓		packt1	Course One		
2	✗		packt2	Course Two		Could not resolve category by ID number
3	✗		packt3	Course Three		Could not resolve category by path
4	✓		packt4	Course Four		
5	✗		COMP-3			Cannot delete a course that does not exist

Upload courses results

Line	Result	ID	Short name	Full name	ID number	Status
1	✓	9	packt1	Course One		Course created
2	✗		packt2	Course Two		Could not resolve category by ID number
3	✗		packt3	Course Three		Could not resolve category by path
4	✓	10	packt4	Course Four		Course created
5	✗		COMP-3			Cannot delete a course that does not exist

- Courses total: 5
- Courses created: 2
- Courses updated: 0
- Courses deleted: 0
- Courses errors: 3

Figure 4.25 – Uploading courses

There is also a CLI tool to perform course uploads from the command line. You can find it in `admin/tool/uploadcourse/cli/uploadcourse.php`. You will see all the supported parameters by calling the `help` mode:

```
sudo /usr/bin/php admin/tool/uploadcourse/cli/uploadcourse.php
--help
```

Here is an example of its usage:

```
sudo /usr/bin/php admin/tool/uploadcourse/cli/uploadcourse.php
--mode=createall --updatemode=dataordefaults --file=./courses.
csv --delimiter=comma
```

There is an entire section on the Moodle CLI in *Chapter 17, Working with Moodle Admin Tools*.

This completes the first part of this chapter, where we dealt with the management of courses and categories. The second part deals with how users get access to courses via enrolment.

Understanding course enrolment

In the introductory chapter, *Chapter 3, Exploring Courses, Users, and Roles*, we have already touched upon enrolment. Now, we will go into more detail and look at the different mechanisms that can be set up to grant users access to courses. You may recall the basic enrolment workflow presented in the third chapter. Let's have a look at a more detailed version:

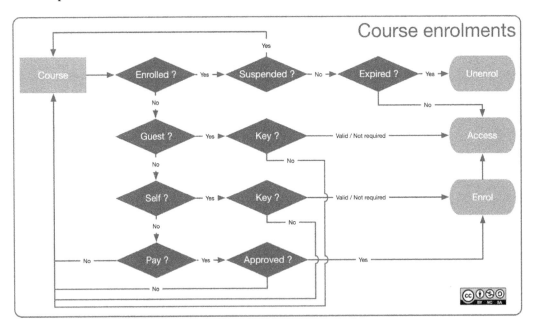

Figure 4.26 – Forms of enrolment

Let's start from the top left, where a user attempts to access a course. Access will be granted if the enrolment has already taken place. If the user is suspended, access will be denied. If enrolment has expired, the user will be unenrolled; otherwise, access will be granted. If the user is not enrolled, Moodle checks whether guest or self-enrolment access is allowed. If either is the case, the enrolment key will be checked. If the key is correct or not required, enrolment will take place for self-enrolment, and access will be granted. As a last option, Moodle checks whether a payment is accepted and, if approved, the user will be enrolled in the courses. You might want to return to this diagram when dealing with a specific enrolment mechanism.

Students need to be given access to a course before they are allowed to use it – or, in Moodle-speak, users need to be assigned a role in the course context. They can be assigned the role automatically via cohorts or external enrolment facilities, by self-enrolling, or manually via the **Participants** tab inside the course.

> **Important note**
> Granting access to a course is performed via an enrolment mechanism.

The actual enrolment of students does not require administrator rights and is a task that teachers can carry out. The role of the administrator is to set up the enrolment mechanisms available sitewide. Moodle supports a wide range of enrolment options, discussed in the remainder of the chapter.

You can access the course enrolments configuration page via **Site administration | Plugins | Enrolments | Manage enrolment plugins**. Each supported enrolment mechanism is represented by an enrolment plugin that can be enabled and configured separately:

Manage enrol plugins
Available course enrolment plugins

Name	Instances / enrolments	Version	Enable	Up/Down	Settings	Test settings	Uninstall
Manual enrolments	3 / 74	2021052500	👁	↓	Settings		
Guest access	3 / 0	2021052500	👁	↑ ↓	Settings		Uninstall
Self enrolment	3 / 1	2021052500	👁	↑ ↓	Settings		Uninstall
Cohort sync	1 / 28	2021052500	👁	↑ ↓	Settings		Uninstall
Enrolment on payment	2 / 0	2021052500	👁	↑	Settings		Uninstall
Category enrolments	0 / 0	2021052500	👁		Settings		Uninstall
External database	0 / 0	2021052500	👁		Settings	Test settings	Uninstall
Flat file (CSV)	0 / 0	2021052500	👁		Settings		Uninstall
IMS Enterprise file	0 / 0	2021052500	👁		Settings		Uninstall
LDAP enrolments	0 / 0	2021052500	👁		Settings		Uninstall
Publish as LTI tool	0 / 0	2021052500	👁		Settings		Uninstall
Course meta link	0 / 0	2021052501	👁		Settings		Uninstall
MNet remote enrolments	0 / 0	2021052500	👁		Settings		Uninstall
PayPal	0 / 0	2021052500	👁		Settings		Uninstall

Figure 4.27 – Enrolment plugins

For every plugin, the number of instances and enrolments are shown. Each plugin can be enabled or disabled separately.

> **Important note**
>
> Moodle supports multi-enrolment; that is, multiple plugins can be enabled simultaneously.

The arrangement of plugins determines in which order user enrolments are checked when a user attempts to enter a course. It is recommended to give the plugins used by the majority of users higher priority over those only used sporadically, as this will benefit system performance.

All active plugins must be configured; we will deal with these settings when covering individual enrolment mechanisms. While it is possible to uninstall plugins, it is not recommended. If they are required at a later stage, they will have to be re-installed, and the preference is to simply leave them disabled.

> **Important note**
>
> Users need to have a user account before they can be enrolled in a course.

Each enrolment type is covered in some detail, except MNet remote enrolments, which are covered in *Chapter 19, Setting Up Moodle Networking*, and **Publish as LTI** tool, which we deal with in *Chapter 9, Configuring Educational Features*. We are also not covering the two legacy solutions **Category enrolments** (replaced by cohort synchronization) and **PayPal** (now a gateway in **Enrolment on payment**). The enrolment mechanism you choose depends entirely on the infrastructure you have in place – that is, where and in what format the enrolment data of learners is stored.

Once an enrolment form has been set up, it must be configured inside the course in which it will be used. Select the **Enrolment methods** options from the dropdown on the **Participants** tab, where you will see a list of all the active (shown) and inactive (hidden) enrolment plugins. Each enrolment method comes with a number of settings, which we will cover as part of the plugin itself:

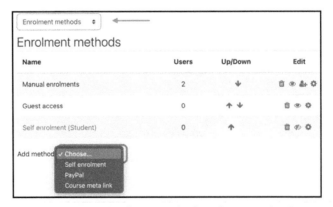

Figure 4.28 – Enrolment methods at the course level

Any non-database enrolment method enabled and configured at the site level can be added via the **Add method** drop-down menu. Whether a plugin automatically appears in the list of new courses depends on the **Add instance to new courses** parameter. Some plugins, for example, **Self enrolment** and **PayPal**, can be added multiple times in the same course, which is helpful if you need to support multiple roles.

So far, we have covered enrolment plugins in general. Now, it is time to kick off with the first type of course enrolment: internal.

Internal enrolment

Internal enrolment means that Moodle handles all enrolment without any other systems involved. Moodle supports three types of internal enrolments:

- **Manual enrolment**
- **Self enrolment**
- **Guest access**

We are going to cover these three internal enrolment types in separate subsections.

Manual enrolment

Manual enrolment is the default enrolment mechanism when Moodle is installed. The sitewide settings are configured at **Site administration | Plugins | Enrolments | Manual enrolments**:

Option	Description
Enrolment expiration action	The action to be taken when a user enrolment expires.
Hour to send enrolment expiry notifications	The time when the enrolment expiry notification will be sent out to the user.
Add instance to new course	Every newly-created course will contain this plugin by default.
Enable manual enrolments	The plugin is enabled by default.
Default role	The role that manually enrolled users will have by default.
Default enrolment start	The three options when the enrolment is to commence are **Course start**, **Today** (default), and **Now**.
Default enrolment duration	The default time for how long users are enrolled in a course.
Notify before enrolment expires	You can opt to notify only the enroller or the enrolled user and also the affected user.
Notification threshold	The time before expiration users will be notified.

Figure 4.29 – Manual enrolment options

Once the plugin has been set up, you will see a very similar-looking screen under **Enrolment methods | Manual enrolments | Settings** on the **Participants** tab inside a course:

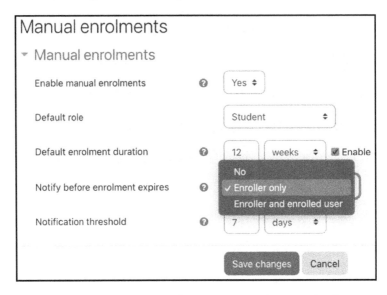

Figure 4.30 – Manual enrolment options at the course level

The actual enrolment of users takes place in **Participants,** as we have already covered in the previous chapter. What we haven't covered yet is the suspension and expiry of enrolments. You can change these individually via the **Edit** symbol in the **Status** column of your enrolled course users:

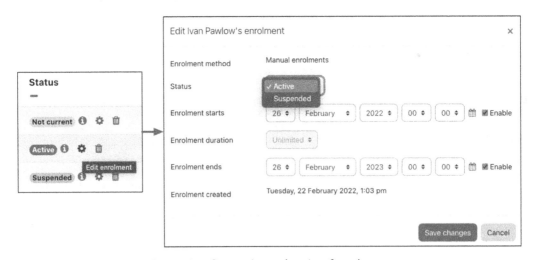

Figure 4.31 – Suspension and expiry of enrolments

To modify the enrolment data of multiple users, select them in the list of participants and choose **Edit selected user enrolments** from the correct section in the **With selected users…** dropdown. Equally, unenrol individual users via the standard **Delete** icon or in batch via the **Delete selected user enrolments** option.

A teacher can carry out all these steps, but you might decide that these tasks should be performed centrally for consistency and also to simplify their workflows. If this is the case, their role should be modified so that only administrators or dedicated users can deal with enrolments.

Self-enrolment

The concept of self-enrolment is relatively simple: users choose which courses they want to participate in. A course can contain a password, known as the enrolment key. Anyone who knows this key is allowed to add themselves to a course. An open door icon is shown beside courses that allow guest access without a password; otherwise, a closed door icon is displayed.

The enrolment key is set at the course level. The teacher must inform the students about the key and ideally limit the enrolment period to an appropriate time frame to avoid misuse.

Once the enrolment key has been set, learners must enter it when they try to access the course for the first time. Access will be granted if the key is entered correctly; otherwise, it will be denied.

> **Important note**
> Self-enrolment requires manual enrolment to be enabled.

You find the sitewide settings for self-enrolments in **Site administration | Plugins | Enrolments | Self enrolment**:

Setting	Description
Require enrolment key	If set, new courses must have an enrolment key. Enrolment keys set in the existing courses cannot be removed but can be modified.
Use password policy	If set, the password policy (see *Chapter 12, Security*) will be applied to enrolment keys.
Show hint	If set, the first letter of the enrolment key is shown.
Enrolment expiry action	The action to be taken when a user enrolment expires.
Hour to send enrolment expiry notifications	The time when the enrolment expiry notification will be sent out to the user.
Add instance to new courses	Every newly-created course will contain this plugin by default.
Enable existing enrolments	If set, all the existing enrolments will be suspended, and new users cannot enrol.
Allow new enrolments	If set, new users can enrol in the course.
Use group enrolment keys	If set, users can self-enrol via a group enrolment key, making them members of that group.
Default role assignment	The role self-enrolled users will have by default.
Enrolment duration	The default time for how long users are enrolled in a course.
Notify before enrolment expires	You can opt to notify only the enroller or the enroller and also the affected user.
Notification threshold	This is the time before expiration a user will be notified.
Unenrol inactive after	The number of days after users will be unenrolled after being logged in to the course.
Max enrolled users	The maximum number of users who can enrol in the course (0 equals unlimited).
Send course welcome message	If set, a welcome message will be sent to the user by email.

Figure 4.32 – Self-enrolment options

Once the plugin has been set up, you will be able to instantiate it at **Enrolment methods | Self enrolment | Settings** on the **Participants** tab inside a course:

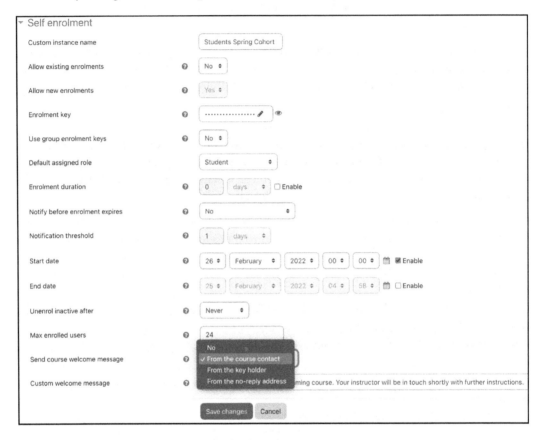

Figure 4.33 – Self-enrolment options at the course level

The settings are mostly identical to the sitewide settings described in the preceding table. The help icons next to each parameter display more details for each setting.

You can create multiple instances of the self-enrolment method, which is why you need to assign a distinguishing **Custom instance name**. This is useful if you need to give different user groups access to the same course – for instance, students of different cohorts or learners from multiple customers.

Guest access

Guest access can be seen as temporary enrolment. Whether authenticated on the system or not, users will be granted controlled (read-only) access to a course. Non-authenticated users will get there via the **Login as a guest** button on the login screen. Internally, they are being allocated a temporary user ID, which will be discarded afterward. The guest icon is shown beside courses that allow guest access.

The sitewide settings for guest access are found in **Site administration | Plugins | Enrolments | Guest access**:

Guest access

Guest access plugin is only granting temporary access to courses, it is not actually enrolling users.

Require guest access password enrol_guest	requirepassword	☐ Default: No
	Require access password in new courses and prevent removing of access password from existing courses.
Use password policy enrol_guest	usepasswordpolicy	☐ Default: No
	Use standard password policy for guest access passwords.
Show hint enrol_guest	showhint	☐ Default: No
	Show first letter of the guest access password.

Enrolment instance defaults

Default enrolment settings in new courses.

Add instance to new courses enrol_guest	defaultenrol	☑ Default: Yes
	It is possible to add this plugin to all new courses by default.
Allow guest access enrol_guest	status	No ⬍ Default: No ☐ Advanced
	Allow temporary guest access by default.

Figure 4.34 – Guest access options

You can specify a password in the course settings for guest access. If you wish to make this compulsory, select **Require guest access password**. For newly-created courses, a random password will be generated (unmask the password in the course settings to view it). Removing guest access passwords from courses is not possible, but they can be modified.

The **Enrolment instance defaults** settings are the same as the first two of the manual and self-enrolment methods.

You can allow or disallow guest access at **Enrolment methods | Guest access | Settings** on the **Participants** tab inside a course. Here, you can also specify the password mentioned previously:

> **Important note**
>
> For guest access to work for users without a login, ensure the **Guest login** button is set to **Show** in **Site administration | Plugins | Authentication | Manage authentication**. Otherwise, guest access will only work for authenticated users.

There are two good Moodle Academy videos featuring guest access at docs.moodle.org/en/ Guest_access. Additional information is also available on topics such as auto-login guests.

This concludes the subsection on internal enrolment methods. Next up is an interesting enrolment method for enrolling the same group of users in multiple courses: cohort enrolment and synchronization.

Cohort enrolment and synchronization

Cohorts are sitewide or global groups. We will cover cohorts in detail in *Chapter 5, Managing Users, Cohorts, and Authentication*, so for now, let's simply assume that they are a collection of users.

Once cohorts have been created and members have been allocated, it is possible to enrol an entire cohort in a course or synchronize a cohort's membership with a course. The two variants are shown in the following diagram:

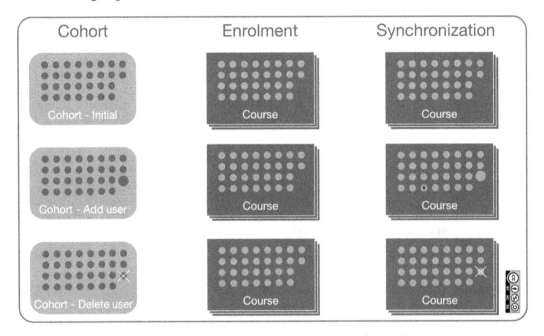

Figure 4.35 – Cohort enrolment versus cohort synchronization

Let's use an example to explain the figure, starting with **enrolment**: assume you have a class called 7c with 30 students, in a school. The same class must be enrolled in eight different courses, where each course represents a subject. We only have to create cohort 7c once and then we can enrol all cohort members in each course one by one.

Alternatively, we can activate cohort **synchronization** with the eight courses, and Moodle will take care of the rest. If new pupils join the class, we only have to add their account to the cohort and the enrolment will be done automatically. Similarly, the pupil will be unenrolled if a cohort member is removed.

So, when do you use one-off enrolment and when do you use permanent synchronization? If the cohort is likely to remain static and enrolment is a one-off, cohort enrolment is sufficient. If, however, the cohort is likely to have a high turnover and courses have to be kept in sync, you are better off using synchronization. Beware that the removal of a cohort membership not only triggers unenrolment from a course but also the deletion of certain learning progress data.

Cohort sync is also great for organizations where groups move together between classes, such as an elementary school. Instead of moving individual users from one year to the next, you will only be dealing with cohorts of users, which is less time-consuming and more fault-tolerant.

The **Cohort sync** plugin (**Site administration** | **Plugins** | **Enrolments** | **Cohort sync**) only contains two parameters – the **Default role** value that is given to users when they are enrolled and what action to take when users are removed from an external enrolment source:

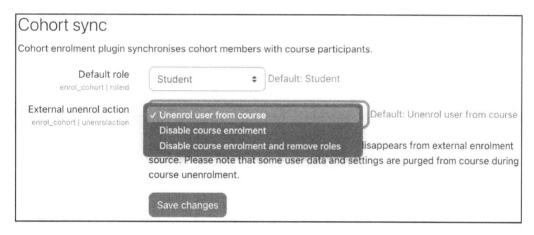

Figure 4.36 – Cohort synchronization options

We have to create a cohort and assign some members to see cohort synchronization in action. Go to **Site administration** | **Users** | **Accounts** | **Cohorts** and add a cohort by clicking on the **Add new cohort** tab. Give the cohort **Name** (in our case, **7c**) and, from the **Context** drop-down menu, select the category in which all the courses belong to class **7c**. Select **System** if that doesn't apply. **Cohort ID** and **Description** are optional fields; ensure that **Visible** is checked. Once saved, you must assign members to the cohort by selecting the **Assign** icon beside it.

Once this has been successful, we can enrol the cohort (that is, all cohort members) in our course. Inside the course, go to the **Participants** tab, click on the **Enrol users** button, and select cohort **7c**:

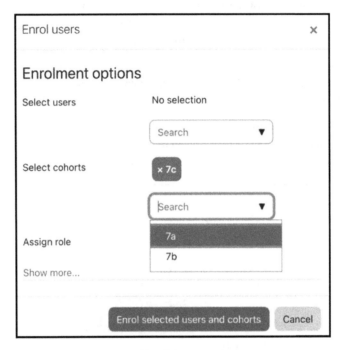

Figure 4.37 – Cohort enrolment

Once you select **Enrol selected users and cohorts**, all cohort members will be enrolled in the course, similar to manual enrolment. However, no further synchronization is carried out – it is effectively the same as manually enrolling all 30 users, but in a single step.

An alternative to this one-off exercise is a permanent arrangement where we set up an enrolment method instance via the familiar **Enrolment methods** link in the **Participants** tab and then select **Cohort Sync** from the **Add method** dropdown:

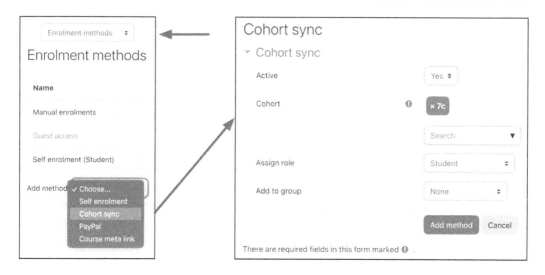

Figure 4.38 – Cohort synchronization

Once added, all users of the cohort will be enrolled. Moodle will automatically keep track of the cohort going forward—if users are added to the cohort, they will also be enrolled in the courses; if users are removed from the cohort, they will be unenrolled. As with self-enrolment, cohort synchronization allows multiple instances inside a course.

Cohort synchronization is a great way to organize your users if you have groups that must be enrolled in multiple courses. Another method that avoids manual enrolments is database-driven enrolment, which we will cover next.

Database-driven enrolment

In larger organizations, storing certain user-related information in a separate database or directory is common. If this information contains course-related information, it should be utilized for enrolment. In doing so, you minimize the necessary effort when using manual enrolment.

> **Important note**
> Unlike internal enrolment methods, database-driven enrolment cannot be configured at the course level. They are applied across the site once set up.

Four enrolment methods fall into the database-driven enrolment category, which we will cover in the following order: LDAP, external databases, flat files, and IMS Enterprise files.

LDAP

Lightweight Directory Access Protocol (**LDAP**) is an application standard for querying and modifying directory services. It is used by many organizations to store learner details and is, therefore, well-suited as an enrolment source for Moodle.

> **Important note**
> The PHP LDAP extension must be installed on the server for the enrolment to work.

If it is not installed, Moodle will display an error message. The module supports Microsoft's implementation of LDAP, called **Active Directory**, and OpenLDAP, an open source implementation of the authentication mechanism. It is common for sites that use LDAP for enrolment to also use LDAP for authentication, which is discussed in detail in *Chapter 5, Managing Users, Cohorts, and Authentication*.

The principle of the enrolment method is rather simple but effective. The information stored in the data source about students, teachers, and courses is mapped to the Moodle counterparts. Enrolments are updated when a user logs in. All we have to provide are the mappings.

Moodle makes several assumptions when working with LDAP enrolment:

- Your LDAP tree contains groups that map to courses
- Each group has multiple membership entries to map to students
- Users have a valid **ID number** field

The LDAP settings are located at **Site administration** | **Plugins** | **Enrolments** | **LDAP enrolments**. They have been annotated with detailed explanations, hence we will not repeat them; instead, we will provide additional information where applicable. Contact your system administrator if you are unsure where to locate some of the required information.

There are seven sections of parameters that have to be provided:

- **LDAP server settings** establish the connection to the directory. LDAP servers with TSL encryption are also supported.
- **Bind settings** specify details about the credentials to access the LDAP server – that is, the provided username and password.
- **Role mappings** specify how user-related information is stored in the LDAP server. The roles must be set, containing a context (usually the same as the one in the server settings) and the member attribute (user IDs). It is crucial to set **Search subcontexts** correctly. If it is set to **No**, subcontexts will not be searched, but the search is potentially faster, and vice versa. Also, ensure that the **User type** setting matches the type of server you use – for example, **MS Active Directory**.

- **Course enrolment settings** specify how course and module information is stored on the LDAP server. It also provides options for different forms of unenrolment.

- **Automatic course creation** is a potentially time-saving feature. A course is created for each entry on the LDAP server in the category specified. To expedite the process and guarantee consistency among courses, you should create a course with the preferred settings and use it (its course ID) as a template for all the newly-created courses.

- **Automatic course update settings** let you specify which fields to update when the CLI script, `enrol/ldap/cli/sync.php`, is run.

- **Nested groups settings** let you configure support for groups of groups inside your LDAP server:

LDAP server settings

Host URL	ldaps://ldap.openumlaut.com	Default: Empty
enrol_ldap_host_url	Specify LDAP host in URL-form like 'ldap://ldap.myorg.com/' or 'ldaps://ldap.myorg.com/'	
Use TLS	Yes ⊕	Default: No
enrol_ldap_start_tls	Use regular LDAP service (port 389) with TLS encryption	
Version	3 ⊕	Default: 3
enrol_ldap_ldap_version	The version of the LDAP protocol your server is using	
LDAP encoding	utf-8	Default: utf-8
enrol_ldap_ldap_encoding	Specify encoding used by LDAP server. Most probably utf-8, MS AD v2 uses default platform encoding such as cp1252, cp1250, etc.	
Page size	250	Default: 250
enrol_ldap_pagesize	Make sure this value is smal...	

Figure 4.39 – LDAP enrolment options

Working with LDAP enrolments often requires a degree of trial and error. Creating a number of sample courses and enrolments in a playpen is recommended before applying the mechanism to your production server.

If you need to access multiple LDAP systems with different settings, there are two options:

- You will need to duplicate the enrolment plugin at the system level and modify the source code accordingly. A programmer must carry out this task, as source code changes are required in the copied module.

- You will need to upgrade to Moodle Workplace, which supports multi-tenancy authentication. Details on this powerful feature can be found at `docs.moodle.org/en/Multi-tenancy_authentication`.

External databases

Many organizations use a management information system, either proprietary or developed in-house, that holds information about staff and learners and the courses in which they are enrolled. It makes perfect sense to utilize this data for enrolment to Moodle. As all the information systems use a database at their core, all we have to do is to get access to the relevant data.

The bad news is that there is a plethora of database systems out there that need to be supported, from the two big commercial players, Oracle and Microsoft SQL Server, to the popular open source systems Maria DB and Postgres. The good news is that a layer called **ActiveX Data Objects (ADO)** exists, which does all the hard work for us. We only have to talk to the ADO layer and its internals will deal with the rest, no matter to which database it is talking.

The database must contain information on the course ID and the user ID. These two fields are compared with their counterparts you choose in the local course and user tables.

> **Important note**
> Getting your database administrator to set up a read-only view of the relevant data is highly recommended. That way, your enrolment mechanism is nicely decoupled from the database itself.

To configure database-driven enrolment, go to **Site administration** | **Plugins** | **Enrolments** | **External database connection**:

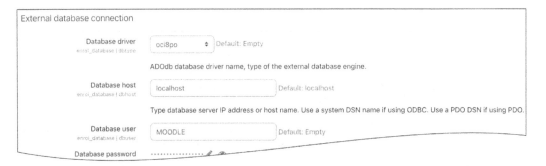

Figure 4.40 – External database enrolment options

The database connection settings have been annotated on the screen with good explanations, which we will not repeat here. Contact your database administrator if you are unsure where to locate some of the required information.

> **Important note**
>
> Some databases, such as Oracle, are case-sensitive; that is, field names must be provided with the correct casing for the database link to work correctly.

It is possible to test your external database settings via the respective link at **Site administration | Plugins | Enrolments | Manage enrolment plugins**. The thrown error messages will help you debug your settings until a valid connection is established.

Flat files

Moodle provides a flat file enrolment mechanism configured at **Site administration | Plugins | Enrolments | Flat file (CSV)**. The method will repeatedly (via the Moodle cron process) check for and process a specially-formatted CSV file in the location that you specify. The format of the file is as follows:

Field	Description
operation	**add** (to add an enrolment) or **del** (to remove it)
role	See **Flat file role mapping** in the lower part of the same screen, for example, student or teacher
user idnumber	The ID number of the user to be enrolled
course idnumber	The ID number of the course in which the user is to be enrolled
start time/end time	The optional start/end time in seconds since epoch (January 1, 1970)

Figure 4.41 – CSV enrolment file format

The following is a sample file snippet:

```
add, teacher, 5, Psychology1
add, student, 12, Psychology1
del, student, 17, English2
add, student, 29, English, 1207008000, 1227916800
```

The start and end times have to be provided together. It is recommended to use an online converter to generate the numbers since epoch.

In the text file settings at **Site administration | Plugins | Enrolments | Flat file (CSV)**, you have to provide the absolute file location on the server. Moodle has to be able to read the file and delete it once it has been processed! You can choose to send a log file to the administrator and a notification to the user responsible for enrolments and students. **External unenrol action** specifies what happens when a user has been removed from the source file. Similarly, **Enrolment expiration action** specifies what happens to users once their enrolment has expired. The default roles in the **Flat file role mapping** section can be overridden with other values if required:

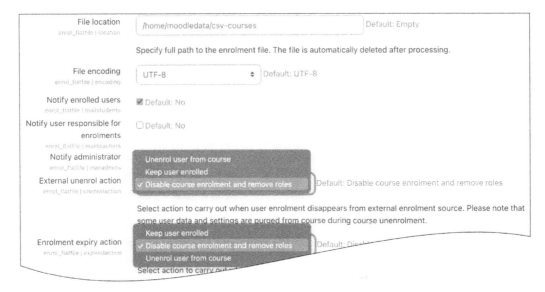

Figure 4.42 – CSV enrolment options

The IMS Enterprise file

The IMS Global Learning Consortium has specified an XML file format representing student and course information. Moodle can use any file that conforms to the format as its enrolment source. As with the flat file format, Moodle regularly checks for its presence; if found, it will process the file and delete it. You find details of its basic structure at docs.moodle.org/en/IMS_Enterprise.

The plugin can also create user accounts if they aren't yet created or change user details if requested. Furthermore, new courses can also be created if they are not found on Moodle.

All other fields, including role mappings, are well-explained on screen and can be accessed at **Site administration | Plugins | Enrolments | IMS Enterprise file**.

This concludes the section on database-driven enrolment. Next up is a unique form of enrolment via so-called meta courses.

Meta courses – sharing enrolment across courses

Meta courses are courses that take their enrolment from other courses. They populate many courses from one enrolment or one course from many enrolments. There are two main scenarios when this is useful:

- Multiple courses want to share information or resources (meta course)

- A course is part of a qualification where students have to be enrolled in a number of courses; each course is set up as a meta course

Both scenarios are depicted in the following diagram:

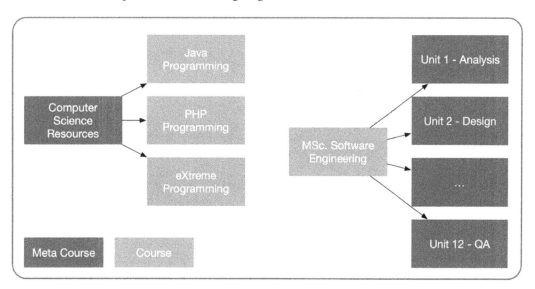

Figure 4.43 – Meta course scenarios

Go to **Site administration** | **Plugins** | **Enrolments** | **Course meta link**. The list contains any roles that are not synchronized; that is, users with those roles in child courses will also be given access to their parent courses. **Synchronise all enrolled users** means that users will also be enrolled if they do not have a role in any parent courses. **External unenrol action** specifies what happens when a user has been removed from the external enrolment source – for instance, a CSV file or LDAP. The **Sort course list** parameter determines whether courses are being ordered as specified at **Site administration** | **Courses** | **Manage courses and categories** or by one of the selected sort criteria:

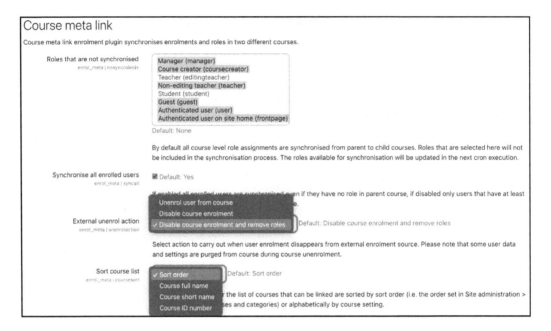

Figure 4.44 – Course meta link enrolment options

Teachers have the right to set up meta courses and manage their dependents via **Course meta link** under **Enrolment method** in the **Users** section of a course. While it is the role of the teacher to manage meta courses, experience has shown that the administrator is frequently asked to set these up on behalf of others.

> **Important note**
>
> A child course gives its enrolments to the parent course. Create a link from the parent course to the child course.

To set up the first scenario, as shown in the earlier diagram, where the meta course holds shared resources, you have to create all the four courses first and create a new course meta link instance from within the **Computer Science Resources** course (via **Enrolment methods** on the **Participants** tab). This instance has to link to all child courses – in our case, the three mentioned programming courses:

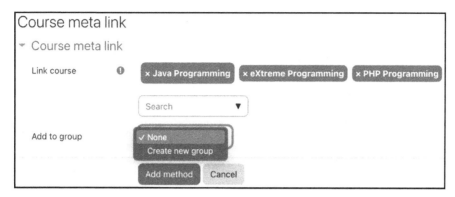

Figure 4.45 – Configuring child courses

To model the second scenario, you will have to create all 13 courses (one course for **MSc Software Engineering** and a course for each unit) and add a course meta link method in each of the 12 parent courses to the **MSc Software Engineering** course.

Meta courses are a great way to synchronize users across courses. There are scenarios where you can achieve the same with cohorts and cohort synchronization. If this is the case, working with cohorts is usually the preferred option, as they are easier to manage, particularly on larger sites.

Another alternative to meta courses is **Programs** in Moodle Workplace, where courses can be bundled flexibly via sets, including support for hierarchical sequences of courses. You will find a good introduction to programs at docs.moodle.org/en/Programs.

So far, all enrolment methods have been driven by organizational parameters, such as course access, passwords, or time. The last type of enrolment we want to dedicate some time to is payment.

Enrolment with payment

Moodle comes with a basic payment mechanism that allows you to charge users for courses via different payment systems. The concept behind Moodle payments is as follows:

- A **payment gateway** represents a payment service – for instance, PayPal, Stripe, or Alipay
- A **payment account** supports one or many payment systems
- **Paid course enrolment** is tied to a payment account

The following table visualizes the three mentioned mechanisms:

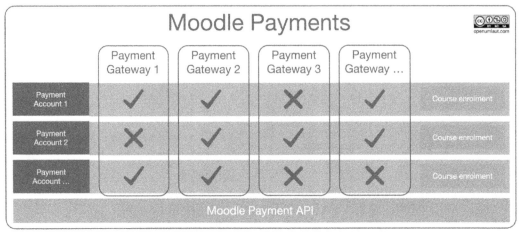

Figure 4.46 – Moodle payments

To create your first payment account, navigate to **Site administration | General | Payments | Payment accounts**, and press the **Create payment account** button. You must provide an **Account name** that will be used when the enrolment instance is set up later. Optionally, you can also provide an **ID number**, which is only necessary when the account is matched against an external system.

You can create multiple payment accounts if your organization requires separate payment gateways for different courses. On our system, we have also created a test account, which has been disabled:

Account name	Payment gateways	
Payments Courses	✘ Alipay , ✔ PayPal, ✔ Stripe	Edit ⌄
Payments Other	✔ Alipay , ✔ PayPal, ✘ Stripe	Edit ⌄
Payments Testing **Not available**	✔ Alipay , ✔ PayPal, ✔ Stripe	Edit ⌄
		Show archived
Create payment account		

Figure 4.47 – Payment accounts

Moodle ships with a single payment gateway, namely PayPal. Additional gateways can be installed via `moodle.org/plugins/?q=type:paygw`. We will deal with installing plugins in *Chapter 8, Understanding Moodle Plugins*.

For each payment account, all payment gateways are shown, including ticks or crosses, to indicate whether a gateway has been configured or not. So, how do you configure a payment gateway? You simply click on the gateway's name, which gets you to the configuration for this particular payment account. Here, we are only going to cover the PayPal gateway since it ships with Moodle:

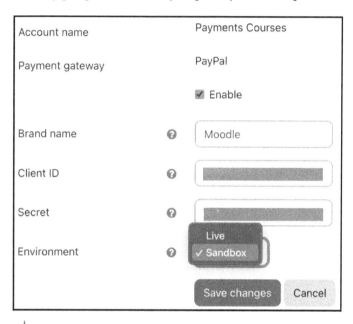

Figure 4.48 – PayPal gateway configuration

Brand name is optional and overrides the business name on the PayPal site. PayPal provides the **Client ID** and **Secret** information via `developer.paypal.com/api/rest`. You will be shown the two values once you have logged in. Bear in mind that you require a PayPal business account to go live. Finally, you can change **Environment** from **Live** to **Sandbox** for testing purposes.

Before payment plugins can be used for enrolment, you must enable them in **Site administration | Plugins | Enrolments | Manage enrolment plugins**. Technically, this is all you have to do to set up payment accounts and gateways as an administrator.

For completeness, here is the final step to create a payment instance inside a course (as usual, via the **Enrolment methods** option **Enrolment on payment** in **Participants**):

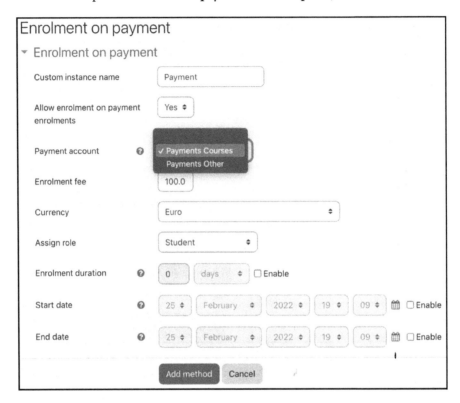

Figure 4.49 – Enrolment on payment configuration

The only fields that deviate from the standard fields of other enrolment methods are the following:

- **Payment account**: Select one of the payment accounts you have set up.
- **Enrolment fee**: The amount you charge for the course.
- **Currency**: The currency of your fee. You must create separate enrolment method instances for each currency to charge users in different currencies.

Multiple instances can be created for the **Enrolment on payment** method. This setup is useful if you wish to charge different amounts in different currencies or roles or if you have a mixture of paying and non-paying learners.

Once a user wants to enrol in a pay-for course, the following dialogue will appear (our chosen payment account also includes the third-party payment gateway, Stripe):

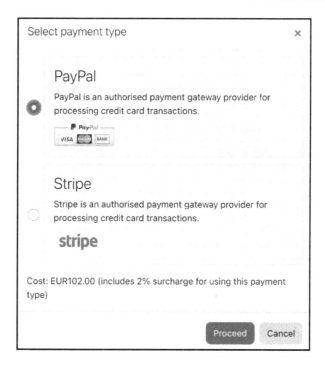

Figure 4.50 – User's payment selection

Once the payment has been successful, the user will be enrolled in the course. You might have spotted the 2% surcharge displayed at the bottom. You can specify the surcharge for each payment gateway at **Site administration** | **Plugins** | **Payment gateways** | **Manage payment gateways** | **Settings**. On this screen, you can also see the currencies each payment gateway supports.

Enrolment by payment provides a flexible means to offer a mix of chargeable and non-chargeable courses. If you require a more advanced shopping cart solution to be integrated into Moodle, you might want to consider commercial services such as Course Merchant or Magento. These systems support more sophisticated workflows, such as bulk purchasing, payment on tax invoice, and price bandings.

This concludes the comprehensive section on enrolments, where we introduced enrolment principles and covered enrolment plugins. By now, you should be able to set up and configure the mix of enrolment mechanisms that is right for your organization and Moodle system.

Summary

Phew! That was a lot to take in. The complexity of courses, their management, and various facets of enrolments demonstrate a typical Moodle conundrum: the features are very powerful and flexible, but this versatility comes at a price in the form of complexity. Moodle has done a great job in mastering this balancing act, but nonetheless, there is usually a steep learning curve to be mastered.

In this chapter, you learned everything about courses and categories. As we have discovered, courses are fundamental to Moodle, as they contain all the learning activities and content prepared by teachers and used by students. Even Moodle's home page is a course, but we will deal with this later when we customize the look and feel of your LMS.

While it is possible to delegate many course-related tasks to non-administrators – we will deal with this in *Chapter 6, Managing Permissions, Roles, and Capabilities* – you, as the administrator, are often required to set up the overall course and category structure. There are also plenty of course- and category-related settings that we deliberately did not deal with in this section but will cover throughout the book. Examples are various options in **Site administration** | **Appearance** | **Navigation** that drive what is shown in the navigation bar, and **Site administration** | **Appearance** | **Courses** where there is information about how the course catalog is structured. Both topics will be discussed in *Chapter 7, Enhancing Moodle's Look and Feel*.

Closely related to courses is the enrolment of users; it is important to understand the difference between enrolment, which we covered in this chapter, and authentication, which we will discuss in detail in the next chapter dealing with user management.

5
Managing Users, Cohorts, and Authentication

This chapter will teach you how to manage users in your Moodle system. We will first look at what information is stored for each user and how we can extend their profiles. We will then perform several standard user actions before dealing with cohorts. Finally, we will deal with a wide range of user authentication mechanisms. We will cover the following topics:

- Understanding user profiles
- Performing standard user actions (manual and bulk)
- Creating user accounts manually (including batch upload)
- Managing cohorts (including batch upload)
- Configuring user authentication (internal, external, service providers, and system)

The following diagram shows a high-level overview of the aforementioned topics (users, cohorts, and authentication) and how they are connected:

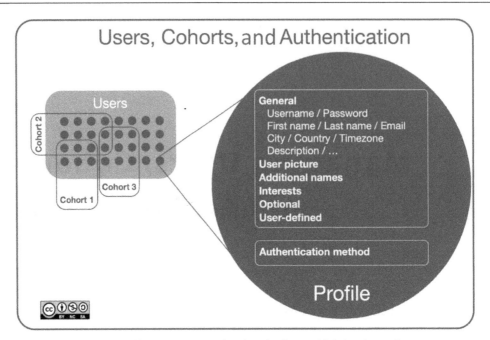

Figure 5.1 – Users, courses, and authentication – a high-level overview

By the end of this chapter, you will be able to manage all aspects of user accounts and user authentication. This is a lot to take in, so we'd better get going!

Understanding user profiles

Other than guests, each user has a profile containing information about them. We will first deal with the information stored for each user and how it is organized in Moodle.

You can view your own profile by selecting the **Profile** item in the drop-down menu beside your name at the top of the screen. Click on the **Edit profile** link in the **User details** section to change your profile details. To modify the profiles of other users, click on the **Edit** icon beside their name by navigating to **Site administration | Users | Accounts | Browse list of users**.

Profile fields

Moodle user profiles are divided into pre-defined categories, which cannot be changed via the Moodle user interface:

- **General**: Standard user fields
- **User picture**: Image of the user
- **Additional names**: Phonetic name, middle name, and alternate name

- **Interests**: Tags for networking activities

- **Optional**: Additional user information

In addition to these static profile field categories, Moodle allows us to create user-defined profile categories and fields. Before dealing with custom profile fields, we will cover the pre-defined fields grouped by the aforementioned categories.

User profile fields – General

The following screenshot shows the profile fields of the **General** category:

Figure 5.2 – User profile fields – General

Most of these items are self-explanatory, but there are a few things you need to know about each of them. Here is a brief description of each profile element, along with tips to use them effectively:

- **Username**: A unique username has to be provided. By default, only alphanumeric lowercase characters, underscores (_), hyphens (-), periods (.), or the *at* symbol (@) are allowed. Suppose you also want to use other characters in usernames, such as umlauts (¨). In that case, you will have to enable these by going to **Site administration | Security | Site security settings** and turning on **Allow extended characters in usernames**. It is important to remember that you ought to have administrator rights to change the username.

  If you wish to use the email address as the username, consider the **Allow login via email** option (at **Site administration | Plugins | Authentication | Manage authentication**). That way, users have two alternatives to log in, their username and their email address.

> **Important note**
>
> If your users don't already have a unique identifier that can be (re)used as their Moodle username, such as an email address or a staff ID, it is highly recommended to develop a consistent naming scheme for usernames, for example, `firstname.lastname` for smaller institutions or `startyear.firstname.lastname.index` for larger organizations.

- **Choose an authentication method**: This menu allows changes to the user's authentication method. While useful for testing and development purposes, it is highly recommended that you do not select any disabled option from this menu. You cannot change the `auth` method of the main admin account. We'll look at authentication methods in detail in the second half of this chapter.

> **Important note**
>
> An incorrect authentication method prevents users from logging in, or even completely deletes their account!

- **Suspended account**: Select this option to prevent a user from logging in. This is useful as a disciplinary measure or in case of a more prolonged absence, for instance, a sabbatical term. There is no expiry date on the suspension, so you must manually change this back.

> **Important note**
>
> Account suspension is not the same as enrolment suspension. The former affects users and the latter, individual course enrolments.

- **New password**: When creating manual accounts, a password must be provided for security reasons. If the user ought to change the given password on their first login, the **Force password change** option has to be selected. You can unmask (reveal) your own password but not that of other users. However, administrators can override the existing passwords of users.

If **Password policy** is enabled (in **Site administration | Security | Site security settings**), the password must adhere to this policy. Refer to *Chapter 13*, *Ensuring Moodle Security*, for more details on password policy.

- **First name** and **Surname**: These are compulsory fields for users, for which diacritical marks (ä, â, à, á, …) are fully supported.

- **Email address**: This is a compulsory field and should be unique. Ensure the address is correct since Moodle makes regular use of it, for example, to notify users who have forgotten their username or password.

  Some organizations still do not make use of email addresses. As it is a mandatory field, there are two typical workarounds in this scenario.

  The first option is to develop a unique dummy email address scheme or void email addresses solely used for identification purposes. While this solves the problem technically, it limits the user experience significantly because communication among users or notifications generated by Moodle cannot be sent.

  The second alternative is to activate **duplicate email addresses** (enable **Allow accounts with same email** in **Site administration | Plugins | Authentication | Manage authentication**) and have users with an email address responsible for groups of learners, for example, a teacher for a class or a supervisor for workers. While this approach is not ideal from a privacy perspective – user-specific messages could potentially be read by multiple persons – at least somebody knows what is going on and can then communicate it to the intended recipients.

- **Email display**: Choices can be made as to who can see the user's email address. The self-explanatory choices are **Hide my email address from non-privileged users**, **Allow everyone to see my email address**, and **Allow only other participants to see my email address** (default). Administrators and teachers (with editing rights) will always see email addresses, even if they are hidden.

- **MoodleNet profile**: Link to the user's MoodleNet profile, which has to be a WebFinger-compliant URI. We will deal with MoodleNet in *Chapter 19*, *Setting Up Moodle Networking*.

- **City/town** and **Select a country**: These are used to further identify users by their geographical location.

- **Timezone**: This is used to convert time-related messages on the system (such as assignment deadlines) from the local time (typically, the server time) to the correct time in whichever zone the user has selected. It is necessary as your users may be geographically spread across multiple time zones. The default city, country, and time zone can be specified by navigating to **Site administration | Location | Location settings**.

- **Description**: This provides additional information about the user. As an administrator, you can leave the field empty.

Additional fields might appear in the user's profile, for example, **Preferred theme** or **Email charset**, but this requires the settings to be changed elsewhere. We will mention these when the respective topics are being dealt with.

User profile fields – User picture

The second category is called **User picture**, and, as the name suggests, it deals with the image attached to a user's profile.

Simply drag it to the **New picture** pane or select the image from the file picker to upload a new picture. The image cannot be larger than the maximum size listed; if your image is too large, it is recommended to reduce its size to a minimum of 100 x 100 pixels. The supported formats are GIF, PNG, and the JPEG family; however, be careful with transparent backgrounds as they might cause issues in some browsers.

The **Picture description** field is used as an alt tag, a description of the image used for nonvisual browsers; it is in conformance with accessibility guidelines.

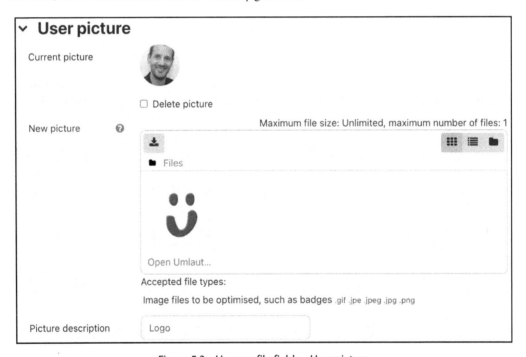

Figure 5.3 – User profile fields – User picture

Once a picture has been assigned, it will be shown in place of the **None** label. To remove the picture, check the **Delete** checkbox, and the picture will be removed when the profile information is updated.

Moodle will automatically crop the image to a square and resize it to 100 x 100 pixels for the larger view and 35 x 35 pixels for the smaller thumbnail view.

> **Important note**
> Two thumbnails are created automatically during the upload process, which reduces the file size to approximately 4 KB. An administrator can view all the uploaded user pictures via the `<moodleurl>/userpix` URL.

Moodle also supports **Gravatars**, so-called globally recognized avatars. Once you select the **Enable Gravatar** option on **Site administration | Users | Permissions | User policies**, Moodle will attempt to fetch a user profile picture from `gravatar.com` if the user has not uploaded an image.

If you suspect that your learners will likely misuse this feature by uploading inappropriate images, you can disable the functionality. Go to **Site administration | Security | Site security settings** and tick the **Disable user profile images** checkbox. Remember that once this feature is disabled, pictures cannot be assigned to any users (except the administrator), nor will it be possible for teachers to represent groups in courses with images.

User profile fields – Additional names

This **Additional names** section comprises the following fields:

- **First name – phonetic** and **Surname – phonetic**: The primary use case for the field pair is in Far East languages where users have an original and a Romanized version or a phonetic name displayed (for instance, Pinyin).

- **Middle name**: In some cultures, it is common to have three or more names that are displayed.

- **Alternate name**: This can be a nickname, a handle, or an alias used in specific pedagogical settings, for example, in gamification or role-playing scenarios.

User profile fields – Interests

Interests, such as hobbies or professional activities, can be entered one by one. To remove a tag, select its label. The given **List of interests** represents tags displayed in the user's profile. You can find more information on tagging at `docs.moodle.org/en/Tags` and in *Chapter 9, Configuring Educational Features*.

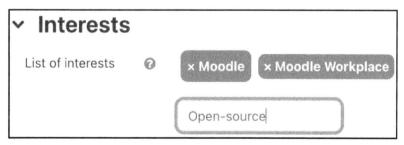

Figure 5.4 – User profile fields – Interests

User profile fields – Optional

More personal details are grouped under the **Optional** category:

- **ID number** can contain a student or staff number and is usually used in synchronization tools, such as HR systems.

- **Institution** and **Department** might be used for campus and faculty in a university. If you are using Moodle Workplace, do not confuse these two fields with departments that are part of the organization structure, including department frameworks, positions, job assignments, and managers.

- **Phone**, **Mobile phone**, and **Address** should be self-explanatory.

Some organizations rename unused fields to ones required in their setup. For more information on this, refer to the *Localization* section in *Chapter 10, Configuring Technical Features*.

This concludes the explanation of pre-defined user profile fields. The list can be extended by custom fields covered in the following section.

Creating user-defined profile fields

Moodle allows new arbitrary fields to be added to user profiles. We have already described the management of user-defined fields in the previous chapter when we dealt with custom course fields. Since the exact mechanism is used for user profile fields, we only deal with account-specific idiosyncrasies.

We just learned that profile fields are organized into categories (for instance, **General**, **User picture**, **Interests**, and **Optional**). Additional categories can be created, and user-defined fields can be placed within these new categories. This feature can be found by navigating to **Site administration | Users | Accounts | User profile fields**.

Unlike in custom courses, a default category, called **Other fields**, is already present, which can be deleted or renamed via the standard Moodle icons. To create a new category, click the **Create a new profile category** button at the bottom of the user profiles once the profile fields have been added.

The five profile field types in courses (checkbox, date/time, drop-down menu, text area, and text input) exist for users, plus one more: social. Let us go through the differences in the field-specific settings:

- **Checkbox**: This is the same as in custom course fields.

- **Date/time**: Instead of minimum and maximum value, the two date boundaries are **Start year** and **End year**, respectively. There also exists an **Include time?** option, though you cannot specify a default time.

- **Drop-down menu**: This is the same as in custom course fields.

- **Social**: This new field type lets you specify social network IDs, such as the user's Skype handle. The options you can see in the **Network type** list were formerly hard coded in the user profile.

Let's hope the list will be updated to the 21st century soon to support social media platforms such as Facebook, Twitter, Instagram, and TikTok, instead of outdated services such as ICQ and AIM.

If you upgrade from Moodle 3.x and any of these services are populated, they will be retained and converted automatically.

Figure 5.5 – User profile fields of type social

- **Text area**: This is precisely the same as in custom course fields.

- **Text input**: This is the same as the **Short text** field in courses, but some fields have been renamed: **Form input size** is now **Display size**, and **Maximum number of characters** is now **Character limit**. Why? I have absolutely no idea!

Each field type in user-profile fields has the same parameters as custom course fields with three notable differences:

- The fields are arranged slightly differently, and the common field settings **Locked** and **Visible** have been moved to the **General** section.

- The options in **Who is field visible to?** have been adjusted as follows. Instead of **Teachers**, there are now two options to choose from, namely **Visible to user** and **Visible to user, teachers, and admins**.

- The only additional setting available is **Display on signup page?**. When self-registration is enabled, several default fields must be provided at signup. If a custom field should also be displayed on the signup page, the option must be set to **Yes**. This feature can be helpful in commercial training settings when additional information, such as the learner's address or previous qualifications, is required.

To demonstrate how user profile fields work, let's assume a school where you wish to extend the user profile with a new profile category called **Parental responsibilities** comprising fields such as **Contact person** and **Relationship**:

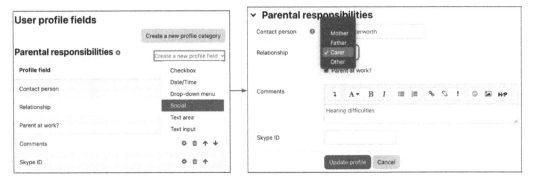

Figure 5.6 – User profile fields example

This completes the subsection dealing with custom user profile fields, extending standard user profiles. The third and last component of user profiles is user preferences, which we will cover next.

User preferences

Some more fields technically belong to the user profile, but they have been placed in the **Preferences** section, which can be accessed via the drop-down menu beside the user icon in the toolbar. The reason why this has been done is that you can disallow users from editing their profile altogether (via the `moodle/user:editownprofile` capability) and let them specify preferences via dedicated forms:

- **Preferred language:** The default language of the system is shown and can be changed to the user's preferred language. We will deal with localization in *Chapter 10, Configuring Technical Features*.

- **Forum preferences**: **Email digest type** determines how a user receives posts from forums to which a subscription exists. There are three possible choices, which are **No digest (single email per forum post)**, which is the default, **Complete (daily email with full posts)**, or **Subjects (daily email with subjects only)**. The **Forum auto-subscribe** setting dictates whether users are automatically subscribed to forums to which they post. The **Use experimental nested discussion view** option makes available a new discussion view; at the time of print, the feature is still in trial mode.

- If **Forum tracking** is enabled, posts that have not yet been read will be highlighted, which improves forum usability. When sending forum post notifications, users can choose whether they should mark the post as read or not to impact forum tracking.

- **Editor preferences**: This option determines which editor should be used when entering information in text areas. Unless the user has special requirements or preferences, this should be left as the **Default editor** option. In *Chapter 7, Enhancing Moodle's Look and Feel*, you'll learn more about editors.

- **Calendar preferences**: The user's choice of calendar and event-related settings. Calendars will be discussed in a dedicated section in *Chapter 10, Configuring Technical Features*.

- **Content bank preferences**: This setting determines the visibility of content the user has created (public or unlisted). We will cover content as part of the *H5P integration* section in *Chapter 8, Understanding Moodle Plugins*.

- **Message preferences**: These settings control privacy and notification preferences. We will deal with messaging as part of the *Communications* section in *Chapter 10, Configuring Technical Features*.

- **Notification preferences**: The user can choose the channels for different notification types. We will deal with messaging as part of the *Communications* section in *Chapter 10, Configuring Technical Features*.

The default preferences of some settings (email, forums, and content bank) can be specified by navigating to **Site administration | Users | Accounts | User default preferences**.

This completes the section on user profiles, where we covered standard and custom profile fields and briefly looked at various user preferences. Now that we know what a user profile looks like, let's start interacting with users.

Performing standard user actions

So far, you have learned what type of user information Moodle holds and how to extend the data stored in each profile. Now, it is time to work with existing users on your system, which consists of browsing and filtering user accounts and applying bulk actions.

Browsing users

The quickest way to view your Moodle user accounts is by navigating to **Site administration | Users | Accounts | Browse list of users**. Initially, a list of users is displayed, ordered by **First name**. Thirty users are shown at a time, and, if applicable, you can navigate via the « and » links or jump directly to another page by selecting a number. Each column can be sorted in ascending or descending order by clicking on the column header.

Figure 5.7 – Browsing user accounts

You can view an individual's profile by clicking on a user's name. In addition to the fields we introduced in the first section of this chapter, you can see **Login activity** showing **First access to site**, **Last access to site**, and the **Last IP address** login took place from.

You can specify which identity information (username, ID number, email address, phone numbers, department, institution, city, and country) about the users is shown in this list and other places. Go to **Site administration | Users | Permissions | User policies** and select the fields that should be shown in the **Show user identity** list. This only applies to users with the moodle/site:viewuseridentity capability.

> **Important note**
> To masquerade as another user, use the **Log in as** option in a user's profile.

When you look at the profile of another user account, you will see a **Log in as** link in the **Administration** pane, which lets you masquerade as another user. This feature is useful when tracking down issues you cannot locate as an administrator. To view all the user profile fields of a user or modify any of them, as discussed earlier, click on the **Edit profile** link. To modify any of the user's preferences, select the respective link.

Go back to the user list and click on the standard **Delete** icon in the rightmost column to delete a user. A confirmation screen has to be answered before the user is irreversibly removed. Actually, the user is only removed from Moodle's user interface. Internally, the user is retained in the database with the deleted flag turned on, which is necessary so that certain user contributions don't disappear, for instance, forum posts. Technically, a user account can be reinstated by changing the delete flag manually in the database.

To **suspend** a user account, toggle the **Show/Hide** icon, which triggers the account suspension, as discussed in the *User profile fields* section.

Related to browsing accounts is filtering, which narrows down the number of user entries you are dealing with. This refinement mechanism is particularly helpful on sites with a large number of user accounts.

Filtering users

We may often be required to search for a particular user or a set of users. Moodle provides a flexible filtering mechanism to refine the list of displayed users. In basic mode, you can filter by the user's full name, which is the first and last name combined. The following filter operations are available, all of which are case insensitive:

- **Contains**: The provided text has to be contained in the field
- **Doesn't contain**: This is the opposite of contains
- **Is equal to**: The provided text has to be the same as the value of the field
- **Starts with**: The field has to begin with the provided text
- **Ends with**: The field has to end with the provided text
- **Is empty**: The field has to be empty

For example, when adding a filter, such as **User full name starts with "cl"**, all users whose name begins with *cl* are displayed. Take a look at the following screenshot:

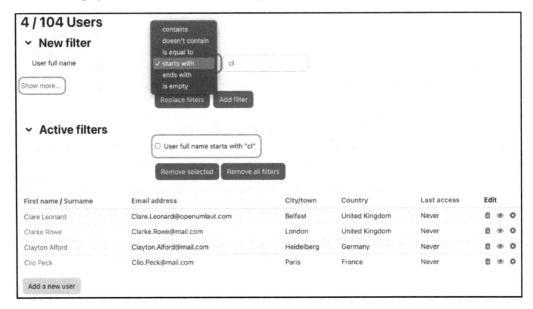

Figure 5.8 – Filtering user accounts I

You can see that the added filter is now active, which becomes more useful once multiple filters have been added (switch to advanced mode via the **Show more…** link). Now, we can apply filters to a wide range of fields:

Figure 5.9 – Filtering user accounts II

For instance, in the preceding screenshot, we look for all users whose username starts with **22** (assuming the naming scheme starts with the year of entry) and whose account has been suspended. Using this mechanism, it is possible to add as many filters as required.

Every time a filter is added, it will be shown in the **Active filters** frame and applied to the user data in Moodle.

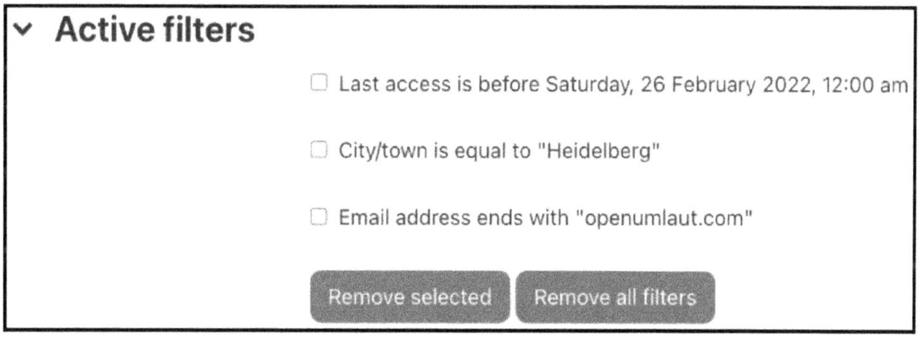

Figure 5.10 – Filtering user accounts III

Here, three self-explanatory filters have been added. It is now possible to delete individual filters (select the filter and click on the **Remove selected** button) or **Remove all filters**.

The filter criteria for text fields have been described earlier in this section. Depending on the field type, some additional operations can be used, as listed in the following table:

Filter operation	Field type	Description
is any value	Lists	All values are acceptable; the filter is disabled
is equal to	Lists	The list value has to be the same as the one that's been selected
isn't equal to	Lists	This is the opposite of **is equal to**
any value	Yes/No	The value can be either **Yes** or **No**; the filter is disabled
Yes	Yes/No	The value has to be **Yes**
No	Yes/No	The value has to be **No**
is defined	Profile fields	The field has to be defined for the user
isn't defined	Profile fields	This is the opposite of **is defined**
is after	Date	This contains all dates after the specified day, month, and year
is before	Date	This contains all dates before the specified day, month, and year

Figure 5.11 – Filtering operations

The **Authentication** criterion offers a selection of all the supported authentication methods. We will deal with these later in the chapter. If user profile fields have been specified, an additional **User profile fields** criterion is shown, offering a choice of all the user-defined fields (as specified earlier).

The current filter settings are saved and can be used the next time you log in. Not only that but they are also saved for bulk user actions, which are covered in the next section.

Bulk user actions

Bulk actions allow an administrator to perform a single action on multiple users, for example, forcing a password to change or sending a message. To illustrate how bulk user actions work, have a look at the user actions funnel depicted in the following diagram:

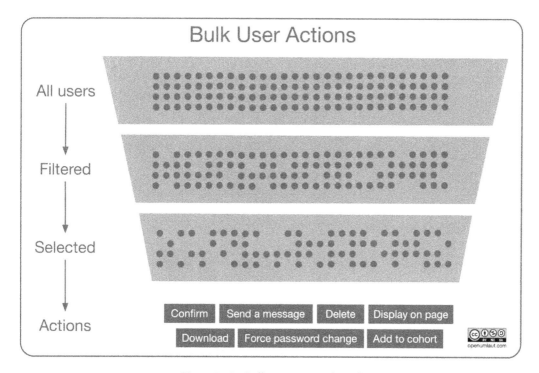

Figure 5.12 – Bulk user actions funnel

The three layers of the funnel have the following characteristics:

- The top layer shows all users in the system (tenant in Moodle Workplace)
- The middle layer contains all users after active filters have been applied
- The bottom layer comprises any users left after you have narrowed down the list by selecting users manually

Various bulk actions can then be applied to this group of chosen user accounts by going to **Site administration | Users | Accounts | Bulk user actions**.

> **New filter**

> **Active filters**

∨ **Users in list**

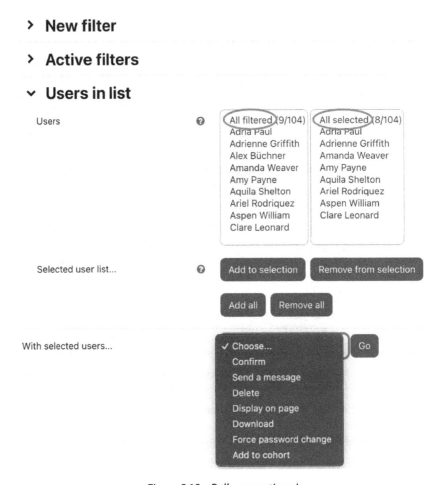

Figure 5.13 – Bulk user actions I

The screen contains three main sections. The first two parts are the familiar **New filter** and **Active filters** sections. Interestingly, filters already created will also show up on this screen since they have been saved.

The third part displays the users that match the specified filter criteria in the **All filtered** list. Before you can do anything with the users, you must move them to the **All selected** list using the **Add to selection** button. In the preceding screenshot, all users except one have been moved across. To move them back to the **All filtered** list, select the users and click the **Remove from selection** button. Two shortcut buttons exist, which allow you to add all users from the **All filtered** list to the **All selected** list and use **Remove all** to move them in the opposite direction.

The advantage of this approach is that you can apply several filters in succession and select the respective users, for example, in a setting where the usernames start with the year of entry. Suppose you wish to select all the users from 2022 and 2023, filter for all usernames that start with **22**, and select all the entries that show up in the results. You can then delete the filter and repeat the filtering with the value 23.

When the **Go** button for the **With selected users...** drop-down menu is clicked, the operation selected will be performed on the users from the **All selected** list. The available operations are shown in the following table:

Action	Description
Confirm	After a confirmation screen, pending user accounts will be confirmed. This is only applicable to email-based self-registrations.
Send a message	You are asked to write a message body, which will be sent to the selected users.
Delete	After a confirmation screen, users will be irreversibly removed from the system (refer to the information on user deletion in the *Browsing users* section).
Display on page	The user information is shown on the screen. By default, the fields displayed are Full name, Email address, City/town, Country, and Last access (take a look at the **Show user identity** setting by going to **Site administration I Users I Permissions I User policies** for more details).
Download	You can choose between the following download formats: CSV, XLSX, HTML, JSON, ODS, and PDF. In addition to user profile fields (standard and custom), the list of fields also includes Moodle's internal user ID.
Force password change	Users will have to change their password the next time they log in to Moodle.
Add to cohort	Select a cohort that users will be added to. Cohorts will be dealt with in detail in the next section.

Figure 5.14 – Bulk user actions II

Now that we know how to deal with existing users, let's look at how they are added to the system.

Creating user accounts manually

There are two ways to manually create accounts for users to get access to your system:

- Adding individual users

- Uploading users in bulk, including their user pictures

In the following three sections, you will learn how to perform and support each type.

Adding individual users

To add user accounts manually, go to **Site administration | Users | Accounts | Add a new user**. Alternatively, you can navigate the list of users and select the **Add a new user** button at the bottom of the screen. You will see the same form you saw earlier when you edited the user's profile.

> **Important note**
> Adding users manually should be the exception, not the rule. It is highly recommended to automate the process.

You should avoid adding individual users manually as much as possible, as it is a very time-consuming, cumbersome, and potentially error-prone procedure. However, there are situations when you cannot avoid it, for example, when a student joins a school halfway through the term or an external trainer requires access to Moodle but is not part of the organization's staff database.

If you have more than one user to add, use Moodle's batch uploading facility, which we will look at next.

Bulk uploading and updating user data

Uploading users in bulk allows importing multiple user accounts from a text file or updating user accounts that already exist in your system.

Learner information is often available in existing applications, such as the internal student management information system or HR database, which can export data to an Excel spreadsheet or directly to a text file. The data represented in the CSV file is then loaded to the Moodle database, and, if specified, users are enrolled in courses and added as members to cohorts. This process is shown in the following workflow diagram:

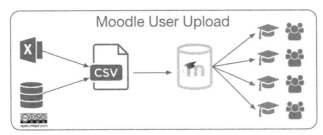

Figure 5.15 – Bulk user upload

You will find excellent and detailed instructions on uploading and updating users in batch mode at docs.moodle.org/en/Upload_users. We will focus on the key elements and upload workflows to supplement the well-documented feature.

The text file format

Before uploading users, you must generate a text file conforming to a specific format. Its general format is a **Comma Separated Value** (**CSV**) file, a flat text file format. While creating CSV files manually (using a plain text editor or a spreadsheet application) is possible, the files are usually generated automatically by a system hosting the user data.

The format of a text file is as follows:

- Each line of the file must contain a single record
- Each record must be a series of data that are separated by delimiters
- The first record of the file must contain the list of field names defining the structure of the rest of the file

An example of a valid input file is as follows:

```
username, password, firstname, lastname, email
galmond, pwd, Graham, Almond, galmond@openumlaut.com
earmstrong, pwd, Eleanor, Armstrong, earmstrong@openumlaut.com
jarnold, pwd, Joanne, Arnold, jarnold@openumlaut.com
```

The first line contains the list of provided fields, while the remaining three lines represent individual users to be uploaded.

Moodle's upload function supports the following types of data fields:

- **Required**: Compulsory fields that must be included
- **Password**: Password fields
- **Optional**: If no value is provided, specified default values will be used
- **Custom**: User-defined profile fields
- **Enrolment**: Dealing with courses, roles, and groups
- **Cohort**: Adding users as members to cohorts
- **System**: Assigning and unassigning system roles to and from users
- **Special**: Modifying and deleting user accounts

We will be going through each field type to understand better how Moodle's user batch upload works and how you can use it in your setting.

Required fields

When adding new users, only `firstname` and `lastname` are compulsory. When updating records, only `username` is required. You might recall that the user profile has a few more compulsory fields, such as the username or email address. A default value must be specified via a template if these fields are not provided. We will deal with templates later in this chapter.

The sample file is an example of an input file containing five fields, including the required `firstname` and `lastname`.

Password

The `password` value is required unless **Create password if needed and send via email** has been enabled. If this is the case, a welcome email with a one-off password will be sent to the respective user the next time the `cron` process runs.

Note

If you set `password` to changeme, the user will be forced to change the password when they log in for the first time. A better way to do this is using the **Force password change** option.

Optional fields

As the name suggests, optional fields do not have to be specified—if they are not included in the text file, default values are taken, if present. These optional fields are as follows:

Type	Fields

Text	The values of these fields are in plain text:
	`address,department,description,icq,idnumber,institution,interests,phone1,`
	`phone2,timezone,url`
	If any fields contain commas, you must encode them as , the upload function will automatically convert them back to commas.

Numeric	The options are numbered in the same order as they appear in the Moodle interface—the numbering starts with 0: `autosubscribe:` 0 = No, 1: Yes `htmleditor:` 0 = Standard web forms, 1: HTML Editor `maildisplay:` 0 = Hide, 1 = Allow everyone, 2 = Allow course members `mailformat:` 0 = Pretty, 1 = Plain `maildigest:` 0 = No digest, 1 = Complete digest, 2 = Digest with just subjects
List	These fields have to be populated with pre-defined values `auth:` Each authentication method is represented by its shortname, for instance, **manual**, **ldap**, **oauth2**, or **nologin**. `country:` Two-letter ISO country code in UPPER CASE, for instance, GB, DE, UA, ES, or US. `lang:` Shortname of the language pack, such as es, es_mx, es_ve, and es_co. You can find the complete list in **Site administration I General I Language I Language packs**. `theme:` Shortname of the user theme. Options are **boost** and **classic**, plus any installed third-party themes. `timezone:` The region of the user's time zone, for example, Europe/Berlin. Case sensitivity is critical, so check out the available values in the **Default timezone** list in **Site administration I General I Language I Location settings**.

Figure 5.16 – User upload (optional fields)

It is crucial to include empty fields when the default setting has to be used. These must be left empty even if it is the last field in each record. An empty field is represented by two consecutive commas, as shown in the sample file:

```
username, password, firstname, lastname, email, city

galmond, changeme, Graham, Almond, galmond@openumlaut.com, Kyiv

earmstrong, , Eleanor, Armstrong, ermstrong@openumlaut.com,

jarnold, , Joanne, Arnold, jrnold@openumlaut.com, Doha
```

A `city` field has been added in the preceding sample file, and the default city has been set to **Paris**. After uploading the file, the `city` value for **Graham Almond** is set to **Kyiv**, and that for **Joanne Arnold** is set to **Doha**. The `city` value for **Eleanor Armstrong** has been left empty and will be set to the default value of **Paris**. Some `password` fields have also been left empty.

Custom profile fields

Any user-defined fields you have specified (in our case, those for parental responsibilities) can also be used as part of the batch upload process. Each field must be preceded by `profile_field_`; for instance, the field representing the Skype ID would be labeled `profile_field_skype_id`.

Custom fields are treated in precisely the same way as optional fields. If specified, the values are taken; otherwise, default values will be used, if present.

Enrolment fields

Enrolment fields allow you to assign roles to users; you can enrol them in courses and assign them to groups. Roles will be covered in detail in *Chapter 6*, *Managing Permissions, Roles, and Capabilities*.

Each course has to be specified separately by `course1`, `course2`, `course3`, and so on. The course name is the course's short name and the only compulsory enrolment field. Each corresponding type, role, group, enrolment start time, enrolment period, and enrolment status must have the same postfix: `type1`, `role1`, `group1`, `enroltimestart1`, `enrolperiod1`, and `enrolstatus1` correspond to `course1`.

It is further possible to set a user's role in a course. Each role has a role short name and a role ID, either of which can be specified. If the type is left blank or no course is specified, the user will be enrolled as a student. The enrolment period sets the enrolment duration in terms of days; the enrolment status suspends a user from a course when it's set to `1`.

If you want to assign users to groups in a course (`group1` in `course1`, `group2` in `course2`, and so on), you have to specify the group name or ID. If a specified group does not exist, it will be created automatically.

The following example demonstrates some of the enrolment features:

```
username, course1, role1, course2
galmond, Advanced, editingteacher, Staff
earmstrong, Advanced, examiner, Staff
jarnold, Basic, 3, Staff
```

The `course1` field and its corresponding `role1` and `course2` are optional enrolment fields. Graham Almond (`galmond`) will be assigned the `editingteacher` role in the `Advanced` course, and Eva Armstrong (`earmstrong`) will be assigned the `examiner` role. Jonny Arnold (`jarnold`) will be `editingteacher` (the role ID is 3) in the `Basic` course. All three users will be assigned the `student` role in the `Staff` course (no role has been specified, hence the default is set).

Cohort fields

Cohort fields allow you to add users as members to cohorts. Like enrolments and groups in courses, the field name has to be suffixed by a counter: `cohort1`, `cohort2`, and so on. An example file snippet is as follows:

```
username, firstname, lastname, cohort1, cohort2
pupil1, Pupil, One, 7a, drama
pupil2, Pupil, Two, 7a, archery
```

Users can be added to system cohorts as well as context cohorts. Cohorts will be dealt with after this main section.

System role

If you need to assign users a system role, you must specify this via `sysrole1`, `sysrole2`, and so on. The field's value has to be `shortname` of the role, for instance, `manager` or `coursecreator`.

You can also unassign a system role from a user by preceding the role name with the minus symbol, for example, `-manager` or `-coursecreator`.

Special fields

The following special fields are supported:

- `oldusername`: When changing a username, you must provide the current value
- `deleted`: When removing a user, you will set `deleted` to 1
- `suspended`: When suspending a user, set `suspended` to 1; to activate, set it to 0

Special fields are the last category of text file format. Once you have created your user file, it is time to upload users to Moodle, which we will tackle next.

Uploading users

Uploading users is a four-step process, as shown in the following diagram:

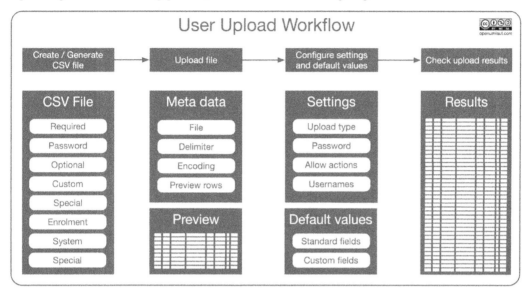

Figure 5.17 – User upload workflow

The workflow comprises the following four steps:

1. Creating or generating the CSV file
2. Uploading the file, specifying metadata, and viewing the data preview
3. Configuring upload settings and default values
4. Checking upload results

We already covered *step 1* in the previous subsection, so let's jump straight to the second and third phases. To upload or update users in batch mode, go to **Site administration | Users | Accounts | Upload users,** where the following settings are available:

- **File**: The name of the text file.

- **CSV delimiter**: Specify whether the delimiter is a comma (default), semicolon, colon, or tab. In most European locales, for instance, German, French, and Dutch, the default delimiter is a semicolon!

- **Encoding**: The encoding scheme of your uploaded file specifies the locale in which it has been saved (the default is **UTF-8**).

- **Preview rows**: The number of rows displayed on the preview screen.

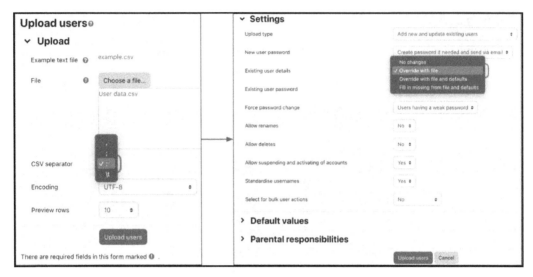

Figure 5.18 – Upload users configuration

Once this screen has been confirmed, you will see the following four sections:

- **Upload users** preview: A sneak peek of the specified number of rows that will be uploaded. Records that are to be skipped will not be shown.

- **Settings**: Different options, which depend on the selected upload type.

- **Default values**: All the user fields for which default values can be set.

- **Custom values**: Any user-defined fields grouped by category, if present.

Remember that not all settings exist for all upload types; they will remain hidden if they are not applicable. The following table shows which settings are available for which upload type:

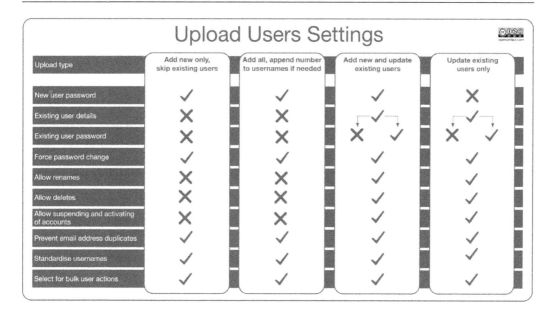

Figure 5.19 – Upload users settings

Here is a brief description of each **Upload users** setting:

- **New user password**: Moodle requires either a password in the file (**Field required in file**) or the cron process will generate a one-off password automatically if none is specified (**Create password if needed and send via email**).

- **Existing user details**: Specifies what action is performed on the existing user details when an account is updated. The options are **No changes**, **Override with file**, **Override with file and defaults**, and **Fill in missing [fields] from file and defaults**.

- **Existing user password**: Specifies what happens with users' passwords when the user details are updated. The password can be left unchanged (**No changes**) or overridden (**Update**).

- **Force password change**: Specifies when to tag accounts requiring users to change the password (**Users having a weak password**, **None**, and **All**).

- **Allow renames**: Specifies whether the changing of usernames is allowed. This only applies to the special oldusername field.

- **Allow deletes**: Specifies whether removing user accounts is allowed. This only applies to the special deleted field.

- **Allow suspending or activating of accounts**: Specifies whether deactivating or activating user accounts s is allowed. This only applies to the special suspended field.

- **Prevent email address duplicates**: Multiple users can have the same email address (as discussed in the *Understanding user profiles* section). This setting will only show if **Allow accounts with same email** on **Site administration | Plugins | Authentication | Manage authentication** is enabled.

- **Standardise usernames**: Removes any invalid characters from usernames (extended characters, unless allowed, as well as spaces) and ensures that all characters are lowercase.

- **Select for bulk user operations**: You can specify whether **New users**, **Updated users**, or **All users** should be selected for bulk operations. You will see the names in the user list for **Bulk user actions**.

Default values have been mentioned a few times so far; now, it is time to deal with them alongside templates.

Setting default values and templates

Moodle's user batch upload function supports default values that are used if no value has been set. Default values cover all user profile fields that can be uploaded as well as user-defined custom fields.

Each text-based field can be populated using a template. This feature is helpful for optional fields, such as the URL of students' websites, and is compulsory for required fields if they're not specified in the CSV file, for example, `username` and `email`. Moodle will warn you if the latter is the case. For example, in the following screenshot, **Username template** has not been provided, which is indicated by the red warning message:

Figure 5.20 – Template missing

The template (or pattern) will create a value based on the values of other fields and the standard characters you specify. A template can comprise the following content:

- **Replacement values**: The value is substituted by the corresponding profile field

- **Template modifiers**: The value is converted or truncated based on the modifier

- **Standard text**: Plain text is included without any modification

The following table hopefully clarifies the preceding concepts:

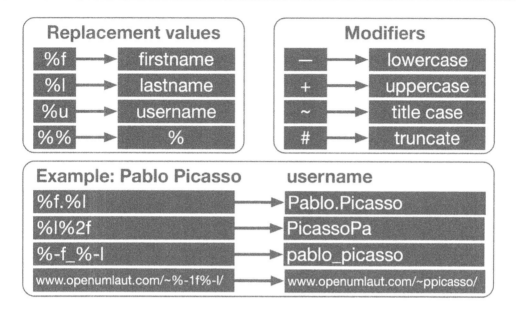

Figure 5.21 – Template content

There are four replacement values, indicated by a percentage. For example, if the username should be the first name of a user, followed by a period, and then the surname, the template would look like %f.%l.

Four modifiers can be included between the % sign and any of the three code letters (l, f, and u), where the hash represents a decimal number. The last template is an example embedding the replacement values inside other text; in this case, it is a URL representing a user's home page.

This completes the third step of our user upload workflow. The last step is to load and review the actual user data.

Loading of data

Once all the settings have been specified, the default values have been provided, and the **Upload users** button has been pressed, Moodle will finally start the actual importing process.

> Important note
> It is highly recommended that you create a test file with a smaller number of dummy records first to ensure that the syntax is correct.

Moodle displays a large table that contains all the user fields that have been added and/or changed. It also shows the status of each field, including any problems or errors that have occurred.

A message is displayed at the end of the results screen, summarizing the upload process. It contains the number of users created and updated, those with a weak password (according to the password policy), and the number of errors. Take a look at the following screenshot:

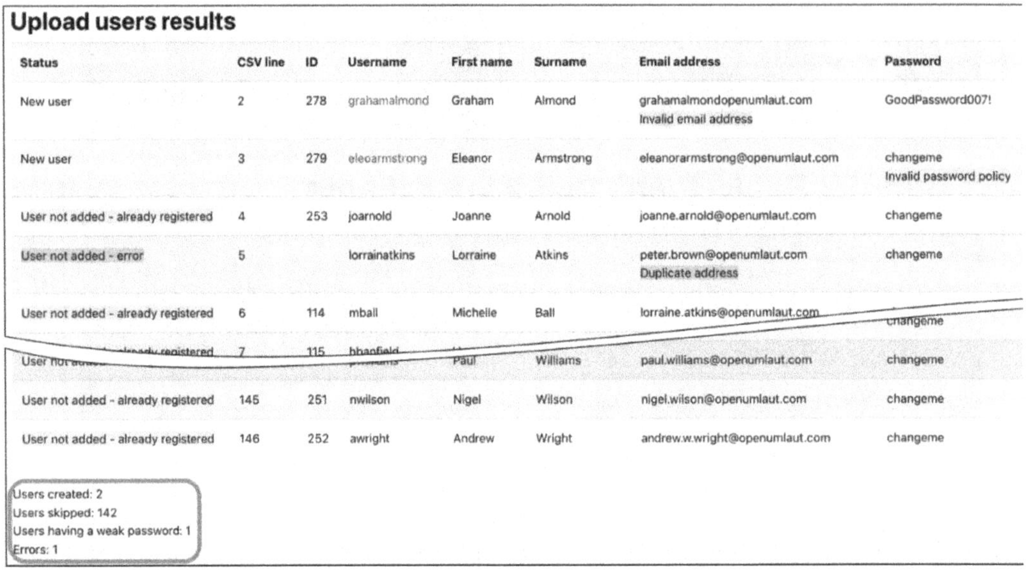

Upload users results

Status	CSV line	ID	Username	First name	Surname	Email address	Password
New user	2	278	grahamalmond	Graham	Almond	grahamalmondopenumlaut.com Invalid email address	GoodPassword007!
New user	3	279	eleoarmstrong	Eleanor	Armstrong	eleanorarmstrong@openumlaut.com	changeme Invalid password policy
User not added – already registered	4	253	joarnold	Joanne	Arnold	joanne.arnold@openumlaut.com	changeme
User not added – error	5		lorrainatkins	Lorraine	Atkins	peter.brown@openumlaut.com Duplicate address	changeme
User not added – already registered	6	114	mball	Michelle	Ball	lorraine.atkins@openumlaut.com	changeme
User not added – already registered	7	115	bbanfield	Paul	Williams	paul.williams@openumlaut.com	changeme
User not added – already registered	145	251	nwilson	Nigel	Wilson	nigel.wilson@openumlaut.com	changeme
User not added – already registered	146	252	awright	Andrew	Wright	andrew.w.wright@openumlaut.com	changeme

Users created: 2
Users skipped: 142
Users having a weak password: 1
Errors: 1

Figure 5.22 – Reviewing upload results

It is recommended that you immediately identify invalid user accounts and modify their user settings manually or fix the upload file and do a re-run.

Bulk user operations provide a versatile means to create and update textual user data. However, one type of user information that CSV files cannot process exists: profile images. Moodle comes with a dedicated feature that deals with user pictures. Let's take a look at it in the next section.

Uploading user pictures

As described so far, the process of uploading users does not support profile images; instead, user pictures must be uploaded separately. The workflow to upload user images is simple yet effective, as depicted in the following diagram:

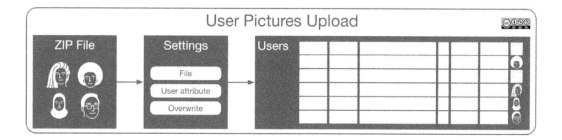

Figure 5.23 – User pictures upload workflow

The upload user picture tool can be found at **Site administration | Users | Accounts | Upload user pictures**. The images to be uploaded have to be archived in a ZIP file. Each image filename inside the compressed file must conform to the following format: `attribute.ext`.

The **User attribute to use to match pictures** field is set to any of these values: **username**, **idnumber**, or (the internal user) **id**. This attribute is used to match the picture to an existing user, and you have to select the attribute in the respective pull-down menu. `ext` is the filename extension (`.jpg`, `.gif` or `.png`). The image filenames are not case sensitive.

Figure 5.24 – Upload user pictures

For example, if the username consists of the first name's initial and a surname (`%1f%1`, if expressed in template style), the valid filenames are `psmith.png`, `lcohen.png`, and `mstripe.png`. If the users exist, the pictures will be added to their profiles; otherwise, they will be ignored. If a picture already exists for a user, it will only be replaced if you have enabled the **Overwrite existing user pictures?** option.

So far, we have only looked at individual users on an account-by-account basis. Moodle thrives on being a learning system that supports communication and collaboration among learners and teachers. To support working together, users can be arranged in two ways: groups and groupings at the course level, and cohorts at the system or category level. We have already come across groups in the previous chapter and during the user batch upload, so let's have a closer look at cohorts now.

Managing cohorts

We have already come across cohorts in *Chapter 4*, *Managing Courses and Enrolment*, and in the introductory diagram of this chapter.

> **Important note**
> Cohorts are groups that are used to logically cluster related users.

So far, we mainly mentioned cohorts in the context of enrolments; however, cohorts are utilized by Moodle in various places, such as the following:

- Course enrolments and synchronization
- Cohort themes provide a user experience to a pre-defined group of users, for example, visually impaired learners
- Report audiences to limit access of a report to cohorts
- Execute actions automatically, such as notifying or issuing a certificate to a cohort as part of dynamic rules (Moodle Workplace only)

Zooming in on the cohort element, we can see its structure and properties:

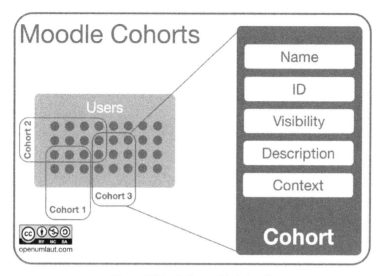

Figure 5.25 – Cohorts (high-level)

Let's have a closer look at how to create and manage cohorts. To do this, navigate to **Site administration | Users | Accounts | Cohorts**.

System: available cohorts (4)

System cohorts   All cohorts   Add new cohort   Upload cohorts

Search   🔍

Category	Name	Cohort ID	Description	Cohort size	Source	Edit
System	7a 🖉	7a 🖉	All students from class 7A	0	Created manually	👁 🗑 ⚙ 👥
System	7b 🖉	7b 🖉	All students from class 7B	0	Created manually	👁 🗑 ⚙ 👥
System	7c 🖉	7c 🖉	All students from class 7C	0	Created manually	👁 🗑 ⚙ 👥 Assign
Test	Temp 🖉	temp 🖉	Used as a placeholder	0	Created manually	⌀ 🗑 ⚙ 👥

Figure 5.26 – Available cohorts

The details of each cohort and its standard actions (hide, delete, edit, and assign) are provided. The **All cohorts** tab provides an almost identical view, displaying system and category cohorts.

To create a cohort, select the **Add new cohort** tab and specify the cohort's properties. **Context** is the scope of the cohort that indicates where the cohort can be used; the options are **System** (global or site-wide) and a selected category. **Cohort ID** is optional, but it is good practice to set this as it will be used for different operations, such as when adding bulk users.

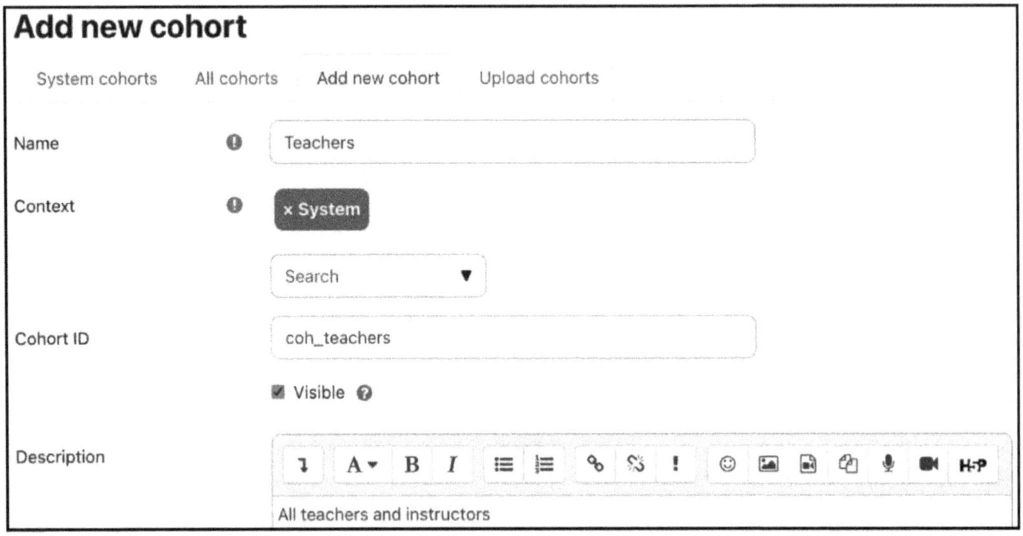

Add new cohort

| System cohorts | All cohorts | Add new cohort | Upload cohorts |

Name ❶ Teachers

Context ❶ × System

Search ▼

Cohort ID coh_teachers

☑ Visible ❓

Description 1 A▾ B I ≡ ≣ % ✂ ! ☺ 🖼 🖾 📑 🎤 🎥 H-P

All teachers and instructors

Figure 5.27 – Adding a cohort

Once you have added a cohort, you will return to the list of all cohorts. Now, you should add members to it by selecting the **Assign** icon, which will display the familiar user selection screen to add or remove cohort memberships.

> **Important note**
> Removing users from a cohort will unenrol them from all courses where cohort synchronization has been enabled!

Instead of adding cohorts manually, you can perform this task in a batch via the **Upload cohorts** tab. The principle is the same as adding users in batch mode, as described in the previous section. Here is a sample file representing the cohorts used earlier:

```
name, contextid, idnumber, description, visible

7a, 1, 7a, All students from class 7a, 1

7b, 1, 7b, All students from class 7b, 1

7c, 1, 7c, All students from class 7c, 1

Temp, , , Used as a placeholder, 0
```

You can find details on uploading cohorts, including optional and additional fields, at `docs.moodle.org/en/Upload_cohorts`.

Now that you know everything about user accounts and the information stored about them, let's look at how to authenticate them with Moodle.

Configuring user authentication

Authentication is the process of getting access to a system. Moodle supports a significant number of authentication types. Furthermore, Moodle supports **multi-authentication**, that is, concurrent authentication from different authentication sources. For example, your organization might use an LDAP server containing user information for all your staff, and OAuth2 for students, but it wishes to manage part-time users locally.

In the second half of this chapter, we will explore user authentication and the overall management of authentication plugins before covering common authentication settings. Then, we will deal with all authentication methods, which have been grouped into four categories: internal, external, provider, and system.

Exploring user authentication

Remember the basic authentication workflow we looked at in *Chapter 3*, *Exploring Courses, Users, and Roles*. Now, we can have a look at a more complete picture, as shown in the following diagram:

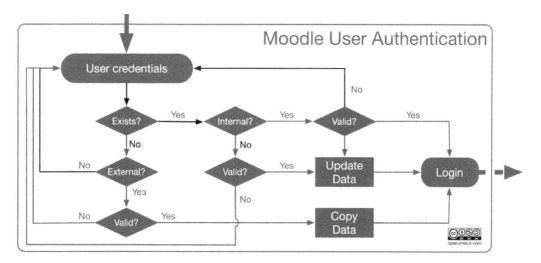

Figure 5.28 – Authentication workflow

Let's start from the top, where the user enters their user credentials, for example, username and password. Bear in mind that this could take place automatically, for example, in a single sign-on setup or via a service provider login. Moodle checks whether a profile exists for the user. If it does and the account is authenticated via an internal mechanism, Moodle only has to check whether the credentials are valid.

If the user profile doesn't exist, which is often the case the first time a user attempts to log in, Moodle checks for any enabled and configured external provider-based authentication mechanisms. If there is a valid entry, an account will be created, any existing data for which a mapping exists will be copied to the local user profile, and access will be granted.

Once the profile exists and authentication is external or via a provider, Moodle checks whether the credentials are valid for the set authentication method. If this is the case, any modified data in the source will be updated, and access will be granted.

Managing user authentication

To access all the authentication plugins, go to **Site administration | Plugins | Authentication | Manage authentication**. You will see a list of available authentication plugins. Each plugin can be activated/deactivated by toggling the **show/hide** icon. The settings for each type discussed in this section are accessed by their respective links or directly through the link in the plugins menu once the authentication method is active.

You can also change the order in which Moodle attempts to authenticate users via the up and down arrows.

> **Important note**
> The order in which authentication plugins are applied will impact how long it takes for users to log in, so make sure that the main ones are at the top.

The **Users** column gives you an indication of the number of registered users for each authentication mechanism.

Manage authentication

Available authentication plugins

Name	Users	Enable	Up/Down	Settings	Test settings	Uninstall
Manual accounts	274			Settings		
No login	0					
Email-based self-registration	2	👁	↓	Settings		
OAuth 2	30	👁	↑ ↓	Settings		
LDAP server	12	👁	↑	Settings	Test settings	
CAS server (SSO)	0	👁⃠		Settings	Test settings	Uninstall
External database	0	👁⃠		Settings	Test settings	Uninstall
LTI	0	👁⃠				
MNet authentication	0	👁⃠		Settings	Test settings	
No authentication	0	👁⃠		Settings		Uninstall
Shibboleth	0	👁⃠		Settings	Test settings	Uninstall
Web services authentication	0	👁⃠				

Figure 5.29 – Authentication plugins

Additional authentication methods are supported by external plugins on `moodle.org/plugins/?q=type:auth`, for example, **OpenID** and **SAML2**. Once installed (refer to the *Installing third-party add-ons* section in *Chapter 8, Understanding Moodle Plugins*), they will appear in the list alongside all the core authentication methods. It is not recommended that you remove plugins via the **Uninstall** option—delete them at the system level instead.

The following diagram illustrates a clustering of Moodle authentication plugins:

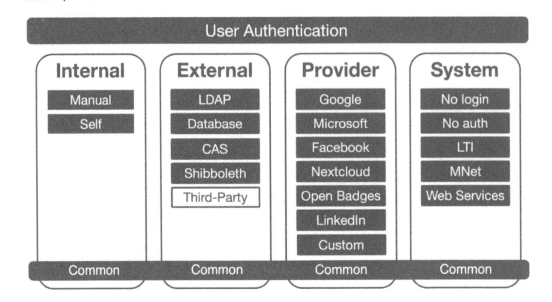

Figure 5.30 – Authentication plugins grouping

This grouping also forms the structure of the remainder of the chapter, starting with common authentication settings all mechanisms share.

Common authentication settings

First, let's look at the common authentication settings, which you will see under the list of available plugins. Whatever your preferred authentication system(s) is, several common settings apply across all methods:

- **Self registration**: Specify which plugin, if any, is used for self-registration (refer to the next section for details).

- **Allow login via email**: Users can log in via their username or email address as long as the latter is unique.

- **Allow accounts with same email**: In some settings, users will have to share the same email address. We discussed this topic in the *Understanding user profiles* section.

- **Prevent account creation when authenticating**: Some authentication mechanisms, for instance, LDAP, support the creation of new accounts. If this is prevented, you must ensure that the accounts are created by other means.

- **Autofocus login page form**: When enabled, the cursor on the login page will always jump directly to the username input field if it is empty or to the password field otherwise.

- **Guest login button**: By default, guest access to your Moodle system is allowed. If you disable this, which is recommended for most educational and commercial sites, the guest login button will not be shown on the login screen.

> **Important note**
> Ensure to disable guest access to your Moodle system to prevent unwanted registrations.

- **Limit concurrent logins**: You can specify the number of simultaneous browser logins. Once the number has been exceeded, the oldest session will be terminated. This limitation is useful in exam scenarios where you might allow only a single concurrent login.

- **Alternate login URL**: By default, users have to log on to Moodle via the standard login screen. However, to change the source of the login credentials (username and password), enter the correct URL here. This redirect is necessary if you wish to have a login block on a separate web page, such as your home page. Details of this mechanism are shown in the *Customizing the login* subsection in *Chapter 7, Enhancing Moodle's Look and Feel*.

- **Forgotten password URL**: Moodle has a built-in mechanism to deal with lost or forgotten passwords. You should enter its URL here if you use an authentication method with its own password-recovery system.

- **Instructions**: It is good practice to provide information on how to sign up for the system and what format the username should have (this only applies to self-registration). There are default instructions if it's left blank.

- **Allowed/Denied email domains**: You can restrict the email domains for self-registration that are allowed/not allowed on your system when new user accounts are created, for example, `openumlaut.com` or `.edu`.

- **Restrict domains when changing email**: If enabled, the allowed/denied email domain settings will also be applied when an email address is changed.

- **ReCAPTCHA public/private key**: This is the key to display the reCAPTCHA element on the signup form/to communicate with the reCAPTCHA server (refer to the *Email-based self-registration* section).

Some common authentication settings will make more sense once we have dealt with the authentication methods they impact. Let's start with internal authentication methods.

Internal authentication methods

Internal authentication methods handle all authentication within Moodle; no other system is connected. There are two internal authentication methods: manual accounts and email-based self-registration.

Manual accounts

Manual account authentication is simply the verification at login that the entered user credentials (username and password) stored in Moodle are correct.

> **Important note**
> The main Moodle administrator account is always a manual account.

There are two types of settings for all manual accounts created: password expiry and the locking of user fields. Both can be changed by navigating to **Site administration | Plugins | Authentication | Manual accounts**.

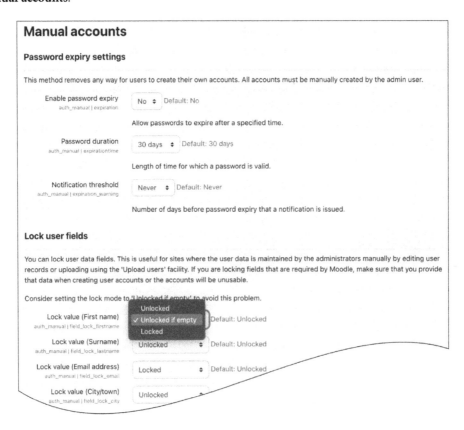

Figure 5.31 – Manual accounts settings

Password expiry lets you choose how long a password is valid via the **Password duration** setting before it has to be changed by a user. **Notification threshold** lets you specify when a user is notified of the password rotation.

You can lock fields for accounts that are manually created or uploaded via batch files. This locking mechanism is helpful whenever you do not want users to be able to change specific data in their user profiles—young students may misuse the **Description** field, the ID number may be used internally to link to other systems, the company might have provided the email address, and so on.

By default, all fields are **Unlocked**. If a field is **Locked**, the user will not be able to change its value. If you lock any compulsory fields, you either have to ensure they are populated correctly, or you set their lock state to **Unlocked if empty**. The latter will force the user to enter the value the next time they log in and lock the field afterward.

Accounts verified by the manual authentication method are usually created manually or via user batch upload. Both operations have been described in detail in the first part of this chapter, where the latter effectively automates manual account creation. Two other authentication mechanisms mimic adding user accounts manually: web services, which we deal with in the *System authentication methods* section later on, and *Email-based self-registration*, which we cover next.

Email-based self-registration

Moodle supports a mechanism that allows users to create accounts without any intervention or knowledge of the administrator. When new users sign up with Moodle via the **Create new account** button on the login screen, they can choose their new username and password. Once this step has been completed, a confirmation mail is sent to the user's email address, containing a secure link that must be confirmed to activate the account. The signup screen looks like this:

Figure 5.32 – Self-registration signup screen

We explained how to add more items to the signup screen (via the **Display on signup page** option) when dealing with user-defined profile fields. This feature is often invaluable in commercial training settings when additional data, such as the learner's address, a participant's dietary requirements, or a customer number, has to be gathered.

Moodle supports a **reCAPTCHA** mechanism activated on the pictured signup screen. The facility is used to avoid automated signups by bots. To enable this facility, you must sign up for an account at `www.google.com/recaptcha`, add the public and private key in **Common settings** in the **Manage Authentication** area, and enable the **reCAPTCHA** element.

> **Important note**
> The PHP cURL extension must be installed for reCAPTCHA to work.

The same locking settings can be set for self-registration as for manual accounts (go to **Site administration | Plugins | Authentication | Email-based self-registration**). Also, the same restrictions apply as described earlier. Additionally, you have the **Enable reCAPTCHA element** option.

If a user policy has been specified when you navigate to **Site administration | Users | Privacy and policies | Policy settings**, a link to the agreement with the confirmation checkbox is shown on the signup screen. We will deal with more complex user consent handling as part of the GDPR set up in *Chapter 14, Complying with Data Protection Regulations*.

If the confirmation email cannot be sent, for instance, because of technical issues, go to the list of users, where you will find two links beside the account entry: one to confirm the account and one to resend the email.

Before we move on to the next authentication method, here is a short checklist for setting up self-registration (apart from enablement, all steps are optional):

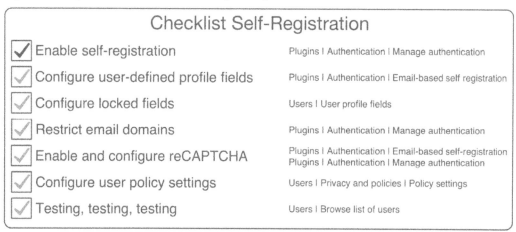

Figure 5.33 – Checklist for self-registration

Allowing users to register accounts on your site comes with a degree of risk since you have no control over who – humans or bots – is coming to your site (assuming it is publicly accessible). Therefore, it is highly recommended to test self-registration thoroughly and regularly check your new users list.

Now that we have covered internal authentication, it is time to look over the (Moodle) fence and deal with external methods.

External authentication methods

External authentication methods require a separate, connected system to handle authentication. We will cover two external authentication methods in detail (LDAP and databases) and two more we only briefly describe (CAS and Shibboleth).

LDAP server

In the previous chapter, we had already seen a basic introduction to LDAP when dealing with course enrolment. Now, let's look at how it can be utilized for **single sign-on** (**SSO**) authentication. We will only cover the basic LDAP settings and exclude advanced setups, such as multiple LDAP servers and secure LDAP. These configurations are documented in great detail at docs.moodle.org/en/ LDAP_authentication.

The principle of the LDAP authentication method is relatively simple but effective—if the entered username and password are valid, Moodle creates a new user account in its database if it doesn't already exist. Once it does exist, that is, from the second login onwards, the credentials are checked against LDAP for validity.

> **Important note**
> The PHP LDAP extension must be installed on the server for LDAP authentication to work.

Go to **Site administration | Plugins | Authentication | LDAP server** to see the settings, which also cover **Active Directory** (Microsoft's implementation of LDAP). There is a significant number of parameters that you must set to communicate with an LDAP server. The settings have been amended with detailed explanations (which I will not repeat). Instead, additional information is provided wherever applicable. Contact your system administrator if you are unsure where to locate some of the required information.

Two parts must be populated to make Moodle work in your LDAP setup: **server settings** and **data mappings**, discussed in the following paragraphs.

There are ten sections of **LDAP server settings** that have to be provided:

- **LDAP server settings**: These establish the connection to the directory. LDAP servers with SSL encryption are also supported.

- **Bind settings**: These specify details about the credentials needed to access the LDAP server. If you have multiple bases, it is recommended that you put them in order of importance as Moodle stops searching once it has found an entry. For example, if you have `ou=Students` and `ou=Staff` and your students make up 90% of the logins, it is recommended that you put them before their lecturers unless staff is given priority.

- **User lookup settings**: These describe how and where user details are stored on your LDAP directory. Make sure you select the correct user type. The same applies to the distinguished name in the bind settings for multiple contexts. It is crucial to set **Search subcontexts** correctly. If it is set to **No**, subcontexts will not be searched, but the search is potentially faster, and vice versa.

- **Force change password**: This specifies whether and how users must change passwords when accessing Moodle for the first time.

- **LDAP password expiration settings**: These are concerned with password lapsing and how this is being dealt with.

- **Enable user creation**: This lets you activate a mechanism that is similar to self-registration, but, in addition to this, an account is created with the values from your LDAP.

- **System role mapping**: This specifies which LDAP user groups will have manager and course creator permissions in Moodle, respectively.

- **User account synchronization**: This setting specifies what Moodle should do with local user accounts when these have been deleted on the LDAP server.

- **NTLM SSO**: This describes how, in a Windows-based environment with MS-AD and NTLM active, users can log in via the Windows domain without re-entering their credentials when accessing Moodle. Check out `docs.moodle.org/en/NTLM_authentication` for details.

The second half of the admittedly very long screen contains the LDAP data mapping. It is common for user profile information to be stored in the LDAP server. To connect user profile fields and the Active Directory, a mapping has to be provided by specifying their counterparts in the directory for each field in Moodle (including user-defined profile fields). All the fields are optional. Default values are used if you leave any of the fields blank:

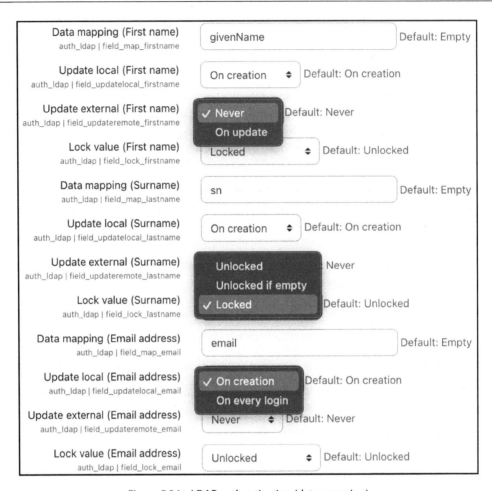

Figure 5.34 – LDAP authentication (data mapping)

If you provide the field information, you will have to set four parameters for each data field, as follows:

- **Data mapping:** This is the field name in the external database representing the value in Moodle.

- **Update local:** For each external user, information is stored locally. You can update this information using **On creation** (this is faster but potentially not up-to-date) or **On every login** (this is a bit slower, but it's always up to date).

- **Update external:** If a user updates the data field's value in Moodle, you can decide whether you want to write this information back to the external database (**On update**) or not (**Never**). Often, the external database is a read-only view, preventing Moodle from updating data in it.

- **Lock value:** You can specify whether the user can modify the value. As explained earlier, the settings (**Unlocked**, **Unlocked if empty**, and **Locked**) are identical to the lock field.

If you use Microsoft's Active Directory MS-AD, check out the data mapping section in `docs.moodle.org/en/LDAP_authentication` for details.

Setting up LDAP authentication can be a bit of trial-and-error. Verifying that the connection works can be assisted by the **Test setting** facility located in the list of available authentication plugins. More detailed error messages will be displayed, which will help you identify any SSO connection issues.

When using LDAP, you might encounter a situation where you wish to assign courses to users before they have logged in to the system for the first time. This scenario regularly applies before the start of the academic year. The problem is that the local user accounts do not exist yet, and you cannot access this information as it is only stored in the external directory. There are two ways around this conundrum:

- Create the user accounts via batch files and set the `auth` field to `ldap`; that way, you effectively mimic the initial logging in of each user.

- Set up the **LDAP users sync job** scheduled task. Tasks are covered in *Chapter 15, Optimizing Moodle Performance*.

LDAP is effectively a specialized and lightweight database for authentication purposes. Authentication against LDAP is very similar to authentication against external databases, which is the topic of the following subsection.

External databases

Most large organizations use a student or management information system—either open source (good), proprietary (bad), or developed in-house (worst)—which holds information about staff and learners. It makes perfect sense to utilize this data for authorization to Moodle. Since all information systems use a database at their core, all we have to do is to get access to the relevant data.

IT departments are usually not too keen for external systems to connect directly to their database. A mechanism that has proven valuable is the **read-only view**, which has several advantages:

- A view can be prepared for Moodle usage; only required fields are shown in the required format

- There's no write-access to the database

- If the database schema of the information system ever changes, only the view has to be adapted, not the Moodle configuration

The external database authentication method contains two types of parameters that you have to provide by going to **Site administration | Plugins | Authentication | External database: connection settings** and **data mappings**.

External database

This method uses an external database table to check whether a given username and password is valid. If the account is a new one, then information from other fields may also be copied across into Moodle.

Host auth_db | host	db.openumlaut.com	Default: 127.0.0.1

The computer hosting the database server. Use a system DSN entry if using ODBC. Use a PDO DSN entry if using PDO. Multiple hosts OR addresses can be specified (eg host1.com;host2.com;host3.com) or (eg xxx.xxx.xxx.xxx;xxx.xxx.xxx.xxx)

Database auth_db | type	mysqli ◆	Default: mysqli

The database type (see the documentation ADOdb - Database Abstraction Layer for PHP for details).

Use sybase quotes auth_db | sybasequoting	No ◆	Default: No

Sybase style single quote escaping - needed for Oracle, MS SQL and some other databases. Do not use for MySQL!

DB name auth_db | name	MIS	Default: Empty

Name of the database itself. Leave empty if using an ODBC DSN. Leave empty if your PDO DSN already contains the database name.

DB user auth_db | user	moodle	Default: Empty

Username with read access to the database

Password auth_db | pass	.... 🖉 👁	

Password matching the above username

Table auth_db | table	USERS	Default: Empty

Name of the table in the database

Username field auth_db | fielduser	ID	

Figure 5.35 – External database authentication

The database connection settings have been amended with good explanations. Contact your database administrator if you are unsure where to locate some of the required information.

> **Important note**
>
> Some databases, such as Oracle, are case sensitive, and field names must be provided with the correct casing for the database link to work correctly.

The second half of the settings screen contains the data mapping. User profile information is stored in the external database. To connect the user profile fields and the database, a mapping has to be provided where a counterpart in the external store has to be provided for each field in Moodle, including user-defined profile fields. All the fields are optional, and default values are used if you leave any fields blank.

Most facilities covered in the LDAP section are also available for external database authentication:

- Creating user accounts via batch files (set the auth field to db)
- Automating synchronization via the task scheduler, **Synchronise users task**
- Testing the database connection

To sum up the topic, here is a checklist for external authentication methods:

Checklist External Authentication

- ✓ Install PHP extension
- ✓ Enable authentication method — Plugins I Authentication I Manage authentication
- ✓ Configure server settings — Plugins I Authentication I LDAP server / external database
- ✓ Configure data mappings — Plugins I Authentication I LDAP server / external database
- ✓ Enable users sync job — Server I Tasks I Scheduled tasks
- ✓ Configure user policy settings — Users I Privacy and policies I Policy settings
- ✓ Testing, testing, testing — Plugins I Authentication I Manage authentication / Users I Browse list of users

Figure 5.36 – Checklist for external database authentication

Hopefully, the previous two subsections gave you an insight into how external authentication mechanisms work in Moodle. Two more methods fall in the same category: CAS and Shibboleth.

Other external authentication mechanisms

Moodle supports some additional external SSO authentication methods that are not utilized as often as LDAP, external databases, and OAuth 2; we only briefly touch upon them:

- **CAS Server (SSO)**: **Central Authentication Service (CAS)** is an open source authentication server based on Tomcat and supports single sign-on in a web environment. CAS is particularly popular in environments that comprise multiple authentication sources and consumers. It utilizes LDAP and, therefore, requires the PHP LDAP modules to be installed.

- **Shibboleth**: Shibboleth is SAML-based open source middleware that provides single sign-on across organizational boundaries. Privacy, security, and flexibility in terms of multi-setups are at the heart of Shibboleth. However, the price to pay is a complicated setup process detailed in the local readme file at `<YOURSITE>/auth/shibboleth/README.txt`. More information on Shibboleth can be found at `www.internet2.edu/products services/trust-identity-middleware/shibboleth`.

All authentication mechanisms covered so far are either internal to Moodle (manual accounts and self-registration) or usually local to the organization but external to Moodle (LDAP or database). Moodle also supports provider-based authentication services via **OAuth 2**, which we will cover next.

Service provider-based authentication (OAuth 2)

OAuth 2.0 is the de facto industry standard protocol for user authorization. OAuth 2 authentication enables users to access Moodle via buttons on the login page using their credentials from popular service providers, such as Google, Microsoft, Facebook, and LinkedIn.

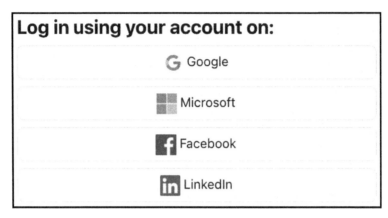

Figure 5.37 – Authentication via OAuth 2 service providers

Before we dive into the configuration of service provider-based authentication, have a look at the interaction diagram, which illustrates how OAuth 2 works in a Moodle context:

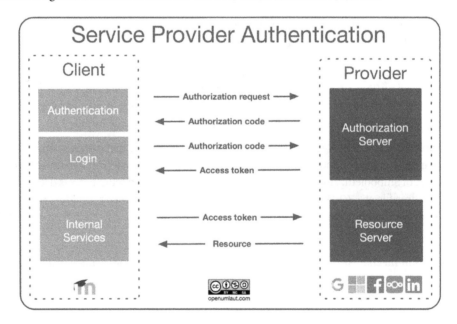

Figure 5.38 – OAuth 2 interactions

An OAuth service provider is an external system ("in the cloud") that provides identity (via the authorization server) and API access (via the resource server) by issuing OAuth access tokens to a client (Moodle). Let's go through the interactions from top to bottom:

1. A user sends an **authorization request**; that is, a user logs in to the service provider via the client. This step is initiated via the service provider buttons on the Moodle login screen.

2. The authorization server issues an **authorization code** if the entered credentials are valid. Once this has taken place, the user is authenticated with Moodle. If account creation is enabled (the **Prevent account creation when authenticating** setting), a new account will be created. Otherwise, the user will be prompted to link the authorization to an existing account with the same email address. An entry can be found in the **Linked logins** section in the user's preferences.

3. An **access token** will be issued when the user logs in using the stored authorization code. A scheduled task exists to regularly update the OAuth 2 tokens (`\core\oauth2\refresh_ system_tokens_task`).

4. Moodle uses this access token for any internal services that require a **resource** from the service provider, for instance, a link to files in a repository. Some internal services require a system account to be connected.

The preceding interaction process is a very crude summary of how OAuth 2 authentication works in Moodle, but this should be sufficient to understand the overall concept. OK, enough of the high-level stuff; let's start setting up service provider authentication.

The first step is to configure OAuth 2 services in **Site administration | Server | Server | OAuth 2 services**.

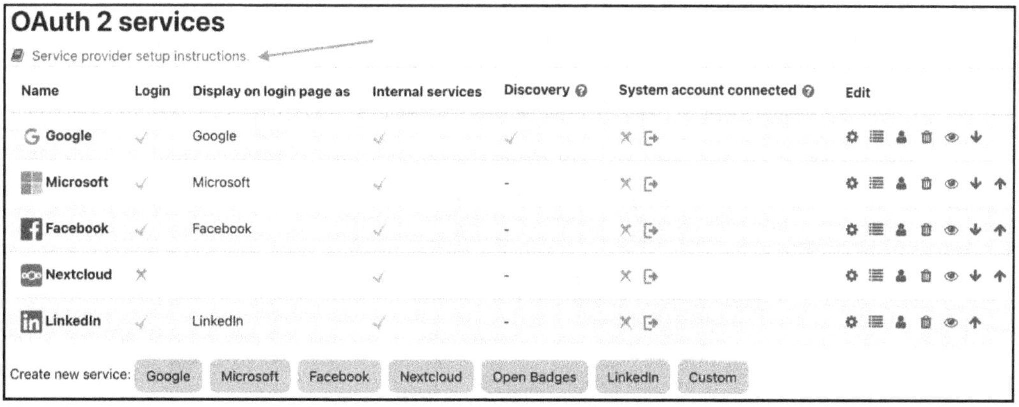

Figure 5.39 – OAuth 2 services

At the bottom, you can see all supported service providers. Select the respective button to add a preconfigured service, which will direct you to the form to create a new service. The service specifications are already populated – all you must do is add the **Client ID** and the **Client secret** details of the respective service provider.

How do you get the client ID and secret? The issuer provides these, so setup must be done at their end, not in Moodle. There is a **Service provider setup instructions** link for the six supported prominent OAuth 2 providers at the top of the screen.

> **Important note**
>
> It is recommended to leave all fields at their default values for pre-defined service providers, except **Client ID**, **Client secret**, and **Service base URL**.

If you wish to set up a service provider not listed, you can create a **Custom** service. The form is identical to the pre-defined services but without any pre-populated values. You find details about the purpose of each parameter at docs.moodle.org/en/OAuth_2_services.

Once the service has been created (pre-defined or custom), the standard actions are available in the **Edit** column, plus two more actions that require some more explanation:

- **Configure endpoints**: Endpoints are the URLs that Moodle uses to make OAuth 2 authentication requests. These have already been added for pre-defined services and shouldn't be changed; for custom services, the mandatory endpoints are authorization_endpoint, token_endpoint, and userinfo_endpoint.

- **Configure user field mappings**: Here, you define how the provider's response from userinfo_endpoint should be mapped to Moodle user fields. It is recommended to at least configure firstname, lastname, and email since these are compulsory fields in Moodle's user profiles.

Once the service provider has been configured properly, it can be used by the OAuth 2 authentication plugin, which has to be enabled at **Site administration | Plugins | Authentication | Manage authentication**. Like all other authentication plugins, OAuth 2 lets you configure any locked fields, and there are no additional configuration options as the service provider setup controls all behavior.

As with other authentication methods, let's conclude the section with a checklist, which hopefully comes in useful when you have to configure OAuth 2 authentication:

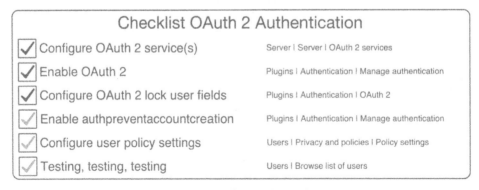

Figure 5.40 – Checklist for OAuth 2 authentication

We have now covered all the authentication mechanisms that ship with Moodle and belong to the first three pillars of our authentication plugin grouping. The fourth category comprises system authentication methods, which we are covering next.

System authentication methods

Moodle contains authentication methods, which are required by certain features to function correctly:

- **No login**: This plugin has no settings and cannot be disabled or uninstalled. Its sole purpose is to suspend users from logging in to your Moodle system, which takes place in the user's profile by selecting the authentication method in the **Choose an authentication method** drop-down list.

- **No authentication**: When this method is enabled, users can create accounts without any kind of authentication or email-based confirmation. It is highly recommended that you do not use this method since it creates a very insecure Moodle site and should only be used for testing or development purposes. Only user fields can be locked in the same way as described earlier.

- **MNet authentication**: Moodle networking allows the connection of multiple Moodle sites in a peer-to-peer or hub style. See *Chapter 19*, *Setting Up Moodle Networking*, for details.

- **LTI**: This plugin has the sole purpose of facilitating the login to LTI producers. LTI will be discussed in *Chapter 9*, *Configuring Education Features*.

- **Web services authentication**: This plugin authenticates users via external clients communicating with Moodle via web services (see *Chapter 18*, *Integrating External Systems Using Web Services*, for details). The authentication plugin has no settings.

This concludes the section on user authentication. While there has been a lot of content, you are highly likely only to require information on manual accounts plus the method(s) you are utilizing in your organization. Since no two authentication setups are the same, you will soon be familiar with all the quirks and idiosyncrasies of your authentication infrastructure and the plugin(s) that connect it.

A last piece of advice: be on good terms with your system, database, and network admins. They will grant you access to your LDAP directory or the organization's authentication database system and open up the ports you need to connect to service providers and web services. Buy them a coffee or bribe them with other niceties!

Summary

Phew! That was a lot to take in for one chapter.

The first part of this chapter demonstrated the different ways Moodle provides to manage users. We first looked at what information is stored for each user account and how their profiles can be extended. We then performed several standard manual and bulk user actions before dealing with cohorts.

In the second part, we dealt with different types of user authentication, namely internal, external, service providers (via OAuth 2), and system. Due to the variety and complexity of authentication methods, we covered prominent plugins in more detail than others.

Authentication has become a complex topic, and we only touched upon methods supported in Moodle core. Other methods such as Microsoft Azure AD or Open ID as well as mechanisms such as two-factor authentication, one-time passwords, and user key authentication are beyond the scope of this already packed chapter and are catered for via plugins at moodle.org/plugins/?q=type:auth.

One aspect of authentication we didn't mention at all is **multi-tenancy**. Assume a setup where different users have to connect via different authentication mechanisms of the same type; for instance, staff authenticates via SAML_internal, and customers and partners via SAML_external. There are two options for how this can be facilitated:

- Duplicate the authentication plugin at the system level and modify the source code accordingly. A programmer must carry out this task as source code changes are required in the copied module. Be careful with this approach, as this might not work when Moodle is updated to a newer version.

- Consider Moodle's big brother, Moodle Workplace, which supports multi-tenancy authentication. To get a feel for how this works, have a look at docs.moodle.org/en/Multi-tenancy_authentication. At the time of writing, the following authentication methods support multi-tenancy: manual, email-based self-registration, OAuth 2, and SAML 2 (as a third-party plugin).

The next step is to grant user roles, that is, the rights as to what they are allowed to do and what they are not. This will be dealt with in the next chapter.

6
Managing Permissions, Roles, and Capabilities

Permissions are complex yet powerful and can be seen as the backbone of Moodle. In this chapter, we will cover contexts, roles, and capabilities, which define what users can and cannot see and do in your Moodle system.

In this chapter, we will cover the following topics:

- Exploring Moodle's predefined roles
- Understanding contexts
- Assigning roles to users
- Understanding capabilities
- Roles and context management

We will start with a short definition that should be kept in mind when managing permissions.

> **Important note**
> A role is a collection of capabilities with corresponding permissions and risks. A role is assigned to a user in a context.

Let's have a look at the following high-level diagram, which visualizes the preceding definition before we cover all permission-related topics in detail:

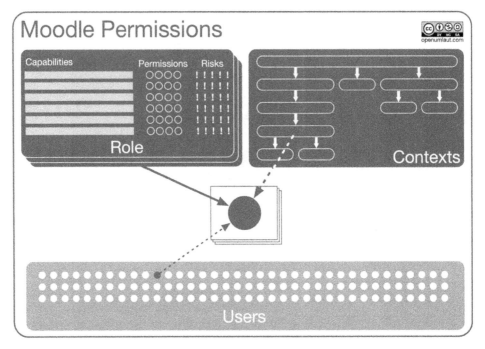

Figure 6.1 – High-level permissions overview

Every user in your Moodle system is assigned one or many roles, and a role comprises many capabilities with associated permissions and risks. Each role assignment takes place in a particular context, representing a hierarchically organized ring-fenced area.

We will begin this chapter by exploring the standard roles of Moodle before covering the slightly abstract concept of contexts. It will get more practical when we assign roles in different contexts. Next, we will look at how roles are structured and modified before creating our own roles. We will conclude this chapter with role management and some best practice advice.

By the end of this chapter, you will have understood the core concepts of the Moodle permission system, which comprises roles, contexts, capabilities, and the management thereof.

Exploring Moodle's predefined roles

Moodle comes with several predefined roles. These standard roles are suitable for most educational setups, but some institutions require modifications to be made to the roles system to tailor Moodle to their specific needs.

Each role has capabilities for several actions that can be carried out. For example, an administrator and a course creator can create new courses, whereas all the other roles are denied this right. Likewise, a teacher is allowed to moderate forums, whereas students can only contribute to them.

The description of each standard role and the short names that are used, internally and in operations, such as user batch upload, are listed in the following table (taken from **Site administration | User | Permissions | Define roles**):

Role ⓘ	Description	Short name
Manager	Managers can access courses and modify them, but usually do not participate in them.	manager
Course creator	Course creators can create new courses.	coursecreator
Teacher	Teachers can do anything within a course, including changing the activities and grading students.	editingteacher
Non-editing teacher	Non-editing teachers can teach in courses and grade students, but may not alter activities.	teacher
Student	Students generally have fewer privileges within a course.	student
Guest	Guests have minimal privileges and usually can not enter text anywhere.	guest
Authenticated user	All logged in users.	user
Authenticated user on site home	All logged-in users in the site home course.	frontpage

Figure 6.2 – Moodle's predefined roles

Moodle Workplace has various extra roles to handle its business-oriented audience, such as tenant administrator, certification manager, dynamic rules manager, organization structure manager, program manager, and report builder manager.

Before we can do anything with roles, we need to understand the concept of contexts, which will be dealt with next.

Understanding contexts

A role (remember, a collection of capabilities with corresponding permissions) can be assigned within different contexts. So, what are contexts?

> **Important note**
>
> **Contexts** are the areas in Moodle where roles can be assigned to users.
>
> A user has a role in any given context.

A context can be a course, a category, an activity, a user, a block, or Moodle itself. Moodle comes with seven contexts, each with a given scope:

- **System**: Moodle itself – that is, the entire system, also known as the core or global context
- **Course category**: A category and its sub-categories
- **Course**: A single course
- **Activity module**: A course activity or resource
- **Block**: A sidebar block
- **User**: A user account
- **Site (Front page)**: The home page and files that can be accessed outside courses (often referred to as the front page context)

> **Important note**
> Each context has a **scope**. A scope is a ring-fenced area or boundary in which specific actions can be carried out

This arrangement is compared to a large building with multiple floors and rooms. A floor manager has certain rights and responsibilities for every room on a level, but these do not apply to rooms on other floors of the property.

Role assignments must be made at the correct context level to implement, such a structure. For example, the teacher role should be assigned at the **Course** context level, the moderator for a particular forum at the **Activity** context level, the administrator at the **System** context level, and so on. While it is technically possible to assign any role in any context, some roles just don't make sense. Unfortunately, Moodle doesn't warn you about this since it cannot distinguish between intentional and inadvertent assignments.

Contexts are hierarchical; that is, permissions are inherited from higher to lower contexts. Rights in a higher context are more general, whereas those in a lower context are more specific. The same applies to our building analogy – a manager at the building level would have the same rights at the floor or room level, whereas the opposite is not true.

The following diagram shows the contexts that exist in Moodle and how they are arranged hierarchically:

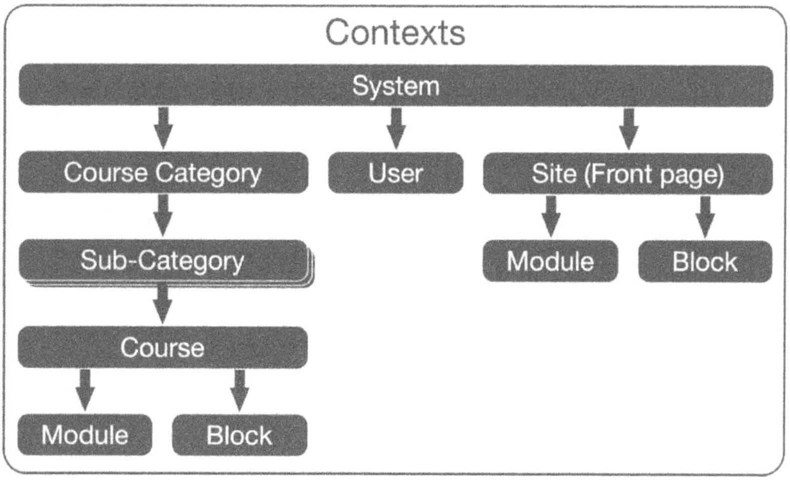

Figure 6.3 – Moodle context hierarchy

The **System** context is the root node of the hierarchy; every role assigned in this context will apply to any other context below it. The **Course Category** context on the next level acts as a parent to the **Course** context. If **Sub-Category** and **Sub-Sub-Category**, and so on, have been created, respective contexts will exist. You can see the **Module** and **Block** contexts on the lowest level. Like the **Course** context, the **Site** context has a **Module** and **Block** sub-context. **Site** refers to the home page and is often referred to as the **Front page** context for legacy reasons. Internally, **Site** is treated as a course (with course ID 1). The **User** context is a standalone entity with no children in the hierarchy.

For example, Jim is a teacher in a course. He is assigned the **Teacher** role in the relevant context (the class he is teaching), and he will have this role throughout the course, including blocks and activity modules (activities and resources). If, however, Jim had been assigned the **Teacher** role in the **Course Category** context instead, he would have the same rights in all the courses in this category and all its sub-categories. Jim will receive emails about all the assignments in all the courses, even if he doesn't teach them. Not only that, but he will also become a teacher in all future courses created in this category!

Organizing contexts hierarchically has several advantages that will sound familiar to those who know of object-oriented technologies:

- **Inheritance**: Rights and permissions set at one level are passed down to lower levels, which simplifies maintenance

- **Overriding**: Rights and permissions can be changed at lower levels

- **Extensibility**: New contexts might be added in future versions of Moodle, when and if required, without changing any of the existing roles in the system

Now we know what roles look like and which roles Moodle ships with, it is time to assign some roles.

Assigning roles to users

The process of role assignment is similar for each context. What is different is the location of each context and its access method. The process of assigning roles to users will be described first before we outline how and where to assign them in individual contexts:

1. Navigate to any **Assign roles** screen for the required context – for example, **Home | Participants | Assigned roles** in the **Permissions** section of the pull-down menu. On our system, you can see that **2** teachers and **18** students have been assigned (only up to 10 names can be displayed):

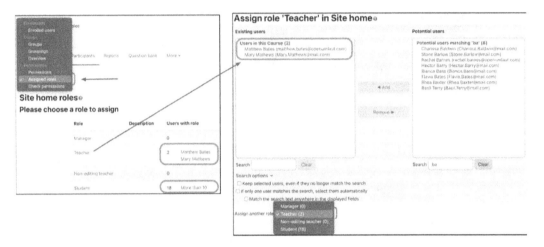

Figure 6.4 – Assigning roles to users

2. Select the role you wish to assign a user to by clicking on the role's name. If there are more than 10 assignees, click on the **More than 10** link. You will see the screen shown in *Figure 6.4* throughout Moodle whenever you wish to assign users to a role (except in courses, where a different modal interface has been developed).

3. Assign the role to users by selecting their names from the **Potential users** list and moving them to the respective category using the **Add** button.

4. Hold down the *Shift* key to select a range of users and the *Ctrl* key (*Command* key on macOS) to select multiple users.

5. To revoke users' role assignments, select the person from the **Existing users** list and move them back to the **Potential users** group by clicking on the **Remove** button.

> **Important note**
>
> Once a user has been assigned a role, permissions will be granted immediately. There is no need to save any changes.

If your list of potential users contains more than 100 entries, no user names will be shown, and you will have to use the **Search** box to filter the list of accounts (you can change this value via the **maxusersperpage** setting in **Site administration | Users | Permissions | User options**). Moodle uses a live search; as soon as you start typing, the list of users is updated immediately. There are three self-explanatory **Search options** underneath the left **Search** box. You might have to expand the area if it is collapsed:

- **Keep selected users, even if they no longer match the search**
- **If only one user matches the search, select them automatically**
- **Match the search text anywhere in the user's name**

You can switch to the assignments of another role in the current context via the drop-down at the bottom.

> **Important note**
>
> Assigning roles in an incorrect context is a common source of problems. It is highly recommended that you check the current context regularly to ensure no unintended rights have been granted. In other words, test your role assignments thoroughly.

So far, we have dealt with the general concept of contexts and looked at how to assign roles to users within a context. We will now deal with each context, following our Moodle context hierarchy. Let's start at the top with the **System** context.

System context

The **System** context covers the entire Moodle system. Assignment takes place from **Site administration | Users | Permissions | Assign system roles**. In our system, only two roles appear that can be assigned. We already mentioned that assigning certain roles in certain contexts doesn't make sense. Inside a role, it is possible to specify in which context roles may be assigned. Only the **Manager** and **Course creator** roles have been selected, which is the reason for the limited choice:

Assign roles in System⊙

Warning: Any roles you assign from this page will apply to users throughout the entire system, including the site home and all courses. ✕

Please choose a role to assign

Role	Description	Users with role	
Manager		1	Sonia King
Course creator		0	

Figure 6.5 – System context

You will see a familiar screen that allows you to assign roles to users. The only difference from the generic screen outlined earlier is the warning, which I can only repeat: **Any roles you assign from this page will apply to the assigned users throughout the entire system, including the front page and all the courses.**

In most Moodle systems with predefined roles, it only makes sense to assign the **Manager** role if you wish to allow read-only access to a user for all the courses, such as an inspector, business manager, or school principal. Assigning the **Course creator** role to a user allows you to create new courses in any category. If, for example, a **Teacher** role is assigned in the **System** context, the user is allowed access to every single course on the site and all the courses created in the future!

There are scenarios when global roles are justified, such as in very small organizations or if Moodle hosts only a small number of courses attended by all users. Also, some new user-defined roles, such as school inspector, are designed to be assigned at the global level.

One role that can only be assigned at the system level is the **Administrator** role. This task has been given a dedicated area under **Site administration | Users | Permissions | Site administrators**. A primary administrator was created when you installed Moodle, which cannot be modified or deleted. You can, however, create additional administrator accounts. This procedure is identical to assigning users in any other context, except that you must confirm the assignment. Furthermore, you can make any site administrator the main site administrator (via the **Set main admin** button).

> **Important note**
> Make sure you keep the number of Moodle administrators to a minimum! This restraint improves the consistency of your system, increases security, and avoids potential mismanagement of the site.

Moving down one level in the context hierarchy, we reach the **Course Category** context, which is the topic of the following subsection.

Course Category context

The **Course category context** covers all the courses within a category and its sub-categories. The role assignment takes place under **Site administration | Courses | Manage courses and categories**. You must select **Permissions** in the respective **Settings** drop-down menu and **Assign roles** from the familiar dropdown. The same mechanism applies to sub-categories, sub-sub-categories, and so on.

A typical role that's assigned in the **Course category** context is the **Course creator** role. It allows a dedicated user to create new courses within the specified category, often a department or division. The standard **Course creator** role does not include teacher capabilities; that is, a course creator cannot edit any course content. In smaller organizations, it may be required to grant the **Teacher** role access to all the courses within the category.

Moving down a level, we reach the **Course** context.

Course context

As the name suggests, all role assignments in a course are granted in the **Course** context. The assignment takes place in the actual course, which we already came across in *Chapter 4*, *Managing Courses and Enrolments*, when we dealt with enrolments.

> **Important note**
> Enrolments in courses are treated as roles in the **Course** context.

As enrolments contain some unique options (start date, end date, and the suspension option), and because these enrolments are often carried out by (non-technical) teaching staff, a different user interface has been implemented. However, within a course, when you go to **Participants | Enrolment methods** and then click on the **Enrol users** icon in the **Edit** column of the **Manual enrolments** method, you will see a familiar-looking screen. We covered the additional expiry options shown in the center of the screen when we covered enrolments:

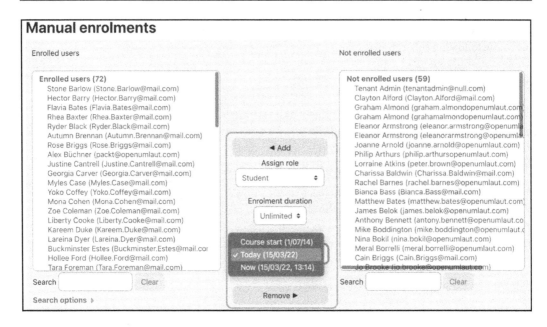

Figure 6.6 – Course context I

When a student is enrolled in a course, either by self-enrolment or any other enrolment mechanism, Moodle automatically assigns the **Student** role in the relevant **Course** context. This also applies if you upload users in batch mode and specify a course to which a user has to be enrolled.

If you have to assign roles to users who are not enrolled but have a role in the course, select **Other users** from the drop-down in the **Participants** menu and click on the **Assign roles** button. This applies to the **Manager** role, for instance, or a newly-created role, such as supervisor teacher. You will see a list of users who are not enrolled in the course but have inherited or assigned roles:

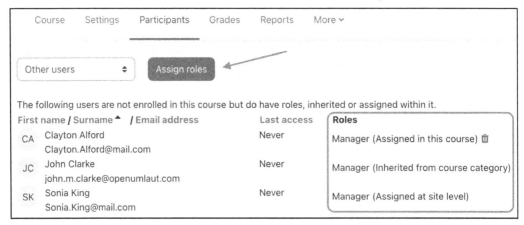

Figure 6.7 – Course context II

There is one level missing in the context level hierarchy, which deals with modules and blocks.

Module context

Once you are inside a course, it is possible to assign roles to users for individual modules – that is, resources and activities. When you select a module, there is a **Permissions** link in the **More** menu with three roles-related options. **Locally assigned roles** will lead to the familiar screen to **Assign roles**. **Permissions** and **Check permissions** let you change the inherited roles and verify the roles of the individual users. We will deal with this later in this chapter:

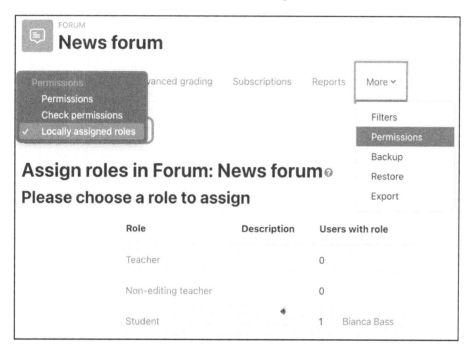

Figure 6.8 – Module context

Teachers often use role assignments in the **Module context** to grant or revoke additional rights to their students. A regularly cited example is that of a forum moderator. If you wish to put students in charge of a forum to help them learn how to moderate discussions, they require the rights to edit and delete posts (among others). These rights are part of the **Teacher** role, and it is perfectly feasible to assign a **Teacher** role to a student in a single activity. Just make sure they cannot grade any exams!

By default, users with a **Teacher** role have the right to assign roles in the **Module** context. However, it is often up to the Moodle administrator to carry out the task on their behalf due to the complexity of the roles system. The same applies to the **Block** context, which will be covered next.

Block context

The **Block** context allows the rights to be assigned at the block level, which is located within a course's block drawer. You will see an **Assign roles in <blockname> block** link in the drop-down menu (editing must be turned on):

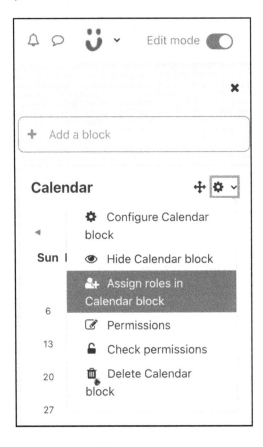

Figure 6.9 – Block context

By default, your system doesn't contain a role that has been granted rights to be assigned in the **Block** context; as a result, the link will be hidden. We will deal with modifying roles later on.

It is possible to control the users who can view blocks. Suppose there is a block that guests are not allowed to see. To hide that block, access the **Permissions** link in the block menu, and delete the **Guest** role from the `moodle/block:view` capability. Alternatively, you can select the **Guest** role from the **Advanced role override** drop-down list and the mentioned capability to **Prevent**. We will deal with capabilities later in this chapter.

The same mechanism also applies to blocks throughout the system, whether on the dashboard, the profile page, a course, or inside activities. It also applies to blocks on the home page, which is covered by the **Front page** context.

Front page context

In Moodle, the home page is covered by the **Front page** context. The front page is like a course and, at the same time, not like a course. In other words, it is a special course! This idiosyncrasy is also the reason why the **Front page** context is referred to as the **Site course** context.

The **Front page** context has the **System** context as the parent and, like the **Course** context, **Module** and **Block** as the sub-contexts. This familiar interface can be accessed via the **Assigned roles** link in the **Permissions** drop-down in the **Participants** section.

A typical user in the **Front page** context is a designer, who is responsible for the layout and content of the front page of the Moodle system. When assigned, only the **Front page** menu and its submenus are accessible. Most sites apply either the **Teacher** role or create a dedicated designer role.

User context

The **User** context is a standalone context with only the **System** context as the parent. It deals with all the issues relating to users outside courses, and it includes the user's profile, learning plans, forum posts, blog entries, notes, reports, logs, and grades.

Roles are assigned in the user's profile, where you must select **Preferences** from the **Administration** pane. The **Assign roles relative to this user** link *does not appear by default!* You need to have a role that can be assigned in the **User** context. None of the predefined roles make sense to be applied in such a way, which is why this only applies to user-defined roles. An often-cited example of a custom role to be applied in the **User** context is the **Parent/Mentor** role, which we will deal with in the *Creating custom roles* section later in this chapter:

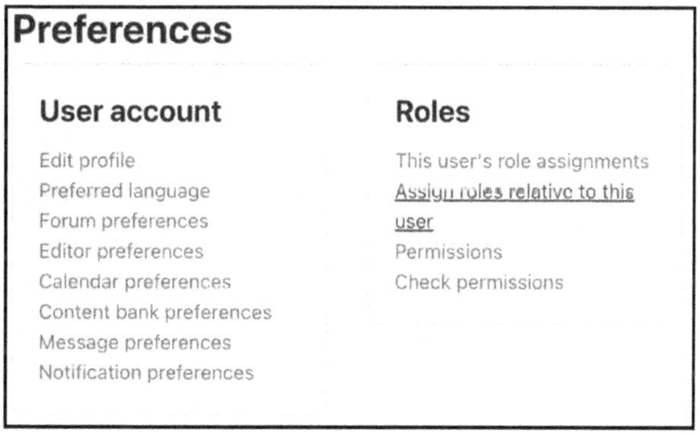

Preferences

User account

Edit profile
Preferred language
Forum preferences
Editor preferences
Calendar preferences
Content bank preferences
Message preferences
Notification preferences

Roles

This user's role assignments
Assign roles relative to this user
Permissions
Check permissions

Figure 6.10 – User context

Roles assigned in the **User** context will only have access to information that's accessible from the user screen. They will not have access to any courses.

Moodle also supports assigning roles to cohorts (**Site administration | Users | Permissions | Assign user roles to cohort**), which effectively automates manually assigning roles in the **User** context. This feature is useful in setups where supervisors are responsible for groups of learners.

Multiple roles

It is common for users to be assigned to more than one role. For example, a class teacher is also made course creator for the year group they are responsible for (the **Course category** context), they are in charge of the Moodle administration (**Site**), they act as a support teacher in a different class (**Course**), or they are the parent of a child (**User**). Every logged-in user is automatically assigned the **Authenticated user** role in the **System** context. We will deal with this later in this chapter.

A significant part of the roles infrastructure in Moodle is the ability to simultaneously assign multiple roles to a user. In our initial building example, the equivalent is a floor manager in charge of a particular floor level, temporarily covering the ground floor during holidays.

As discussed earlier, the actual context has to be selected to specify an additional role. You will then be able to assign additional roles as necessary.

The problem is the potential for conflicts, which Moodle has to resolve. For example, if one role can delete a forum post and another one doesn't, but a user has been assigned both roles in the same context, which right applies? While Moodle has a built-in resolution mechanism for these conflicts, it is best to avoid such scenarios altogether.

It is technically possible to assign two or more roles to the same user in the same context. It is hard to think of situations where such a setup would make sense.

> Tip
>
> The inner workings of the built-in permission resolution mechanism are well-documented in the *Conflict resolution of permissions* section at `docs.moodle.org/en/Override_permissions`.

This concludes this section on role assignments. Roles are made up of capabilities, which we will tackle next.

Understanding capabilities

So far, we have assigned existing roles to users in different Moodle contexts. In the following few pages, we will look inside a role where capabilities dictate what functionality is allowed and what isn't. Remember, a role is a collection of capabilities with corresponding permissions. Once we have understood capabilities, we can modify existing roles and create entirely new ones.

Role definitions

The existing roles can be accessed via **Site administration | Users | Permissions | Define roles**. The screen shown is the one from earlier when we explored Moodle's predefined roles. When you click on a role name, its composition is shown. You might recall the role element shown in *Figure 6.1*. Let's zoom in on the role to see what its elements are:

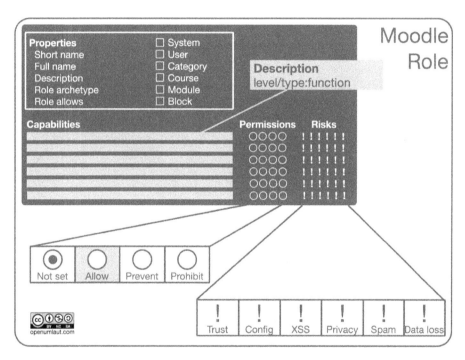

Figure 6.11 – Role structure

Each role contains a unique **Short name** (utilized in batch operations), a **Custom full name**, and an optional **Custom description**. The **Role archetype** field specifies which permissions are set if the role is reset to its default value. This setting further determines what values any new permissions will have when introduced in future versions of Moodle. These settings will then be applied during the update process.

The **Context types where this role may be assigned** field is set to the context in which the role will be allowed as an option. This restriction reduces the risk of assigning roles in contexts where they shouldn't. We encountered this when we tried to assign roles in the **Block** or **User** context, and Moodle prevented us from doing so.

The next four fields (**Allow role assignments**, **Allow role overrides**, **Allow role switches**, and **Allow role to view**) show which roles users assigned the current role are allowed to assign, override, switch, and view, respectively. The **Role risks** field indicates which of the six available dangers the current role has. All this information will make more sense once we have dealt with roles in more detail.

In addition to these parameters, each role consists of a large number of capabilities. Moodle's role system currently has approximately 450 (!) of them, and Moodle Workplace adds another 50+. If you have installed plugins, this number might even be higher.

> **Important note**
> A capability is a permissible action of a particular Moodle feature.

Each capability represents a legitimate Moodle action and is displayed as a single row in the list of all the capabilities. To simplify searching for capabilities, use the **Filter** option so that only the capabilities that match the filter criterion are shown (covering the name as well as the description):

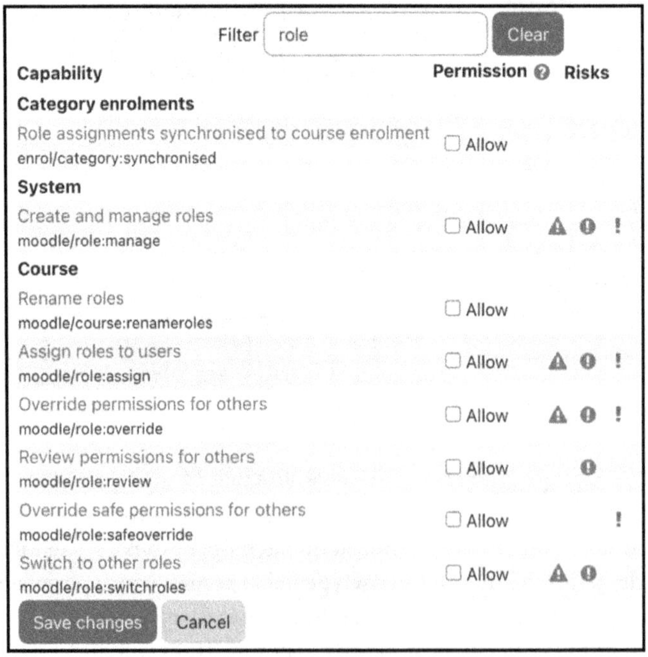

Figure 6.12 – Capabilities

Each capability has the following components:

- **Description**: The description, for example, **Upload new users from file**, provides a short explanation of the capability. Clicking a capability opens the online Moodle documentation for that capability in a separate browser window.

- **Name**: The name, for example, `moodle/site:upload users`, follows a strict naming convention, `level/type:function`, which identifies the capability in the overall role system. The level states which part of Moodle the capability belongs to (such as `moodle`, `mod`, `block`, `tool`, `enrol`, or `wp`). The type is the capability class, and the function identifies the actual action.

- **Permission**: The permission of each capability has to have one of the four values explained in the following table:

Permission	Description
Not set	All permissions for a new role are set to this value by default. The value in the context where it will be assigned is inherited from the parent context. Moodle searches upward through each context to determine this value until it finds an explicit value (**Allow**, **Prevent**, or **Prohibit**) for this capability; the search terminates when an explicit permission is found.
	Example: If a role is assigned to a user in a Course context and a capability has a **Not set** value, then the actual permission will be whatever the user has at the category level or, failing to find an explicit permission, at the site level. If no explicit permission is found, then the value in the current context is set to **Prevent**.
Allow	To grant permission for a capability, set the permission to **Allow**. It applies in the context in which the role will be assigned and all contexts below it.
	Example: When assigned in the **Course** context, students can start new discussions in all forums in that course unless some forum contains an override or a new assignment with a **Prevent** or **Prohibit** value for this capability.
Prevent	To remove permission for a capability, set the permission to **Prevent**. If granted in a higher context (no matter at what level), it will be overridden, and the value can be overridden again in a lower context.
Prohibit	This is the same as the **Prevent** permission, but the value cannot be overridden again at a lower context. The value is rarely needed but useful when an administrator wants to prohibit a type of user from certain functionality throughout the site. The capability is set to **Prohibit** and then assigned in the site context. A situation where this applies is when a user is a lousy student who is not allowed to post to the forums.

Figure 6.13 – Permissions

Important note

Principally, permissions at lower contexts override permissions at higher contexts. The exception is **Prohibit**, which, by definition, cannot be overridden at lower levels.

- **Risks**: Moodle displays the risks associated with each capability – that is, the risks that each capability can potentially raise. They can be any combination of the following six risk types:

Risk	Icon	Description
XSS		Users can add files and texts that allow cross-site scripting (potentially malicious scripts which are embedded in web pages and executed on the user's computer)
Privacy		Users can gain access to private information of other users
Spam		Users can send spam to site users or others
Data loss		Users can destroy a large amount of content or information

Figure 6.14 – Risks

> **Important note**
>
> Risks are only displayed; it is impossible to change these settings since they only act as warnings. The **Risks** documentation page is opened in a separate browser window when clicking on a **Risk** icon.

Moodle's default roles have been designed with the following capability risks in mind:

- **Administrator**: All capabilities, with a few exceptions
- **Teacher**: Certain capabilities with XSS and privacy risks, mainly adding and updating content
- **Student**: Certain capabilities with spam risks
- **Guest**: Only capabilities with no risks

Now that we have covered the ingredients of roles, let's start modifying them.

Modifying roles

To edit a role, click on the **Edit** button at the top of the view role details screen or select the appropriate icon in the **Edit** column on the main roles screen:

Figure 6.15 – Role operations

You can change the standard fields and their permissions when editing a role. For example, some schools change the **Student** role name to **Pupil**, while some training organizations change **Teacher** to **Instructor**. In Moodle Workplace, the two roles have been relabeled to **Learner** and **Trainer**, respectively. Bear in mind that this only changes the name of the role, not the corresponding labels used throughout Moodle. You will learn how to do this in the *Managing localization* section in *Chapter 10, Configuring Technical Features*.

When you change capabilities in a role derived from a **Role archetype**, its original values are highlighted when you click on the **Show advanced** button. For example, if your organization decides not to allow users to see the profiles of other users due to privacy or other reasons, you would edit the **Student** role, search for the moodle/user:viewdetails capability, and change it from **Allow** to **Not set**. Now, **Not set** is selected, but the **Allow** value remains highlighted; do not forget to save your role changes once applied:

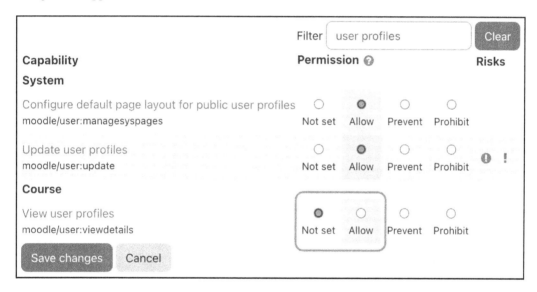

Figure 6.16 – Role operations

Unless you are confident with role modifications, it is recommended to duplicate a role first (via the **Export** functionality at the top of the screen in *Figure 6.16* and by creating a new role described further down) and then edit it. Keeping the default roles untouched makes maintenance more manageable if multiple administrators work on the same system or a third party provides support.

Important note

It is not possible to modify the **Administrator** role via the Moodle interface.

Modifying roles can often be avoided using the role's overriding mechanism, which we will cover in the next section.

Overriding roles

It is possible to override the permissions of a role in a given context. Picture the context hierarchy where a role definition has taken place at the top level. At a lower level, say category or course, you now wish to modify the permissions of that role. Role overrides facilitate precisely that.

> **Important note**
>
> Overrides are permissions designed to change a role in a specific context, allowing you to tweak your permissions as required. Tweaking involves granting additional or revoking existing rights.

Using the **Permissions** link in the familiar dropdown with the same name, you can see which role has been given or has inherited which permission for any of the capabilities of the current context (here, an assignment in the Module context):

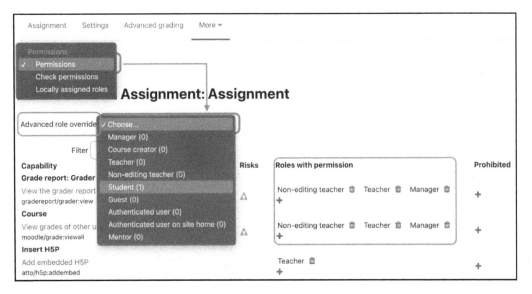

Figure 6.17 – Overriding roles I

The number shown in brackets indicates the number of overrides for each role. In the **Roles with permission** column, you can remove a role for each capability (using the standard **Delete** icon) or select a role to be added to the list of allowed roles (via the + symbol). The same applies to the **Prohibited** column.

Once you select a role from the **Advanced role override** dropdown, you will see a screen that shows details of each activity capability for this particular role. Overrides can now be used to open up areas in that context to grant extra permissions to users. Suppose you want to experiment with giving students the ability to grade some assignments; you would change the corresponding capability (mod:assign/grade) from its inherited value of **Not set** to **Allow**:

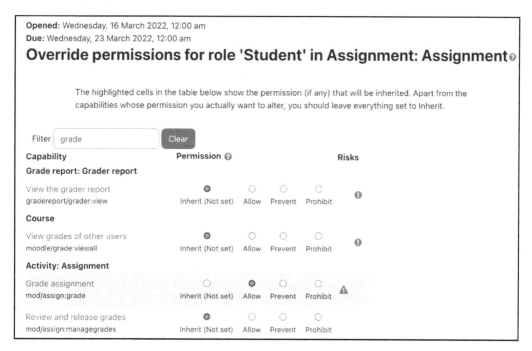

Figure 6.18 – Overriding roles II

Any changes to the roles system are highlighted, and datetime stamps are shown at the top of the screen.

Overrides can also be used to deny functionality in that context and remove permissions from users. For example, while learners with the role of student in a course are usually allowed to start new discussions in forums, there is one particular forum for which you want to restrict that capability: you can set an override that prevents the capability for students to start new threads in this forum (mod/forum:startdiscussion).

So far, we have understood the composition of roles and learned how to modify and override capabilities at different levels in the context hierarchy. Now, it is time to create our first custom role.

Creating custom roles

Moodle allows you to create new roles. Examples of such custom roles are parent, teaching assistant, secretary, inspector, and librarian in an educational setting and training coordinator, assessor, mentor, or staff manager in a business context. New roles can be defined by going to **Site administration | Users | Permissions | Define roles** and using the **Add a new role** button.

Before you get to the familiar role-editing screen, you have three options to choose from:

- **Use role or archetype**: Using an existing role or role archetype as a basis is commonly used to create a new role. It minimizes the amount of work required and reduces errors in creating new roles.

- **Use role preset**: Import a role (in XML format) that has been exported either in your Moodle instance or another system (using the **Export** button when viewing role details).

- **No selection**: Create a role from scratch without any presets or inherited archetypes:

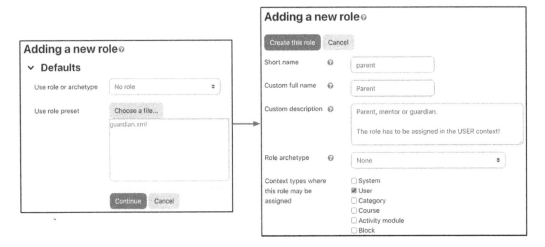

Figure 6.19 – Adding a new role

Make sure that you specify **Context types where this role may be assigned**. If you miss a context, assigning the role will not be possible. If you allow a context that is not suitable for the role, you run the risk that it will potentially cause problems.

Let's look at some example roles you might want to add to your Moodle system.

Example roles

Moodle Docs has provided several sample roles that might be relevant to your organization (docs. moodle.org/en/Creating_custom_roles). If not, they offer a good starting point for you to create other roles. Some valuable examples are as follows:

- **Calendar editor**: This role enables users to add site events to the calendar (for more details, refer to docs.moodle.org/en/Calendar_editor_role)

- **Demo teacher**: This role is used to provide a demonstration teacher an account that has a password and profile that cannot be changed (docs.moodle.org/en/Demo_teacher_role)

- **Forum moderator**: This role is used in a particular forum and allows users to edit or delete forum posts, split discussions, and move discussions to other forums (docs.moodle.org/en/Forum_moderator_role)

- **Learning plan viewer**: This role allows teachers to view their students' learning plans (docs.moodle.org/en/Learning_plan_viewer)

- **Question creator**: This role enables students to create questions for use in quizzes (docs.moodle.org/en/Question_creator_role)

- **Question sharer**: This role allows teachers to access and share questions at the category or site level (docs.moodle.org/en/Question_creator_role)

One prominent entry that's missing from the list is the infamous parent or mentor role, which we will be creating step by step in the following subsection.

The parent/mentor role

One of the most popular and sought-after custom roles in Moodle is the one of a parent, guardian, or mentor. The idea is to grant permission to users to view certain profile information, such as activity reports, grades, learning plans, blog entries, and forum posts regarding their children, wards, or mentees. It also allows the assignee to consent to policies on someone's behalf (see *Chapter 14, Complying with Data Protection Regulations*). Furthermore, the specially-introduced **Mentees** block has to be placed on the front page to give users who have been assigned the role access to the **User** context.

To create a new role, follow these steps:

1. Go to **Site administration | Users | Permissions | Define roles**.

2. Click **Add a new role**, continue to the next screen, and name it **Parent** or **Mentor**. Provide an appropriate **Short name** and **Custom description**.

3. Leave the **Role archetype** type set to **None** and select the **User** checkbox for the **Context types where this role may be assigned** field.

4. Change the capabilities shown in the following screenshot to **Allow**:

Capability	Permission ⍰	Risks
User		
View all learning plans moodle/competency:planview	Allow Default: Not set	
View all user blogs moodle/user:readuserblogs	Allow Default: Not set	
View all user forum posts moodle/user:readuserposts	Allow Default: Not set	
View user full information moodle/user:viewalldetails	Allow Default: Not set	❶
See user activity reports moodle/user:viewuseractivitiesreport	Allow Default: Not set	❶
Policies		
Give consent for policies on someone else's behalf tool/policy:acceptbehalf	Allow Default: Not set	❶
Course		
View user profiles moodle/user:viewdetails	Allow Default: Not set	

Figure 6.20 – Modified capabilities for the parent role

5. Save the role using the **Create this role** button.

6. Each parent requires a separate user account, which must be created either manually or in bulk. In our example, the caring and loving father is **Ozzy Harris**, and his children are **Kelly Harris** and **Jack Harris**:

First name ▾ / Surname	Email address	City/town	Country
Ozzy Harris	ozzy.harris@openumlaut.com	Los Angeles	United States
Kelly Harris	kelly.harris@openumlaut.com	Los Angeles	United States
Jack Harris	jack.harris@openumlaut.com	Los Angeles	United States

Add a new user

Figure 6.21 – Parent and children accounts

7. Each parent must be linked to each child (again, manually or in batch). To do so, follow these steps:

I. Access the first child's profile page, select the **Preferences** link in the **Administration** pane, and click on **Assign roles relative to this user**.

II. Choose **Parent** as the role to assign.

III. Select the parent (**Ozzy Harris**) from the **Potential users** list and add him to the **Existing users** list. Repeat these steps for all kids.

If a mentor has many mentees, you can add them to a cohort and automate the role assignment (**Site administration | Users | Permissions | Assign user roles to cohort**). While this is unlikely to happen in a family context, it might be helpful in other setups, such as supervision. We covered this option when we dealt with user contexts earlier.

8. A special **Mentees** block has been introduced to facilitate access to user information:

I. Go to your home page and switch to **Edit mode**.

II. Add the **Mentees** block to the block drawer (it can also be added on the default dashboard) and change its title to **Parent access** via the **Configuration** icon.

III. Log in as **Ozzy Harris**; you should see the following block:

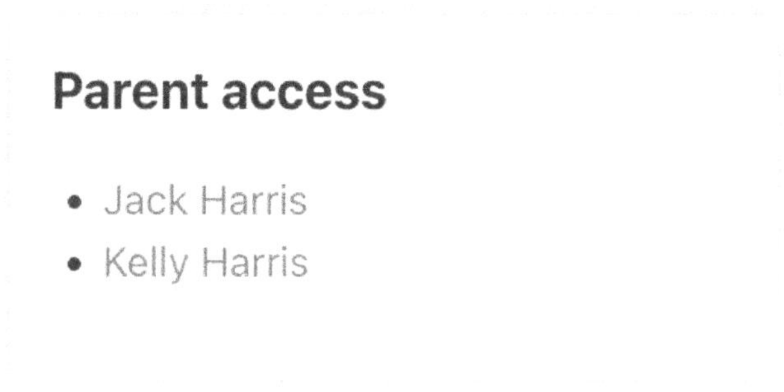

Parent access

- Jack Harris
- Kelly Harris

Figure 6.22 – Mentees block

When a name is clicked, the respective user profile will be shown, including posts sent to forums, learning plans, blog entries, and activity reports, including logs and grades.

The creation of the parent role hopefully demonstrates not only the potential but also the versatility and complexity of custom roles. Therefore, you must test new roles diligently.

Testing new roles

After creating a new role, it is recommended that you create a test account and assign the new role to it in all supported contexts. Log out as an administrator and log in as the newly created user to test the new role or use the **Login as** function to masquerade as the test user. Alternatively, use a different browser to test the role without logging out as an administrator.

> **Important note**
> It is highly recommended to test new roles thoroughly before assigning them to any users.

If you have modified a predefined role and would like to roll it back to its factory settings, go to **Site administration** | **Users** | **Permissions** | **Define roles**, select (do not edit) a role, and click the **Reset** button. This will replace its existing values with the ones from the built-in capabilities.

The complexity of the roles system and the ability to assign multiple roles to multiple users in multiple contexts calls for a mechanism to verify the correctness of the permissions set. This problem is amplified by the fact that permissions can be inherited and then overridden at lower levels again.

Moodle has a built-in **permission checker** that displays the values of any capability in the context in which the checker has been initiated. You can access this facility via the **Check permissions** link in a specific context. For example, in the following screenshot, we have called the permission checker in the **User** context of **Kelly Harris** and showed the permissions of user **Ozzy Harris** (go to Kelly's profile, follow the **Preferences** link in the **Administration** block, and select the **Check permissions** link in the **Roles** block. Then, select Ozzy and **Show this user's permissions**). It confirms the settings of the previously created **Parent** role:

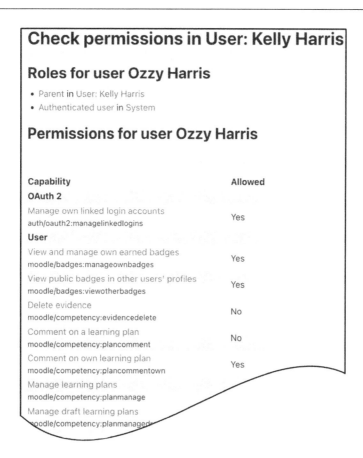

Figure 6.23 – Permission checker

At the site level, two additional mechanisms help identify any potential issues with roles. The capability report (**Site administration | Users | Permissions | Capability overview**) shows, for a selected capability, what permission it has in the definition of one or many selected roles. It also shows if the capability has been overridden anywhere in the system, which is a great help when you are trying to locate local modifications.

In the example screenshot, I have picked the mod/assign:grade capability, selected **All** roles, and filtered the results to **Show differences only**. The following report shows the capability's values in all the roles. Of particular interest is the **Student** role in the assignment context, where it has been overridden:

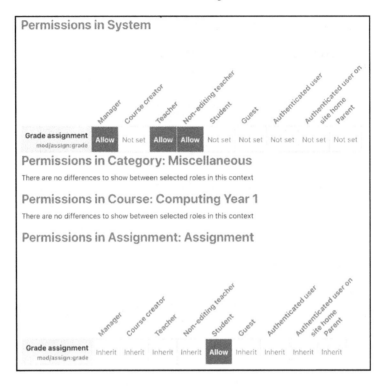

Figure 6.24 – Capability overview

The second tool can be found at **Site administration** | **Users** | **Permissions** | **Unsupported role assignments**. As the name suggests, it lists any invalid role assignments that can occur when upgrading from a previous version of Moodle. If any assignments are listed, you will have to modify or remove them manually.

This ends this section on creating and testing new roles. We will conclude this chapter with some miscellaneous roles-related features that didn't fit any of the previous sections.

Roles and context management

We have now dealt with the essential tools so that we can use, modify, and create roles. Moodle offers some crucial features when working extensively with roles, which we will cover in this section. We will deal with role assignments and override allowances before assigning default roles. Then, we will learn about context freezing and conclude with best practice advice.

Allowing roles assignments and overrides

By default, some roles have the right to allow other roles to assign roles. For instance, a teacher is allowed to assign **Non-editing teacher** and **Student** roles, whereas the manager is allowed to assign all the roles except the **Guest**, **Authenticated user**, and **Authenticated user on site home** roles (these are automatically assigned when a user signs in for the first time). There will be instances when you wish to change the default settings; for example, a teacher should be allowed to assign roles to other teachers or when the newly created roles have to be managed. To achieve this, select the **Allow role assignments** tab by navigating to **Site administration | Users | Permissions | Define Roles**:

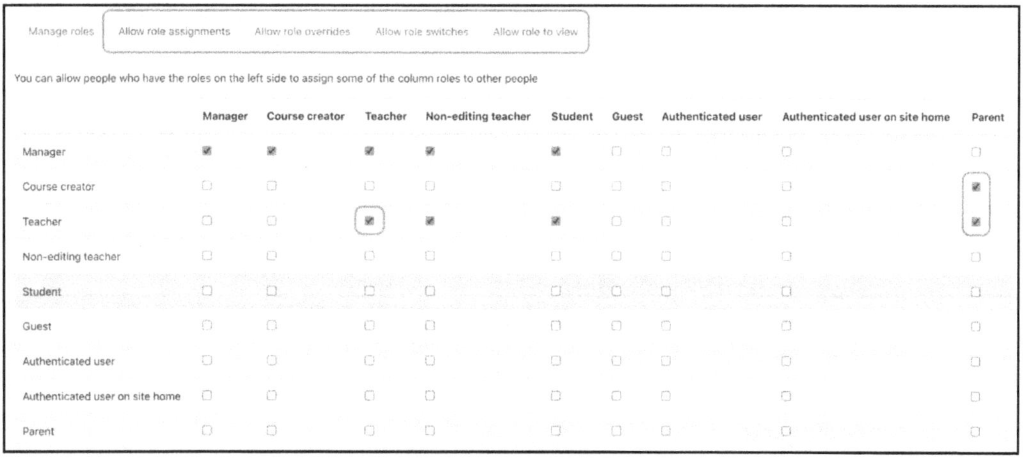

Figure 6.25 – Allowing role assignments

In the preceding screenshot, the modified allowances have been highlighted. Teachers can assign the **Teacher** role, and both course creators and teachers can assign the new **Parent** role.

An identical mechanism exists for role overrides, role switches, and role viewing. They can be accessed via the **Allow role overrides**, **Allow role switches**, and **Allow role to view** tabs on the same screen, respectively.

Assigning default roles

In certain situations, standard roles are assigned automatically. These can be specified in the **User policies** section under **Site administration | Users | Permissions**:

User policies

Role for visitors notloggedinroleid	Guest (guest) ⬍ Default: Guest (guest)
	Users who are not logged in to the site will be treated as if they have this role granted to them at the site context. Guest is almost always what you want here, but you might want to create roles that are less or more restrictive. Things like creating posts still require the user to log in properly.
Role for guest guestroleid	Guest (guest) ⬍ Default: Guest (guest)
	This role is automatically assigned to the guest user. It is also temporarily assigned to not enrolled users that enter the course via guest enrolment plugin.
Default role for all users defaultuserroleid	Authenticated user (user) ⬍ Default: Authenticated user (user)
	All logged in users will be given the capabilities of the role you specify here, at the site level, in ADDITION to any other roles they may have been given. The default is the Authenticated user role. Note that this will not conflict with other roles they have unless you prohibit capabilities, it just ensures that all users have capabilities that are not assignable at the course level (eg post blog entries, manage own calendar, etc).
Creators' role in new courses creatornewroleid	Teacher (editingteacher) ⬍ Default: Teacher (editingteacher)
	If the user does not already have the permission to manage the new course, the user is automatically enrolled using this role.
Restorers' role in courses restorernewroleid	Teacher (editingteacher) ⬍ Default: Teacher (editingteacher)
	If the user does not already have the permission to manage the newly restored course, the user is automatically assigned this role and enrolled if necessary. Select "None" if you do not want restorers to be able to manage every restored course.

Figure 6.26 – Default role assignments

The preceding screenshot shows the assignment of the default **Role for visitors** (users who are not logged in) and **Role for guest**.

Moodle comes with a predefined role called **Authenticated user** – that is, **Default role for all users**. It is assigned to *every* logged-in user, in addition to any other roles. This role has been created to grant users access to certain functionality, such as posting blog entries, managing personal calendar entries, changing profile fields, and so on, even if they are not enrolled in a course.

You can further specify what role is given automatically (via the **Creator's role in new courses** drop-down list) to users who have created a course but don't have any permissions yet in the course. An equivalent setting exists for users restoring courses from backups called **Restorers' role in courses** (see *Chapter 16, Avoiding Sleepless Nights – Moodle Backup and Restore*).

> **Important note**
> Changing the **User policies** settings can significantly impact what new users are allowed to do on your Moodle system, so double-check the default roles before they are applied!

In addition to the default roles in the **User policies** section, it is possible to specify a default home page role, which can be set by going to **Site administration | General | Site home | Site home settings**. The **Default site home role** field can be set to enable logged-in users to participate in activities on the front page, usually **Student** or **Teacher**. It is also possible to allow the logged-in users to participate in these activities by setting an authenticated user role override.

Next up is context freezing, which effectively puts content in a context in read-only mode.

Context freezing

Context freezing allows administrators or those with the relevant capability to make course categories, blocks, courses, or modules **read-only**; that is, users cannot modify or add to the content anymore.

Go to **Site administration | Development | Experimental | Experimental settings** and enable this feature to enable context freezing. Administrators can always modify frozen content unless the **Context freezing applies to administrators** setting is enabled:

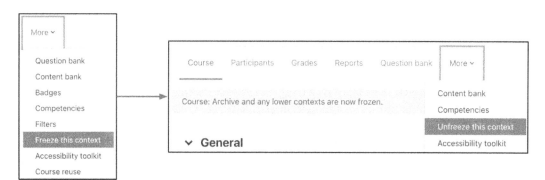

Figure 6.27 – Context freezing and unfreezing

Once a user has been granted the `moodle/site:managecontextlocks` capability, they can use the context freezing feature in the course, front page, and category context. For example, teachers may lock courses once they are over, or they may close forums when discussions are to be ended. This locking can also be reversed via the unfreeze option.

At the time of writing, context freezing has been an experimental feature, but it is expected to leave its trial phase shortly.

Moodle role assignment – best practices

Roles sometimes cause problems in Moodle sites, and it is therefore advised to follow some recommendations regarding roles:

- Only touch the roles once you have understood them thoroughly

- Never grant users a role that is beyond their competence

- Avoid assigning multiple predefined roles to users when possible

- Avoid system roles as much as possible

- Avoid creating too many new roles

- Avoid role assignments that don't make sense

- Keep track of role assignments to ensure maintainability in the future

- Do not change the permissions of predefined roles

- Test role modifications and new roles intensively

This list also serves as a good summary of this chapter as it touches upon the most covered topics.

Summary

In this chapter, you learned what roles are and how they are applied in different contexts. We covered modifying existing roles before creating custom roles such as parent, inspector, and librarian. Finally, we looked at managing administrative role-related settings, including context freezing.

Getting your head around the concept of roles is vital if you wish to add, modify, or remove functionality for a distinct group of users. There is always a trade-off between the complexity of such a system and its flexibility. While you can argue about the user-friendliness of the roles system, it has undoubtedly proven to be one of the most powerful concepts in Moodle.

The interconnectedness between courses, users, and roles is crucial. Once this has been set up and configured correctly, your Moodle is technically ready to take off. However, before that, you probably want to change its look and feel first. This is what the next chapter is all about.

7

Enhancing Moodle's Look and Feel

Your system is now fully operational with users, courses, and roles in place. It is now time to change its look and feel to create a more engaging user experience and ensure compliance with your corporate branding.

There is a wide range of building blocks that impact the look and feel of your Moodle system, as demonstrated in the following diagram:

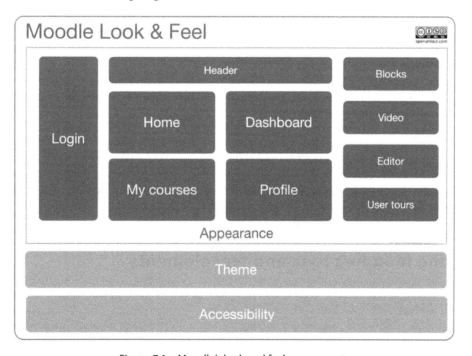

Figure 7.1 – Moodle's look and feel components

We have divided Moodle's look and feel components into three parts, which also form the structure of this chapter:

- **Appearance**: These are modifications that can be configured in administration settings. You will learn how to change the layout of key pages (Home, Dashboard, My courses, and user profiles) before we deal with different login workflows and how to adjust the header. We will then cover some appearance tools that impact the look and feel throughout the site: the block drawer, the Atto HTML editor, video and audio, and finally, user tours.

- **Themes**: These are modifications that require CSS styling. The main topics are theme selection, theme types, and theme customization.

- **Accessibility**: These are modifications required to be compliant with accessibility regulations relevant to you. To support users with different types of accessibility issues, we will equip you with tools to ensure system, theme, and content accessibility.

> **Tip**
> Theme creation is not covered in this book as it is not the task of an administrator but a designer with good CSS skills. *Moodle Theme Development* by *Silvina Paola Hillar, Packt Publishing*, is a good book to familiarize yourself with the basics of Moodle's themes and designs.

In this chapter, we will be covering the following main topics:

- Exploring Moodle's look and feel elements
- Customizing Moodle's appearance
- Moodle video and audio
- Creating walk-throughs with user tours
- Moodle themes
- Accessibility

By the end of this chapter, you will be familiar with Moodle's visual elements that you can customize via the administrator interface. Before we start customizing the appearance of our site, let's explore Moodle's look and feel elements first.

Exploring Moodle's look and feel elements

Moodle can be fully customized in terms of layout, branding, and device support. It has to be stressed that certain aspects of changing the look and feel require advanced design skills. While you, as an administrator, can make some adjustments, getting a professional frontend designer involved will be necessary, especially when it comes to styling.

Before covering the three pillars of Moodle's look and feel, let's explore some key visual elements. It is not always obvious which page elements can be adjusted via settings (appearance) and which ones require styling (theme). Have a look at the following screenshot of the home page:

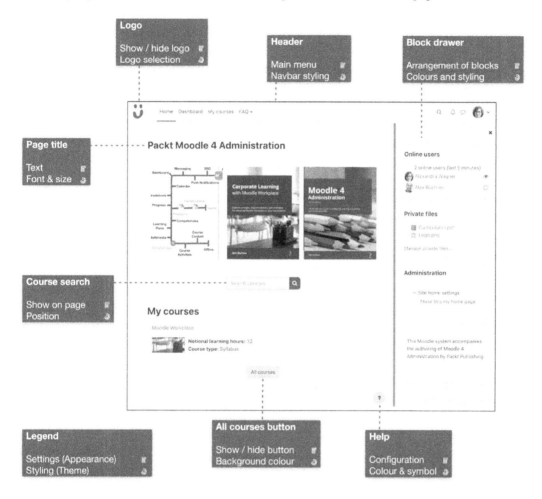

Figure 7.2 – Sample home page (Boost theme)

We have highlighted a few selected visual elements and annotated them with a feature that can be customized via appearance settings and one that can be adjusted by the theme (indicated by the color palette symbol). While this list is by no means complete, it hopefully gives you an idea that various elements drive the site's look and feel. It should also give you an idea about the elements that can be modified via appearance settings and that require theme changes.

In short, appearance (such as home page settings and menu configuration) dictates what content users will see. In contrast, themes are responsible for the design scheme or branding, that is, the header and footer, colors, fonts, icons, and so on.

Now that you are familiar with some key elements of Moodle's look and feel, let's get started by customizing the appearance of our site.

Customizing Moodle's appearance

We will kick off the customization of your Moodle system by covering its appearance elements. As shown in the overview of the chapter's introduction, we have divided this part into six elements we will customize: login, home page, my courses, dashboard, user profile, and header.

Customizing the login

There are three (and a half) pathways to log in to Moodle. What's that got to do with the look and feel of the LMS? The chosen workflow potentially impacts the layout and design of the home page because it can be shown before and after login.

Have a look at the pathways shown in the following diagram:

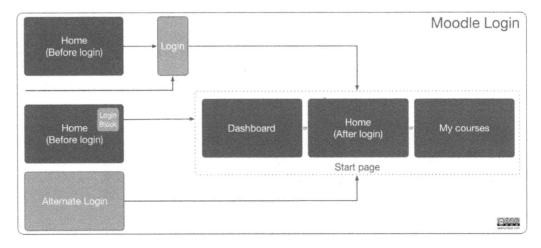

Figure 7.3 – Moodle login pathways

In the **standard login** workflow that has been activated by default, users navigate to the home page, select the **Login** link at the top right, log in to the site, and end up at the start page. To jump directly to the **Login** page, go to <yoursite>/login/index.php. We have discussed various login mechanisms in *Chapter 5, Managing Users, Cohorts, and Authentication*, when dealing with authentication, including the option to bypass the **Before login** page and force the **Login** page.

The second login option is to place the **Login block** in the block drawer, effectively moving the dedicated login page inside the home page. Once authenticated, the users will be directed to the start page.

The **alternate login** option is to log in to Moodle from a different website, maybe your organization's home page, effectively avoiding Moodle's onboard login screens. To implement this, you will have to add some HTML code on the remote page from which you wish the user to log in:

```
<form class="loginform" name="login" method="post"
   action="https://[yourmoodlesite]/login/index.php">
   <p>Username <input size="10" name="username" /> </p>
   <p>Password <input size="10" name="password"
       type="password" /> </p>
   <p><input name="Submit" value="Login"
       type="submit" /></p>
</form>
```

The form will pass the credentials to your Moodle system. You will have to replace the URL of `[yourmoodlesite]` with the URL of your Moodle instance; this address must be entered in the **Alternate Login URL** field by navigating to **Site administration | Plugins | Authentication | Manage authentication**.

By default, authenticated users will see the **Dashboard** screen after they have logged in. You can change the **start page** in **Site administration | Appearance | Navigation**, where you have the option to specify **Start page for users**. The options are **Site**, **Dashboard** (default), **My courses**, and **User preference**. If the latter is chosen, users can choose it in the **Start page** setting in **Preferences** in their user profiles.

Which login pathway is best depends on your existing infrastructure and personal preference. Whatever option you choose, users will always have access to the home page, which we will customize next.

Customizing the home page

The home page is identical for all users. Well, its structure is static, whereas its content changes depending on the user who is logged in. For example, every home page might contain a block that displays the courses a user is enrolled in, which is unlikely to be the same for every user. This page is also known as **Site home** or, for legacy reasons, front page.

As we just mentioned, Moodle's home page is shown before a user has logged in, and changes after authentication has taken place. The content and layout of the page before and after login can be customized. Look at the following screenshot. It is the same site that was shown in the preceding screenshot, but before a user had logged in:

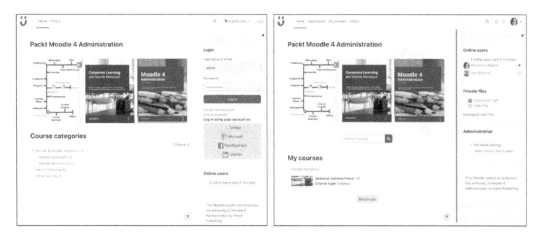

Figure 7.4 – Sample home page before and after login

In this particular example, the **Login** block is shown in the block drawer, and **Course categories** are displayed in the center. Once logged in, the **Login** block is hidden, the **Private files** block is shown, the language selector has been replaced with the user profile menu, and two more items appear in the main menu. I am sure you can spot a few more differences!

To change the home page's appearance before and after login, we need to change the Site home settings.

Modifying the Site home settings

To customize the home page, select **Settings** on the home page or go to **Site administration | General | Site home | Site home settings**:

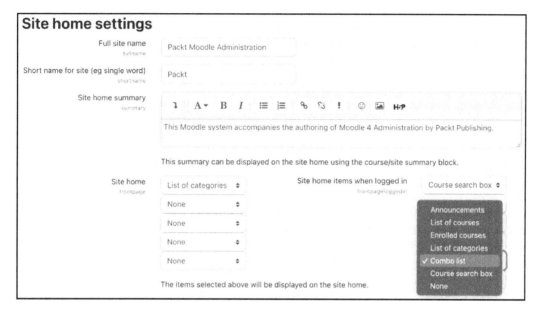

Figure 7.5 – Home page settings

The following parameters are available on the **Site home settings** page:

- **Full site name**: This is the name displayed on the home page and in the browser's title bar. It is usually the name of your organization or your Moodle system.

- **Short name for site**: This is the internal name of your site that is used at various places, for instance, as part of the backup name or when networking the site.

- **Site home summary**: This site description can be displayed via the **Course/Site summary** block. The description text is also picked up by the Google search engine crawler if allowed.

- **Site home**: Moodle can display up to five elements in the center column of the home page when not logged in: **Announcements**, **List of courses**, **List of categories**, **Combo list** (categories and courses), and **Course search box**. The order of the elements is the same as the one chosen in the pull-down menus.

- **Site home items when logged in**: This is the same as **Site home**, but it's used after a user is logged in. A sixth item is provided to be displayed, namely, **Enrolled courses**, which wouldn't make any sense before users have been authenticated.

- **Maximum category depth**: This setting specifies how many hierarchy levels are displayed when course categories are shown. Limiting this if your category hierarchy's depth exceeds three or four is recommended.

- **Maximum number of courses**: This setting determines the number of courses shown on the home page. If more courses are available, the **More courses** link is shown.

- **Include a topic section**: If ticked, an additional topic section (just like the topic block in a course) appears in the home page's center column. It can contain any mix of resources or activities available in Moodle. It is often used to provide information about the site or show an image or trailer video.

- **Number of announcements**: This includes the number of news items displayed.

- **Comments displayed per page**: This setting dictates how many entries are shown in the **Comments block** if used on the front page.

- **Default site home role**: A default front page role should be set if logged-in users need to be allowed to participate in home page activities.

The Moodle home page is treated like a course (internally, it has course ID=1). Therefore, most available settings are identical to their course counterparts: reports, question bank, content bank, filters, and course reuse. The same holds for the **Participants** menu item: the home page has its own context in which groups can be created, and roles can be assigned to users. This allows a dedicated user to design and maintain the home page without accessing any other elements in Moodle. Since the home page is treated like a course, a **Teacher** role is usually sufficient.

Moodle provides a great set of tools to customize the home page. Sometimes, you might want to replace this with a custom front page, which we deal with in the following subsection.

Replacing the home page

To replace the home page, Moodle lets you add a custom script. To implement this feature, you will have to add the following line to your `config.php` file:

```
$CFG->customfrontpageinclude="<dirroot>/local/<yourfrontpage>";
```

Bear in mind that this will display the output of the `<yourfrontpage>` PHP file at the top of the content area, in addition to any elements of the home page. This way, you have the best of both worlds: the Moodle elements (disable the ones you don't require) and your custom elements.

While users cannot modify the home page itself, its content is personalized for each user, for example, calendar entries or private files. The same holds for the **My courses** page, which we will customize in the following subsection.

Customizing My courses

As the name suggests, the **My courses** tab shows the courses a user is enrolled in by displaying the **Course overview** block in the content area (center of the page). In the **My courses** view, users can star and archive courses; they can also reduce the number of displayed courses they are enrolled in by applying any combination of the following filters:

- **Status**: **All**, **In progress**, **Future**, **Past**, **Starred**, and **Archived**

- **Text**

- **Ordering**: **Sort by course name** and **Sort by last accessed**

- **Details**: **Card**, **List**, and **Summary**

The following screenshot shows the **My courses** page I see on my Packt demo system:

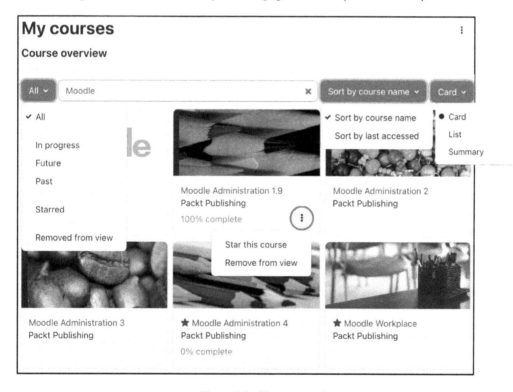

Figure 7.6 – My courses view

You can specify appearance settings and available filters by navigating to **Site administration | Plugins | Blocks | Course overview**. The **Display categories** setting shows the course category name underneath the course name. You can further customize **Available layouts** and **Available filters**. Specifying the **Custom field** option lets you add your own items to the **Status** filter, a great way to align the user experience to the subjects taught in your organization.

Figure 7.7 – Course overview block settings

The **Future** and **Past** statuses can be adjusted by two grace period settings in **Site administration | Appearance | Navigation**: **Grace period for future courses** and **Grace period for past courses**.

Courses can (and ideally should) have a course image. If the optional picture is missing, it will be replaced with a patterned course card. The colors used in those cards can be specified in **Site administration | Appearance | Course card colours**:

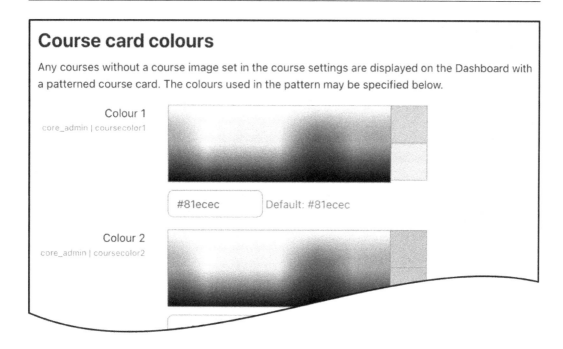

Figure 7.8 – Course card colors

You can use the standard color picker to select ten colors, which are applied to course images in random order.

In **Site administration | Appearance | Courses**, some settings let you specify how courses are presented to users and what level of course detail is displayed:

- **Course contacts**: The users that are shown alongside the course description. **Teacher** is the most often used choice here.

- **Display extended course names**: If enabled, short and long course names will be displayed; otherwise, only the long name is shown.

- **Courses per page**: This is a threshold setting used when displaying courses within categories. If there are more courses in a category than specified, the page navigation will be displayed at the top of the page. Also, when a combo list is used, course names are only displayed if the number is less than the specified threshold.

- **Courses images file limit**: By default, only one file can be attached to a course; you might need to increase this limit, especially if you want to add PDF to the list of valid **Course image file extensions**, for instance, to attach a curriculum.

The **My courses** page is concerned with courses that users are enrolled in. What about navigating through courses and categories users are not enrolled in? We will look at this in the following subsection.

Course navigation

The list of courses seen throughout Moodle can be overwhelming, and it might be difficult for users to navigate through the entire category hierarchy. Examples of where courses and categories are visible to users are the **All courses** link in the **Courses** block, by selecting **List of categories** or **Combo list** in the site page settings, or through the **Courses** listing in the **Navigation** block.

Some settings in **Site administration | Appearance | Navigation** deal with the level of detail shown in courses and categories. Bear in mind that these mainly apply to the **Navigation block** and some navigational features in **Classic**-based themes:

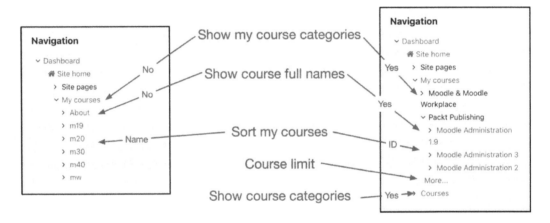

Figure 7.9 – Course navigation settings

Once course selection has taken place – either in **My courses** or via **Navigation** – users will be inside a course where two look and feel elements can be configured.

Inside a course

Courses are where learning takes place, and course creators are responsible for their content, structure, and layout. There are two tools that you should set up to ensure an enjoyable experience for your content creators:

- **Course formats**: A course format dictates how course content will be presented to the learner; we already looked at them in *Chapter 4, Managing Courses and Enrolments*. You can configure or disable course formats at **Site administration | Plugins | Course formats | Manage course formats**. Additional course formats can be installed, which we will cover in *Chapter 8, Understanding Moodle Plugins*. Popular course formats are **Tiles**, **Collapsed topics**, and **Designer**.

- **Activity chooser**: The activity chooser appears when in editing mode inside a course and content creators wish to add an activity or resource. You can determine which tabs should be displayed in the activity chooser in **Site administration | Courses | Activity chooser | Activity chooser settings**. Here, you can also show or hide the link to MoodleNet in **Activity chooser footer**. Popular activities and resources can be added to the **Recommended** tab via **Site administration | Courses | Activity chooser | Recommended activities**. Bear in mind that these settings apply to all (editing) users across the system.

To ensure consistency across courses and to simplify course authoring, it is recommended to implement a course templating mechanism. There are two ways such course skeletons can be provided:

- **Course templates via on-board tools**: Moodle doesn't provide a dedicated facility, but you can mimic a course template workflow using several different tools, namely course backup, course restore, and course upload. All three operations have been covered in the *Managing courses in bulk* section in *Chapter 4, Managing Courses and Enrolments*.
- **Course templates via third-party plugins**: There are various options available, Kickstart (`moodle.org/plugins/format_kickstart`) being my favorite.

The home page and **My courses** are predefined by the administrator (or a user with appropriate permissions). The intention is that the two pages are static and identical for all users. On the other hand, dashboards and the profile page have been designed to be adjusted by users to match their personal preferences. Let's look at dashboards next.

Customizing dashboards

Dashboards are like personal home pages that each user can customize. For legacy reasons, this top-level page is sometimes referred to as **My Moodle** or **My home** (even the URL is <YOURSITE>/my).

Important note

A **dashboard** is a personal page that each user can customize.

So, what's the role of the administrator when users have permission to create their own dashboards? There are two main obligations you have:

- Create a default dashboard
- Set up and configure dashboard elements that users cannot change or delete

Once logged in, users can edit the dashboard by adding blocks to the respective areas and changing any blocks that have already been added by default. They also can reposition certain elements. You, as the administrator, can specify what these default blocks are and where they are positioned, and control how much customization can be carried out. Users can reset the respective pages to these defaults when they customize their dashboards.

By default, the dashboard shows three blocks: **Timeline**, **Calendar**, and **Recently accessed items**. The default **Dashboard** page can be found by navigating to **Site administration | Appearance | Default Dashboard page**, where you must switch to **Edit mode**. Any blocks you place on the default page will appear on the users' pages. Using the standard **Move** handle, you can place blocks freely on the page; the allowed locations (left, center, and right) depend on the active theme—more on block handling shortly.

There might be blocks that you wish to display on every page, effectively making them compulsory blocks that cannot be modified or deleted. To facilitate these **sticky blocks**, go to the block configuration and change the **Select pages** setting from **This specific page** to **Any page matching the above**. The block will appear on all subpages, that is, all user dashboards, and cannot be deleted, effectively making the block sticky.

One impactful feature is **Reset Dashboard for all users**. As the name suggests, all user dashboards in your system will be reset to your default layout. This action is useful if you have changed the default dashboard and wish to push it out to all users.

To prevent users from editing their dashboard, adjust the `moodle/my:manageblocks` capability in the **Authenticated user** role. To completely disable dashboards, untick the **Enable dashboards** parameter in **Site administration | Appearance | Navigation**. To prevent guests from accessing the dashboard, you must untick the **Allow guest access to Dashboard** parameter.

The second page that users can modify is the profile page, where the customization is similar to that of dashboards. Let's look at it in the following subsection.

Customizing the user profile page

The **user profile page** provides information about the user. We already came across this view when looking at user profile details in *Chapter 5*, *Managing Users, Cohorts, and Authentication*.

To change the profile page layout, go to **Site administration | Appearance | Default profile page** and turn on editing mode. By default, this page is empty, and you can decide which blocks you wish to add, if any.

The information shown on the user profile page (user details, course details, etc.) cannot be changed. These pseudo-blocks are hard-coded and cannot be modified like standard blocks.

There are three capabilities to impact the level of customization of user profiles. These self-explanatory values are shown in the following filtered list of capabilities in the **Authenticated user** role:

Figure 7.10 – User profile capabilities

We have now covered the main non-course pages in Moodle: **Home**, **My courses**, **Dashboard**, and **User profile**. A quick summary from a user's perspective is shown in the following table:

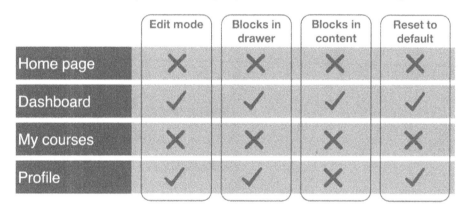

	Edit mode	Blocks in drawer	Blocks in content	Reset to default
Home page	✗	✗	✗	✗
Dashboard	✓	✓	✓	✓
My courses	✗	✗	✗	✗
Profile	✓	✓	✗	✓

Figure 7.11 – Home vs Dashboard versus My courses versus User profile

There is one key layout element missing: the header.

Customizing the header

The Moodle header is shown on *every* page in Moodle and comprises different navigational elements, as shown in the following annotated toolbar:

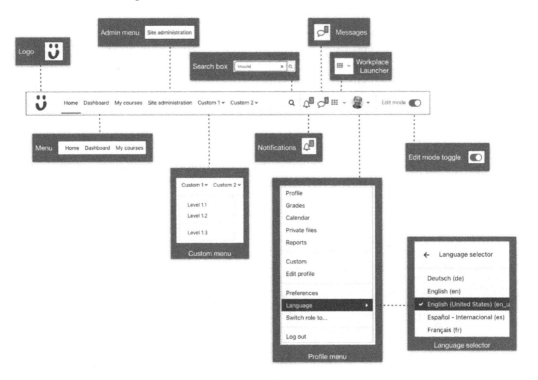

Figure 7.12 – Moodle header

The different header items include the following (from left to right), including pointers on where to change their appearance:

- (Compact) logo of your site (**Site administration | Appearance | Logos**), where you can also specify **Favicon**. If no logo is provided, the site name is displayed instead (**Site administration | General | Site home | Site home settings**).

- Main menu items (**Dashboard** is hidden when disabled in **Site administration | Appearance | Navigation**).

- Admin menu (only site administrators see this).

- Custom menu (additional menu items can be added via the **custommenuitems** setting in **Site administration | Appearance | Themes | Theme settings**. Each entry represents a menu item in the form of `<Indent><Text>[|<URL>] [|<Tooltip>] [|<Language>]`.

<Indent> is a series of hyphens: no hyphens indicate a top-level menu; one hyphen, a submenu; two hyphens, a sub-submenu; and so on. The Boost theme does not support submenus; other themes may overcome this restriction. <Text> is the label of the menu item, <URL> is the internal or external link, and <Tooltip> is the optional balloon help. You can add a <Language> code or a separated list of code as the last item, which will only be shown if the user has currently selected the listed language. ### creates a separator.

- The following sample **Custom menu items** entry will generate the menu shown in the Moodle header image:

```
Custom 1
- Level 1.1|URL
- Level 1.2|URL
-###
- Level 1.3|URL
Custom 2
- Language 2.1|URL EN||en, en_us
- Sprache 2.1|URL DE||de, de_du, de_kids
- Level 2.2|URL|Shown in Boost
-- Level 2.2.1|URL|Not shown in Boost
-- Level 2.2.2|URL|Not shown in Boost
```

- Search box (enable **Global search** in **Site administration | General | Advanced features**).

- Notifications indicator and notification menu toggle (always shown).

- Messaging indicator and messaging toggle drawer (always shown).

- Workplace launcher (Moodle Workplace only).

- Profile menu (menu items can be hidden via the **customusermenuitems** setting in **Site administration | Appearance | Themes | Theme settings.** You can specify which menu items will appear in the top part of the profile menu. The syntax for each entry is as follows: <Item><URL>.

  <Item> is either a text entry (in our example, **Custom**) or a pair <langstringname><componentname>. The former is the language pack entry, and the latter is the name of the Moodle component, for example, to provide a direct link to edit a user's profile: editmyprofile, core|/user/edit.php.

- Language selector (**Display language menu** and **Languages on language menu** in **Site administration | General | Language | Language settings**).

- Edit mode toggle.

This concludes the customizing of appearance pages and the header. Next up are the visual elements that appear across the entire system, starting with blocks.

Configuring blocks

Every page we have come across so far contains blocks. In fact, bearing a few exceptions, every page in Moodle can contain blocks. You must switch to **Edit mode** and open the block drawer to configure blocks. Once turned on, you will see the **Add a block** item, which lets you add all the available blocks to the home page (except the ones that have already been added and only allow a single instance):

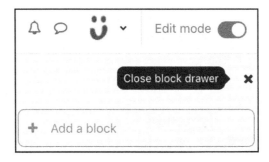

Figure 7.13 – Adding blocks to the block drawer

Every block has a purpose usually tied to a particular Moodle feature, for instance, showing deadlines in the calendar, getting access to the user's private files, or showing the latest announcements. An exception is the **Text** block that lets you add any HTML code, useful for content that cannot be displayed using standard Moodle blocks.

Throughout the book, we deal with specific blocks whenever they are relevant to the covered topic. Here, we focus on the block configuration.

Blocks have up to three types of settings, which can be accessed through the **Configuration** icon:

- **Block settings**: These are unique to the block, and not all blocks provide configuration parameters. For example, the Mentees block we used when we created the Parents role in the previous chapter allows you to specify a block title.

- **Where this block appears**: Where the block will be displayed and what the default properties are.

- **On this page**: Properties in the current context.

A sample block configuration (of the Mentees block) is shown in the following screenshot:

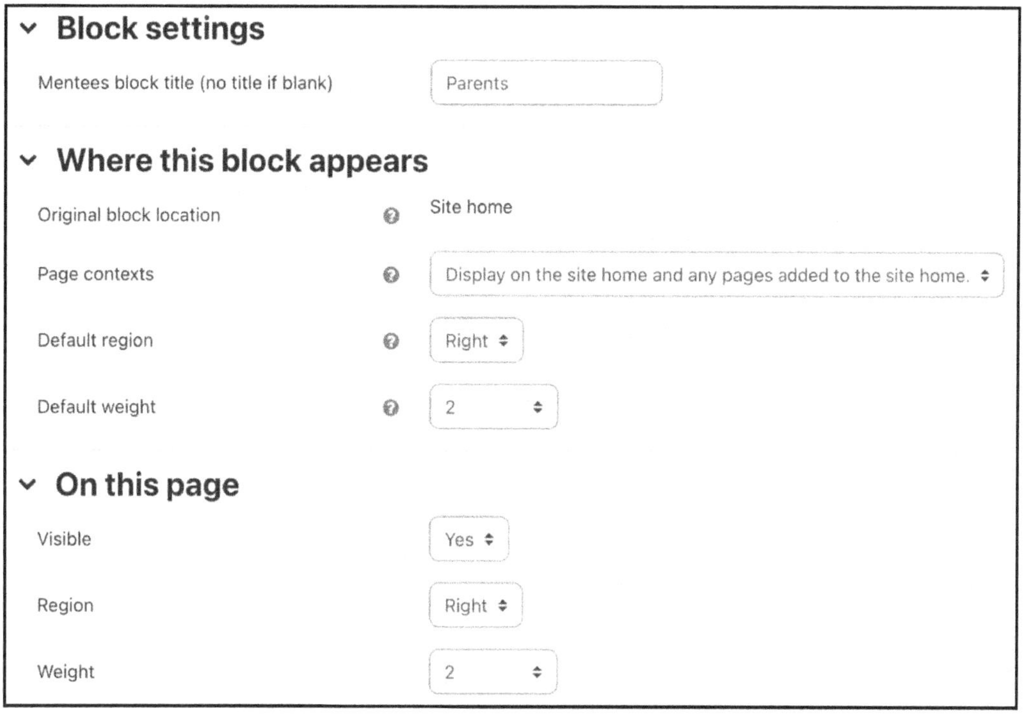

Figure 7.14 – Block configuration

The following parameters are available:

- **Original block location**: This shows the context in which the block has been created (here, **Site home**). As with roles, pages may inherit blocks from a parent context.

- **Page contexts** (not available in all contexts): This setting determines on which pages the block will be shown; the self-explanatory options that are available are: **Display on the site home only**, **Display on the site home and any pages added to the site home**, and **Display throughout the entire site**. In other contexts, such as Courses, other (context-sensitive) options are available, depending on the original block location and your current location.

- **Display on page types** (unavailable on the home page): The available options depend on the block's context. Examples in the **Courses** context are **Any page**, **Any course page**, and **Any type of course main page**.

- **Default region**: This determines the block's position, and the options available depend on how they have been defined in the theme. Usually, the options are **Left** (or **side-pre**), **Content**, and **Right** (or **side-post**).

- **Default weight** (-10 to 10): Think of a block as a balloon – the lighter the weight of the block, the higher up its position, and the heavier the weight, the further down it will be placed.

- **Visible** (**Yes** or **No**): This determines whether the block is shown or hidden.

- **Region** (**Left** or **Right**): This is the same as **Default region**. On pages that allow the positioning of blocks in the center column, for example, Dashboard and the user profile page, **Content** is offered as a third option.

- **Weight** (-10 to10): This is the same principle as **Default weight**.

The concepts of blocks weight and region have been illustrated in the following (block) diagram:

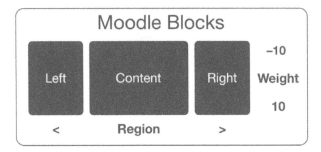

Figure 7.15 – Moodle blocks weight and region

While teachers have permission to configure blocks inside their courses, it often requires some support since the concepts of weight and region are not super-intuitive.

The editor covered next is another visual element that users will use throughout the site.

The Moodle editor

The editor is central to any user experience in Moodle since it is used throughout the site for a wide range of operations. These include posting in forums (learner), providing feedback to submissions (teacher), and editing content (editing teacher). You, as the administrator, should ensure that the editor is configured to facilitate your users' requirements.

Moodle's default editor is called **Atto**, which has been developed by Moodle for Moodle. Atto has been designed to work with responsive themes, support left-to-right as well as right-to-left strings, provide accessibility support, and is fully configurable.

TinyMCE used to be Moodle's standard editor, which is still supported but uses an outdated version. Moodle HQ has communicated the following text editor strategy: the latest version of TinyMCE will be incorporated into Moodle, and all Atto plugins will be ported across. Once this process has been completed, Atto is expected to be phased out over future releases. So, in this book, we will only cover Atto since this is currently the best Moodle editor available; soon, you will be dealing with TinyMCE, and all essential features are expected to be available and, hopefully, some more.

Additionally, Moodle contains a built-in plain text editor implemented to enter any text that does not require formatting, for instance, source code.

To get access to the available editors and their settings, go to **Site administration | Plugins | Text editors | Manage editors**:

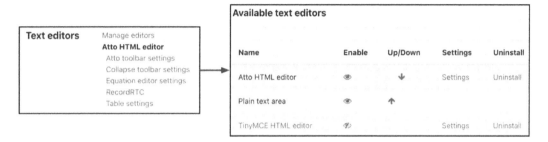

Figure 7.16 – Managing text editors

The idea of the **Text editors** plugin area is that additional editors can be installed and utilized throughout Moodle (refer to *Chapter 8*, *Understanding Moodle Plugins*). These can either be replacements for default editors or editors that enter specialized content. Furthermore, each button in Atto is implemented as a Moodle subplugin, which allows for the flexible extension of editor functionality.

> **Tip**
>
> It is recommended that you use Atto as the default editor as this is the one that will be maintained in the future and also fully supports mobile devices.

You can enable/disable each editor, change the order (in which they will be displayed when choosing an editor), and adjust the editor's settings through the **Settings** link.

By default, the editor toolbar is configured to look like this (when expanded):

Figure 7.17 – Atto editor toolbar (default)

The toolbar can be configured in the **Toolbar config** setting under the list of Atto plugins:

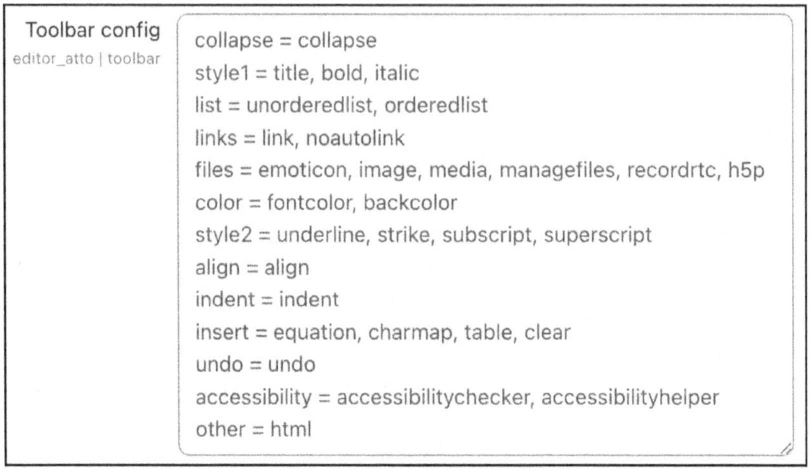

Toolbar config	collapse = collapse
editor_atto | toolbar	style1 = title, bold, italic
	list = unorderedlist, orderedlist
	links = link, noautolink
	files = emoticon, image, media, managefiles, recordrtc, h5p
	color = fontcolor, backcolor
	style2 = underline, strike, subscript, superscript
	align = align
	indent = indent
	insert = equation, charmap, table, clear
	undo = undo
	accessibility = accessibilitychecker, accessibilityhelper
	other = html

Figure 7.18 – Atto toolbar configuration

Toolbar buttons are organized in groups, for example, `collapse`, `style1`, and `list`. Group names must be unique, and the order determines in which order button groups are arranged. The format of each entry is as follows:

`group = button1[, button2][,button3] [...]`

For example, the `color` group contains two buttons: `foreground` and `background`.

When you navigate to **Site administration | Plugins | Text editors | Atto HTML editor | Collapse toolbar settings**, you can specify via the **Show # first groups when collapsed** option which buttons are shown when the editor toolbar is not expanded.

You can install Atto's editor plugins, adding additional buttons to your editor. Examples of `moodle.org/plugins/?q=type:atto` are word counter, inline corrections, and MS Word import.

Atto autosaves its content in predefined intervals, which is helpful if users close their page by accident since the content will be restored the next time they return to the same form. You can adjust this **Autosave frequency** setting by navigating to **Site administration | Plugins | Text editors | Atto toolbar settings**. Beware, a very high frequency, such as a second, will potentially harm the performance of your system.

There exists a wide range of options to expand Atto's functionality without installing any add-ons:

- **Extending the functionality of tables**: Atto contains a powerful table mode, which supports the formatting and customization of tables. To equip your users with the full functionality, you might turn on the available features by going to **Site administration | Plugins | Text editors | Atto HTML editor | Table settings**.

- **Supporting mathematical equations**: If some of your users use mathematical equations regularly, you have two options. The first is **Equations via TeX**, a typesetting language supporting a wide range of mathematical operations. The second is **Equations via MathJax**; MathJax is a JavaScript library that displays a mathematical notation in web browsers using various markups, including TeX. You will need to enable the filters in **Site administration | Plugins | Filters | Manage filters**. Once you have activated one or both filters, you can specify their details in the filter settings and the toolbar options by navigating to **Site administration | Plugins | Text editors | Atto HTML editor | Equation editor settings**.

- **Giving a smile ;-)**: Whether you like them or not, emoticons have come to stay, and educational settings make no exception. To configure or add emojis, go to **Site administration | Appearance | HTML settings**, where you will find the list of emoticon values, alongside a good explanation at the bottom of the table. Ensure that the **Emoji picker** setting in **Site administration | General | Advanced features** is enabled.

- **Adding some awesomeness**: FontAwesome is a font icon toolkit that, at the time of writing, contains more than 2,000 fully scalable vector icons. To support this great set of features, you will have to install the **Font Awesome Icon Filter** plugin from `moodle.org/plugins/filter_fontawesome`. Refer to *Chapter 8*, *Understanding Moodle Plugins*, on how to do this. Alternatively, you can add **FontAwesome** via Mustache templates. Once you have activated the filter in **Site administration | Plugins | Filters | Manage filters**, your users will be able to add icons via a text input like this:

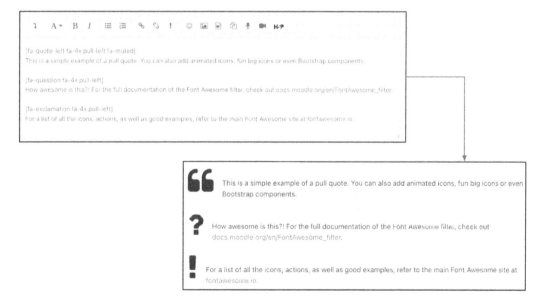

Figure 7.19 – Filter FontAwesome

Atto is utilized throughout Moodle whenever content has to be entered. So far, we have mainly focused on textual content and ignored multimedia; this is going to change in the following section when we deal with video and audio.

Enabling Moodle video and audio

Video and audio content are essential for building engaging learning experiences. Moodle supports **playing** various media formats as well as the **recording** of audio and video.

We will cover both modes: first, we will look at media players before dealing with media recorders.

Media players

Users nowadays expect to incorporate media formats in their teaching and learning content. Whether it is teachers providing videos as learning resources or learners embedding audio clips in their assignments, it is taken for granted that different media formats are supported. Your job as a Moodle administrator is to ensure that these media files are played correctly.

So how does Moodle handle media content in different formats? In simple terms, every time Moodle detects a link that points to a multimedia resource or `<video>` and `<audio>` HTML tags, it replaces them with an appropriate media player code. A multimedia filter is used to facilitate this conversion process (more on filters in *Chapter 10, Configuring Technical Features*), as shown in the following visualization:

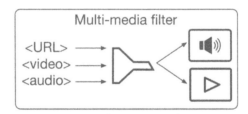

Figure 7.20 – Multimedia filter in action

Moodle does a pretty good job playing media formats, and most setups require little or no tweaking. You can see the players supported in **Site administration | Plugins | Media players | Manage media players**:

Manage media players

Available players

When players are enabled, media files can be embedded using the multimedia plugins filter (if enabled) or using a file or URL resource. When not enabled, these formats are not embedded and users can download or follow links to these resources.

Where two players support the same format, enabling both increases compatibility across different devices such as mobile phones. It is possible to increase compatibility further by providing multiple files in different formats for a single audio or video clip.

Name	Supports	Version	Enable	Up/Down	Settings	Uninstall
VideoJS player ❓	Video: **.mov**, **.mp4**, **.m4v**, **.ogv**, **.webm** Audio: **.mp3**, **.aac**, **.flac**, **.m4a**, **.oga**, **.ogg**, **.wav** YouTube videos	2021052503	👁	↓	Settings	Uninstall
YouTube ❓		2021052500	👁	↑		Uninstall
Vimeo ❓		2021052500	👁			Uninstall
HTML5 video ❓	Video: .fmp4, .mov, .mp4, .m4v, .ogv, .webm	2021052500	👁			Uninstall
HTML5 audio ❓	Audio: .aac, .flac, .mp3, .m4a, .oga, .ogg, .wav	2021052500	👁			Uninstall

Figure 7.21 – Media players

Out of the box, Moodle uses **VideoJS**, a popular open source player, supporting HTML5 video, audio, and streaming services, such as YouTube and Vimeo. VideoJS also delivers content to users with accessibility issues. Due to its pluggability and simplicity to style, it has become the de facto standard for web applications. VideoJS is sufficient to play all content unless your users have specific media format requirements.

There are a couple of checks you should carry out to ensure media can be played on your site:

- Ensure **Multimedia filter** is enabled in **Site administration | Plugins | Filters | Manage filters**.

- Double-check **VideoJS Settings**. In **Video file extensions** and **Audio file extensions**, you can specify which file formats are supported. While there is a dedicated YouTube media player, VideoJS also supports **YouTube videos**. You can disable the standalone player if your users don't use playlists. **CSS class for video** and **CSS class for audio** lets you customize the player. Check out the available classes on docs.videojs.com. The **Limit size** option defines whether **Default width** and **Default height** are applied when no dimensions are specified or the video is stretched to its maximum possible width.

- Enable Vimeo support in the list of available players if the streaming service is in use.

There are various ways to spice up your site with video-related third-party plugins. One highly-recommended example is **Video Time** (`moodle.org/plugins/mod_videotime`). The Video Time product family contains a set of plugins to integrate videos into Moodle. Videos can be hosted locally in Moodle, externally, and on YouTube or **Vimeo**. Supported features are simplified video embedding, an adjustable and customizable tab interface, activity completion, video tracking, resume, interactive transcript, and many more.

Media recorders

In Moodle, everyone can be a content creator. Teachers can record assignment feedback by voice, and students might want to add recorded videos to forum posts. Some users will use their desktop PC or Mac; others might want to use their mobile devices for recording.

Moodle fully supports media recording through its Atto text editor. Internally, **RecordRTC** is utilized, an open source JavaScript library using WebRTC for audio and video recording. You can configure its settings in **Site administration | Plugins | Text editors | Atto HTML editor | RecordRTC**:

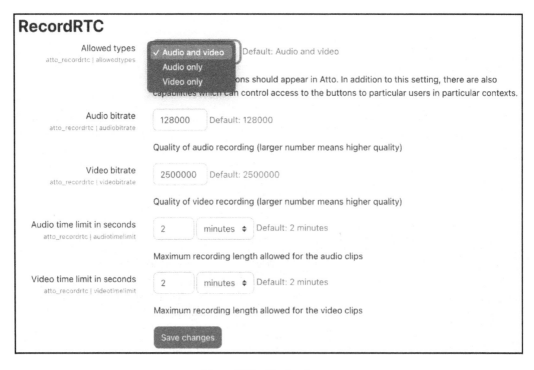

Figure 7.22 – Media players

The options are worth looking at since they have an impact on server resources, both in terms of bandwidth and disk usage:

- **Allowed types**: You can specify whether **Audio and video** recording are supported or **Audio only** or **Video only**. There are two capabilities to control access to the Atto buttons: `atto/recordrtc:recordaudio` and `atto/recordrtc:recordvideo`.

- **Audio bitrate** and **Video bitrate**: The lower the bitrates, the smaller the file sizes, and vice versa. The default bitrate for recorded audio (**128000**) should generate files of about 15 KB per minute; the default bitrate for recorded video (**2500000**) to files of approximately 20 MB per minute.

- **Audio time limit in seconds** and **Video time limit in seconds**: The default time limit is **2 minutes** for audio and video recording. Again, the longer the maximum recording length, the bigger the resulting files.

Recordings are stored in subdirectories of `$CFG->dataroot>/filedir`. You might want to double-check the section on files and upload limits in *Chapter 2*, *Exploring the Moodle System*.

> **Important note**
> Make sure `post_max_size` and `upload_max_filesize` are configured in line with your expected maximum recording sizes.

This concludes the section on audio and video. Next up are user tours to assist your learners and teachers while familiarizing themselves the first time they encounter a page or a feature.

Creating walk-throughs with user tours

User tours allow you to create simple walk-throughs, highlight key areas, or demonstrate new features with on-screen step-by-step guides. The following is a sample mini-tour we are going to create in this section:

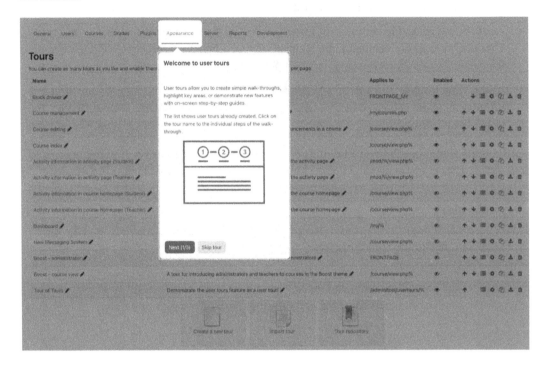

Figure 7.23 – Managing user tours

A **tour** comprises multiple **steps**, each being associated with a **target**. A target is a page element that is one of the following three **target types**:

- **Block**: A Moodle block to display the step next to it

- **Selector**: A CSS selector on the page where the step is displayed next to

- **Middle of the page**: General information not associated with any elements on the page

Each tour step has a title, some content, and a target. Each target is associated with a block, a CSS selector, or the page center. There is no limit to the number of pages in a tour. The structure of a user tour is shown in the following diagram:

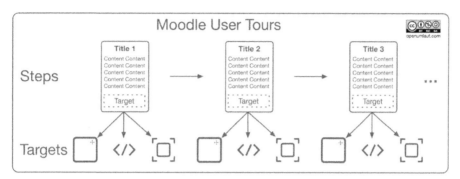

Figure 7.24 – User tours overview

Our sample tour contains three steps where the first one is associated with the **Appearance** menu, which is of target type **Selector**.

Enough of the theory; let's create your first user tour.

Creating a tour

To get to the user tours feature, go to **Site administration | Appearance | User tours**. Moodle ships with a number of user tours, which you will see listed. Let's make our first guide using the **Create a new tour** button.

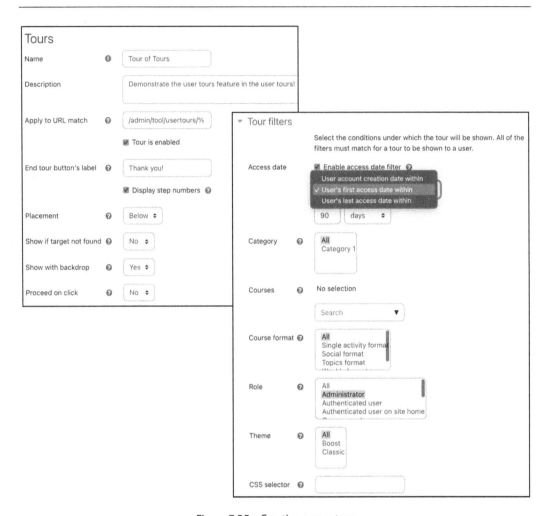

Figure 7.25 – Creating a user tour

While **Name** and **Description** should be self-explanatory, the other settings require some explanation:

- **Apply to URL match**: Tours will be displayed on any page in Moodle whose URL matches the specified path value. The percentage sign is used as a wildcard to catch multiple pages, for instance, `/admin/tool/usertours/%` in our "Tour of Tours" tour. The wildcard can also be preceded with any URL fragment, for example, `%add=scorm%`, for a user tour explaining the various aspects of setting up a SCORM activity.

    Other useful URLs to match are `/my/%` (dashboard), `/course/view.php%` (all courses), `/course/view.php?id=x` (course with id x), and `/user/profile.php%` (user profile). To match the home page, the `FRONTPAGE` value has to be used.

- **Tour is enabled**: Initially, a tour is disabled. You can have multiple tours for the same page destination, but you should only have one per page enabled at a time.

- **End tour button's label**: By default, the button on the last step is labeled **Got it** for single-step and **End tour** for multi-step tours. You can specify a custom label if you wish.

- **Display step numbers**: Whether to display a step counter, such as 2/4, to indicate the tour length. Such an indicator is handy on longer tours.

- **Placement**: The step can be placed **Above**, **Below**, **Left,** or **Right** of the target (matching block or CSS selector). The two horizontal options should be avoided since this may cause issues on mobile devices. If the size exceeds the available space, Moodle will auto-position the step.

- **Show if target not found**: There are cases when the specified target is not displayed, for example, when the user's capabilities won't allow it. In such cases, the step is not shown unless this setting is changed.

- **Show with backdrop**: When ticked, this option will cause the target to be highlighted and the rest of the screen to be dimmed down. We have applied this setting in our example. Some parts do not support backdrops, for instance, the main menu bar.

- **Proceed on click**: If enabled, the next step will be shown when the user clicks the target, mimicking a learning-by-doing feature.

Additionally, you can specify several **Tour filters**, which are conditions that must be met for the tour to be displayed. The available filters are the following:

- **Access date**: The filter restricts a user tour according to account creation, first access, and last access. This is useful if you wish to limit the tour to new users or users who haven't accessed the site for a specified period.

- **Category**: Only show the tour on pages within courses in the selected categories.

- **Courses**: Only show the tour on pages within any selected courses.

- **Course format**: Only show the tour on pages within courses where the selected course format has been applied.

- **Role**: Only show the tour to users who have a selected role in the context where the tour is shown.

- **Theme**: Only show the tour when the selected theme is in use by the user.

- **CSS selector**: Only show the tour when the specified CSS selector is on the page. More on CSS selectors when we add steps, which we will cover next.

Adding steps to your tour

A tour comprises multiple steps, simulating a simple walk-through. In the screenshot, you can see the three steps of our Tour of Tours tour:

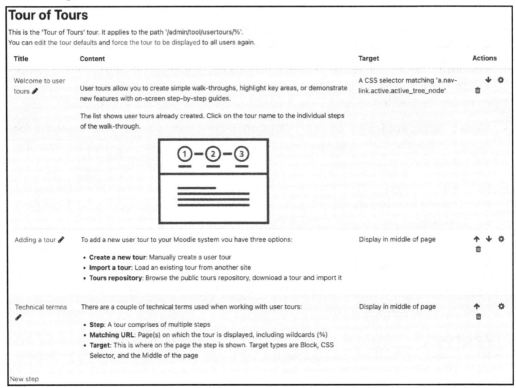

Figure 7.26 – Tour steps

A step contains the following three main elements:

- **Target**: This is the page element the step is associated with. There are three target types:

  - **Block** indicates that the step is displayed next to a Moodle block. You can select one of the many Moodle blocks from the drop-down list.

  - The **CSS selector** target is the most versatile but also the least intuitive approach since you need to identify the relevant CSS selector using the inspector in the browser's development tools. Every browser has implemented its dev tools differently, so you will need to consult your browser's help page. In our case, the CSS selector that must be matched is `a.nav-link.active.active_tree_node`, representing the active tab of the admin menu.

  - Use the **Middle of the page** option to display general information not associated with any elements. The last two steps in our Tour of Tours tour use this target type.

- **Content**: This element comprises a title and the step's explanatory text; the latter can also contain images and even instructional videos. Both compulsory fields will be shown to the user.

  To display your step in the language the user has selected, use **language string IDs**, which can be entered once you have selected the option from the **Content type** menu instead of **Manual**. The standard format for the language string ID is `identifier,component` (see the *Managing localization* section in *Chapter 10, Configuring Technical Features*, for more details, including how to incorporate images in string texts).

  All tours that ship with Moodle make use of the language string feature. Bear in mind that when modifying any of these onboard tours, they may be overridden during the next upgrade.

- **Options**: The available step settings (**Placement, Show if target is not found, Show with backdrop**, and **Proceed on click**) are identical to those specified in the tour settings. You can override each, for instance, when the backdrop doesn't display correctly or stick to the inherited default values.

When you add a new step to your tour via the **New step** link at the bottom, you will find the mentioned elements on the following form:

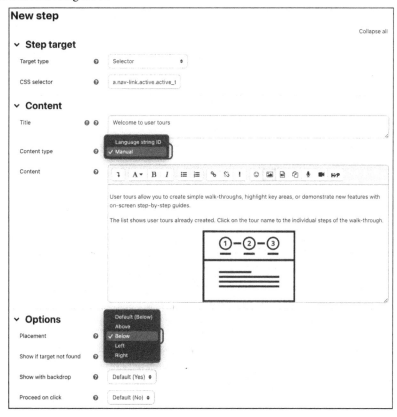

Figure 7.27 – Adding a tour step

After saving the form, you can add as many steps to your user tour as required. You can also amend a tour at a later stage or simply modify any existing content. When the structure of the tour changes, Moodle will recognize this and display the tour to all users, including those who have already viewed the previous version. When you only change small parts of the tour, you can use the **force the tour to be displayed** link at the top of the screen to reset the internal store that records who has already viewed the tour.

Now that you are familiar with creating tours with multiple steps, let's look at sharing tours by importing and exporting them.

Importing and exporting tours

You can download a tour using the **Export** button in the list of tours. Moodle creates a JSON file that can be imported to another Moodle site. The **Import tour** button takes you to the standard upload feature of Moodle.

A valuable resource for mostly high-quality user tours is the **tour repository**. Once you have selected its button, you will be directed to the public **User tours** site on `moodle.net`. At the time of writing, there have been approximately 100 user tours in different languages, which might interest you. All you need to do is select the chosen file and click on the JSON filename, which will download the user tour, which you can then load to your Moodle site using the import mechanism already explained. Ensure that the user tour matches your Moodle version to avoid any inconsistencies.

If you feel that you have created a useful user tour that might be of interest to others, feel free to share it in the tour repository. All you need to do is to export your tour and, using your Moodle account, upload it to the repository on `moodle.net`.

This concludes the section on user tours, the last building block of appearance elements. Next up are Moodle themes, which have an impact across the entire Moodle site.

Using Moodle themes

Moodle provides a flexible skinning mechanism to brand your site to follow corporate design guidelines. As mentioned in the introduction, we will only cover the theme settings that can be accessed from the Moodle administration menu. For details on how to create Moodle themes, refer to *Moodle Theme Development* by *Silvina Paola Hillar, Packt Publishing*, or contact your Premium Moodle Partner, who will be able to offer professional theme design services. There are also some good pointers at `docs.moodle.org/dev/Themes`, which assumes that you have a good understanding of HTML and CSS.

While Moodle supports fixed-width and fluid themes, utilizing (or developing) responsive themes is highly recommended. We exclusively cover responsive themes here.

> **Important note**
>
> The future of e-learning is mobile, as reflected by Moodle, which only ships two responsive themes: Boost and **Classic**.

Responsive themes automatically adapt to the device, screen resolution, and screen orientation. Additionally, responsive themes adjust to the learning content that is displayed and the navigation that is used. Moodle themes are based on **Bootstrap 4** and fully support SASS.

> **Important note**
>
> All modern browsers (the latest versions of Firefox, Edge, Chrome, and Safari) are fully supported by Moodle.
>
> Internet Explorer 11 and other legacy browsers are not supported!

In this themes section, we first select a theme for your site before looking at different theme types. We then customize your theme, a topic categorized in general, advanced, and feature theme settings.

Selecting a Moodle theme

Standard or custom themes can be selected by going to **Site administration | Appearance | Themes | Theme Selector**. On our site, you can see the two core themes (**Boost** and **Classic**) as well as the two most popular third-party themes according to the statistics on moodle.org, **Moove** and **Adaptable**:

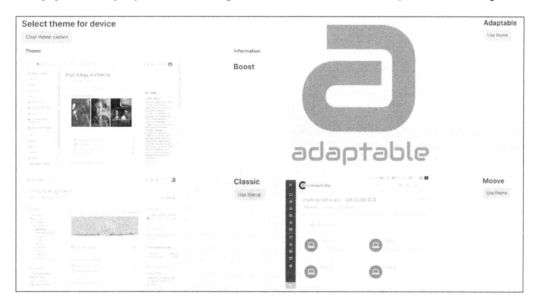

Figure 7.28 – Theme selection

The new skin will be applied immediately by selecting a theme via the **Use theme** button. However, some of your users might experience issues after a theme change, so it is recommended to clear theme caches when a new theme has been applied or an existing theme has been updated.

> **Important note**
> Ensure that the selected theme is compatible with your version of Moodle. Older themes will not be rendered correctly by the Moodle 4 theme engine.

So far, we have applied a single theme for the entire Moodle system. To apply different themes in different contexts, we need to grasp the concept of theme types, which is the topic of the following subsection.

Understanding theme types

To understand most theme settings, we require a little bit of background. Like roles, themes are assigned in different contexts: **Site** (system), **User** (covering **Cohort**), **Category**, and **Course**. Two additional areas, **Session** and **Page**, are supported by Moodle. These **theme types** are explained in the following table:

Type	Description	Configuration
Site	Theme is applied throughout the site. Default when you first install Moodle.	Theme selector
User	Personal theme is selected in the user profile and applied throughout the site.	User profile
Cohort	Theme is applied to all cohort members.	Cohort settings
Category	Theme is applied to all courses within the category and all sub-categories.	Category settings
Course	Theme only applies to the course in which it is set.	Course settings
Session	Temporary theme applies until user is logged out. Set via URL (`?theme=x`).	URL
Page	Page themes are set in code. Added for completeness only.	Code

Figure 7.29 – Theme types I

The table briefly describes each theme scope and where configuration takes place. As a side note, you can change the precedence order (priority of themes) by modifying the `$CFG->themeorder` parameter in `config.php`. The default is set to `array('course', 'category', 'session', 'user', 'cohort', 'site'`.

To force themes to be applied in different areas, two configurations must be carried out:

- Different theme types have to be enabled, which takes place in **Site administration | Appearance | Themes | Settings**. You will see a tick box for each theme type, except site themes, which cannot be disabled, and page themes, which have been preserved for developers.

- A theme has to be selected for the respective theme type via the **Force theme** option. This selection can be made by users who have sufficient permissions in that context; for example, editing teachers are allowed to change a course theme.

The two configurations are shown in the following figure:

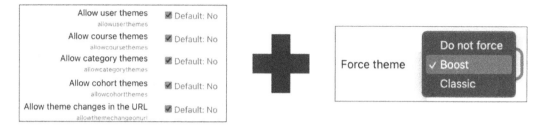

Figure 7.30 – Theme types II

There is a trade-off when allowing theme types other than the site theme: while allowing different theme types, additional processing is required that will add some overhead to your system and place an increased demand on your server. However, not allowing these themes limits the level of customization that can be carried out on your site. To assist you in resolving this uniformity versus personalization balancing act, here are some scenarios where the theme selection feature might be helpful:

- Provision of themes for users with accessibility issues (a high-res theme in the user profile)

- Branding of courses of a qualification (category themes)

- Creation of a theme gallery (session theme via URL: `<yoursite>/?theme=<themename>`)

There are two remaining theme parameters in **Site administration | Appearance | Themes | Theme settings** that are worth mentioning in the context of theme types:

- **Theme list**: To limit the number of available themes, name them in the textbox, separated by commas, and with no spaces.

- **Theme designer mode**: This setting is relevant to designers and developers, effectively turning off theme caching. Do not use this on a production site, as it will slow down your system significantly!

Now that we have the skill set to work with themes, it is time to customize the existing themes.

Customizing themes

As an administrator, you are unlikely to be involved in creating a full-blown custom theme as this task requires strong design skills and deep knowledge of CSS and HTML. However, you will be able to make basic modifications to existing themes.

Theme customizations can be grouped into three categories. While not all themes follow this approach, it gives a good indication of what types of customizations you can carry out via theme settings:

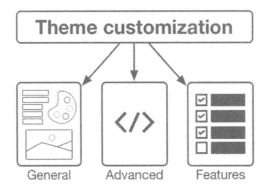

Figure 7.31 – Theme customizations

General settings deal with some basic parameters, images, and colors; advanced settings let you add custom CSS code, and feature settings add new functionality to your system. We are going to cover the three types in the following subsections.

General theme settings

General theme settings let you specify a few basic options, background images, and brand colors. We cover the two core themes (their settings are almost identical) since many custom themes are based on them. Third-party themes will likely have additional settings, for example, more color fields, font sizes, or button styles.

Go to **Site administration | Appearance | Themes** and select either **Classic** or **Boost**, where you can configure the following options:

- **Use a dark style navbar**: Toggle between dark and light style navigation bars (Classic only).

- **Unneeded blocks**: Some blocks are not needed or supported in certain themes. Here, you can disable them without having to hide them for other themes.

- **Theme preset** and **Additional theme preset files**: Presets contain SCSS instructions used to generate the new stylesheets for the theme. More on presets and SCSS in the following subsection.

- **Background image** and **Login page background image**: These two settings should be self-explanatory.

- **Brand colour**: Menu items and buttons are changed to the selected color.

General theme settings are usually insufficient to style a site to your needs. CSS gives you more flexibility, which we are covering next.

Advanced theme settings

Moodle uses **Cascading Style Sheets** (**CSS**) to describe the presentation of each element that is displayed. CSS defines different aspects of the HTML presentation, including colors, fonts, layouts, and so on.

To learn more about theme basics, go to `docs.moodle.org/dev/Themes_overview`, where you will find a well-documented and detailed help section. Ensure you are familiar with your browser's **Inspect** tool to identify CSS styles and attributes.

Moodle uses consistently plain English for the naming of styles. For the login page elements that are displayed in the following two screenshots, a few sample styles have been labeled (original on the left original and modified version on the right):

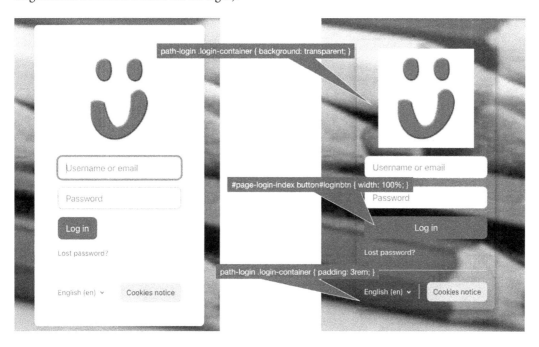

Figure 7.32 – CSS style samples

You can see that a style represents each element of Moodle. There are literally thousands of styles in Moodle, which gives designers a high degree of freedom.

Moodle supports **Sassy CSS** (**SCSS**), a superset of CSS providing additional features such as variables and nesting. SCSS is a preprocessor language that is converted to CSS before it is applied to any site. For the sake of simplicity, we are going to stick to CSS throughout this chapter.

> **Tip**
> If you already have any SCSS code or libraries, feel free to use these for your visual customizations.

Any code you wish to inject side-wide should be applied directly in the theme at **Site administration | Appearance | Themes | <Theme>**. On the **Advanced settings** tab, you will find two settings that let you override the initial SCSS variables and add new SCSS to themes without modifying any code in the backend: **Raw initial SCSS** (code injected before any other code) and **Raw SCSS** (injected at the end of the style sheet). In the following example, we have added three variables to add some weight to all fonts throughout the site:

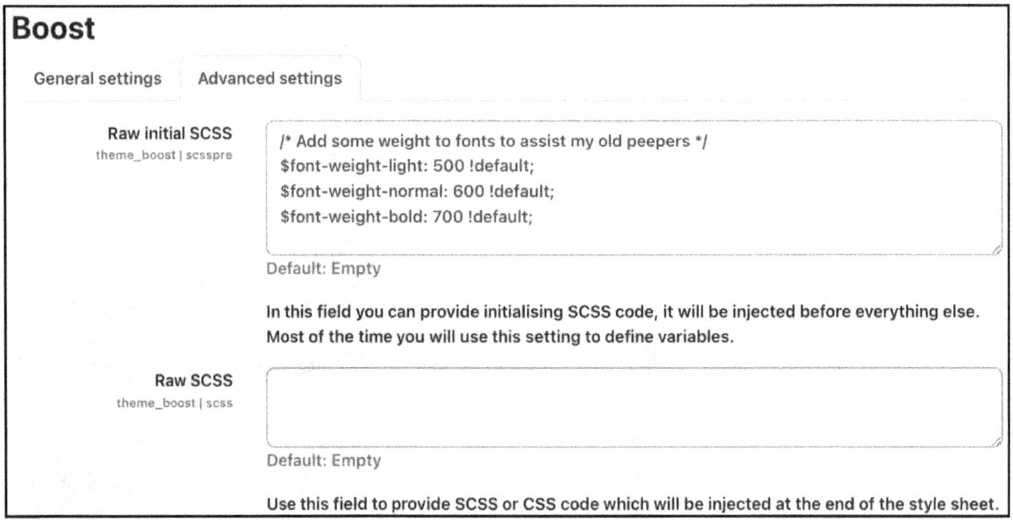

Boost

General settings   Advanced settings

Raw initial SCSS
 theme_boost | scsspre
	`/* Add some weight to fonts to assist my old peepers */`
	`$font-weight-light: 500 !default;`
	`$font-weight-normal: 600 !default;`
	`$font-weight-bold: 700 !default;`

Default: Empty

In this field you can provide initialising SCSS code, it will be injected before everything else. Most of the time you will use this setting to define variables.

Raw SCSS theme_boost | scss	

Default: Empty

Use this field to provide SCSS or CSS code which will be injected at the end of the style sheet.

Figure 7.33 – Advanced theme settings

The second concept we already came across in the general settings is **theme presets**. According to the developer documentation, a preset is an SCSS file designed to be added to the Boost theme or a child of it. It combines the Bootstrap 4 SCSS files with the required Moodle SCSS files and adds a layer of customization. Preset files can be uploaded into the admin settings for the theme and then chosen from a list of installed presets.

Moodle also supports **Mustache** templates to render HTML output. For more information on Moodle's use of Mustache, check out the Moodle developer documentation at `docs.moodle.org/dev/Templates`.

Technically, you can customize your entire site using SCSS and theme presets. However, unless there are only a handful of adjustments, its usage is cumbersome and its maintenance potentially tricky. Third-party or custom themes overcome this shortcoming and also have the potential to introduce new features.

Feature theme settings

The beauty of themes is that they can't just control the look and feel elements but also add new functionality. All popular themes make use of this ability and add new features.

There is a plethora of themes on `moodle.org/plugins/?q=type:theme`. There are also plenty of design and development companies that offer paid-for Moodle themes via their websites. According to the statistics on `moodle.org`, the three most popular themes are **Moove**, **Adaptable**, and **Fordson**. To give you an idea of what the configuration options in a professional theme can look like, have a look at the snippet from the **Adaptable** theme:

Figure 7.34 – Adaptable theme

Just have a look at the sheer volume of menu items! The theme provides a plethora of customization options, ranging from custom menus, front page slide shows, news tickers, and marketing spots to social networking icons and analytics support. Refer to *Chapter 8, Understanding Moodle Plugins*, for how to install third-party themes.

The topic of themes and customization is hugely complex, and Moodle administrators are usually not involved in the design and branding process. We have covered theme basics that can be customized via the admin interface and, hopefully, this gave you a little insight into the topic. Closely related to theme customization is accessibility, which has to be ensured on your site.

Ensuring accessibility

In most educational settings, accessibility is now a legal requirement. So, it is crucial to ensure compliance of your system with the respective standards.

> **Important note**
> Accessibility is the ability for users with certain disabilities to access Moodle's functionality.

An area has been dedicated to Moodle accessibility in Moodle Docs, which you can access at `docs.moodle.org/en/Accessibility`. It provides useful links to standards, guidelines, legislation, and subject-related tools and resources.

Three main accessibility areas affect accessibility in Moodle:

- System accessibility
- Theme accessibility
- Content accessibility

We will cover all three accessibility types in the following subsections.

System accessibility

Moodle fully complies with major accessibility standards and has obtained WCAG 2.1 level AA Accreditation. Moodle enforces XHTML 1.0 Strict, which only allows the usage of compliant HTML constructs and the implementation of the Moodle forms library. These restrictions guarantee consistency across pages and ensure support for standard screen readers without further configuration.

Moodle provides links to external validation sites, checking the current page for standard compliance. Go to **Site administration | Development | Debugging** and check the **Show validator links** box to activate these. Links to **Validate HTML** and **Web Content Accessibility Guidelines (WCAG) check** will be displayed at the bottom of your page (if supported by your theme):

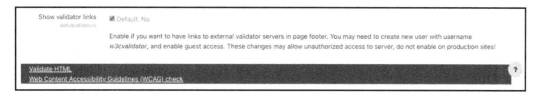

Figure 7.35 – Validator links

External validation sites will be opened with the URL as a parameter when selecting the respective links. For the validation sites to be able to check pages on your Moodle system, you need to create a new user with username w3cvalidator and enable guest access to your site. Only do this on a staging or test site since these settings potentially compromise the security of your system.

The validation sites not only check for any page issues but also for theme problems, which are covered next.

Theme accessibility

CSS is Moodle's representation layer independent of the system layer, represented in XHTML 1.0 Strict. Thus, accessibility also has to be ensured in the theme itself.

Once you have implemented your accessibility styles, either directly in the theme or through custom CSS, ensure these have been validated against any issues.

One popular choice is to incorporate accessibility options and offer them in the theme as options, such as different color schemes, font styles, text sizes, and readability choices. You can install the **Accessibility tool** from github.com/sharpchi/moodle-local_accessibilitytool, and the following selection will be available to all users via their **Preference** menu (if supported by your theme):

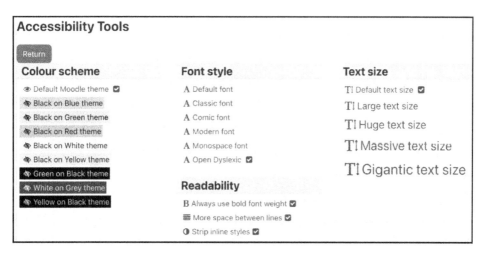

Figure 7.36 – Accessibility tool

System and theme accessibility are issues you, as an administrator, have full control over; content accessibility, on the other hand, is more difficult to achieve since you are relying on content creators. How to assist them will be covered in the following subsection.

Content accessibility

Accessibility compliance is only guaranteed for Moodle pages (assuming that the theme follows all standards) but not for your teachers' and instructors' newly created and uploaded content.

Moodle has some basic built-in tools that assist your content creators:

- The **HTML tidy** text filter checks whether the HTML code is XHTML-compliant, tidying it up wherever necessary. You must activate the filter by navigating to **Site administration | Plugins | Filters | Manage filters**. Ensure that PHP has been compiled with the `libtidy` option.

- The **Accessibility checker** button in Atto carries out some basic checks against the entered HTML code to ensure conformity with accessibility guidelines.

- The **Screenreader helper** button in Atto checks whether images have been tagged correctly to ensure screenreader compatibility.

While these tools provide some basic assistance, they are insufficient in helping content creators to ensure accessibility compliance. To achieve full accessibility conformance, the **Accessibility toolkit** should be facilitated. To understand the principle behind the tool, have a look at the following diagram:

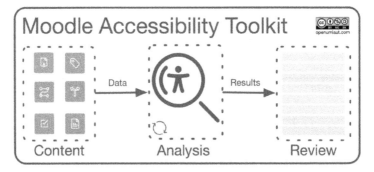

Figure 7.37 – Accessibility toolkit process

The accessibility toolkit comprises the following steps:

1. The course content is preprocessed, and the data required for analysis is extracted. This data contains any relevant content for analysis and information about the content, such as HTML tags.

2. Data analysis takes place on your Moodle server in the background; no content is transferred off your site. (The only data being transferred off the Moodle site is for one purpose only: to send a regular summary of overall data for statistical and progression purposes, such as the number of courses, the number of users, analysis check errors, and so on.)

3. The results are available via the **Accessibility review** block and, in more detail, on different data breakdown pages in the toolkit.

The beauty of the system is that every time content is updated, only the delta of the data is analyzed. This mechanism reduces the load on your Moodle site and performs analyses faster on your server.

As an administrator, you have to ensure that the tool has been configured correctly, which requires the following steps:

1. Ensure accessibility tools are enabled in **Site administration | General | Advanced features**.

2. Register the accessibility toolkit with Brickfield Education Labs. Go to **Site administration | Plugins | Admin tools | Accessibility | Brickfield registration** and follow the registration link. You will need to create an account and add your site details before receiving your API key and Secret key. These keys will enable your toolkit once submitted on the registration page on your Moodle site.

3. Go to **Site administration | Plugins | Admin tools | Accessibility | Accessibility toolkit settings** and **Enable analysis requests**. The analysis is updated automatically for requested courses on an ongoing basis with course content edits; **Delete historical checks results** allows the toolkit to delete older analysis records that have been superseded by newer records. **Batch limit** sets the limit of analysis batches run periodically by scheduled tasks:

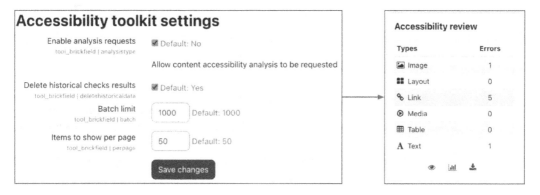

Figure 7.38 – Accessibility toolkit settings and review block

4. Go to **Site administration | Plugins | Blocks | Accessibility review** and ensure the **What to show on the course page**, **Display errors in this format**, and **Toolkit page to show** settings are appropriately configured.

5. Go to **Site administration | Server | Tasks | Scheduled tasks**, search for tool_brickfield, and change the first four tasks to be run every minute (change the **Minute** settings to *). The default has been set to 5 minutes to avoid potential overloading during the initial analysis. Check out the *Cron management and scheduled tasks* section in *Chapter 15, Optimizing Moodle Performance*, for more details.

The accessibility starter toolkit that ships with Moodle contains some helpful tools to assist content creators in producing accessibility-compliant learning materials. The **Enterprise Accessibility Toolkit** has a complete set of features to help your organization improve the accessibility of your courses. Check out www.brickfield.ie/brickfield-accessibility-toolkit for details.

This concludes the section on the complex task of accessibility and ends the chapter on configuring Moodle's appearance.

Summary

In this chapter, we tackled the not-so-appealing look and feel of a vanilla Moodle site and touched upon a significant number of areas supporting customization.

We first looked at pages that can be customized by the administrator: login, home, dashboard, my courses, and the user profile. We then covered appearance elements visible or usable throughout the site: the header, blocks, video and audio, the Atto editor, and user tours.

The second part of the chapter was concerned with the customization of themes. Before customizing your theme via general, advanced, and feature theme settings, we looked at different theme types.

The last topic covered was accessibility, a legal requirement in most educational settings. We dealt with system, theme, and content accessibility.

> **Important note**
> Double-check what your site looks like when you are not logged in. Ensure no information is visible that should only be accessible to logged-in users.

The main objective of adapting the look and feel of your Moodle system is to ensure a consistent user experience alongside ease of use. However, the level of customization is constrained by two factors, as shown in the following triangle:

Figure 7.39 – Level of customization

The appearance of your site is subject to restrictions, usually the corporate design guidelines of your organization and accessibility regulations. Also, the higher the level of customization, the higher the potential maintenance effort when you upgrade the site to a newer version. It is recommended to consider these aspects when you modify any visual Moodle elements or outsource the task to a Moodle Partner.

Now that your Moodle looks (hopefully) the way you want it to, it is time to enable all the functionalities you wish to offer your users. Plugins are a versatile way to add new features to your Moodle system, which we will deal with in the following chapter.

8
Understanding Moodle Plugins

Your system is fully operational and has a look and feel that reflects your organization's branding. As with all complex web-based applications, a significant number of configuration activities can be carried out to bring Moodle in line with your organization's needs and requirements.

In this chapter, we will first provide an overview of plugins. Then, we will explore some third-party plugins and learn about their powers. We will then understand how to install, update, and delete plugins before we conclude with plugin evaluation criteria, popular plugins, and organizational decisions.

One of the many strengths of Moodle is its pluggable architecture. Moodle supports a wide range of plugins, which we are going to shed light on by covering the following topics:

- Moodle plugins – an overview
- The power of third-party plugins
- Managing third-party plugins (install, update, and delete)
- Good plugins and bad plugins (plugin evaluation criteria, popular plugins, and organizational decisions)

A word on terminology: we will use plugin, module, and add-on interchangeably in this chapter.

Let's start with an overview of plugins and integrations.

Moodle plugins – an overview

Moodle is a (very) modular system – that's what the *M* in Moodle stands for, after all – and most of Moodle's functionality has been implemented as modules, called plugins.

> **Important note**
> Moodle plugins are modules that provide some specific, usually ring-fenced, functionality.

Navigate to the **Plugins** tab in the **Site administration** area. You will find two menu items dealing with installing and managing plugins before all plugin types are shown underneath.

Let's get started with **Plugins overview**, which displays a list of all the installed plugins. The information shown for each plugin includes the following:

- **Plugin name**: The official name of the plugin.

- **Component name**: A unique internal identifier, shown underneath the plugin name.

- **Version**: The plugin version number, in date format. Some third-party plugins also show the supported Moodle version.

- **Availability**: Enabled or disabled.

- **Actions**: A link to the plugin settings, if available.

- **Uninstall**: An option to delete the plugin; unavailable for some core plugins.

- **Notes**: Additional information, usually in the form of dependencies or errors.

The **Plugins overview** window shown in *Figure 8.1* is helpful to get a quick overview of what has been installed on your system and what functionality is available. You can also perform a check for available updates via the button at the top of the screen.

Select the **Additional plugins** link to see which third-party plugins have been installed. There are 16 additional plugins on my Moodle system. We utilized some in *Chapter 7, Enhancing Moodle's Look and Feel*; we will install the other plugins later in this chapter.

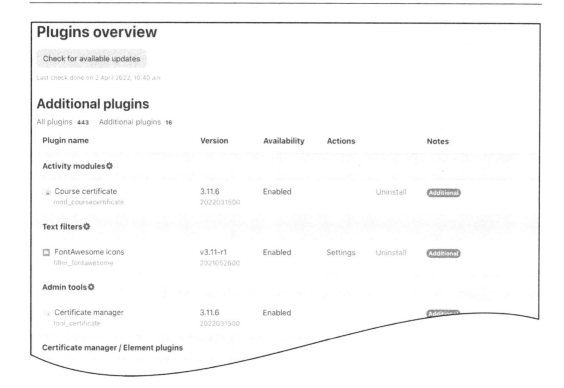

Figure 8.1 – Installed plugins

You can also see that each plugin has been placed in a category, a so-called plugin type, which is a good filter criterion when searching for third-party plugins, as we will see later.

> **Tip**
> Plugins are grouped into **plugin types** and **plugin subtypes**. For more technical information, check out `docs.moodle.org/dev/Plugin_types`.

As you can see from your instance's long list of entries, Moodle already ships with over 400 plugins. Most plugins work within the realm of Moodle itself; that is, they do not need to communicate with any other systems. However, some plugins – **integration plugins** – require some sort of data exchange with other systems or services. We have **system plugins** at the other end of the spectrum, which need some internal configuration to function correctly.

Our plugins overview diagram follows the same structure and order as Moodle's list of plugin types:

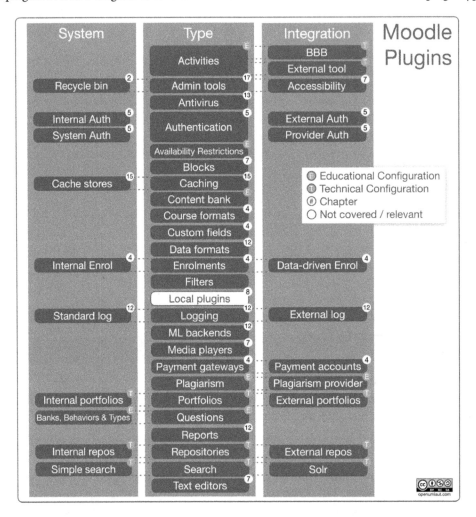

Figure 8.2 – Moodle plugins overview

Some plugin types have not been listed in this diagram. They either represent a niche type, for example, document converters and development tools, such as web service protocols, or are treated differently, such as themes.

The tiny bubbles attached to each plugin in *Figure 8.2* indicate in which chapter the plugin is covered. The *E*-bubbles will be dealt with in *Chapter 9, Configuring Educational Features*, and the *T*-bubbles in *Chapter 10, Configuring Technical Features*.

We haven't mentioned one type of plugin called **local plugins** yet. The directory is the recommended place for customizations that do not fit the plugin types we already mentioned. These customizations can be changed according to the existing functionalities or the introduction of new features. For more information on local plugins, check out the `readme.txt` file in the `local` directory located in `dirroot`.

A plugin stores data in up to three locations:

- It always stores **code** in `dirroot`. This is the plugin itself.

- It might store data in the **database**, such as configuration settings or user data.

- It can store **files** in `dataroot`, for example, images or videos.

The following diagram visualizes these dependencies:

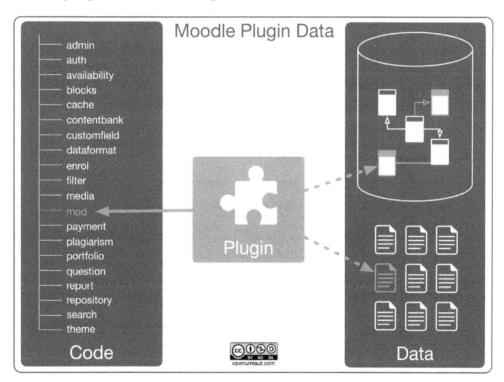

Figure 8.3 – Plugin data

If you delete any plugin – core or custom – used anywhere in Moodle, all of its already-created instances will be deleted, including any associated user data! Deleting a plugin cannot be undone; it has to be installed from scratch.

> **Important note**
> Do not delete any core plugins unless you are 100% sure you will never need them again. If you wish to prevent the usage of a core plugin, it is better to hide it instead of remove it.

With that stark warning, let's extend your Moodle system with third-party plugins.

The power of third-party plugins

A plethora of third-party Moodle software exists that adds new functionality, fixes shortcomings, or integrates Moodle with external systems and cloud services. Let's start with an overview of third-party software.

Moodle ships with a comprehensive set of core plugins. While the provided functionalities sufficiently satisfy a majority of use cases, there is a growing demand for additional software. Also, requirements change over time, and new functionalities are needed in your Moodle system.

Due to Moodle's open source nature and modularity, it is relatively straightforward for developers to add new functionality or modify existing features. These can range from minor modifications (patches) or hacks to full-blown modules. You can access the **plugin directory** by visiting `moodle.org/plugins`, which contains all the approved non-core plugins (and themes).

You have three options to navigate through the plugin directory:

- Using **Search** with the help of a keyword
- Using **Plugin types** combined with other criteria, such as version or purpose
- Using **Navigation** in the side block where you can also contribute new plugins

Either way, you should always end up with a list of add-ons. Once you click on the plugin's name, you will see details such as a description, installation instructions, statistics, and translations.

At the time of writing, there are over 2,000 third-party Moodle plugins, and the number is growing continuously. You will find all kinds of add-ons, from the weird and wonderful to the very powerful.

Now that we know where to locate plugins, let's see how to install, update, and delete them in the next section.

Managing third-party plugins

The management of third-party plugins comprises the basic standard operations of add, change, and delete. There are four different ways to install, update, and uninstall plugins, which we will cover in this section:

- Installation via the **web interface**
- **Manual** installation
- Installation via **Git**
- Installation via the **command line**

Once you have added, modified, or removed a plugin via any of the four methods, you need to trigger the Moodle updater from **Site administration** | **General** | **Notifications**, which will manage the data stored in the database and `moodledata`. These processes are shown in the following diagram:

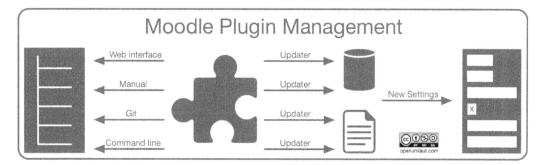

Figure 8.4 – Plugin management

If the updater has added any configurable settings, they will be displayed on a separate **New settings** page. This screen will be skipped if the plugin doesn't contain any new parameters.

> **Important note**
>
> Installing, updating, and removing plugins should always be done in maintenance mode, which is activated from **Site administration** | **Server** | **Maintenance mode**. While it is possible to add most plugins while Moodle is in use, it is not recommended as this can lead to unforeseen problems.

In the following subsections, we will deal with the three standard management operations to install, update, and delete plugins by installing some popular third-party add-ons.

Installing third-party add-ons

Installing plugins to your Moodle system can greatly enhance the set of features and, consequently, your users' experience. However, we recommend avoiding experimenting with new add-ons on your production site(s). Most organizations set up a shadow site of their live server to be used as a sandbox. Once the installation has been successful, the procedure is reapplied on the production site.

> **Important note**
>
> Try out new plugins on a staging or test site first. Back up your production site before installing new plugins.

Additionally, it is recommended that you make a complete site backup before installing any third-party software. This way, you can roll it back in case of a disaster. We will deal with backups in *Chapter 16, Avoiding Sleepless Nights – Moodle Backup and Restore*.

> **Important note**
>
> Ensure the plugin version is compatible with the version of Moodle you are running.

Most add-ons are structured in a very similar way. However, some modules either don't follow this standardized approach or require other steps, particularly when the module communicates with other software systems. Each plugin should contain a file (usually) called README, and it is important to read the instructions inside it before starting the installation process.

We will demonstrate each installation type (web interface, manual, Git, and command line) by adding a popular plugin, starting with Video Time, which we already mentioned in the previous chapter.

Installing the Video Time plugin via the web interface

The easiest way to install a plugin is by going to **Site administration** | **Plugins** | **Install Plugins**. However, you must ensure that the target directory on your server is writable, which is not recommended in production sites for security reasons but is usually acceptable on test sites. There are two options for using the web-based plugin installer:

- **Install plugin from Moodle plugins**

  This option will direct you to the familiar plugins section at moodle.org/plugins, where you must log in, to perform installations. Also, bear in mind that your site's full name, URL, and Moodle version will be transferred to ensure a smooth installation process. Once you have located the plugin you wish to install (here, Video Time), you will see an additional **Install now** button appear:

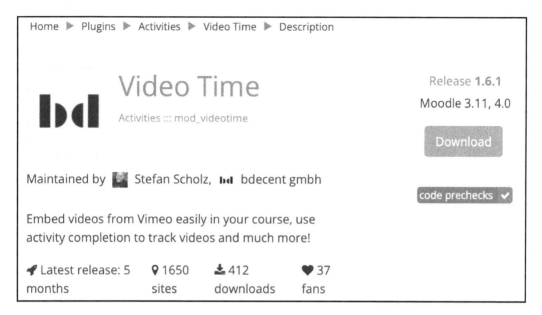

Figure 8.5 – Installing plugins from Moodle plugins I

Once selected, a list of your sites will be shown, and you need to select **Install now** again. You will be redirected back to your Moodle site, where a message will indicate whether the plugin can be installed or a problem has arisen; for instance, the target directory is not writable. Once this has been confirmed, the plugin validation will be carried out, and the already-familiar **Plugins check** screen has to be confirmed before the installation is carried out.

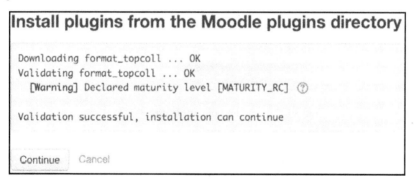

Figure 8.6 – Installing plugins from Moodle plugins II

Once **Upgrade Moodle database now** has been clicked, the updater will be started, and the standard installation process will kick off.

• **Install plugins from a ZIP file**

Alternatively, you can download and upload the plugin by navigating to the **Site administration | Plugins | Install Plugins** interface. You will have to confirm the validation screen before the installation is performed.

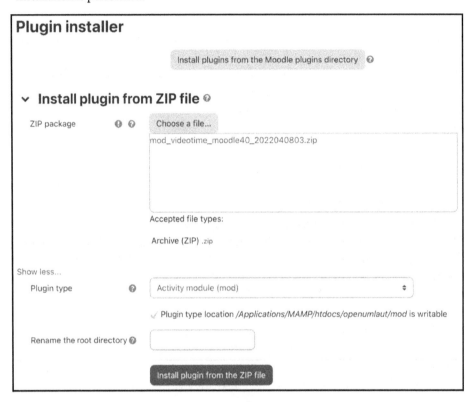

Figure 8.7 – Installing plugins from a ZIP file

The installer automatically detects the type of plugins that correctly declare their component's name. If auto-detection fails, choose the correct plugin type manually. The installation procedure can fail if an incorrect plugin type is specified! If you need to change the root directory for the plugin installation, change the **Rename the root directory** setting.

The installation via ZIP files lets you add plugins not only from the public plugin repository on moodle.org but also from other sources, such as trusted developers or (Premium) Moodle Partners.

The advantage of the two covered web-based installation methods is their simplicity; the price to pay is compromised site security. The following plugin installation method overcomes this restriction.

Installing the Zoom meeting plugin manually

You can perform these installation tasks manually as an alternative to installing plugins via the admin interface. To demonstrate these steps, we have chosen the **Zoom meeting** plugin, which became very popular during the pandemic when working from a home office was the norm for many and the demand for video conference calls increased significantly.

After locating the add-on in the plugins repository (`moodle.org/plugins/mod_zoom`), download the version of the software that fits the version of your Moodle system (here, 4.0). Next, put Moodle in maintenance mode (**Site administration | Server | Maintenance mode**).

The module follows the standardized structure of add-ons; it uses Moodle's predefined directory hierarchy and naming convention. It is best to copy the ZIP file to the `$CFG->dirroot/mod` directory and unpack the file via the `unzip` command. You might have to change the user and group attributes of the folder. Depending on their type, other plugins must be placed in other directories in `$CFG->dirroot`.

Now, go to **Site administration | General | Notifications**, where the module behind this page will recognize that a new module has to be installed and kick off the updater.

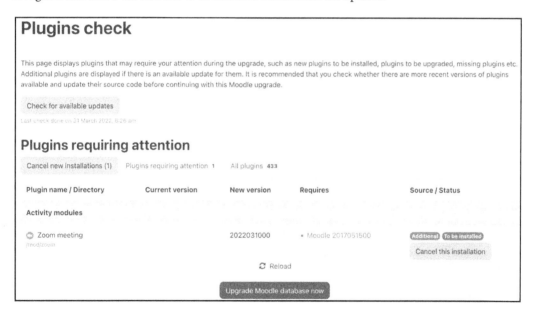

Figure 8.8 – Installing plugins manually

You will see a new entry in the **Activity modules** plugin types called `/mod/zoom` with the **To be installed** status. Once you confirm this via the **Upgrade Moodle database now** button, database tables with fields are created and populated with values. The overall success of the installation will be displayed.

If a new plugin contains settings that can be configured via the admin interface, they will be displayed on a separate **New settings** page. The **Zoom meeting** plugin has over 40 new parameters, which can be entered straight away (or left at their defaults), or later via the **Plugin** tab. In the case of our **Zoom** plugin, you must provide `apikey`, `apisecret`, and `zoomurl` for the module to function.

That's it! All you have to do now is ensure the module works as expected. In the case of **Zoom meeting**, go to **Site administration** | **Plugins** | **Activity modules** | **Zoom meeting**, and you will see an entry for the newly installed add-on. You can find detailed information at `github.com/ncstate-delta/moodle-mod_zoom/wiki`.

Finally, don't forget to disable Moodle's maintenance mode and let your users know the new functionality is available!

An alternative to manually installing third-party plugins is to install and update them via Git, which we will cover in the following subsection.

Installing the Workplace certificate manager via Git

Developers are encouraged to maintain their personal Git repositories, which might contain multiple Moodle extensions. We will use the popular **Workplace certificate manager** to demonstrate how to install a contributed extension from its Git repository. As the name suggests, the plugin is part of Moodle Workplace and has been made available to work in Moodle LMS. Check out the Moodle Docs page at `docs.moodle.org/en/Certificates` and the *Managing certificates* section in *Chapter 9*, *Configuring Educational Features*, for details about the tool.

When you browse the plugin page, you will see a link to **Source control URL**, which will direct you to the GitHub entry of the plugin. GitHub (now owned by Microsoft) is the de facto standard site for managing Git repositories.

Figure 8.9 – Installing plugins via Git I

Workplace certificate manager is an admin tool. To install the plugin, you have to execute the following steps:

1. Change to the $CFG->dirroot/admin/tool directory (this is where admin tools are stored).

2. Execute the following git command, which adds a new subdirectory called certificate and creates a local copy of the plugin code repository:

```
git clone https://github.com/moodleworkplace/moodle-tool_
certificate.git certificate
```

When executing the git command, progress is displayed as shown in the following screenshot:

```
root@debian:/var/www/packt/mod# git clone https://github.com/markn86/moodle mod_certificate.git certificate
Cloning into certificate...
remote: Reusing existing pack: 1979, done.
remote: Total 1979 (delta 0), reused 0 (delta 0)
Receiving objects: 100% (1979/1979), 3.46 MiB | 811 KiB/s, done.
Resolving deltas: 100% (1009/1009), done.
```

Figure 8.10 – Installing plugins via Git II

3. Go to the **Site administration | General | Notifications** page and run through the upgrade screens for the plugin to be added to your Moodle system. Once this last step has been successfully executed, the plugin will be available by navigating to **Site administration | General | Certificates | Manage certificate templates**.

A second plugin works in tandem with **Workplace certificate manager**. The **Workplace course certificate** activity (`moodle.org/plugins/mod_coursecertificate`) automatically issues digital certificates to course participants. Feel free to install the plugin yourself and check its documentation at `docs.moodle.org/en/Course_certificate_activity`.

The installation via Git has the advantage that you have a version history and can potentially roll back in case of any problems. A further benefit is that Git commands can be placed in shell scripts to automate plugin maintenance. However, some may find the Git syntax a bit cryptic or the usage of Git overkill. An intuitive alternative to Git is the MOOSH command-line tool, which might work better in some environments.

Installing plugins via the command line

Moodle itself does not support the installation of plugins via its CLI, but there is a utility called **MOOSH** that does exactly that. You will find the tool in the Moodle plugins database (`moodle.org/plugins/view.php?id=522`). To install MOOSH, extract the downloaded package and set a symbolic link to your programs folder:

```
sudo ln -s $PWD/moosh.php /usr/local/bin/moosh
```

You should now be able to execute MOOSH from the command line. For further installation options, have a look at `moosh-online.com`.

MOOSH is a bit different; that is, it is not a plugin as such but a command-line tool supporting over 150 commands, two of which are relevant in the context of installing plugins:

- `moosh plugin-list`: This command lists all the plugins (full name, short name, available Moodle versions, and a short description) available at `moodle.org/plugins`; it makes sense to apply some filters, such as the module name, since the list is enormous.

- `moosh plugin-install mod_coursecertificate 1`: This command downloads and installs the current version of the **Workplace course certificate** activity we mentioned in the previous subsection. It doesn't get any easier than this! To obtain the version number, use the aforementioned `plugin-list` command (`moosh plugin-list | grep "Course certificate"`).

You can use the `config_plugins` command to configure the settings of the plugin. To get an overview of all the plugins installed on your Moodle instance, use the `info-plugins` command.

You will come across MOOSH at various places in this book, and an entire section has been dedicated to the tool in *Chapter 17, Working with Moodle Admin Tools*.

So far, we have worked our way through alternative plugin installation procedures. Regular updates are published for most plugins, and the topic of the following subsection is how to keep your add-ons up to date.

Keeping plugins up to date

One main challenge that Moodle administrators face is to keep plugins up to date. The preceding steps are sufficient for a one-off installation but do not cater to plugin maintenance.

How do you know that new plugins are available? You can either be notified automatically by email (go to **Site administration | Server | Update notifications**, as covered in *Chapter 1, Installing Moodle*), you can check manually for updates at **Site administration | Plugins | Plugins overview** (see *Figure 8.1*), or you can go to **Site administration | General | Notifications**, where you might see the following notification:

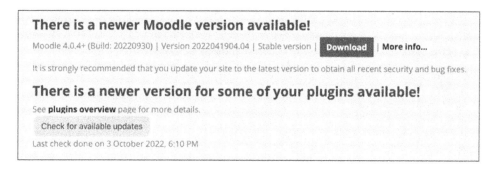

Figure 8.11 – Plugin upgrade required?

Keeping plugins up to date depends on the installation method you chose initially:

- **Web interface**: Go to **Site administration | Plugins | Plugins overview**, where the **Install available updates** button will initiate the update process of any available plugins (download and installation).

- **Manually**: You will have to download the latest version at `moodle.org/plugins` and re-install, as described previously.

- **Git**: To keep the plugin up to date over time, you will have to create a local module branch of the module that is synchronized with the remote branch on GitHub. You will find detailed instructions on how to do this at `docs.moodle.org/en/Git_for_Administrators`.

- **Command line**: All you need to do is rerun the same command you used during installation: `moosh plugin-install <plugin> <moodle_version>`.

Plugins might become obsolete, or a better alternative might get published. Removing plugins from your Moodle system will be dealt with in the following subsection.

Uninstalling third-party add-ons

Moodle plugins usually comprise two parts: the plugin code, located in a subdirectory of `$CFG->dirroot`, and data associated with the plugin, located in the database and/or Moodledata. When deleting a plugin, you must ensure that both parts have been removed. If the code is removed, but there is still some data in the database or filesystem, inconsistencies might occur; if the data is gone, but the plugin is still present, it will be re-installed the next time the updater is initiated.

The removal of a plugin depends again on the installation method you chose initially:

- **Web interface**: Go to the **Site administration | Plugins | Plugins overview**, where you must follow the **Uninstall** link. Once the deletion has been confirmed, all data associated with the plugin will be removed. To prevent the plugin from re-installing itself, its code must be removed from your server, which can be done by confirming the second screen.

- **Manually**: The procedure is the same as the uninstallation via the web interface. The only step unlikely to work is deleting the plugin code from Moodledata due to a lack of permissions. If that is the case, you must remove the folder(s) at the shell level.

- **Git**: To remove the plugin code, you have to run the following command:

  ```
  git rm <plugin>
  ```

- While this command keeps your local git repository up to date, it doesn't remove the data associated with the plugin. As before, you need to do this manually via the **Uninstall** option at **Site administration | Plugins | Plugins overview**.

- **Command line**: All you need to do is run the MOOSH `plugin_uninstall` command: `moosh plugin-uninstall <plugin>`. This command removes both the plugin code and the plugin data.

You are not tied to a single method for maintaining plugins; you can install an add-on via the command line and remove it manually. The only method that requires consistency is Git, as the repository has to be kept in sync with the code base of your Moodle instance to avoid inconsistencies.

Important note
Deleting an add-on will also irreversibly remove all the user data associated with the module!

This concludes the section on managing third-party plugins. The following table provides a summary of the four described plugin management types, highlighting key features and restrictions:

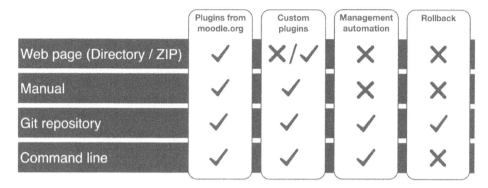

	Plugins from moodle.org	Custom plugins	Management automation	Rollback
Web page (Directory / ZIP)	✓	✗ / ✓	✗	✗
Manual	✓	✓	✗	✗
Git repository	✓	✓	✓	✓
Command line	✓	✓	✓	✗

Figure 8.12 – Plugin management options

So far, we have not distinguished between good and not-so-good plugins, which is the topic of the following section.

Good plugins and bad plugins

Every module that is part of the core of Moodle has gone through a thorough quality assurance procedure. Moodle has implemented a tight process of accepting third-party plugins to its database. While this practice does not guarantee the add-on's functionality, security, or integrity, it evaluates the code at a high level. Once this stage has been passed, it will be accepted in the plugin database. The potential problem with third-party add-ons is that you don't know anything about the quality of the software.

While it is possible to uninstall modules if they don't fit your purpose, you will have to ensure that you don't put barriers in place for future updates. If an add-on is not maintained correctly, it is unlikely that it'll be able to support any upcoming versions of Moodle. You will have to delete the module that's already in use, or you won't be able to upgrade your system. Also, a module might cater to some required functionality but can compromise your system's security.

Plugin evaluation criteria

Several criteria indicate whether a plugin is trustworthy or not. They are as follows:

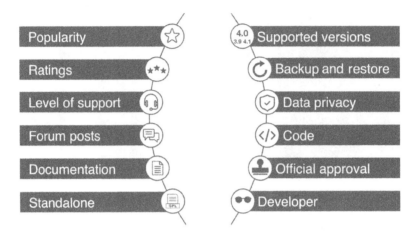

Figure 8.13 – Plugin evaluation criteria

The following enumeration provides a brief explanation for each item in the diagram:

- **Popularity**: Moodle maintains statistics on usage and downloads, which can be found in the **Stats** tab of each plugin. While there is no guarantee, the more popular a module, the more likely it is to be of a high standard.

- **Ratings**: Each plugin page allows users to mark a plugin as their favorite. Again, there's no guarantee here, but the more admins who are fans of a plugin, the more likely that this is a good plugin.

- **Level of support**: Some of the most valuable third-party add-ons have vanished because they are unsupported. Your best bet is if a major stakeholder supports the add-on in Moodle, that is, a (Premium) Moodle Partner. The maintainer should have been active in the community during the past 60 days.

- **Forum posts**: Users are encouraged to post comments, problems, and praise about each module. Read through the posts to get an idea about what other users have experienced. Be suspicious about modules that are not talked about at all. Also, check whether there are any bad reviews in the **Reviews** section.

- **Documentation**: Each add-on should have a dedicated page in Moodle Docs. It is usually not a good sign if the page does not exist or is only a wiki stub. Also, it is a good practice if a changelog is kept for the developed software.

- **Standalone**: Third-party add-ons mustn't modify any core code (known as patches supplied in the form of patch files). This restriction is essential as the changes will be overridden with every Moodle update, and the modifications must be reapplied.

- **Supported versions**: Support for current and all supported versions of Moodle shows that the software is being actively maintained. You can look at any of the existing versions in the **Versions** tab.

- **Backup and restore support**: If applicable, the add-on should be supported by the course backup and restore facility. Otherwise, what good is an activity if it is not included in your archives?

- **Data privacy**: If the plugin stores any data, Moodle's data privacy features (data requests, data registry, and data deletion) must be fully supported. More details can be found in *Chapter 14, Complying with Data Protection Regulations*.

- **Code**: If you can read PHP code, look at the actual source code of the add-on. Try to find answers to the following questions: Is the code well structured, and can it be easily followed? Is the source code well commented? Does the module follow the Moodle coding guidelines (`docs.moodle.org/dev/Coding`)? Beware if the answer to any of these questions is no.

- **Official approval**: Add-ons stored outside the official Moodle plugin repository, for example, on a developer's home page, should only be trusted if they come from a well-known source.

- **Developer**: Some developers are known to produce very well-written Moodle add-ons. Programmers affiliated with a (Premium) Moodle Partner are usually a good bet, as are core developers, Moodle documenters, and particularly helpful Moodlers.

Sound quality is a non-negotiable criterion, but many good third-party plugins are still available. We have put together a list of popular plugins to get you started, which you will see in the following subsection.

Popular plugins

The following is a list of some popular third-party Moodle add-ons, available through the plugin directory at `moodle.org/plugins`, alongside brief descriptions (excluding themes and course formats, which we already covered in *Chapter 7, Enhancing Moodle's Look and Feel*):

- **Adminer**: This is a repackaged version of Adminer. Once installed, you will see a new **Moodle Adminer** item in the **Server** menu. This tool can handle all database-related operations, including creating database backup dumps.

- **Attendance**: The plugin allows an attendance log to be kept in blended-learning environments and includes a block for easy access to relevant functions.

- **Checklist**: This plugin, containing an activity module and a block, allows teachers to create a checklist to benefit their students. The teacher can monitor all their students' progress as they tick off each item on the list, and items can be indented and marked as optional. Students are presented with a progress bar, and they can add their private items to the list.

- **Completion progress**: This block is a time management tool for students that visually shows what activities and resources a student should interact with within a course.

- **Dash**: Dash is an interface and report builder that lets you create flexible course catalogs, team dashboards, and progress reports, among others.

- **Level Up**: This provides a great way to add various gamification elements to your Moodle system, supporting (experience) points, (configurable) levels, leaderboards, targets, rewards, and many more.

- **Microsoft Office 365**: Microsoft has developed a suite of plugins to allow Microsoft Office 365 usage within Moodle. The set includes logging in via OpenID, access to OneDrive, integration with Office resources, and Outlook calendar synchronization.

- **Zoom**: To strengthen our love-hate relationship with Zoom, we can add the plugin to our Moodle instance, as described earlier in this chapter. We will discuss the built-in web conferencing system BigBlueButton in detail in *Chapter 10, Configuring Technical Features*.

Keep monitoring the list of **Recently added** plugins at `moodle.org/plugins` or via the Twitter handle `@moodleplugins`. There are always great new plugins that might be useful for your site. However, before adding every plugin to your site that could be useful to some users sometime in the future, please consider some organizational criteria, which we will discuss next.

Organizational decisions around plugins

Before you go wild and bombard your Moodle system with dozens of plugins, sit back and reflect on the following questions:

- *Who is the plugin for?*

  Does the plugin cater to the needs of a wide range of users or only a handful of trainers with very specific needs? Is it a nice-to-have gimmick or a must-have feature? Neither is a problem; just be aware of this.

- *What are the requirements of your users?*

  It has proven very useful to gather your staff's requirements from a representative group of users. Math teachers have needs that are different from language coaches, novices need tools separate from experts, and course authors request features dissimilar to those required by course coordinators. Gather all the requirements first, and then decide which plugins are needed to cater to the majority.

- *What is the impact on your users?*

  Adding new activities, question types, and course formats is a great way to equip your teachers with new tools to build engaging learning content. However, take into account the skills of your staff and the time they would have to invest in mastering these add-ons.

- *What is the impact on your infrastructure?*

  Some plugins require access to other systems, for instance, authentication plugins or cloud services. Other plugins rely on a commercial service, for example, video conference tools or plagiarism detection systems. Ensure that the plugin suits your infrastructure and that there is a sustained budget in case regular fees must be paid.

- *Is there an alternative?*

  Ensure that onboard tools cannot cater to the requirements. If this is not the case, trawl Moodle's plugin directory for alternative options.

Be very selective with the plugins you add to your system – the fewer add-ons you have to maintain, the less work and potential hassle you face in the long term.

Summary

In this chapter, we learned the basics about Moodle plugins. We first provided an overview of plugins, before covering the essentials of managing third-party Moodle add-ons. Plugin management comprised installation, update, and removal; for each operation, we offered four methods: web interface, manual, Git, and command line.

After that, we offered some advice on good plugins and not-so-good plugins. We provided some plugin evaluation criteria you might want to apply, presented some popular plugins, and gave you a list of organizational decisions you should take into account.

You've hopefully experienced a flavor of the breadth and depth of additional functionalities available for Moodle. It demonstrates the extensibility and significant benefit of open source software, that is, programmatically enhancing a system to a user's requirements. The consistent manner in which plugins have been implemented demonstrates the modular architecture of Moodle and flattens the learning curve when additional modules are added in the future and must be administered.

Now, let's move on to configuring Moodle plugins. Due to the high volume of available plugins, we divided the topic into two chapters: educational configuration and technical configuration.

9

Configuring Educational Features

Moodle supports a wide range of tools and features that require administrative attention, some only once, others regularly. Due to the volume of configuration areas, we have divided the topic into educational and technical configurations, each represented by a dedicated chapter:

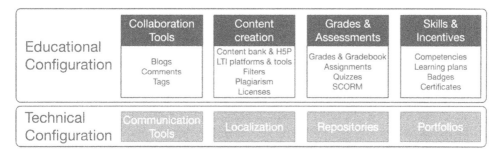

Figure 9.1 – Educational configuration topics

This chapter deals with configuring educational settings. Therefore, we will cover the following topics:

- Configuring collaboration tools
- Configuring content creation features
- Configuring grades and assessments
- Managing skills and incentives

Configuring educational settings usually requires input from domain experts, such as curriculum planners, content creators, or assessors. It has proven beneficial to liaise with these specialists to ensure the optimal setup for your Moodle system.

By the end of this chapter, you should be in a good position to approach your colleagues, ask the right educational questions, and implement their requirements.

Configuring collaboration tools

One of Moodle's many advantages is its built-in support for collaboration among learners and instructors. This ranges from several collaborative course activities, such as **Forum**, **Wiki**, **Glossary**, and **Database**, the ability to run activities in group mode, and support for groupings. Additionally, there are three social tools in Moodle that have to be configured by the administrator: **blogs**, **comments**, and **tags**. We will discuss these in the following subsections.

Configuring blogs

The blogging mechanism provided to users in Moodle allows them to create personal and public entries and posts relating to courses.

> **Important note**
> Blogs are a means for users to express themselves either in the form of a learning journal or as a personal account of events.

As an administrator, you must ensure that **Enable blogs** is turned on in **Site administration** | **General** | **Advanced features**. Next, you should navigate to **Site administration** | **Appearance** | **Blog** to configure the following settings, which apply to all blog users:

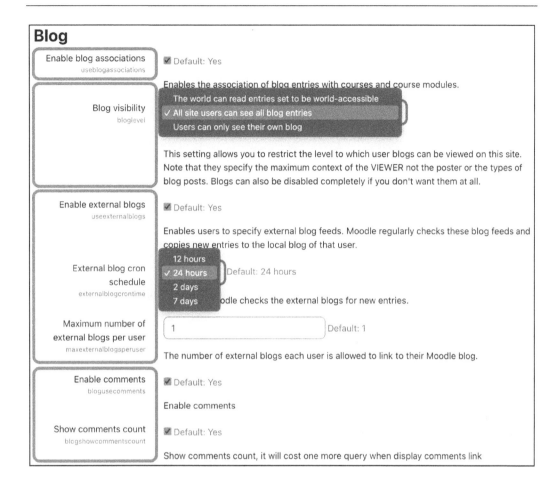

Figure 9.2 – Configuring blogs

There are four types of settings that you should double-check:

- **Enable blog associations**: If checked, course and activity blogs become available, which allow learners to choose link entries to a course or course module. If unchecked, all blog posts will be converted into user blog posts. This setting can be overridden locally via the `moodle/blog:associatecourse` and `moodle/blog:associatemodule` capabilities.

- **Blog visibility**: What you choose here depends on your organization's policy and how blogs are used as part of the learning process.

- **External blogs**: Moodle supports external blogs, such as those from WordPress. If enabled, users can link external blogs via the **Register an external blog** link in the **Preferences** menu. The entries will be shown as if they had been entered in the Moodle blog but cannot be modified.

- **Blog comments**: If enabled, others can provide comments on blog posts; for instance, a teacher can leave private or public feedback on a journal entry. You can further specify whether the comments count should be shown.

We have just come across comments in blogs, which are the second collaboration tool to be configured.

Configuring comments

Moodle comes with a generic comments functionality independent of the one in the blogging tools. It allows you to place the **Comments** block in any context of the system, such as in a course or an individual activity.

> **Important note**
> Comments are remarks that can be attached to various Moodle artifacts.

This feature is enabled by default but can be disabled via the **Enable comments** parameter under **Site administration** | **General** | **Advanced features**.

There are several areas where additional comment-related settings can be set; for instance, when they are included in backups or supported by certain activities. You can also look at a report by going to **Reports** | **Comments**, where you will see all the comments throughout the system. You might want to check this frequently in case anything offensive or inappropriate has been entered.

You can search for comments using the **Search** box to see these settings. As always, these options can be overridden locally via the respective role capabilities.

The third and last collaboration activity in Moodle is tagging, which we deal with in the following subsection.

Configuring tags

Tagging is the process of describing artifacts or users using keywords. These tags are then harnessed to search for, share, and perform various collaborative activities to match interests.

> **Important note**
> Tagging is the process of describing artifacts or users using keywords.

Users create their own tags that represent their personal or educational interests. However, as an educational institution, you might want to create site-wide tags that can be used in addition to the user-defined tags or even limit tagging to a set of standard tags. Examples of global tags include organization-related keywords, topics your entity specializes in, campaigns your company runs, and newsworthy topics relevant to your institution.

As with blogs and comments, tags can be enabled (default) and disabled for the entire site via the **Enable tags functionality** parameter under **Site administration** | **General** | **Advanced features**. The following diagram illustrates how tags are organized in Moodle:

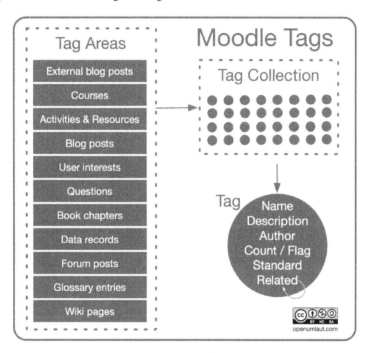

Figure 9.3 – Moodle tags

Tags are organized in **tag collections**. A tag belongs to one collection; a tag cannot belong to more than one collection. There are several predefined tag areas, each representing Moodle features that support tags. Each **tag area** has an associated tag collection; one tag collection can be associated with multiple tag areas. To see the tags, tag areas, and tag collections in action, navigate to **Site administration | Appearance | Manage tags**, where you will see the following:

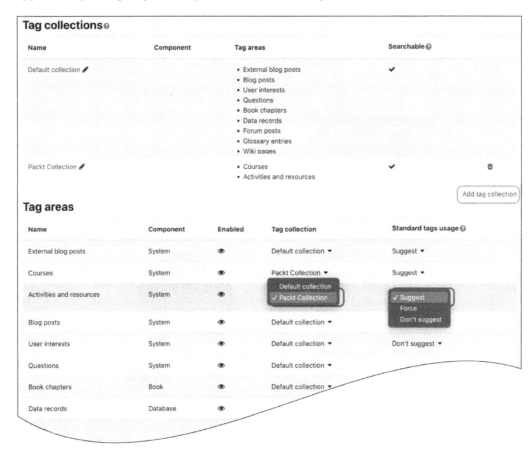

Figure 9.4 – Managing tags I

There are two tag collections at the top of the screen, one of which has been added via the **Add tag collection** link. To associate a tag collection with a tag area, you need to select it in the respective column in the tag areas table. The **Standard tags usage** setting indicates how tags are being dealt with when entered in the tag area: they can be proposed once you start typing (**Suggest**), only standard tags can be selected (**Force**), or no tags are shown (**Don't suggest**).

Disabling a tag area (via the standard eye symbol) completely hides the tagging functionality from this component. For example, when turning off tagging in **User interests**, the respective entry in the user profile won't be available anymore.

When you select the name of a tag collection, you will see all tags of that collection:

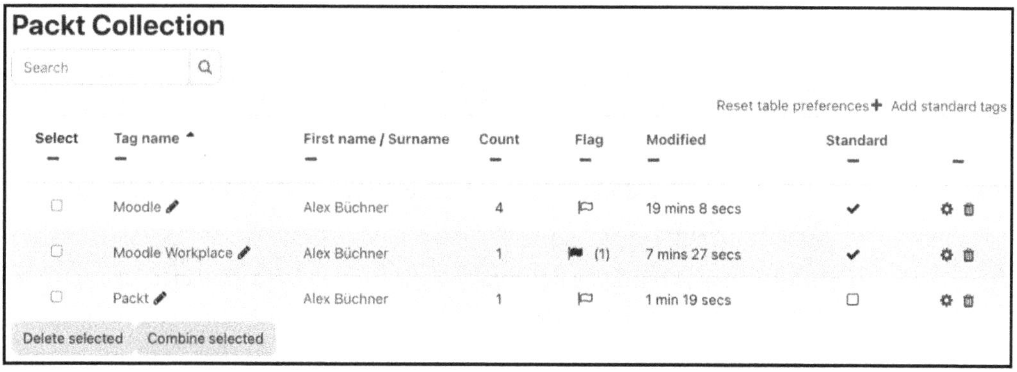

Packt Collection

Select	Tag name ▲	First name / Surname	Count	Flag	Modified	Standard	
☐	Moodle ✏	Alex Büchner	4	🏳	19 mins 8 secs	✔	⚙ 🗑
☐	Moodle Workplace ✏	Alex Büchner	1	🏴 (1)	7 mins 27 secs	✔	⚙ 🗑
☐	Packt ✏	Alex Büchner	1	🏳	1 min 19 secs	☐	⚙ 🗑

Reset table preferences ✚ Add standard tags

Delete selected   Combine selected

Figure 9.5 – Managing tags II

For each tag, the following settings/actions are available:

- **Tag name**: When selected, you see which users have been tagged with this tag.
- **First name / Surname**: Tag creator.
- **Count**: This is the number of times the tag has been used throughout the site. This will be used as a basis for tag cloud sizes in the **Tag** block.
- **Flag**: This shows whether the tag has been flagged as inappropriate and the number of times in brackets.
- **Modified**: This shows the last time the tag was edited.
- **Standard**: Standard tags are available to all users.
- **Edit**: You can alter the tag's name, change its description, and select any related tags.
- **Delete**: This removes the tag from the system.

You can add standard tags via the **Add standard tags** link. If you identify any tags that should be combined, such as when a tag name has been misspelled, use the **Combine selected** button and select the tag that should be kept.

If you need to block users from tagging, you will need to create a separate role and adjust the two relevant capabilities, `moodle/tag:create` and `moodle/tag:edit`. If you want tag names to keep the original casing as entered by the users who created them, ensure that the **Keep tag name casing** setting is ticked under **Site administration | General | Security | Site security settings**.

This concludes this subsection on configuring tags and, thus, the section on administering collaborative Moodle tools. Next up is configuring the features required by your content creators.

Configuring content creation features

Course authors heavily rely on the content creation tools made available to them. Moodle allows you to create content with built-in tools, incorporate content from external applications, and add structure and conditions among content items.

In this section, you will learn how to configure different content creation features, namely the content bank and H5P, LTI platforms and tools, filters, plagiarism prevention, and licenses. First, let's configure some generic content creation settings.

Configuring content creation settings

Several site-wide settings impact content creation, which are as follows:

- **Require activity description**: Activities and resources do not require a description by default. To enforce a descriptive explanation, you must enable the parameter in **Site administration | Plugins | Activity modules | Common activity settings**.

- **Completion tracking**: Course and activity completion allows authors to set completion criteria for activities and courses. It is recommended to leave the feature enabled in **Site administration | General | Advanced features**, where you can also find the **Default completion tracking** option.

- **Restricting access**: Inside Moodle courses, a course author can restrict access to individual activities or resources. The types of available restrictions can be configured by navigating to **Site administration | Plugins | Availability restrictions | Manage restrictions**:

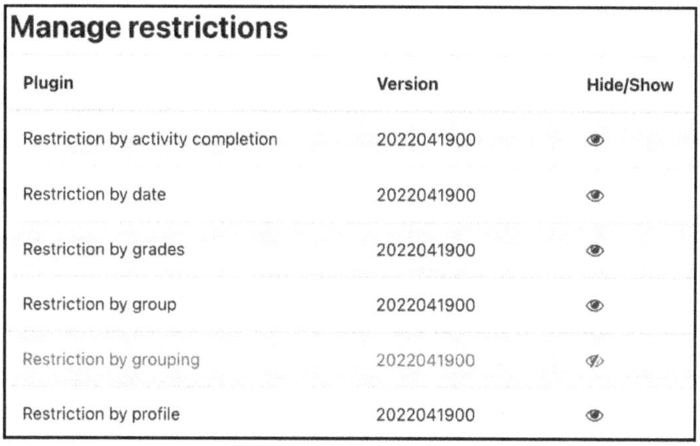

Manage restrictions

Plugin	Version	Hide/Show
Restriction by activity completion	2022041900	
Restriction by date	2022041900	
Restriction by grades	2022041900	
Restriction by group	2022041900	
Restriction by grouping	2022041900	
Restriction by profile	2022041900	

Figure 9.6 – Managing availability restrictions

You only have the option to show and hide each restriction; by default, all the plugins are enabled. Some restrictions require other elements to be present or configured, respectively. For example, groups and groupings only appear in a course's **Access restriction** when they exist in a particular course. Ensure **Enable restricted access** is turned on in **Site administration** | **General** | **Advanced features**.

A popular third-party availability restriction is **Restriction by language** (`moodle.org/plugins/availability_language`), which will be described in more detail in the *Managing localization* section of *Chapter 10, Configuring Technical Features*.

- **Stealth activities**: These are available but invisible activities, previously known as orphans. These are useful if course creators wish to hide activities and provide links from elsewhere, such as a page resource or a text block.

Each activity or resource has a settings page in **Site administration** | **Plugins** | **Activity modules**. The majority of settings are default values that are often accompanied by the following additional value states, if applicable:

- **Enabled**: If set, the standard setting will be ticked; otherwise, it will be unticked
- **Advanced**: If set, the teacher has to select the **Show more...** link to see them, which is recommended for settings used infrequently
- **Locked**: If set, the teacher cannot alter the setting; for example, if you wish to enforce a description for all activities across the system

The following is an example from the **Assignment** activity where all three states are shown on the right-hand side:

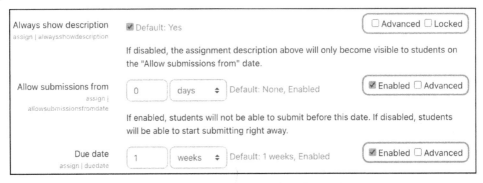

Figure 9.7 – The Enabled, Advanced, and Locked states

Once you have checked and configured these general course and activity settings, we can configure the content bank in general and H5P in particular.

Configuring the content bank and H5P

H5P lets your course authors create, share, and reuse rich, interactive, and mobile-friendly HTML5 content. In Moodle, a content bank has been implemented to incorporate H5P content, as illustrated in the following diagram:

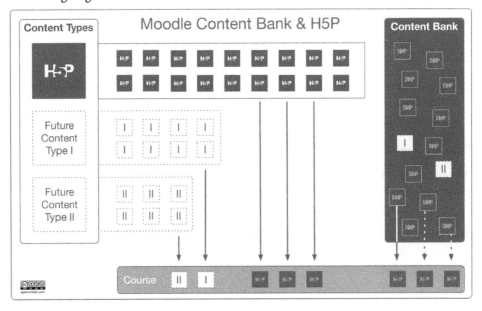

Figure 9.8 – Content bank and H5P

Moodle supports the concept of **content integrations**, where each integration is represented as a separate entity. Only a single content integration – H5P – has been implemented at the time of writing. Go to **Site administration | Plugins | Content bank | Manage content types** to manage content integrations. Expect additional types to be published in the future at moodle.org/plugins/?q=type:contenttype.

Each content integration comprises one or many **content types**, where each type represents a feature. In the case of H5P, you can view all available content types by going to **Site administration | General | H5P | Manage H5P content types**:

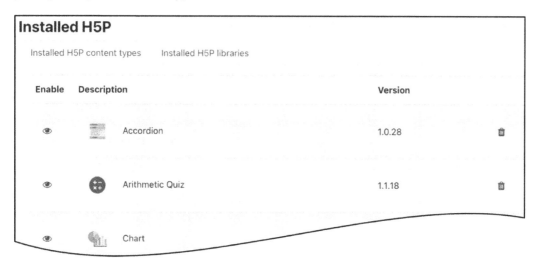

Figure 9.9 – H5P content types

H5P content can be embedded in courses in different ways:

- **Directly via the H5P activity**: Ensure the activity is enabled at **Site administration | Plugins | Activity modules | Manage activities**.

- **Inside text authored via the Atto editor**: Ensure the **Insert H5P** plugin is installed at **Site administration | Plugins | Text editors | Atto HTML editor | Atto toolbar settings**.

- **Using a URL representing H5P content (by default, from** h5p.com**)**: The **Display H5P** filter must be enabled at **Site administration | Plugins | Filters | Manage filters**.

- **Linked from the content bank**: Content to be reused can be stored in the content bank and linked to activities or courses. Any changes in the content bank are automatically updated inside courses since no copies are stored but linked entries. Other users can share content placed in the content bank if they have access to the folder where .h5p is stored.

- **From a repository**: H5P content is copied or linked from a repository. For more details, see the *Managing repositories* section in *Chapter 10, Configuring Technical Features*.

A short checklist is available at **Site administration | General | H5P | H5P overview** with links to the respective configuration pages, as shown in the following screenshot:

Feature	Status	Description
Insert H5P button	Enabled	The Insert H5P button in the Atto editor enables users to insert H5P content by either entering a URL or embed code, or by uploading an H5P file.
Display H5P filter	Enabled	The Display H5P filter converts URLs into embedded H5P content.
H5P scheduled task	Enabled	The H5P scheduled task downloads available H5P content types from h5p.org.

Figure 9.10 – H5P overview

We have already mentioned the first two entries; the last entry – **H5P scheduled task** – is important as it automatically downloads any new content types from h5p.org. Since the task only runs once a month, check that it has been executed after installing or updating your Moodle system. If not, temporarily change all time values of the task to *, trigger cron.php, and reverse any changes back to their defaults. More on tasks will be covered in the *Scheduled tasks* section in *Chapter 15, Optimizing Moodle Performance*. If it is not possible to use this scheduled task, then **Site administration | General | H5P | Manage H5P content types** allows you to upload the necessary files manually.

H5P represents interactive content that's been stored, edited, and created in Moodle. Another type of content integration is LTI, which will be dealt with in the following subsection.

Configuring LTI platforms and tools

According to IMS, **Learning Tools Interoperability** (**LTI**) is a standard for learning tool interoperability to allow remote tools and content to be integrated into a Learning Management System. Moodle supports depreciated versions of LTI and the latest **LTI Advantage** (core LTI 1.3 packaged with some essential services). Moodle can act as an LTI platform (external content can be used in Moodle) and LTI tool (Moodle content can be used in other LTI platforms).

> **Important note**
> Legacy LTI uses the terms **Consumer** and **Provider**, whereas LTI Advantage uses **Platform** and **Tool**.

We will use these new terms going forward, starting with Moodle operating as an LTI platform.

Moodle as an LTI platform

For Moodle to act as an LTI platform, course authors must use the **External tool** activity. The simplified data flow between Moodle (LTI platform) and an external system (LTI tool) is depicted in the following diagram:

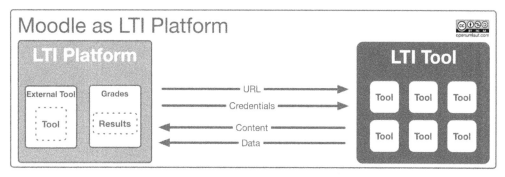

Figure 9.11 – Moodle as an LTI platform I

The tool has to be connected to Moodle via a URL and some credentials; the latter can be a consumer key/shared secret pair, an RSA key, or a keyset URL. Once the connection has been established, learning content is embedded via the aforementioned external tool activity. Additional data might be transferred, which are usually results to be stored locally in the gradebook.

As an administrator, you have to configure external content providers, which will then appear in the **Preconfigured tool** dropdown in the activity inside a course. Go to **Site administration** | **Plugins** | **Activity modules** | **External tool** | **Manage tools**, where you have multiple options to add new providers:

- **Add LTI Advantage**: If the provider supports this workflow, enter a **Tool URL**; you will be directed to the tool registration page, where you will be guided through the registration steps.

- **Add Legacy LTI**: Moodle supports deprecated LTI versions; depending on the current version, either a key/secret pair has to be provided (version 1.1), or a registration process similar to LTI Advantage will be kicked off (version 2.0).

- **Configure tool manually**: If neither of the preceding two options works, you must provide the tool parameters manually. The external tool settings are well documented at `docs.moodle.org/en/External_tool_settings`.

Added tools will first be given a pending state, which allows you to review the tool configuration and the privacy and services granted, and apply possible modifications before activating the tool via the **Manage preconfigured tools** link.

> **Important note**
>
> For a tool to appear as a separate item in the activity chooser, change the **Tool configuration usage** setting to **Show in activity chooser and as a preconfigured tool**.

In our demo system, two LTI tools have already been registered successfully:

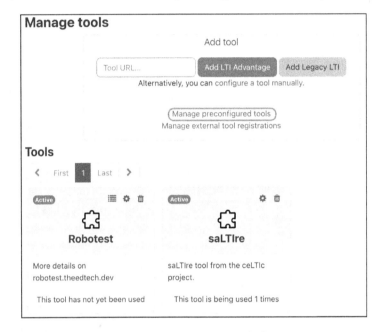

Figure 9.12 – Moodle as an LTI platform II

Now that we have configured Moodle to act as an LTI platform, let's look at the opposite, where Moodle is the LTI tool, provisioning content for other systems.

Moodle as an LTI tool

For Moodle to operate as an LTI tool, it is essential to understand the simplified data flow between an external platform (LTI consumer) and Moodle (LTI producer), as shown in the following diagram:

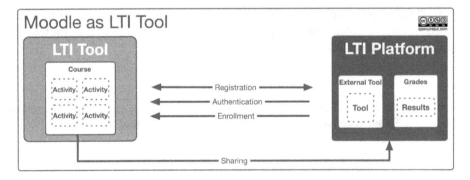

Figure 9.13 – Moodle as an LTI tool I

The LTI tool and the LTI platform must register with one another; they effectively sign a security contract that allows communication and data exchange between the two systems. Content (an entire course or a single activity) and, optionally, grades are shared by the LTI tool and utilized in the LTI platform. When both LTI sites are Moodle systems, this process is identical to the Moodle as LTI platform workflow. For users of the LTI platform to access published content in the LTI tool, an authentication and enrolment mechanism have to be activated. These two steps and further configurations to enable Moodle as an LTI tool are outlined here:

1. Go to **Site administration** | **Plugins** | **Authentication** | **Manage authentication** and enable the **LTI** plugin.

2. Go to **Site administration** | **Plugins** | **Enrolments** | **Manage enroll plugins** and enable **Publish as LTI tool**. Configure the user default values in the plugin settings with your details.

3. Go to **Site administration** | **Plugins** | **Enrolments** | **Publish as LTI tool** | **Tool registration** and select **Register a platform**.

   After providing a name, Moodle will automatically generate tool details, which must be entered into the LTI platform. Once the tool has been set up in the platform, details must be recorded on the **Platform details** tab to complete the registration. For dynamic registrations, this information is entered automatically; for manual registrations, it must be copied and entered manually.

   We have registered two platforms on the right-hand side of the following screenshot (one active and one pending). You can see the tool details for dynamic and manual registration on the left:

Figure 9.14 – Moodle as an LTI tool II

4. Inside a course, teachers can publish content (the entire course or an individual activity) via **Published as LTI tools**. Here, grade and user synchronization must be configured. **User synchronization mode** determines how the enrollment of remote users has to be handled.

5. When remote users access a shared activity or course for the first time, Moodle will either use an existing account or create a new one. How this user account provisioning is carried out (automatic or user-prompted) is determined by the settings in **Teacher first launch provisioning mode** and **Student first launch provisioning mode**.

While teachers carry out *steps 4* and *5*, they usually require assistance with this partly technical procedure. The preceding list only crudely outlines the setup steps of the LTI tool when using dynamic registration. At docs.moodle.org/en/Publish_as_LTI_tool, you can find very well-written documentation on other LTI setups, such as manual registration, sharing access, and user provisioning, as well as information on legacy LTI.

> Tip
>
> It is recommended that the **Allow frame embedding** setting is enabled by going to **Site administration** | **General** | **Security** | **HTTP security** so that tools are displayed within a frame rather than in a new window.

LTI is a powerful standard that opens up your Moodle system to grant access to and from external content. Filters, which we will cover next, transform content inside your Moodle instance.

Configuring filters

Filters scan any text entered via the Atto editor and automatically transform it into different and often more complex forms. For example, entries or concepts in glossaries are automatically hyperlinked in text, URLs pointing to MP3 files become an embedded audio player, mathematical equations are represented as visual formulae, uploaded videos are given play controls, and so on.

Moodle ships several filters, which can be accessed by navigating to **Site administration** | **Plugins** | **Filters** | **Manage filters**:

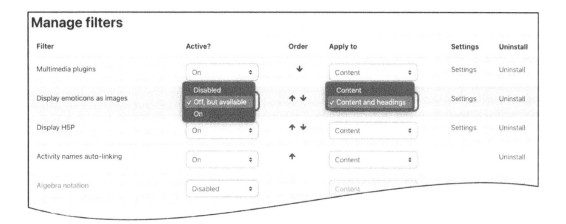

Figure 9.15 – Filter configuration

By default, all the filters are disabled. You can enable them by changing the **Active?** status from **Disabled** to **On** or **Off, but available**. If the status is set to **On**, the filter is activated throughout the system but can be deactivated locally. If the status is set to **Off, but available**, the filter is not activated but can be enabled locally. Managing local filter settings requires the `moodle/filter:manage` capability, which is allowed by default for the **Manager** and **Teacher** roles.

Filters used throughout the LMS and by most of your users should be turned on. Typical candidates are **Multimedia plugins**, **Display H5P**, **Display emoticons as images**, and **Multi-language content**. Filters that are only used by some users should not be activated but made available locally, such as **TeX notation**, to deal with mathematical or scientific notation. Enabled filters might also be switched off temporarily at the activity level, for instance, **Glossary auto-linking** in an online exam. Activating some filters might trigger the appearance of an editor button, such as **Display emoticons as images** (emoji selection) or **TeX notation** (equation editor).

You can change the order in which the filters are applied to text using the up and down arrows in the **Order** column. If a particular filter isn't working, try moving it higher up the list.

> **Important note**
> The filtering mechanism operates on a first-come, first-served basis; if a filter detects a text element that has to be transformed, it will do this before the next filter is applied.

Each filter can be configured to be applied to **Content and headings** or **Content** only; that is, filters will be ignored in the names of activity modules.

> **Important note**
> Applying filters to headings as well as content can significantly increase the load on your server, so use them sparingly.

Some filters provide settings that either indicate to which text format the filter should apply or are specific to the filter; the latter is described in detail in the respective Moodle Docs. In addition to filter-specific settings, Moodle provides several settings that are shared among all filters. These can be accessed via **Site administration** | **Filters** | **Common filter settings** and are as follows:

- **Filter uploaded files**: By default, only text entered via the Moodle editor is filtered. If you wish to include uploaded files, you can choose any of them from the **HTML files only** and **All files** options.

- **Filter match once per page**: Enable this setting if the filter should stop analyzing text after it finds a match; that is, only the first occurrence will be transformed.

- **Filter match once per text**: Enable this setting if the filter should only generate a single link for the first matching text instance found in each text item on a page. This setting is ignored if the **Filter match once per page** parameter is enabled.

- **Filter navigation within system context**: Filters are context-sensitive, which might cause performance issues when filtering is enabled for headings. Selecting this option should reduce the number of filter operations to pages.

The following diagram provides a summary of how filters are applied, considering the order of filters, filter matching, and what text the filter is applied to (content and heading or content only):

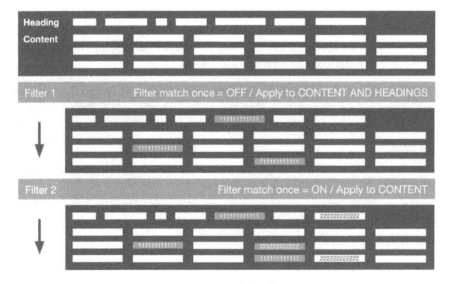

Figure 9.16 – Applying filters

Filter 1 has matching turned off (all matches are transformed) and is applied to both content and headings. **Filter 2** has matching turned on (only the first match is transformed) and is only applied to content; that is, the matching text in the heading is ignored.

Plagiarism prevention is next on the (long) list of content creation topics that require admin attention.

Configuring plagiarism prevention

The idea behind plagiarism prevention is to check students' submitted content against others' work – the higher the overlap, the more likely the content has been plagiarized. This detection can either be for users' content in Moodle or through public resources.

Plagiarism prevention must be enabled by selecting the **Enable plagiarism plugins** parameter at **Site administration** | **General** | **Advanced features**. Once this occurs, you can access any installed plagiarism prevention plugins when navigating to **Site administration** | **Plugins** | **Plagiarism** | **Manage plagiarism plugins**.

At the time of writing, about a dozen plugins are available at `moodle.org/plugins/?q=type:plagiarism` that cater to plagiarism prevention. The two most popular are **Turnitin** and **Ouriginal** (previously **Urkund**). Both systems are commercial tools and require a paid subscription. Once installed and configured, the plagiarism prevention functionality will be available as part of the **Assignment** and **Forum** modules inside courses.

Another topic that requires agreement across the site and organization is which licenses are available in your Moodle system; this is the topic of the following subsection.

Managing licenses

A license can be selected when adding a file via **File picker**. This information will then be attached to the metadata of the file. To configure the licenses that are available to your users, go to **Site administration** | **General** | **License** | **License manager**, where all available licenses are listed:

License manager

Create license

Enable	License	Version	Order	Edit	Delete
👁	License not specified (unknown)	2010033100	↓		
🔒	All rights reserved (allrightsreserved) https://en.wikipedia.org/wiki/All_rights_reserved	2010033100	↑ ↓		
👁	Public domain (public) https://en.wikipedia.org/wiki/Public_domain	2010033100	↑ ↓		
👁	Creative Commons (cc) https://creativecommons.org/licenses/by/3.0/	2010033100	↑ ↓		
👁	Creative Commons - NoDerivs (cc-nd) https://creativecommons.org/licenses/by-nd/3.0/	2010033100	↑ ↓		
👁	Creative Commons - No Commercial NoDerivs (cc-nc-nd) https://creativecommons.org/licenses/by-nc-nd/3.0/	2010033100	↑ ↓		
👁	Creative Commons - No Commercial (cc-nc) https://creativecommons.org/licenses/by-nc/3.0/	2010033100	↑ ↓		
👁	Creative Commons - No Commercial ShareAlike (cc-nc-sa) https://creativecommons.org/licenses/by-nc-sa/3.0/	2010033100	↑ ↓		
👁	Creative Commons - ShareAlike (cc-sa) https://creativecommons.org/licenses/by-sa/3.0/	2010033100	↑		

Figure 9.17 – Managing licenses

You can create new licenses via the **Create license** button, where you have to provide the following information:

- **License short name**: Internal license name
- **License full name**: Display license name
- **License source**: The URL where the license's terms and conditions can be found
- **License version**: Publication date of the license version being utilized

The license manager can edit and delete manually added licenses; those that ship with Moodle can't. Except for the default site license, all licenses can be disabled (hidden).

> **Important note**
> The license attached to an uploaded file does not affect its visibility; it simply creates the default when it's reused elsewhere.

You can select **Default site license** under **Site administration | General | License | License settings**. By default, the last license selected by a user is pre-selected when uploading a file via the file picker. If the **Remember user license preference** setting is disabled, the default site license is pre-selected.

This concludes this section on content creation features, where we covered configuring the content bank and H5P, LTI platforms and tools, filters, plagiarism prevention, and licenses. One particular type of content – assessments and grading thereof – has been ignored so far and will be covered in the following dedicated section.

Configuring grades and assessments

In addition to learning per se, assessment is a critical requirement in educational settings. Moodle offers a wide range of tools to facilitate formative, interim, and summative assessments and handles the inevitable grades that go with it.

In this section, we will cover the administrative elements of the gradebook before we deal with assessments, where we will cover how to configure assignments, quizzes and the question bank, and SCORM packages.

Configuring grades and the gradebook

The gradebook is one of the most important constructs in any LMS, and Moodle is no exception. The Moodle gradebook is a powerful, flexible, and accurate grade management system. Its flexibility and customizability result in a very high degree of complexity. Consequently, a considerable number of administrative settings are at your disposal that affect how teachers, trainers, and assessors use grades throughout the system.

Most parameters are tightly linked to the gradebook, and teachers at the course level deal with the related reports. A site-wide agreement on default values and global settings for grades should be in place for your organization.

> **Important note**
> A **gradebook** is a container that holds grades for all the learners in Moodle.
>
> A **grade** is an item in the gradebook.

The following is a high-level overview of grades and all relevant gradebook elements:

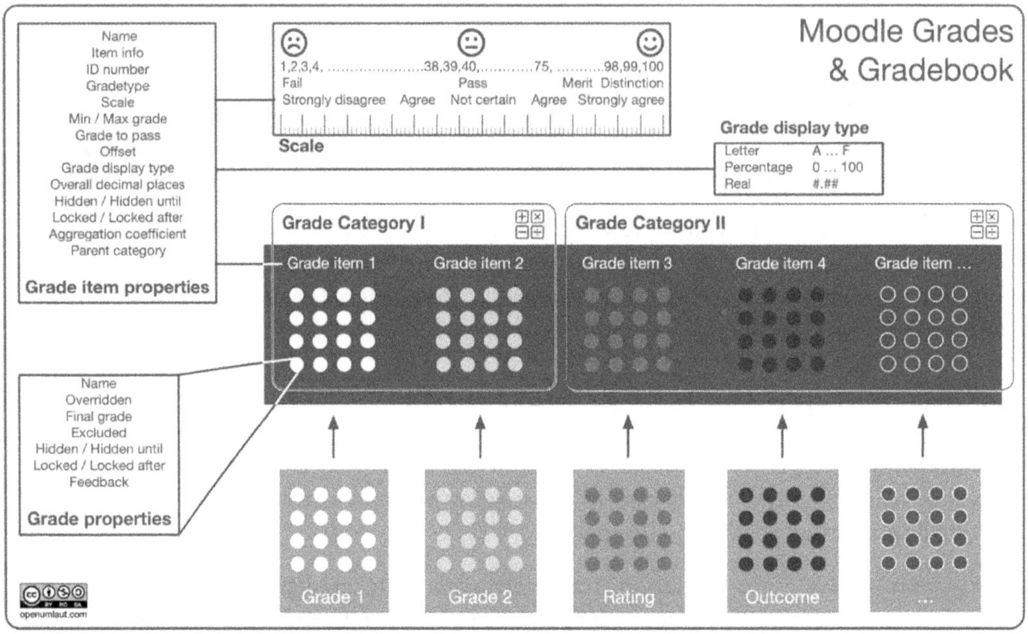

Figure 9.18 – Grades and gradebook

Additionally, the inline help for each setting is very comprehensive, as is the accompanying area in the Moodle Docs at docs.moodle.org/en/Grader_report, which contains several pages dedicated to administrators. We will only briefly describe each element in the **Grades** tab and highlight some key parameters, which are listed as follows:

- **General settings**: These parameters influence the gradebook and grades in general. **Enable publishing** (the ability to publish results via external URLs) is a setting that is turned off by default and is required regularly. Another setting that is changed frequently is **Navigation method**, in which most users prefer the **Tabs** option as it is consistent with the rest of Moodle.

- **Grade category settings**: Grades are organized into categories; you can set the relevant settings here. Different grading strategies can be leveraged with the gradebook's aggregation system, such as sum-of-points or percentage-category.

- **Grade item settings**: These are settings that impact individual grades and grade items.

- **Scales**: Here, you can specify site-wide scales used for grading and rating. The global scales are often linked to qualifications offered by your organization.

- **Outcomes**: Outcomes are used by most vocational and some academic curricula to specify the expected competencies or goals of a subject being taught. Outcomes have to be enabled by going to **Site administration | General | Advanced features**. Most organizations prefer to use the more powerful competencies instead of outcomes.

- **Letters**: Many education systems use letters (A, A-, B+, …, and F) to grade items. Here, you specify which percentage range corresponds to which grading letter.

Moodle comes with several predefined gradebook reports. **Report settings** determines the appearance and content of the reports. If additional user-defined reports (plugins) are installed, this list is likely to have a separate configuration page for each report type (a good tutorial on creating custom reports can be found at `docs.moodle.org/dev/Gradebook_reports`). The different types of reports are as follows:

- **Grader report**: This setting includes whether to show calculations, show or hide icons, column averages, and so on. Teachers can override most of the settings in the **My report preferences** tab.

- **Grade history**: The gradebook keeps track of all the changes that are made to the gradebook entries. Here, you can specify how many entries will be displayed on the page. You can **Disable grade history** by going to **Site administration | Server | Cleanup**. On the same page, you can also specify the length of time the grade history should be kept (**Grade history lifetime**).

- **Overview report**: This consists of two settings that determine whether the ranking information is shown and how to deal with totals containing hidden grades, respectively.

- **User report**: This shows the settings that determine whether the ranking information is shown and how to deal with hidden items.

We have only touched upon the customization options of the gradebook since the complete gradebook management heavily depends on grading strategies deployed in your organization.

Next, we will deal with administering the three most used assessment tools in Moodle: assignments, quizzes, and SCORM.

Configuring assignments

According to MoodleDocs, the *assignment activity allows students to submit work to their teacher for grading*. A simplified assignment workflow is shown in the following diagram:

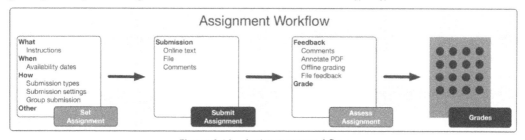

Figure 9.19 – Assignment workflow

The assignment workflow consists of the following three steps:

1. When an assignment is set by the teacher, a range of assignment settings have to be provided, covering instructions (**What**), various availability dates such as the start, due, and cut-off date (**When**), submission types, submission settings, and whether group submissions are supported (**How**), plus various **Other** settings, such as notifications.

2. The students then submit their work via one of the required submission types: online text, uploaded file(s), and/or an auxiliary commentary.

3. Finally, the teacher provides feedback via one of the supported channels: comments, PDF annotations, offline grading sheets, and feedback via files. As described in the previous section, any given grades will automatically be transferred to the gradebook for the student to review.

The elements that require administrator input are assignment settings, submission plugins, and feedback plugins:

- **Assignment settings**: In **Site administration | Plugins | Activity modules | Assignment | Assignment settings**, you should specify the fields based on the requirements of your powers to be – for example, the wording of submission statements. In the second part of the screen, you can specify default values for the assignment activity.

- **Submission plugins**: Activated submission plugins dictate how students can submit their work. By default, the available options are online text, file, and comments. To configure each type, go to **Site administration | Plugins | Activity modules | Assignment | Submission plugins | Manage assignment submission plugins**.

- **Feedback plugins**: Activated feedback plugins dictate how teachers can grade, rate, and comment on submitted work. By default, the available options are comments, PDF annotations, offline grading worksheets, and file. To configure each type, go to **Site administration | Plugins | Activity modules | Assignment | Submission plugins | Manage assignment submission plugins**.

Additional submission and feedback plugins can be found at `moodle.org/plugins/?q=type:assignfeedback` and `moodle.org/plugins/?q=type:assignsubmission`, respectively. Further plugins can be installed to convert uploaded assignment submissions into PDF format for teachers to annotate. The list of available converters is available at **Site administration | Plugins | Document converters | Manage document converters**. At the time of writing, two **document converters** are available as standard plugins: Google Drive (requires OAuth 2 Google service to be enabled) and Unoconv (requires Unoconv to be installed on a server).

> **Important note**
> For PDF annotations to work correctly, **Path to ghostscript** must be set in **Site administration | Server | System paths**.

The second popular assessment module in Moodle is the quiz activity, which is the topic of the following subsection.

Configuring quizzes

The quiz activity enables teachers to create quizzes comprising questions of various types, including multiple-choice, matching, short-answer, numerical, and drag and drop.

Creating a quiz is a two-step process. In the first step, content authors populate the question bank with questions. In the second step, teachers create the quiz activity, set its options that specify the rules for interacting with the quiz, and add questions from the question bank.

> **Important note**
>
> Moodle stores questions used in quizzes in a question bank. Within the question bank, questions are organized into categories.

Learners take quizzes in their standard browser or, if configured, in the Safe Exam Browser. The specified question behavior determines how submitted questions are dealt with. Grading takes place automatically (except for Essay type questions), and results are pushed to the gradebook as usual. A simplified quiz workflow is shown in the following diagram:

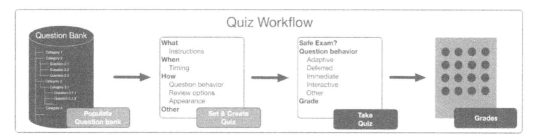

Figure 9.20 – Quiz workflow

Two parts of this process require configuration by the administrator: customizing the question bank and quiz activity and enabling the Safe Exam Browser.

Customizing the question bank and quiz activity

Moodle has a powerful question engine that supports a wide range of features, question types, and question behaviors. All three elements can be configured separately:

- **Question bank features**: At **Site administration** | **Plugins** | **Question bank plugins** | **Manage question bank plugins**, you can see all the available question bank features. You can change the column sort order and add question custom fields if required.

- **Question types**: At **Site administration** | **Plugins** | **Question types** | **Manage question types**, you should disable any question types that are not in use and might want to change the default values for the multiple-choice type.

- **Question behaviors**: At **Site administration** | **Plugins** | **Question behaviors** | **Manage question behaviors**, you should hide any methods through which submitted questions are dealt with that are not in use in your organization.

In the following figure, you can (hopefully) see parts of the three question-related elements:

Figure 9.21 – Question bank plugins, question types, and question behaviors

In true Moodle style, all three constructs are handled as plugins, and it is possible to add additional question bank plugins, question types, and question behaviors to the system.

There is one more setting you should have a look at, namely the **Auto-save delay** parameter in **Site administration** | **Plugins** | **Activity modules** | **Quiz** | **General settings**. The specified value determines how often students' work is automatically saved during quiz attempts.

> **Important note**
> The short **auto-save delay** increases the server load but reduces the chance that students lose their work.

All other settings on this screen are default values for the quiz activity and do not require further explanation. The Safe Exam Browser is often utilized when quizzes are used for examinations, as covered in the following subsection.

Enabling the Safe Exam Browser

The **Quiz** activity is used frequently for exams. Depending on the physical setup and the importance of the examination, different levels of security may be required. The **Quiz** activity offers some built-in settings in the **Extra restrictions on attempts** section:

- **Require password**: The password must be entered before access to the quiz is granted

- **Require network address**: Access to the quiz is restricted to the specified IP address(es) on your LAN or the internet

- **Browser security**: When the **Full screen pop-up with some JavaScript security** option is enabled, the quiz will only work in a JavaScript-enabled browser, shown full-screen, and, if technically possible, disallow certain operations such as copy and paste

If these facilities are insufficient for specific exam setups, whether classroom-based or invigilated online, Moodle offers **Safe Exam Browser** (**SEB**) support. According to its website, `safeexambrowser.org`, SEB is as follows:

> *"a web browser environment to carry out e-assessments safely. The software turns any computer temporarily into a secure workstation. It controls access to resources like system functions, other websites, and applications, and prevents unauthorized resources being used during an exam."*

The architecture and components of SEB in connection with Moodle are shown in the following schematic illustration (partly borrowed from `safeexambrowser.org`):

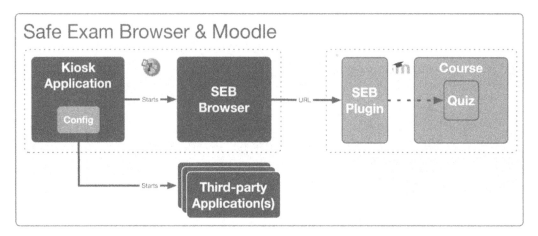

Figure 9.22 – Safe Exam Browser architecture and components

Kiosk Application locks down the computer or tablet and starts the SEB plus optional third-party applications. The **Config** file specifies the browser's behavior, such as disabling features such as shortcuts, stopping audio, or hiding screen elements, and which external applications can be launched. **SEB Browser** loads and displays the Moodle quiz using a preset URL and hides any navigation elements such as the address bar, search engine field, and more. **SEB Plugin** is an extension to Moodle to facilitate the interaction between SEB and the **Quiz** activity.

From a Moodle administrator's point of view, you need to configure the following components to ensure SEB support for quizzes:

- **Safe Exam Browser templates**: A SEB template is effectively a configuration file. The easiest way to create a SEB file is to create a quiz, configure the SEB settings manually, and download the configuration file. Then, go to **Site administration** | **Plugins** | **Activity modules** | **Quiz** | **Safe Exam Browser templates**, where you can create new templates (using the downloaded SEB file) and manage existing ones:

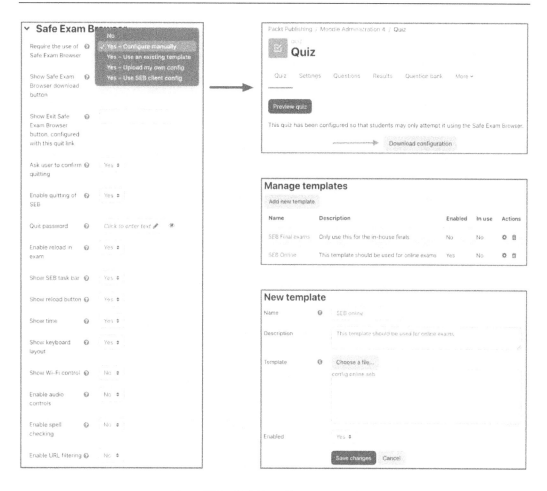

Figure 9.23– Safe Exam Browser templates

Any enabled SEB templates will be available in the **Quiz** activity.

- **Safe Exam Browser access rules**: At **Site administration** | **Plugins** | **Activity modules** | **Quiz** | **Safe Exam Browser access rules**, you can specify several general SEB settings, all of which have been well documented at docs.moodle.org/en/Safe_Exam_Browser.

Important note

SEB requires students to download the browser on their computer or tablet. Doing a trial run with everybody's equipment is recommended to avoid panic attacks minutes before an important exam.

The third popular assessment module in Moodle is the SCORM activity, which is the topic of the following subsection.

Configuring SCORM

Shareable Content Object Reference Model (**SCORM**) is the de facto standard for exchanging learning objects across different learning management systems. Like assignments and quizzes, SCORM packages are incorporated into courses via a dedicated activity. Unlike the other two assessment tools, the SCORM activity requires little administrative configuration.

In **Site administration | Plugins | Activity modules | SCORM package**, there are two types of parameters:

- **Default settings**: These have been grouped into three categories (display, grade, and others) and are described in detail at `docs.moodle.org/en/SCORM_settings`.

- **Admin settings**: The first four settings directly impact the features available to users and are all disabled by default. SCORM standards mode enforces strict compatibility with version 1.2, whereas the other three settings allow/disallow different package types:

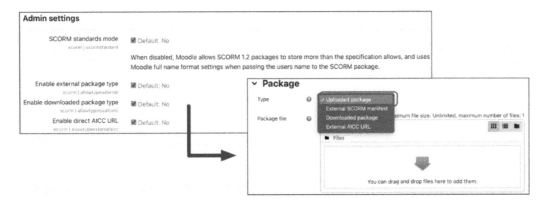

Figure 9.24 – SCORM configuration

The remaining admin settings present internal data (sessions, timeout, user ID) or debugging features. Only adjust these settings if your users experience technical issues with their SCORM packages.

This completes this section on configuring assignments, quizzes, and SCORMs. Other activities are classified as educational, such as Book, Database, Workshop, and Glossary, which haven't been covered here. Almost all administrative settings are default values, appearance settings, or file upload limits. The tricky job of a Moodle administrator is to find a consensus among all their staff on what these parameters should be. We recommend leaving those activity-related settings at their default values unless specific requirements exist to adjust them.

Closely related to assessments are skills and incentives, which we will deal with in the following section.

Managing skills and incentives

Skills and incentives are at the heart of each assessment strategy. Since Moodle is a strategic building block of a modern learning environment, we feel the two concepts deserve a dedicated section.

> **Important note**
>
> A **skill** is the ability to perform a particular action to solve a given problem. Skills are represented in Moodle as competencies.
>
> An **incentive** is a motivator to acquire a skill. Incentives are represented in Moodle as grades, feedback, badges, and certificates.

We will now focus on three skills and incentives tools being offered in Moodle, as depicted in the following diagram:

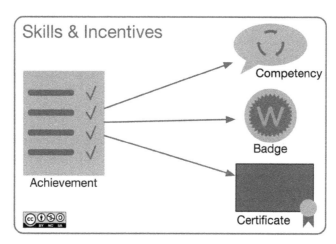

Figure 9.25 – Moodle skills and incentives

The left part of the diagram covers **achievements** in the form of completions at different levels, such as activity and course (or program and certification in Moodle Workplace). Various components support a range of award mechanisms; for instance, attaching a **Competency** once a certain number of points have been achieved in a quiz, issuing a **Badge** when completing a course, or awarding a **Certificate** after completing a program.

This section focuses on administrative tasks for the aforementioned components – competencies, badges, and certificates.

Managing competencies

Competencies describe the learner's proficiency or level of understanding in specific subject-related skills. Moodle has powerful competency management that fully supports modeling and awarding competencies. The main components and issuing mechanisms of competencies are depicted in the following diagram:

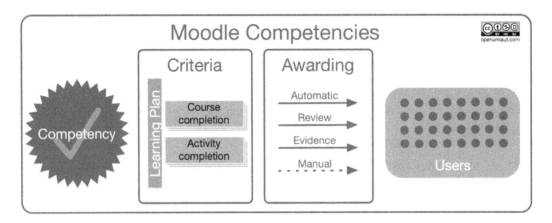

Figure 9.26 – Moodle competencies

A **competency** has specific properties such as name, scale (for instance, not competent, competent with supervision, competent), the competency framework it belongs to, and a parent to model competency hierarchies. A competency is usually tied to course and/or activity completions. Competencies can be part of a **Learning Plan** (template) that's assigned to users or cohorts. Moodle supports different awarding mechanisms, namely **Automatic** upon completion, following a **review** process after providing additional **Evidence**, or **Manual**. In Moodle Workplace, competencies can also be awarded via dynamic rules, where competencies can be configured via the rule action.

Detailed information on competencies can be found at docs.moodle.org/en/Competencies. We will focus on the main mechanisms of how to model competencies and configure awarding mechanisms since this is done site-wide and thus requires administrative permissions.

We will use the **Common European Framework of Reference for Languages** (**CEFR**) as an exemplar competency framework since it is used across Europe and, increasingly, in other countries to measure a learner's language skill sets. First, you need to create a competency framework at **Site administration | General | Competencies | Competency frameworks**, as shown in the following screenshot:

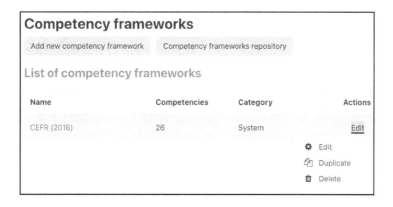

Figure 9.27 – Competency frameworks

For simplicity, we have imported the **CEFR** framework from the public Moodle **Competency frameworks repository** (via the respective button at the top). The result of the framework and its competencies (**A1**, **A2**, **B1**, **B2**, **C1**, and **C2**), along with its sub-competencies, is shown in the following screenshot:

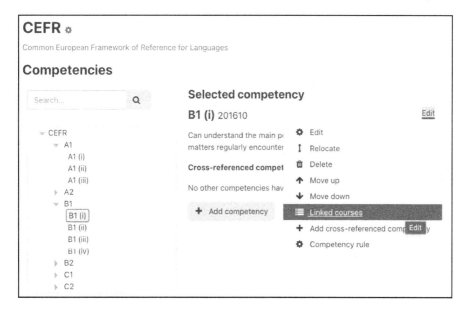

Figure 9.28 – CEFR competency framework

Once competencies have been modeled in a competency framework, the next step is to configure how to award competencies to users once they are proficient in the skill to be acquired. There are two options regarding how to award a competency to learners:

- Via **course and activity completion,** where proficiency is achieved by completing defined tasks. The most straightforward option is competency **completion,** which concludes the user's process of achieving the competency. Attaching **evidence** allows users to submit a testimony of training received outside of Moodle – for instance, a link to a public webinar or a certificate of participation in an external seminar. The last option is for the learner to request a **review** by the instructor.

  As an administrator, you do not need to configure course and activity completion since teachers or course authors do this. All that is required are the aforementioned competencies inside competency frameworks.

- Via **learning plans,** to ensure that groups of users achieve competency – for instance, all data protection officers. **Learning plans** are a means to ensure that all of your learners have targeted learning based on their goals and training needs and that it has been delivered in a structured way based on learning plan templates, which themselves are based on competencies. You can create learning plans based on the learning plan template, either manually for individual users or automatically via cohorts.

> **Important note**
> A learning plan template defines a set of competencies assigned to users.

Go to **Site administration | General | Competencies | Learning plan templates** and select the **Add new learning plan template** button to add a learning plan template. We have already created some templates, as shown in the following screenshot:

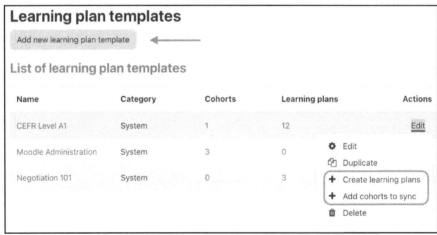

Figure 9.29 – Learning plan templates

When you select a learning plan template, you will see the already familiar competency view and also have the option to add more competencies via the **Add competencies to learning plan template** button.

Once a learning plan template has been finalized, you can create individual learning plans one by one via the **Create learning plans** option in the **Edit** menu or automatically via **Add cohorts to sync**. Users can view their learning plans via the **Learning plans** link in their respective user profiles, where they also have the option to provide evidence of prior learning – for instance, documentation of prior learning.

Moodle Workplace supports a third option via dynamic rules to award competencies based on flexible criteria, such as cohort membership. This awarding mechanism is described in detail at docs. moodle.org/en/Dynamic_rules.

This concludes our quick run-down of Moodle's robust and flexible implementation of competencies, which included modeling competency frameworks and configuring awarding mechanisms via activity and course completion, as well as via learning plans. Next up is the second incentive type: badges.

Managing badges

Badges are a good way of celebrating achievement and showing learning progress. Moodle allows you to manage badges and gives you different ways to award badges. Moodle badges are fully compatible with Open Badges and can be published in any Open Badges-compatible backpack.

Badges are awarded based on various chosen criteria and will be displayed on a user's profile. The main components and issuing mechanisms of badges are depicted in the following diagram:

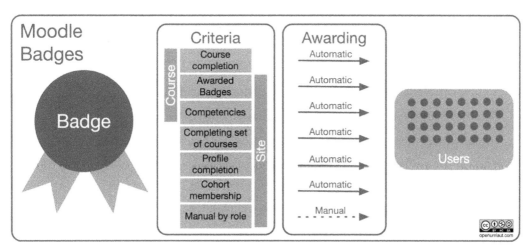

Figure 9.30 – Moodle badges

A badge has specific properties such as name, expiry date, and issuer. Additionally, badges have one or many **criteria** to be fulfilled to trigger their award. Some criteria only exist at the **course level**, while others exist at the **site level**. The **awarding** itself is automatic, except for manual assignment.

Detailed information on badges can be found at `docs.moodle.org/en/Badges`. We will now focus on the main mechanisms of managing and awarding badges.

Once you or some creative whiz kid in your marketing department has created the badges to be awarded to your learners, you will need to add and manage these in your learning management system. In Moodle, there are two types of badges:

- **Course badges** are assigned at the course level and are related to the activities and completions inside a course

- **Site badges** are assigned site-wide and are related to achievements, such as completing a set of courses in Moodle or a certification in Moodle Workplace

As an administrator, you are only concerned about site badges, which are managed under **Site administration** | **General** | **Badges** | **Manage Badges**. Once you have added a badge and provided its properties, you must specify the **badge criteria**. There are different types of course badge criteria and site badge criteria, as shown in the following screenshot comparison:

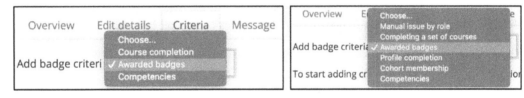

Figure 9.31 – Course badge criteria versus site badge criteria

The following badge criteria are available:

- **Course completion** (course): The user has completed the current course

- **Awarded badges** (both): The user has been awarded the selected badge(s)

- **Competencies** (both): The user has been awarded the selected competencies

- **Manual issue by role** (site): To be awarded manually by users with a particular role within the site or a course

- **Completing set of courses** (site): The user has completed the selected course(s)

- **Profile completion** (site): A user profile field has a specific value

- **Cohort membership** (site): The user is a member of the selected cohort(s)

As with competencies, there are two options regarding how to award a badge to a learner:

- **Automatic**: All preceding criteria, except **Manual issue by role**, trigger awarding a badge to the users who have successfully fulfilled the respective criteria

- **Manual**: When the **Manual issue by role** criterion has been selected (site badges only), a user with the correct permissions can award a badge to another user

In Moodle Workplace, badges can also be awarded via dynamic rules, where badges can be configured via the rule action. This awarding mechanism is described in detail at `docs.moodle.org/en/Dynamic_rules`.

Users can view their awarded badges in the **Badges** section of their user profile.

This completes our brief introduction to badges, where we covered Moodle's management and awarding mechanisms. Next up is the third and last incentive type: certificates.

Managing certificates

Certificates are an excellent incentive for both formal and informal training. However, at the time of writing, they are not (yet?) part of Moodle, but they are of Moodle Workplace. However, the module works without a glitch in Moodle. We installed the **Workplace certificate manager** in *Chapter 8, Understanding Moodle Plugins*. Moodle HQ has developed the plugin, so it is safe to assume that it is here to stay. As always, we will concentrate on the administrative elements of the tool. You find the full documentation at `docs.moodle.org/en/Certificates`.

The certificate manager allows you to design engaging certificates and then award them to users in different ways. The tool comes with a certificate generator, which lets you design templates so that diplomas or certificates of participation can be issued. The basic workflow is shown in the following diagram:

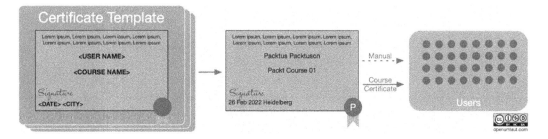

Figure 9.32 – Basic certificate workflow

Certificate templates act as a blueprint and contain **static elements** (organization name or logo), **dynamic elements** (username or certification title), and **verification elements** (code or digital signature). Based on the template, individual **certificates** are generated and assigned to users, which can be done manually or via the course certificate activity. Moodle Workplace also supports certificate issuing via dynamic rules.

We will mainly deal with the basics of certificate template management as teachers or instructors usually trigger the awarding via the aforementioned course certificate activity. Most of this content has been borrowed from *Chapter 7, Skills and Incentives* of *Corporate Learning with Moodle Workplace*, published by Packt Publishing.

You can manage certificate templates via **Site administration | General | Certificates | Manage certificate templates**, where you will see a list of certificate templates. In our demo instance, we have already created three certificate templates. On the right of each item, you will see several actions, some of which are the usual Moodle icons (**Edit**, **Details**, **Preview**, **Duplicate**, and **Delete**), while others are specific to certificates (**Certificates issued** and **Issue certificates**). We will discuss these in due course:

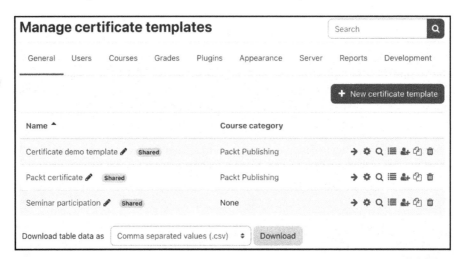

Figure 9.33 – Certificate templates

To create a new certificate template, select the + **New certificate template** button; you will then be greeted with a pop-up screen and the following mostly self-explanatory settings:

- **Name**: This doesn't have to be unique, but it is recommended not to use the same name more than once.

- **Course category**: The certificate is available in the selected course category; it is also **Available in sub-categories and courses** if the option is enabled. When no course category is selected, the certificate is available across the site.

- **Page width** and **Page height**: The default values depend on your server locale. For reference, the dimensions of A4 are 297 mm and 210 mm; the ones for letter size are 279 mm and 216 mm, respectively.

- **Left margin** and **Right margin**: These are for the edge width on the left and right in mm. The default is 0.

As soon as you save the certificate template, you will be directed to the certificate designer, which we will work with next.

Certificate designer

The **certificate designer** lets you interactively create multi-page, multi-language certificate templates. The canvas, which has an already (very poorly) designed certificate, has the following user interface:

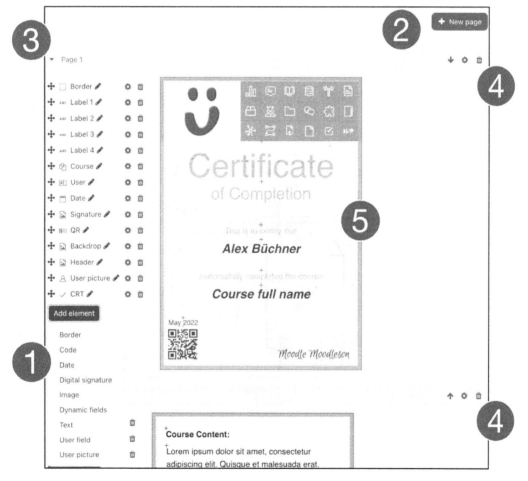

Figure 9.34 – Certificate designer

The following controls are available in the certificate designer:

1. **Adding elements** to the certificate template. These will be covered subsequently.

2. **Adding a new page**. You will have to set the page height and width, as well as the page margins. The default values are the ones for the current page.

3. **Expand** and **collapse** the current page.

4. **Page actions**. Here, you have the option to **Move** up and down (only multi-page certificates), access various **Settings** (dimensions of the page), and **Delete** (only multi-page certificates).

5. **Certificate canvas**, which fully supports dragging and dropping elements.

Once some elements have been added to a template, each item will be listed on the left. Each item can be renamed via the **Inline Editing** option beside the element name or by simply clicking the label. The **Settings** symbol opens the parameters pop-up window for each item, while the **Delete** icon removes the entry. Changing the elements' order using the standard **Move** icon will change which element is displayed in front of another.

> **Tip**
> To modify the element values, simply click the element on the canvas.

Now, let's go through the different elements that can be added to a certificate template.

Adding certificate elements

To add an element to the certificate template, select it from the **Add element** drop-down, which opens up a pop-up menu containing element options. Each element contains the following settings:

- **Element name**: This identifies an element when editing a certificate. Note that this will not be displayed on the certificate.

- **Element-specific settings**: These, mostly self-explanatory options, depend on the added element type. For example, a text string has a font and size, whereas the date field also has a format.

- **Element dimension(s)**: Every element has a **Width**, while some elements (for example, images) also have a **Height**.

- **Element position**: When you select **Show more…**, two more settings – **Position X** and **Position Y** – will be shown, with the apex at the top left of the certificate template. Usually, you position your image by dragging and dropping it onto the canvas; however, sometimes, it is useful to position elements manually, especially when you need to align multiple items horizontally or vertically.

We have grouped the available element-specific certificate settings into three categories – static, dynamic, and validation – which will be covered in the following subsections.

Adding static certificate elements

Static elements are fixed for every certificate issued from the certificate template, and they will be identical on every certificate that will be generated. The three static elements that are available are **Border**, **Image**, and **Text**:

- The **certificate border** is the only element that cannot be moved around on the canvas.

- You will need to upload a **certificate image** that has been prepared elsewhere. The supported image file types are GIF, JPE, JPG, JPEG, PNG, SVG, and SVGZ. Alternatively, you can select a **shared image**, which is managed centrally and acts as a simple repository for assets used on multiple certificates; for instance, your company logo or the signatures of certificate signees. You can manage shared images by going to **Site administration | General | Certificates | Certificate images**. If you tick the **Use as a background image** box, the picture will be stretched across the entire certificate and shown behind all other elements. It is recommended that you use an image with added transparency when it is used as a background.

- **Certificate text** is effectively a label for which you can specify **Font**, **Size** (in **pt**), and **Colour**. You also have three **Text alignment** options: **Left**, **Centre**, and **Right**. Right alignment of the text means that the element coordinates' **Position X** and **Position Y** will refer to the top-right corner of the text box; in center alignment, they will refer to the top middle, and in left alignment, they will refer to the top-left corner:

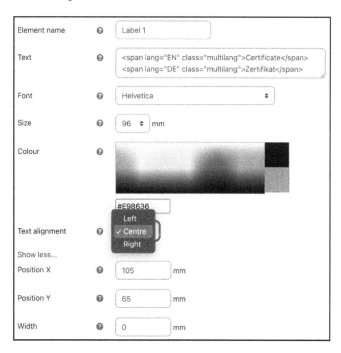

Figure 9.35 – Certificate text element

Text supports multi-lingual content to generate certificates in the user's language via so-called lang tags. Ensure the **Issue certificate in user language** setting in **Site administration** | **General** | **Certificates** | **Certificates settings** is ticked, the multi-language content filter is enabled, and text fields contain multi-language tags. This generic feature will be dealt with in the *Managing localization* section of *Chapter 10, Configuring Technical Features*; you can see a brief example in the sample screenshot.

Now that we have added all the required static elements, namely **Border**, **Image**, and **Text**, let's look at the different dynamic elements that can be placed on a certificate template.

Adding dynamic certificate elements

Dynamic elements will be replaced with specific data for every certificate issued from the certificate template. Thus, each dynamic element acts as a mini placeholder on the certificate template. Typical dynamic values include the receiver's name, the course title, or simply the date when the certificate will be issued. The four dynamic elements available are **Date**, **Dynamic fields**, **User field**, and **User picture**:

- The **certificate Date** element adds a date field to the template, either **Issued date** (when the PDF will be generated) or **Expiry date** (when the certificate's validity ends). You can further choose from one of the seven available **Date format** options. Please note that the **Date format** options will be adjusted according to the active language pack while editing the certificate template. While there is no limit to the number of date elements you can put on a certificate template, usually, one item is placed on the document.

- The **certificate Dynamic fields** element type is effectively a placeholder for several course fields: short name, full name, URL, completion grade, and, if present, custom course fields. In our example, we have selected the course's full name, which will be displayed on the PDF once generated. In Moodle Workplace, additional program and certification fields are at your disposal.

- The **certificate User field** displays textual information on the certificate, which supports all plain text fields (that is, no rich text/HTML text fields) in the user profile, including custom profile fields. We have added the user's full name on our certificate, which is almost always part of a personalized certificate.

- The **certificate User picture** type adds the user's image to the template. User pictures are handled the same way as elements of the **Image** type; the only difference is that the picture cannot be selected since it is already set in the user profile.

This concludes this subsection on dynamic certificate elements, where we covered **Date**, **Dynamic fields**, **User field**, and **User picture**. Next up are validation elements.

Adding validation certificate elements

Certificates are regularly issued in settings where their validity is critical; for example, diplomas, compliance documents, and qualification credentials. To ensure that the certificates have been generated by the Moodle system, two validation mechanisms are offered:

- **Certificate code**: Every issued certificate contains a unique **code**, made up of 10 digits plus two uppercase letters; for instance, 0123456789AB (The last two letters are the user's initials). This code can be displayed on the certificate in four different formats: **Code only** (default), **Code with link**, **Verification URL** (code without a link), and **QR Code** (as used in our example).

To verify the certificate's validity (code), Moodle offers a dedicated form that can be reached via one of the four described display options. It is also possible to enter codes manually via **Site administration | General | Certificates | Verify certificates**, as shown in the following screenshot:

Figure 9.36 – Certificate validation

Once you select **Verify**, information regarding the certificate metadata is displayed. You can also access the document's PDF version by selecting the **View certificate** link at the bottom.

- **Digital signatures** can be added to a certificate (template) based on self-signed CRT certificates that follow the X.509 standard. They offer a higher degree of security than the code element by electronically signing the generated PDF file with a self-signed certificate to prevent forgery and falsification of certificates.

It is common to sign an image in a document using a logo, a signature, or a seal, although creating signed PDFs with no in-document visualization is possible. The only compulsory field is the digital signature itself, represented as a CRT file. You will either have to use an existing CRT file from your organization or generate a self-signed certificate. Follow these three steps via the Linux command line:

```
openssl req -x509 -nodes -days 365000 -newkey rsa:1024
-keyout moodle.crt -out moodle.crt
openssl pkcs12 -export -in moodle.crt -out moodle.p12
openssl pkcs12 -in moodle.p12 -out moodle.crt -nodes
```

The first command creates a self-signed signature that's valid for 10 years (365,000 days) and is RSA-encrypted with 1,024 bytes. It contains both the private key and the certificate part. The second step is to export the CRT file in P12 format before converting it into a PEM file. You will need to provide the CRT file – here, `moodle.crt` – to the digital signature on your certificate, which uses the standard key part to tag the certificate as valid and verifiable. Internally, the PDF generator uses functionality in the TCPDF library.

With that, we have listed the supported certificate elements, all of which have been utilized in our sample certificate, as shown in the following figure:

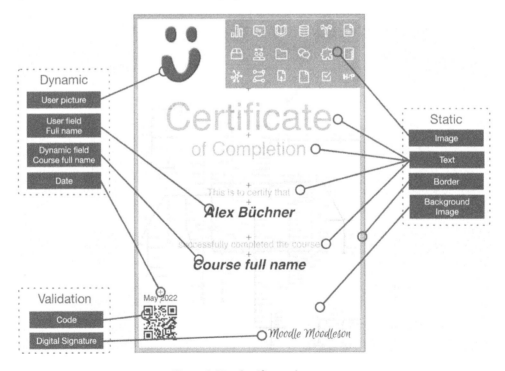

Figure 9.37 – Certificate elements

By default, all available certificate plugins are shown in alphabetical order in the certificate designer menu. If you wish to change the order of the elements or hide any elements that are not in use in your organization, go to **Site administration** | **Plugins** | **Admin tools** | **Manage certificate element plugins** and configure the list as required. It is also possible for developers to create new certificate element plugins, which will appear in this list and be treated like core elements.

Now that we have dealt with creating certificate templates, let's look at administrative tasks for certificate issuing.

Issuing certificates

The key objective of certificates is to be awarded to users once they have completed a specific task or solved a given problem. Certificates can either be issued manually or via the course certificate activity.

To **manually issue a certificate**, you have to select the **Issue certificates from this template** icon to the right of the certificate template. This will open a pop-up form where you have to choose at least one user and, optionally, specify an expiry date or period. In the following screenshot, two users have been selected:

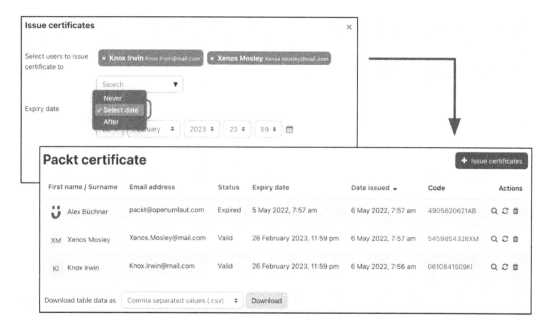

Figure 9.38 – Manually issuing certificates

For every issued certificate, no matter how it has been generated, metadata will be stored in the underlying Moodle database. Select the **Certificates issued** icon beside the certificate template to view this data. In addition to self-explanatory standard fields, the table shows the certificate code and a link to the verification page. In the **Actions** column, a **Preview** of the generated PDF file can be viewed, the PDF file can be regenerated on the fly and re-issued to the user (the award date and time remain unchanged), and the certificate can be revoked.

To use the **Course Certificate activity**, you must install **mod_coursecertificate** from moodle.org/plugins/mod_coursecertificate. This activity allows teachers to choose from certificate templates. Learners will then be able to download a PDF copy of the certificate themselves, and there are options to email PDF copies automatically. As all this takes place at the course level, you, as the administrator, don't have to worry about this. More details on this activity can be found at docs.moodle.org/en/Course_certificate_activity.

One last certificate-related admin setting might be relevant: users can see their certificates on the **My certificates** page in their user profile. If the **Show share on LinkedIn** option is ticked in **Site administration** | **General** | **Certificates** | **Certificates settings**, an additional column labeled **Share on LinkedIn** will be shown. When users select the LinkedIn icon, the certificate will be added to their feed. You need to follow the instructions shown to receive your **LinkedIn organization ID** for this to work.

This completes our look at the trio of skills and incentives covered in this chapter, where we covered competency management, badge configuration, and creating and issuing certificates.

Summary

This chapter taught you how to administer any Moodle tools and features classified as educational.

First, we configured collaboration tools while covering blogs, comments, and tags. Next, we dealt with various content creation features and looked at the Moodle content bank and H5P, LTI platforms and tools, filters, plagiarism prevention, and licenses. We then configured grades and assessments, namely the gradebook and the configuration of the three activity types – assignment, quiz, and SCORM. Finally, we managed skills and incentives in the form of competencies and learning plans, badges, and certificates.

You should now be in a good position to approach all organizational stakeholders to gather relevant input to ensure a suitable setup of educational components.

Due to the high volume of configuration areas, we have divided the configuration topic into two separate chapters – educational configuration, which we dealt with in this chapter, and technical configuration, which we will cover in the next chapter.

10

Configuring Technical Features

Moodle supports a wide range of tools and features that require administrative attention – some only once, others regularly. Due to the volume of configuration areas, we have divided this topic into educational and technical configurations, each represented by a dedicated chapter:

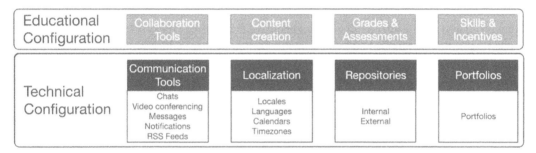

Figure 10.1 – Technical configuration topics

This chapter deals with configuring technical settings.

First, we will configure synchronous and asynchronous **communication tools** while covering chats, video conferencing (BigBlueButton), messaging (messages and notifications), and RSS feeds.

Next, we will learn how to configure **localization** features while dealing with different locales represented as language packs, multi-languages, calendars, and time zones.

We will then configure internal and external **repositories**, enabling users to add files to courses and other locations via the file picker.

Finally, we will configure **portfolios**, allowing data to be exported to external (portfolio) systems.

In this chapter, we will cover the following topics:

- Configuring communication tools
- Managing localization
- Managing repositories
- Managing portfolios

Configuring technical settings usually requires input from other techies, such as mail, system, or network administrators. It has proven beneficial to liaise with these experts to ensure the optimal setup of your Moodle system.

By the end of this chapter, you should be in a good position to approach your colleagues, gather the technical information needed, and implement these accordingly.

Configuring communication tools

Communication is a key feature in Moodle as it enhances the learning experience of all users involved. Moodle supports synchronous and asynchronous communication, which has to be configured by the administrator and is the topic of this section. We have also added a small section on contacting support since it is perceived as a relevant communication topic in the Moodle administration context. Let's start with synchronous communication.

Synchronous communication

We will cover two types of synchronous communication in Moodle: **instant messaging** and **web conferencing**, both of which will be discussed in the following subsections.

Configuring instant messaging (Chat)

Moodle's inbuilt facility for instant messaging is the **Chat** activity, which is used in courses or on the home page. The configuration of the module is presented – I couldn't resist – as a Moodle chat:

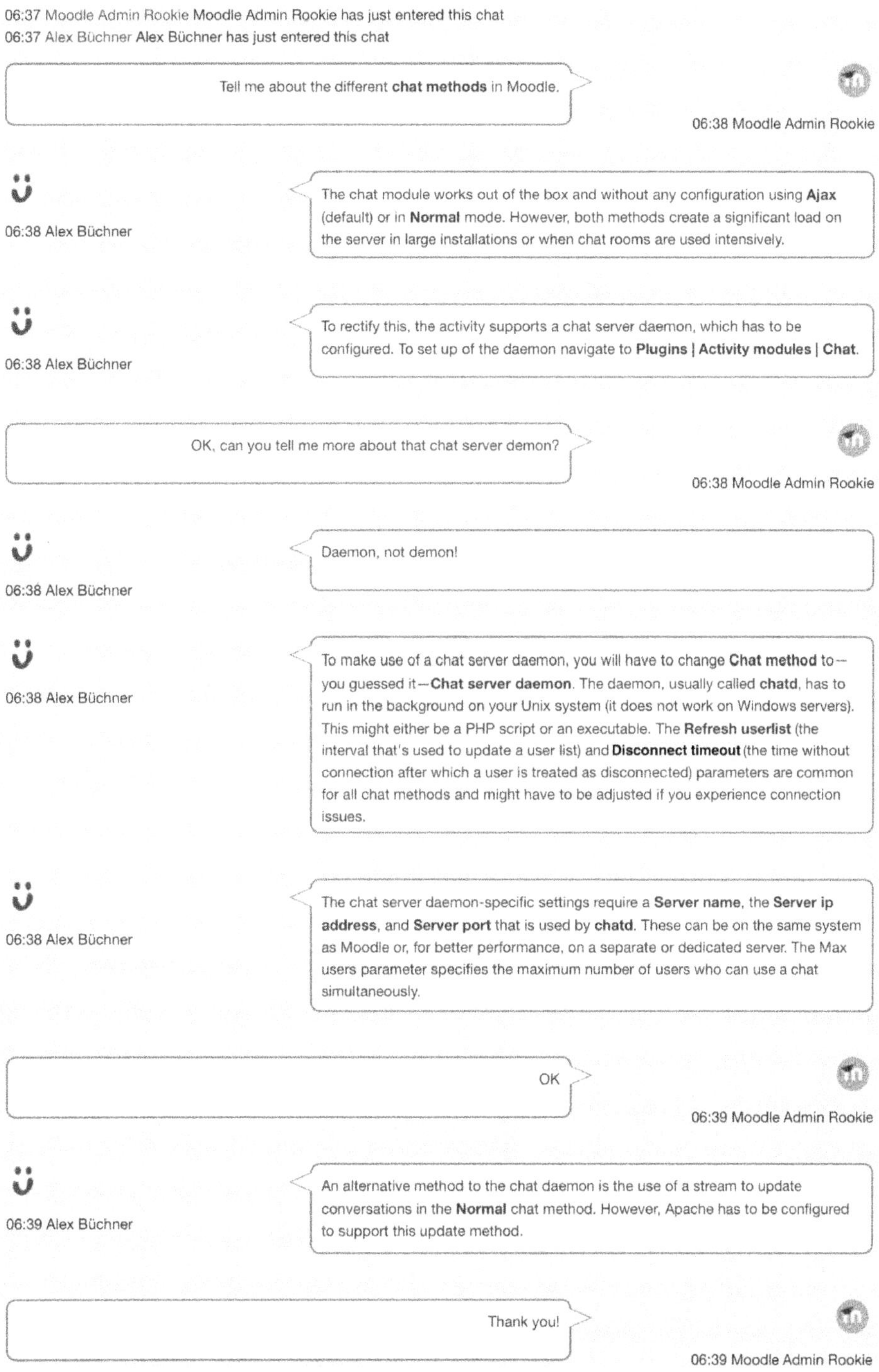

06:37 Moodle Admin Rookie Moodle Admin Rookie has just entered this chat
06:37 Alex Büchner Alex Büchner has just entered this chat

> Tell me about the different **chat methods** in Moodle.
>
> 06:38 Moodle Admin Rookie

> The chat module works out of the box and without any configuration using **Ajax** (default) or in **Normal** mode. However, both methods create a significant load on the server in large installations or when chat rooms are used intensively.
>
> 06:38 Alex Büchner

> To rectify this, the activity supports a chat server daemon, which has to be configured. To set up of the daemon navigate to **Plugins | Activity modules | Chat**.
>
> 06:38 Alex Büchner

> OK, can you tell me more about that chat server demon?
>
> 06:38 Moodle Admin Rookie

> Daemon, not demon!
>
> 06:38 Alex Büchner

> To make use of a chat server daemon, you will have to change **Chat method** to — you guessed it — **Chat server daemon**. The daemon, usually called chatd, has to run in the background on your Unix system (it does not work on Windows servers). This might either be a PHP script or an executable. The **Refresh userlist** (the interval that's used to update a user list) and **Disconnect timeout** (the time without connection after which a user is treated as disconnected) parameters are common for all chat methods and might have to be adjusted if you experience connection issues.
>
> 06:38 Alex Büchner

> The chat server daemon-specific settings require a **Server name**, the **Server ip address**, and **Server port** that is used by chatd. These can be on the same system as Moodle or, for better performance, on a separate or dedicated server. The Max users parameter specifies the maximum number of users who can use a chat simultaneously.
>
> 06:38 Alex Büchner

> OK
>
> 06:39 Moodle Admin Rookie

> An alternative method to the chat daemon is the use of a stream to update conversations in the **Normal** chat method. However, Apache has to be configured to support this update method.
>
> 06:39 Alex Büchner

> Thank you!
>
> 06:39 Moodle Admin Rookie

Figure 10.2 – Chat configuration

The **Chat** activity can significantly impact server performance when used heavily. We have presented some chat optimization strategies in the *Optimizing Moodle activities* section in *Chapter 15, Optimizing Moodle Performance*.

The **Chat** activity is sufficient for basic group exchanges; however, a web conferencing tool is needed for more advanced collaborative activities, which we will cover in the following subsection.

Setting up web conferencing (BigBlueButton)

Since the COVID-19 pandemic has made the home office become the new normal, web conferencing has become a must in every working and learning environment. Typical requirements are meeting rooms for sessions such as live online classes, virtual office hours, or group collaboration with remote learners.

BigBlueButton (**BBB**) is an open source web conferencing system for online learning. According to its website, www.bigbluebutton.org, its key features are "*real-time sharing of audio, video, presentation, and screen – along with collaboration tools such as chat (public and private), whiteboard, shared notes, polling, and breakout rooms. BigBlueButton can record your sessions for later playback.*"

BBB has been integrated into Moodle and offers a free service provided by Blindside Networks with the following restrictions:

- The maximum length for each session is 60 minutes
- The maximum number of concurrent users per session is 25
- Recordings expire after 7 days and are not downloadable
- Student webcams are only visible to the moderator

BBB is a Moodle activity that's set up and configured by teachers within a course. You, as an administrator, should ensure that the site-wide configuration is in line with the typical usage of the web conferencing tool. BBB comes with a significant number of configuration options, which is reflected by the number of menu items at **Site administration** | **Plugins** | **Activity modules** | **BigBlueButton**:

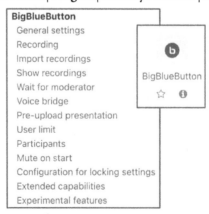

Figure 10.3 – BigBlueButton configuration

The configuration options in each sub-menu are well described and commented on. Instead of repetition, we will briefly describe the purpose of each of these settings areas:

- **General settings**: The BBB server details are specified in addition to default welcome messages. If the offered free service is too restrictive for your organization, you can either install a local BBB instance, engage with a Moodle Partner, or use a commercial BBB hosting provider for a more advanced setup and update the server settings accordingly.

- **Recording**: Various recording-related settings and default values.

- **Import recordings**: Enable these settings so that recordings can be imported from other courses.

- **Show recordings**: Specify how recorded sessions should be presented to learners – for instance, with or without preview.

- **Wait for moderator**: Define the behavior of the BBB activity before the moderator joins the session.

- **Voice bridge**: How a voice bridge is handled as part of the BBB setup.

- **Pre-upload presentation**: BBB lets moderators pre-upload presentations in various formats. Here, you can configure this feature.

- **User limit**: Specifies the number of users allowed in a session.

- **Participants**: The rule to be used by default when a new room is added.

- **Mute on start**: Sets whether microphones are muted when joining a session.

- **Configuration for locking settings**: Enables and disables various BBB features such as webcams, microphones, chats (private and public), or shared notes.

- **Extended capabilities**: Specifies whether a notification should be sent out once the recording link is available.

- **Experimental features**: At the time of writing, the only beta feature available was to automatically support activity completion for BBB.

For more information on BBB, refer to `docs.moodle.org/en/BigBlueButton`.

If your organization already uses an alternative web or video conferencing system such as **Zoom** or **WebEx**, a third-party plugin should be available at `moodle.org/plugins`; its installation was covered in *Chapter 8, Understanding Moodle Plugins*.

This completes this section on synchronous communication. Next up is its counterpart, asynchronous communication.

Asynchronous communication

There are two types of asynchronous communication options in Moodle – messaging and **RSS** feeds. We will cover both tools to equip you with the information needed to configure asynchronous communication.

Messaging configuration

Moodle comes with a flexible messaging facility that can be seen as a basic multichannel communication system that supports **messages** and **notifications**.

> **Important note**
>
> **Messaging system = Messages + Notifications**
>
> **Messages** contain information and are sent from a sender to a receiver. **Notifications** let users know that a message has been sent or an event has been triggered.

A learner might send a message to the teacher, who receives a notification (user to user). An activity or Moodle itself might also send messages: you, as an administrator, might be notified when updates are available, and a learner might get notified when an assignment is due. Not only this, but users can also reply to forum posts via email or send attachments to their private files. The different messaging channels are summarized in the following table:

Sender	Receiver	Direction
User	User	Outbound
Activity	User	Outbound
Sytem	User	Outbound
External	Activity	Inbound
External	Private files	Inbound

Figure 10.4 – Messaging communication channels

We can distinguish between **inbound** and **outbound** messaging, as seen from the perspective of Moodle: a message sent from one (Moodle) user to another (Moodle) user is seen as outbound, as the sending takes place within Moodle. A file sent via email by a learner to their private files is seen as inbound, as Moodle receives the attachment. We will be dealing with both direction types, starting with outbound messaging.

Outbound messaging

Before configuring outbound messaging, ensure the **Enable messaging system** checkbox is ticked in **Site administration | General | Advanced features**. For each notification type (such as subscribed forums, posts, or feedback reminders), the following message outputs are available:

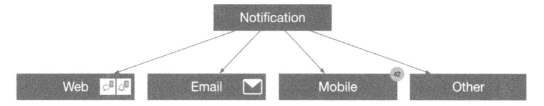

Figure 10.5 – Message outputs

Let's look at these in more detail:

- **Web**: This uses the built-in notifications mechanism and does not require any customization. The default theme displays notification indicators in the toolbar.

- **Email**: Messages will be forwarded to an email address. Moodle's email works without any configuration using its internal PHP-based method. To improve its performance and make use of your existing email infrastructure, go to **Site administration | Server | Email | Outgoing mail configuration**, where you will find all the relevant mail-related settings. The page is divided into the following six categories:

  - **SMTP**: Settings for sending emails

  - **No-reply and domain**: No-reply address and allowed email domains

  - **Email diverting**: For use in development environments

  - **DKIM**: Email signing

  - **Test outgoing mail configuration**

  - **Email display settings**: You can find well-documented instructions at docs.moodle. org/en/Mail_configuration

- **Mobile**: Messages will be sent to the mobile Moodle app. The setup is described in more detail in the *Configuring mobile notifications* subsection of *Chapter 11*, *Enabling Mobile Learning*.

- **Other**: A separate column is shown for each installed third-party message output. At moodle. org/plugins/?q=type:message, you will find additional notification plugins, including those for Jabber, Telegram, Slack, and SMS.

Users can (via **Notification preferences** in the **User account** section of their **Preferences**) configure how to receive notifications, depending on whether they are online or offline. The defaults for each notification type and channel can be configured by going to **Site administration | General | Messaging | Notification settings**. You can also lock the settings for each notification type; in the following screenshot, we have locked **Assignment notifications** for the **Web** and **Email** channels to make sure nobody can claim they didn't know about that upcoming deadline:

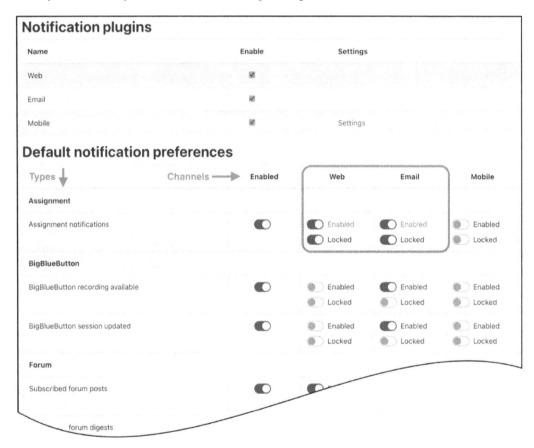

Figure 10.6 – Notification preferences

System notifications only apply to you, the administrator; all others apply to all users, including the three notification types in **Inbound message configuration**, which is the topic of the following subsection.

Inbound messaging

Moodle allows users to reply to forum posts via email and send attachments to their private files. Incoming messages are processed by **message handlers**, as illustrated in the following diagram:

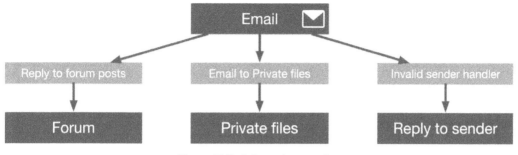

Figure 10.7 – Inbound messaging

To support incoming messages, the following settings have to be configured:

- Make sure **Enable incoming mail processing** is turned on in **Site administration | Server | Email | Incoming mail configuration**.

- **Mailbox configuration**: Specify the **Mailbox name** and **Email domain on the same screen** details. For packt@openumlaut.com, the former would be packt and the latter openumlaut. com.

> **Important note**
> It is highly recommended that you use a dedicated address for inbound messaging and not your day-to-day email.

- **Incoming mail server settings**: On the same page, configure your IMAP server – check with your mail administrator for details.

- **Configure message handlers**: To specify which types of emails will be processed by Moodle, go to **Site administration | Server | Incoming mail configuration | Message handlers**. Here, you need to configure the message handlers, which have been implemented as plugins:

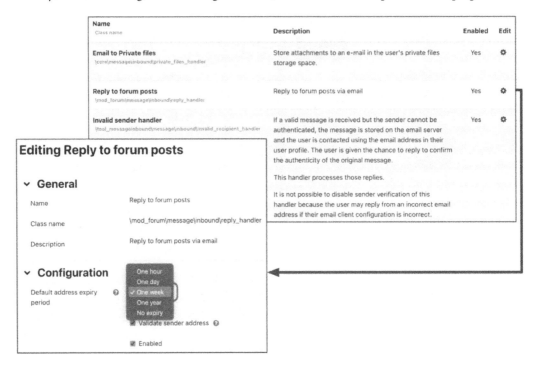

Figure 10.8 – Message handlers

Three message handlers come with Moodle: **Email to Private files**, **Reply to forum posts**, and **Invalid recipient handler**. The first two have already been mentioned and should be self-explanatory. The invalid recipient handler deals with messages from senders that do not match the user's email address and cannot be disabled.

Select the **Configuration** icon in the **Edit** column and tick the **Enabled** setting to enable any of the other two handlers. It is recommended that you leave the expiry setting as-is. You can find a good explanation of incoming email configuration with hints for other email servers at `docs.moodle.org/en/Mail_configuration`.

Messaging in Moodle provides versatile inbound and outbound communication among users, but also between system entities. As an administrator, you must guarantee that all supported channels work correctly and in line with your organization's guidelines. You will likely have to liaise with the mail admin to ensure proper configuration.

The second type of asynchronous communication supported by Moodle is RSS feeds, which will be covered in the following subsection.

Configuration RSS feeds

Really Simple Syndication (**RSS**) is an XML-based format for distributing and aggregating web content, such as news headlines. Moodle supports the consumption as well as the production of RSS feeds, as illustrated in the following diagram:

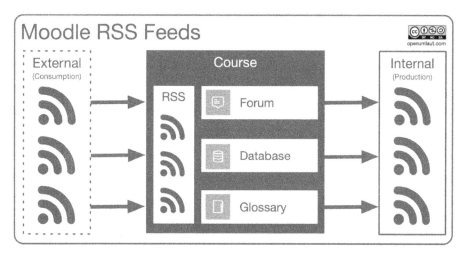

10.9 – Moodle RSS feeds

RSS feeds must be switched on via the **Enable RSS feeds** setting at **Site administration | General | Advanced features**.

External RSS feeds are consumed via the **Remote RSS Feeds** block in Moodle courses or the dashboard. The block is configured and pre-populated at **Site administration | Plugins | Blocks | Remote RSS feeds**. The parameters available are **Entries per feed** (the number of loaded and displayed atoms) and **Timeout** (the amount of time before the feed expires in the cache).

Three Moodle activities – **Forum**, **Database**, and **Glossary** – can be set up as RSS producers; their feeds can be used in other courses. Each module has an **Enable RSS feeds** option in its respective plugin setting. For security and privacy, each RSS feed URL contains an automatically created token for the user. If there is a suspicion that this has been compromised, users can reset this via the **Security keys** link in the **User account** section of their **Preferences**.

RSS feeds are valuable for consuming external feeds and providing certain course data as internal feeds. To conclude this section on communication, we will cover how users can contact your support channels.

Contacting support

A topic remotely related to communication is users of your Moodle system seeking assistance. When you go to **Site administration | Server | Support contact**, Moodle lets you specify a **Support name**, a **Support email** address, and a **Support page**:

Support contact

Support name supportname	Alex Büchner	Default: Alex Büchner

The name of the person or other entity providing support via the support form or support page.

Support email supportemail	support@openumlaut.com	

If SMTP is configured on this site and a support page is not set, this email address will receive messages submitted through the support form. If sending fails, the email address will be displayed to logged-in users.

Support page supportpage	www.openumlaut.com	Default: Empty

A link to this page will be provided for users to contact the site support. If the field is left blank then a link to a support form will be provided instead.

Save changes

10.10 – Support contact

Your contact details are displayed at various places throughout Moodle – for instance, during self-registration. There is no support block you can put on the front page, but you can easily mimic this using a **Text** block.

This concludes this section on communication tools, where we dealt with synchronous tools (chat and web conferencing), asynchronous tools (messaging and RSS), and setting up communication channels for Moodle support. In the following section, we will cover Moodle localization to facilitate the usage of your LMS across locales.

Managing localization

Localization is concerned with adapting software to be used in different locales. A locale is linked to a region where certain cultural aspects apply, such as language, formatting of dates and times, calendric representation, and so on.

As Moodle is used worldwide and given that many educational establishments span continents and cultures, localization must be fully supported.

> **Important note**
>
> If the main language of your Moodle system is anything other than (UK or US) English, make sure you select this during installation. This way, locale settings, as well as role names and descriptions, will be adequately localized.

The key areas that can be configured in Moodle are language-related settings and calendric information. Languages and calendars are the topics of the following two subsections.

Languages, idiomas, 语言, and اللغات

Moodle supports over 80 languages, including Latin and Esperanto! The Unicode standard has been adopted to represent the character sets of multiple languages as it covers most modern scripts that are used throughout the world. Moodle supports left-to-right writing systems, as used in this book, and right-to-left writing systems too, such as Arabic:

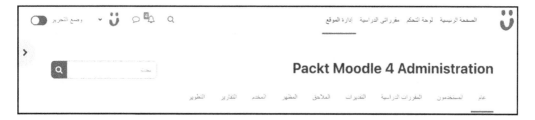

Figure 10.11 – Support for right-to-left writing

Language packs are utilized to support different locales.

Understanding language packs

In Moodle, a **language pack** contains information about the locale and all translations. Technically, the term "language pack" is a bit of a misnomer – they should be called "locale packs."

> **Important note**
>
> Every locale is represented as a language pack.

The following diagram illustrates the fundamental concepts of language packs:

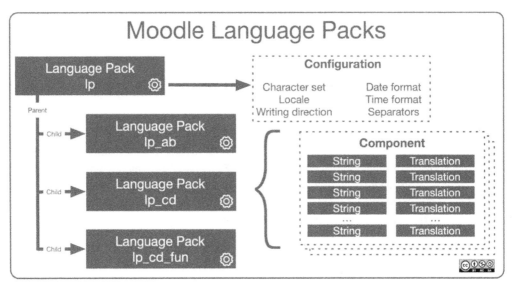

Figure 10.12 – Language packs

Each language pack contains two essential parts:

- **Language configuration**: This contains localization information about the locale – for instance, the character set to be used, the writing direction, various date and time formats, and separators for different data types

- **Language strings**: These are grouped by Moodle components (for example, core, module, third-party), and translations are provided for each language string

Standardized two-letter region codes characterize locales. For example, **pt** represents Portuguese, as spoken in Portugal, whereas **pt_br** represents Brazilian Portuguese. Internally, **pt** is the parent language, whereas **pt_br** is the child language, which only contains strings that are different from the parent language pack. This approach reduces the size of child language packs significantly.

Some packs of non-standardized languages have made their way into Moodle, which partly explains why there are over 200 (!) language packs to choose from. For these specialized packs, new codes have been made up by their creators, including **de_kids**, **en_us_k12**, and **es_mx_kids** (for young learners), **da_rum** (courses have been renamed rooms), and, most importantly, **en_ar** (pirate language – ahoy!). You may also come across language packs with a **wp** suffix; they represent strings from Moodle Workplace.

To support a locale, you have to install its language pack, which Moodle will download automatically from `download.moodle.org`. Go to **Site administration | General | Language | Language packs** to include new packs via Moodle's language import utility:

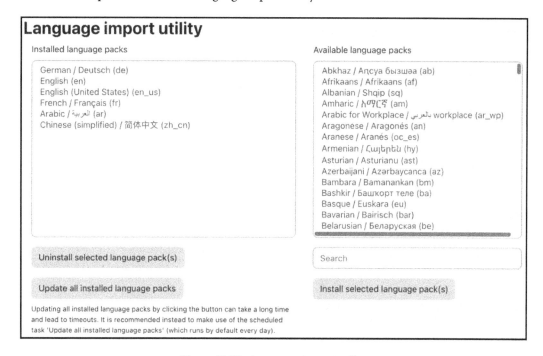

Figure 10.13 – Language import utility

Six language packs, consisting of Arabic, English (**en** and **en_us**), French, German, and simplified Chinese, have been installed in the preceding screenshot. Select one or many locales on the right-hand side and click the **Install selected language pack(s)** button to add more language packs. To reverse this operation, select a single or multiple language packs in the list on the left-hand side and click on the **Uninstall selected language pack(s)** button.

> **Tip**
> If your firewall doesn't allow connections to Moodle's download server, you need to download the required language packs from `download.moodle.org/langpack`, copy them to `$CFG->wwwroot/lang`, and unzip the file(s) manually.

The **English (en)** language pack cannot be uninstalled. It is used as a reference language in cases where strings in other languages are not translated. Some language packs are incomplete, and sometimes, only non-admin features have been translated.

Once installed, the user can choose a language (if configured) from the language menu located in the profile menu. Bear in mind that only terms and phrases that are part of Moodle will change. Any content that's created will not be translated unless it is configured to make use of the multilingual feature (refer to the *Customizing languages* subsection of this chapter):

Figure 10.14 – Language selector

Language packs are kept and maintained at `download.moodle.org/langpack/4.x` (where **x** is the current release version number). Some packs are updated more frequently than others, and Moodle automatically updates language packs daily. If you're impatient like me, clicking on the **Update all installed language packs** button performs this task immediately.

Once you have installed all the required language packs, you should configure the language-related settings.

Configuring language settings

Moodle offers several language-related parameters that you can find at **Site administration | General | Language | Language settings**:

- **Language auto detect**: By default, Moodle detects the language from the used web browser locale. If you wish to override this and use the default site language instead, untick this checkbox.

- **Default language**: This allows you to select the language used throughout the site unless individual users override it via the language menu or from their profile. Only those languages for which a language pack has been installed appear and are shown in the language menu.

- **On account creation set user's browser language as their preferred language**: If enabled, it does what it says on the tin; otherwise, the configured default language is used. The default language will also be set if the user's browser language is not installed.

- **Display language menu**: If enabled, the language menu will be displayed in the profile menu. Users will always be able to change the language in their profile, no matter the setting. Bear in mind that some themes do not support this feature.

- **Languages on language menu**: If left empty, all the installed languages will appear in the language menu. To narrow down the number of available languages, specify a comma-separated list of locale codes.

- **Cache language menu** and **Cache all language strings**: Unless you add or remove language packs, it is recommended that you leave both settings enabled, as they cache language menu items and strings, respectively, rather than loading them dynamically.

- **Site wide locale**: The localization operations are internally driven by system locales based on the chosen language pack. If you wish to change this (which is hardly ever required), select the site-wide locale in its operating system format, such as en_US.UTF-8. The corresponding file has to be installed at the system level.

- **Excel encoding**: Moodle uses the Unicode format when downloading data in Microsoft Excel (such as in gradebook reports or log files). Leave this setting unchanged unless your teachers or learners use a dinosaur version of Excel.

- **Task status**: This entry is for information purposes only and cannot be modified. It informs you of whether installed language packs are updated regularly via scheduled tasks (more on tasks in *Chapter 15, Optimizing Moodle Performance*).

Three additional language-related settings are placed elsewhere:

- The **Full name format** option in **Site administration** | **Users** | **Permissions** | **User policies** defines how names are displayed when the full name is shown. If the **language** placeholder is entered, the format of the full name is decided by the current language pack. This way, you can cater to local sensitivities concerning first names.

- The **Alternative fullname format** option, in **Site administration** | **Users** | **Permissions** | **User policies**, is the same as **Full name format** but defines how names are shown to users with the moodle/site:viewfullnames capability.

- The **Allow extended characters in usernames** parameter, which you can see by going to **Site administration** | **General** | **Security** | **Site security settings**, removes the limitation of only using alphanumeric characters in usernames – for instance, alex.büchner.

So far, we have worked with language packs provided by Moodle and its community-based translators. Next, let's deal with customizing language strings and phrases.

Customizing languages

Every phrase, term, and string used in Moodle is represented in language files, tied to specific Moodle modules (located in the `lang` directory). There are over 30,000 (!) language strings, demonstrating the system's scale. You can change any word or phrase; for example, you may want to change Grades to Marks, Outcomes to Work indicators, Teacher to Instructor, and so on.

To customize a language file, go to **Site administration** | **General** | **Language** | **Language customization**, where you first have to choose a language to be customized. Clicking on the **Open language pack for editing** button will lead to the checkout step; this might take a few seconds. Once this has been done, you can click on the **Continue** button.

> **Important note**
>
> Moodle creates a `local` directory inside `$CFG->dataroot`, where it stores your edited phrases. Ensure you have write access to the `lang` directory to avoid error messages.

Moodle keeps a separate language file for each module. This separation is beneficial as it frees the underlying code (developed by programmers) from the localization (worked on by translators). However, the disadvantage is that you need to know where (that is, in which PHP module) the respective strings are located. However, Moodle offers a good filtering mechanism to simplify the search for strings that are to be modified.

Let's say you wish to change the term *Guest* to *Visitor*. As it is likely that the term *Guest* appears in several modules, it is safe to select all the items in the **Show strings of these components** list.

The filter criteria you can choose from includes **Customised only** for strings that have been changed in previous sessions, **Help only** for balloon help tooltips, and **Modified in this session only** for phrases that have been changed in the current session. The **Only strings containing** parameter requires the word or phrase you are looking for (in our case, *Guest*). Internally, Moodle uses string identifiers, which can also be used to search for content. Just enter the string ID in the **String identifier** textbox to do this. Once the search has been successful, the following information is shown for each string that matches the filter:

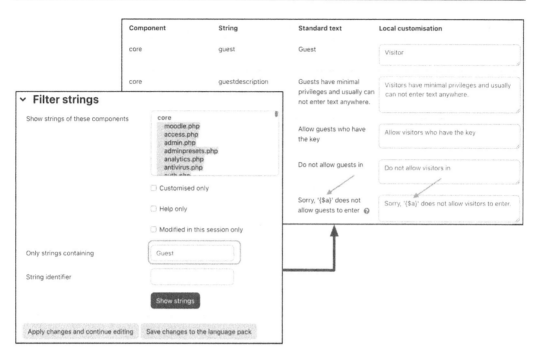

Figure 10.15 – Language customization

You might have spotted the $a parameter in the fifth phrase from the top. This is a placeholder, which is substituted on the fly; in this instance, it is substituted with the name of a course. These codes must be included in the local customization – you must keep them to avoid any problems. Some placeholders will contain a parameter, such as $a->id or $a->query.

Ensure you click the **Save changes to the language pack** button to reflect the changes on your Moodle site. These modifications will be maintained when you update your site.

You can grant users access to the **Language customization** menu for translators via the report/customlang:edit and report/customlang:view role capabilities.

There is a helpful setting called **Show origin of languages strings**, which you can see by going to **Site administration** | **Development** | **Debugging**, which is useful when you customize a language pack. If this setting is enabled, it shows the file and string identifier besides each string as the output on the screen if `?strings=1` or `&strings=1` is appended to the page URL, as demonstrated in the following sample:

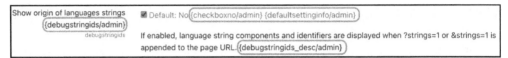

Figure 10.16 – Displaying the language string components and identifiers

If you wish to contribute translated strings to a language pack, go to the Moodle languages portal at `lang.moodle.org`. You will find information on utilizing the AMOS translation tool and the AMOS Moodle block (for details, check out `docs.moodle.org/dev/AMOS_manual`).

Now that we have localized some textual elements of the user interface, let's deal with multilingual content.

Supporting multilingual content

If some of your users deal with multilingual content, turning on the **Multi-Language Content** filter is recommended by going to **Site administration** | **Plugins** | **Filters** | **Manage filters**. The **Multi-Language Content** filter supports the `<span lang="xx"class="multilang">` tag, which lets your course designers and content creators support multiple languages in all text areas entered via the Atto editor.

The multilang HTML syntax changed a while ago and is not supported anymore. If any of your users still use the old format, you will need to run the **Multilang upgrade** admin tool (`admin/tool/multilangupgrade`) once. You will find more details on admin tools in *Chapter 17, Working with Moodle Admin Tools*.

An additional plugin, which was mentioned in the previous chapter when we dealt with availability restrictions, is **Restriction by language** (`moodle.org/plugins/availability_language`). Once the add-on has been installed, users can restrict individual activities and resources based on the selected language. In addition to the available standard restrictions, such as activity completion, course authors can also specify a language as the criteria.

This concludes this section on language-related topics in Moodle. The second part of localization is calendric information, which will be covered in the following subsection.

Calendric information

Different cultures represent calendric information – dates, times, and time zones – in different formats. The following high-level diagram illustrates the main components of a Moodle calendar:

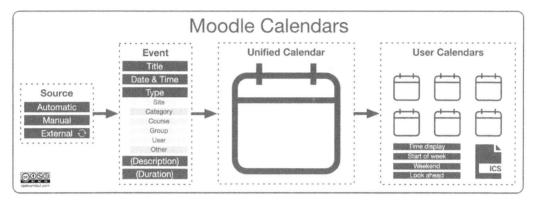

Figure 10.17 – Moodle calendars

The built-in calendar is fed by multiple sources, which can be **Automatic** (for example, assignment deadlines or grading cut-off dates), **Manual** (for instance, a fire drill announcement), or an **External** calendar feed that's updated frequently.

Each calendar entry is represented as an **Event**, which comprises several fields: title, date, time, description, duration, and type. Additional fields might make up the event, depending on the calendar type (site, category, course, group, user, or other).

The centralized **Unified Calendar** aggregates all the events in the system and acts as the source for user calendars. **User Calendars** display events in the format specified in the selected locale (language pack) and the parameters specified in the calendar settings.

> **Important note**
>
> Locales have to be installed for non-English calendars to work correctly. On Unix systems, you can check this with the `locale -a` command. Otherwise, your days in the calendar will be displayed in English.

We will configure calendars first before we deal with time zones in Moodle.

Configuring calendars

By default, Moodle formats dates and times according to the set locale for Gregorian calendars. Other calendars are supported, but they must be installed as a plugin. To do so, follow the instructions in *Chapter 8*, *Understanding Moodle Plugins*, and browse the **Calendars** section in the public plugins database at moodle.org.

Calendar settings can be changed by going to **Site administration** | **Appearance** | **Calendar**:

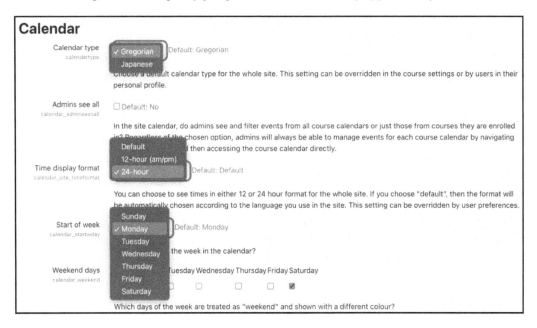

Figure 10.18 – Calendar configuration

The fields that are most relevant to calendar localization are shown in the preceding screenshot (I have installed the Japanese calendar plugin):

- **Calendar type** is the default setting for the site and its users, which can be overridden in the user's **Preference** section via the **Preferred calendar** option.

- If you need to see all the calendar events, turn on **Admins see all**; otherwise, you will only see your events.

- Times are displayed according to the selected locale; **Time display format** can be overridden by a 12-hour or a 24-hour clock.

- Different countries have different starting days for the week – for instance, in North America, the week starts on Sunday, whereas in Europe, it starts on Monday (**Start of week**).

- Not all countries use the default values of Saturday and Sunday as the weekend days. For example, in Islamic countries, the weekend is on Friday and Saturday, whereas Sunday is a normal working day. This can be specified via the **Weekend days** option.

A few more settings on this page mainly deal with look-ahead values and calendar export options. These settings are rather well explained on screen.

Configuring time zones

Moodle supports systems that span across time zones, which happens in three scenarios:

- In countries that cover more than a single time zone

- On sites that have learners from multiple countries/time zones

- In a situation where the server is hosted outside the time zone of the organization – for example, with an internet service provider

To modify the default time zone parameters, go to **Site administration | General | Location | Location settings**:

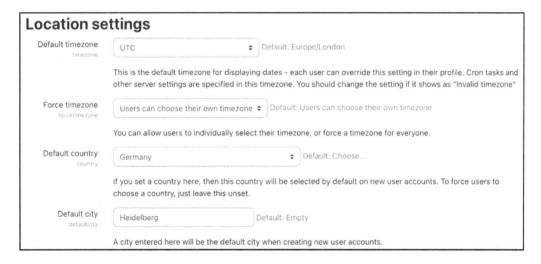

Figure 10.19 – Time zone configuration

The value selected in the **Default timezone** parameter is used throughout the system. The default value is set during installation, but this might not reflect your local time. Each learner can change this setting in their user profile unless **Force timezone** has been set. Displayed times, such as for assignment deadlines, are adjusted to the selected time zone. **Default country** and **Default city** are used for new user accounts if specified.

Every so often, rules in certain time zones (there are almost 2,300 separate ones!) change – for instance, the adjustment of daylight savings time. In this case, you should update your system as new versions of Moodle always contain the latest version of the time zone rules.

This completes this section on localization. Next, we will look at repositories and the management thereof.

Managing repositories

The **file picker** is central to most file operations in Moodle. Files can be selected from a wide range of sources, known in Moodle as **repositories**.

> **Important note**
>
> Repositories enable users to add files to courses and other locations in Moodle.

The following diagram shows which repositories are available in Moodle core and a high-level view of how they work in conjunction with the file picker:

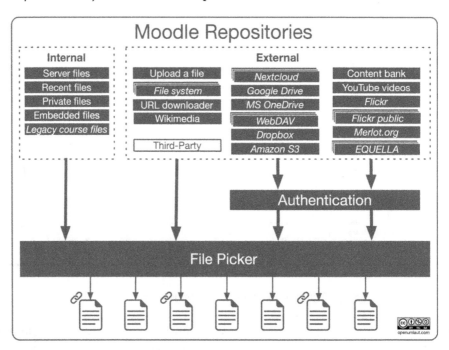

Figure 10.20 – Moodle repositories

For the sake of simplicity, we will distinguish between internal and external repositories. An **internal repository** accesses internal Moodle files. An **external repository** is located outside Moodle, on some local or remote media, in another application's data storage, or the cloud. All repositories are accessed via the file picker – some directly, others with an added layer of authentication. Files can be copied or linked, although not all repository types support linking.

You can configure Moodle repositories by going to **Site administration** | **Plugins** | **Repositories** | **Manage repositories** (the order of the repos on your system might differ from this view):

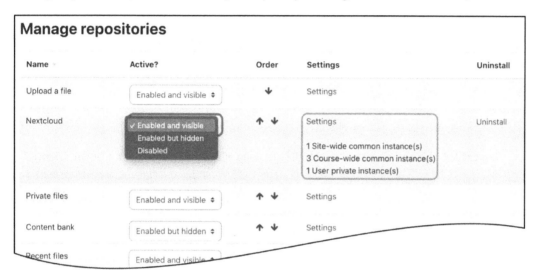

Figure 10.21 – Managing Moodle repositories

Each repository plugin has one of the following three states:

- **Enabled and visible**: The repository plugin is always available via the file picker

- **Enabled but hidden**: The repository plugin is unavailable via the file picker, but already created instances are kept

- **Disabled**: The repository is unavailable in your Moodle system, and all instances will be deleted

> **Important note**
>
> When you disable a repository plugin, its settings and all of its instances will be removed. You have the option to download any content or references to Moodle.

The order in which the repositories are listed reflects the order in which they appear in the file picker. This arrangement can be changed using the up and down arrows. A **Settings** link will be displayed for almost all repository types as soon as a repository has been enabled. Every repository has a **repository plugin name** parameter that lets you override its default name. Some repositories also have additional plugin-specific settings, which will be discussed in due course.

All repository types support **copying** files, but only some also support **linking** of files. If you wish to enable linking, make sure **Allow external links** is checked at **Site administration | Plugins | Repositories | Common repository settings**. Some institutions don't allow linking for data integrity and security reasons.

In the following subsections, we will cover the different types of internal and external repositories in more detail.

Internal repository plugins

There are several internal repository plugins to choose from:

- **Server files**: These are files on your Moodle system to which a user has access. Files are arranged in a hierarchy reflecting Moodle contexts (refer to *Chapter 2, Exploring the Moodle System*).

- **Recent files**: These are recently used and uploaded files. You can specify **Number of recent files** (the default is **50**) and a **Time limit** in the settings.

- **Private files**: These are the personal files of a user and can be accessed throughout Moodle. You can specify the user quota via the **Private file space** parameter by going to **Site administration | General | Security | Site security settings**.

- **Embedded files**: This allows users to reuse the files embedded in the current text area.

- **Legacy course files**: This gives access to files after they've been migrated from (ancient) Moodle 1.9. You can find details about this repository type at docs.moodle.org/en/ Legacy_course_files. Legacy course files are intended to be a temporary measure, and the objective is to discontinue their use once all the files have been migrated. You can find two self-explanatory settings related to legacy files at **Site administration | Plugins | Repositories | Common repository settings**: **Legacy course files in new courses** and **Allow adding to legacy course files**.

Internal repository plugins are handled by Moodle and usually don't require any configuration or management. This is not the case for their external counterparts, which we will cover next.

External repository plugins

External repository plugins will let your users add (copy, stream, or link) new files or data to your Moodle system. Content may be uploaded from your local computer, a USB pen drive, network drive, cloud storage, or external applications, including streaming services. As always, additional repository types can be installed via the plugins database at `moodle.org/plugins/?q=type:repository`.

The following table lists all the external repository plugins that are part of Moodle's core:

Plugin	Instances	Authentication	Format	Access to ...
Upload a file	Single	None	All	... files manually uploaded from your local PC or Mac. This will be used a lot by all users.
File system	Single	None	All	... subdirectories in `$CFG->dataroot/repository`.
URL download	Single	None	All	... a file via a URL link. This can be an internal or external web address.
Wikimedia	Single	None	Media	... the Wikimedia Commons platform.
Nextcloud	Multiple	OAuth 2	All	... Nextcloud's universal file access and sync platform.
Google Drive	Single	OAuth 2	All	... users' documents in Google Drive. Additionally, you can configure the default import formats from Google.
MS OneDrive	Single	OAuth 2	All	... users' documents in MS OneDrive.
WebDAV	Multiple	WebDAV	All	... a WebDAV server.
Dropbox	Single	OAuth 2	All	... a single Dropbox folder, not one for each user.
Amazon S3	Single	Access / Secret	All	... the Amazon S3 storage service, including the choice of the geographical region your data will be stored.
Content bank	Single	Internal	H5P	... local H5P content.
YouTube	Single	API key	Video	... the YouTube video platform. Videos will be streamed to Moodle, not copied.
Flickr	Single	API key / Secret	Image	... the personal accounts of Flickr, a photo sharing site. A login required when accessing it the first time.
Flickr public	Multiple	API key	Image	... the public area of the Flickr photo sharing site.
Merlot.org	Single	License key	All	... to MERLOT (Multimedia Education Resource for Learning and Online Teaching).
EQUELLA	Multiple	Secret	All	... the EQUELLA repository.

Figure 10.22 – External repository types

Some external repository types support multiple **instances**. The number of existing site-wide, course-wide, and private user instances are displayed under the plugins' **Settings** link. These can then be configured in the relevant context:

- **Site-wide instance**: You, as the administrator, can create global instances that all users in the system can then access. Site-wide instances are created as part of **Settings** when managing a plugin – for example, the **Nextcloud** repository:

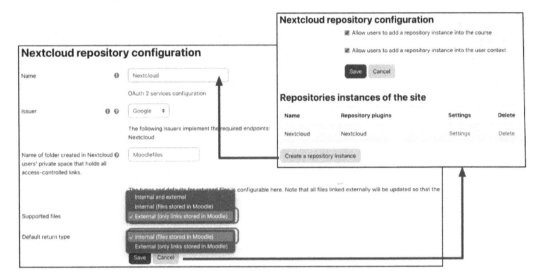

Figure 10.23 – Creating site-wide instances

- **Course-wide instance**: You can add instances via the **Repositories** link in the **More** menu if the **Allow admins to add <repository plugin> instance to a course** option is selected. Everybody enrolled in the course who has the `repository/filesystem:view` capability can access the instance in their file picker.

A popular example is the **File system** repository type, where a readable directory must be selected for each instance. A typical use case is to create a dedicated directory for file upload, which can then be accessed in a particular course. How to set up the course repository is shown in the following annotated screenshot:

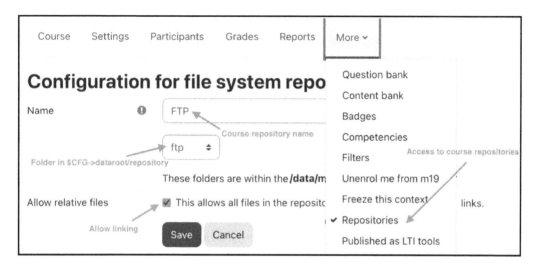

Figure 10.24 – Configuring the course repository

- **User private instance**: You can create a personal instance via the **Manage instances** link in the **Repositories** pane in **Preferences** if the **Allow admins to add <repository plugin> instance for personal use** option is selected.

You can find the following three types of **authentication** when configuring external repository plugins:

- **No authentication**: Files or content can be accessed directly without any credentials.

- **OAuth 2 services**: Access to the repository requires authentication via OAuth 2. How to configure its services was covered in the *Service provider-based authentication* section in *Chapter 5, Managing Users, Cohorts, and Authentication*. The Nextcloud screenshot (*Figure 10.23*) shows a typical setup for a repository plugin that's been done via OAuth 2.

- **Plugin-dependent**: Repository types that do not (yet) support OAuth 2 have implemented their own authentication mechanism. This might be an access/secret key pair, an API key, or simply a license.

While most external repository types support all **file formats**, some only host particular ones; for example, YouTube only provides video streams, and the content bank (currently) only stores H5P files. Streaming content repositories (for instance, YouTube and the third-party plugin for Vimeo) only appear in the file picker when initiated from Atto's audio/video icon.

Additional information on all the mentioned Moodle repositories can be found at docs.moodle.org/en/Repositories.

> **Hint**
>
> Once the repository setup has been completed, it is best to test the access from several contexts (users, sites, and courses) and ensure that no users have access to sources they shouldn't have and vice versa.

To wrap up this section, let's have a look at a fully populated file picker that supports a significant number of repository types:

Figure 10.25 – File picker with various repositories

Repositories are concerned with getting internal and external content into Moodle. To achieve the opposite – pushing content out of Moodle – you can use portfolios, which is the topic of the final section of this chapter.

Managing portfolios

According to Moodle Docs, Moodle portfolios enable data, such as forum posts or assignment submissions, to be exported to external systems. The following diagram illustrates the high-level workflow for this:

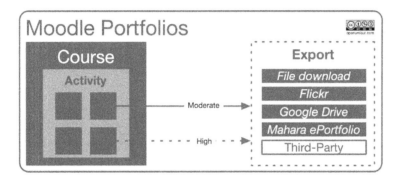

Figure 10.26 – Moodle portfolios

The data that users can export is very granular – for instance, a chat session, one glossary entry, or an individual forum post. Depending on the size of the file to be exported, the portfolio export is executed straight away (moderate file size) or queued (high transfer file size).

> **Important note**
> Supported export formats are HTML, LEAP2A, images, text, and files.

Moodle portfolios must be enabled by selecting the **Enable portfolios** parameter by going to **Site administration** | **General** | **Advanced features**. Once done, you have access to all the available portfolio plugins at **Site administration** | **Plugins** | **Portfolios** | **Manage portfolios**:

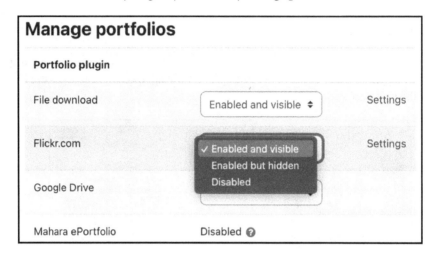

Figure 10.27 – Managing portfolios

Each portfolio has one of the following three states:

- **Enabled and visible**: The portfolio will be available throughout the system

- **Enabled but hidden**: Portfolios have to be activated to be used

- **Disabled**: The portfolio is unavailable in your Moodle system

Like repositories, each portfolio plugin has a **Name** setting, where the default plugin label can be changed. Unlike repositories, multiple instances do not exist, nor is it possible to change the order of the plugins.

The following core portfolio plugins can be activated and configured:

- **File download**: Supported export formats are HTML and LEAP2A (a specification for e-portfolio portability).

- **Flickr.com**: Follow the on screen instructions to obtain an **API key** and a **Secret string**. Authorization is required at first use.

- **Google Drive**: Follow the on screen instructions to register your site with Google using OAuth 2.0 to obtain the **Client ID** and **Secret** details. Permission has to be granted at first use. An HTML file will be created automatically in the users' **Documents** area.

- **Mahara ePortfolio**: This repository type is only available if a valid network connection to the open source e-portfolio system Mahara has been established and the **MNet authentication** plugin has been enabled. In *Chapter 19*, *Setting Up Moodle Networking*, we will briefly cover MNet.

- **Third-party**: Additional plugins can be found at `moodle.org/plugins/?q=type:portfolio` – for example, Box.

Once at least one portfolio type has been set up, users will see an **Export to portfolio** option at various places inside activities in their courses. When selecting this option, they must choose one of the existing destinations from the **Available export formats** drop-down menu. Depending on the chosen portfolio type, additional actions might have to be taken – for example, logging into the site, confirming the file type, or granting access to the external application.

Users can select which available portfolios are presented in their **Export to portfolio** list. Once they navigate to the **Configure** option in the **Portfolios** pane in **Preferences**, they have the option to hide any configured portfolio plugins.

Furthermore, when they navigate to **Transfer logs** in the **Portfolios** pane, they will be shown a list of any **Currently queued transfers** and **Previous successful transfers**. The former lists all the pending exports, which can either be continued (using the play button) or canceled (via the stop button). The latter displays details about all the recent transfers that have been made.

The three mentioned user actions – manage portfolios, export portfolios, and view transfer logs – are shown in the following screenshot arrangement:

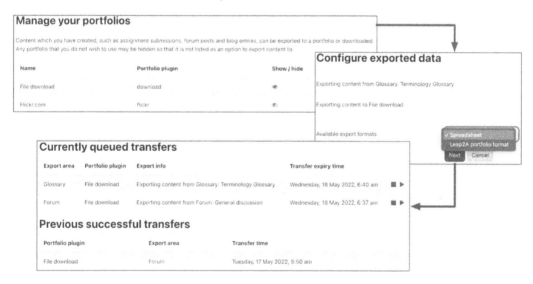

Figure 10.28 – Portfolio user actions

Some settings apply to all portfolios and they can be accessed at **Site administration | Plugins | Portfolios | Common portfolio settings**. They include two thresholds for file sizes (**Moderate transfer filesize** and **High transfer filesize**) and two for the number of database records (**Moderate transfer dbsize** and **High transfer dbsize**). If the actual values exceed the threshold values, users will be warned that the export might take some time.

> Hint
>
> Additional information on all the mentioned Moodle portfolios can be found at `docs. moodle.org/en/Portfolios`.

Portfolios are the last of the four building blocks that make up this technical configuration chapter. While not used heavily, they are a valuable feature for learners to export their data to external (portfolio) systems.

Summary

This chapter taught you how to administer any Moodle tools and features that are classified as technical.

First, we configured synchronous and asynchronous communication tools by covering chats, video conferencing (BigBlueButton), messaging (messages and notifications), and RSS feeds. Next, we dealt with various localization creation features, locales, multi-languages, calendars, and time zones. We then configured internal and external repositories to enable your users to add files to courses and other locations via the file picker. Finally, we configured portfolios to let your learners export data to external (portfolio) systems.

You should now be in a good position to approach all stakeholders in your organization and gather any relevant input to ensure that all technical components have been set up appropriately.

Now, let's move on to another exciting chapter, where we will cover mobile learning and the Moodle app.

11
Enabling Mobile Learning

In most organizations, mobile learning is becoming the norm for e-learning and forms a crucial part of curriculum delivery. Mobile learning gives learners more flexibility whenever and wherever learning takes place; it offers self-directed and independent learning, supports on-the-job training, and boosts micro-learning. Mobile devices are typically used for consumption and communication rather than authoring and administration.

Moodle has released an app for iOS and Android that allows users to interact with a Moodle system. The app is most suited for learners and supports key functionality for participants to access course content, receive notifications, upload data, monitor progress, and interact with other users. The app is an alternative to accessing Moodle via a web browser on a smartphone or tablet and has the advantage of being specifically designed for mobile usage, both online and offline.

By the end of this chapter, you will know how to prepare, configure, and customize the Moodle app. This chapter comprises the following main sections:

- **Understanding Moodle's app plans**: You will be familiar with the different subscriptions Moodle offers, including the branded mobile app.

- **Preparing to use the Moodle app**: You will learn about preparatory steps you must take before your learners can use the app. We distinguish between accessing Moodle from mobile browsers and the app. We will then go through the centrally managed settings to enable the app and configure different authentication types. We will also briefly look at installing the app on mobile devices.

- **Configuring the Moodle app**: We will look through options on how the Moodle app can be configured to provide learners with a suitable mobile learning experience, including mobile features, notifications, and the app policy.

- **Customizing the Moodle app's appearance**: You will learn how to adapt the app's look and feel, which includes changing the login logo, modifying the app's theme, and configuring app banners.

Understanding Moodle's app plans

In this section, you will learn about the different app subscriptions offered by Moodle. The choice depends on the features you require, the number of active devices, and, as always, your budget.

> **Important note**
> The Moodle iOS and Android apps are free without any in-app purchases or hidden costs.

Moodle offers four plans to support different features and restrictions:

- **Free**: Basic feature set, almost no customization options, limited to 50 active devices for push notifications per month, up to two offline courses per device, and no branding options.

- **Plus**: Full feature set, some customization options, limited to 500 active devices for push notifications per month, up to four offline courses per device, and no branding options.

- **Premium**: Full feature set and customization options, unlimited push notifications and offline courses per device, and basic branding options. Sites on moodlecloud.com and instances hosted by Moodle Partners are on this tier.

- **Branded Moodle App**: As the name suggests, its main aim is to provide you with an app where the look and feel aligns with your corporate brand. However, on top of supporting your organization's visual identity, the branded app comes with several additional advantages:

  - A separate entry in the Apple and Google Play app stores.

  - A static URL site is embedded in the app, so there is no need for your users to enter the URL of your Moodle instance when they use the app for the first time.

  - Separate hosting space is provided, and advanced privacy is ensured in Moodle's **General Data Protection Regulation** (**GDPR**)-compliant push notifications infrastructure.

  - Tracks mobile engagement analytics to better understand behaviors and improve your mobile-friendly learning experience. It also gets insights into how learners use your app with personalized access to mobile engagement data.

  The branded app is a subscription service provided by Moodle. Contact your local Premium Moodle Partner or check out moodle.com/app for more details.

You will find a full feature comparison table with up-to-date prices at apps.moodle.com.

To find out about your site's plan, navigate to **Site administration** | **General** | **Mobile app** | **Mobile app subscription**. Here are screenshots from a **Free** and a **Premium** plan, also listing all features, except the ones for the branded app:

Moodle app subscription

Name	Free
Description	Free subscription
Start date	19 July 2022

For details of the various app plans, and to access Moodle app usage

Subscription features

QR Login	Not included
This feature is configured on your site but it is not included in your Moodle app plan.	
Multimedia push notifications	Not included
Custom site listing in search results	Not included
Basic branding	Not included
Site logo	Not included
This feature is configured on your site but it is not included in your Moodle app plan.	
Active devices for push notifications	2/50
Offline access to content	?/2
Custom menu items	3/1 – Subscription limit exceeded
Disabled features	0/1
Custom strings	1/10

Notifications

For details of the various app plans, and to access Moodle app usage statistics, please visit the **Moodle Apps Portal**. Moodle app notification statistics could not be retrieved. This is most likely because mobile notifications are not yet enabled on the site. You can enable them in Site Administration / Messaging / Mobile.

Moodle app subscription

Name	Premium
Description	Premium subscription
Start date	19 July 2022

For details of the various app plans, and to access Moodle app usag statistics, please visit the Moodle Apps Portal.

Subscription features

QR Login	Included
Multimedia push notifications	Included
Custom site listing in search results	Included
Basic branding	Included
Site logo	Included
Active devices for push notifications	Unlimited
Offline access to content	Unlimited
Custom menu items	Unlimited
Disabled features	Unlimited
Custom strings	Unlimited

Figure 11.1 – Moodle app plans

We will describe the features of the **Premium** plan in this chapter as they cover all customizations that administrators can carry out. Before we start, some preparatory steps must be undertaken, as explained in the following section.

Preparing to use the Moodle app

Before users can access learning content, cooperate with others, or monitor progress from a mobile device, there are several things to consider. First, a decision must be made on accessing the LMS, either from a mobile web browser or a dedicated app. This chapter focuses on the mobile app, which has to be enabled centrally. Second, users must download and install the app before the first login. And third, users must authenticate via the mobile app. This section will cover all of these items, starting with a short introduction about ways to access the Moodle app from a mobile device.

Accessing Moodle from mobile devices

Generally, there are two ways that learners can access Moodle via a mobile device—directly via a web browser on a cell phone or a tablet, or via Moodle's app for iOS and Android.

The **web browser** view is effectively the same as we have seen throughout the book, only it is optimized via responsive design for smaller screen sizes. There are three main arguments relating to using Moodle via a mobile browser—users have the same functionality available as on a desktop device, the handling is identical, and users won't have to install an extra app on their mobile device.

The **Moodle app** provides an alternative view of the same data, and interactions have been optimized for mobile usage. Furthermore, offline usage and synchronization are supported, indicated by a little cloud symbol. Another advantage of the mobile app over the browser view is the support of push notifications, which we have all become accustomed to.

The following two screenshots show the difference between the two usage types when accessing the same dashboard, with the browser view on the left and the app view on the right:

Figure 11.2 – Browser view versus app view

The following diagram shows a simplified process of what happens when Moodle is accessed from a mobile device (details for web browser access are at the top, and for app access at the bottom):

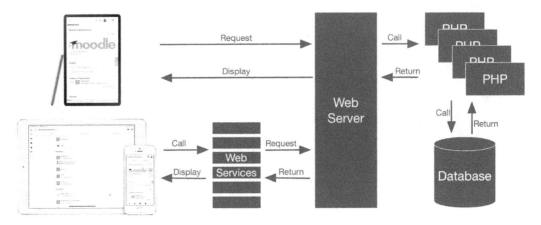

Figure 11.3 – Accessing Moodle via the browser and the app

Let's go through the preceding diagram from left to right and back again. When a user makes requests via the web interface, the browser passes the request to the web server, which calls the responsible PHP module. The PHP module calls the database with an action (a query, update, insert, or delete operation), which returns the requested data. Based on this information, the PHP module returns data (usually in HTML or JavaScript) to the web server, which passes the information to be displayed back to the user's browser.

When accessing a Moodle instance via the app, the process is precisely the same except for the first step, which involves calling web services requesting data from the web server. The same applies to the returning information, which is also passed through web services. Web services are the standard communication protocol between web and mobile applications. You will find more information on this topic in *Chapter 18, Integrating External Systems Using Web Services*.

We will be exclusively focusing on the Moodle app in this chapter. Before your learners can use the app, however, the following prerequisites must be fulfilled:

- App usage must be enabled on your site
- Users must download and install the app on their mobile devices
- Users must authenticate via the app

We will run through all three steps, starting with the app's enablement.

Enabling the app

The process of enabling the Moodle app to interact with your Moodle site has been greatly simplified. Go to **Site administration** | **General** | **Advanced features** and tick the **Enable web services for mobile devices** option, which also activates the **Enable web services** setting on the same page if it isn't already ticked:

Figure 11.4 – Enabling the Moodle app

That's it. No other steps are required. Well, almost. You should also enable the **Mobile** notification option, which you can find under **Site administration** | **General** | **Messaging** | **Notification settings**. We will cover the settings of the mobile notifications plugin later in the app configuration section.

> **Important note**
> It is highly recommended that you enable HTTPS with a valid certificate. The Moodle app will always try to use a secured connection first.

Now that the app usage has been enabled, let's look at how your users can install the app on their snazzy mobile devices.

Installing the Moodle app

Your learners must download and install the app from Apple's App Store or Google Play. There is no charge for the app. Screenshots of both apps on the Apple App Store (on a tablet) and Google Play (on a phone) are shown as follows:

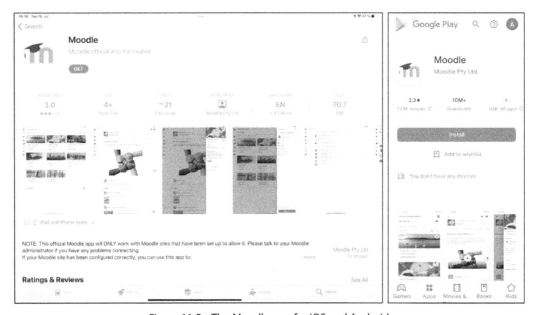

Figure 11.5 – The Moodle app for iOS and Android

To install the app, users need to follow the usual steps on their mobile devices (starting with **GET** on iOS and **Install** on Android).

Note there is also a Moodle Workplace app, which is based on the official Moodle app. It has the same functionality plus some extra features to cater for Workplace-specific features such as programs and teams.

> **Important note**
> The Moodle app only works with Moodle. The Moodle Workplace app only works with Moodle Workplace.

Don't be discouraged by negative reviews since almost all poor feedback comes from users who expected the app to work standalone without access to an existing Moodle system. This misunderstanding leads nicely to the next enablement step—accessing your Moodle system via the app and authentication.

Authenticating on the Moodle app

Once the app has been installed and launched for the first time, each user must authenticate with the Moodle instance. Moodle supports three different login types, which have to be selected by the administrator at **Site administration | General | Mobile App | Mobile authentication,** as in the following screenshot:

Mobile authentication

Please note that some features may be restricted depending on your Moodle app subscription. For details, visit the **Moodle Apps Portal.** ✕

Type of login		
tool_mobile | typeoflogin	Via the app	Default: Via the app
	✓ Via a browser window (for SSO plugins)	
	Via an embedded browser (for SSO plugins)	

If the site uses a SSO authentication method, then select via a browser window or via an embedded browser. ...better user experience, though it doesn't work with all SSO plugins.

QR code access
tool_mobile | qrcodetype

Access via QR code disabled
QR code with site URL
✓ QR code with automatic login   Default: QR code with automatic login

A QR code can be provided for mobile app users to scan. This can be used to fill in the site URL, or where the site is secured using HTTPS, to automatically log the user in without having to enter their username and password.

QR authentication key duration
tool_mobile | qrkeyttl

10   minutes ⇕   Default: 10 minutes

The length of time for which a QR code for automatic login is valid.

URL scheme
tool_mobile | forcedurlscheme

moodlemobile   Default: moodlemobile

If you want to allow only your custom branded app to be opened via a browser window, then specify its URL scheme here. If you want to allow only the official app, then set the default value. Leave the field empty if you want to allow any app.

Minimum app version required
tool_mobile | minimumversion

Default: Empty

If an app version is specified (3.8.0 or higher), any users using an older app version will be prompted to upgrade their app before being allowed access to the site.

Minimum time between auto-
login requests
tool_mobile |
autologinmintimebetweenreq

6 minutes ⇕   Default: 6 minutes

The minimum time between auto-login requests from the mobile app. If app users are frequently asked to enter their credentials when viewing content embedded from the site, then set a lower value.

Save changes

Figure 11.6 – Authentication types

The **Type of login** field provides the following three options:

- **Via the app** (default): This is the default authentication mechanism that applies to all manual accounts.

- **Via a browser window (for SSO plugins)**: If your site uses an **SSO** authentication method, such as **Microsoft Active Directory (MS-AD)**, **Lightweight Directory Access Protocol (LDAP)**, or **Open Authorization (OAuth)**, this mechanism opens a separate browser window where the login credentials have to be provided.

- **Via an embedded browser (for SSO plugins)**: This is effectively the same as the previous option but provides a better user experience. However, not all authentication plugins will work in an embedded browser—for instance, when JavaScript popups are required.

QR code access is an alternative way to let users access the site by scanning the matrix barcode. QR login is unavailable on the free plan. This mode can be configured with a site URL (users must enter their credentials) or via automatic login. The **QR authentication key duration** parameter determines how long the QR shown in the user profile is valid. If the **QR authentication same as IP check** setting is ticked, users are forced to use the same network to generate and scan a QR code for login. This added security measure should remain enabled unless users report problems:

Figure 11.7 – QR login

If your organization uses a custom branded app and the **Type of login** field is set to one of the two SSO types, then the **URL scheme** option may be set. This will result in only the custom-branded app working for the site, whereas the official Moodle app will not work.

The **Minimum app version required** option can usually be left empty and should only be set if you want or need to force users to update to an up-to-date version of the Moodle app.

The **Minimum time between auto-login requests** parameter lets you specify a threshold for creating an auto-login key for the current user. The security measure will nag users with their login credentials if this threshold is set too high.

The three different login types will show up for users differently, as shown in the following sequence of screenshots:

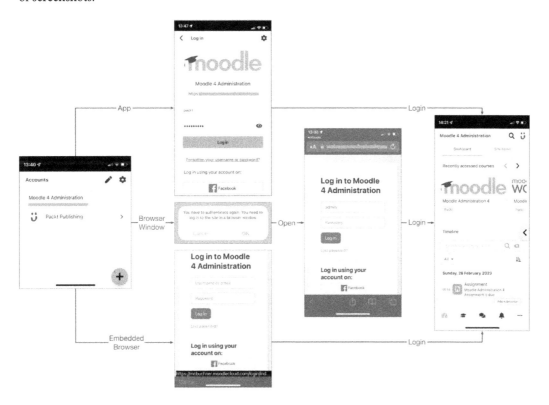

Figure 11.8 – Different mobile login types and authentication

During the initial launch, the URL must be entered; on subsequent launches, this will be pre-filled. The same applies to the login credentials unless the administrator has selected the **Forced log out** setting in **Site administration** | **General** | **Mobile App** | **Mobile features**. No URL has to be entered on the branded app since it is hardcoded.

Logging in via the app displays a login window as part of the app. When logging in via a browser, a notification will be displayed telling the user that the default browser on the mobile device will be opened before the redirection takes place. Once the credentials have been entered, Moodle redirects the user back to the app. The embedded browser view looks the same, but no external browser will be opened.

This concludes the section on the preparatory steps you must take before the Moodle app can be used. We first discussed two options for accessing your Moodle system from a mobile device before focusing on the mobile app for iOS and Android. Next, we enabled the app and configured authentication. We also briefly covered the installation of the app on users' devices. Now that these steps have been completed, we will customize the app from within Moodle.

Configuring the Moodle app

The beauty of the Moodle app is that it can be customized "from the outside"—that is, by configuration only. In this chapter, you will learn how to tailor the app to your learners' needs. The three main areas of customization are as follows:

- Mobile features
- Mobile notifications
- Mobile app policy

It is also possible to extend the mobile app's functionality via development, which is beyond the scope of this book since programming skills are needed. More details can be found at `docs.moodle.org/dev/Mobile_support_for_plugins`. Let's get started with the mobile app features.

Configuring mobile features

The Moodle app lets you customize some basic features under **Site administration | General | Mobile App | Mobile features**, as shown in the following screenshot:

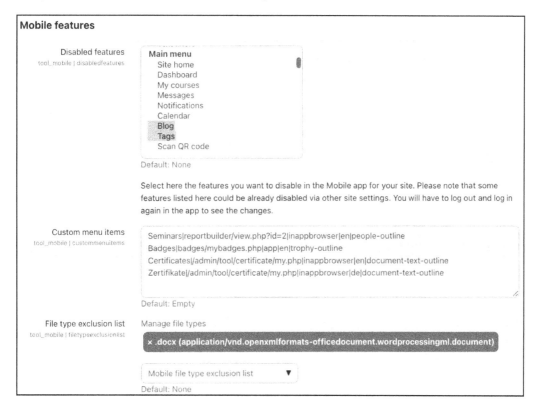

Figure 11.9 – Mobile features

The **Disabled features** list lets you remove features from the mobile app. It is recommended that you hide any features that are not being used to reduce the app's complexity and improve your learners' learning experience.

The opposite of removing features is adding items to the app's main menu. These items have to be specified with **Custom menu items**. The format of each entry is as follows (all entries have to be separated by the pipe symbol):

```
item text|link|opening method|[language code]|[icon]
```

`item text` is the label that will appear in the app. The `link` parameter sets the URL that the user will be directed to. The app supports four different **opening methods**:

- **app**: For linking to items supported by the app. For instance, the link to **Badges** is supported since badges can also be accessed via the user's profile.

- **inappbrowser**: For opening the link in a browser without leaving the app.

- **browser**: For opening the link in the device default browser outside the app.

- **embedded**: For displaying the link in an **iframe** on a new page on the app (no scrolling possible).

The optional **language** field only displays the item to users of the specified language. The link to certificates has also been provided in our sample in German.

The optional `icon` field is the name of an icon from `ionicons.com`.

The following is a screenshot from the Moodle app, where the site blog and tags have been removed, and the three custom menu items have been added. The before-and-after screenshots demonstrate the impact of custom menu changes:

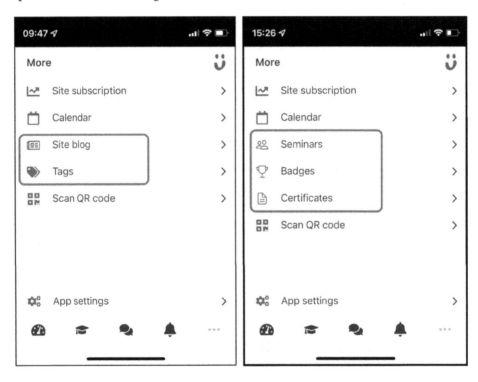

Figure 11.10 – Mobile custom menus

The **File exclusion list** setting lets you specify for which files a warning should be displayed if learners attempt to open them from within a course.

The app's standard terminology is aimed at educational establishments, which might not suit your setting. The **Custom language strings** setting lets you modify strings used in the app. For instance, you might want to change the term student to learner or course to module, as in the following screenshot:

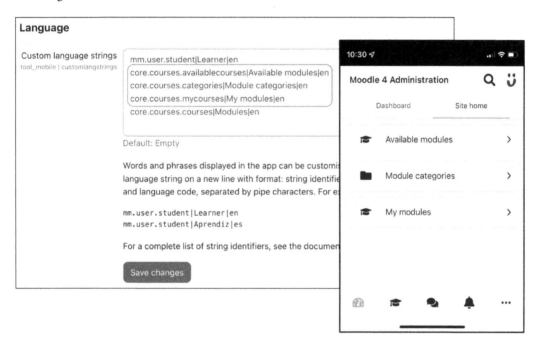

Figure 11.11 – Custom language strings

Words and phrases displayed in the app can be customized by adding a separate line for each entry using the following notation:

```
string identifier|custom string|language code
```

A complete list of **string identifiers** can be found under the *Custom language strings* section at docs. moodle.org/en/Moodle_app_guide_for_admins. **custom string** is the replacement text for the language set via the **language code**.

Ensure you sync the app to apply the configured changes (**Site administration** | **Menu** | **App settings** | **Synchronization**).

We already mentioned the built-in push notifications mechanism that should be activated, which we will cover in the following subsection.

Configuring mobile notifications

The Moodle app supports push notifications for both mobile platforms. We already enabled mobile notifications in **Site administration | General | Messaging | Notification settings** when we activated the app in the first section. To configure mobile notifications, navigate to the form shown in the following screenshot via **Site administration | General | Messaging | Mobile**:

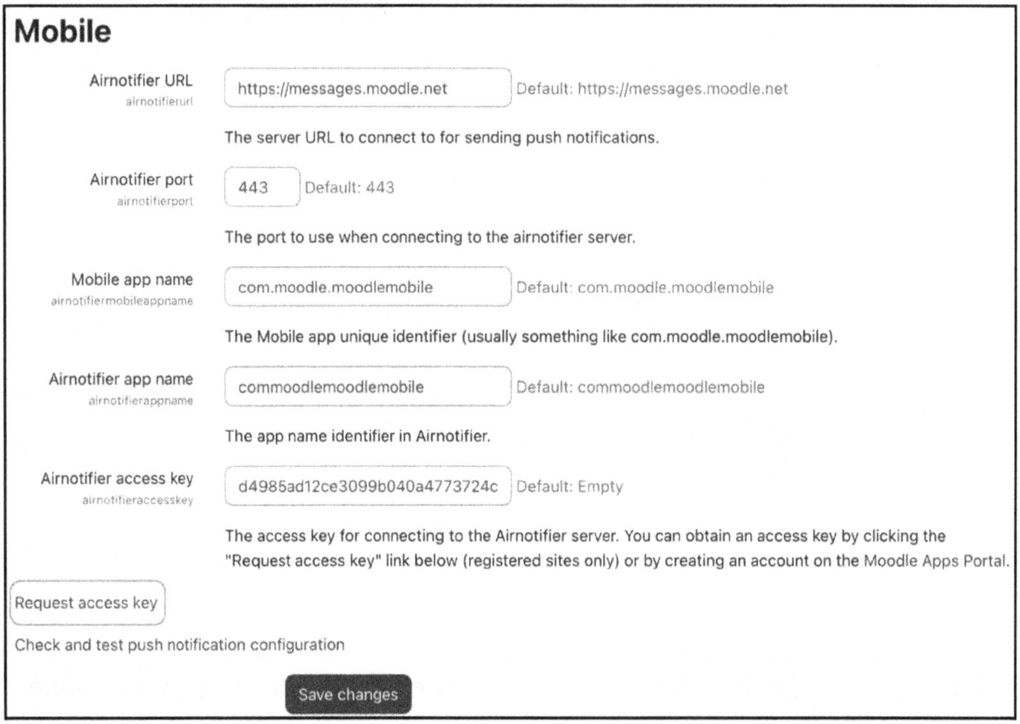

Figure 11.12 – Mobile messaging settings

The default values connect to the public Moodle messaging server. All you need to do is click on **Request access key** (the link at the bottom), which requires your site to be registered on the Moodle app portal at `apps.moodle.com`.

Select the **Check and test push notification configuration** link to test your mobile messaging configuration. You will see a checklist indicating the statuses of all required steps, like the one in the following screenshot:

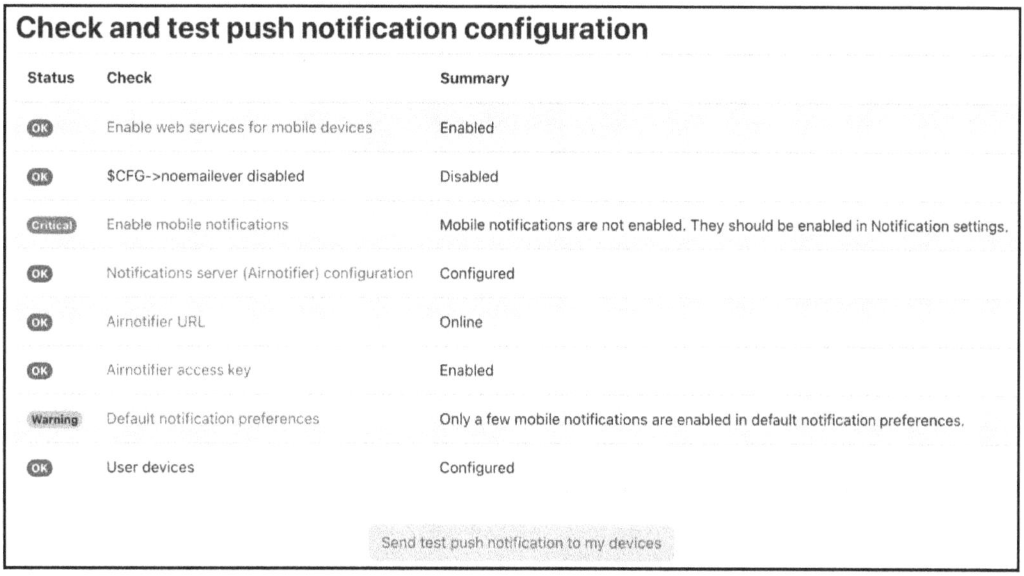

Check and test push notification configuration

Status	Check	Summary
OK	Enable web services for mobile devices	Enabled
OK	$CFG->noemailever disabled	Disabled
Critical	Enable mobile notifications	Mobile notifications are not enabled. They should be enabled in Notification settings.
OK	Notifications server (Airnotifier) configuration	Configured
OK	Airnotifier URL	Online
OK	Airnotifier access key	Enabled
Warning	Default notification preferences	Only a few mobile notifications are enabled in default notification preferences.
OK	User devices	Configured

Send test push notification to my devices

Figure 11.13 – Mobile messaging check and test push notification

There are eight items on the checklist:

- **Enable web services for mobile devices**: We already did this at the start of the section
- **$CFG->noemailever disabled**: The configuration setting to disable sending any notifications and messages mustn't be enabled
- **Enable mobile notifications**: We enabled these at the start of the section; on my system, they were only turned off during configuration
- **Notifications server (Airnotifier) configuration**: We just went through its configuration
- **Airnotifier URL**: Indication of whether the messaging server is live or not
- **Airnotifier access key**: Again, we just requested this
- **Default notification preferences**: We dealt with those in the *Messaging* subsection in *Chapter 10, Configuring Technical Features*, where you can enable and lock all or some notification types in the **Mobile** channel
- **User devices**: At least one user must have logged in to your site from a mobile device

Once there are no critical statuses, you can send a test push notification to the devices that connect to the site, as illustrated in the following screenshot. Ensure that your devices are connected to the internet and that the mobile app is not open since push notifications are usually only displayed when received in the background:

Figure 11.14 – Push notification test

The following is a schematic overview of how push notifications work. **Apple Push Notification service (APNS)** and **Google Cloud Messaging** are the respective gateways for relaying push notifications on iOS and Android devices:

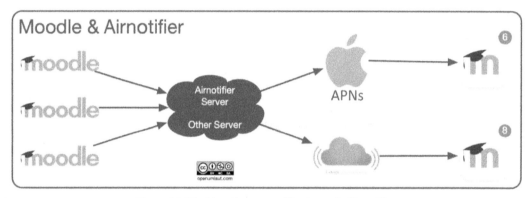

Figure 11.15 – Moodle app notifications via Airnotifier

Moodle's messaging server is a public Airnotifier system and, therefore, carries a (small) degree of risk. This approach will not be acceptable for some privacy-conscious organizations, so it is possible to set up your own notification infrastructure, which involves setting up a local Airnotifier server. You will find instructions on how to do this and links to related resources at docs.moodle.org/en/Moodle_app_notifications.

Whether you use a public or a local notification server, you should let your users know which data the messaging facility transfers, which should be part of your mobile app policy, covered in the following subsection.

Configuring the mobile app policy

When a user logs in for the first time, any specified site policies must be consented to. The same applies when a new version of a site policy has been released. This data protection feature works the same on the web version and in the app of Moodle. For more details on data privacy, refer to *Chapter 14, Complying with Data Protection Regulations*.

In **Site administration** | **General** | **Mobile app** | **Mobile settings**, you configure what the user will see when navigating to the **About** page in the app. If the **App policy URL** field is left empty (default), the main site policy will be shown; if set, as in the following screenshot, the specified page will be listed:

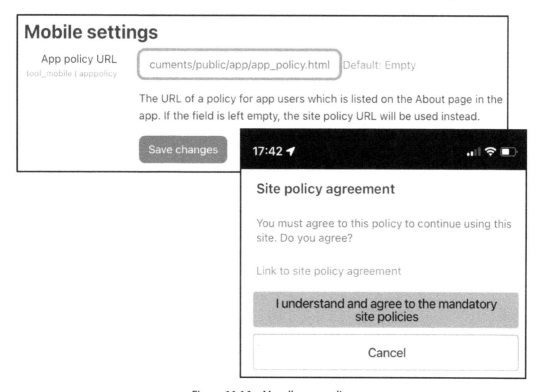

Figure 11.16 – Moodle app policy

This concludes the section on customizing the Moodle app, which dealt with various mobile features, setting up mobile notifications, and configuring the mobile app policy.

Next up is the customization of the app's look and feel.

Customizing the Moodle app's appearance

Most organizations use the app as is, but some wish to change the app's look and feel. The beauty of the Moodle app is that its appearance can also be adapted from the outside—that is, from Moodle itself. The following three aspects can be adjusted:

- The app's login logo

- The app's look and feel via remote themes

- The app banner behavior when accessing the site via a mobile browser

Changing the app's login logo

The app's login screen displays the standard Moodle logo. If the site's logo has been configured at **Site administration** | **Appearance** | **Logos**, it will be shown on the user's login screen. To compare the two versions, check out the following screenshots:

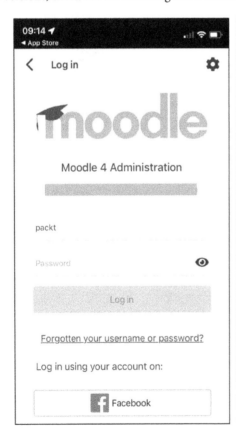

Figure 11.17 – Moodle app login logo (standard and custom)

Bear in mind that this feature is only available on the **Pro** and **Premium** app plans, respectively.

Changing the app's look and feel via remote themes

The app makes use of **remote themes**; that is, the styles are specified elsewhere—in Moodle itself—and loaded dynamically to each mobile device.

A single CSS file must be provided at **Site administration | General | Mobile app | Mobile appearance**, which overrides the styles from the default theme; your new CSS file should contain the styles you wish to modify. Once the CSS file has been created, load it to a location where it can be accessed from your Moodle server. This can either be a public URL or locally in your Moodle instance, ideally in your custom theme or inside a local plugin. In the following screenshot, a new `packt.css` file has been created and uploaded to our `theme` folder:

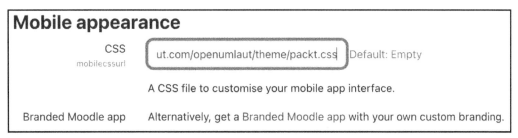

Figure 11.18 – Mobile appearance

Here is a sample CSS file that only changes a single style to modify the app toolbar's background color to orange:

```
/* Change toolbar background color to orange */
.toolbar-background
{
  background: orange;
}
```

How do you know which elements to style in your mobile CSS file? For basic customization, check out `moodledev.io/general/app/customisation/remote-themes`, where some common customizations are described. For more serious app theme development, you will need to create an environment where you can run the app in a browser—for instance, Chromium. Using the browser's developer tools allows you to inspect the HTML and identify styles you wish to change.

> **Important note**
>
> You must clear the cache and restart the app to apply new styles.

As with the custom CSS for the browser version of Moodle, there is virtually no limit to what can be done in the mobile CSS. To tweak your app further, you'd best involve an experienced Moodle designer or a Premium Moodle Partner.

Configuring app banners

App banners let users know that a dedicated mobile app is available when accessing the site using a mobile browser. In the following screenshot, you can see two app banners for the Moodle iOS app—the one on the left is displayed when the app has not yet been installed; the one on the right is displayed when the app has been installed:

Figure 11.19 – App banners in action

App banners are disabled by default. To activate them, tick the **Enable app banners** checkbox at **Site administration | General | Mobile app | Mobile appearance**. Bear in mind that currently in iOS, app banners are only shown in the Safari web browser. App banners for Android devices are only displayed on the Chrome browser when the app is not installed and when the conditions for its engagement heuristic have been met.

If you are using a branded mobile app, you need to provide a **unique identifier** for the iOS and Android app; if you are using the Moodle app, the settings may be left at their defaults, as shown in the following screenshot:

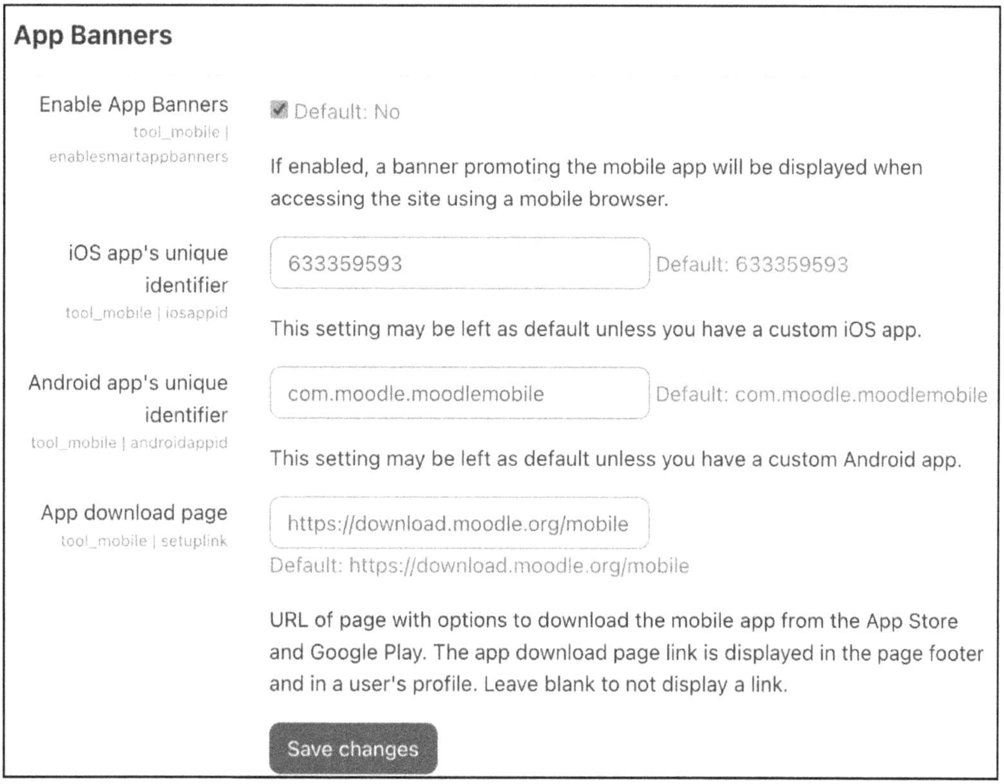

App Banners

Enable App Banners
tool_mobile |
enablesmartappbanners

☑ Default: No

If enabled, a banner promoting the mobile app will be displayed when accessing the site using a mobile browser.

iOS app's unique
identifier
tool_mobile | iosappid

633359593

Default: 633359593

This setting may be left as default unless you have a custom iOS app.

Android app's unique
identifier
tool_mobile | androidappid

com.moodle.moodlemobile

Default: com.moodle.moodlemobile

This setting may be left as default unless you have a custom Android app.

App download page
tool_mobile | setuplink

https://download.moodle.org/mobile

Default: https://download.moodle.org/mobile

URL of page with options to download the mobile app from the App Store and Google Play. The app download page link is displayed in the page footer and in a user's profile. Leave blank to not display a link.

Save changes

Figure 11.20 – App banners configuration

The last setting in the **App Banners** section is labeled **App download page** and indicates the URL displayed in the page footer and the user's profile. Creating a dedicated page on your website that links to your app's iOS and Android downloads is highly recommended if you have a branded Moodle app.

This concludes the section on customizing the app's look and feel, which covered the login logo, remote themes, and app banners.

Summary

This chapter taught you how to prepare, configure, and customize the Moodle app.

First, we familiarized ourselves with the different subscription plans Moodle offers, including the branded mobile app.

Next, we went through the required preparatory steps before your learners can use the app. We reviewed the settings to enable the app and configured different authentication types. We also briefly looked at installing the app on mobile devices.

Then, we configured the app to provide learners with a suitable mobile learning experience, which included mobile features, notifications, and the app policy.

Last, we customized the app's appearance, adapting the app's look and feel by changing the login logo, modifying the app's theme, and configuring app banners.

The paid app version has significantly more features than the free version, so it is well worth budgeting for the annual fee if your organization encourages mobile learning. If e-learning is a central part of your learning culture, you might consider the branded app. Another feature of the deluxe version is the provision of usage statistics, which brings us to the next chapter's topic: reporting and analytics.

12

Gaining Insights through Moodle Reporting and Analytics

Moodle collects usage data from various activities from when users log in until they log out. This data can be utilized for a range of reporting and analytics activities, all of which will be dealt with in this chapter.

To get an overview of the topics that will be covered, have a look at the following diagram:

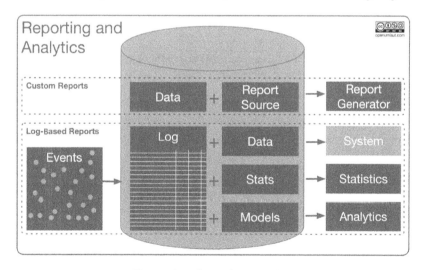

Figure 12.1 – Reporting overview

There are two types of reports in Moodle: **custom reports** created with the report generator and **log-based reports**, hardcoded in Moodle.

The first part of this chapter will provide an overview of the **report generator** and cover data sources, report building, report audiences, and schedules. We will also briefly cover a more technical third-party report generator: Configurable reports.

The second part of this chapter deals with log-based reports. After a detailed overview of the underlying **Moodle logging framework** and its components, events, and log stores, you will learn how to interact with Moodle logs.

Finally, we will deal with two more reporting techniques that use logs as their basis: **Moodle statistics** and **Moodle analytics**.

We won't cover **system reports** in this chapter – that is, reports that deal with a particular topic; they will be dealt with when the relevant topics are covered. For instance, backups reports will be described in *Chapter 16, Avoiding Sleepless Nights – Moodle Backup and Restore*.

In this chapter, we will cover the following topics:

- Creating custom reports with the report generator
- Understanding Moodle's logging framework
- Interacting with log-based reports
- Gathering statistics
- Making predictions with Moodle Analytics

OK, let's start with the first part of this chapter and create custom reports with the report generator.

Creating custom reports with the report generator

The **report generator** was initially implemented as part of Moodle Workplace, Moodle's powerful and flexible learning platform for corporate training and workplace learning. Due to its popularity in Moodle's commercial edition and its applicability across sectors, it was decided to port the report generator to Moodle 4. The stripped-down version has been adopted by Moodle and has proven to be a valuable addition to creating custom reports.

So, before we deal with data sources and report building, let's explore the report generator.

Exploring the report generator

You might not have realized it, but you have already used reports in the previous 11 chapters! How? Well, Moodle has done something very smart: it uses internal reports for key features in Moodle. For example, the list of certificate templates in the *Skills and incentives* section in *Chapter 9, Configuring Educational Features*, is a report. The report on config changes? You guessed it, yet another report. Every time you see a table list view in any Moodle tool, it is likely to be a built-in system report.

Moodle distinguishes between two types of reports:

- **Internal reports**: Embedded, predefined reports that are part of Moodle. Internal reports cannot be modified or removed since Moodle relies on them.

- **Custom reports**: User-generated reports made available to other users.

This section exclusively deals with custom reports, so let's see how Moodle's report builder works. The following diagram illustrates the high-level elements of the reporting workflow:

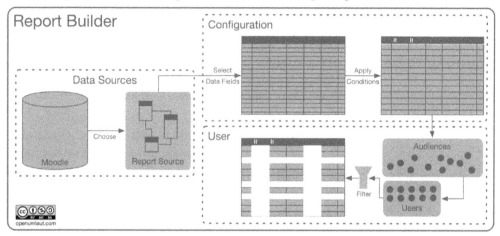

Figure 12.2 – Report builder workflow

Moodle stores its data relevant to reporting in the **Moodle database**. External data sources might be added in future versions, but at the time of writing, this is the only data source available.

The most flexible reporting tool would let you select individual fields from every entity in the underlying database. However, this would require users to be familiar with the entire database model, which contains well over 100 tables and even more relationships among them. Instead, Moodle offers some report sources to simplify the usage of the report builder.

> **Important note**
> A **report source** contains a predefined set of fields and relationships available when building a report.

Based on the selected record source, a certain amount of data will be available, which can be reduced by the following mechanisms: **Selecting data fields** lets the report creator decide which columns are being made available – for example, student name, course name, and completion status. **Applying conditions** lets the report creator decide which rows will be made available – for instance, all records from a particular faculty. Access to reports is granted via audiences – for example, all users with the Manager role or all users who are members of a particular cohort.

The report viewer can then reduce the amount of data further via filters. A **filter,** which has to be configured by the report creator, allows you to select one or more criteria – for instance, by course category or by country.

> **Important note**
> A report isn't static; it is an interactive view of your data.

The following subsections are dedicated to each building block of the reporting workflow. Let's start with the first part of the diagram: data and report sources.

Selecting data and report sources

In this subsection, we will deal with the input options for the report builder – you will learn what they are and when to use each option.

The database is the underlying **data source** where Moodle stores its data. Courses, users, course completions, grades, and other data – such as information about learning resources added by authors, forum posts contributed to by learners, and system settings configured by the administrator – are mostly stored in the database.

A **report source** implicitly defines which elements (tables and relationships) of the data source will be used in a report. The set of available report sources includes data such as user profile information, course data, or cohort membership. Additional report sources can be created by Moodle developers programmatically, and the number of record sources is expected to go up in upcoming releases.

Before exploring the report builder, ensure the **Enable custom reports** setting is enabled under **Site administration | General | Advanced features**.

Let's look at the report sources available in Moodle to date. You can manage reports via **Site administration | Reports | Report builder | Custom reports**, where you will see a list of available reports – actually, what you will see is a report. A report of reports! In our example instance, we have already created some reports, as shown here:

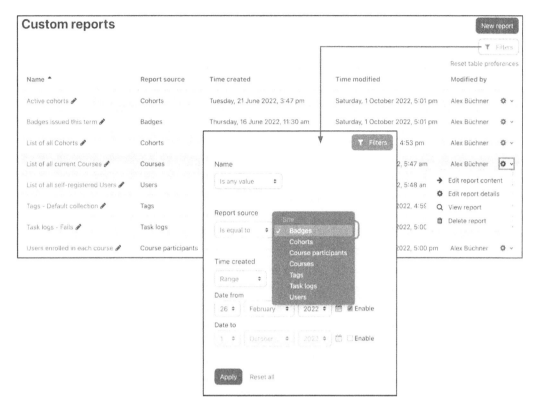

Figure 12.3 – Custom reports and filters

The self-explanatory fields shown in the report table are **Name**, **Report source**, **Time created**, **Time modified**, and **Modified by**. The standard actions available are **Edit report content**, **Edit report details**, **View report**, and **Delete report**. There are filters available on the right-hand side that let you limit the number of reports shown by **Name**, **Report Source**, and **Time created**.

> **Important note**
> Each report has one report source.

The selected report source cannot be changed once a report has been created. To use a different report source, a new report must be created.

Select the **New report** button on the **Reports** page to create a new report. You will then be greeted with a pop-up screen, as shown here:

Figure 12.4 – Creating a new report

A report contains the following two compulsory settings: **Name** (displayed whenever the report is made available to users) and **Report source** (defines where the data for the report will come from). The following report sources are currently available in Moodle:

- **Badges**: Badge details linked to recipients (users) and courses
- **Cohorts**: Cohort data and user membership details
- **Course participants**: Courses, users, and their enrolments and course completions
- **Courses**: Course and category details
- **Tags**: Tags and tag categories
- **Task logs**: Data regarding scheduled and ad hoc tasks
- **Users**: User details

The following report sources are already in the pipeline and are likely to be available by the time you read this book: Notes, Blogs, Groups, Comments, and Files. Existing report sources may also be extended by adding more data fields, relations to other entities, conditions, and filters.

There are two more settings when creating a new report that require some attention:

- **Include default setup**: When enabled, the report will already be populated with several predefined columns, conditions, and filters. When you get started, it is recommended that you leave this option ticked since it simplifies the process of building reports, which we will cover next.
- **Remove any duplicate rows**: When enabled, any duplicate rows will be removed from the report.

By default, there is no limit to the number of reports you or anybody with the `reportbuilder:edit` (edit your own custom reports) or `reportbuilder:editall` (edit all custom reports) capabilities can create. If you need to restrict the number of custom reports, go to **Site administration | Reports | Report builder | Custom report settings** and adjust the **Custom reports limit** setting accordingly.

Another setting on the same screen that potentially improves performance is **Custom reports live editing**. If disabled, the preview of data while editing the report will be deactivated; otherwise, it will be kept up to date:

Custom report settings

Custom reports limit	0	Default: 0
customreportslimit		
	The number of custom reports may be limited for performance reasons. If set to zero, then there is no limit.	
Custom reports live editing	☑ Default: Yes	
customreportsliveediting		
	If enabled, users can view report data while editing the report. This may be disabled for performance reasons.	

Save changes

Figure 12.5 – Custom report settings

When you **Save** the report, you will be redirected to the actual report builder, which we will cover next.

Building reports

In this subsection, we will deal with the various facilities the report builder has to offer. You will learn what these are and how to apply them in real-world scenarios.

The report generator allows you to build and customize reports with drag and drop, instant preview, inline column editing, grouping, and aggregation. The following annotated screenshot shows the key elements of the Moodle report generator:

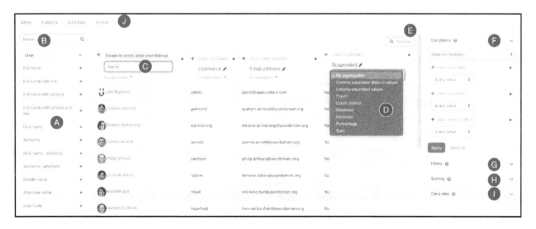

Figure 12.6 – The report builder interface

The following actions are available in the report generator:

- **A – Data fields panel**: List of data fields, grouped by entities
- **B – Data fields panel**: Live search fields
- **C – Preview panel**: Inline editing of column names and headings
- **D – Preview panel**: For selecting the field aggregation method
- **E – Preview panel**: Preview toggle
- **F – Settings panel: Conditions**
- **G – Settings panel: Filters**
- **H – Settings panel: Sorting**
- **I – Settings panel: Card view**
- **J – Report builder menu**: Access to report tabs

For the database boffins among you, it might be helpful to map the report elements to their SQL counterparts:

- Selected data fields: **SELECT … FROM …**
- Conditions: **WHERE**
- Aggregation and grouping: **GROUP BY**
- Sorting: **ORDER BY**

Now that you have had a first glimpse of the report creation interface, let's look closely at the various elements, which can be grouped into two categories: configuring fields (columns) and configuring settings (rows).

Configuring fields (columns)

This subsection deals with available options to customize the columns in a report.

In the left-hand side panel of the Moodle report generator, you will see all available fields for the selected report source, which have been grouped into entities. Each entity can be expanded or collapsed for better usability. You can also search for field entries to limit the number of displayed items. These items have been labeled **A** and **B** in the previous screenshot.

To add columns to the report, click on the selected field on the left list. The column will be added automatically as the rightmost column in the table. You can then rearrange the column order via the standard **Move** handle. To remove a column, click on the standard delete icon.

Two field types are available that can be added as columns to a report:

- **Text fields**: For example, surname, department, or course name
- **Image fields**: For example, user picture or badge image

Most text fields reflect a value from the underlying Moodle database. However, some text fields are preprocessed by the report generator to support additional functionality:

- **Hyperlinked text fields**: Mainly to directly view data entries – for example, to a user profile or a course
- **Calculated text fields**: To provide a numeric value – for instance, the number of courses in a category
- **Grouped text fields**: To provide multiple data points as a single cell – for example, the members in a cohort

Custom fields, such as custom user profile fields or custom course fields, are fully supported by the report generator. They will appear in the list of available fields, just like any built-in variable.

One of the most powerful features of the report generator is its support for **aggregation**. Have a look at the following three reports, all with the same fields but different aggregation methods applied to the **Badge recipient** column:

Figure 12.7 – Aggregation

In the first report, **No aggregation** has been applied, so all data entries are shown. In the second report, the **Comma separated values** option has been selected, which displays multiple usernames in a single cell. In the last report, the **Count** method was chosen, which shows the number of recipients per badge.

Depending on the data field selected, different methods are at your disposal, as shown in the following table, including the SQL function used internally:

Aggregation Method	Description	SQL Function
Average	Average of all (numeric) values	AVG()
Count	Number of values in column	COUNT()
Count distinct	Number of unique values in column	COUNT DISTINCT()
Comma separate values	List of data points, separated by comma	GROUP_CONCAT()
Comma separate distinct values	List of unique data points, separated by comma	GROUP_CONCAT(DISTINCT)
Maximum	Biggest (numeric) value in column	MAX()
Minimum	Smallest (numeric) value in column	MIN()
Percentage	Ratio of (numeric) values in percent	AVG()
Sum	Sum of all (numeric) values in column	SUM()

Figure 12.8 – Aggregation operations

An aggregate function calculates a set of values and returns a single value. For example, **Count** takes a list of values and returns – you guessed it – the number of items. The **Remove any duplicate rows** setting has no effect if columns are aggregated.

Using the **Course participants** record source in conjunction with aggregation methods, you can create powerful reports, such as the following:

- Number of users enrolled in each course: **Course full name (No aggregation)**, **User Full name (Count)**

- Users enrolled in each course: **Course full name (No aggregation)**, **User Full name (Comma separated distinct value)**

- Number of completions of each course: **Course full name (No aggregation)**, **Course completion (Distinct count)**

There is no system behind what methods are available for which field type. For each data field, a set of possible aggregation methods is offered by Moodle.

Viewers also have the option to download the table data in various formats, namely CSV, XLSX, HTML, JSON, ODS, and PDF. You can reduce or rearrange the options in that list by going to **Site administration | Plugins | Data formats | Manage data formats**. The XLSX format is useful for visualizing data using Excel's charting tools.

Now that we have exhausted all the options for customizing columns in a report, let's look at how to configure the second dimension in a table: rows.

Configuring settings (rows)

This subsection deals with the available options for customizing or limiting the rows in a report. This can be done via the **Settings** panel on the right-hand side, where you can access the **Conditions**, **Filters**, **Sorting**, and **Card view** accordion panels. These configuration options will be described in the following four subsections.

Conditions

Conditions let you limit the amount of data that is being presented to the report viewer. For example, you might want to exclude any suspended users from your reports.

> **Important note**
> Conditions are a predefined set of criteria that are always applied when viewing a report. Conditions cannot be changed in viewing mode.

Depending on the selected report source, the list of available conditions might differ slightly from the list of available fields.

An interesting condition available in most report sources is **Select user**, which has three options:

- **Any user**: All users are shown.
- **Current user**: The report only shows data about the report viewer. Using this powerful mode, you can create reports that display personalized data, depending on who is viewing the report. For example, if you wish to create a report showing the progress of the report viewer in each course, select the **Course full name** and **Student progress** fields and set the **Select user** condition to **Current user**. When students view the report, they will only see the progress in the courses they are enrolled in.
- **Select**: The same principle as **Current user**, but you can select one or many users.

Two more conditions let you select values: **Select course** and **Select category**, including an option to **View all subcategories**.

Filters

The following two screenshots show configuring filters (left) and what the first three entries look like from a user's perspective when viewing the report (right):

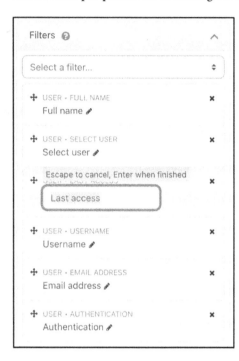 

Figure 12.9 – Report filtering

We described the **Current user** option in the **Select user** filter, which creates a unique report for each viewer. This type of filter also impacts reports created automatically and sent out to users via schedules (see the *Scheduling reports section* further down).

You can add as many filters as you wish. Furthermore, the list of filters is not limited to the fields shown in the report. For example, in a user report, you might add a filter to narrow the search down to individual authentication methods, even though the field is not available in the report itself.

Sorting

The penultimate of the four settings deals with the order in which the data is presented.

> **Important note**
> Sorting defines the initial order in which the fields are being ordered.

In the following screenshot, the data is ordered by **Category name** (in ascending order), **Course short name** (in descending order), and **Course full name** (in ascending order):

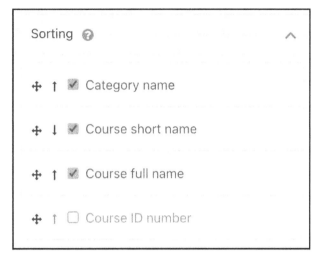

Figure 12.10 – Report sorting

When in viewing mode, the preceding order will initially be applied. Once a user clicks on a column name, the data will be sorted by this field; the sort order will be reversed when the same column is clicked again.

Card view

The card view feature supports responsive layout design in the report builder. Card view allows you to configure the report layout for narrow views when the block is in the sidebar or a smaller device is used. A report will automatically switch to card view when displayed on small screens.

Report audiences

Report audiences indicate which users have access to the report. They can also be used as recipients in scheduled reports. To access audiences, select the **Audiences** tab of a report, where you can create the following audiences:

- **All users**: Use this audience to give access to all users
- **Assigned system role**: Select at least one system role
- **Manually added users**: Select at least one user (via name or email address)
- **Member of cohort**: Select at least one cohort
- **Site administrators**: Moodle admins – that is, you and everybody who is also an admin

To confirm which users now have access to the report, switch to the **Access** tab, which is, as you might have guessed by now, yet another system report. Now that we know who has been granted access to the report, let's configure when a report is sent to the specified audiences.

Scheduling reports

By default, all reports are available as pull reports; that is, users have to select and view a report proactively. This section provides instructions on configuring the automatic delivery of reports via the report scheduler, known as push reports. Having users log in to see a report is less effective than having the report land directly in their inbox.

To access the scheduler, select the **Schedules** tab of a report. And yes, the list of schedules is yet another system report with a predefined filter:

Figure 12.11 – Scheduling reports I

Select the **New schedule** button at the top right to create a new report schedule. You will then be presented with a pop-up window containing the following four sections:

Figure 12.12 – Scheduling reports II

These four sections contain the following settings:

- The **General** part of the screen contains information about the schedule, including what report to send, in which format the report should be sent, and the timing settings.

  Name is only used in the list of schedules. The **Format** dropdown lets you pick the file format of the report. The options are CSV, XLSX, HTML, JSON, ODF, and PDF. You can reduce or rearrange the options in that list by going to **Site administration | Plugins | Data formats | Manage data formats**.

  The **Starting from** setting specifies when the report will be sent for the first time. The **Recurrence** option lets you specify whether the report should be sent once (**None**) or frequently. The repeating options are **Daily, Daily (Weekdays only), Weekly, Monthly**, and **Annually**. The cron process triggers the execution of the report being sent.

  The last setting in this section is **View report data as**, which has three options: **Schedule creator, Schedule recipient**, or **Select user**. If a user or the schedule creator is selected, the attached report data will be included as if viewed by this masquerading user; that is, all recipients will receive the same report. If left empty, the report's recipient will be used; individual reports will be sent out, depending on how the report has been configured. The reportbuilder:scheduleviewas capability determines whether reports can be scheduled to be viewed as others.

- In the **Audience** section, you specify who the recipients are. You need to select at least one audience, as specified previously. If no audiences have been specified yet, a warning will be shown.

- The **Schedule** section contains the custom message, which includes the two standard elements of any email message: **Subject** and **Body**. At the time of writing, no placeholders are supported, so you will have to tailor the message text accordingly.

- In the **Advanced** section, there is only a single option, which lets you specify what happens *If the report is empty*. The self-explanatory options are **Send message with empty report, Send message without report**, and **Don't send message** (default).

With that, we have provided an overview of the report generator, a potentially powerful tool for generating custom reports. However, it has some limitations, which we will discuss in the following section.

Report generator limitations and an alternative

The report builder is a powerful tool for creating reports based on predefined report sources. At the time of writing, the number of report sources available is rather small, but it is expected that this limitation will change in the very near future. Moodle Workplace (docs.moodle.org/en/Report_builder) already contains significantly more report sources than Moodle, so watch out for new sources being added soon.

We mentioned earlier that the report creator's main advantage is that you don't have to be familiar with Moodle's underlying database schema. However, some administrators find the concept of report sources too restrictive and wish to create more flexible reports. **Configurable reports** (moodle.org/plugins/block_configurable_reports) is a popular third-party plugin for Moodle, which appears as a block once installed. The plugin supports the following five types of reports:

- **Course reports**: Reports that use course data
- **Category reports**: Reports that use category data plus optional embedded course reports
- **User reports**: Reports that use user data and their course activities
- **Timeline reports**: Reports across time for courses, users, and their activities
- **SQL reports**: Any valid SQL statement can be used to query the Moodle database

Depending on what type of report has been chosen, different selection criteria (fields, conditions, ordering, and calculations) are offered. Additionally, filters for drill-down can be specified, the layout can be created, and permissions for who is allowed to run the report can be set. Furthermore, the plugin can plot different types of graphs.

The unique feature of Configurable reports is that you can create reports based on **Custom SQL**. If you are familiar with the SQL language and the underlying Moodle database schema, you can add queries, such as the one shown in the following screenshot arrangement:

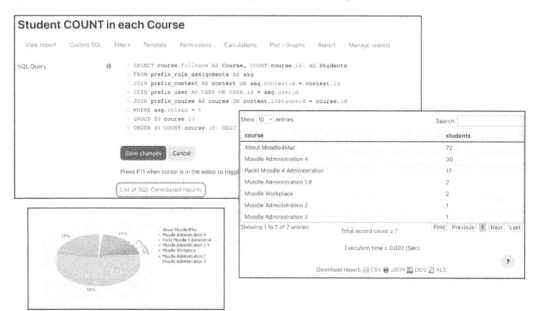

Figure 12.13 – Configurable reports sample

In the preceding screenshot, you can also see a link to **List of SQL Contributed reports**, which is a very good starting point for creating reports (this is where I got the SQL query of the sample report).

This concludes this section on custom reporting based on Moodle's report builder, where we covered the tool's workflow, the available data sources, and configuration. In addition to creating flexible custom reports, Moodle ships with several predefined reports that make use of the logging framework, mentioned in this chapter's introduction.

Understanding Moodle's logging framework

Moodle has a powerful built-in logging framework that is, as expected, fully customizable and extensible. The idea behind the logging mechanism is as follows:

- A user performs an action that triggers an **Event**. An example is a student who posts a reply on a forum.

- The **Log manager** entity monitors the event and decides whether it will be logged or ignored. Site-wide log manager settings determine this behavior.

- The log manager sends the data to the active **Log store plugin**, which filters or enriches the information. The passed-on data might be augmented with an IP address and a timestamp.

- The data is then written to the configured **Log store**.

The top half of the diagram shows this logging workflow:

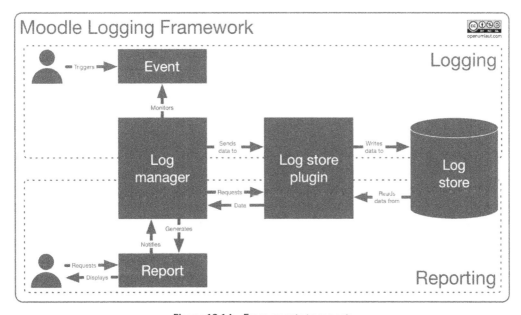

Figure 12.14 – From events to reports

Now, let's take a look at what happens when a user requests a report, which is represented in the bottom half of the diagram:

- The reporting module notifies the log manager, who passes on the request to the log store plugin. If more than one log store has been set up, the user must select one.

- The log store plugin reads the relevant data from the log store and passes it back to the log manager.

- The report module generates the report, which is then displayed to the user.

Now, let's look at the individual components of Moodle's logging framework in more detail, starting with events.

Understanding events

Two closely related elements deal with events in Moodle – the events list and event monitoring rules:

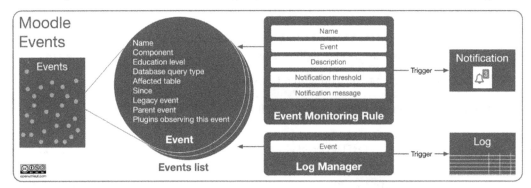

Figure 12.15 – Events, events list, and event monitoring rules

These concepts have been illustrated in the preceding diagram and will be described in detail in the remainder of this subsection, starting with the events list.

Events list

Most actions in Moodle trigger an event. You can look at the list of all the available events by going to **Site administration | Reports | Events list**. This list will grow over time, with internal and external events being added. Each event comprises the following elements:

- **Event name**: The name of the event and a unique internal identifier

- **Component**: The Moodle component that the event belongs to; for instance, Core, a course module, or some other part, such as statistics or logs

- **Education level**: There are three levels: **Participating**, **Teaching**, and **Other**

- **Database query type**: Four query types can occur, namely **create, read, update, and delete (CRUD)**

- **Affected table**: The database table that is being affected

- **Since**: The Moodle version when the event was introduced

- **Legacy event**: The event that was triggered in the legacy log store (this only contains events from version 2.6, when events were introduced)

The following screenshot shows some events filtered by **user**:

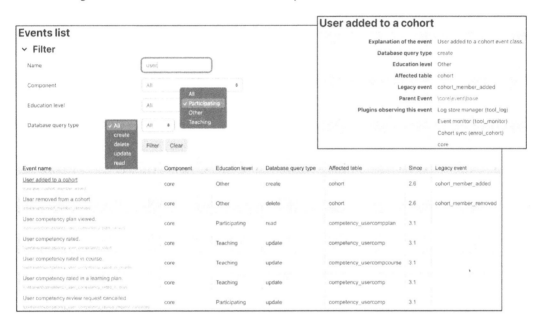

Figure 12.16 – Events list (filtered by user)

You can filter the list by **Name, Component, Education level**, and **Database query type**. You will see a more detailed presentation of the same information by clicking on an event name. In the screenshot arrangement, we have selected the **User added to cohort** event. In addition to fields already familiar from the events list, the screenshot shows two additional items of information:

- **Parent Event**: Internally, events are organized hierarchically, but the information is relevant mainly to developers.

- **Plugins observing this event**: These are the plugins that monitor the event. Here, we have a log store manager (`tool_log`); the event monitor itself; the Cohort sync module, which ensures that every time a user is added to a cohort, they will also be enrolled in linked courses; and the core system itself.

The information about events is for administrators, mostly for information purposes. However, it is relevant when setting up event monitoring rules.

Event monitoring rules

Administrators (and users with the `tool/monitor:managerules` capability) can define events that you can subscribe to. These patterns of activities are represented as rules that contain an event as well as a frequency. Once such a pattern has been detected, an event will be triggered, sending a message to all subscribers.

While users with editing teacher rights can set up their own rules at the course level, you, as the administrator, are more likely to define a set of required rules to which educators will subscribe.

First, you must enable event monitoring by navigating to **Site administration | Reports | Event monitoring rules**.

Let's add our first event rule via the **Add a new rule** button. Once you have entered **Rule name**, select **Area to monitor**. The values in the list are identical to those you came across in the **Component** dropdown, as seen in the preceding events list. Once chosen, the **Event** list will be populated with all the available events that the component supports. The description is optional, but it is recommended that you provide this for potential subscribers. The **Notification threshold … in minutes** combo specifies the number of events within a specified period that are required for the **Notification message** property to be sent. The body of this message can include any or all of the placeholders explained in the sample message text shown in the following screenshots:

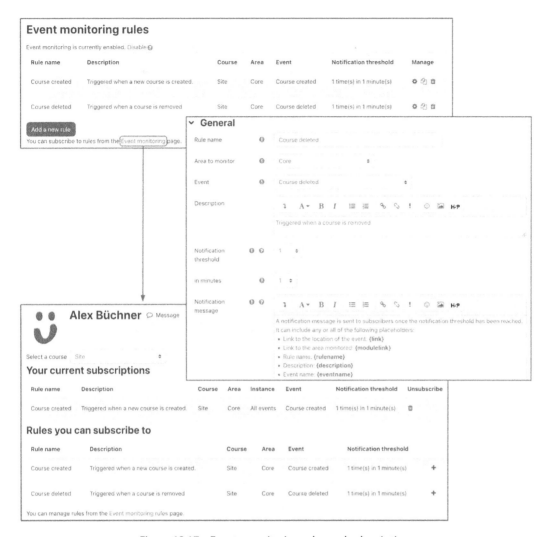

Figure 12.17 – Events monitoring rules and subscriptions

Any user with the `tool/monitor:subscribe` capability can subscribe to event rules via the **Event monitoring** link in the **Miscellaneous** section under **Preferences**. Once an event rule has subscriptions, rules editing is limited.

Before subscribing to a course, you must **Select a course** that is monitored (**Site** covers all courses). From now on, a notification message will be sent when the subscribed rule is triggered.

Now that we have covered events in detail, let's have a look at the logging components of our diagram.

Logging and log stores

Logging involves three components: the log manager, log store plugins, and physical log stores.

The **log manager** is an internal component that monitors events and passes data to all enabled log store plugins. Moodle comes with a predefined log manager; however, this may be replaced by other log manager plugins in the future. For now, as an administrator, you have no means of configuring the log manager itself.

A **log store plugin** is associated with a physical log store and determines what data is stored and read. Navigate to **Site administration | Plugins | Logging | Manage log stores** to see Moodle's three core log store plugins: **Standard log**, **External database log**, and **Legacy log**. We will ignore legacy logs as they will be discontinued over time.

The **standard log store** has replaced the legacy log; it supports all new logging concepts and provides better performance. In its **Settings**, you can specify whether to **Log guest access**, whether to store in **JSON format** (instead of serialized PHP), how long to **Keep logs for**, and its **Write buffer size**.

You can configure an **external database log** store if you wish to write logging information to a database separate from Moodle. This additional data storage is useful if you wish to collect data for more detailed analysis or data warehousing operations. This is shown in the following screenshot:

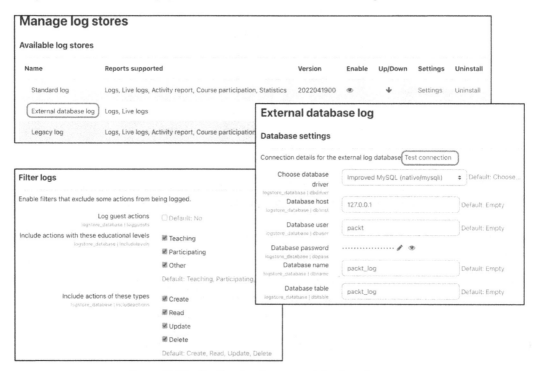

Figure 12.18 – Configuring the external database log store

By default, the same databases are supported as when we installed Moodle. The database host, user, password, and name settings are identical to the ones we covered in *Chapter 1*, *Installing Moodle*. Additionally, you have to specify a **Database table**, the structure of which has to be identical to the one stored in `mdl_logstore_standard_log`. Ensure you test the connection (the link is at the top of the screen); if successful, the check will display the columns that the external table contains. You can also specify various settings for a persistent database connection if you have a lot of logging traffic on your site and performance is an issue.

Now comes the exciting part of the external log store plugin. You can specify filters, which will then be applied when storing the data:

- **Log guest actions**: This tells you whether guest actions are stored or not. Usually, this is not required unless you wish to log all users' traffic.

- **Educational levels**: These are the three types that we came across in the events section, namely **Teaching**, **Participating**, and **Other**.

- **Database query types**: These are the four CRUD types we came across in the events section, namely **Create**, **Read**, **Update**, and **Delete**.

Filtering logs is useful when privacy regulations do not allow you to store actions of certain users or types (refer to *Chapter 14*, *Complying with Data Protection Regulations*) and when reporting from the log store does not require specific actions; this will also have a beneficial impact on performance.

> **Important note**
> External database logs supplement the standard log, not replace them. Disabling the standard log will cause log-based system reports to malfunction.

You can add additional log stores from `moodle.org/plugins/?q=type:logstore`. An interesting option is **Logstore xAPI**, which emits xAPI statements (also known as Tin Can) to an LRS of your choice.

This concludes this subsection on logging components, which covered the log store manager, log store plugins, and the log store itself. The last element in our process diagram covers log-based reports, which we will cover next.

Interacting with log-based reports

There are two types of built-in reports in Moodle: ones supplied with data from a log store and others generated on the fly without log store input. You can view the list of reports by going to **Site administration | Plugins | Reports | Manage reports**, as shown in the following annotated screenshot (the icons on the left indicate whether it is a course, system, or another type of report):

Reports				
Plugin	Log stores that support this report	Version	Uninstall	**Capability**
Activity completion	Log store not required	2022041900	Uninstall	report/progress:view
Activity report	Legacy log, Standard log	2022041900	Uninstall	report/outline:view
Backups report	Log store not required	2022041900	Uninstall	
Competency breakdown	Log store not required	2022041900	Uninstall	
Config changes	Log store not required	2022041900	Uninstall	
Course completion	Log store not required	2022041900		report/completion:view
Course overview	Log store not required	2022041900	Uninstall	report/courseoverview:view
Course participation	Legacy log, Standard log	2022041900	Uninstall	report/participation:view
Events list	Log store not required	2022041900	Uninstall	
Infected files	Log store not required	2022041900	Uninstall	
Insights	Log store not required	2022041900	Uninstall	moodle/analytics:listinsights
Live logs	External database log, Legacy log, Standard log	2022041900	Uninstall	report/log:view
Logs	External database log, Legacy log, Standard log	2022041900	Uninstall	report/log:view
Overview statistics	Log store not required	2021050500	Uninstall	report/overviewstats:view
Performance overview	Log store not required	2022041900	Uninstall	report/performance:view
Question instances	Log store not required	2022041900	Uninstall	report/questioninstances:view
Security checks	Log store not required	2022041900	Uninstall	report/security:view
Statistics	Legacy log, Standard log	2022041900	Uninstall	report/stats:view
System status	Log store not required	2022041900	Uninstall	report/status:view
User sessions report	Log store not required	2022041900	Uninstall	report/usersessions:manageownsessions

Figure 12.19 – System reports

Here, you can see when a report requires a log store and, if so, which ones are supported. We will focus on (live) logs since they form the basis for log-based reporting, before moving on to statistics and analytics.

Remember that most information you retrieve from log-based reporting is also available to teachers at the course level. While educators use this information mainly in a pedagogical context (to monitor progress and measure performance), your role as an administrator is to view this data in a site-wide context. Furthermore, you are the one who is likely to be approached if any claims, problems, or other anomalies occur, for example, if a student insists on having submitted an assignment that is not on the system or a teacher is unable to log in from home. Given the sensitivity of such data and your organization's policies, access to some operations has to be deactivated via roles and capabilities (added to the right of each report, if available).

Depending on your setup and configuration, Moodle records a detailed log of each action that users perform. By default, each record (or hit) in the standard log contains data about the following:

- **Who** (user)
- **What** (action)
- **When** (date and time)
- **Where** (IP address)

Site-wide logs can be accessed by going to **Site administration | Reports | Logs**. At the top of the page, you can interactively drill down to the data via filters, which is useful if you need to locate data about an individual, an activity, or a course. For example, if pupils claim that they have submitted an assignment, which cannot be located, the tracking log will be able to shed light on this. The available filters are as follows:

- **Courses**: Select a specific course or the entire Moodle site (site logs).
- **Groups**: Select a specific group or **All groups**. This filter is only displayed if group mode is enabled in the selected course.
- **Participants**: Select a specific user or **All participants**.
- **Date**: Specify a particular day or all days of activity. Unfortunately, it is not (yet) possible to specify date ranges.
- **Activities**: Select whether you wish to run a report of **All activities** or **Site errors** – this list changes when a course has been selected.
- **Actions**: You can choose among **All actions**, **Create**, **View**, **Update**, **Delete**, and **All changes**.
- **Educational levels**: You can choose from **All events**, **Teaching**, **Participating**, and **Other**. We came across the latter three options when looking at events.
- **Log store**: If more than one log store has been set up, you must select the one from which the data is being read.

Once you have selected a course and clicked on the **Get these logs** button, the content in each dropdown menu changes context-sensitively. For example, the **Participants** menu contains all the names of users who have a role in the course, and the **Activities** menu is populated with activities and resources. If you watch Moodle's submenu, you will see what happens internally. Moodle temporarily redirects the reporting tool inside the selected course where the course log viewer is called, which is identical in appearance. Once you have selected your filtering criteria, a report is displayed, as follows:

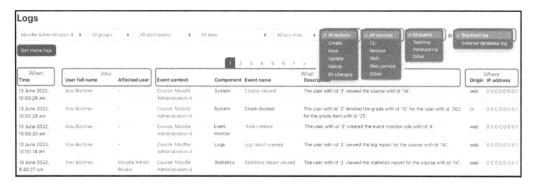

Figure 12.20 – Log data

This tabular information is displayed in the reverse order of a user's access date and time; that is, the last hit is displayed first. The columns of the table represent the following information:

- **Time**: Date and time of the hit.

- **User full name**: Name of the user – if a particular user is selected, the same value will be displayed in each row.

- **Affected user**: This will display if the action impacts another user.

- **Event context**: The context in which the event has been triggered. A link directs you to the context, for instance, a course.

- **Component**: The event component (refer to the *Events* section earlier in this chapter).

- **Event name**: The event that has been triggered. When selected, a pop-up window containing the event will open.

- **Description**: A short description of what the user has been doing – this is very useful for seeing what resources are being accessed or checking whether an individual has viewed a course. Internal IDs are used, such as user ID, course ID, or forum ID.

- **Origin**: Indicates whether the hit came from a CLI script (`cli`), a restore operation (`restore`), Moodle itself (`web`), a web service (`ws`), or any other origin (`other`).

- **IP address**: The (unresolved) IP address; this is useful for identifying where the user accessed the page (for example, from home or within the organization).

At the bottom of the results page, you can download table data in several formats (CSV, XLSX, HTML, JSON, ODS, or PDF). You can reduce or rearrange the options in that list by going to **Site administration | Plugins | Data formats | Manage data formats**.

When you click on the IP address in the log, a new page will open that displays the registered location of the user's IP as a pin on the world map (this is not the case for local or private IP addresses), as shown in the following figure:

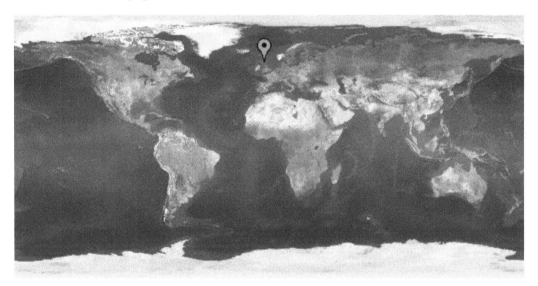

Figure 12.21 – Geographical location of an IP address

The default lookup tool that's used is called **NetGeo** (www.geoplugin.com). For more accurate results, you will need to install a local copy of the **MaxMind GeoLite** database (dev.maxmind. com) or specify a Google Maps API key. Both settings can be found in the IP address lookup section at **Site administration | General | Location | Location settings**.

Moodle provides **live logs** of activities in the last hour, which can be accessed by navigating to **Site administration | Reports | Live logs**. It is a prepared report that shows activities that took place in the previous 60 minutes; it is updated automatically every 60 seconds. You can **Pause live updates** via the button beside the log reader selector. Live logs are helpful if you have changed the configuration, for instance, an authentication or enrolment plugin, and want to ensure that it is working correctly. Alternatively, you can just sit back and watch what is happening on your site. The format of the screen is identical to the preceding standard log. Note that the first entry in the live log is you looking at the live log!

When selecting **site errors** from the activities dropdown menu, all the errors (mainly failed logins) are displayed. For example, the report that is shown in the following screenshot displays two invalid logins, as well as two failed attempts to send an email to users:

Time	User full name	Affected user	Event context	Component	Event name	Description	Origin
13 June 2022, 4:42:42 pm	-	-	System	System	User login failed	Login failed for user 'root'. User does not exist (error ID '1').	web
13 June 2022, 4:38:43 pm	Alex Büchner	-	System	System	User login failed	Login failed for user 'admin'. Most likely the password did not match (error ID '3').	web
13 June 2022, 9:56:18 am	Alex Büchner	Buck Futin	System	System	Email failed to send	Failed to send an email from the user with id '2' to the user with id '63' due to the following error: "Invalid address: (From): noreply@localhost".	cli
13 June 2022, 9:56:18 am	Buck Futin	Buck Futin	System	System	Email failed to send	Failed to send an email from the user with id '63' to the user with id '63' due to the following error: "Invalid address: (From): noreply@localhost".	cli

Figure 12.22 – Error log

It is a good practice to check the error logs regularly to identify problems on your site and potential unauthorized access attempts. These reports can also be set up to be sent by email to the site administrator (refer to *Chapter 13, Ensuring Moodle Security*).

You should now be equipped to interact with Moodle logs fully. Statistics has been mentioned a few times in this section; we'll look at what statistical analysis Moodle supports and how we can benefit from it in the next section.

Gathering statistics

This section will teach you how to set up and interpret **Moodle statistics**.

Moodle has a built-in Statistics module, which is deactivated by default because the component is very resource-hungry in terms of disk space usage and, more importantly, memory usage.

> **Important note**
> Only use the Statistics module if you require the information and can accept some potentially significant performance reduction.

Select **Enable statistics** under **Site administration | General | Advanced features** and configure it by navigating to **Site administration | Server | Statistics**, where the following parameters are available:

- **Maximum processing interval**: After enabling the Statistics module, Moodle utilizes the logs to derive statistical information. Here, you need to specify the time that Moodle should go back by to gather the stats. Be aware that this is quite a resource-intensive operation.

- **Maximum runtime**: You can limit the time the statistics gathering process is allowed to run; this is another mechanism that helps you avoid putting too much burden on the system.

- **Days to process**: The number of days that will be processed in each statistics execution.

- **User threshold**: Here, the Statistics module can be instructed to ignore courses with less than a certain number of enrolled users.

Statistics calculations take place in the background via the `\core\task\stats_cron_task` scheduled task. It is highly recommended that its execution time does not clash with the site backup as both operations are potentially very resource-intensive.

Let's look at some statistics by going to **Site administration** | **Reports** | **Statistics**. Once you have selected **Course**, **Report type** (views, posts, logins, or all of these), and **Time period**, a graph and some tabular information will be displayed. The data that's shown represents the number of *hits* on a particular day, broken down by roles:

Figure 12.23 – Statistics report

If no data is displayed, you might have to readjust the settings of your statistics. Also, while statistics gathering is in progress, a message might be displayed stating that the module is in catch-up mode. If this is the case, you must wait until the processing has been completed.

A report that shows some basic statistics on courses over a period of interest that make use of the statistics data is located at **Site administration | Reports | Course overview**. The options are as follows (you can find the report measure calculations at docs.moodle.org/en/Course_overview_report):

- **Most active courses**
- **Most active courses (weighted)**
- **Most participatory courses (enrolments)**
- **Most participatory courses (views/posts)**

Each report shows a table, and a graph visualizes the course data.

I don't know about you, but the information provided by these two Statistics reports is highly unsatisfactory. Given the module's burden on our system and the amount of available data, this seems like a very simplistic – some would say useless – way to display statistics.

An extension to the Statistics module is a plugin called **Overview Statistics** (moodle.org/plugins/report_overviewstats), which provides you with more analyses on users who are logging in, user countries, preferred languages, and some course stats. While this is an improvement over the Statistics facility, it is still far from ideal.

If the described statistics facilities do not satisfy your hunger for usage data, you might consider using tools such as **Matamo**, **Piwik** (both privacy-focused and open source), and **Google Analytics**. These web log analyzers are feature-rich services that track any traffic to your Moodle site and offer an abundance of statistics on visitors, traffic sources, content, user-defined goals, and much more.

You have two options for adding web traffic analysis support to your Moodle system:

- A dedicated plugin that supports any or all of the tools mentioned previously, for example, **Web Analytics** (moodle.org/plugins/tool_webanalytics).
- A theme that supports web log analyzers. The two most popular third-party themes, which were mentioned in *Chapter 7, Enhancing Moodle's Look and Feel*, provide different levels of integration: while **Moove** only supports your Google Analytics V4 code, **Adaptable** has a dedicated **Analytics** tab where you can customize your Google Analytics, Matamo, and Piwik settings, respectively.

Piwik, Matomo, and Google Analytics run sophisticated statistics against historical browsing data. Moodle Analytics, on the other hand, applies machine learning techniques and models to make predictions of future outcomes, which is the topic of the final section of this chapter.

Making predictions with Moodle Analytics

In this section, you will learn about **Moodle Analytics**, including how to create learning analytics models.

Custom and log-based reports are descriptive; they tell viewers what happened but not why, and don't predict outcomes or advise users on how to improve. While reporting tells us about *who, what, when,* and *where,* learning analytics aims to explain *why* and *how well.*

> **Important note**
> Moodle Analytics predicts or detects unknown aspects of learning based on (historical) log data and current behavior.

There are two types of models that Moodle Analytics supports:

- **Machine learning-based models**: Sophisticated models use mathematical tools to make predictions; for instance, students with a high likelihood of failing a course
- **Static models**: Simple models are based on assumptions and do not require sophisticated analyses; for example, students who have not enrolled in a course

The following diagram illustrates the key components of the Moodle Analytics workflow (adapted from `docs.moodle.org/dev/Analytics_API`):

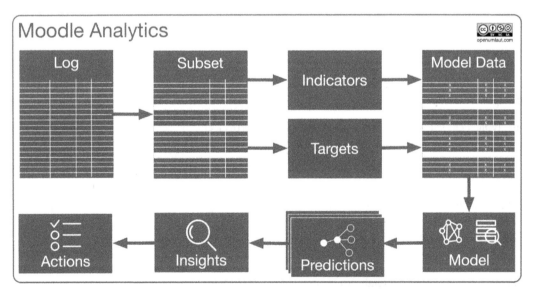

Figure 12.24 – Moodle Analytics components and workflow

Let's circle through the workflow, starting from the top left:

1. **Log** is the selected log file we covered earlier. A **Subset** of the log will be created based on the analytics model and the selected analysis interval.

2. **Indicators**, also known as predictors or features, are what you think will lead to an accurate target prediction. An indicator might be forum participation or teacher availability. **Targets**, also known as classes, represent the event the model is attempting to predict. A popular target is "students at risk of dropping out."

3. The filtering and augmentation outcome from the first three steps results in **Model Data**, which is used for the prediction model at hand.

4. The **Model** itself is created using **machine learning** (**ML**) algorithms that carry out all the heavy computation behind the scenes. We can treat this element as a black box and rely on the of the machine learning backend working correctly.

5. **Predictions** are patterns found in data – the bigger and more diverse the model data, the more accurate the predictions. A prediction might be in the form of a rule such as "if forum participation is low and teacher availability is low, then students at risk of dropping out is high."

6. **Insights** are generated by predictions when certain thresholds are met (a particular student is at risk of dropping out). Based on the insights, **Actions** should then be taken.

One of the most popular machine learning techniques is **classification**. The objective of classification is to predict a target by building a model based on a training dataset and then utilizing that model to predict the target in the test data. In our learning analytics context, a typical target is a prediction of whether students will pass or fail, or whether they are likely to drop out.

This type of learning is known as supervised learning because the learning process is guided toward the targets while building the model. Staying with the pass-fail scenario, the modeler (you!) would decide which data should be considered as indicators; for instance, course progress, grades, and participation levels.

Some typical classification applications include loan approval, churn prediction, medical diagnoses, and spam detection. Learning analytics usually deals with classification problems with one target (for example, pass or fail) to be predicted. Moodle Analytics currently only supports this type of binary classification.

We have only touched upon the very basics of the inner workings of Moodle Analytics. If you wish to dive deeper into this fascinating topic, some excellent resources are available online, such as `docs.moodle.org/en/Using_analytics` and `docs.moodle.org/dev/Analytics_API`.

OK, enough of all the abstract machine learning and learning analytics theory. However, before we can create our first Moodle analytics model, some initial configuration is required, which we are going to cover first.

Setting up Moodle Analytics

First, ensure that the **Analytics** option under **Site administration | General | Advanced features** is turned on. Setting up Moodle Analytics requires configuring two types of settings: educational domain knowledge and some technical parameters.

Under **Site administration | General | Analytics | Site information**, you should provide information about how most educators and learners use your Moodle site. This educational domain knowledge can be taken into account by machine learning algorithms. The self-explanatory fields to be configured are shown in the following screenshot:

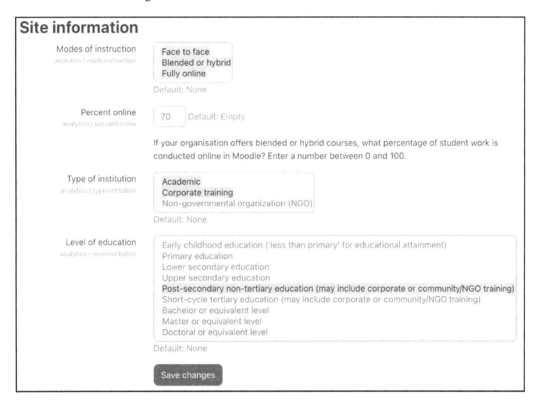

Figure 12.25 – Analytics site Information

You can find the technical configuration by going to **Site administration | General | Analytics | Analytics settings**, where the parameters have been explained in detail:

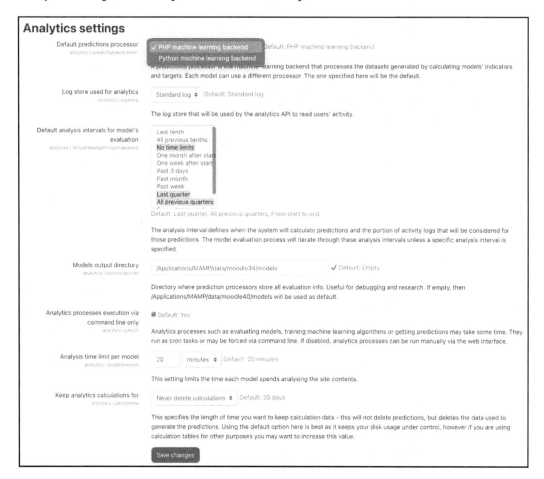

Figure 12.26 – Analytics settings

Most of these settings can easily be mapped onto the Moodle Analytics workflow presented earlier. Two scheduled tasks (\tool_analytics\task\train_models and \tool_analytics\task\predict_models) iterate through enabled models to train models and generate predictions, respectively. While you can allow these processes to be executed manually by disabling the **Analytics processes execution via command line only** setting, this is only recommended for testing purposes and not in production environments.

Once the domain and technical setup has been completed, we can create analytics models.

Creating analytics models

Analytics models are managed under **Site administration | General | Analytics | Analytics models**, as shown in the following screenshot:

Figure 12.27 – Analytics models

For each model, the three relevant fields are **Indicators**, **Analysis interval**, and **Insights**:

- **Indicators**: There are nearly 60 predefined indicators available, based on an empirical model of student engagement among many Moodle instances and some Moodle Partner sites. These indicators are divided into two types: cognitive depth and social breadth. You can find more details on Moodle Analytics indicators at docs.moodle.org/en/Learning_ analytics_indicators.

- **Analysis interval**: This time-splitting method defines when Moodle will calculate predictions and the portion of logs that will be considered for those predictions.

- **Insights**: These are the "interesting" prediction outcomes. The selection depends on the model type, for instance, users who are at risk of dropping out. These insights also trigger events, for example, notifications to course teachers or messages to students. Here is an **Insights** sample provided to course teachers, where they can also provide feedback, which will then be taken into account during the subsequent analysis:

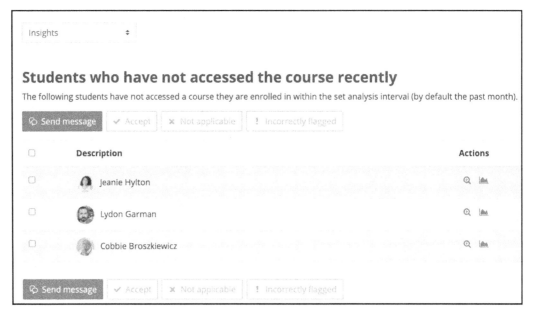

Figure 12.28 – Insights example

To adjust the settings of a model, select the standard **Edit** option in the **Action** menu. Here is an example of the **Students at risk of dropping out** model:

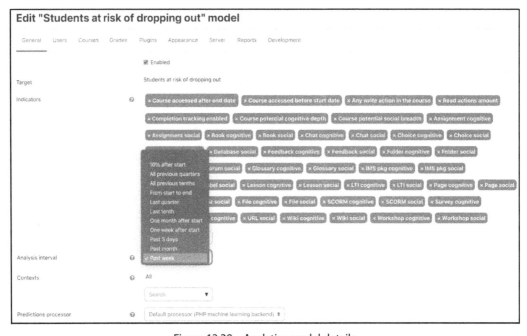

Figure 12.29 – Analytics model details

You can modify the list of **Indicators** and **Analysis interval**. Additionally, you can restrict the model-building to **Contexts** – that is, selected course categories and courses.

> **Important note**
> When a model is modified, all previous predictions will be deleted.

You must configure the same parameters when creating a new model after selecting the target. The following targets (what the model will predict) are available in Moodle:

- Students at risk of not achieving the competencies assigned to a course (ML)

- Students at risk of not meeting the course completion conditions (ML)

- Students at risk of dropping out (ML)

- Students at risk of not achieving the minimum grades to pass the course (ML)

- Courses at risk of not starting (static)

- Students who have not accessed the course recently (static)

- Students who have not accessed the course yet (static)

- Upcoming activities due (static)

At the beginning of this section, we mentioned that Moodle Analytics supports machine learning-based and static models. In static models, the indicators are fixed; you cannot modify these as you can in machine learning-based models.

There are several other analytics-specific commands in the **Actions** menu (some of those options only appear if the **Analytics processes execution via command line only** setting under **Site administration | General | Analytics | Analytics settings** is disabled):

- **Execute scheduled analysis**: Train machine learning algorithms with the new data available on the system and get predictions for ongoing courses

- **Insights report**: Depending on the model, report insights will be shown about what insights have been found and information about the individual targets

- **Export**: Moodle Analytics models can be exported in JSON format and imported via the **Import model** option upon selecting the **New model** button

- **Invalid site elements**: A list of the elements that cannot be analyzed by this model

- **Clear predictions**: Clears all the model predictions and training data

Moodle Analytics is one of the most powerful tools in Moodle but also one of the least utilized. Whether it is due to its complexity or lack of trust in machine learning algorithms, I don't know. Hopefully, we have shed some light on this topic and have equipped you with the skills to offer Moodle Analytics to your learners and educators.

Summary

Moodle offers a wide range of reporting facilities for teachers and administrators. In this chapter, we focused on reporting tools admins interact with or have to configure and provide to users. Even if you are not a data nerd, I hope the reporting facilities presented are helpful in your day-to-day administrative work.

The newly introduced report generator is a versatile tool for creating flexible and interactive custom reports. You got to know the report generator, including data sources, report building, audiences, and schedules. The more report sources that are made available in the future, the less likely you will need third-party tools, such as Configurable reports, which we briefly dealt with.

In the second part of this chapter, you learned everything about Moodle's logging framework in terms of its components, events, and log stores. You also interacted with Moodle logs, one of the most often used tools in the administrator's day-to-day job.

The logging framework provides the foundation for statistics and learning analytics, which we covered in dedicated sections.

Moodle reporting, particularly the newly introduced report generator, has recently undergone a significant makeover. Expect more features to be introduced shortly. Another constantly improved topic is Moodle's security, which is the next chapter's topic.

13
Ensuring Moodle Security

Moodle, like any other web application, has the potential to be misused. Moodle has dedicated an entire section to security settings that administrators can use to fine-tune its safety. After an overview of Moodle's security, you will learn about the following topics:

- **Security notifications**: You will learn how to set up Moodle's notification mechanisms that warn you about potential security issues and inspect the built-in security report.

- **User security**: We will look at the configuration of Moodle passwords, protection of user details, and spam prevention.

- **Content security**: We will deal with potential issues in content created within Moodle and the visibility thereof. You will learn how to restrict content created within Moodle, set up content visibility, and configure the antivirus scanner.

- **System security**: We will discuss configuration settings (location of the data `root` directory and cron execution), supporting HTTPS, and working with the IP blocker.

Before we cover the four aforementioned topics, let's provide an overview of Moodle security, touching upon all layers of the technology stack.

Moodle security – an overview

Moodle takes security extremely seriously, and any potential issues are given the highest priority. Fixed vulnerabilities of serious issues usually trigger the release of minor versions, emphasizing the subject's importance.

The following diagram illustrates the layers of a typical Moodle setup where the security of each component has to be ensured:

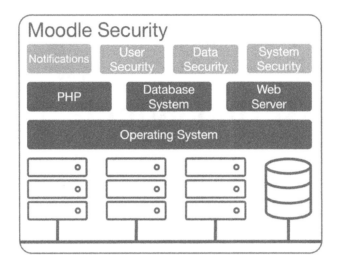

Figure 13.1 – Moodle security

The security of a system is as good as its weakest link. Since Moodle relies on underlying software, hardware, and network infrastructure, security can potentially be compromised in several areas. As this book focuses on Moodle administration, we only cover the security elements of Moodle per se. The following areas are **not** dealt with, and it is necessary to consult the respective documentation and experts on security issues:

- **Software**: As described in *Chapter 2*, *Exploring the Moodle System*, Moodle's key components comprise a **web server** (usually Apache or Microsoft IIS), a **database server** (MySQL, Microsoft SQL Server, PostgreSQL, MariaDB, or Oracle), and a programming language (**PHP**). Additional PHP and operating system extensions are required, for instance, to support the aforementioned database systems.

- **Operating system**: An operating system's security is under the constant threat of exploitation for malicious purposes. The hardening of the operating system is a crucial task of a system administrator.

- **Hardware**: Moodle runs on (physical or virtual) servers hosted internally or externally. There are ongoing safety and security improvements in such systems, reflected by ever-extending precautions taken by data centers and hosting providers.

- **Network**: Any system that is part of a network is potentially vulnerable. Configuration of firewalls, proxy servers, and routers, as well as general network security, are key aspects of protecting your system from attacks.

A number of these topics are covered at docs.moodle.org/en/Security.

> **Important note**
> One rule that applies to all elements is that the latest software updates should be installed regularly.

With the increasing complexity and growing popularity of Moodle, it is imperative that you ensure that all possible measures are taken to prevent any security issues. Let's get started with security notifications.

Configuring security notifications

Moodle has set up a dedicated site at `moodle.org/security` that deals with security issues. If you register your Moodle instance, which is highly recommended, your email address will automatically be added to the security alerts mailing list, which gives you advanced notice of vulnerabilities and updates a couple of days prior to public release. To set this up, go to **Site administration | General | Registration**, fill in the required information, and click on the **Register your site** button.

Alternatively, follow the `@moodlesecurity` Twitter handle to be notified of any Moodle security announcements.

Once you are up to date with general security issues, it is time to focus on being aware of any potential issues on your Moodle system. In the remainder of this section, we will deal with setting up Moodle notifications and inspecting the built-in system report.

Setting up Moodle notifications

When you navigate to **Site administration | General | Notifications**, Moodle will display any potential issues with your site. This link also initiates the installed Moodle updates and plugins (refer to *Chapter 8, Understanding Moodle Plugins*).

Four messages are displayed in the following screenshot; the second and third issues would clearly fall into the security category:

Figure 13.2 – Moodle notifications

Moodle monitors failed login attempts in its log file, as described in *Chapter 12, Gaining Insights through Moodle Reporting and Analytics*. Repeated login failures can indicate that unauthorized users are trying to access your system. In addition to checking your log files regularly, you should consider monitoring these activities by configuring the settings when you navigate to **Site administration | General | Security | Notifications**:

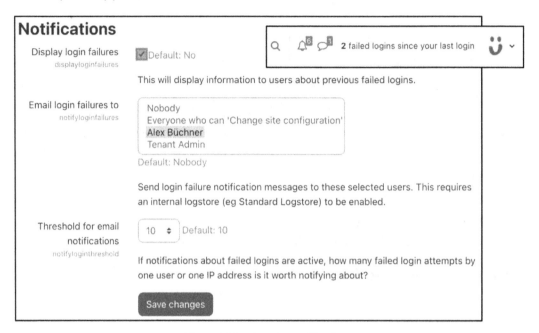

Figure 13.3 – Security notifications

You can specify whether users will see messages displayed on their screens about previously failed logins and who will be emailed about login failures. You can further set the number of failed logins from the same IP address that will trigger these notifications.

While this is not a foolproof threat alert, it can potentially highlight some problems within your system, and it is therefore recommended that you activate it. Another benefit of receiving these notifications by email is the customer care aspect of getting back to legitimate users who have felt frustrated when trying to access your site.

Inspecting security checks

Another mechanism that we already mentioned in *Chapter 12, Gaining Insights through Moodle Reporting and Analytics*, is the security report you find at **Site administration | Reports | Security checks**:

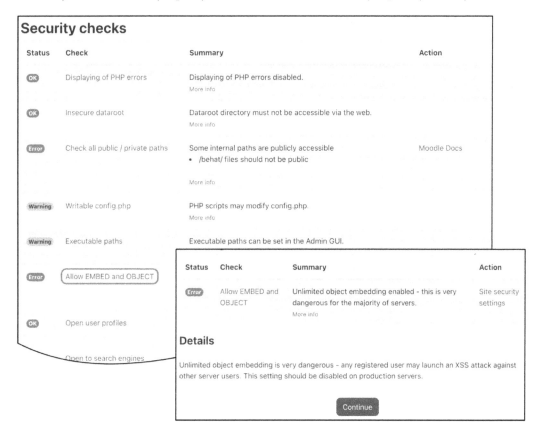

Figure 13.4 – Security checks

The report shows several potential key security issues, their status (**OK, Info, Warning, Critical**, or **Error**), and a summary. When you click on an issue name, you will be redirected to a page that provides more information about the problem and, if available, a further **Action** link to the settings page where you can rectify the situation.

The **Security checks** page is a good starting point to identify some potential issues. However, it does not replace a full security audit, penetration test, or health check offered by some Moodle Partners.

Awareness of what is going on in your Moodle system is as critical as ensuring the security of critical components. Let's start with the weakest link in any IT setup – users.

Ensuring user security

A critical security aspect lies in ensuring that only privileged users can access your system and, once they are authenticated, they only have access to their privileged areas in Moodle.

Here is a quick recap of the key elements concerning security in the magic Moodle triangle – users, courses, and roles:

- Ensuring the correct **authentication** setup is critical to ensuring a secure Moodle system, especially when self-registration or guest access has been activated. We dealt with internal, external, provider-based, and system authentication methods in *Chapter 5, Managing Users, Cohorts, and Authentication*.

- Once users have authenticated with Moodle, you have to ensure that they can only enrol in courses where they should have permission to do so, which is controlled by **enrolment** methods, as discussed in detail in *Chapter 4, Managing Courses and Enrolments*.

- When users are enrolled in courses or access any other area of Moodle, it is crucial that they are granted the correct **permissions**, which are controlled via roles and capabilities, a topic covered at length in *Chapter 6, Managing Permissions, Roles, and Capabilities*. The six risk types of capabilities – **Trust**, **Configuration**, **XSS**, **Personal**, **Spam**, and **Data loss** – provide a good indication of the damage that can be caused.

In this section, we will focus on three topics impacting users' security:

- Moodle passwords, dealing with password policies, and recovering the admin password
- Protection of user details
- Prevention of spam

Let's start with Moodle passwords, a topic impacting all Moodle users.

Configuring Moodle passwords

Moodle offers a password policy feature that applies to manual accounts, which can be configured by going to **Site administration | General | Security | Site security policies**, as shown in the following screenshots:

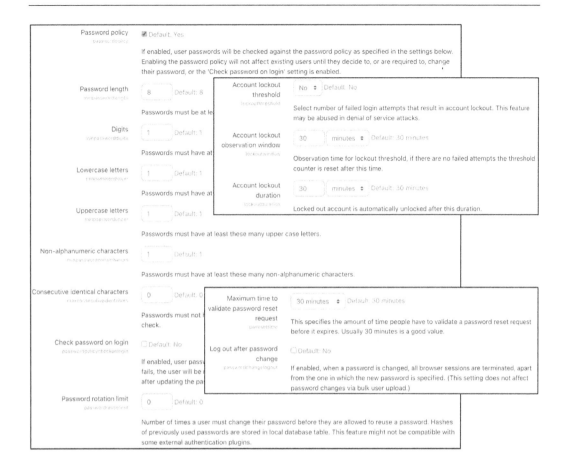

Figure 13.5 – Password policy

Moodle's password policy supports the following configuration option types:

- **Complexity**: All common password requirements are supported, namely **Password length**, **Digits**, **Lowercase letters**, **Uppercase letters**, **Non-alphanumeric characters**, and **Consecutive identical characters**.

- **Validity**: Password expiry can be specified for manual accounts at **Site administration | Plugins | Authentication | Manual accounts**, where you can configure **Enable password expiry**, **Password duration**, and **Notification threshold**. Related settings are **Password rotation limit** (the number of times before a user can reuse a password), **Maximum time to validate password reset request** (when password recovery is being triggered), and **Log out after password change** (all browser sessions except the current one).

- **Consequences**: You can lock out user accounts after too many failed logins. **Account lockout threshold** lets you specify the number of failed logins required to trigger a reactivation email to the user, the **Account lockout observation window** setting lets you specify the period during which further failed logins will be included in the current suspension, and **Account lockout duration** lets you specify the time after which the account will be unlocked automatically.

Bear in mind that the password policy only applies to manual accounts. If you use a different authentication method, the lockout thresholds will be defined elsewhere – for instance, within the **Lightweight directory access protocol (LDAP)** instance.

> **Important note**
>
> It is highly recommended that you use a strong password (long, complex, and random) for the Moodle administrator account(s), even if the password policy has been deactivated.

Moodle stores passwords in a cryptographic hash using `bcrypt` (Blowfish). To further improve password security, Moodle supports **password salting**, which adds a separate random string to the hash of each user's password. The password stored in the Moodle database has the following format:

```
$<hash_id>$<cost>$<secure salt><hash>
```

`<hash_id>` is the ID of the hashing algorithm used (2y for bcrypt), and `<cost>` is the cost of using that algorithm (two digits). `<secure salt>` is a randomly generated 22-character salt; you can find more details on salting at `docs.moodle.org/en/Password_salting`. `<hash>` is a 31-character hash of the actual password.

If you ever lose your admin password and have no means of recovering it, you have two options:

1. **Overriding the password in the database**: You can manually override the password field in the `mdl_user` table in the SQL database by manually replacing the old hash with the MD5 value of the new password; it will be upgraded to the strong hash value after the first login. For example, to set the password to `'newpassword'`, you need to use the following SQL statement:

   ```
   UPDATE mdl_user
       SET password = MD5('newpassword')
       WHERE username = 'admin';
   ```

   If your database does not support the MD5 function, you must set the password to the actual MD5 hash tag. For example, this would be `5e9d11a14ad1c8dd77e98ef9b53fd1ba` for 'newpassword'. Use one of the many available online generators to find out the tag.

2. **Overriding the password via the command line**: The `reset_password.php` CLI script sets the correctly salted password for any given user. The syntax to change the admin password to `'newpassword'` is as follows:

```
sudo -u www-data /usr/bin/php admin/cli/reset_password.
php --username=admin --password=newpassword --ignore-
password-policy
```

The passwords prevent users from unauthorized access to Moodle. Once users have identified themselves, the next step is to protect their user details, which is the topic of the following subsection.

Protecting user details

Identity theft is a common problem on the internet, and Moodle is no exception. To avoid the possibility of fraudsters gathering details about authenticated users, a number of settings can be seen by navigating to **Site administration** | **General** | **Security** | **Site security policies**:

- **Protect usernames**: If users cannot remember their username or password, Moodle provides a **Forgotten password** screen. By default, the message displayed reads **If you supplied a correct username or email address then an email should have been sent to you**. If the protection is turned off, however, the message reads **An email should have been sent to your address at ******@<domain name>**, which could allow a guess at the username.

- **Force users to login**: By default, Moodle's front page is visible to everyone, even if they are not logged in to the site. Change this parameter if you wish to force users to log in before they see the front page. As a result, your users will only see the login screen when they enter your site.

- **Force users to login for profiles**: When set to **Yes** (the default setting), users will have to log in with an authentic account before accessing other users' profile pages.

- **Force users to login to view user pictures**: If disabled (default), guests will be able to see pictures of other users in their profile. Otherwise, the default user image will be shown. Some organizations disable user profile images altogether, which can be achieved via the **Disable user profile images** option.

- **Open to search engines**: Moodle can be configured to allow search engines to crawl through courses with guest access and add content to its search engine database. This functionality is turned off by default.

- **Allow indexing by search engines**: The self-explanatory options are **Everywhere except login and signup pages**, **Everywhere**, and **Nowhere**. Note that these settings cannot be enforced because a tag header is added to each site to ask search engines to respect it.

- **Profile visible roles**: Any selected role will be visible on user profiles and participation pages.

There are two more related parameters further down in the **Site security settings** screen. You can activate **Email change confirmation**. If set to **Yes**, users will be sent an email to confirm that their change of email address in their profile is genuine. Moodle offers a means to remember usernames via cookies, which will be entered in the login form when opened. While this is convenient for the end user, it poses a potential security risk. To prevent this feature from being supported, configure the **Remember username** parameter by going to **Site administration | General | Security | Site security policies**. Since usernames are stored in a permanent cookie, this potentially infringes user privacy (see *Chapter 14, Complying with Data Protection Regulations*).

By default, Moodle triggers a notification when a login has taken place by a user from a new device. To avoid users deactivating this security measure, you might want to change the **New Login notifications** status to **Locked** in **Site administration | General | Messaging | Notification settings**.

Related to the protection of user details is the prevention of profile spam, which we will cover in the last topic of the user security section.

Preventing spam

If Moodle is not configured correctly, it allows spammers to insert content into user profiles of accounts created via self-registration.

> **Important note**
> Only use email-based self-registration if it is indispensable.

If you must use self-registration, ensure to undertake the following measures:

- Enable **reCAPTCHA** in **Site administration | Plugins | Authentication | Manage authentication**. On the same page, configure **Allowed email domains** and **Denied email domains**. Refer to the *Common authentication settings* section in *Chapter 5, Managing Users, Cohorts, and Authentication*. Many public online lists contain domains for disposable and temporary email addresses, which you might want to use for the denylist.

- Keep **Email change confirmation** enabled in **General | Security | Site security policies**.

- Configure the IP blocker, as described further on in this chapter.

To prevent **profile spam**, also make sure that the following settings in **General | Security | Site security policies** are set correctly (which they are, by default):

- Keep the **Force users to login for profiles** parameter enabled (refer to the *Protection of user details* section). This way, you can prevent anonymous visitors and search engines from seeing user profiles.

- You further limit access to changing profiles to only those users who are enrolled in a course via the **Profiles for enrolled users only** setting.

Also, be aware that legit users can be the cause of spam. Ensure that no user has any unnecessary capabilities in their roles that allow for this (refer to spam risk in *Chapter 6, Managing Permissions, Roles, and Capabilities*).

If your site has been victim to spam, go to **Site administration | Reports | Spam cleaner**. You can either let Moodle autodetect common spam patterns (the list makes for some interesting reading!) or search for your own keywords:

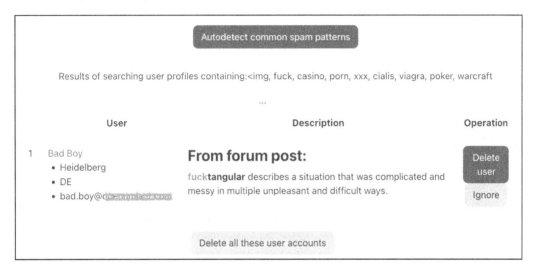

Figure 13.6 – Spam cleaner

Any user profiles where the **Description** field contains any of the listed keywords are shown. You then have the option to delete the user account(s). For more information on spam prevention in Moodle, check out `docs.moodle.org/en/Reducing_spam_in_Moodle`.

This concludes the section on user security, where we have covered the configuration of Moodle passwords, protection of user details, and spam prevention. Next up is content security.

Ensuring content security

Content by learners and teachers can potentially contain malicious code, and once created, it needs to be protected from unauthorized access. This section will ensure content security (namely, content created within Moodle), content visibility, and antivirus scanners.

Limiting content created within Moodle

Users can create Moodle content by using the Atto editor or uploading files. Two settings are available in **Site administration** | **General** | **Security** | **Site security policies** to partly prevent the misuse of these:

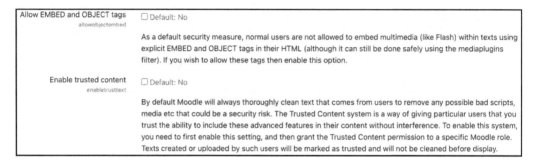

Figure 13.7 – Content security settings

The two parameters are as follows:

- HTML allows embedding code that uses the explicit <EMBED> and <OBJECT> tags. Potentially, malicious code can be put in embedded scripts, which is why its support is deactivated by default. To activate it, enable the **Allow EMBED and OBJECT tags** parameter.

- The Atto editor automatically removes any unwanted HTML elements and attributes. You can bypass this cleansing mechanism for individual users. First, you must set the **Enable trusted content** parameter, as shown in the preceding screenshot. Second, you will have to allow the moodle/site:trustcontent capability for each user you trust to submit JavaScript and other potentially malicious code. Texts created or uploaded by those users will be marked as trusted and will not be cleaned before display.

If you wish to censor obscene or other unwanted words entered by learners in activities such as forums, Moodle has developed a **Word censorship** filter and made it available as a plugin (moodle. org/plugins/filter_censor). Once installed and enabled, you can enter a list of censored words and phrases to be blacked out in **Site administration** | **Plugins** | **Filters** | **Word censorship**. Alternatively, you can edit the badwords language string in filter_censor.php (be careful, as this list is far from G-rated). Also, bear in mind that the filter picks up words within words and marks valid terms, such as cocktail, sextant, sparse, and altitude.

Okay, before your imagination runs completely wild, let's set up content visibility next.

Setting up content visibility

Blogging, tagging, and commenting are Moodle social networking activities. Blog entries, tags, and comments are harnessed for searching, sharing, and performing other collaborative activities to match interests. The potential issue is that the content is visible to users who should not be able to share or view entries. Moodle has catered for this by providing several settings, which we have already dealt with in the *Configuring collaboration tools* section in *Chapter 9, Configuring Educational Features*. Here is a list of areas where the respective functionalities need to be turned on and off:

- **Site administration | Appearance | Blog | Blog visibility**
- **Site administration | Advanced features | Enable tags functionality**
- **Site administration | Appearance | Blog | Enable comments**

If you deactivate any mechanisms, tags, comments, and blog entries that are already on the system or kept hidden, they will reappear when the functionality is turned on again. In other words, there is no risk of data loss when turning the functionality off and back on.

You might also consider creating a dedicated role on your system – for example, a Blogger role utilizing the `moodle/blog:create` capability. This will limit blogging to specific users only – those who have been assigned the new role. You can find more details on the Blogger role in the Moodle Docs at `docs.moodle.org/en/Blogger_role`.

The last component of content security is the configuration of virus scanners, which is dealt with in the following subsection.

Configuring antivirus scanners

Moodle supports the scanning of uploaded files for viruses, which can be configured at **Site administration | Plugins | Antivirus plugins | Manage antivirus plugins**:

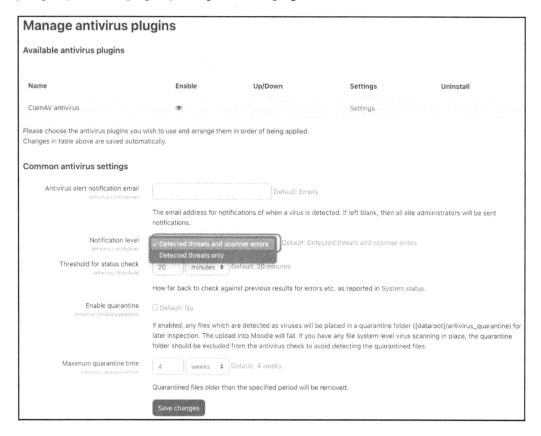

Figure 13.8 – Managing antivirus plugins

There are some common antivirus settings applicable to all antivirus plugins. The three-step process behind Moodle's (and most other) antivirus scanning mechanism is as follows:

1. **Detection**: Files are scanned for potential threats, where the antivirus plugin determines the detection method.

2. **Quarantine**: Any potentially malicious or infected files will be isolated. They are placed in the `$CFG->dataroot/antivirus_quarantine` quarantine folder for later inspection.

3. **Removal**: Detected files will be deleted immediately after detection when quarantine is disabled, after inspection of the quarantine folder, or when the maximum quarantine time has been exceeded.

ClamAV is available as a standard scanner; more antivirus plugins are available from the Moodle plugins directory at moodle.org/plugins/?q=type:antivirus. ClamAV is an open-source antivirus engine. Refer to www.clamav.net for more details, downloads for different operating systems, and how to keep the virus definition database up to date. You must install ClamAV on your system before the scanner can be configured via the **Settings** link.

There are two running methods for ClamAV:

- **Via command line:** This is the default method for which you need to specify the path where ClamAV has been installed.

- **Via system sockets:** On Unix systems, better performance can be obtained using either a Unix domain socket or a TCP socket. You need to contact your system administrator for configuration details on these parameters.

ClamAV has two limitations. First, ClamAV does not exist for Windows servers, and you will need to install a Windows-based virus scanner to provide this functionality and monitor any quarantined files separately. Second, ClamAV will impact your system's performance, which becomes an issue if the file upload facility is plentifully used. If this is the case, you might have to allocate 10–20% more RAM to your server(s).

This concludes the section on content security, where we covered content created within Moodle, content visibility, and antivirus scanners. The last section deals with ensuring system security.

Ensuring system security

In the last section of this Moodle security chapter, we deal with configuration settings impacting system security, covering access to dataroot, cron execution, secure HTTP, and the IP blocker.

Configuring access to dataroot

In the **Notifications** screenshot earlier in the chapter, you probably spotted the warning that the dataroot directory is directly accessible via the internet. Moodle requires additional space on a server to store uploaded files, such as course documents and user pictures. The directory is called dataroot and must not be accessible via the web. If this directory is accessible directly, unauthorized users can get access to content.

> **Important note**
> $CFG->dataroot must not be accessible via the web!

To prevent dataroot from being accessible, move the directory outside the web directory (ensure not to mangle permissions) and modify config.php accordingly by changing the $CFG->dataroot entry.

In externally hosted environments, it is often not possible to locate the directory outside the web directory. If this is the case, create a file called .htaccess in the data directory and add a line containing denyfromall.

The second system security measure is the protection of the execution of the cron process, which is covered next.

Protecting cron execution

We have already described the **cron** process in *Chapter 1*, *Installing Moodle*, and will go into more detail about this in *Chapter 15*, *Optimizing Moodle Performance*. cron is a script that regularly runs to perform certain operations, such as sending notifications, processing statistics, and cleaning up temporary files. Scripts that run at the operating system level can potentially contain malicious code.

It is possible to run a script via a web browser by simply typing in the following URL: <yourMoodlesite>/admin/cron.php. Two mutually exclusive settings can be set in **Site administration** | **General** | **Security** | **Site policies** to prevent this:

Figure 13.9 – Configuring cron execution

If you only allow the cron process to be executed from the command line, running the script via a web browser will be disabled, and a message will be displayed, saying **Sorry, internet access to this page has been disabled by the administrator**. The cron process can still be executed automatically if it's set up correctly.

If the **Cron password for remote access** parameter is set, Moodle requires that executing the cron script via a web browser requires the provision of a password in the form of a parameter, such as <yourMoodlesite>/admin/cron.php?password=yourpassword. If the password is not provided or is incorrect, an error message, which is the same as the one we saw earlier, is displayed.

Next up is the configuration of HTTP security.

Configuring HTTP security

Moodle offers full HTTPS support, which runs HTTP requests over SSL (a more secure but slightly slower socket layer). Given the rapid advance in hacking technology and the negligible cost of SSL certificates, every public-facing web page containing user data should run over HTTPS.

> **Important note**
>
> Repeat after me: every public-facing Moodle site should run over HTTPS, with no exception.

To ensure that all data transferred from a user's browser to the server that hosts Moodle is encrypted, HTTPS must be enabled on your web server. You will also have to purchase or generate an SSL certificate. Every web server has a different method to enable HTTPS, so you should consult your server's documentation. A good starting point for setting up SSL/TSL for Apache can be found at `httpd.apache.org/docs/current/ssl/ssl_howto.html`.

Once the web server has been configured to work with HTTPS, the Moodle installation script will work with those details (see *Chapter 1*, *Installing Moodle*). If you need to transition from HTTP to HTTPS, we recommend that you follow the instructions on Moodle Docs (`docs.moodle.org/ en/Transitioning_to_HTTPS`) and make use of the **HTTPS conversion tool** provided by Moodle at the bottom of **Site administration** | **General** | **Security** | **HTTP security**:

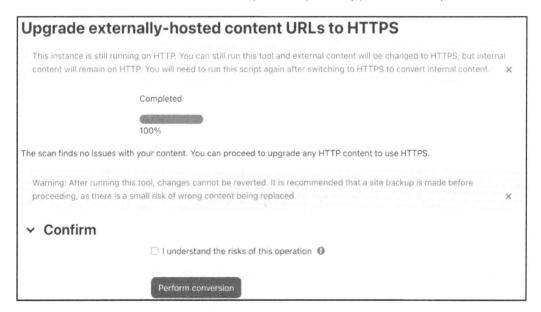

Figure 13.10 – HTTPS conversion tool

The tool performs two tasks. First, it scans any course content and notifies you if there are any potential issues or conflicts. Second, once you have ticked the confirmation box, an irreversible conversion is performed; all HTTP links are changed to HTTPS.

The tool can also be executed in CLI mode using the following syntax:

```
sudo -u www-data /usr/bin/php admin/tool/httpsreplace/cli/url_
replace.php --replace --confirm
```

For more details on the tool, consult `docs.moodle.org/en/HTTPS_conversion_tool`.

> **Important note**
>
> If you turn on HTTPS without the relevant system components installed – that is, the PHP extension added along with the correct web server configuration – you will lock yourself out of your system!

There are a number of related settings in **Site administration | General | Security | HTTP security** that you should double-check:

- **Secure cookies only**: Web servers can be configured in a way that they only accept HTTPS URLs. If this is the case on your system, you should enable this parameter.

- **Only http cookies**: Moodle supports instructing web browsers to send cookies only with real requests, which prevents some XSS attacks.

- **Allow frame embedding**: See the tip in the *Moodle as LTI tool* section in *Chapter 9, Configuring Educational Features*.

- **cURL blocked hosts list**: Block hosts for Moodle's cURL implementation – for example, `localhost` variants.

- **cURL allowed ports list**: Restrict Moodle's cURL implementation to specific web ports. The defaults are the standard ports, `80` and `443`.

HTTP security defines over what protocol your Moodle instance is accessed and the related settings. The last system security topic deals with allowing and blocking IP addresses accessing your site.

Allowing and blocking IP addresses

Users will access your system from stationary and mobile devices. What they all have in common is that they will access your site via an IP address. You can limit this access by specifying an allowlist and a denylist at **Site administration | General | Security | IP blocker**:

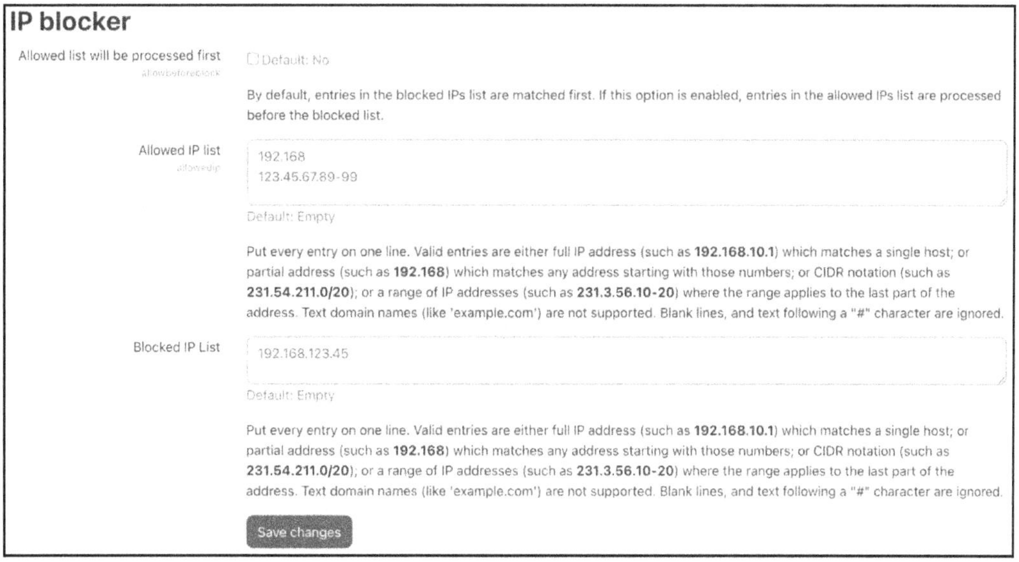

Figure 13.11 – IP blocker

The allowlist (**Allowed IP list**) can contain IP addresses in several formats (the full IP address, partial address, ranges of IPs, and the CDIR notation). The same applies to the denylist (**Blocked IP list**). By default, the denylist has priority over the allowlist. If you wish to reverse this, select **Allowed list will be processed first**.

> **Important note**
>
> Be aware that with any entries in the allowlist, the effect is to allow ONLY those IP addresses and block all others. Exercise care with this setting, as it is possible to lock yourself out of Moodle.

For example, you might want to add 192.168.*.* to your allowlist, and denylist a particular IP – say, 192.168.123.45 – that was trying to guess your admin password multiple times.

This concludes the section on system security, in which we dealt with access to dataroot, cron execution, HTTPS, and IP blockers.

Summary

This chapter taught you how to protect your Moodle system from potential misuse and to keep a regular check on its security. To summarize, here is a short list of best practices in the following checklist. While this list is by no means complete, it gives an indication of the elements you are responsible for as a Moodle administrator:

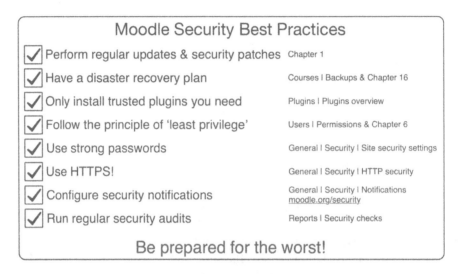

Figure 13.12 – Moodle security best practices

It is important to stress that Moodle's security is only a single variable in the overall equation. Ensure that all other underlying software, infrastructure, and hardware components are set up correctly as well.

It is also important to stress the importance of an emergency plan if a security threat arises. This includes a strategy for identifying the problem, measures to resolve the situation, and a list of users to notify, among others.

Most Moodle systems run on the LAMP platform, which has proven to be very secure if configured correctly. Moodle's developers are very conscious that security is vital when dealing with personal user data, such as grades, assignments, and competencies. Hence, the topic has been given the highest priority. However, there is no guarantee that your system is 100% protected against misuse. New hacking techniques will emerge in today's world of cyber threats, and users will continue to be careless with their credentials (you have all seen the Post-it notes under the keyboard). So, ensure security patches and updates on your entire system, not just Moodle, are always up to date, and keep educating your users about the dangers. Also, consider undergoing a regular security audit or health check, which some Moodle Partners offer.

Now that your system is secure, let's ensure that its privacy setup complies with data protection regulations.

14
Complying with Data Protection Regulations

Data privacy is all about the protection of personal data. Depending on its setup, Moodle potentially stores a significant amount of sensitive data such as IDs, addresses, grades, and exam submissions. With the introduction of the **General Data Protection Regulation** (**GDPR**), a legally binding framework has been introduced and is fully supported in Moodle.

This chapter will teach you the tools to configure your Moodle site to comply with data protection regulations.

> **Important note**
>
> *Disclaimer*: The advice in this chapter is provided for informational purposes only and not be construed as legal or professional advice.

After some legal background on the GDPR, you will learn about the following topics:

- **Designating a privacy officer**: You will learn how to set up a privacy officer role and activate the privacy officer functionality.

- **Managing policies**: We will look at the configuration of Moodle's policy handler before creating and updating versioned policies. We will further monitor user agreements and deal with minors in your Moodle system.

- **Configuring the data registry**: We will set up data registry categories and purposes before assigning them to contexts.

- **Managing data requests**: Finally, we will manage subject access requests to deal with data rectification (message), data access (export), and data erasure (deletion).

We will conclude the chapter with a Moodle privacy checklist. Before we cover the mentioned topics, let's get used to some legal terminology.

Understanding Moodle privacy

May 25, 2018: GDPR applies to all **European Union (EU)** residents.

One week earlier: Moodle 3.5 is released, supporting some but not all GDPR features.

It was the first time that Moodle was forced to implement a set of features to comply with legislative regulations (gdpr-info.eu). The implementation of all required features was completed in version 3.6, and the functionality was backported to three releases—another first for Moodle.

While GDPR only applies to EU residents or sites that are hosted in the EU, there are two reasons why the regulations are potentially relevant to all Moodle systems:

- If a single user on your system (student, employee, supplier, and so on) is or will be from the EU, you are obliged to comply with the regulation. Or, in more legalese: any individual or organization that stores or processes personal information on an identifiable person from an EU member state (regardless of whether the processing or storage of information occurs in the EU or not).

- The EU's data protection laws have long been regarded as the gold standard and have been wholly or partly adopted by numerous countries outside the EU.

Before we configure the privacy and policy settings in your Moodle system, I need to bore you with some GDPR fundamentals. There is some terminology used throughout the GDPR that you will come across when configuring Moodle privacy, as presented in the following screenshot:

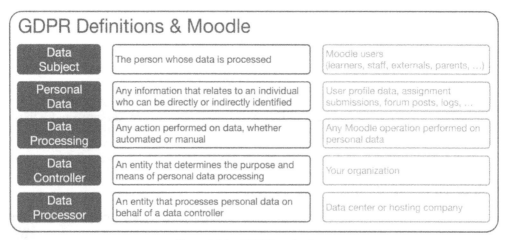

Figure 14.1 – GDPR terminology

To summarize *Figure 14.1*, a data subject's personal data is processed by a data processor on behalf of a data controller. In Moodle speak, user-related data is stored in your data center or by a third-party hosting company, as instructed by your organization.

> **Important note**
> The main objective of GDPR is the protection of personal data.

Moodle stores personal and non-personal data, and it is the personal data GDPR is concerned about and that we need to protect. Data subjects (Moodle users) have far-fetching rights concerning their stored and processed data, which have been summarized in the following screenshot, alongside the respective Moodle feature:

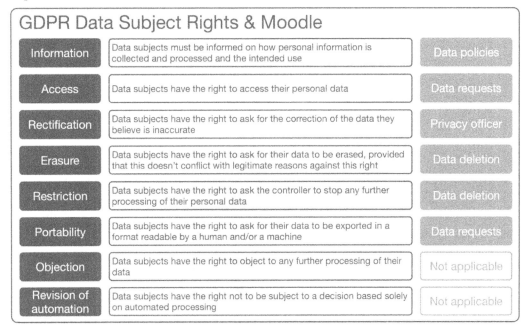

Figure 14.2 – GDPR data subject rights

From a Moodle user's—sorry—from a data subject's perspective, access to these rights can be gained via the **Privacy and policies** section in the user profile and might look like this:

Privacy and policies

Contact the privacy officer

Data requests

Export all of my personal data

Delete my account

Data retention summary

Policies and agreements

Figure 14.3 – GDPR data subject rights (Moodle user profile)

So, why couldn't Moodle just implement GDPR in its core and label the product as GDPR-compliant? Unfortunately, such a hardcoded approach is impossible since different factors must be considered and hence configured. Examples are the users' ages (kids are better protected than adults), the type of data that is stored (age or gender, for example, might be acceptable in one Moodle system but not another), and local or internal regulatory constraints overruling GDPR—in particular, retention periods of data.

> **Important note**
>
> There is no one-size-fits-all Moodle GDPR setup. Correct configuration and implementation of processes and procedures are required.

What might be perceived as a shortcoming of GDPR is actually its strength because it caters to all kinds of setups in different contexts. For Moodle administrators, this has two key implications:

1. You need to liaise with a legal expert. You know, the people in grey suits who charge by the minute.

2. You need to configure Moodle's privacy settings, policies, and processes in line with what the grey suit told you.

The GDPR also specifies seven principles for the lawful processing of personal data. Furthermore, privacy implementations must be supplemented by required documentation in case of an audit, infringements, or complaints. Both items are beyond the scope of this book and will not be dealt with in this chapter, but the grey suit will be able to assist you on these matters.

Enough legal speak, so let's get started. Moodle has dedicated an entire **Privacy and policies** section to the topic, which we will cover in the remainder of the chapter. First, we need to designate a privacy officer, which is dealt with in the following section.

Designating a privacy officer

Once the Moodle privacy features have been set up, someone will have to deal with the day-to-day requests from users and any other privacy-related issues. Moodle has named this function **privacy officer**, and we are sticking to this term here.

The Moodle administrator regularly takes on this role for smaller instances, often a separate function in larger systems. Either way, we recommend setting up a dedicated user account to deal with any privacy-related tasks.

To establish a privacy officer in Moodle, the following three steps are required:

1. Create a new **Privacy Officer** role.

2. Assign the role to your designated privacy officer(s) in the **System** context.

3. Activate Moodle's privacy officer functionality.

The context type where the role may be assigned must be set to **System**. The following screenshot arrangement shows the capabilities that must be set to **Allow**. The simplest way to find them is to search for dataprivacy and policy, respectively:

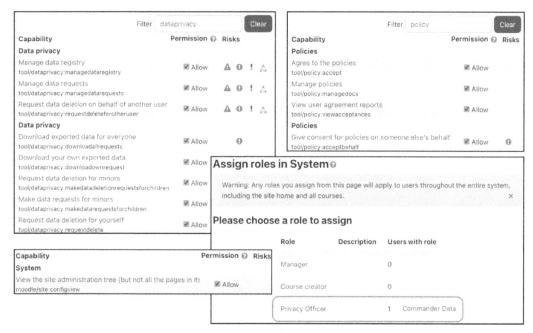

Figure 14.4 – Privacy Officer role definition

For more details on creating and assigning roles, refer to *Chapter 6, Managing Permissions, Roles, and Capabilities.*

The new role must be selected in **Privacy officer role mapping** in **Site administration | Users | Privacy and policies | Privacy settings**. This role mapping and the moodle/site:configview capability will grant assigned privacy officers access to the relevant site administration menu items as shown:

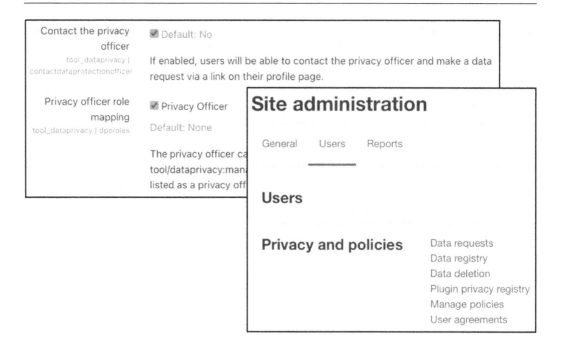

Figure 14.5 – Activating Privacy Officer functionality

Once the **Contact the privacy officer** option has been enabled, users will have access to the feature via the **Privacy and policies** section in the user profile, as shown in *Figure 14.3*. It is recommended to keep this feature deactivated until you have configured all required privacy elements. We'll start with the right to be informed, implemented in Moodle as policies.

Managing policies

Moodle has implemented a policy tool that lets you define multiple policies, supports policy versions, tracks user agreements, and can deal with the consent of minors.

To give you an initial understanding of how Moodle policies are structured, have a look at the following diagram:

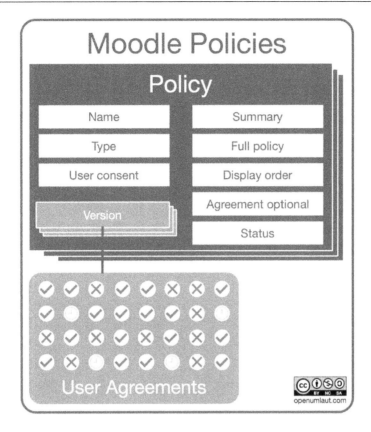

Figure 14.6 – Moodle policies

A site can have multiple policies; for example, you might have three policies: one handling user data privacy, one dealing with cookies, and one covering third-party plugins and external data.

Each policy can have multiple versions. Every time there is a change in a policy, a new version is created, which might have to be consented to by your users. For each version that is not labeled as a minor change (typos or cosmetic adjustments), Moodle keeps track of user agreements.

In this section, you will learn how to configure and monitor the following policy features:

- Choosing a site policy handler
- Creating and updating policies, including policy versions
- Monitoring user agreements
- Dealing with minors (in Moodle, not in life)

Before we create our first policy, we first need to choose a site policy handler.

Choosing a site policy handler

The Moodle site policy handler determines how data policies and user consent are managed. Moodle ships with the following two policy handlers:

- **Default (core)**: You can specify a **Site policy URL** parameter, which has to be agreed to by all registered users, and a **Site policy URL for guests** parameter

- **Policies (tool_policy)**: You can manage multiple site, privacy, and other policies, including policy versions, and monitor different types of user consent

The `core` policy handler is a one-size-fits-all method and does not support advanced policy functionality. We recommend not using this "old" tool. The remainder of this chapter focuses on `tool_policy`, which you must enable at **Site administration** | **Users** | **Privacy and policies** | **Policy settings** by selecting the **Site policy handler** type, as illustrated in the following screenshot:

Figure 14.7 – Site policy handlers

A separate privacy policy can be specified for the Moodle app in the **App policy URL** parameter in **Site administration** | **General** | **Mobile app** | **Mobile settings**. If left empty, the global **Site policy URL** parameter will be used instead. We have dealt with the app policy in *Chapter 11, Enabling Mobile Learning*.

Site policy handlers have been implemented as plugins. Technically, future data protection frameworks from other regulations may be developed and made available in Moodle.

Now that we have chosen the correct policy handler, let's create our first policy.

Creating policies

Policies are managed in **Site administration** | **Users** | **Privacy and policies** | **Manage policies**. In our system, we have already created three policies—one is active, and two are in draft status, as seen here:

Figure 14.8 – Policies and agreements

Every user who logs on to your Moodle site for the first time must agree to any active privacy notice; two users have already done so, and the others are still missing.

When you select the **New policy** button, you will be presented with the following screen:

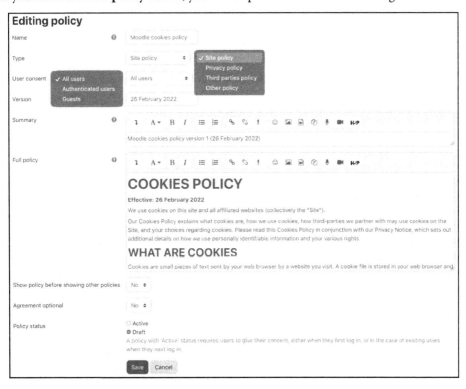

Figure 14.9 – Creating a new policy

In addition to the self-explanatory **Name** field, the following fields have to be provided:

- **Type**: The available options are **Site policy**, **Privacy policy**, **Third parties policy**, and **Other policy**. The policy type does not impact the policy behavior and is for display purposes only.

- **User consent**: Does the policy apply to **All users**, **Authenticated users**, or only **Guests**? Guest policies don't have to be given consent to; instead, if a user browses the site or logs in as a guest, a modal notice window is shown at the bottom of the page with links to all policies that have been defined for guests or all users:

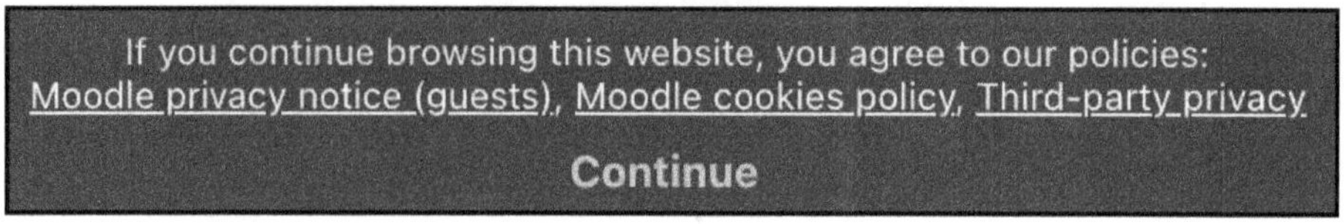

> If you continue browsing this website, you agree to our policies:
> Moodle privacy notice (guests), Moodle cookies policy, Third-party privacy
>
> **Continue**

Figure 14.10 – Guest policies

- **Version**: You should come up with your own versioning convention. Most sites use the date, a version number, or a combination thereof. If the version of an edited policy hasn't been changed, Moodle automatically appends a version number to it.

- **Summary**: A short description of the policy, which will be shown on the acknowledgment screen.

- **Full policy**: That's the policy's full (legal) text.

- **Show policy before showing other policies**: Should this be the first policy to be shown when multiple policies are present? An alternative way to change the order of policies is by using the up and down arrows on the **Policies and agreements** screen.

- **Agreement optional**: Optional agreements are displayed but can be declined by users without consequences.

- **Policy status**: As soon as you switch the status from **Draft** to **Active**, users (except administrators) have to consent to the policy at login.

Be careful with creating too many try-out policies: as soon as you have set a policy to **Active** once, it cannot be deleted anymore! All you can do is change its status back to **Draft**, but it'll be in your system indefinitely unless you manually remove it at the database level.

If you modify a policy, Moodle creates a new version, which we will cover in the following subsection.

Updating policies (versioning)

Due to the fact that data protection is a legal requirement, a history of the entire policy trail must be kept. This auditability applies to policies (covered first) and user agreements (covered next).

> **Important note**
> When you edit a policy, Moodle will create a new version.

When editing a user policy, you will likely change its name and/or content (summary or full policy). Either way, two fields are relevant for the handling of the policy:

- **Version**: Each version number within a policy trail has to be unique. If you don't change it, Moodle will automatically amend it with a version number.

- **Policy status**: If the status of the policy is active, you can choose whether the edited version is a minor or major change. Minor changes do not have to be consented to by users; major ones do.

You can view the version trail of a policy via the **View previous versions** option in the **Actions** column on the **Manage policies** page. Users can also view current and out-of-date versions via the **Policies and agreement** link in the **Privacy and policy** block in their profile. Here is a sample where our cookies policy has three versions:

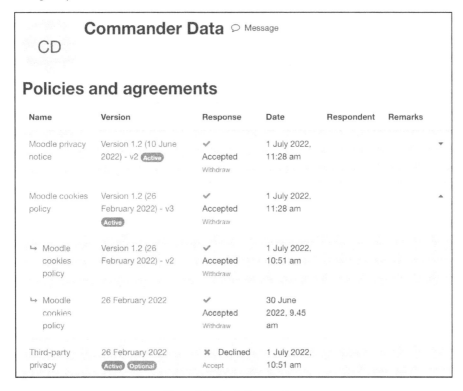

Figure 14.11 – Policy versions

Once you have created and updated your policies, you can manage their user agreements, as covered in the following subsection.

Monitoring user agreements

A user agreement spells out the rights and responsibilities of all involved parties.

> **Important note**
>
> A user agreement is a **legally binding contract** between a data subject (Moodle user) and the site's owner, operator, or provider (data controller or data processor).

Given the contractual nature of user agreements, you, the privacy officer, or anybody who has been granted permission (`tool/policy:viewacceptances`) must keep track of user agreements. You can view the status of each agreement in **Site administration** | **Users** | **Privacy and policies** | **User agreements**:

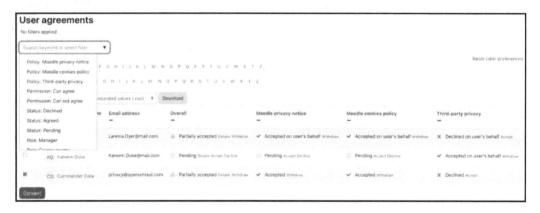

Figure 14.12 – User agreements

User agreements for a particular policy may also be viewed via the **Manage policies** page by clicking the link in the **Agreements** column. You can filter the table by **Policy** (and its versions), **Permission**, **Status**, and **Role**. For each user and each policy, one of the following statuses is shown:

- **Accepted**: The user has consented to the policy.

- **Pending**: The user has not (yet) consented to the policy.

- **Declined**: The user has rejected the policy. This status only exists for optional agreements.

Any user with the `tool/policy:acceptbehalf` capability can give consent **on a user's behalf**. This operation is relevant in scenarios where written consent has been obtained offline or consent has to be given on behalf of minors, which we will deal with next.

Dealing with minors

The GDPR attaches particular importance to protecting children's personal data. Minors (users younger than the age of digital consent) may be prevented from consenting to privacy policies. Instead, someone (usually a parent or guardian) must give consent on their behalf.

To deal with users agreeing to policies, you need to make use of the `tool/policy:accept` capability. Depending on the percentage of minors on your site, you can choose between two different approaches, as outlined next (partly borrowed from `docs.moodle.org/en/Policies#Minors`).

Sites with minors as the majority of users

This approach prevents all users from accepting policies except those you explicitly grant permission to—for instance, teachers or staff. Here are the steps you would need to take:

1. Set the `tool/policy:accept` capability to **Prohibit** in the **Authenticated user** role.
2. Create a new role with the `tool/policy:accept` capability set to **Allow**, and set **context type where the role may be assigned** to **System**.
3. Assign the new role to all users who are allowed to agree to policies.

For instructions on modifying and creating roles, refer to *Chapter 6, Managing Permissions, Roles, and Capabilities.*

Sites with minors as the minority of users

The approach is the opposite of the previous one and prevents nobody from accepting a policy except individually selected users (minors). Follow these steps:

1. Create a new role with the `tool/policy:accept` capability set to **Prohibit**, and set **context type where the role may be assigned** to **System**.
2. Assign the new role to all users who are NOT allowed to agree to policies.

To avoid the overhead of dealing with paper-based policies and signatures that must then be accepted on their behalf in Moodle, consider the **Parent** role we covered in *Chapter 6, Managing Permissions, Roles, and Capabilities.*

The scenario we covered dealt with minors already authenticated on your site. When you expect minors to sign up for new accounts, you also need to verify their digital age of consent, which we will cover in the following subsection.

Verifying the digital age of consent

If you have self-registration activated and anticipate minors signing up to your site, you should enable the **Digital age of consent verification** setting at **Site administration | Users | Privacy and policies | Privacy settings**, as illustrated in the following screenshot:

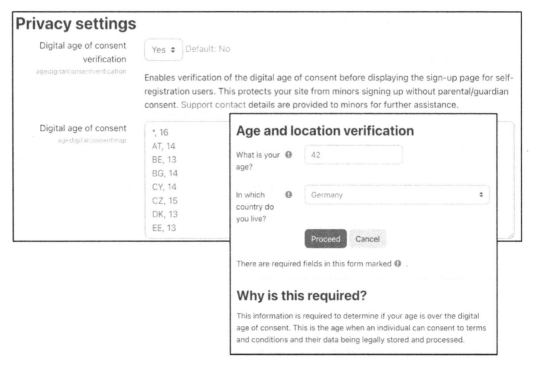

Figure 14.13 – Digital age of consent

You can further specify the **Digital age of consent** setting and the age in any country where it differs from the default. Enter each age on a new line with the format `country code, age`. The default age is indicated by * in place of the country code. The two-letter country codes are as specified in ISO format.

Once enabled and configured, users will have to provide their age and select a country of residence before they are allowed to proceed.

This concludes the section on privacy policies. The second part of the chapter deals with the data registry, which is needed for managing data requests.

Configuring the data registry

One of the information types that users can request under the GDPR is a list of all data processing and the reasoning behind it, including its retention period. The data registry contains that information, represented in categories and purposes.

Important note

Categories are used to organize the data in Moodle.

Purposes describe the usage (legal reason and retention period) of the data.

You will find the data registry in **Site administration** | **Users** | **Privacy and policies** | **Data registry**, which displays the following explanation:

The data registry enables categories (types of data) and purposes (the reasons for processing data) to be set for all content on the site – from users and courses down to activities and blocks. For each purpose, a retention period may be set. When a retention period has expired, the data is flagged and listed for deletion, awaiting admin confirmation.

This note perfectly sums up the objective of the data registry. The structure of the data registry is depicted in the following diagram:

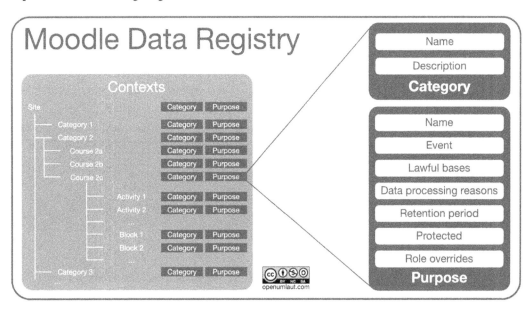

Figure 14.14 – Data registry

Every context in the system, from **Site** to users and categories, all the way down to individual course activities and blocks, is assigned a category and a purpose. Before we can manage data requests, we first need to configure these categories and purposes, which we will cover in the following two subsections.

Managing data registry categories

Select the **Categories** item from the **Edit** menu in **Site administration** | **Users** | **Privacy and policies** | **Data registry** to access data registry categories. Use the plus button to add new entries; we have already created three data registry categories, as follows:

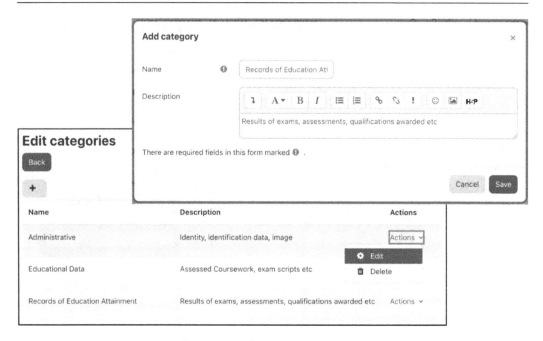

Figure 14.15 – Data registry categories

Before you can assign added categories to contexts, we need to create data registry purposes.

Managing data registry purposes

Select the **Purposes** item from the **Edit** menu in **Site administration | Users | Privacy and policies | Data registry** to access data registry categories. Use the plus button to add new entries; we have already created some data registry purposes, as follows:

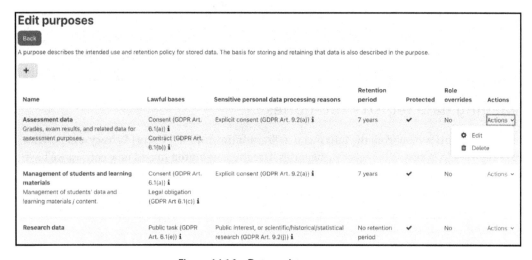

Figure 14.16 – Data registry purposes

Each purpose has the following properties:

- **Name** and **Description**: These should be self-explanatory.

- **Lawful bases**: Select at least one of the available options that serve as the lawful basis. Lawfulness is one of the seven GDPR principles.

- **Sensitive personal data processing reasons**: Select at least one of the available reasons that exempt the prohibition of processing personal data. Purpose limitation is another GDPR principle.

- **Retention period**: The retention period for course content is measured from the course end date an activity is in. For a user, it is from the last login time for any user who is no longer enrolled or has already been deleted.

- **Protected**: Specify whether this data is protected from erasure by the user or not. If set, the retention of this data has a higher legal precedent over a user's request to be forgotten. This data will only be deleted after the retention period has expired.

- **Role overrides**: This option is only available when you edit a purpose. The default retention policy can be overridden for specific user roles, allowing you to specify a longer or shorter retention policy. A user account is only expired when all of their roles have expired.

The options, including their GDPR articles for lawful bases and sensitive personal data processing reasons, are shown in the following screenshot:

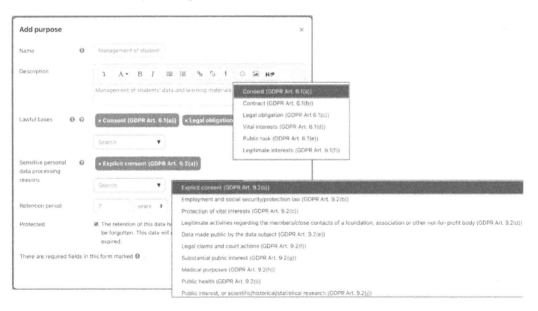

Figure 14.17 – Data registry purpose

Now that you have created data registry categories and purposes, you can assign them to contexts, as shown in the following subsection.

Assigning categories and purposes to contexts

In the data registry, for every context in your Moodle site, a category and purpose must be set, and thus the data retention period for that context. You should set the category and purpose at the site level; once this is set, all lower contexts will inherit from that level.

You can then set different categories and purposes for different context levels, such as having a specific course with a longer or shorter retention period, thus overriding the inherited values.

The **Data registry** interface is shown in the following screenshot:

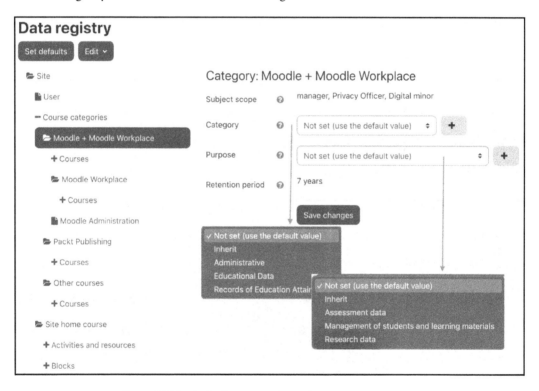

Figure 14.18 – Assigning categories and purposes to contexts

For each context, the following values are stored:

- **Subject scope**: The roles that may be assigned in this context
- **Category**: In addition to the categories specified, you have the **Not set (use the default value)** and **Inherit** (use the category from the parent context) options

- **Purpose**: In addition to the purposes specified, you have the **Not set** (**use the default value**) and **Inherit** (use the purpose from the parent context) options

- **Retention period**: The period is displayed as specified in the selected purpose

To specify default values, select the **Set defaults** button, where you can edit the default values for course categories, courses, individual activities, and blocks. The hierarchy of contexts is—from top to bottom—site, category, course, activity, and block. We covered contexts in great detail in *Chapter 6, Managing Permissions, Roles, and Capabilities*.

All Moodle core plugins fully comply with the Moodle Privacy API (docs.moodle.org/dev/Privacy_API). It is highly recommended that you only install third-party plugins that also support the Privacy API, which you can verify in the **plugin privacy compliance registry** at **Site administration** | **Users** | **Privacy and policies** | **Plugin privacy registry**. All installed Moodle plugins are listed alongside information on personal data stored and whether they comply with the Privacy API or not. Any flagged plugins storing personal data will not be able to be exported or deleted through Moodle's privacy system. Privacy-friendly plugins are labeled as such in the Moodle plugins database at moodle.org/plugins. You can see an example of this here:

Awards

Privacy friendly

Figure 14.19 – Privacy-friendly plugins

Users can view the data registry information (core and third-party) via the **Data retention summary** link in their profile. You can remove this link by unticking the **Show data retention summary** option in **Site administration** | **Users** | **Privacy and policies** | **Privacy settings**.

Once the data registry has been completed, it will be used by data deletion processes, which are part of the data requests covered in the following section.

Managing data requests

Users have different options to request information or amendments to their data via their profile menu:

- Contact the privacy officer (**Message**)
- Request a copy of their personal data (**Export**)
- Request the deletion of their personal data (**Delete**)

The following diagram illustrates the workflow of data requests, also known as subject access requests:

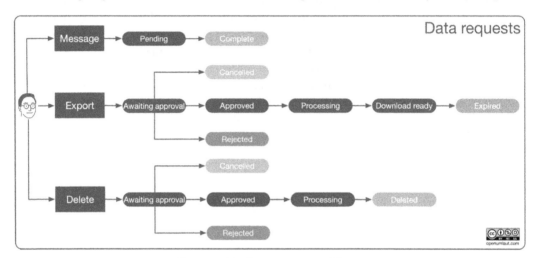

Figure 14.20 – Data request workflows

To manage all data requests, go to **Site administration** | **Users** | **Privacy and policies** | **Data requests**, where you see a screen like this:

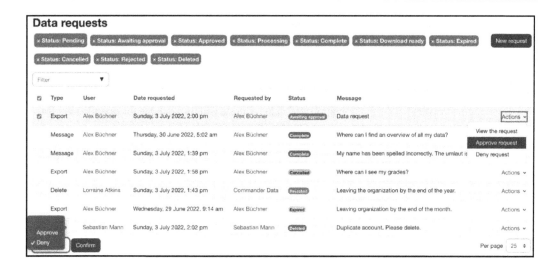

Figure 14.21 – Data requests

The message workflow is straightforward: a user contacts the privacy officer via the contact form in their user profile. The privacy officer will be notified, and can then act upon the message and mark the request as complete. This option covers the data subject's right to rectification—that is, the right to ask for the correction of data they believe is inaccurate.

The other two workflows—export and deletion—require a little more attention and will be dealt with in the following two subsections.

Data export

Data subjects have the right to access their personal data, and the data export feature facilitates this GDPR right.

User requests to export all their data are initially labeled as **Awaiting approval**. As long as no action has been taken, users can **Cancel** their requests. The privacy officer either has to **Approve** or **Deny** the export requests; once approved, requests will be queued and processed during the next cron run (**Processing**). When completed, the user will be notified that the data export status has been changed to **Download ready**. When the specified period has passed, the status will change to **Expired**, and downloading will be disabled.

The data export format is **JSON** and complies with the GDPR right to portability, where the data has to be in a structured, commonly used, and machine-readable format. The download comprises a zipped bundle of files, including field descriptors.

Three parameters have an impact on the data export workflow, which you can configure at **Site administration | Users | Privacy and policies | Privacy settings**:

- **Automatic data export request approval**: The approval step is skipped, and the export is approved automatically.

- **Data request expiry**: The time that approved data requests will be available for download before expiring. If set to zero, then there is no time limit.

- **Include logs when exporting**: Whether or not user-related log entries are included in the export.

Data export covers the right to access in the GDPR. The right to erasure is covered by data deletion, which is the topic of the following subsection.

Data deletion

Data subjects have the right to ask for their data to be erased, provided that this doesn't conflict with legitimate reasons against this right. The latter half of this sentence is tricky, as "legitimate reasons" might differ not only between organizations but also between Moodle instances, user types (roles), courses, and even individual activities. We specified this information in the data registry, which is taken into account during data deletion processing.

The initial stages of the data deletion process are identical to the data export workflow: requests are put in a holding area where they wait for approval; they can then be approved or denied by the privacy officer unless the user has canceled the request.

The data erasure is processed during the next `cron` run considering data retention periods specified in the data registry. Depending on how granular you have specified data retention values, this might trigger the removal of some data straightaway, whereas other data might not be deleted for years. The following basic timeline illustrates when data is erased during the deletion processing and when it is kept until the end of the expiry period:

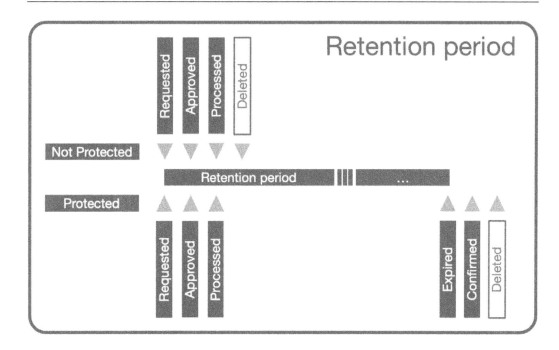

Figure 14.22 – Retention period – protected versus not protected

You can view data for which the retention period has expired by navigating to **Site administration |
Users | Privacy and policies | Data Deletion** and choosing a context (**Course, User, Activities and
resources**, and **Blocks**). In my system, the retention period for personal data is 7 years. I didn't want to
wait that long, so I created a test retention period of a single day to demonstrate its behavior, as follows:

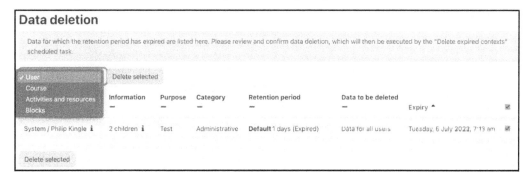

Figure 14.23 – Data deletion

Each entry shows privacy-related information about the data to be deleted—here, it is a user. You
need to confirm the irreversible data deletion, which will be executed during the next `cron` run.

Three parameters have an impact on the data deletion workflow, which you can configure at **Site administration | Users | Privacy and policies | Privacy settings**:

- **Automatic data deletion request approval**: The approval step is skipped, and the deletion is approved automatically

- **Create automatic data deletion requests**: When users are deleted manually, a data deletion request will be created automatically

- **Consider courses without end data as active**: This option has been explained in detail in the inline help and details nicely how the retention period for course users is calculated:

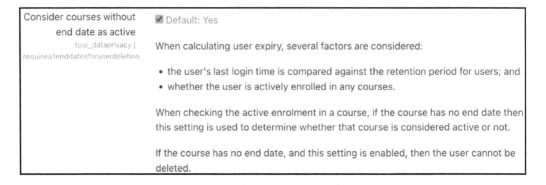

Figure 14.24 – Data retention calculation for user expiry

This concludes the section on managing data requests, where we covered Moodle's data privacy tools to deal with the following GDPR user rights:

- Right to rectification (**Message**)
- Right to access (**Export**)
- Right to erasure (**Delete**)

To conclude the chapter, we have summarized its content and provided its key messages in a Moodle privacy checklist.

Summary

May 25, 2018: The GDPR applies to all EU residents.

One week earlier: Moodle 3.5 is released, supporting some but not all GDPR features.

We started the chapter on Moodle privacy with those two events in May 2018. Now that you have read through the chapter and hopefully realized the complexity of ensuring the compliance of all IT systems, can you imagine the hectic week all stakeholders had to configure Moodle systems? For those old enough to remember, dealing with the Y2K bug was peanuts compared to complying with GDPR.

This chapter introduced some legal background on the GDPR. We then designated a privacy officer by setting up a dedicated role and activating the **Privacy Officer** functionality.

Next, you learned all you need to know to manage policies. We configured Moodle's policy handler before creating and updating versioned policies. We then monitored user agreements and dealt with minors in your Moodle system.

Then, we configured your data registry, setting up data registry categories and purposes before assigning them to contexts.

Finally, we managed data requests, dealing with data rectification (**Message**), data access (**Export**), and data erasure (**Delete**).

As a summary, here is a short Moodle privacy checklist. While this enumeration is by no means complete, it gives an indication of the elements you are responsible for as a Moodle administrator and/or Moodle privacy officer:

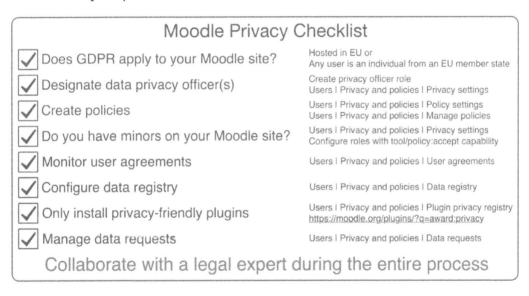

Figure 14.25 – Moodle privacy checklist

Now that your system hopefully complies with data privacy and all the grey suits are happy, let's ensure Moodle performs to its full potential. In the following chapter, we will optimize Moodle to guarantee adequate scalability and hence, a good user experience.

Optimizing Moodle Performance

The performance of web-based systems is a critical issue, and it is the key responsibility of an administrator to configure, monitor, and fine-tune the LMS for maximum speed. While Moodle has the potential to scale to tens of thousands of simultaneous users, good performance management is required to guarantee adequate scalability.

After providing an overview of the subject, we will cover the most relevant topics related to Moodle's performance and optimization:

- **Optimizing Moodle feature performance**: We will look at performance issues in Moodle functions and Moodle activities. Optimizing their performance is often a trade-off between improved speed and potentially reduced functionality, which is discussed.

- **Moodle Universal Cache (MUC)**: We cover the different elements of the powerful MUC, namely cache types, cache stores, and cache definitions. We will then run you through some MUC performance testing and various caching options.

- **Optimizing Moodle system performance**: A range of system-related performance settings are dealt with, namely session handling, cron management and scheduled tasks, configuring global search, and setting system paths.

We will conclude the chapter with a short Moodle performance profiling and monitoring section.

Understanding Moodle performance

Web applications in general, and Moodle in particular, have very distinct application layers consisting of an operating system, web server, database server, and an application developed in a programming language. Each layer has its idiosyncrasies when it comes to optimization. We will exclusively focus on the *application layer*, which is the focus of this book, as shown in the following diagram:

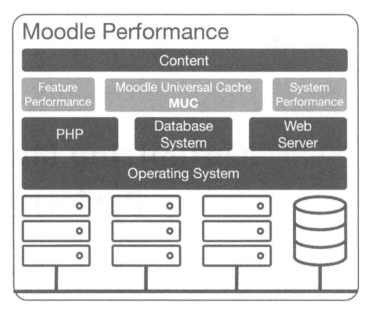

Figure 15.1 – Moodle performance

The following areas are *NOT* dealt with in any detail, and it is necessary to refer to the respective documentation with regard to performance and optimization issues:

- **Operating system performance**: The choice of operating system and configuration will significantly impact how Moodle performs. In principle, Linux or any other Unix derivative performs better than any other operating system. PHP applications, such as Moodle, run significantly slower in a Windows environment than on Linux. Some aspects of this were covered in *Chapter 1, Installing Moodle*, when we dealt with the installation of Moodle.

- **Database performance**: The database is a major bottleneck since it requires disk access, which is slower than memory access. Entire books and conferences have been dedicated to database optimization, with indexing, caching, buffering, querying, and connection handling as the primary candidates for discussion. The two techniques that significantly impact database performance are enabling query caching and increasing buffer sizes. You should consider running the database on a dedicated server or a cluster. The former is relatively straightforward: once set up, all you need to do is to change the $CFG->dbhost entry in config.php from localhost to the IP address of your database. The latter is significantly more complex and requires strong database administration skills.

  There is also much debate about which database is best suited for Moodle. While the open source camp is divided between MySQL, MariaDB, and PostgreSQL, corporates are split between MS SQL Server and Oracle. Whichever your choice of system, a well-set-up and tuned database will always perform better than one used with out-of-the-box settings—"The best database system is the one you know."

- **Web server performance**: Each web server (Apache, **Internet Information Services** (IIS), nginx, and so on) offers an array of optimization settings that include memory handling, caching, process management, and other minor tweaks.

- **PHP performance**: There are several ways in which PHP can be forced to execute code significantly faster. The key to doing this is using a PHP accelerator in combination with good memory management and caching techniques. Moodle supports **Zend OPcache**, which is precompiled by default. Zend OPcache speeds up PHP execution by opcode caching and optimization. It stores precompiled script byte code in shared memory. You can check whether OPcache is working correctly by going to **Site administration** | **Server** | **Environment**, as illustrated in the following screenshot:

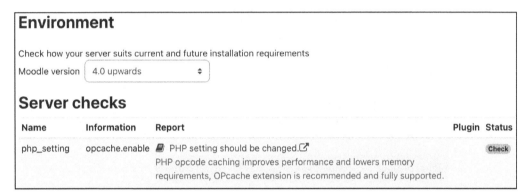

Figure 15.2 – Zend OPcache check

Your `php.ini` file is likely to contain the following entries (for details, refer to `docs.moodle.org/en/OPcache`):

```
[OPcache]
  opcache.enable = 1
  opcache.memory_consumption=128
  opcache.interned_strings_buffer=8
  opcache.max_accelerated_files=8000
  opcache.revalidate_freq=60
  opcache.fast_shutdown=1
  opcache.enable_cli=1
; Required for Moodle
opcache.use_cwd = 1
opcache.validate_timestamps = 1
opcache.save_comments = 1
opcache.enable_file_override = 0
```

There is a handy plugin available at `moodle.org/plugins/tool_opcache`, adding a PHP OPcache management GUI to Moodle, a CLI tool to reset PHP OPcache, and a Nagios check for PHP OPcache.

- **Hardware performance**: We already mentioned in *Chapter 1, Installing Moodle*, that there is no one-size-fits-all approach to the ideal hardware setup. For single-server systems, the key is RAM: the more, the better. It's as simple as that. Once the level of concurrency increases above a certain level, it is inevitable to use multiple web servers in a load-balanced environment.

- **Network performance**: Networks are the backbone of most IT infrastructures and thus a potential performance bottleneck. Your topology, software, and hardware must be configured correctly to ensure a well-performing network without typical issues such as packet losses.

- **Content performance**: The content that is created and uploaded by your course creators or home page designers will have an impact on the performance of your system. While you cannot dictate which learning sources are added to Moodle, you might want to recommend two main strategies to reduce the load content has on your system: First, the content volume in courses and the home page should be kept to a manageable size, avoiding the infamous *scroll of death*. Second, content should be optimized, especially office docs (for instance, PDFs instead of Word files), images (resolution and color depth), and audio/video (sample rate and resolution).

While all the preceding criteria apply, some elements can be changed on the fly. For example, during exam week, you might consider increasing the memory available for Moodle, while during the summer break, you can reduce the number of servers to carry out maintenance. More sophisticated setups let you specify load and usage thresholds, which dynamically trigger resource allocation.

For each area mentioned, profile tools, monitoring systems, benchmarks, and stress tests are available to help you gauge which performance bottlenecks are present and whether they have been reduced after optimization has been carried out.

An entire area has been dedicated to performance and optimization in the Moodle docs. You can find most of the relevant information and links to relevant sites at `docs.moodle.org/en/Performance`.

You should remember that Moodle's performance cannot be viewed independently. For example, improving security comes at a price in terms of performance reduction; running your entire site over HTTPS is highly recommended, but it slows down certain operations. Some typical trade-offs are shown in the seesaw depicted here:

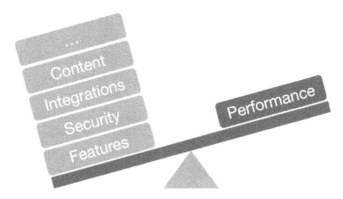

Figure 15.3 – Performance versus the rest of the world

Another trade-off you will face regularly is performance versus functionality, where certain features harm how speedily your system performs. Moodle comes with an elementary performance report (**Site administration** | **Reports** | **Performance overview**), showing some of those trade-offs.

We will kick off the list of performance optimizations by looking at some of those Moodle features that can be optimized but will impact some or all of your users.

Optimizing Moodle feature performance

The title of this section is slightly misleading because optimizing Moodle features effectively means limiting its functionality. Suggestions in this section have a positive impact on performance but a potentially negative impact on user functionality. While some features might be dispensable (for instance, statistics), others should be non-negotiable, such as backups.

We have grouped Moodle features in the performance optimization context into Moodle functions and Moodle activities.

Optimizing Moodle functions

In this subsection, we have collected some Moodle tools that impact the performance of your LMS. Most of the following functions have been dealt with elsewhere in this book, and we provide links to the respective chapters:

- **Course backups**: As you will learn in the next chapter, course backups hurt performance during execution, especially on larger systems. If possible, schedule the backup procedure when the load on the overall system is low. If you turn off site-wide course backups and use system-level backups instead, you reduce performance problems but lose the ability to recover individual items. A compromise is to include only essential data and leave out less relevant information, such as log files. All this will be dealt with in *Chapter 16, Avoiding Sleepless Nights – Moodle Backup and Restore*.

- **Log files**: In *Chapter 12, Gaining Insights through Moodle Reporting and Analytics*, we looked at Moodle logging, reporting, and analytics. Keeping track of user behavior can potentially harm your server performance, as logs must be created and kept up to date. The recommended approach is only to log data that will be analyzed and reported on. Three parameters determine the volume of logs: the number of log stores, the number of fields stored, and the time logs are being kept.

- **Statistics**: If you have enabled the statistics functionality, be aware that it is likely to have a profound impact on the performance of your system whenever statistical information is updated. Go back to the *Gathering statistics* section in *Chapter 12, Gaining Insights through Moodle Reporting and Analytics*, and ensure that the configuration has minimum impact on your system.

- **Home page courses**: The home page is likely to be accessed frequently by all users. On sites with many courses, displaying all of them every time the home page is called is unlikely to be a pleasant user experience. You can limit the **Maximum number of courses** and **Maximum category depth** parameters by going to **Site administration | General | Site home | Site home settings**.

- **Roles and users**: We dedicated an entire chapter to roles (*Chapter 6, Managing Permissions, Roles, and Capabilities*). The robust flexibility of Moodle's roles system comes at a price, which is a minor drop in performance if a lot of lookups are required in the context hierarchy (avoid global roles) and the override mechanism is applied frequently.

- **User selector**: The user selector is displayed in various places throughout Moodle. If you experience speed problems in courses with a large number of users, adjust the **Maximum number of users per page** settings by navigating to **Site administration | Users | Permissions | User policies**.

Next up are Moodle activities, which offer some performance tweaking settings.

Optimizing Moodle activities

While optimizing Moodle activities will positively impact performance, they should only be implemented if the loss of functionality is acceptable to your users. The following are some modules that can be tweaked:

- **Gradebook optimization**

    Due to the complexity of the gradebook, some settings in the **Grades** menu will impact performance. In general, when more aggregation and other calculations have to be carried out, the population of the gradebook data store becomes slow. For example, the **Aggregate including subcategories** parameter in **Site administration | Grades | Grade category settings** will add minor overhead to calculating grades.

    A second gradebook-related area that impacts performance is the gradebook history, which forces Moodle to keep track of any changes in grades. Go to **Site administration | Server | Cleanup**, and you will see two gradebook history settings at the bottom:

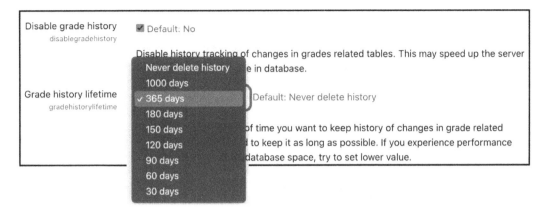

Figure 15.4 – Gradebook history settings

The gradebook history is turned on by default, and values are kept forever. You can either turn the facility off entirely or limit the time you wish to keep the grade entries.

You will find more details on the gradebook in the *Configuring grades and the gradebook* section of *Chapter 9, Configuring Educational Features*.

- **Chat optimization**

By default, Moodle chat uses the **AJAX** method, which, like the **Normal** method, contacts all participating clients regularly. The upside of both approaches is that they require no configuration and work on any system; the downside is that they have a significant performance impact on the server, especially when the chat activity is used regularly. A solution is to use the **Chat server** daemon, which ensures a scalable chat environment. However, the daemon, a small system-level program that runs in the background, has to be installed on the operating system level and only works on Unix (check your administration guide for how to do this).

To change the chat method Moodle uses and to configure some performance parameters, go to **Site administration | Plugins | Activity modules | Chat**. We dealt with these in the *Synchronous communication* section of *Chapter 10, Configuring Technical Features*.

The following table lists the performance-related settings and the methods to which they apply:

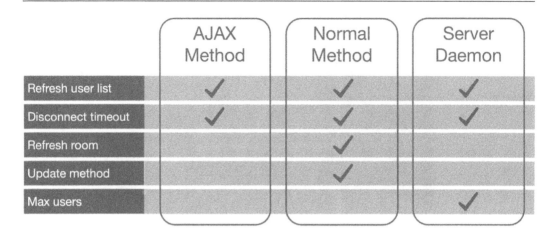

Figure 15.5 – Chat performance settings

- **Forum optimization**

  On systems with large forums, tracking unread posts can slow down the activity. Though the impact is relatively minor, the tracking can be turned off by going to **Site administration | Plugins | Activity modules | Forum**, where you will find the **Track unread posts** and **Allow forced read tracking** parameters.

- **Moodle's filter settings**

  We focused on filter functionality when we looked at the feature in *Chapter 9, Configuring Educational Features*. Now, let's look at filters again, highlighting some performance issues. The following is a list ordered by priority when setting up filters by going to **Site administration | Plugins | Filters | Manage filters**:

  I.   Activate all the filters that course creators need but not more than those. Too many active Moodle filters affect the server load, especially on lower-end systems. The number of active filters will increase the time it takes to scan each page since filters are applied sequentially, not in parallel.

  II.   Configure as many active filters as possible using the **Off, but available** setting. They can then be activated locally at any course or activity level.

III.   Place the filters used most often (usually multimedia plugins) at the top of the list, as filters are applied on a first-come-first-serve basis.

IV.   Caching is applied to pages that use text filters, a topic discussed later in the *MUC* section. Additionally, you should optimize the generic filter settings in **Site administration | Plugins | Filters | Common filter settings**: only turn on **Filter uploaded files** if required. Also, change **Filter match once per page**, **Filter match once per text**, and **Filter navigation within system context** to **On** if the resulting behaviors are acceptable. We have discussed these parameters in the *Configuring filters* section of *Chapter 9, Configuring Educational Features*.

There are other minor tweaks in Moodle activities and modules—for example, timeout values—and you'll need to adjust those when and if you encounter any performance issues.

A bigger problem than feature performance is scalability, caused by concurrent users. We will spend the rest of the chapter dealing with this issue, starting with exploring the powerful MUC.

Moodle Universal Cache (MUC)

Caching stores frequently accessed data in transient storage and expedites its access using a cached copy instead of prefetched (from disk) or recomputed (in memory) data.

> **Note**
>
> Caching has proven to be one of the most efficient performance optimization techniques, and Moodle is no exception.

Moodle contains a powerful caching framework called MUC, which allows certain functions to take advantage of different configured caching services (`docs.moodle.org/en/Caching`).

Understanding MUC

Before we look at how MUC works, let's explore some basic concepts: cache types (modes), cache stores, and cache definitions. The following diagram shows all three concepts and how they work together in MUC:

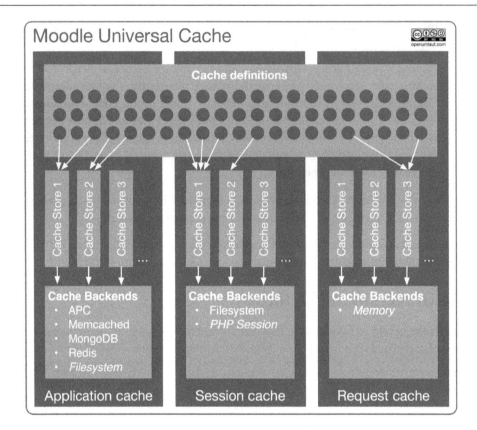

Figure 15.6 – Moodle Universal Cache

Moodle has nearly 100 cache definitions—for example, fetching of language strings, config settings, or processed CSS. Cache definitions are mapped onto cache stores, which act as connectors to the cache backend for different cache types. This all will make more sense by the end of this section.

Let's go through each component, starting with cache types.

Cache types

There are three different **cache types** in Moodle, often referred to as cache modes:

- **Application cache**: The application cache deals with Moodle-specific operations—for example, caching of language strings or configuration settings. This is the most commonly used cache as it has the highest impact on Moodle performance.

- **Session cache**: This is basically the same as your PHP session cache. It is only used in very few scenarios; we do not need to cover this in further detail.

- **Request cache**: As the name suggests, this type of caching is only stored for the lifetime of a request and allows developers to optimize code. Again, this is not a cache type we, as administrators, must worry about.

Here's an overview of the different cache types:

	Application Cache	Session Cache	Request Cache
Lifetime	Persistent	Session	Request
Applicable to	All users	User	User
Performance impact	High	Medium	Low
Default cache store	Filesystem	PHP session	Memory

Figure 15.7 – Cache types (modes)

The last entry in *Figure 15.7* describes the default cache stores. What these are and why they are critical in Moodle are covered in the following subsection.

Cache stores

In Moodle, cache stores are plugins that talk to MUC's backend.

> **Important note**
> A **cache store** connects Moodle to physical storage, where the cached data gets stored.

As mentioned previously, the default cache stores are in the form of a filesystem (for application caches), a PHP session (session caches), and memory (request caches). For most setups, these are sufficient, but for larger sites, it is beneficial to consider a dedicated application cache store.

Moodle ships with the following four application cache store plugins (the descriptions have mostly been taken from their respective websites, not some techie buzzword-bingo):

- **APC user cache (APCu)**: The alternative PHP cache is an in-memory key-value store for PHP

- **Memcached**: An in-memory key-value store for small chunks of data from results of database calls, API calls, or page rendering

- **MongoDB**: A NoSQL database system that can be configured to run like an in-memory database

- **Redis**: An in-memory data structure store, used as a distributed, in-memory, key-value database, cache, and message broker, with optional durability.

Plugins for other cache backends can be found in the **Cache Stores** section at `moodle.org/plugins/?q=type:cachestore`.

All the supported cache stores can be found at **Site administration | Plugins | Caching | Configuration**. On our system, all cache stores have been installed and configured at the system level except APCu, hence the ticks in the **Ready** column. The **Supports** column indicates which features are supported by the cache store; the options are **ttl** (time-to-live), **data guarantee**, **key awareness**, **multiple identifiers**, and **searching by key**, as illustrated in the following screenshot:

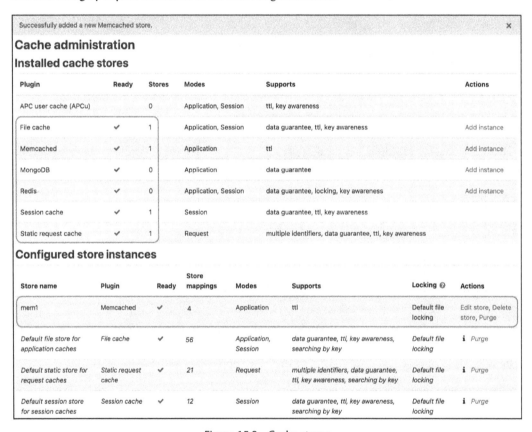

Figure 15.8 – Cache stores

For each configured cache type, you can add instances via the respective link in the **Actions** column. Each cache store has different settings, depending on the cache backend's supported features. Here are the parameters of the popular **Memcached** store, which are documented at docs.moodle. org/en/Caching#Memcached:

Figure 15.9 – Adding Memcached cache store

Once you have set up your cache store and cache instance(s), you must add **store mappings**, which are part of the cache definitions we will cover next.

Cache definitions

Different features in Moodle support caching. Years ago, there was a single monolithic cache that was either harnessed by a feature or wasn't. Now, via MUC, each feature is represented via **cache definitions**, which can be configured individually. At the time of writing, over 90 cache definitions are available, and it is expected that this number will increase with each version. For each definition, the following information is available:

- **Definition**: Name of the feature that is being cached.
- **Mode**: Cache types (**Application**, **Session**, or **Request**).

- **Component**: The Moodle component that the definition belongs to (**core** or module).

- **Area**: The section the feature belongs to—only relevant to developers.

- **Store mappings**: If no customization has taken place, this will be the default cache store of the cache mode; otherwise, the newly set value.

- **Sharing**: By default, this will be **Site identifier**. When modified, the possible values are **Everyone**, **Version**, and **Custom key** (see next bullet list).

- **Can use local store**: Only relevant on multi-server systems.

In the **Actions** column, you have **Edit mappings** and **Edit sharing** options, as well as a **Purge** option to purge the cache for this specific definition.

Edit mappings lets you specify which cache store is being used as the primary store and, for some definitions, as the final store. This is where you specify which store is used for a particular feature (cache definition).

By default, each cache definition is shared across the instance of the site. However, there are scenarios where you might want to change this to any of the following sharing options:

- **Everyone**: Every user in the system.

- **Site with the same ID**: If you run a single version of Moodle on a single server, this is identical to the preceding point. If you run Moodle on a multi-server setup, all systems will be included.

- **Sites running the same version**: If you run multiple Moodle instances from one wwwroot, only sites with identical version numbers will be included.

- **Custom key**: If you run multiple Moodle instances from one wwwroot, you can group them via a custom key. For example, you might want to cache all the instances of one country in one store.

To clear the cache of a specific definition, simply select the **Purge** option. The following screenshot shows some cache definitions and the described values:

Known cache definitions

Definition	Mode	Component	Area	Store mappings	Sharing	Can use local store	Actions
Accumulated information about modules and sections for each course	Application	core	coursemodinfo	Default file store for application caches	Site identifier	Yes	Edit mappings, Edit sharing, Purge
Activity completion status	Application	core	completion	Default file store for application caches	Site identifier	No	Edit mappings, Edit sharing, Purge
Allowed content bank course categories for current user	Session	core	contentbank_allowed_categories	Default session store for session caches	Site identifier	No	Edit mappings, Purge
Allowed content bank courses for current user	Session	core	contentbank_allowed_courses	Default session store for session caches	Site identifier	No	Edit mappings, Purge
Allowed extensions and its supporter plugins in a content bank context	Request	core	contentbank_context_extensions	Default static store for request caches	Site identifier	No	Edit mappings, Purge

Figure 15.10 – Cache definitions and mappings

There are two more elements on the **Site administration | Plugins | Caching | Configuration** page we haven't covered yet:

- **Summary of cache lock instances**: There are different locking mechanisms in shared environments, caches being no exception. By default, Moodle ships with a default file locking mechanism, and it would be possible to install additional lock instances. However, at the time of print, no such plugins are present for Moodle 4.x at `moodle.org/plugins`.

- **Stores used when no mapping is present**: You can specify which default mappings will be used for which cache type.

Now that we have covered all the relevant concepts of MUC, let's look at the items to consider when optimizing your Moodle site.

Configuring and testing MUC

We have already explored the complexity of MUC. While this provides enormous flexibility in terms of granular optimization, it makes it impossible to come up with a one-size-fits-all configuration. Somebody in the Moodle community once compared the MUC control panel with a big mixing desk at a concert: it gives you a lot of knobs to play with, but unless you know what each of them does and how they work together, you are unlikely to get good results.

Several factors impact the configuration of MUC:

- Usage of the system (volume, diversity, functions, and type)
- Underlying infrastructure (single server, multiple servers, virtualization, and so on)
- Types of cache stores used

In particular, when talking about the usage of the system, it is almost impossible to quantify this since it's constantly changing. During the summer break, there will be minimal usage; during exam time, the load on the system is likely to rise, and so on.

Performance optimization is an ongoing exercise that is accompanied by regular performance testing. Moodle provides a basic performance test for different cache types (**Site administration | Plugins | Caches | Test performance**). Here is an example where you can see the results of 100,000 unique requests; the file cache is significantly slower than the session cache, a behavior that is not unexpected:

Cache store performance reporting - 100000 unique requests per operation.

Test with 1, 10, 100, 500, 1000, 5000, 10000, 50000, 100000 requests

Store requests when used as an application cache.

Plugin	Result	Set	Get - Hit	Get - Miss	Delete
APC user cache (APCu)	Invalid plugin	-	-	-	-
File cache	Tested	13.9968	3.4031	0.4103	2.5716
Memcached					
MongoDB					
Redis					
Session cache					
Static request cache					

Store requests when used as a session cache.

Plugin	Result	Set	Get - Hit	Get - Miss	Delete
APC user cache (APCu)	Invalid plugin	-	-	-	-
File cache	Tested	17.5921	3.4271	0.4053	2.6069
Memcached	Untestable	-	-	-	-
Session cache	Tested	0.1593	0.0227	0.0119	0.0734

Store requests when used as a request cache.

Plugin	Result	Set	Get - Hit	Get - Miss	Delete
APC user cache (APCu)	Invalid plugin	-	-	-	-
File cache	Unsupported mode	-	-	-	-
Static request cache	Tested	0.0872	0.0281	0.0167	0.0777

Figure 15.11 – Cache store performance testing

While it is nice to have a built-in performance test tool in Moodle, it has two significant shortcomings: first, some plugins are classed as **Untestable**, for instance, **Redis** and **Memcached**; second, the test runs only mimic some unique requests but do not mirror their behavior if users are on your system. To overcome these drawbacks, proper profiling and monitoring are required, which will be dealt with at the end of this chapter.

There are several caching-related settings spread across the administration area, which you should tailor to your requirements:

- **Language caching**: We dealt with localization in detail in *Chapter 10, Configuring Technical Features*, where we covered the configuration of Moodle's ability to handle multiple languages. In addition to keeping the number of languages to a minimum, language caching should be utilized.

  Language packs are cached to speed up the retrieval of language strings. You will find the **Cache language menu** and **Cache all language strings** parameters by going to **Site administration | Languages | Language settings**. Unless you modify a language pack, it is highly recommended that you leave both settings enabled as they cache all the language strings rather than load them dynamically.

- **Theme caching**: Moodle caches the images and style sheets of themes either locally in a web browser or on a server. Unless you are in the process of designing or modifying a theme, which you shouldn't be doing on a live system anyway, the **Theme designer mode** setting, at **Site administration | Appearance | Themes | Theme settings**, should remain off.

  You can clear the theme cache using the **Clear theme caches** button by going to **Site administration | Appearance | Themes | Theme selector**.

- **JavaScript caching**: Moodle makes use of JavaScript and AJAX. The **Cache JavaScript** setting at **Site administration | Appearance | AJAX and Javascript** should be kept on unless you are a developer. The same applies to **YUI Combo loading** on the same page.

- **RSS caching**: RSS feeds are cached locally. You can modify the time after the cache is refreshed by changing the **Timeout** parameter at **Site administration | Plugins | Blocks | Remote RSS feeds**.

- **Networking caching**: Moodle uses cURL to fetch data from remote sites. The **cURL cache TTL** setting can be modified by going to **Site administration | Server | Performance**. The larger the time-to-live value, the better the performance. More on networking in *Chapter 19, Setting Up Moodle Networking*.

- **Repository caching**: When browsing external repositories, such as Nextcloud or Google Drive, the file listing is kept in a local cache. The amount of time the listing is kept can be changed via the **Cache expire** parameter by going to **Site administration | Plugins | Repositories | Common repository settings**. We covered repositories in *Chapter 10, Configuring Technical Features*.

You can purge all these caches in a single operation by pressing the **Purge all caches** button when you navigate to **Site administration | Development | Purge caches**. Effectively, this clears out all the defined cache stores—for instance, the directories in $CFG->dataroot/cache for the file cache. While this feature is more relevant to developers, it is recommended after installing updates or when your system behaves oddly. You can see an illustration of this in the following screenshot:

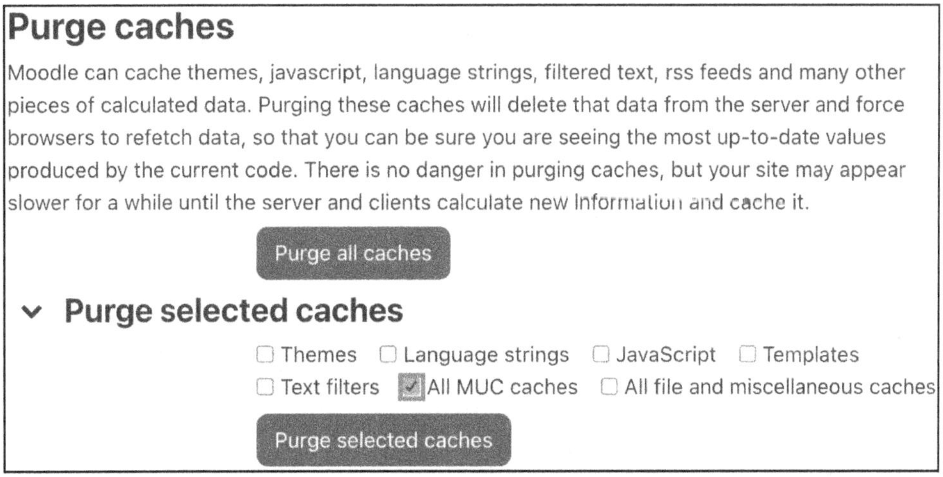

Purge caches

Moodle can cache themes, javascript, language strings, filtered text, rss feeds and many other pieces of calculated data. Purging these caches will delete that data from the server and force browsers to refetch data, so that you can be sure you are seeing the most up-to-date values produced by the current code. There is no danger in purging caches, but your site may appear slower for a while until the server and clients calculate new information and cache it.

> Purge all caches

⌄ Purge selected caches

☐ Themes   ☐ Language strings   ☐ JavaScript   ☐ Templates
☐ Text filters   ☑ All MUC caches   ☐ All file and miscellaneous caches

> Purge selected caches

Figure 15.12 – Purging caches

There is also a CLI script to purge caches: `php admin/cli/purge_caches.php`.

Once you have set up cache stores and configured all available caching options correctly, you should then move on to check that performance-related system settings have been configured properly.

Optimizing Moodle system performance

In this section, we have grouped settings that potentially impact performance without compromising any Moodle features. The topics covered are session handling, cron management and scheduled tasks, global search, and system paths.

Handling sessions

A session is initiated for each user that authenticates against Moodle, which also applies to guests. There are several well-explained settings relevant in a performance optimization context, which can be found by going to **Site administration | Server | Session handling**:

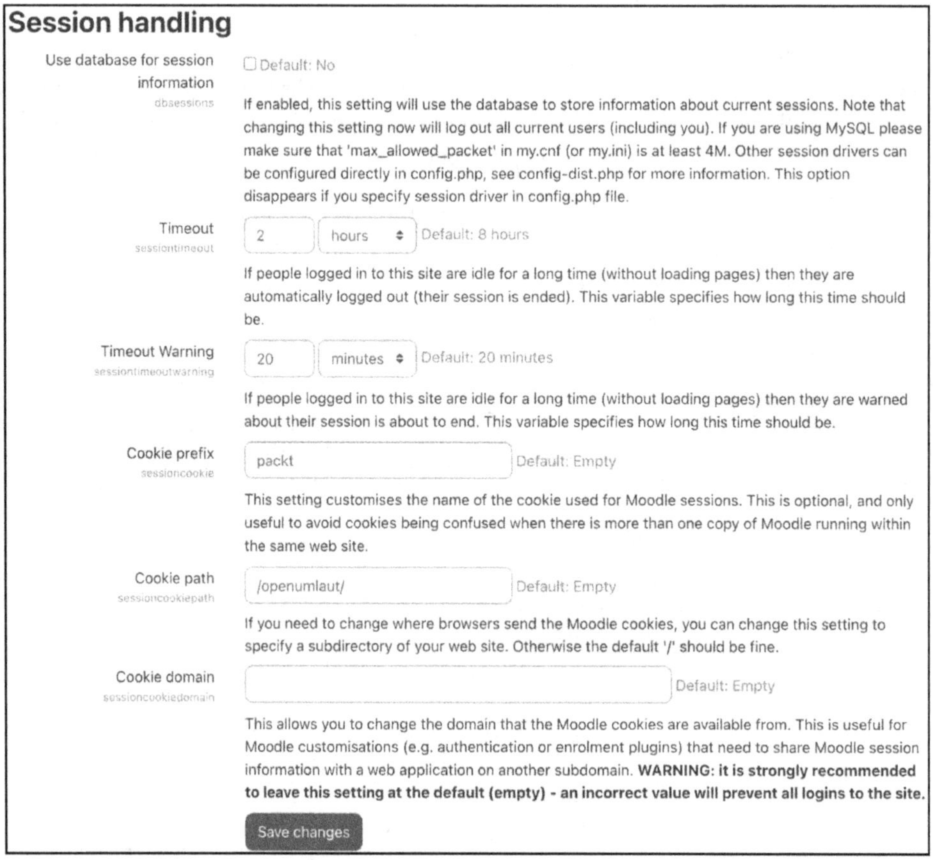

Figure 15.13 – Session handling

Moodle manages sessions and cookies very well. However, when problems occur, it is sometimes necessary to intervene manually. This should be done locally in the web browser if a specific user experiences issues (clear cache and cookies) or on the server if the problem affects multiple users. The latter is done by clearing the `mdl_sessions` table if sessions are stored in the database or emptying the `$CFG->dataroot/sessions` directory if the sessions are stored in files. Bear in mind that all logged-in users will be logged out.

You can also kill all user sessions via a CLI script that performs the preceding steps via a single command: `php admin/cli/kill_all_sessions.php`.

Cleaning up old sessions is done in the background by a so-called scheduled task. Cron management and scheduled tasks are the topics of the following subsection.

Managing cron and scheduled tasks

Moodle performs a significant number of background tasks regularly. The system script that performs these tasks is known as a **cron script** and is executed by the **cron process**.

> **Important note**
> The Moodle cron script runs different tasks at differently scheduled intervals.

The following diagram illustrates when scheduled tasks are executed in Moodle:

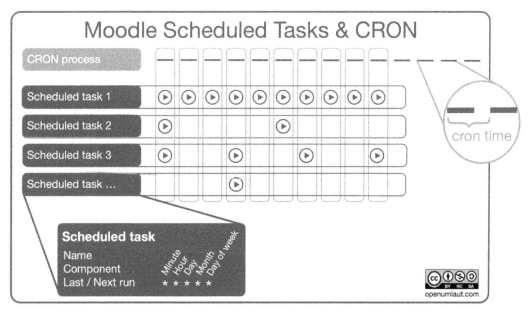

Figure 15.14 – Scheduled tasks and the cron process

Cron is a system process that triggers Moodle's cron script, which determines which tasks are executed at a particular time slot.

> **Important note**
> The cron process should run every minute.

Moodle comes with a task scheduler (**Site administration | Server | Scheduled tasks**) that lets you precisely configure which routine job runs when and how often. The following screenshot shows some selected tasks (I hope your eyesight is better than mine):

Scheduled tasks

Name	Component	Edit	Logs	Last run	Next run	Minute	Hour	Day	Day of week	Month	Fail delay	Default
CAS users sync job \auth_cas\task\sync_task	CAS server (SSO) Disabled auth_cas	⚙	📄	Never	Plugin disabled	0	0	*	*	*	0	Yes
Unused H5P files cleanup \core\task\h5p_clean_orphaned_records_task	Core	⚙	📄	Never Run now	ASAP	* Default: *	* Default: *	*	*	*	86400 Clear	No
Download available H5P content types from h5p.org \core\task\h5p_get_content_types_task	Core	⚙	📄	Saturday, 28 May 2022, 6:13 pm Run now	Task disabled	31	10	1	*	*	60 Clear	No
Legacy cron processing for plugins \core\task\legacy_plugin_cron_task	Core	⚙	📄	Thursday, 7 July 2022, 1:15 pm Run now	ASAP	*	*	*	*	*	0	Yes
Process bulk caching \tool_brickfield\task\bulk_process_caches	Accessibility toolkit tool_brickfield	⚙	📄	Thursday, 7 July 2022, 1:15 pm Run now	ASAP	*/1 Default: */1	*	*	*	*	0	No
Process bulk batch accessibility checking \tool_brickfield\task\bulk_process_courses	Accessibility toolkit tool_brickfield	⚙	📄	Thursday, 7 July 2022, 1:15 pm Run now	ASAP	*/1 Default: */2	*	*	*	*	0	No
Task to check for any invalid checkids \tool_brickfield\task\checkid_validation	Accessibility toolkit tool_brickfield	⚙	📄	Thursday, 7 July 2022, 1:15 pm Run now	ASAP	01 Default: 06	9	*	*	*	0	No
Process content analysis requests \tool_brickfield\task\process_analysis_requests	Accessibility toolkit tool_brickfield	⚙	📄	Thursday, 7 July 2022, 1:15 pm Run now	ASAP	*/1 Default: */5	*	*	*	*	0	No

Figure 15.15 – Scheduled tasks

The following information is provided for each scheduled task:

- **Name**: Name and internal location of the task

- **Component**: Moodle component that triggers the task

- **Logs**: Details on each task execution, including duration and database reads/writes

- **Last run**: Date and time of the previous task execution or **Never**

- **Next run**: Date and time of subsequent task execution or **ASAP**

- **Minute, Hour, Day, Day of week, Month**: Schedule information in Unix cron format:

    - *: every minute, hour, day, day of the week, and month

    - */**x**: every *x* minutes, hours, and so on

- x-y: every minute between *x* and *y* past the hour or every hour, between *x* and *y*

- 0 = Sunday, 1 = Monday, and so on

- **Fail delay**: Number of seconds to wait before reattempting a failed task

- **Default**: Specifies whether the task has been modified

You must select the configuration icon in the **Edit** column if you wish to change the schedule for any tasks. As an example, we have picked the **Check for updates** task, which is executed at 10:48 every day, every month, and every day of the week:

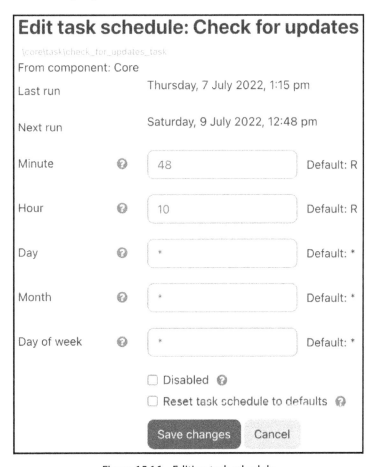

Figure 15.16 – Editing task schedule

In addition to the already covered scheduling settings, you can pause a task (**Disabled**) and revert the original settings (**Reset task schedule to defaults**). The default settings have been set with performance in mind. However, you might want to fine-tune these, considering any idiosyncrasies in your setup.

There are some things worth mentioning when dealing with scheduled tasks and the cron process:

- Tasks can be kicked off manually using the **Run now** option. For this action to appear underneath each enabled task, the **Allow 'Run now' for scheduled tasks** option in **Site administration | General | Security | Site security settings** must be set, and **Path to PHP CLI** in **Site administration | Server | System paths** has to be configured correctly.

- Multiple tasks can run in parallel. The concurrency limits for scheduled and ad hoc tasks can be configured at **Site administration | Server | Tasks | Task processing**.

- A cron run can take longer than the specified time between two executions, and the new tasks will be queued and executed at the next run if this is the case. The task lifetime before the task is freed can also be scheduled, and ad hoc tasks can be configured at **Site administration | Server | Tasks | Task processing**:

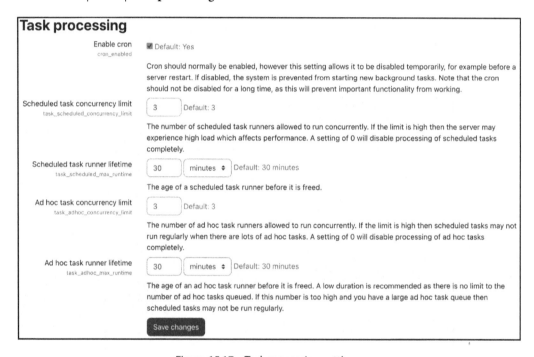

Figure 15.17 – Task processing settings

To view which tasks are running, go to **Site administration | Server | Tasks | Tasks running now**. Any processes in progress will be listed, including the time the process has already run.

Details of each task are logged in Moodle and can be viewed at **Site administration | Server | Tasks | Task log**. Via the report filters, you can drill down to processes that have taken a long time or tasks that have failed to complete. The settings at **Site administration | Server | Tasks | Task log configuration** let you reduce the number of log entries that are written to the log table:

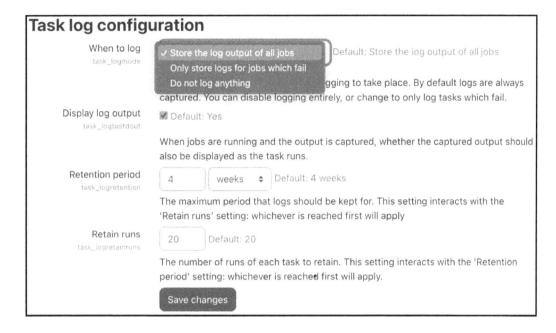

Figure 15.18 – Task log configuration

We have already covered this as part of the installation, but it is worth reiterating that the method by which you call the Moodle cron job can have a significant impact on your system performance, especially on larger installations. If the cron.php script is invoked over HTTP (either using wget or curl), more memory is used than calling directly via the php –f command.

Moodle's memory management has proven to be very efficient. However, there are scenarios when extra memory is required to execute complex PHP scripts, and cron is a candidate for such a complex script. To increase the memory limit, change the **Extra PHP memory limit** setting by going to **Site administration | Server | Performance**.

An operation that relies heavily on scheduled tasks and that potentially has a significant impact on system performance is global search, which we are configuring in the following subsection.

Configuring global search

Moodle comes with a powerful global search facility, supporting different content types, content areas, access permissions, and pluggable search engines.

> **Important note**
> Global search lets users search everywhere in Moodle they have access.

The following diagram is a simplified illustration of how global search works in Moodle:

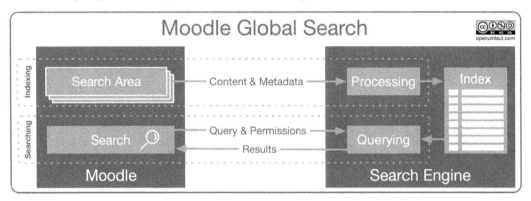

Figure 15.19 – Moodle global search

The **indexing** process (top) is triggered by a scheduled task, during which any **content and metadata** created, updated, or deleted since the last run is sent to the search engine. The search engine never requests anything from Moodle; there is no content crawling. Moodle global search can be limited to **search areas**, such as assignment activity information, text block content, or received messages. The search engine processes the received data and stores it in its index.

The **searching** process (bottom) is initiated by a user keying in a search word or phrase. The query is sent to the search engine alongside the user's access permissions, which are taken into account by the **querying** mechanism in the search engine. This last point is critical to ensure that users are only presented with results they have access to. The results are returned to Moodle and displayed to the user.

Moodle ships with one internal and one external search engine plugin:

- **Simple search**: A built-in search engine supporting basic search operations.

- **Solr**: According to `solr.apache.org`, "*Apache Solr is the popular, blazing-fast, open source enterprise search platform built on Apache Lucene.*" **Solr** supports file searches and advanced search operations, such as Boolean operators, wildcards, prefixing, proximity searches, and boosting.

You will find additional search engine plugins at `moodle.org/plugins/?q=type:search`, for example, **Elastic** or **Azure Search**.

To manage global search, go to **Site administration | Plugins | Search | Manage global search**, where you should see a table of setup steps to go through:

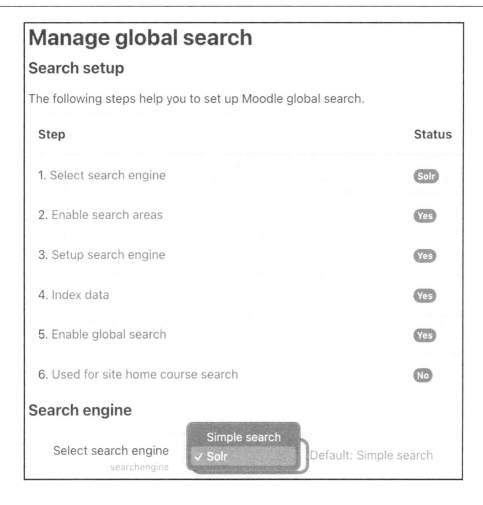

Figure 15.20 – Moodle global search setup

Let's go through the six actions step by step:

1. **Select search engine**: The options are **Simple search** and **Solr** unless you have installed third-party search engine plugins.

2. **Enable search areas**: Search areas are content groups that are indexed separately. By default, global search indexes all search areas; however, you can enable and disable individual search areas in **Site administration** | **Plugins** | **Search** | **Search areas**. By disabling a search area, you improve search speed but exclude its content from appearing in search results. You might choose to disable the **User** search area to exclude links to user profiles from global search.

3. **Setup search engine**: Simple search does not need any configuration; others do.

4. **Index data**: Indexing is triggered by the **Global search indexing** scheduled task. Alternatively, there are multiple indexing actions in **Site administration | Plugins | Search | Search areas**, namely updating, reindexing, and deleting the entire index or indices of an individual search area.

5. **Enable global search**: You enable global search in **Site administration | General | Advanced features**. Before enabling the feature, you should first configure global search and index the site contents. Otherwise, searches can return incomplete results.

6. **Used for site home course search**: If enabled, search results will include course information visible to users, even if they don't have access to the course content.

You will find the last setting underneath the list of setup steps among various configuration options dealing with search options, search scopes (for instance, only courses the users are enrolled in), and display preferences. These settings are well explained onscreen, so we are not repeating them here.

Some more parameters are grouped under **Search management** at the bottom of the global search configuration screen. These options are helpful when making changes on sites with extensive search indexes that take a long time to rebuild.

Since the **Solr** plugin ships with Moodle, here are some pointers that will help you use the powerful search engine as part of your setup:

- Solr must be installed separately, either on the same or on a dedicated server.

- Solr configuration in Moodle is located in **Site administration | Plugins | Search | Solr**. There are three groups of parameters: configuration (Solr host information and **SSL** support), file indexing, and query-only alternate settings.

- Solr installation and configuration in Moodle have been well documented at docs.moodle. org/en/Global_search.

The last configuration options in the system performance section are system paths, which we will set in the following subsection.

Setting system paths

An operation that Moodle performs regularly is the listing of directories. The operation can either be run using Moodle's internal routine coded in PHP or a native version of the function provided by the host operating system. The latter approach is significantly faster since it reduces the load on your server, but it is only supported in Unix environments.

You can specify the path for the du command by navigating to **Site administration | Server | System paths**, as shown in the following screenshot. On most systems, the location of the executable is /usr/bin/du. Once specified correctly, this will accelerate the displaying of the directory content, especially if it contains many files:

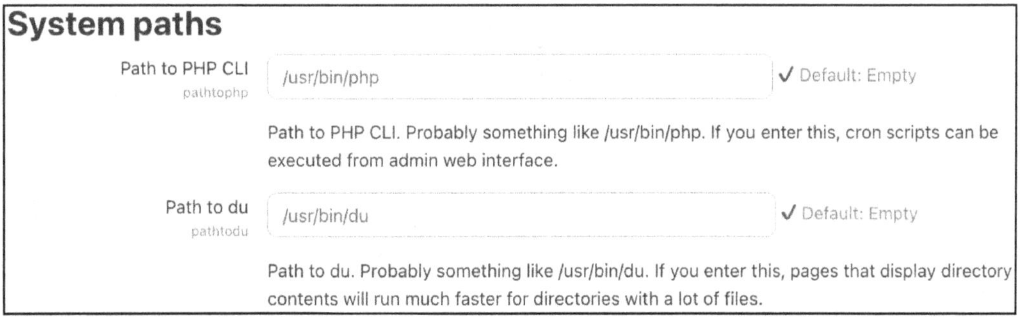

System paths

| Path to PHP CLI | /usr/bin/php | ✔ Default: Empty |
| pathtophp | | |

Path to PHP CLI. Probably something like /usr/bin/php. If you enter this, cron scripts can be executed from admin web interface.

| Path to du | /usr/bin/du | ✔ Default: Empty |
| pathtodu | | |

Path to du. Probably something like /usr/bin/du. If you enter this, pages that display directory contents will run much faster for directories with a lot of files.

Figure 15.21 – System paths

This concludes the section on system performance. To ensure that any optimization leads to better performance and user experiences, you need to profile and monitor your Moodle system, which we will deal with in the last section of the chapter.

Moodle performance profiling and monitoring

When you set up your Moodle system, you can take some initial precautions to optimize the performance of your LMS. However, the real test is when Moodle is in full operation—that is, when the system is under load ("There is no test like production!").

We will be looking at Moodle's built-in profiling tools to let you monitor your Moodle system regularly. While application monitoring cannot be seen as a standalone exercise, we won't be dealing with system profiling since this is beyond the scope of this book.

We will cover three supported tools: **Performance info**, Tideways, and JMeter.

Performance info

Moodle provides some basic profiling information you can activate in **Site administration | Development | Debugging**, where you have to enable the **Performance info** option. This feature displays the execution time, RAM usage, the number of files in use, CPU usage and load, session size, and various filter and caching measures (less information will be shown on a Windows-based installation).

Performance info further displays information on the caches used on the particular page. For each cache, **hits**, **misses**, and **sets** are shown. The caches are highlighted using traffic light colors: red uses up the most, orange some, and green (or no color) uses up the least resources. These signals are rather good indicators to identify potential performance issues.

The data will be displayed in the footer of Moodle as long as the theme in use supports it—for instance, **Boost**.

You can see an overview of **Performance info** in the following screenshot:

3.601214 secs	RAM: 9.9 MB	RAM peak: 18.0 MB
Included 793 files	Contexts for which filters were loaded: 2	Filters created: 8
Pieces of content filtered: 1	Strings filtered: 35	get_string calls: 1405
DB reads/writes: 2042/0	DB queries time: 0.25692 secs	ticks: 360 user: 315sys: 11 cuser: 0 csys: 0
Load average: 3.33	Session (core\session\file): 6.7 KB	

Mode	Cache item	Static	H	M	Primary store	H	M	S	I/O
App	core/capabilities	** static accel. **	532	1	default_application	1	0	0	156.8 KB
Ses	core/coursecat				default_session	2	0	1	-
Req	core/coursecatrecords				default_request	2	2	2	-
App	core/coursecattree	** static accel. **	0	2	default_application	2	0	0	0.3 KB
App	core/coursecompletion	** static accel. **	0	2	default_application	2	0	0	1.0 KB
App	core/coursemodinfo				default_application	1	0	0	1.2 KB
App	core/databasemeta	** static accel. **	4	11	default_application	11	0	0	45.0 KB
App	core/eventinvalidation	** static accel. **	1	2	default_application	2	1	0	0.1 KB
App	core/fontawesomeiconmapping	** static accel. **	0	1	default_application	1	0	0	22.0 KB
App	core/htmlpurifier				default_application	1	0	0	0.3 KB
App	core/langmenu	** static accel. **	5	1	default_application	1	0	0	0.3 KB
App	core/license				default_application	1	0	0	2.9 KB
App	core/message_processors_enabled	** static accel. **	0	1	default_application	1	0	0	0.0 KB
App	core/plugin_functions	** static accel. **	0	17	default_application	17	0	0	2.6 KB
App	core/plugin_manager				default_application	3	0	0	86.7 KB
Req	core/repositories				default_request	0	20	40	-
App	core/string	** static accel. **	1228	487	default_application	487	0	0	4564.9 KB
App	core/yuimodules				default_application	3	0	0	16.2 KB
App	tool_mobile/plugininfo	** static accel. **	0	1	default_application	1	0	0	5.7 KB
App	tool_usertours/tourdata	** static accel. **	0	1	default_application	1	0	0	3.8 KB

Store name	Cache store	H	M	S	I/O
** static accel. **		1770	527	0	-
default_application	cachestore_file	536	1	0	4909.6 KB
default_request	cachestore_static	2	22	42	-
default_session	cachestore_session	2	0	1	-
Total		2310	550	43	4909.6 KB

Figure 15.22 – Performance info

Performance info provides data on the overall Moodle system and its cache items. If you require more in-depth information, Tideways profiling might be helpful.

Tideways profiling

Moodle supports profiling at the PHP level. While this is mainly targeted at developers, it may be helpful for you to identify bottlenecks in your system. Internal profiling is built on top of **Tideways**, a replacement for **XHProf**, which allows the profiling of PHP pages at a relatively low performance cost.

Once you have installed the `php-tideways` and `php-graphviz` PHP extensions, you will see a new menu item when you navigate to **Site administration | Development | Profiling**:

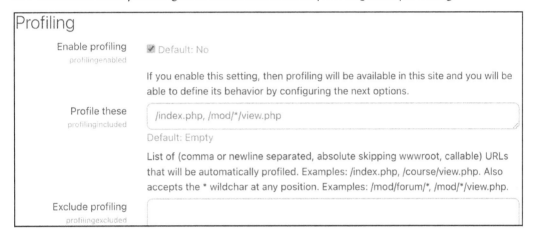

Figure 15.23 – Profiling configuration

The profiler can be configured to run automatically (set the **Automatic profiling** frequency to any value except 0, and specify URLs in the **Profile these** field) or manually. The latter can be **Selective** (you have to initiate the profiling) or **Continuous** (once it starts, you have to stop it).

As soon as profiling has been enabled, yet another menu item will appear when you go to **Site administration | Development | Profiling runs**, which lists summary information on all the profile runs that have been executed:

Profiling runs

[Import]

URL —	Date ▾ —	Execution time —	CPU time —	Function calls —	Memory used —	Comment —
/mod/forum/view.php ➜	11 Jul 2022, 13:10	999.841 ms	955.958 ms	139819	8761.672 KB	
/mod/forum/view.php ➜	11 Jul 2022, 13:10	1012.329 ms	963.126 ms	139827	8761.828 KB	
/mod/forum/view.php ➜	11 Jul 2022, 13:10	1007.753 ms	973.422 ms	139560	8758.586 KB	
/mod/forum/view.php ➜	11 Jul 2022, 13:09	1246.752 ms	1133.049 ms	154488	9446.352 KB	
/index.php ➜	11 Jul 2022, 13:09	1001.941 ms	954.340 ms	106460	8554.750 KB	

Figure 15.24 – Profiling runs

When you click on the URL or date of a single run, you can mark the run as a reference and provide a comment. You can also view its profiling details, where each function call's execution times and memory usage are shown in tabular form. From this table, you can view a call graph. However, this requires dot to be installed (part of the Graphviz package) and **Path to dot** to be specified at **Site administration | Server | System paths**. The result is a scary-looking graph showing each function call's order, dependencies, and details.

The general strategy when dealing with profiling is to identify the functions that take the longest to execute, tweak your setup, and check whether the time has been reduced. The difficulty in doing this is ensuring that the test runs occur under the same or, at least, very similar conditions. You can find more information on PHP profiling at docs.moodle.org/dev/Profiling_PHP.

Tideways helps identify issues at the PHP level. Another external profiling tool supported by Moodle is JMeter, as briefly covered in the following subsection.

JMeter support

Apache JMeter is another tool aimed at developers but potentially helpful when locating Moodle bottlenecks. To create a test plan file, set **Debug messages** to **DEVELOPER** at **Site administration | Development | Debugging**, and go to **Site administration | Development | Make JMeter test plan**. You need to follow the instructions shown in the following screenshot before a test plan can be created:

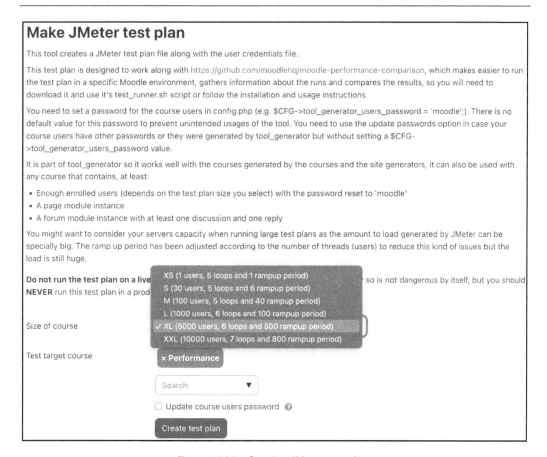

Figure 15.25 – Creating JMeter test plans

The outcome of the performance test run over a Moodle course is a file in JMX format that can then be loaded and analyzed in the JMeter tool, which you need to install separately.

Moodle comes with an unsupported tool that lets you generate random course data, which is helpful in the context of creating JMeter test plans. You have to call the script manually at `<yoursite>/admin/tool/generator`, where you can simulate having hundreds of courses with various levels and types of activities. You can see an overview of this here:

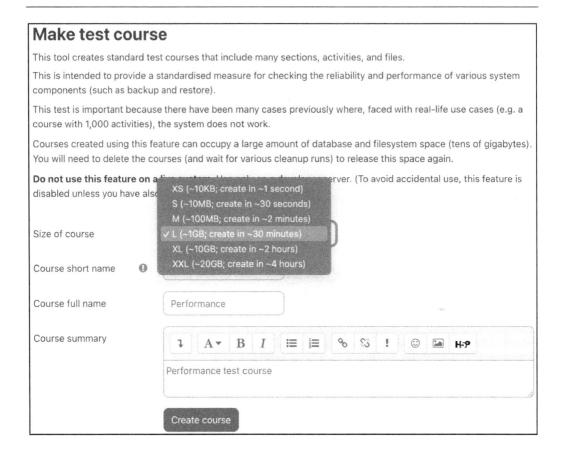

Make test course

This tool creates standard test courses that include many sections, activities, and files.

This is intended to provide a standardised measure for checking the reliability and performance of various system components (such as backup and restore).

This test is important because there have been many cases previously where, faced with real-life use cases (e.g. a course with 1,000 activities), the system does not work.

Courses created using this feature can occupy a large amount of database and filesystem space (tens of gigabytes). You will need to delete the courses (and wait for various cleanup runs) to release this space again.

Do not use this feature on a ⬚⬚⬚⬚⬚⬚⬚⬚⬚ **erver. (To avoid accidental use, this feature is disabled unless you have als**⬚

> XS (~10KB; create in ~1 second)
> S (~10MB; create in ~30 seconds)
> M (~100MB; create in ~2 minutes)
> ✓ L (~1GB; create in ~30 minutes)
> XL (~10GB; create in ~2 hours)
> XXL (~20GB; create in ~4 hours)

Size of course

Course short name   ❶

Course full name   `Performance`

Course summary

> ⬚ A ▾ B I   ☰ ☰   ⧉ ✂ !   ☺ 🖼 H-P
>
> Performance test course

[Create course]

Figure 15.26 – Creating JMeter test plans

You can select **Size of course** as well as **Course short name**, **Course full name**, and **Course summary** options. Beware that the generation of large courses may take hours and significantly negatively impacts your system performance. Do not perform this operation in production environments.

Now that you have been armed with some profiling and monitoring tools, you can tweak the settings as described throughout the chapter. Take a look at what impact, positive or negative, they have on the performance of your Moodle system.

Summary

You learned how to optimize and monitor Moodle's performance in this chapter. We first provided an overview of Moodle performance and briefly mentioned optimizing hardware, networks, databases, web servers, and course content. The key Moodle performance topics have been grouped into the following sections:

- **Moodle feature performance**: We covered performance issues in Moodle functions and Moodle activities.

- **Moodle Universal Cache**: We dealt with the powerful MUC and configured cache types, cache stores, and cache definitions before testing MUC performance and activating various caching options.

- **Moodle system performance**: We optimized session handling, cron management and scheduled tasks, global search, and system paths.

The chapter was concluded with a short Moodle performance profiling and monitoring section.

As you have probably gathered from the chapter, optimization is not always straightforward. It depends on various circumstances, such as the system that Moodle is running on, the hardware it utilizes, the network, the number of concurrent users logged in to the system, the types of activities carried out, and so on. While basic optimization is usually straightforward, fine-tuning is a bit of an art in itself. A lot of trial and error (that is, profiling) will be required to achieve the ideal setup for your Moodle system.

Now that your system is ready to perform to its maximum potential, let's ensure that you have a professional backup and recovery strategy in place, which is covered in the next chapter.

16
Avoiding Sleepless Nights – Moodle Backup and Restore

Your Moodle application will contain important data such as coursework, assignments, grades, and all administrative data, for example, users, cohorts, and roles. Therefore, you must have a good backup strategy in place.

Preparing for the unexpected is always a good strategy when dealing with information systems, and having well-preserved backups allows for full application recovery upon unexpected hardware or software failures. Systems are not expected to fail, but there's always a possibility for failure, and a good strategy for fast recovery ensures a low impact on users. This chapter presents strategies and options for managing backups and auto-backups of your data.

Moodle itself supports two types of backups:

- **Course-level backups**: Course backups are usually ad hoc and only archive the selected course. You will learn how to create course backups, restore courses, and copy course content using the related course import facility.

- **Site-level backups**: The site backup option saves all courses and related data to a specified location at regular intervals. You will learn how to set this up and recover data from it.

Both mechanisms will be covered in detail before we look at **system-level backups**, including Moodle backups (covering the Moodle software and the data stored in it) and snapshot creation (full system images). The three backup types are shown in the following diagram and are at the core of this chapter:

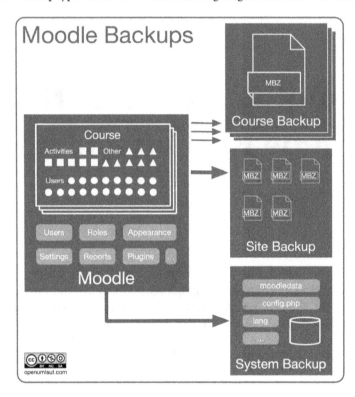

Figure 16.1 – Moodle backups

We will conclude this chapter by looking at two applications that use backup and restore facilities: planning year-end procedures and implementing course templates.

We will cover the following main topics in this chapter:

- Managing course-level backups
- Managing site-level backups
- Managing system-level backups
- Using backup and restore for alternative tasks

Managing course-level backups

Course-level backups allow teachers and administrators to create copies of courses for safekeeping or to pass on to colleagues. If configured appropriately, course backups can save an administrator a lot of hassle and time.

> **Important note**
> Course backups include some or all of the items of a course.

First, we will look at the backup procedure before going into the details of recovering data during the restore operation.

Creating course backups

To back up an individual course, it is best if you are inside that course, where you have to select the **Course reuse** option in the course menu and then select **Backup** from the dropdown.

The backup procedure comprises five steps, illustrated in the following workflow:

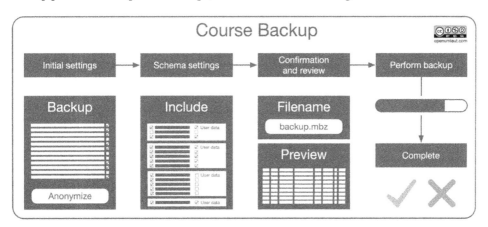

Figure 16.2 – Course backup workflow

You can navigate back to any step via the process links at the top of the screen or the navigation buttons at the bottom. We will go through the steps one by one in the following subsections.

Initial settings

Several settings determine how the backup will be performed and what type of information will be included:

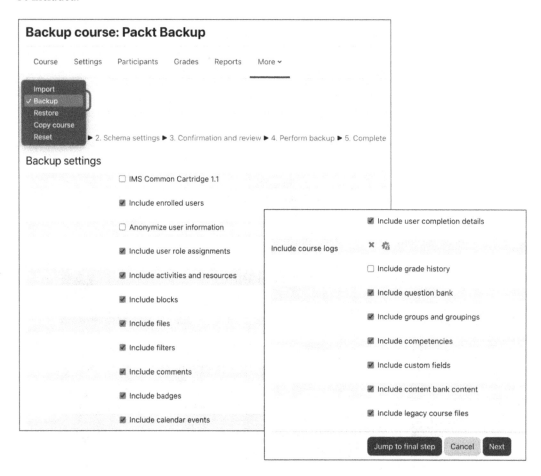

Figure 16.3 – Course backup – Initial settings

Some settings are only available if other settings have been activated; for example, **Include user role assignments** can only be ticked if enrolled users are included. Most options are self-explanatory, but two options require some commentary:

- If **Anonymize user information** is selected (**Include enrolled users** is a prerequisite), user data (username, first name, last name, and email address) will be substituted by aliases. For example, Jonny Walker might become anonfirstname69 anonlastname69.

- In addition to the standard Moodle backup format, **IMS Common Cartridge 1.1** is a special format that's supported. For more information on IMS CC, please consult the Moodle Docs at docs.moodle.org/en/IMS_Common_Cartridge_import_and_export.

By default, all options can be selected for all users who have the appropriate permissions in the course context. If you wish to change the default values and/or lock specific settings (such as **Include course logs**, as shown in the previous screenshot), go to **Site administration** | **Courses** | **Backups** | **General backup defaults**:

General backup settings

Include users backup	backup_general_users	☑ Default: Yes Sets the default for whether to include users in backups.	☐ Locked
Anonymise information backup | backup_general_anonymize	☐ Default: No If enabled all information pertaining to users will be anonymised by default.	☑ Locked
Include role assignments backup | backup_general_role_assignments	☑ Default: Yes If enabled by default roles assignments will also be backed up.	☐ Locked
Include activities and resources backup	backup_general_activities	☑ Default: Yes Sets the default for including activities in a backup.	☐ Locked
Include blocks | backup_general_blocks	☑ Default: Yes	

Figure 16.4 – Course backup default settings

For every setting, there are two checkboxes. The first represents the parameter's default, whereas the second value indicates whether it is locked or not. Locking allows you to force specific settings, for instance, the exclusion of users.

There are usually two types of course backups that you are likely to perform:

- **Content-only backups**

  As the name suggests, this type of backup only contains content that can be passed on to another person without transferring any information about its users, roles, grades, and so on. To perform a content-only backup, you must deselect **Include enrolled users**, which is a prerequisite for all user-related backup options.

A content-only backup is the best option if you wish to pass a course on to other educators or make it available for download. Another use case is to create a new instance of a course for yourself, for example, taking a course backup from one semester to use in a different semester. When you publish courses on a community hub or MoodleNet (refer to *Chapter 19, Setting Up Moodle Networking*), you will also create a content-only backup.

> **Important note**
> By default, users with teaching rights can only perform content-only backups. This restriction can be changed via the `moodle/backup:userinfo` capability, but it should be done carefully.

- **Full-course backups**

  If you wish to back up a course for potential recovery purposes, you should create a full-course backup, which includes user data (for example, forum posts), course data, and user information. To do this, you can leave all the settings at their default values and use the **Jump to final step** button.

If you wish to back up the course logs, the **Include course logs** setting must be enabled. Remember that logs can be massive and often exceed multiple gigabytes when you're backing up several courses.

Before we move on to the next screen, a note of caution: some third-party course-level plugins (activities, blocks, or filters) might not support backups. If you encounter any issues, you will have to exclude items created by these from the backup or, better, avoid the plugin altogether.

Schema settings

All learning resources and activities are shown in the order in which they appear in the course. Resources are only available if the **Include activities** parameter has not been deactivated on the previous screen. By default, all the available elements are selected; if you wish to exclude any individual items, you have to deselect them. Additionally, you can exclude/include all the items of a section by selecting/deselecting the section name itself:

1. Initial settings ▶ **2. Schema settings** ▶ 3. Confirmation and review ▶ 4. Perform backup ▶ 5. Complete

Include:

☑ **General**   ☑ **User data**

☑ News forum 🗩   ☑ -

☑ BBB ⓑ   ☐ -

☑ **Topic 1**   ☑ **User data**

☑ An assignment 🔎   ☑ -

☑ A chat 🗪   ☑ -

☑ A file 🗋   ☑ -

☐ A video 🖹   -

☐ **Topic 2**   **User data**

Figure 16.5 – Course backup – Schema settings

Moodle distinguishes between **course content** and **user data**. For example, the forum description and all its settings are classified as course content in a forum activity. In contrast, all topics, posts, and replies to a forum are classified as user data. If the **Include enrolled users** option has been left activated on the initial setup screen, user data can be included/excluded for each selected activity and resource.

Selecting the **Next** button will take you to the last course backup configuration screen.

Confirmation and review

The third screen lets you choose the backup filename and review the items to be included in the archive. The format of the default **Filename** is as follows:

```
backup-<type>-<format>-<course name/id>-<date>-<time>[-nu|-an].
mbz
```

At the time of writing, `<type>` is always set to **moodle2**, and the only value supported for `<format>` is **course**. The optional `-nu` parameter stands for no users, and `-an` is an indicator for anonymous users.

If you have opted to create **IMS Common Cartridge** as the backup form, the `.imscc` extension will be used instead of `.mbz`:

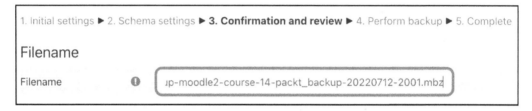

1. Initial settings ▶ 2. Schema settings ▶ **3. Confirmation and review** ▶ 4. Perform backup ▶ 5. Complete

Filename

Filename   ❶   [ɹp-moodle2-course-14-packt_backup-20220712-2001.mbz]

Figure 16.6 – Course backup – Confirmation and review

Moodle creates a bespoke file format for backups, known as the **Moodle Backup Format**, using the `.mbz` extension. A Moodle backup file is a compressed file (in `.tgz` format) that consists of an XML file (which describes the file's content) and the actual content, users, log data, and so on.

The additional **Backup settings** section shows which item has been selected and deselected on the initial settings screen. The **Included items** section indicates, with a green tick, all resources and activities that will be included, as well as any user data that will be part of the course backup. A red cross means that the item has been deselected, whereas a red cross followed by a lock indicates that it wasn't possible to select the item since a prerequisite has not been fulfilled.

Once you press the **Perform backup** button, the Moodle course archive will be created.

Finalizing the backup

The created archive file is saved in the **Course backup** area. This process can take a few minutes, depending on the volume of data being backed up. If the **Anonymize user data** setting was chosen at the beginning, the backup file will be placed in the **User private backup** area.

> **Important note**
> Moodle backups include the course configuration, which contains course settings, activity arrangements, and block positions.

After completion, a brief status message is shown; you will have to take appropriate actions if this contains any errors or warnings.

Backups sometimes fail on large courses, and the cause is usually that the backup process runs out of time or memory. If this happens, you have two options that are not mutually exclusive:

- First, you can increase the **Extra PHP memory limit** setting by going to **Server** | **Performance**.
- Second, you can choose **Enable synchronous backups** by going to **Site administration** | **Courses** | **Backups** | **Asynchronous backup/restore**, which triggers Moodle to execute backups (and restores) as a separate background process:

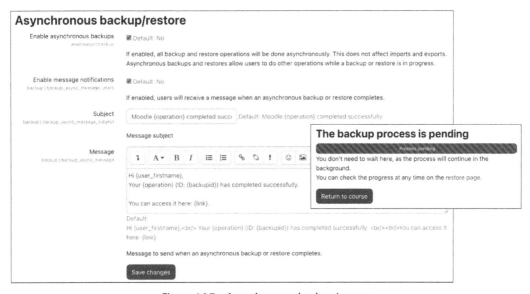

Figure 16.7 – Asynchronous backup/restore

Asynchronous backups only allow a user to have one pending backup for a resource at a time. Multiple asynchronous backups of the same resource can't be queued, as this would likely result in multiple backups that contain the same content.

If you wish to notify the user who initiated the course backup when the process is completed, choose **Enable message notifications** and customize the **Subject** and **Message** properties of the notification that will be sent out.

This concludes this section on creating course backups. The reverse operation – restoring course backups – is the topic of the following section.

Restoring course backups

To wholly or partly restore a previously backed up course, it is best if you are inside that course, where you have to select the **Course reuse** option in the course menu and then select **Restore** from the dropdown. Alternatively, you can navigate to **Site administration | Courses | Restore course**.

Once you have selected a .mbz file, the restore procedure comprises seven steps, illustrated in the following diagram:

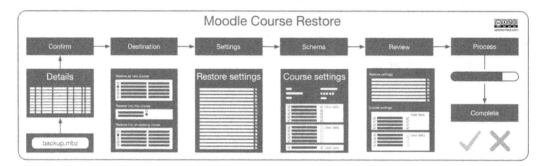

Figure 16.8 – Course restore workflow

As with the backup workflow, you can navigate back to any step via the process links at the top of the screen or using the navigation buttons at the bottom. We will go through the steps one by one in the following subsections.

File selection and confirmation

Moodle stores its backup files in different **backup areas**. There are four locations where you can choose a .mbz file to be restored, as shown in the following screenshot:

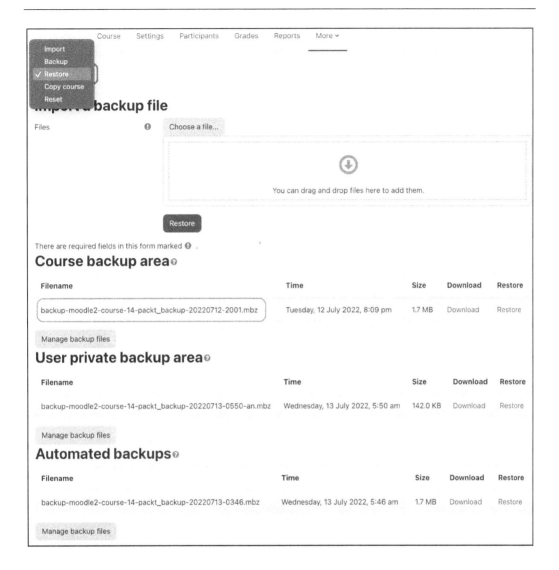

Figure 16.9 – Course backup areas

The four locations for Moodle archives are as follows:

- **Import backup file**: Archives that are usually stored outside of Moodle and selected via the file picker or drag'n'drop

- **Course backup area**: Archives created using default settings are stored in this area

- **User private backup area**: Archives with anonymized users are stored here

- **Automated backups**: Archives that are created automatically (see the *Site backups* section)

In the preceding example, a single course is present in the course backup area, called `backup-moodle2-course-14-packt_backup-20220712-2001.mbz`. From its filename, we already know that the course ID is 14, its name is Packt Backup, and that it was backed up on July 12, 2022, at 20:01.

Select the **Restore** link beside a backup file to start the recovery process. The first screen displays **Backup details** (type, format, mode, backup date/time, Moodle version, backup version, and the URL of the `.mbz` file), **Backup settings** (identical to the initial settings in the backup), and **Course details**. Once you have confirmed this information-only screen, you have to specify where you wish to recover the backup.

Selecting the restore destination

There are various options for restoring a course backup:

- **Restore as a new course**
- **Restore into this course** and merge the backup into this course
- **Restore into this course**, delete the contents of this course, and then restore it
- **Restore into an existing course** and merge the backup into the selected course
- **Restore into an existing course**, delete its contents, and then restore:

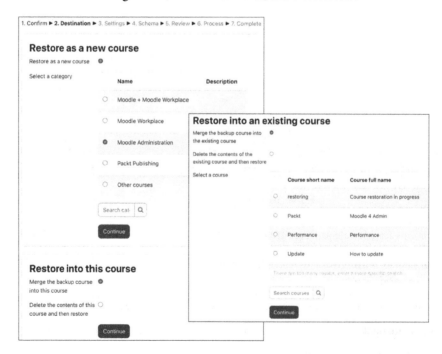

Figure 16.10 – Course restore – Destination

If you wish to **Restore as a new course**, you will have to select a category in which the new course will be created. You must use the provided search facility if the number of categories exceeds 20. Alternatively, you can choose the current course as the destination (**Restore into this course**). You can either combine the current course content with the backup (**Merge the backup course into this existing course**) or replace it (**Delete the contents of this course and then restore**). If you choose the merging option and an activity or resource with the same name exists, both will be kept and not overridden. The third option is to restore the course to another existing course, which you have to select. The same options (merge and replace) exist to restore the backup in the current course. Make sure you click on the correct **Continue** button before you proceed.

Restore settings

The **Restore settings** screen shows all the available options that were selected during the backup process (refer to the preceding *Initial settings* section). As shown earlier, the choices made here determine the types of data that will be recovered, and which type of content will be offered for further selection. Also, most options have prerequisites that are identical to their backup counterparts.

If you wish to change the default values and/or lock specific settings, go to **Site administration | Courses | Backups | General restore defaults**. For every parameter, there are two checkboxes. The first represents the setting's default, whereas the second value indicates whether it is locked or not. Locking allows you to force specific settings, for instance, the exclusion of users.

The backup schema

Depending on your choices on the previous two screens, the schema step lets you specify several course settings. If you restore the backup to an existing course, you have the option to overwrite its settings. These are **Course name**, **Course short name**, and **Course start date**. You can further choose to **Keep current roles and enrolments** (if these are part of the backup), **Keep current groups and groupings** (if stored in the backup), and use the course settings of the backup file instead of the current ones (**Overwrite course configuration**):

Figure 16.11 – Course restore – Schema

You must also choose which content and user data to include in the recovery procedure. The selection mechanism is very similar to the backup equivalent described earlier. By default, all the data that is present is selected. If you wish to narrow down the data to be restored, you must manually deselect items.

Finalizing restore

After the final familiar-looking **Review** screen, the restore process is initiated once the **Perform restore** button is pressed. Any selected data will be recovered to the chosen destination. After completion, a summary message is shown.

If the restored course contains any roles that do not exist on your Moodle system, a role mappings step will be shown, where you must map roles manually to ensure consistency:

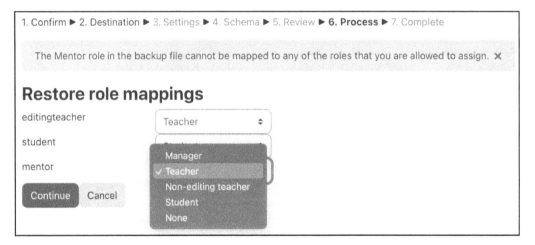

Figure 16.12 – Course restore – Restore role mappings

This completes this section on restoring course backups. Before we move on to site backups, let's cover a feature closely related to course restore: course import.

Importing course data

It is sometimes necessary to copy data from one course to another. To achieve this, Moodle provides the **import course data** feature. However, unlike the backup function, it will not import user data, such as assignment submissions or forum posts – it will only import the structure of activities, blocks, and filters. For example, you might want to import a single quiz from one course to another.

Teachers can import content from courses for which they have editing rights; as an administrator, this restriction does not apply. This mechanism bypasses the requirement for a backup and restore procedure if you want to copy course content from one course to another and do not require user data.

To copy course data, you need to be inside the receiving course, where you have to select the **Course reuse** option in the course menu and then select **Import** from the dropdown.

The import procedure comprises six steps, as illustrated in the following workflow:

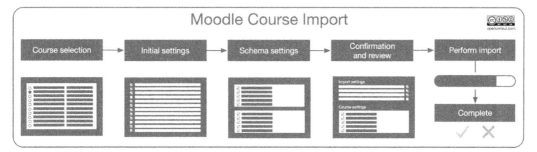

Figure 16.13 – Course import workflow

As with the backup and restore workflows, you can navigate back to any step via the process links at the top of the screen or the navigation buttons at the bottom. Since the course import feature is effectively a subset of the course backup and restore functionality, we will only briefly mention each step in the process:

- **Course selection**: You must select a course from which you wish to import content. Use the provided search facility if the list exceeds 10 courses (default value). You can also select the current course; this way, you can duplicate multiple activities.

- **Initial settings**: Choose which course items you wish to import. Note the absence of user-related options.

- **Schema settings**: A familiar screen for selecting topics and activities.

- **Confirmation and review**: Import settings and included items are shown.

- **Perform import**: Go, go, go!

- **Complete**: A summary message is shown.

If you wish to change the default values and/or lock specific settings, go to **Site administration | Courses | Backups | General import defaults**. There are two checkboxes for every setting, and the same logic applies as for the backup and restore defaults. On this screen, you can also specify the **Maximum number of courses listed for import** option.

Importing concludes this section on course-level archives, where the focus has been on creating and restoring individual course backups. To automate this process across courses, site-level backups are needed, which we will cover in the following section.

Managing site-level backups

So far, we have dealt with backing up single courses. Site-level backups perform the same operation for every course in your system, including hidden courses and the home page.

Before we look at backup reports and notifications, we will configure automated backups. We will conclude this section with some backup strategies.

Configuring automated backups

Go to **Site administration** | **Courses** | **Backups** | **Automated backup setup** to schedule site backups. Here, you will see the following settings:

Setting	Description
Active	Turns automatic backups on and off. Make sure that your backup is activated! The **Manual** option allows the execution via the CLI (refer to the command after this table).
Schedule	Specify the days of the week on which the backup has to run.
Execute at	Specify the time of the day the backup will be executed.
Automated backup storage	By default, backups are stored in the course backup file areas. To store backups centrally, select **Specified directory for automated backups**. If you choose both locations, twice the storage will be taken up.
Save to	If backup storage includes a directory, specify the full (absolute) path to the folder, and ensure access rights are set to writable.
Maximum number of backups kept	Specify the number of backups to be kept. Beware that a large number will have an impact on disk usage. Older versions will be deleted automatically.
Delete backups older than	Backups older than the specified number of days will be deleted automatically.
Minimum number of backups kept	Backups of older or inactive courses will be removed with the previous setting. To avoid this, specify the number of backups you wish to keep.
Use the course name in backup filename	Toggle that switches between the course ID and course name for the default backup filename.
Skip hidden courses	If selected, hidden courses will be excluded from the backup (default).
Skip courses not modified since	Select the number of days to exclude courses that have not been altered since.
Skip courses not modified since previous backup	If selected, only courses that have been changed since the previous backup will be included. This is the most disk space and time-efficient setting. Make sure logging is activated in order to support this mode.

Figure 16.14 – Automated backup configuration

The remainder of the configuration page covers **Automated backup settings**, which specify which elements will be included in the backup. These are identical to the initial backup settings, except for the anonymize option, which has been excluded.

For the backup to start automatically at the specified time, the cron process must be configured correctly, which we covered in *Chapter 1, Installing Moodle*. Alternatively, you can initiate the backup process via the CLI, which executes the same script that's called by the cron process. The command execution from the shell or for the inclusion in scripts is as follows (assuming the Apache user is www-data):

```
sudo -u www-data /usr/bin/php admin/cli/automated_backups.php
```

Recovering courses from an automated backup is identical to restoring data from course-level backup archives.

To ensure that the backups are running correctly, Moodle provides a backup report and notifications, which we will explain in the following subsection.

Backup reports and notifications

As a Moodle administrator, you must ensure that the backup execution has been successful. For this purpose, Moodle provides a backup report, which you can find by going to **Site administration | Reports | Backups**. It shows a log of the last execution:

Last execution log

Course	Time taken			Status	Next backup
Moodle Administration 4	13 Jul, 05:46	-	13 Jul, 05:46	OK	13 Jul, 22:30
Performance	13 Jul, 05:46	-	1 Jan, 01:00	Unfinished	12 Jul, 22:30
Course One	1 Jan, 01:00	-	1 Jan, 01:00	Queued	12 Jul, 22:30
Moodle Administration 3	1 Jan, 01:00	-	1 Jan, 01:00	Queued	12 Jul, 22:30
Moodle Administration 2	1 Jan, 01:00	-	1 Jan, 01:00	Queued	12 Jul, 22:30
Moodle Workplace	1 Jan, 01:00	-	1 Jan, 01:00	Queued	12 Jul, 22:30
Course restoration in progress	1 Jan, 01:00	-	1 Jan, 01:00	Automated backup pending	13 Jul, 22:30

Figure 16.15 – Automated backup configuration

The report provides details for each **Course** being backed up, namely **Time taken** (start and end time), **Status**, and the date and time of its **Next backup**.

Courses in which there hasn't been any activity for 30 days – that is, no changes have been made to the course content, and no users have used the course – are excluded from the automated backup, and the status is shown as **Skipped**.

As a Moodle administrator, you will receive an email after the scheduled site-level backup has been completed. It provides details on the total number of courses backed up and a split of how many course backups were okay, contained errors, were unfinished, and were skipped. Ensure your email settings have been configured correctly (refer to *Chapter 10, Configuring Technical Features*). It is highly recommended that you check the content of this email every day.

To ensure the smooth and reliable execution of your automated backups, you must have an adequate backup strategy in place, which we will discuss next.

The backup strategy

There are several issues to consider when running automatic site-wide Moodle backups:

- **Backup content**: Ensure that everything included in the archives is needed, and anything that is not required is excluded. Do you have to back up the entire logs and gradebook history every night?

- **Backup size**: The size of the backup files can be potentially huge (multiple gigabytes). Ensure that you only keep the number of backups that are required and your setup can cope with.

- **Backup timing**: The backup operation is a CPU and hard disk-intensive operation. Make sure you schedule its execution when the load on the site is relatively low. If you run multiple sites on the same server, it is recommended to time-stagger backups or create a script that uses the described CLI. An alternative approach is to set up a dedicated backup server.

- **Backup frequency**: Do you need seven daily backups, or are weekly backups sufficient? Are there periods (such as weekends) when you can switch off the backup facility altogether?

- **Backup location**: By default, all backup files are saved to the respective courses, which means that the backups are held on the same server as Moodle. If you have to recover multiple courses, you must locate each archive separately, a potentially mind-numbing and time-consuming exercise.

You might want to consider storing your backups on an external device (external disk, NAS drive, SAN, and so on). An alternative to this approach is to mount a backup device and include its content in the organization-wide backup.

Site-level backups are a great way to automate course backups and simplify educators' lives. However, they only back up courses, not the entire system. While this is sufficient if you have to recover a single course or some activities, it is insufficient in a disaster scenario when the entire system has to be recovered.

> **Important note**
> You should not use the course backup facility as your sole backup system.

Instead, system-level backups should be used as a supplement, which we will look at next.

Managing system-level backups

System-level backups cannot be configured or executed from within Moodle. Instead, they must be set up at the system level. If your system is hosted externally, there is a possibility that you will not have access to the system level, which will prevent you from performing this type of backup. Unless the host already runs system-level backups on your behalf, it is time to change to another provider!

There are two types of system backups that are not mutually exclusive:

- **Moodle backups**: These create an archive of Moodle itself, the application data, and any application configuration

- **Snapshots**: These create an image of the system, which is used for disaster recovery if the system has to be rolled back in its totality

We will briefly cover both approaches in the following two subsections.

Moodle backups

Moodle distinguishes between the application software and the data stored in it. The advantage of this separation becomes apparent when creating backups: a software backup is only required when an update has been installed or customization is taking place, whereas data should be backed up more frequently.

Backing up the **Moodle software** itself is straightforward: you must create a copy of the directory and all its subdirectories where the Moodle software is installed (usually called `moodle`). Most administrators would create a single archive of the directory for easier handling (in Unix, simply use `tar -cvf <backupfile>`). This step is usually only required before a system upgrade or when you need to archive your entire system.

Moodle stores its data in two separate locations:

- **Moodle database**: Most content is stored in the Moodle database. You can either use the export feature of phpMyAdmin (if installed) or use the following `mysqldump` shell command for MySQL and MariaDB to create a single backup file:

  ```
  mysqldump -u <username> -p [-h <databasehost>] -C -Q -e
  -a <database> > <backup-file>.sql
  ```

  `<username>` has to be replaced with the database username, `-p` will ask you for a password, and `-h <databasehost>` is only required if the database is located on a separate server. The `<database>` option is the name of the database, and `<backup-file>` is the name of the archive to be created. It is common practice to use the `.sql` extension.

To recover the database dump, use the following `mysql` shell command:

```
mysql -p <database> < <backup-file>.sql
```

For other database types, refer to the respective administration guides.

- **Moodle data directory ($CFG->dataroot)**: This is where all contributed files reside – for instance, submitted assignments, language customizations, user profile pictures, videos, and so on. Like the Moodle system, all you have to do is create a copy of the directory and all its subdirectories. It is crucial to stop Apache while performing the backup to guarantee that the content does not go out of sync.

The advantage of this approach is that it is less resource-intensive, can be scripted, and recovering the entire Moodle system is far more straightforward. However, it is impossible to retrieve individual activities without setting up a temporary server, as is possible with course backups.

Snapshot creation

Creating snapshots is only briefly mentioned here for completeness as it is not a Moodle administrator role but a system administrator task. However, you should ensure that such a mechanism is set up in case of hardware failures or other system issues.

A snapshot is an image of the entire partition(s) on the hard disk(s) that contain(s) the Moodle software itself, as well as all the data (database and data directory). The advantage of the snapshot is that the entire system can be rolled back to the point when the image was created. However, any data that has been added or modified since this point in time will be overridden. Snapshots cannot be used to recover a single course or parts thereof but to fully replace the system.

> **Important note**
>
> No matter what combination of backups you choose, frequently verify that the backup procedure is working. There is nothing worse than a false sense of security – that is, assuming that all your data is backed up when it isn't!

This concludes this section on site-wide backups, which covered Moodle backups and snapshots. The following checklist provides a quick summary of the backup and restore configurations that should be taken care of:

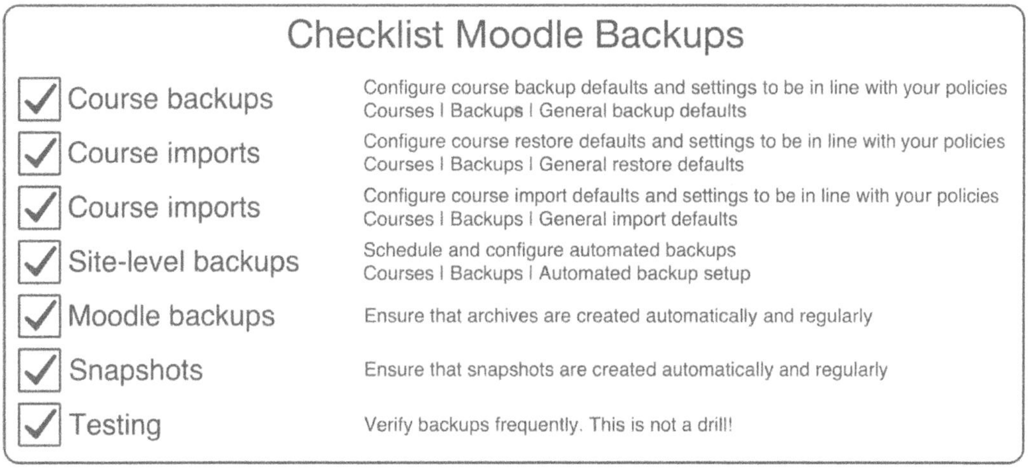

Figure 16.16 – Backup checklist

We will finish this chapter by looking at two use cases that utilize Moodle's backup and restore features.

Using backup and restore for alternative tasks

While the prime purpose of backups is the recovery of data in case of loss, some applications can be carried out using the techniques covered in this chapter. We will briefly describe two of them: year-end procedure and course templates.

Planning the year-end procedure

Most organizations have some sort of year-end procedure in place, which might be at the end of an academic year, a term, the financial year, or, in the case of roll-on-roll-off setups, every month. Given the nature and importance of the procedure, each step should be planned well in advance. The key considerations are as follows:

- When do you run the year-end procedure?
- What has to be done?
- Who is involved?
- Where will the archives go?

The following is a list of typical steps that might or might not apply to your setup. It gives you an idea of how such a procedure may look and demonstrates the importance of the backup facility:

1. **Archive**: Create full backups of all courses and consider including a system backup. Ensure archives are stored on a separate medium.

2. **Grade export**: Export grades course by course to store them on your student management information system.

3. **Course reset**: Use the reset feature at the course level to remove any user data. (Resetting courses can also be done in batch mode. Refer to the *Managing courses in bulk* section in *Chapter 4, Managing Courses and Enrolments.*)

4. **Delete users**: Remove users who have left the organization or disable their accounts.

5. **Next-year preparation**: Hide or delete obsolete courses and add new courses. Add new users and assign roles to courses.

This is only a crude outline of tasks to be considered. Ensure you have a detailed plan for this type of exercise before you kick off the year-end procedure.

Implementing course templates

There is often a requirement to create course templates, which are used as a basis to create multiple courses. This process might be in an organization that emphasizes the homogeneity of course structure and layout or an education establishment that wants to simplify the work of its course creators. The steps to achieve this are as follows:

1. Create a course that will become your course template.

2. Add all the elements (activities, resources, filters, blocks, and so on) to the course, change its settings, and arrange the content as required.

3. Create a content-only backup of the course.

4. You can now use the restore mechanism to create as many courses from this template as you wish. (This operation can also be done in batch mode. Refer to the *Managing courses in bulk* section in *Chapter 4, Managing Courses and Enrolments.*)

5. Alternatively, use the **Copy course** feature in the **Course reuse** menu at the course level instead of performing *Steps 3* and *4*. However, course copying cannot be done in batch mode.

6. Optionally, you can grant users appropriate rights to the course so that they can use the import facility.

The preceding list requires you to perform some manual steps to implement a course templating mechanism. You may find more user-friendly approaches in the Moodle plugin database at `moodle.org/plugins`, such as **Kickstart** (`moodle.org/plugins/format_kickstart`).

Summary

In this chapter, we dealt with various Moodle backup alternatives. You learned how to create course-level, site-level, and system-level backups, as well as how to perform data recovery from each type. Your Moodle backup strategy must fit in with your organization's overall disaster recovery plan. We also saw some applications that use the covered backup and restore facilities.

Moodle offers a good range of backup and restore options. Ensure that they are configured correctly and run test recoveries to be on the safe(r) side. There is nothing worse than a false sense of security – that is, assuming that all your data is backed up when it isn't!

In the next chapter, we will cover a collection of useful and not-so-useful Moodle admin tools.

17
Working with Moodle Admin Tools

Moodle ships with several administration tools that have not been allocated to a particular topic; some are not even directly accessible via the familiar admin web interface.

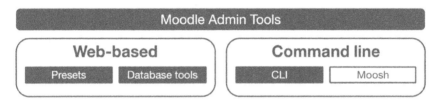

Figure 17.1 – Moodle admin tools

We have grouped the admin tools into the following categories, each presented in a separate section:

- **Site admin presets**: Presets allow you to create backups of site settings that can be rolled back in case something goes wrong.

- **Database tools**: These tools let you apply specific database actions. In addition to the tools part of Moodle core, we will cover a useful external tool called **Adminer** that lets you manage the underlying database directly from within Moodle.

- **Command Line Interface (CLI)**: The CLI is a built-in mechanism that allows us to automate administrative processes via the command line or shell scripts.

- **Moosh**: A powerful alternative to the CLI, Moosh is the third-party Moodle Shell. We will learn how Moosh works and provide some practical examples.

Before we cover these admin tools in detail, let's explore how they are organized in Moodle.

Exploring Moodle admin tools

Moodle's classification of what constitutes an admin tool is a little vague. When you navigate to **Site administration | Plugins | Admin tools | Manage admin tools**, a long list of plugins is shown:

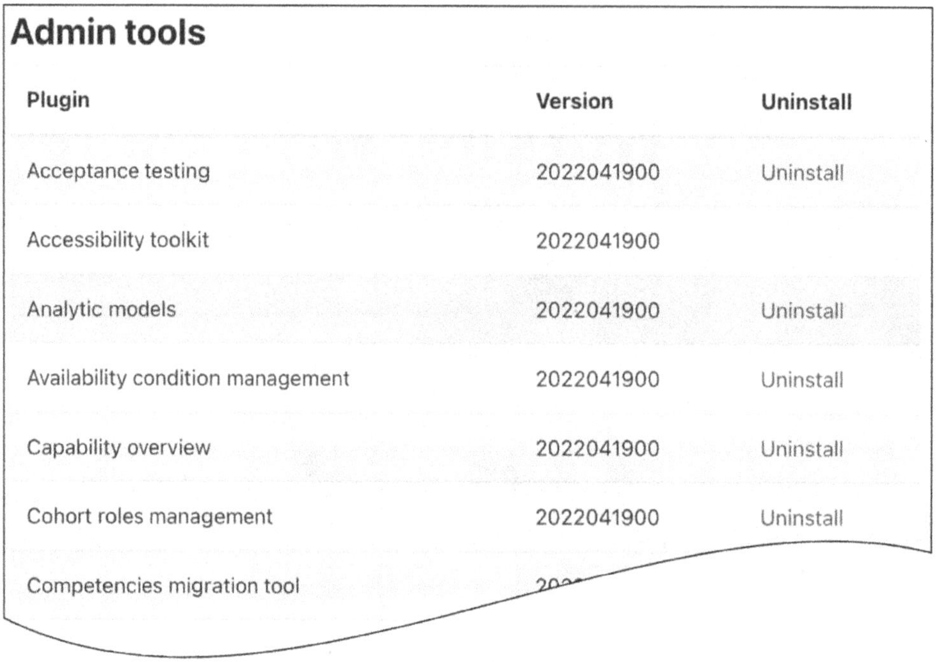

Admin tools		
Plugin	**Version**	**Uninstall**
Acceptance testing	2022041900	Uninstall
Accessibility toolkit	2022041900	
Analytic models	2022041900	Uninstall
Availability condition management	2022041900	Uninstall
Capability overview	2022041900	Uninstall
Cohort roles management	2022041900	Uninstall
Competencies migration tool	202	

Figure 17.2 – Moodle admin tools

We can group admin tools into the following categories:

- **Conversion tools**: These tools are usually only applied once to migrate a feature from an old state to its current counterpart. Examples are the **HTTPS conversion tool** (see *Chapter 13, Ensuring Moodle Security*) and **Multilang upgrade** (see *Chapter 10, Configuring Technical Features*).

- **Database tools**: These are tools to work with Moodle's underlying database. We have dedicated an entire section to database tools in this chapter.

- **Development tools**: These tools are aimed at Moodle programmers – for instance, **Acceptance testing** (Behat), **PHPUnit tests**, and the **XMLDB editor**. You came across a development tool in *Chapter 15, Optimizing Moodle Performance*, when we dealt with profiling and used the course generator. We are not going to deal with development tools here.

- **Design tools**: These tools are aimed at theme designers – for example, the **Template library** or the **UI component library**. We are not going to deal with design tools, either.

- **Standard Moodle features**: Some admin features have been implemented as admin tools, such as the recycling bin, learning plans, or the task scheduler. This way, they could be uninstalled from Moodle if not needed, though this is not recommended.

Many tools of the first four categories are hidden from the Moodle admin web interface and can only be accessed by calling them directly via the URL: `<yoursite>/admin/tool/<tool>`. All core admin tools are located in subdirectories in `$CFG->dirroot/admin/tool`. For details of mostly non-standard admin tools, refer to `docs.moodle.org/en/Admin_tools`.

We are not covering any admin tools classified as standard Moodle features, since they are either dealt with elsewhere in the book or are irrelevant in the administrator context. However, one exception are site admin presets, the only feature that does not belong to any category in the site administration menu. So, let's get started with our first admin tool.

Site admin presets

Presets allow you to create backups of site settings that can then be restored. There are several use cases where this facility comes in handy:

- Experimenting with a set of system settings and rolling back in case they didn't work
- Applying the same set of configurations to multiple sites
- Migrating one Moodle site's settings to another – for instance, your test instance to your production system

The workflow of Moodle admin presets is illustrated in the following diagram – a straightforward but very powerful tool:

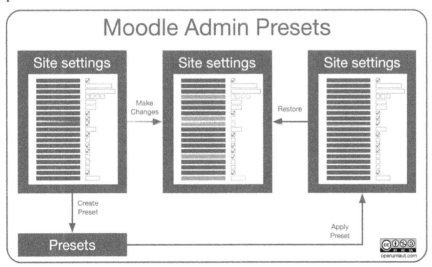

Figure 17.3 – Site admin presets workflow

You find the **Site admin presets** tool in the **General** section of the **Site administration** area. It is the only Moodle feature that has not been placed in a menu category, hence its coverage in this chapter.

Moodle ships with two preconfigured presets that have been labelled **Starter** and **Full**. Details about its content are provided in the respective descriptions, as shown in the following screenshot, which contains a third preset that we will create in this section.

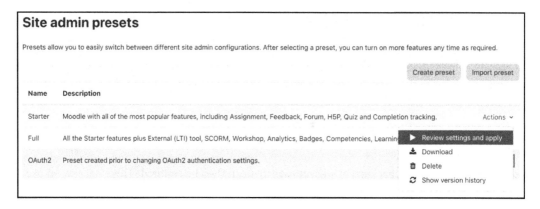

Figure 17.4 – Site admin presets

To make your first preset, click the **Create preset** button, and then you have to provide a name, an optional description, and an author, which is pre-populated with your name:

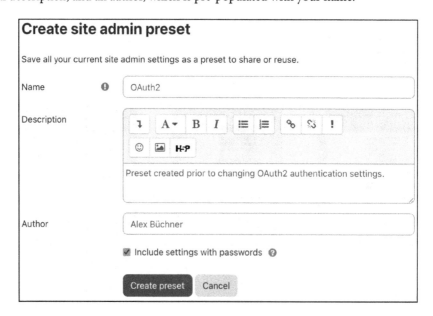

Figure 17.5 – Creating a site admin preset

The **Include settings with passwords** option will add any sensitive information – passwords, keys, and IPs – of your site to the preset, so ensure that this will only be applied internally. You can view and modify the list of fields to be excluded in the **Settings with password** field in **Site administration | General | Security | Site security settings**.

Once the preset has been created, it will appear in the list alongside the two default presets. The following actions are available for each preset:

- **Review settings and apply**: Details about the preset are shown, which include information on who created the preset (author), when (date and time), where (site URL), and on which Moodle version. As soon as you apply the admin preset, any site settings that differ from the preset will be applied, as shown in the following list of setting changes.

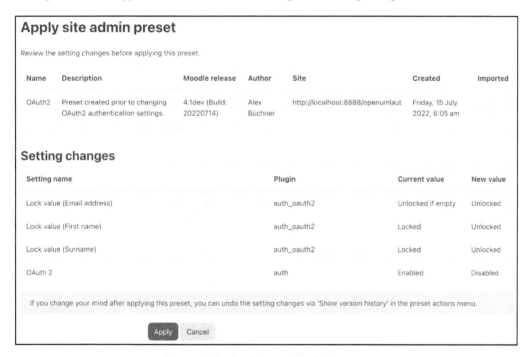

Figure 17.6 – Applying a site admin preset

- **Download**: Moodle exports the settings as an XML file. You can load an exported file via the **Import preset** button.

- **Delete**: Remove the preset permanently. The two default presets cannot be deleted.

- **Show version history**: If you change your mind after applying a preset, you can undo the setting changes via this action.

Site admin presets is a powerful tool during setup, maintenance, and when experimenting with new features.

> **Tip**
>
> It is good practice to store the presets of your production site as part of your system documentation.

Admin presets deal with your site's configuration, stored in the underlying database. A number of dedicated database tools are discussed in the following section.

Database tools

Moodle's database tools transfer databases from one server to another, perform search-and-replace operations on text strings in the entire database, and let you view or change any data in the database itself.

Transferring your Moodle database

If you have to move the database of a Moodle instance from one server to another or migrate to another Moodle system, you have two broad options. You can either create a database dump manually (or via the Adminer tool, which is covered later) or use the built-in **database transfer** facility.

The database migration tool is available at `<yoursite>/admin/tool/dbtransfer`. At the time of writing, the feature can also be accessed via **Site administration** | **Development** | **Experimental** | **Database migration**. As the category name suggests, the tool is experimental and might make it into core or might disappear again from the admin interface in future releases.

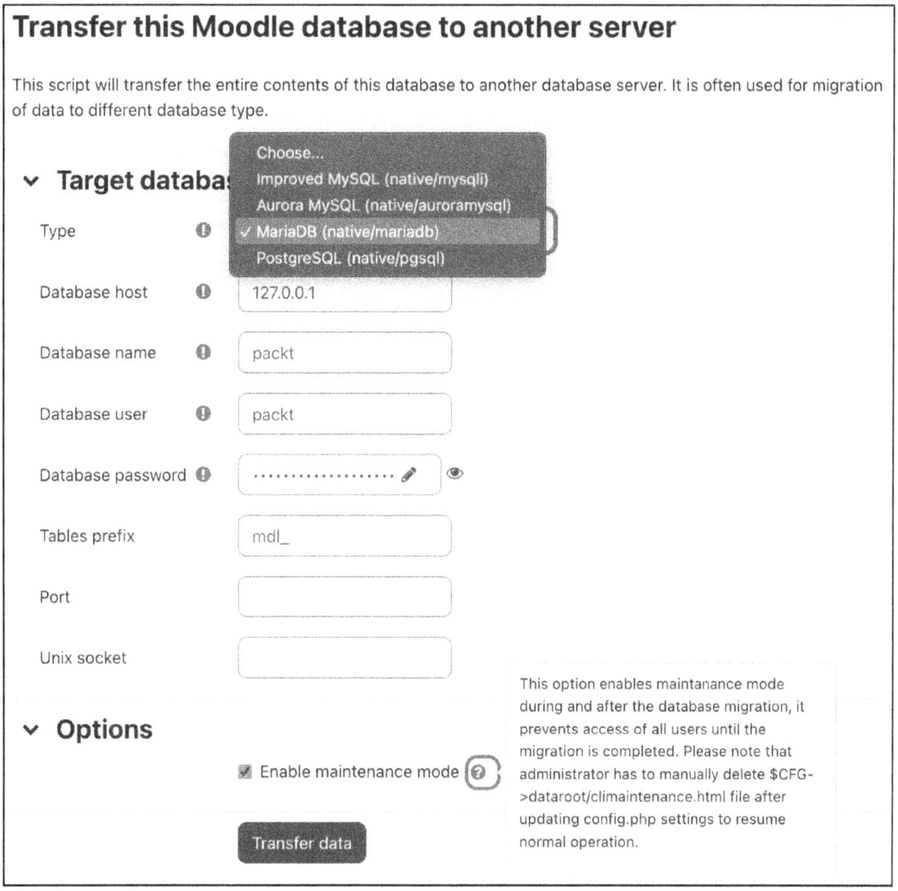

Figure 17.7 – Database transfer

You must provide the details of the database to which the content of the current database will be copied. These settings are identical to the ones applied during installation (see *Chapter 1*, *Installing Moodle*).

You further have the **Enable maintenance mode** option, which will turn on maintenance mode during and after migration. If used, you will have to remove the $CFG->dataroot/climaintenance. html file afterwards manually or via **Site administration** | **Server** | **Server** | **Maintenance mode**.

Searching and replacing database content

A tool related to the database migration facility is **DB search and replace**. After you have moved or copied your system to another location, your URL might have changed. Any user using fixed URLs anywhere in their content now faces dead links. As an administrator, you have a script at hand where you can replace any text in the underlying database, except a few tables, as noted in the second warning. You can find the script at `<yoursite>/admin/tool/replace`.

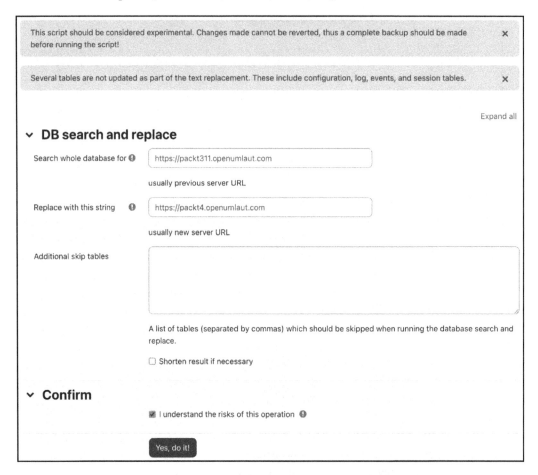

Figure 17.8 – Database search and replace

The last option, labeled **I understand the risks of this operation**, indicates the potential risk of the execution – unless you are 100% certain that the replacements will not have any impact on the system, you had better stay away from it. Once completed, the script will display all executed SQL queries.

Moodle Adminer

Adminer is an open source tool to administer different types of SQL databases. A wrapper has been created that lets you access the tool directly from within Moodle. Moodle Adminer must be installed in your `local` plugins section (see *Chapter 8*, *Understanding Moodle Plugins* for details). You will find the installer at `moodle.org/plugins/local_adminer`.

Once installed, you access the database management console via **Site administration** | **Server** | **Moodle Adminer**, which opens the tool in a modal window:

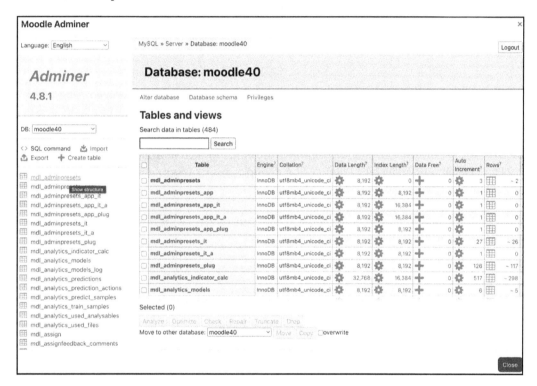

Figure 17.9 – The Moodle Adminer interface

By default, you must select a database. However, you can skip this step if you enable the **Start adminer with current database** setting in **Site administration** | **Plugins** | **Local plugins** | **Moodle Adminer**.

Once a (Moodle) database has been opened, you can perform operations (such as querying, altering data, or creating an SQL dump) without any SQL knowledge.

> **Important note**
> Ensure you only change data if you know what you are doing; otherwise, you might introduce database inconsistencies, and Moodle will not work as expected.

We will not go into using Adminer in detail since this is beyond the scope of this chapter. You can find all the information you are looking for at www.adminer.org.

This concludes the database tools section, where we covered database transfer, database search and replace, and Moodle Adminer. We ignored one tool that only applies to MySQL/MariaDB and is only needed when migrating a database still using the legacy MyISAM format. This tool can be found at `<yoursite>/admin/tool/innodb`, which converts any tables from MyISAM to the InnoDB storage engine.

There are also CLI scripts supporting database-related operations, such as `mysql_engine` and `check_database_schema`. What's a CLI script? Find out in the following section.

CLI

We already encountered the CLI selectively throughout the book and during *Chapter 1, Installing Moodle*, when we dealt with Moodle upgrades. However, the CLI has a few more tricks up its sleeve, which we will deal with in this section.

First, let's look at how you call CLI scripts, which are either located in `admin/cli/*` or in the sub-folder of plugins that offer a CLI option – for example, `auth/ldap/cli`. To call a CLI script, follow the following notation:

```
sudo -u <apache_user> /usr/bin/php admin/cli/<script>.php
[--params]
```

Your `<apache_user>` is usually `www-data`, `httpd`, or `apache`.

> **Important note**
> Always run Moodle CLI scripts under the identity of the web server user.

Every CLI script has a `--help` parameter that offers additional information and also describes calling options and parameters. The following is a list of some useful CLI commands and chapter numbers in which they have been covered. Look in their respective CLI directories or at `docs.moodle.org/en/Administration_via_command_line` for all other commands. We do not list any parameters here, as these are explained well in the `--help` options.

CLI Script	Description	Chapter
adhoc_task	Executes adhoc tasks.	15
automated_backups	Executes automatic backups ignoring the set schedule.	16
backup	Backs up a single course to a named location.	16
cfg	Gets and sets config values.	−
check_database_schema	Validation that the current database structure matches `install.xml`.	−
cron	Executes the cron command.	1
dashboard_reset	Resets all dashboards.	7
fix_course_sequence	Checks and ensures that course modules and sections reference each other correctly. Only run if you experience inconsistencies.	4
fix_deleted_users	Fixes user accounts if they got deleted incorrectly. Only run if you experience inconsistencies.	5
install	Moodle installer that creates `config.php` and prepares the database.	1
install_database	Installs Moodle in an empty database. `config.php` must already exist.	1
kill_all_sessions	Kills all user sessions without warning.	15
maintenance	Enable or disable maintenance mode. Custom messages are stored in `$CFG->dataroot/climaintenance.html`.	1
mysql_engine	Converts MySQL tables to a different engine.	−
purge_caches	Clears all system caches.	15
reset_password	Resets a user's password. Also works for the admin account!	5
restore_backup	Restores a `.mbz` file.	16
scheduled_task	Executes a scheduled task manually.	15
uninstall_plugins	Uninstalls Moodle plugins.	8
upgrade	Upgrades Moodle to a newer version.	1

Figure 17.10 – A selection of Moodle CLI scripts

The real power of the CLI lies in the ability to embed CLI commands in shell scripts, which allows for powerful **automation** of otherwise time-consuming or error-prone routines. We presented a small installation script in *Chapter 1, Installing Moodle*. Here is another sample script that kills all user sessions and clears caches, utilizing some CLI scripts:

```
1  # Script to kill all user sessions and clear caches
2  cd /var/www/html/moodle
3
4  # Enable maintenance message
5  echo '<h1>Sorry, maintenance in progress</h1>' > climaintenance.html
6
7  # Enable maintenance message
8  php admin/cli/maintenance.php --enable
9
10 # Kill all user sessions
11 php admin/cli/kill_all_sessions.php
12
13 # Clear all system caches
14 php admin/cli/purge_caches.php
15
16 # Disable maintenance message
17 php admin/cli/maintenance.php --disable
```

Figure 17.11 – A sample Bash script utilizing the Moodle CLI

While useful for the supported operations, the CLI provides a relatively restricted set of commands. Moosh, which we will cover next, overcomes this limitation.

Moosh – the Moodle Shell

Moosh stands for Moodle Shell and is a command-line tool that allows you to perform the most common Moodle tasks.

Before you can make use of Moosh, you have to install it (see *Chapter 8, Understanding Moodle Plugins*). Once installed, you will have a vast number of commands (at the time of writing, over 150!) at your disposal.

The general syntax of Moosh is as follows:

```
moosh <-params> <command> <options>
```

To give you an idea of the types of things you can do with Moosh, here are a few examples:

- `moosh user-create test`: Creates a user with the username `test`.
- `moosh user-create test{1..10}`: Creates 10 users. This type of enumeration can be used with many Moosh commands.

- `moosh user-create --email packt@openumlaut.com --city "Heidelberg" --country DE --firstname "Alex" --lastname "Büchner" packt`: All user profile values are supported; this is just a sample.

- `moosh info-plugins`: Displays a list of all plugins installed and their locations.

- `moosh file-list course=42`: Outputs information on all files in the course with the ID 42. There are more file-related commands, such as showing the system path of a file or the ability to upload files directly.

- `moosh plugin-install mod_videotime`: Downloads and installs the latest version of the versatile Videotime plugin. How cool is that?

Once you combine Moosh commands with standard shell commands via pipes and streams, you have a powerful arsenal of commands at hand. For example, you might want to find all backups that are larger than 10 GB, archive them, and reclaim the space.

The following example demonstrates the execution and output of three Moosh commands:

```
pi@moodle:/var/www/html/moodle $ moosh course-list
"id","category","shortname","fullname","visible"
"1","0","Home","Home","1"
"2","Top/Computing/Computing Year 1","cpp","C++","1"
"4","Top/Computing","removed course","Removed Course","1"
"5","Top/Computing/Computing Year 1","Cat 2","Cat 2","1"
"6","Top/Computing/Computing Year 1","ALGDS1","Algorithms & Data Structures I","1"
"7","Top/Computing","Test","Test","1"
"8","Top/Computing","abc","abc","1"
pi@moodle:/var/www/html/moodle $ moosh category-list
id              name            idnumber        description     parent          visible
1               Computing       COMP                            Top             1
2               Computing Year 1COMP-1                           Top/Computing  1
3               Computing Year 2COMP-2                           Top/Computing  1
4               Computing Year 3COMP-3                           Top/Computing  0
pi@moodle:/var/www/html/moodle $ moosh user-create testuser{1..10}
150
151
152
153
154
155
156
157
158
159
```

Figure 17.12 – Playing with Moosh

The first (`moosh course-list`) shows the information on all courses; the second (`moosh category-list`) does the same for categories; the last (`moosh user-create test{1..10}`) shows the IDs of the 10 user accounts after they have been created.

For a complete list of over 150 commands and hundreds of options, refer to the Moosh website at `moosh-online.com/commands`. The list is constantly growing, so ensure you have installed the latest version.

This concludes the section on Moosh and the chapter on Moodle admin tools. Hopefully, some facilities will streamline your day-to-day job and optimize some of the routine tasks you need to carry out.

Summary

In this chapter, we have covered a range of admin tools, some hidden and unsupported but nonetheless very useful. We first explored how admin tools are organized, before we covered site admin presets and some database tools, including the external Adminer, the Moodle CLI, and the powerful third-party Moosh tool.

Other ways to extend the reach of Moodle are web services, which we will cover in the following chapter.

18

Integrating External Systems Using Moodle Web Services

In most organizations, the LMS is rarely an isolated, standalone system; instead, it is almost always part of an institution-wide infrastructure containing several best-of-breed components. Web services facilitate exchange and communication among these systems and Moodle is no exception. At the time of writing, Moodle ships with almost 700 web service functions, a number that is growing with every release.

After providing a brief overview of web services and giving some application examples, we will learn about the basic concepts of Moodle web services. Next, we will configure the generic Moodle web services functionality required for different setups. Then, we will learn how to set up the Moodle web service for another application to control Moodle. Lastly, we will learn how to set up the Moodle web service for a user as the client.

We will be covering the following topics in this chapter:

- Understanding Moodle web services
- Configuring Moodle web services
- Enabling web services for external systems
- Enabling web services for users

We will not cover any programming aspects of web services, as this is not an administrative task. You will find good documentation about the topic for users and developers at `docs.moodle.org/en/Web_Services`.

By the end of this chapter, you will know what web services are and how they are configured for external systems and users.

Understanding Moodle web services

This section will familiarize you with web services, how they work, and when to use them.

It has always been possible to extend Moodle via code (PHP and JavaScript). Due to Moodle's open source code base, there is no limitation on what code a developer can modify or extend. As an administrator, this was not a satisfactory situation, as you have no control over what parts of Moodle are being changed as a result, and, equally importantly, what data is being accessed or altered.

Moodle has various APIs that provide abstract layers for certain functionalities. Examples are the Privacy API, Repository API, and File API. These are great for programmers, as they reduce the amount of code that has to be rewritten. In addition to these interfaces, Moodle provides us with an ever-growing number of web services.

> **Important note**
> Web services enable other systems to perform operations inside Moodle, and vice versa.

Why would we want this? Well, there are four scenarios we can think of:

- Other systems in your organization – for instance, the HR system – have to trigger specific actions in your LMS; for example, once new staff has been added to the system, an account must be created in Moodle, and enrolments in several courses should take place. Web services simplify this process greatly.

- Certain information stored in Moodle might have to be transferred to external applications. Examples are course completions, grades, or issued certificates, which have to be recorded in a student information system. Again, web services are predestined for the transfer of such sensitive data.

- The Moodle app we covered in *Chapter 11, Enabling Mobile Learning*, uses web services internally; all communication and data exchange between a mobile device and the Moodle backend takes place via web services.

- The community hub feature requires web services, which we will cover in *Chapter 19, Setting Up Moodle Networking*.

Why should you, as an administrator, care about web services when they have been designed for developers? Well, that's the other advantage of web services. You can control which system can talk to your Moodle system and which features these systems are allowed to use. This way, you can manage who has access to your system and limit what they can do.

The following diagram illustrates a (very) simplistic overview of how Moodle interacts with external applications via web services:

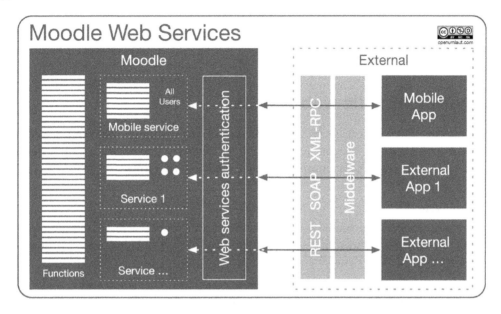

Figure 18.1 – Moodle web services

Let's go through this schema from left to right: many Moodle features are represented as **functions** – for example, creating a user account or enrolling a user into a course. A **service** is a set thereof plus the definition of which user(s) can access the selected functions. For instance, the Moodle app uses a built-in (that is, predefined) service granting all users access to Moodle. In contrast, a custom service might only allow access to a single dedicated account.

> **Important note**
> A service is a set of functions. A service can be user-restricted, token-restricted, IP-restricted, or time-restricted.

External applications must authenticate with Moodle through the web service **authentication** plugin for security. Communication from external apps can be unidirectional or bidirectional, which is implicitly determined by the functions of the service. The supported web service **protocols** are SOAP, REST, and XML-RPC.

Web services return feedback on whether the calls or transactions have succeeded. For instance, if the creation of a user account has failed in Moodle for whatever reason, the HR system will be notified and can repeat the attempt after a predefined period. Most web services-based infrastructure requires some **middleware** to facilitate queueing and error handling.

Now that you have some basic understanding of Moodle web services, it is time to configure protocols, services, and functions.

Configuring Moodle web services

First, you must activate web services via the **Enable web services** setting in **Site administration | General | Advanced features**. The setting is linked to the **Enable web services for mobile devices** parameter on the same page; the latter cannot be enabled without the former.

> Important note
>
> Enabling web services is a potential security risk, as you grant Moodle access to outside users and systems. The mantra should always be "open up as few services and functions as possible."

Second, you have to enable the **Web services authentication** plugin (**Site administration | Plugins | Authentication | Manage authentication**). No configuration is needed, as Moodle handles all handshake operations and communication internally.

Moodle supports two types of external services that can connect via web services:

- **Built-in services**: These are preconfigured services where the set of supported functions cannot be modified. The **Moodle mobile web service** is part of Moodle and lets users of the app interact with Moodle. We covered the app's configuration in *Chapter 11, Enabling Mobile Learning*. Third-party plugins might add further entries to the list of built-in services.

- **Custom services**: These are user-defined services where you configure which functions can be utilized. We will focus on custom services in this chapter, allowing two types of entities to access Moodle: external systems and users as clients with tokens.

When you navigate to **Site administration** | **Server** | **Web services** | **External services**, you see the services for the two described service types. We have installed the `mod_attendance` plugin in our system, which installs a built-in service alongside the mentioned mobile web service. We have also created two custom services, one for testing purposes (which is disabled) and one to connect to our HR system, as shown in the following screenshot:

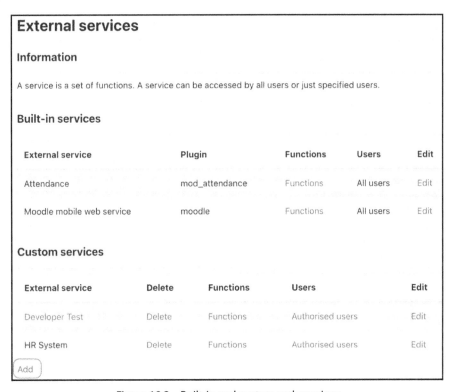

Figure 18.2 – Built-in and custom web services

To configure web services, it is best to go to **Site administration | Server | Web services | Overview**, which acts as a dashboard for setting up Moodle web services. Two checklists are shown, one to **Allow an external system to control Moodle** (dealt with first) and one for **Users as clients with token** (seen shortly):

Allow an external system to control Moodle

The following steps help you to set up the Moodle web services to allow an external system to interact with Moodle. This includes setting up a token (security key) authentication method.

Step	Status	Description
1. Enable web services	Yes	Web services must be enabled in Advanced features.
2. Enable protocols	None	At least one protocol should be enabled. For security reasons, only protocols that are to be used should be enabled.
3. Create a specific user		A web services user is required to represent the system controlling Moodle.
4. Check user capability		The user should have appropriate capabilities according to the protocols used, for example webservice/rest:use, webservice/soap:use. To achieve this, create a web services role with protocol capabilities allowed and assign it to the web services user as a system role.
5. Select a service		A service is a set of web service functions. You will allow the user to access to a new service. On the **Add service** page check 'Enable' and 'Authorised users' options. Select 'No required capability'.
6. Add functions		Select required functions for the newly created service.
7. Select a specific user		Add the web services user as an authorised user.
8. Create a token for a user		Create a token for the web services user.
9. Enable developer documentation	No	Detailed web services documentation is available for enabled protocols.
10. Test the service		Simulate external access to the service using the web service test client. Use an enabled protocol with token authentication. **WARNING: The functions that you test WILL BE EXECUTED, so be careful what you choose to test!**

Figure 18.3 – Allowing an external system to control Moodle

We have already enabled web services (step 1). Moodle supports three web service protocols – **SOAP**, **REST**, and **XML-RPC**. We won't provide details on those standards; for more information, check out `docs.moodle.org/dev/Creating_a_web_service_client`. At least one protocol must be enabled, which depends entirely on the external application, the protocols supported, and the developer's preference. Clicking on the **Enabled protocols** link in the overview table when you go to **Site administration** | **Server** | **Web services** | **Manage protocols** will guide you to this screen. Enable a protocol by toggling the show/hide icon in the **Enable** column. Here, **SOAP** has been enabled, which is common in, but not limited to, Microsoft-based environments, as shown in the following screenshot:

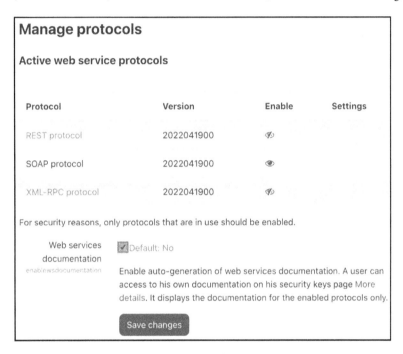

Figure 18.4 – Protocols for web services

Technically, it is possible that more web service protocols will be added in the future, for example, a Java- and .Net-compatible WSDL, but to date, this has not happened.

> **Important note**
> Depending on the protocol chosen, you might have to install the respective PHP extension – for example, `php-soap`.

Now that we have enabled web services and at least one protocol, let's cover the configuration of the two types of web service accesses.

Enabling web services for external systems

An external system is an application that accesses Moodle and its data in one way or another. Eight steps have to be performed to complete the setup, which follows the workflow described on the web services overview screen:

1. **Create a specific user**

    Each application should have a separate user account. This way, you can control the capabilities each external system will use. Our user is aptly called *webservice*.

2. **Check user capability**

    Depending on the protocol you've selected, you must allow specific permissions for the user. You achieve this by creating a new role with any of the three capabilities, `webservice/rest:use`, `webservice/soap:use`, or `webservice/xmlrpc:use`.

    This role has to be assigned to the web service user(s) in the **System** context.

3. **Select a service**

    A service is a defined interface that an external application can connect to, represented by a set of functions (see step 4). Selecting a service takes place at **Site administration | Server | Web services | External service**. You have to add a custom service:

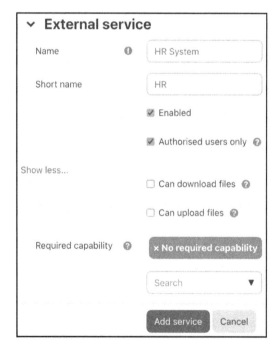

Figure 18.5 – Web services: adding a custom service

Each external service must have a given **Name** and a unique **Short name** and should be **Enabled** once configured. A service has to be accessed via a token. The **Authorized users only** setting restricts this access to selected users. All users with the token permission can access the service if it remains unchecked.

You can also specify download and upload permission for the web service with **Can download files** or **Can upload files**. In our HR role, this would be useful if you also managed profile pictures via web services. You can further restrict access by specifying the required capabilities that users need to have.

Once you have saved the service, select the **Add functions** link shown.

4. **Add functions**

    At the time of writing, Moodle provides almost 700(!) functions that can be accessed via web services, and even more in Moodle Workplace. The function(s) selected depend(s) on what tasks the external system has to perform and should be set up in liaison with the developer in charge. Since we are connecting to an HR system, we will allow the following user-related functions:

Figure 18.6 – Web services – adding functions

Once you have added the selected functions, you will be shown the required capabilities that a user must have to access the service. Ensure these have been allowed in the role assigned to the web services user.

5. **Select a specific user**

   If you selected **Authorized users only** when creating the preceding service, you must select this user(s), which takes place at **Site administration | Server | Web services | External services**, where you see a list of all the services that have been set up. Select the **Authorized users** link, which will guide you to the familiar user selection screen. Select the web services user you created in step 1:

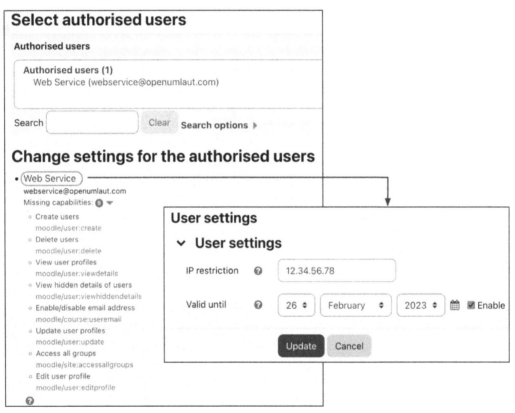

Figure 18.7 – Web services – selecting users

Moodle will check whether the account has sufficient permissions to access the selected functions. If any capabilities are missing, they will be displayed under the user selection screen in the **Change settings for the authorized users** section. Ensure that you add the listed capabilities to your web service's permissions. Clicking on a username will allow you to restrict access to an IP address and set an expiry date.

6. **Create a token for a user**

    Web services use tokens for security. These are created for each user and can be added by going to **Site administration | Server | Web services | Manage tokens**. To add a token, select a user (or multiple users), select the service to be accessed, and optionally specify an IP address (or range) and an expiry date, as shown in the following screenshot:

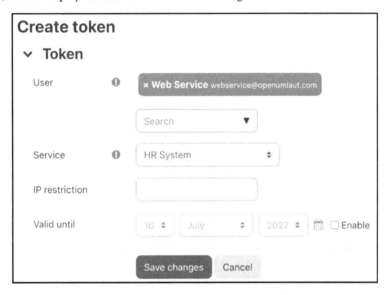

Figure 18.8 – Web services – creating a token

Users can access and reset their web services token by going to **Security keys** in **Preferences** if they have the `moodle/webservice:createtoken` capability.

7. **Enable developer documentation (optional)**

Moodle can be instructed to generate documentation for developers for the selected functions in the selected protocol format. When you set up the protocols (**Site administration | Server | Web services | Manage protocols**), you must tick the **Web services documentation** option. Developers can view the documentation as part of their security keys:

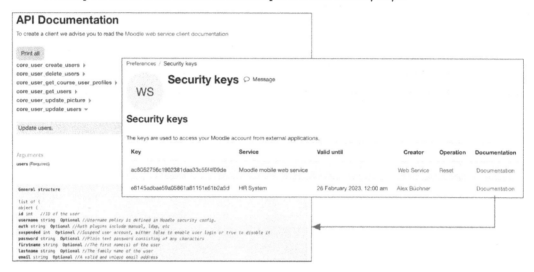

Figure 18.9 – Web services – security keys and API documentation

8. **Test the service**

Once a web service is set up, functions have been selected, and users have been assigned, it is imperative that you test the service to ensure that it works and, more importantly, that the external system has only opened up the required functionality. Web services are tested by navigating to **Site administration | Development | Web service test client**. Unfortunately, the test client only supports some hardcoded functions, not those you have configured. I quote from the Moodle Docs at docs.moodle.org/en/Web_services_test_client: "*The test client is not clever! It lets you choose disabled/unavailable functions (however it behaves well and produces an error in these case). This is normal because clients are going to be bad sometimes so we needed to simulate a bad client!*"

> **Important note**
> Be careful with executing functions via the test client, as they perform them as though they are executed for real!

First, you have to select the **Authentication method** (**simple** for a username and password and **token** for a security key), **Protocol**, and **Function** settings to test. The screen that follows depends on which authentication method has been selected and which function has been chosen. Here, we used **token** and **core_course_create_categories** (you have to temporarily add the moodle/category:manage permission to your web service role for this to work):

Figure 18.10 – Web services testing

Once you have filled in the required values and executed the command, you will see a return value in the XML format. If you press the **Execute** button, your database will be modified, and changes cannot be reverted without manual intervention at the database level. It is also a good practice to try out some functions the web service should not be able to access:

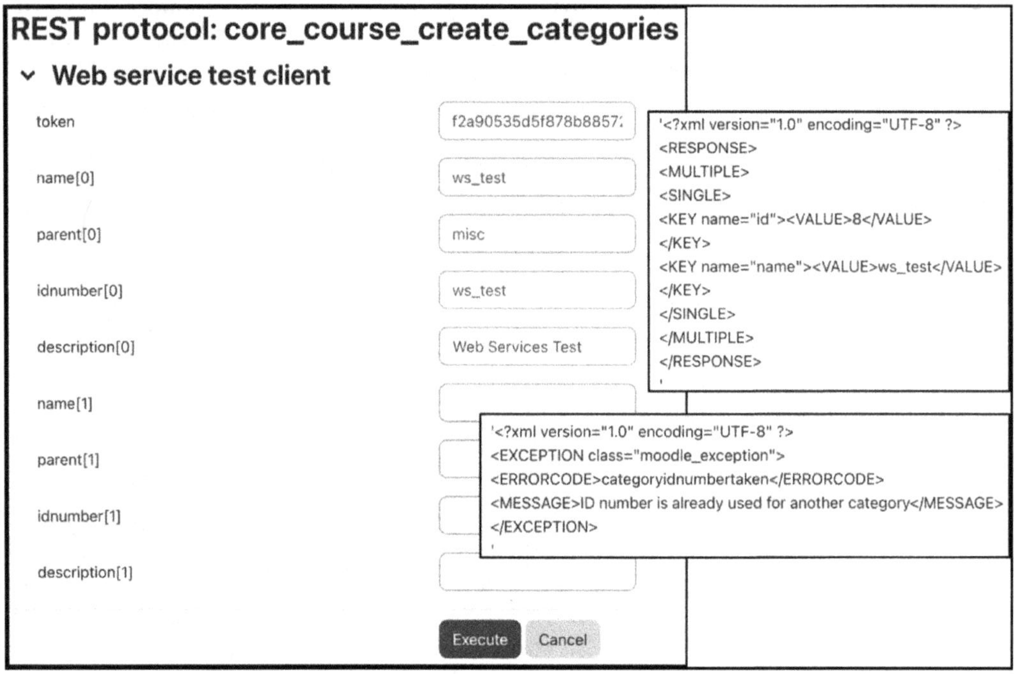

REST protocol: core_course_create_categories

⌄ Web service test client

token	f2a90535d5f878b8857...	
name[0]	ws_test	
parent[0]	misc	
idnumber[0]	ws_test	
description[0]	Web Services Test	
name[1]		
parent[1]		
idnumber[1]		
description[1]		

```xml
'<?xml version="1.0" encoding="UTF-8" ?>
<RESPONSE>
<MULTIPLE>
<SINGLE>
<KEY name="id"><VALUE>8</VALUE>
</KEY>
<KEY name="name"><VALUE>ws_test</VALUE>
</KEY>
</SINGLE>
</MULTIPLE>
</RESPONSE>
'
```

```xml
'<?xml version="1.0" encoding="UTF-8" ?>
<EXCEPTION class="moodle_exception">
<ERRORCODE>categoryidnumbertaken</ERRORCODE>
<MESSAGE>ID number is already used for another category</MESSAGE>
</EXCEPTION>
'
```

[Execute] [Cancel]

Figure 18.11 – Web services testing

To receive a more meaningful message, change the **Debug messages** setting by going to **Site administration | Development | Debugging** and then to **DEVELOPER**. If the result shown contains a line containing a DEBUGINFO element, an error has occurred. Otherwise, you should check that the function performed what it was supposed to when executed. We executed the operation twice; the first run was successful – that is, the category was created. The second run wasn't because the category already existed.

Now that we have covered how to configure web services for external applications, let us briefly look at its little brother – enabling token-based access for users.

Enabling web services for users

It is sometimes necessary for users to have to access web services directly instead of applications – for example, a developer who needs to execute test runs against the system. The process is a subset of steps already covered in the previous section and follows the **Users as clients with token** section on the web services overview screen:

Users as clients with token

The following steps help you to set up the Moodle web service for users as clients. These steps also help to set up the recommended token (security keys) authentication method. In this use case, the user will generate their token from the security keys page via their preferences page.

Step	Status	Description
1. Enable web services	Yes	Web services must be enabled in Advanced features.
2. Enable protocols	rest soap	At least one protocol should be enabled. For security reasons, only protocols that are to be used should be enabled.
3. Select a service		A service is a set of web service functions. You will allow users to access to a new service. On the **Add service** page check 'Enable' and uncheck 'Authorised users' options. Select 'No required capability'.
4. Add functions		Select required functions for the newly created service.
5. Check users capability		Users should have two capabilities - webservice:createtoken and a capability matching the protocols used, for example webservice/rest:use, webservice/soap:use. To achieve this, create a web services role with the appropriate capabilities allowed and assign it to the web services user as a system role.
6. Test the service		Simulate external access to the service using the web service test client. Before doing so, log in as a user with the moodle/webservice:createtoken capability and obtain the security key (token) via the user's preferences page. You will use this token in the test client. In the test client, also choose an enabled protocol with the token authentication. **WARNING: The functions that you test WILL BE EXECUTED for this user, so be careful what you choose to test!**

Figure 18.12 – Web services for users as clients with tokens

These steps should be familiar by now; there are only two minor deviations from the previous scenario when web services were allowed for external systems instead of users.

In step 3, the **Authorized users** option must be unchecked. In addition to the protocol use capabilities, the users must have the `moodle/webservice:createtoken` capability set to allowed (see step 5).

To test the service (see step 6), log in as the user, obtain a security token for testing, and avoid using the simple authentication method in the web service test client.

Summary

In this chapter, you learned the basics about web services and how they are configured from within Moodle. We covered the two main administrative tasks: setting up web services for external applications and enabling token-based web services for users.

All the processes covered in this chapter are identical in Moodle and Moodle Workplace; the only difference is that Moodle Workplace supports significantly more web service functions.

In the following chapter, we will cover another option for Moodle to communicate with other systems, namely via Moodle networking.

Setting Up Moodle Networking

Moodle provides a unique feature that lets you network multiple Moodle sites. This networking functionality is useful in several contexts – for example, when you want to share resources with remote LMSs, partner with another organization, or have a multi-campus setup where each site has its own Moodle instance.

After providing an overview of **Moodle networking** (**MNet**), we will learn which networking components are required and how networking is enabled. Next, we will will learn how to link two Moodle sites, which entails setting up peer-to-peer connections, roaming across instances, configuring remote authentication and enrolment, and using the Networks server block. Lastly, we will learn how to connect multiple Moodle sites to a central MNet hub.

We will finish this chapter with a new platform closely related to MNet known as **MoodleNet**, a platform for finding, sharing, and curating open educational resources. You will learn how to enable MoodleNet so that your educators can make use of it.

We will cover the following main topics in this chapter:

- Configuring Moodle networking prerequisites
- Setting up peer-to-peer networks
- Setting up a Moodle hub
- Enabling MoodleNet

Understanding Moodle networking

Learning management systems are usually standalone systems. But learning is a lot about communication and collaboration, and MNet overcomes this limitation by providing a powerful facility to establish logical links among multiple Moodle sites.

Moodle Docs contains a very well-written page on MNet, and this chapter follows the document in part: `docs.moodle.org/en/MNet`.

The following two networking topologies are supported:

- **Peer-to-peer**: This layout connects two Moodle systems directly. This topology is favorable if you have two partnering organizations or one site that offers courses in which students from another site wish to enrol.

- **Moodle hub**: A hub is a Moodle server (known as the **MNet hub**) that's been configured to accept connections from other Moodle servers and provide services to users of these remote servers. This topology is favorable if you have a portal for sharing learning resources or courses.

The two topologies are not mutually exclusive and can be mixed in the same network, as visualized in the following diagram. All participating Moodle instances connect to a central hub, and the two Moodle systems on the left have established a peer-to-peer connection:

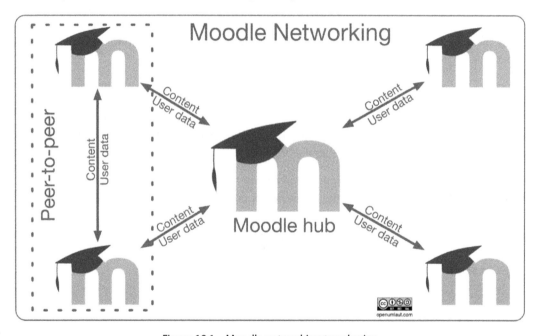

Figure 19.1 – Moodle networking topologies

MNet supports **single sign-on** (**SSO**), which provides seamless integration of multiple Moodle systems. Security is guaranteed by fully encrypting authentication and content exchanges.

> **Information**
>
> **MNet** has been designed for Moodle-Moodle pairing. The plan is to replace MNet in the future with OAuth2 (for authentication) and web services (for communication and data exchange).

Now that we've covered some networking prerequisites and security issues, let's learn how to set up peer-to-peer networks and an MNet hub.

Configuring Moodle networking prerequisites

MNet requires three additional components to be installed on all participating servers that deal with secure communication and safe data exchange.

Checking the required PHP extensions

The following elements must be installed on all Moodle servers participating in the network:

- **curl**: A PHP library of calls designed to safely fetch data from remote sites. If not installed, you must recompile PHP and add `--with curl` when running `configure`.

- **openssl**: The OpenSSL PHP library provides encryption functionality without the need to purchase an SSL certificate (`--with openssl`).

- **xmlrpc**: A PHP library that supports remote procedure calls via XML (`--with xmlrpc`).

  It is possible to add trusted hosts to Moodle, which allows them to execute calls via XML-RPC to any part of the Moodle API. Trusted hosts are potentially very dangerous and are only meant for developers; we will not be dealing with this functionality here:

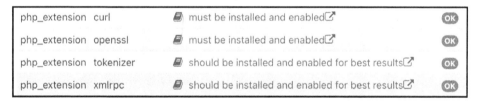

Figure 19.2 – Moodle networking prerequisites

To check that the required PHP extensions have been installed, go to **Site administration | Server | Environment** and ensure the status for all three components is **OK**.

Enabling Moodle networking

The aforementioned PHP extensions ensure secure communication and that data is safely transmitted between participating sites. Moodle will generate a certificate to encrypt the communication, which is done via PHP using the certificate mentioned earlier.

Once networking has been enabled, Moodle generates a public/private key pair using OpenSSL. When you later connect to another Moodle site (which also has a set of keys), the public key is exchanged, and you will have to confirm that your site will trust this public key. When the two sites exchange data, the sender will sign each request using their private key and encrypt the message with the recipient's public key. The receiver, who is the holder of the sender's public key and its private key, will be able to decrypt the message and execute the request. So much for the theory. Now, back to the real world.

To activate Mnet, go to **Site administration** | **General** | **Advanced features** and turn on **Networking**, which will add the **Networking** menu to the site admin menu. This step has to be performed on all participating servers in the Moodle network.

Go to **Site administration** | **Networking** | **Settings**, where you will see the public key created by OpenSSL:

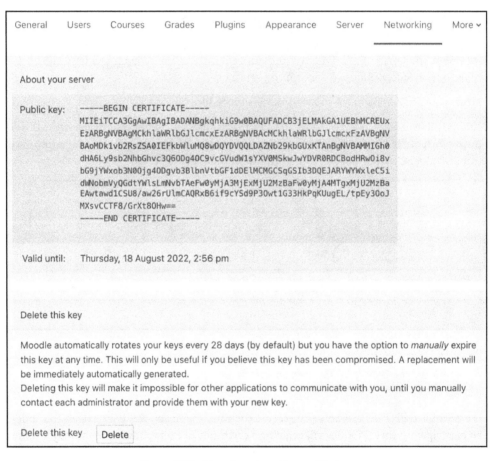

Figure 19.3 – Moodle networking public key

The key has an expiry date that is 28 days from creation; after this, a new key is created (**key rotation**). The key can be renewed manually by using the **Delete** option on the same screen.

> **Important note**
> The key expiry duration cannot be changed via a Moodle parameter; however, it can be changed via a configuration setting (see the *Appendix, Configuration Settings*). Add `$CFG->mnetkeylifetime=365` to `config.php` to increase the expiry period to a full year to avoid regularly having to renew keys.

Now that MNet has been enabled and the public key has been generated, it is time to get the servers talking to each other.

Setting up peer-to-peer networks

This section deals with peer-to-peer networks, where two Moodle servers are connected.

For demonstration purposes, we have set up two local sites (two peers); one is located at `localhost:8888/one` and the other is located at `localhost:8888/two`.

The two sites do not have to be in the same domain or organization. For example, two universities or two high schools might want to offer a collaborative course. They both have their own Moodle system in their domain, and they both control who gets access to which part of their site.

If your two sites are hosted in the same top-level domain, and you are accessing both sites from the same web browser simultaneously, change the cookie prefix of one site (**Site administration** | **Server** | **Session handling**) to avoid any conflicts.

Adding network peers

Go to **Site administration** | **Networking** | **Manage peers** and add a new remote host you want to connect to. We are currently working on `localhost:8888/one`; to establish a link to the remote server, we have to enter `localhost:8888/two`. Then, perform the equivalent step on the other host:

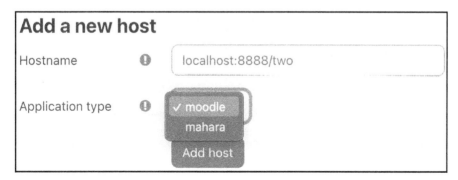

Figure 19.4 – Adding a peer I

The pull-down menu offers an additional **Application type: mahara**. We won't cover the integration with Mahara here and leave this setting as-is (**moodle**).

> **Information**
>
> Mahara is an open source ePortfolio system that can be integrated via MNet. The integration between Moodle and Mahara has been affectionately named **Mahoodle**, which has been documented in great detail at `wiki.mahara.org/wiki/System_Administrator's_Guide/Moodle//Mahara_Integration`.

Once the host has been added, the **Site**, **Hostname**, and **Public key** details are retrieved automatically. The **SSL verification** parameter determines the level of security; it is recommended to leave this at its default value of **Verify host and peer**. Optionally, select **Force theme** that will be used when roaming:

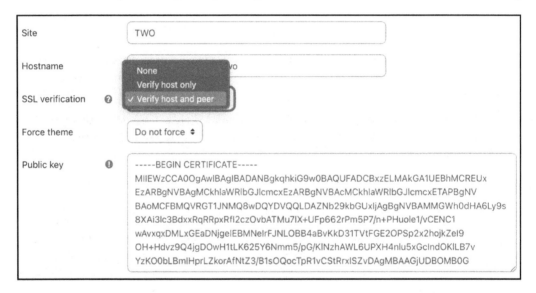

Figure 19.5 – Adding a peer II

Once the peer details have been saved, certificate details of the remote server are displayed. You will also see the following three tabs at the top of the screen:

- **Review host details**: We just dealt with the details of the peer connection. You can always return to this screen by selecting the respective host under **Site administration | Networking | Peers**.

- **Services**: Peer services define what SSO is enabled between the sites.

- **Profile fields**: This determines which fields are populated when users roam from the local to the remote site.

> **Important note**
> Deleted peers are kept on the system and can be reactivated when you attempt to add a new host with the same address.

Now that the two sites are talking to each other, let's start configuring user roaming by configuring the peer services.

Configuring peer services

The SSO supported by MNet avoids the need to log in when roaming to a remote site. The **Services** tab contains four areas. We will focus on the last two, which deal with SSO; the enrolment and portfolio services will be dealt with later.

Two SSO services represent a two-way process, and both services must be set up on both Moodle sites by the respective administrators.

> **Important note**
> Peer services can be published and subscribed to.

It is important to note that the local administrator fully controls publication and subscription. The administrator of the *other* site will never be able to modify any of those settings on *your* site.

You must publish the identity provider service to allow your users to roam to the other site without having to log in again. Subscribe to the identity provider service to allow authenticated users from the other site to access your site without having to log in again.

You must publish the service provider service to allow authenticated users from the other site to access your site without having to log in again. Subscribe to the service provider service to allow your users to roam to the other site without having to log in again there:

	Local users	Remote users
Publish identity provider	Allow roaming	
Subscribe service provider	Allow roaming	
Subscribe identity provider		Grant access
Publish service provider		Grant access

Figure 19.6 – Peer services

Let's look at an example of two collaborating universities. University A will publish the identity provider, while University B will subscribe to it. Students from University A can now access restricted areas at University B's site without having to log in again.

Each service has a reciprocal dependency on the other server, as shown in the preceding table. For example, the subscribed SSO (Service Provider) on the local site requires the SSO (Service Provider) to be published on the remote site. To allow roaming in both directions, all four boxes on both peers in your Moodle network have to be checked by the respective administrator.

Configuring profile fields

When a user from one site roams to another site for the first time, a local user account is created, and specific profile fields are populated by fetching the data from the remote site. You can override the default fields by selecting any of the shown profile fields in the provided list. This setting exists for **Fields to import** (users who roam from a remote site to the local site) and **Fields to export** (vice versa):

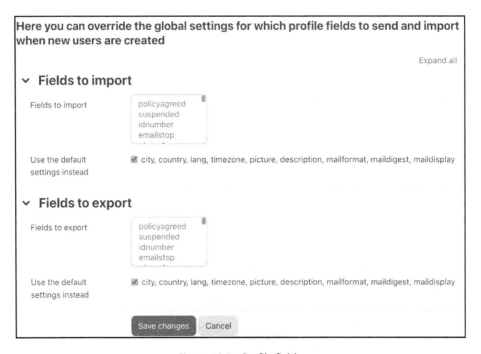

Figure 19.7 – Profile fields

The default fields can be changed under **Site administration | Networking | Profile fields**. Fields included in your import list but excluded from the remote site's export list will be ignored.

Bear in mind that no password will be stored on the remote server. As the authentication mechanism will be set to **MNet authentication**, Moodle checks the credentials every time a user logs in. We will deal with authentication next.

Enabling MNet authentication

To initiate roaming, you must enable the Moodle network authentication plugin on both sites. Go to **Site administration** | **Plugins** | **Authentication** | **Manage authentication** and enable the **MNet authentication** option. Every time a new user from a remote site logs into this site, a user account is created automatically.

When you select the **Test connection** link beside the authentication plugin, you will see a list of which hosts that users are allowed to roam to your site and which local users are allowed to roam out:

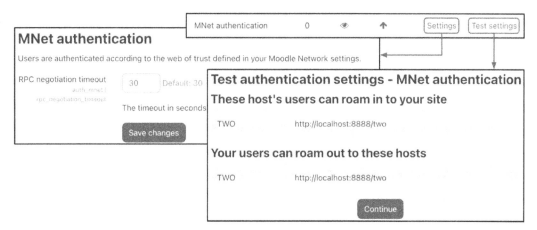

Figure 19.8 – MNet authentication

Only change the **RPC negotiation timeout** parameter on the **Settings** screen if users experience intermittent timeout problems when roaming from one site to another.

Allowing roaming

Only users that have been assigned a role with the `moodle/site:mnetlogintoremote` capability are allowed to roam to other sites. By default, this `Roam to a remote Moodle` capability is turned off and has to be allowed for each role. Revisit *Chapter 6, Managing Permissions, Roles, and Capabilities*, for details on how to do this.

To turn on roaming for all users logged into your site, allow the capability in the **Authenticated user** role. Unless all users are allowed to roam, it is worth considering creating a separate roaming role. Alternatively, if you wish to grant (or deny) access to individual users from a remote host, go to **Site administration** | **Networking** | **SSO access control**. You have to specify a username, a remote host (the **All hosts** option is only relevant for the community hub mode, which will be discussed later), and the access level (**Allow** or **Deny**).

The newly added username does not have to exist on either Moodle site! The remote hub ID is displayed in the list of users, which is the internal ID. This is similar to a user ID, group ID, or role ID:

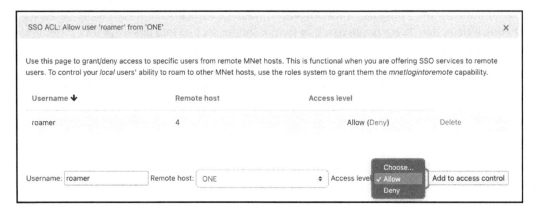

Figure 19.9 – Allowing roaming

Network users can also be assigned via CSV batch upload, which we described in detail in *Chapter 5, Managing Users, Cohorts, and Authentication*; the relevant field in the CSV file is mnethostid.

Adding the Network servers block

Moodle provides a **Network servers** block, which can be added to the home page. This block cannot be configured and is only displayed if the role of the logged-in user has the moodle/ site:mnetlogintoremote capability mentioned previously set to **Allow**:

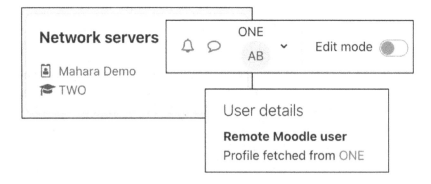

Figure 19.10 – Network servers block

The block acts as a launch pad from which to access remote sites. Here, in addition to our Moodle peer, we have also set up a link to a Mahara instance. Once you click on the remote server, you will be redirected to the selected site, where you can enroll in remote courses.

With that, your first peer-to-peer network has been set up!

Moodle shows the host you logged in from above the user icon, similar to when you masquerade as another user. When you click on your name, you access the profile of the newly created user on the remote server, which cannot be changed. The **Remote Moodle user – Profile fetched from <peer>** message will be displayed.

If you want to deny a remote user access – for example, because of misconduct – go to **Site administration | Users | Accounts | Browse list of users**; you will see that an additional column has been added to the list of users. Remote users cannot be edited locally; only the site they have logged in from is displayed. In the right-hand column, you can select **Deny access** to revoke access to the site. To reverse the operation, select **Allow access**:

First name / Surname	Email address	City/town	Country	Last access	Edit		
Admin User	info@openumlaut.com	Heidelberg	Germany	now	⚙		
Alex Büchner	packt@openumlaut.com			2 mins 29 secs	(Deny access) ⚙	Allow: ONE
Roamer One	roamer@openumlaut.com			2 mins 9 secs	(Allow access) ⚙	Deny: ONE

Figure 19.11 – Remote users

The **Network servers** block adds the final compulsory piece to the Moodle networking puzzle: hosts can talk to each other, and users can roam to remote sites. There is one more goodie in Moodle's networking bag known as remote enrolment, which we will cover in the following subsection.

Configuring network enrolment

This last step is optional and only required if you wish to grant an administrator in one Moodle system permission to enrol local users in remote courses and vice versa. Remote enrolment is helpful if you run a shared course on your server, but learners from the remote site should be participants. To minimize the administrative effort at your end, you can grant the remote administrator the right to take on this task, which is limited to the courses you have specified.

First, on the local site (that is, the one that grants the rights to the remote site), go to **Site administration | Plugins | Enrolments** and enable the **MNet remote enrolments** plugin, which allows the local server to receive enrolments from its remote counterpart. You can change the default role (**Student**) for MNet enrolments on the **Settings** screen.

Now, go to **Site administration | Networking | Peers**, select the remote host, and click on the **Services** tab. **Publish** and **Subscribe** to **Remote enrolment service**, which grants remote administrators the right to enrol students on your site and allows local students to enrol in courses on the remote site, respectively. This step has to be repeated on the peer.

Both Moodle sites have now been configured to allow communication between the two servers, and courses have been set up to enrol remote students. Ensure you activate the **MNet enrolment** method inside your course (see *Chapter 4, Managing Courses and Enrolments*, for details).

When you go to **Site administration | Networking | Remote enrolments client**, you will see a list of remote hosts where local users are enrolled. When you click on a host, courses offered for remote enrolment are displayed. You can then edit the enrolments, just like how you manage users in a local course:

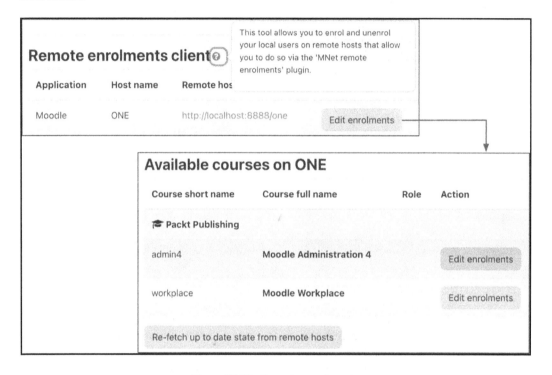

Figure 19.12 – Remote enrolments

This concludes this long section on setting up peer-to-peer connections between Moodle hosts. Next, we will look at another supported networking topology: Moodle hubs.

Setting up a Moodle hub

A Moodle or MNet hub is similar to a peer-to-peer network, with the only difference being that it accepts connections from multiple Moodle (and Mahara) servers. While this could be set up manually using several peer-to-peer connections, hub mode automatically accepts any hosts that try to connect to it. Potentially, this is a big time and maintenance saver, but at the cost of opening up your site to other Moodle instances.

A public learning portal with resources to be shared across many sites is typically implemented using hub mode. Each Moodle instance that wishes to access the portal must be configured to connect to the hub.

Once networking has been turned on, choose the Moodle site that will act as a hub and go to **Site administration** | **Networking** | **Manage peers** to turn on **Register all hosts** (promiscuous mode). Effectively, a hub is a regular Moodle site that operates in a special mode.

All hosts are treated like peer-to-peer sites, except the **Review host details** tab is empty. All the other settings are identical to the peer-to-peer parameters. You might decide that traffic (that is, authentication and enrolment) should only go one way: from the different Moodle sites to the hub. You can control this using the **SSO-Publish** and **SSO-Subscribe** options under the **Services** tab:

	SSO (Identity Provider)	SSO (Service Provider)	Enrolment
Moodle Hub	Subscribe	Subscribe	Publish
Connecting Peer	Publish & Subscribe	Publish & Subscribe	Subscribe

Figure 19.13 – Moodle hub versus connecting peers

The primary use case for setting up an MNet hub is a portal to share resources across sites. A more contemporary alternative to MNet is MoodleNet, which we will cover in the following section.

Enabling MoodleNet

MoodleNet is Moodle's open social media platform for educators that focuses on sharing openly licensed learning resources. MoodleNet forms an integral part of the Moodle ecosystem and can be reached from within Moodle or directly via `moodle.net`.

> **Important note**
> MoodleNet aims to find, share, and curate open educational resources.

While the platform is targeted at teachers and content creators, you, as an administrator, must enable your colleagues to share (appropriate and legal) resources internally and with peers worldwide.

The workflow of MoodleNet's integration is illustrated in the following diagram:

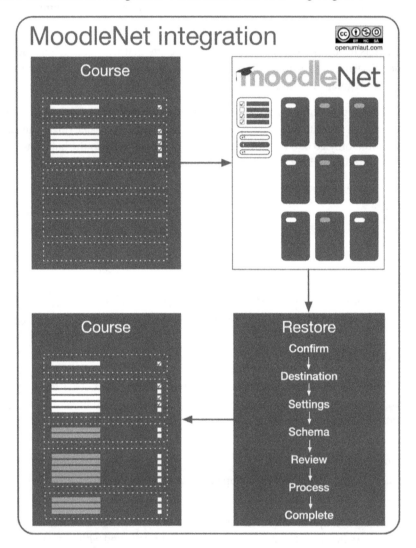

Figure 19.14 – MoodleNet integration

Let's assume you are a course creator who has started developing a module about a particular topic. From within the course (via the activity chooser), MoodleNet is called, and resources are browsed. When an element (from a simple learning nugget to an entire curriculum) is chosen, Moodle's standard restore process is utilized to import the resources into your course. These steps can be repeated multiple times and support effective content curation.

The MoodleNet connection is turned on by default, so ensure that the **Enable MoodleNet integration** option under **Site administration | General | Advanced settings** is ticked.

Users who have permission to create or manage activities can browse the public catalog at moodle. net from the activity chooser and import resources into their courses. Ensure that the **MoodleNet** option has been selected under **Site administration | Course | Activity chooser | Activity chooser settings** for the link to appear at the bottom of the activity chooser:

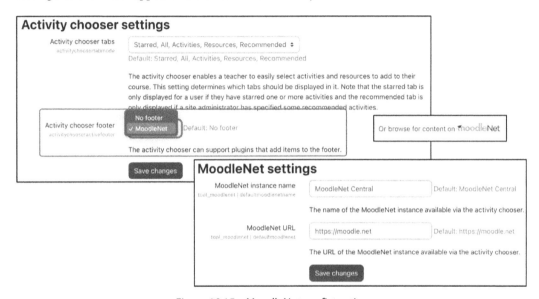

Figure 19.15 – MoodleNet configuration

If you wish to change the name of the MoodleNet instance that's been made available to your users, go to **Site administration | General | MoodleNet | MoodleNet settings**, where you will see two parameters, **MoodleNet instance name** and **MoodleNet URL**. Only change the latter option if you are running your own instance or wish to connect to an alternative MoodleNet system.

Moodle lets you deploy your own secure and scalable MoodleNet instance. MoodleNet has been developed using Node.js and ArrangoDB. You find details on how to set up a local instance at www. npmjs.com/package/@moodlenet/ce-platform.

The integration between Moodle and MoodleNet is planned to be enhanced in the future. The key feature to be looking forward to is the ability for educators to share activities to MoodleNet easily. Check the release notes for upcoming versions to find out what administrative tasks will be available for you to configure this upcoming feature.

This concludes this section on the administrative aspects of enabling your teachers and content creators to share resources via MoodleNet.

Summary

In this chapter, you learned how to network disparate Moodle systems. The setup process required several steps, summarized in the following checklist:

Checklist Moodle Networking	
☑ Install curl, openssl, and xmlrpc	PHP
☑ Enable networking	General I Advanced settings
☑ Generate public key	Networking I Settings
☑ Add peers	Networking I Manage peers
☑ Configure peer services and profile fields	Networking I Manage peers
☑ Enable MNet authentication	Plugins I Authentication I Manage authentication
☑ Allow roaming	Networking I SSO access control
☑ Add Network servers block	Dashboard
☑ Configure network enrolment	Plugins I Enrolment I Manage enrol plugins
☑ Set up a network hub	Networking I Manage peers

Figure 19.16 – MoodleNet checklist

After providing an overview of MNet, we covered the required components and how networking is enabled.

We linked two Moodle sites, which entailed setting up peer-to-peer connections, roaming across instances, configuring remote authentication and enrolment, and using the Networks server block.

Then, we introduced the concept of a central MNet hub to connect multiple Moodle sites.

Finally, we enabled MoodleNet, a platform for finding, sharing, and curating open educational resources.

Moodle's networking facility introduces a new dimension to learning management systems. Disparate systems can be connected logically, and roaming from one Moodle site to another can be facilitated. Networking Moodle hosts opens up entirely new opportunities, whether among entities within your organization or with external sites.

Another setting in which multiple entities are represented is multi-tenancy, which is the topic of the final chapter of this book.

20
Supporting Multi-Tenancy

This chapter discusses different approaches to designing and implementing multi-tenancy in Moodle. If any of the following scenarios are of interest, then this chapter is for you:

- An authority representing multiple schools or colleges in a region or country wishes to provide each school or college with a separate Moodle system but needs to manage the systems centrally

- A private training organization with multiple customers, each needing its own walled area

- A company that has regional offices, each requiring its own learning space

First, we will provide an overview of what multi-tenancy is and why there isn't a one-size-fits-all solution before we present three different types of implementations.

The first approach, multi-tenancy via categories, uses a single Moodle instance with specifically tailored course categories and permissions.

The second implementation, multi-tenancy via a centralized code base, provides separate standalone Moodle instances and delegates all responsibilities to local administrators.

Lastly, we will describe how multi-tenancy has been implemented in Moodle Workplace.

We will cover the following topics in this chapter:

- Understanding Moodle multi-tenancy

- Supporting multi-tenancy via categories

- Supporting multi-tenancy via a centralized code base

- Supporting multi-tenancy in Moodle Workplace

Understanding Moodle multi-tenancy

What exactly is multi-tenancy? In a Moodle context, multi-tenancy can be defined as follows.

> **Important note**
>
> In a Moodle multi-tenancy setup, separate entities or instances (tenants) are administered centrally, where specific features are devolved and managed locally.

The following radial diagram shows a simplistic high-level view of Moodle multi-tenancy:

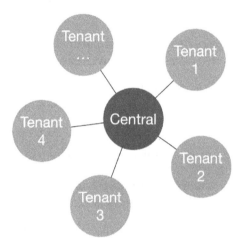

Figure 20.1 – Moodle multi-tenancy: a high-level view

Two critical high-level questions need answering when it comes to multi-tenancy:

- Which features are handled **centrally**, and which are delegated – that is, dealt with at the **tenant level**?

- Which elements can be **shared** across tenants (if any)?

These questions are critical because the answers determine what type of multi-tenancy is suitable for your organization.

Let's drill down further to the two dimensions – features and sharing – in a Moodle context, as illustrated in the following diagram:

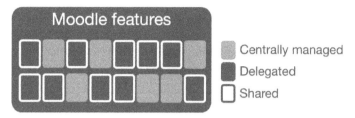

Figure 20.2 – Moodle multi-tenancy: features and sharing

More questions arise when looking at specific Moodle functionality that is potentially impacted by multi-tenancy:

- **Users**: Are user accounts managed centrally and assigned to tenants or can a tenant admin manage users locally? How about authentication? Does each tenant have a separate authentication mechanism or are logins managed site-wide? Do user names have to be unique across tenants? Can users be in multiple tenants? Does every tenant have its own guest account? How about tenant-aware user profile fields? Should there be a user quota per tenant? And what about tenant cohorts and tenant roles?

- **Courses**: Will courses (and categories) be managed centrally, locally, or both? Can courses be sharable across tenants? Should users from multiple tenants be able to enrol in the same course and, vice versa, can users enrol in courses in multiple tenants?

- **Plugins**: Do all tenants have the same plugins or can they be activated and deactivated at the tenant level? Can the configuration of each plugin differ for each tenant or is it identical for all?

- **Admin settings**: Which site-wide settings can be configured individually (if any)? Should the master administrator be able to lock down specific configuration settings to prevent individual tenant admins from changing those values?

- **Admin features**: Which admin tools, such as reporting and backups, can be configured and operated by tenant admins? How about security and privacy setups? Will reporting across tenants be allowed?

- **Themes**: Does the main theme apply to all tenants or can each tenant have its own design? How about one white-labeled theme that can be branded for each tenant?

- **Moodle code**: Is the code base identical for all tenants or can individual tenants have their own code (as in, make modifications)?

The list goes on and on. You can see from the questions that there cannot be a one-size-fits-all approach to multi-tenancy. When you ask three Moodle consultants to come up with a multi-tenancy checklist, you will likely receive four different versions.

Now that we have asked several questions, let us look at three (very) different multi-tenancy approaches to hopefully answer some of them.

Supporting multi-tenancy via categories

The simplest form of multi-tenancy is configuring your Moodle system so that a category represents a tenant. The following diagram illustrates this approach:

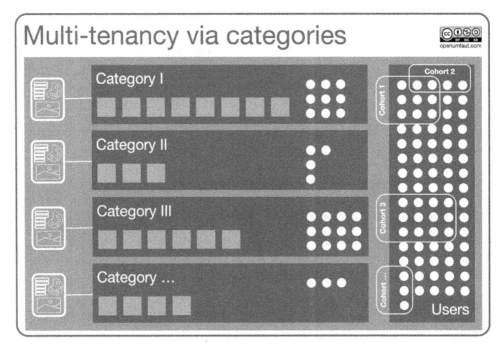

Figure 20.3 – Multi-tenancy via categories

A category represents a ring-fenced area (tenant) where courses are managed locally. Users can be assigned via category cohorts; that is, users can be members of multiple tenants.

You can assign a dedicated theme for each category, as we saw in *Chapter 7, Enhancing Moodle's Look and Feel*. However, users won't see that branding until they have logged in. A new category admin role should be created and the appropriate permissions granted accordingly – for instance, the ability to add subcategories and courses.

One main drawback of the category-based approach is that plugins can only be configured site-wide and not at the tenant (that is, category) level. You can bypass this limitation by using the *addinstance* capability for each module, which allows you to control which activities can be added to which courses. However, this capability only caters to activities, not other plugins, such as authentication, enrolment, or plagiarism. *addinstance* can also only be applied at the course level and not at the category level.

The following checklist summarizes this poor man's approach to multi-tenancy:

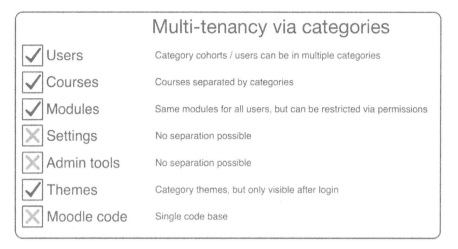

Figure 20.4 – Checklist: multi-tenancy via categories

Multi-tenancy by categories is mainly suitable for sites where users are managed centrally and departments, faculties, or other entities only have control over course content. The approach is unsuitable for sites where a higher degree of autonomy is required at the tenant level. Multi-tenancy via a centralized code base overcomes that restriction, as shown in the following section.

Supporting multi-tenancy via a centralized code base

The principal idea of this multi-tenancy approach is to have a single code base but multiple separate and standalone Moodle instances.

An example where this kind of model is suitable is where each tenant represents a school or college in the region, and each school or college has its own Moodle admin, theme, and administration settings for managing users, courses, privacy, and grades.

The following diagram illustrates this federated approach:

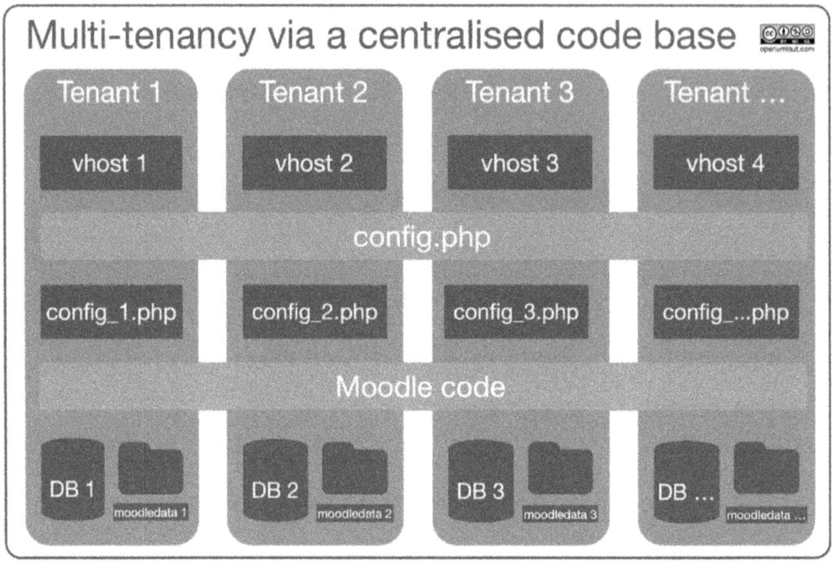

Figure 20.5 – Multi-tenancy via a centralised code base

This solution requires two main configuration steps:

1. **Web server configuration**:

    For each Moodle instance, a separate virtual host is required where the `ServerName`, `ErrorLog`, and `CustomLog` parameters point to the individual instances (tenants), but the `DocumentRoot` variable must be identical in all virtual hosts, ensuring that the same code base (`CFG->dirroot`) is used. A virtual host can either be a separate `vhost` file or a `<VirtualHost>` entry in `httpd.conf`.

2. **Moodle setup**:

    There is one main `config.php` file that acts as the launch pad for all other instances that are represented by individual `config.php` files. These local `config.php` files must be stored in separate locations and have to follow a strict naming convention (in our example, `<domain name>_config.php`). The installation of these config files and their maintenance is usually implemented via scripts to ensure consistency.

    To make this work, the main `config.php` file has to be modified as follows, assuming your local `config.php` files are stored in a dedicated `/tenants` folder:

    ```php
    <?php // Moodle configuration file
    $moodle_host = $_SERVER['HTTP_HOST'];
    ```

```
require_once('/tenants/'.$moodle_host.'_config.php');
```

In each local `config.php` file, `$CFG->dirroot` must be set to the same value specified in `DocumentRoot` in vhost here.

Local config files can be customized further to cater to any idiosyncrasies in a particular tenant. For instance, you might want to freeze specific administration parameters that the tenant administrator must not modify.

Using this setup, you only have to maintain a single code base and provide each tenant with a separate, standalone Moodle instance. The implementation is also suitable for environments where you have to provision Moodle instances on an ad hoc basis – for instance, in a training or development environment.

The following checklist summarizes this centralised approach to multi-tenancy:

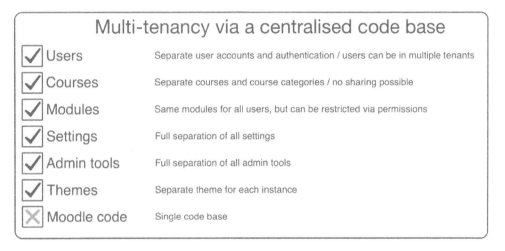

Figure 20.6 – Summary: multi-tenancy via a centralized code base

The approaches presented so far offer very different solutions to multi-tenancy: one uses a single Moodle instance with configured course categories and permissions, while the other provides separate standalone instances and delegates all responsibility to local administrators. The implementation presented in the following section is positioned somewhere between these two: a single Moodle instance with a built-in tenant functionality.

Supporting multi-tenancy in Moodle Workplace

This book is about Moodle administration and all its content applies to Moodle Workplace, too. Since Moodle Workplace provides a unique feature to cater to multi-tenancy, we will make an exception and cover a Moodle Workplace-only feature here. Parts of the section have been borrowed from the *Tenants, Organizations, and Teams* chapter in (advertisement alert!) my book *Corporate Learning with Moodle Workplace* by Packt Publishing.

There are two critical parts to multi-tenancy in Moodle Workplace:

- **Tenants**: Tenants are entirely isolated entities with their own look and feel, structure, users, and learning entities

- **Sharing entities**: Sharing courses and certificates across tenants is supported, as is sharing data such as programs, reports, or organization structures

We will cover both aspects of Moodle Workplace multi-tenancy in the following two subsections by describing how they work in general. For implementation details about Moodle Workplace's powerful yet versatile multi-tenancy feature, check out `docs.moodle.org/en/Multi-tenancy`, also written and maintained by the author.

Understanding Moodle Workplace tenants

In Moodle Workplace, tenants are isolated entities with their own users, hierarchies, roles, dynamic rules, theme settings, reports, custom pages, and learning entities (courses, programs, and certifications).

All Moodle Workplace tools are multi-tenant-aware – depending on the feature, different levels of multi-tenancy are supported. The following diagram shows a high-level view of a tenant and multi-tenant-aware elements:

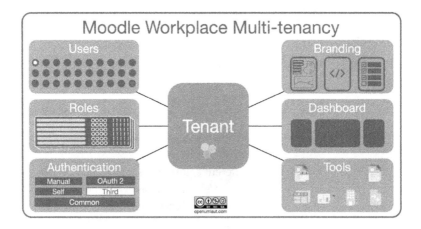

Figure 20.7 – Moodle Workplace multi-tenancy

A single default tenant is created during installation or after upgrading from Moodle LMS to Moodle Workplace. Each tenant has the following properties:

- **Tenant name** and **ID number**: Name of the tenant and unique tenant identifier.

- **Site name** and **Site short name**: These two tenant settings override the **Full site name** and the **Short name for the site** settings respectively in **Site administration | General | Site home settings**.

- **Login URL**: Two selections are available to access the login directly: one containing the ID number and the other an internal numeric tenant ID – for example, `workplace.openumlaut.com?tenant=packt`.

- **Course category**: Courses belonging to a particular tenant must be located in a tenant category. We will elaborate more on that feature later when we deal with sharing content across tenants.

There are two critical rules – some may call them restrictions – when dealing with **tenant users** in Workplace:

> **Important note**
>
> A user is always assigned to a tenant; an account cannot be tenantless.
>
> A user cannot be assigned to more than one tenant; an account always belongs to just one single tenant.

When a new user account is created, whether by self-registration, manual entry, batch upload, or via web services, it is always attached to the default tenant unless specified otherwise. The following diagram illustrates how users are assigned to tenants:

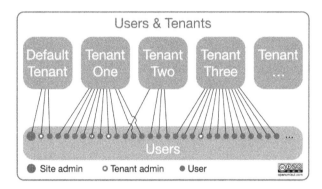

Figure 20.8 – Moodle Workplace: users and tenants

Each user belongs to precisely one tenant, although this is likely to change in the future. Moodle Workplace supports tenant user quotas and lets you specify the maximum number of tenants allowed.

Moodle's user profile fields have been extended to allow the definition of different user profile fields per tenant. When profile fields belong to tenant-specific categories, they will only appear in the profile for users in those tenants; this also includes sign-up and edit forms.

Each tenant can have zero, one, or many **tenant admins** who have devolved administration functions that allow you to fine-tune their level of responsibility. In addition to handling tenant users, a tenant admin has permission to manage tenant roles, configure tenant authentication settings, adjust the tenant branding, and create tenant dashboards by default:

- **Tenant roles**:

  Role assignments to users can be managed separately for each tenant – thus, handling a tenant is almost like context.

- **Tenant authentication**:

  Moodle Workplace supports multi-tenancy for authentication; you can configure different authentication options for different tenants. At the time of writing, supported authentication methods are *manual, email-based self-registration*, and *OAuth 2. SAML* is an explicitly supported, third-party authentication method. For more details, check out docs.moodle.org/en/ Multi-tenancy_authentication.

- **Tenant branding**:

  You can customize the look and feel of the tenant by configuring the multi-tenancy-aware Workplace theme. The branding elements, images, colors, custom SCSS, and footer are described in detail in the Moodle Docs at docs.moodle.org/en/Workplace_theme.

- **Tenant dashboards**

  By default, all tenant dashboards are linked to the content defined in the default site dashboard, and any modifications to this page will appear for the new users in any tenant. Any user with appropriate permissions (site and tenant admins by default) can define a tenant-specific dashboard with the same editing capabilities as the main dashboard. Tenant admins can manage the dashboards of their tenants and reset the configuration for tenant users.

All Moodle Workplace tools, such as programs, certifications, custom pages, dynamic rules, and organization structures (departments, positions, and jobs), are fully multi-tenancy-aware. In addition to defining and managing these features per tenant, Moodle Workplace also supports sharing content and data across tenants, as described in the following subsection.

Understanding Moodle Workplace sharing entities

Moodle Workplace supports two ways that sharing across tenants can be facilitated:

- **Shared content**: Sharing courses and certificates
- **Shared space**: Sharing Moodle Workplace data, such as programs or organization structures

Let's have a brief look at both options.

Sharing content in Moodle Workplace

Typically, each tenant has its own course category, and hence, its own courses. The manual enrolment method has been modified, so the user picker only displays users from the current tenant. However, there are scenarios where you might want to share specific courses among tenants, which is achieved by placing courses in the *shared courses* category.

Multi-tenancy does not apply to course content, which means that if learners or trainers are enrolled in a course, they will see users from other tenants while browsing the course. This behavior is intentional: suppose your organization has some shared courses. It can be assumed that you want the learners to study together and the trainer from one tenant to be a trainer for all learners regardless of their tenant.

If you share courses between different tenants and want users from each tenant to learn independently, they must belong to separate groups. Allocation to separate groups is done automatically when a shared course is part of a program.

The certificates tool we covered in the *Skills and incentives* section in *Chapter 9, Configuring Educational Features*, uses the shared course category feature just described. If a certificate template is placed in a tenant course category, it is limited to this particular tenant; otherwise, it is shared across all tenants.

Custom pages enable site and tenant administrators to create personalized experiences for different audiences by easily adding new pages to the navigation. The content on these pages can be customized using standard Moodle Workplace blocks. While tenant custom pages are specific to a single tenant, global custom pages are shared across all tenants.

Sharing data in Moodle Workplace using Shared space

The **Shared space** feature enables the sharing of entities across all tenants. It works like a special tenant where users can create supported entities available in other tenants.

> **Important note**
> **Shared space** is a special tenant to share Moodle Workplace entities among **all** tenants.

Currently, the following Workplace tools are supported in **Shared space**:

- Programs and certifications
- Organization structure (departments, positions, and jobs)
- Dynamic rules
- Reports

In the following screenshot, you can see a list of custom reports to demonstrate the **Shared space** feature. Moodle Workplace's report generator is the same as the one described in *Chapter 12, Gaining Insights through Moodle Reporting and Analytics*, only with more report sources and the support of **Shared space**:

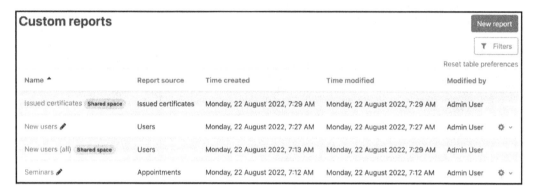

Figure 20.9 – Moodle Workplace: users and tenants

Two reports (**Issued certificates** and **New users (all)**) have a little mark beside them to indicate that they are shared across tenants, while the other two reports are only available in the local tenant.

This concludes the overview on multi-tenancy in Moodle Workplace, which also applies to the Moodle Workplace app. To summarize, we have created a familiar checklist as shown in the following figure:

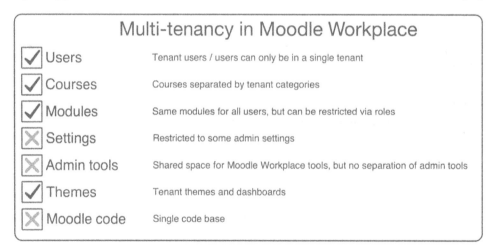

Figure 20.10 – Summary of multi-tenancy in Moodle Workplace

For more interesting reading on multi-tenancy in Moodle Workplace, check out the article at moodle. com/news/lms-multi-tenancy.

Summary

This chapter discussed different ways to support Moodle multi-tenancy. We first defined what multi-tenancy is and showed why there is a need for different types of multi-tenancy implementations. We presented three different approaches, one of which hopefully matches your requirements.

The first model, multi-tenancy via categories, used a single Moodle instance with configured course categories and permissions.

The second approach, multi-tenancy via a centralized code base, provided separate standalone instances and delegated all responsibilities to local administrators.

Lastly, we presented multi-tenancy in Moodle Workplace, the most versatile out-of-the-box implementation currently available.

We covered three representative implementations to facilitate multi-tenancy in Moodle. These solutions can, of course, be extended or further modified to cater to your individual requirements. While some aspects of implementing multi-tenancy might look technical, daunting, and labor-intensive, it will be a relatively pain-free exercise if a solid strategy is followed, possibly assisted by a professional and experienced Moodle Partner.

Appendix
Configuration Settings

This appendix on configuration settings aims to provide you with a list of parameters that can be modified in `config.php` and the impact each value will have.

We will first examine `config.php` and explore what types of parameters are supported by Moodle. After providing this overview, we will look at two types of configuration settings:

- **Administration settings**: These variables are available via the **Site administration** menu but can be locked with values specified in `config.php`.

- **System settings**: We distinguish between default and supplementary configuration values. The former will have been created by the installer and are mostly required for Moodle to function; the latter are parameters that change various Moodle behaviors.

Configuration reference – an overview

The `config.php` configuration file contains several settings and variables that heavily influence how Moodle operates. It is located in the main directory of your Moodle system (`$CFG->dirroot`) and can be edited with any text editor.

> **Important note**
> Be careful when modifying `config.php`! Moodle depends heavily on its content, and any faults can cause the software to malfunction.

You should create a backup of the config file before modifying it, so you can roll back to it in case of problems. Also, ensure the file permissions are correctly set, as the file contains the plain-text database username and password. In a Linux environment, the owner should be `root`, the group also `root`, and the permissions set to `644`. A sample configuration file is shown in the following screenshot:

```php
<?php  // Moodle configuration file

unset($CFG);
global $CFG;
$CFG = new stdClass();

$CFG->dbtype    = 'mysqli';
$CFG->dblibrary = 'native';
$CFG->dbhost    = 'localhost';
$CFG->dbname    = 'packt';
$CFG->dbuser    = 'packt';
$CFG->dbpass    = 'Packt123!';
$CFG->prefix    = 'mdl_';
$CFG->dboptions = array (
   'dbpersist' => 0,
   'dbport' => '',
   'dbsocket' => '1',
   'dbcollation' => 'utf8mb4_unicode_ci',
);

$CFG->wwwroot   = 'https://moodle4.openumlaut.com';
$CFG->dataroot  = '/var/www/packtdata';
$CFG->admin     = 'admin';

$CFG->directorypermissions = 0777;

require_once(dirname(__FILE__) . '/lib/setup.php');

// There is no php closing tag in this file,
// it is intentional because it prevents trailing whitespace problems!
```

Figure A.1 – Sample config.php file

The `config.php` values we are interested in are the ones that start with a dollar symbol. Each parameter has the following information format:

`$<object>-><parameter> = <value>;`

The `<object>` parameter is the part of Moodle in which the parameter is used ($CFG or $THEME). Third-party modules or custom distributions might have introduced their own objects—for example, $TOTARA. We will focus on $CFG objects as these are most relevant to administrators.

`<parameter>` is the name of the configuration setting. Each setting has a unique identifier.

The `<value>` parameter must be of the type the parameter accepts, which depends on the type of the setting. The following table provides information for each of the types:

Type	Moodle field type	Values
Binary	Checkbox	True or 1 and False or 0
Numeric	Number	The number itself
String	Text	Text surrounded by single quotes
Password	Password	Password surrounded by single quotes
List	Pull-down menu	Each value is represented by a number or a string. Unfortunately, there is no consistency for the allocation for the types `List` and `Array`. For example, while the `debug` parameter accepts the values `0`, `5`, `15`, `30719`, and `32767`, the `sitemailcharset`
Array	Multi-select menu	parameter accepts `0`, `EUC-JP`, and `GB18030`! The easiest way to find out what values are valid is to change the values in Moodle and check the config change report. Alternatively, you can check the `mdl_config` table in the database.

Figure A.2 – Data types supported in configuration settings

Each parameter has to be terminated by a semi-colon. To comment out a parameter, precede it with two forward slashes.

Before we deal with the different settings, we'll discuss some tools that might come in useful. As there is no list of available settings, you have to generate your own. To do so, execute the following shell command in your `$CFG->dirroot`:

```
grep -r -h -o '\$CFG->[a-z][[:alnum:]_]*' . | sort -u
```

This concatenated set of commands will generate a list of all available `$CFG` variables in alphabetical order. The `moosh config-get` command (see *Chapter 17, Working with Moodle Admin Tools*) only provides you with a list of all config variables that can be set via Moodle's admin interface and are stored in `mdl_config`; it excludes the *hidden* variables we are interested in here.

Moodle provides a report that lets you monitor all changes to any config settings via the administration interface. You can find the report at **Site administration | Reports | Config changes**.

Config changes					
					▼ Filters
Date ▾	First name / Surname	Plugin	Setting	New value	Original value
Sunday, 14 August 2022, 11:29 am	Alex Büchner	core	hiddenuserfields	city,country	
Sunday, 14 August 2022, 11:27 am	Alex Büchner	core	defaultcity	Heidelberg	
Sunday, 14 August 2022, 11:22 am	Alex Büchner	core	sitemailcharset	GB18030	0
Sunday, 14 August 2022, 11:21 am	Alex Büchner	core	debug	30719	32767
Sunday, 14 August 2022, 11:21 am	Alex Büchner	core	debugdisplay	0	1

Figure A.3 – Config changes report

The table shows any changes made to settings in the **Site administration** section. For each modification, **Date**, **First name / Surname**, **Plugin**, **Setting**, **New value**, and **Original value** are shown.

If you are experimenting with configuration variables, consider using the site admin presets we discussed in *Chapter 17, Working with Moodle Admin Tools*. The tool lets you create backups of site settings, which can then be rolled back if something goes wrong.

Configuration reference – administration settings

Each parameter in the **Site administration** menus can be configured via config.php. If a value has been set via this method, it is effectively hardcoded and cannot be changed via the Moodle interface, not even by the administrator.

For example, you might want to ensure that an administrator does not turn on HTTPS for logins on an internal site, even by accident. Activating this would lock everybody out of the site if no SSL certificate is installed. To do this, enter the following line in config.php:

```
$CFG->loginhttps=false;
```

How do you know what the parameter is called? Go to the respective setting in Moodle (in this case, **Site administration | Security | HTTP security**), and you will see the parameter's name underneath the label.

> **Tip**
>
> You can search for any parameter in the search box of the administration menu.

If the value is specified in config.php, Moodle will display **Defined in config.php** beside the parameter, which indicates that the setting cannot be changed via the admin interface. Invalid values are also shown for these hardcoded settings. In the following screenshot, the **Debug messages** value is incorrect while the **Display debug messages** value is correct:

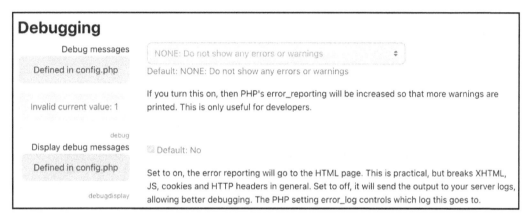

Figure A.4 – Hardcoded configuration settings

If you wish to force plugin settings, you must put them in a special array called forced_plugin_settings (see the reference to optional parameters later).

Configuration reference – system settings

This section contains the actual reference for configuration settings; the explanations have been taken from help pages, forum posts, and comments in the source code.

Default parameters

Default parameters are settings created by the installer, derived from `config-dist.php`. Most settings are compulsory for Moodle to operate, so be careful when modifying them. The parameters are listed in the order in which they appear by default in `config.php`:

Parameter	Description
$CFG->dbtype (String)	The database system that is used. The six valid values are `mysqli` (MySQL), `pgsql` (Postgres), `sqlsrv` (MS SQL Server), `mariadb` (MariaDB), `auroramysql` (Amazon Aurora),and `oci` (Oracle).
$CFG->dblibrary (String)	Currently only `native` is suported as an entry.
$CFG->dbhost (String)	The name of the database host. `localhost` or `127.0.0.1` (if the database is located on the server); or the resolved or unresolved URL, if located on another server.
$CFG->dbname (String)	The name of the database.
$CFG->dbuser (String)	The username of the database account.
$CFG->dbpass (String)	The password of the database account.
$CFG->prefix (String)	By default, all tables in Moodle are prefixed with `mdl_`. This should only be changed if you run multiple Moodle instances using the same database.
$CFG->dboptions (Array)	Values that determine database behavior: `dbpersist` (whether an existing connection can be reused to improve performance, potentially decreasing stability); `dbsocket` (when a UNIX socket is used); and `dbport` (TCP port if different from default).
$CFG->wwwroot (String)	This is the full web address (including `http://` or `https://`) where Moodle has been installed.
$CFG->dataroot (String)	This is the absolute directory name where Moodle's data dictionary is located. The directory has to be readable and writable, but must not be accessible via the Web.
$CFG->admin (String)	The admin pages in Moodle are located in the `admin` directory. If this has to be changed, specify the new directory here as some ISPs don't allow its usage. This approach can also potentially help secure the site from attacks.
$CFG->directorypermissions (Special)	These are the permissions (in Unix format) that are applied for directories Moodle is creating. The default is `0777` (rwx).

Figure A.5 – config.php default parameters

In addition to the default parameters, there are hundreds of optional parameters, some of which we will deal with in the following subsection.

Optional parameters

There are over 300 `config.php` parameters that cannot be modified via the Moodle administrator interface. These hidden settings allow you to modify the behavior of Moodle without the requirement to change any code.

We only cover a representative list of settings, ignoring those that are only relevant to developers and designers. We have also disregarded obsolete and obscure parameters and ones that have a counterpart in the admin settings. Parameters have been listed in alphabetical order, and some have been grouped for simplicity.

Available types are **Array**, **Binary**, **Numeric**, **List**, and **String**:

Name	Type	Description
adhoctaskageerror adhoctaskagewarn	N	Moodle checks how old tasks are in the ad hoc queue and warns at 10 minutes and errors at 4 hours.
admineditalways	B	When set to true, enables admins to edit any post at any time.
apacheloguser	N	Logging Apache: 0 = off, 1 = user id, 2 = full name, 3 = username.
apachemaxmem	N	Memory threshold over which Apache children will be reaped after they complete serving the request.
backuptempdir	S	It is possible to specify a different backup temp directory. Use a local (fast) filesystem for normal web servers. Server clusters must use a shared filesystem for `backuptempdir`. The directory must not be accessible via the web.
bounceratio	N	The default is 20. See `$CFG->handlebounces`.

customfiletypes	A	Adding entries to Site administration | Server | File types, for instance.
		
		``
		$CFG->customfiletypes = array(
		    (object)array(
		        'extension' => 'mobi',
		        'icon' => 'document',
		        'type' => 'application/
		x-mobipocket-ebook',
		        'customdescription' =>
		'Kindle ebook'
		    )
		);
		``

customfrontpageinclude	S	You can replace the home page with your own version. `moodle.org` uses this approach. Only the center area will be replaced, not the header, footer, or blocks.

Name	Type	Description
customscripts	S	Enabling this will allow custom scripts (to be specified with the full path name) to replace existing moodle scripts. For example, if `$CFG->customscripts/course/view.php` exists, then it will be used instead of `$CFG->wwwroot/course/view.php`. Currently, this will only work for files that include `config.php` and are called as part of the URL (`index.php` is implied). Custom scripts should not include `config.php`. Warning: Replacing standard Moodle scripts may pose a security risk and/or may not be compatible with upgrades. However, this is useful when having to patch a particular page without actually overwriting the core code.
debugimap debugsmtp	B	Enable verbose debug information while sending email messages to the IMAP/SMTP server (requires `$CFG->debug` to be set to `DEBUG_DEVELOPER`).
debugusers	S	Comma-separated list of user IDs that always see debug messages.
defaultblocks	A	Default block variables for new courses, for instance, `participants`, `activity_modules`, `search_forums`, `admin`, `course_list`, `news_items`, `calendar_upcoming`, `recent_activity`. This setting can be overridden for different course types, such as `defaultblocks_social`, `defaultblocks_weeks`, and `defaultblocks_topics`.
disablemycourses	B	This setting will prevent the My Courses page from being displayed when users log in. The home page will always show the same (logged-out) view.
disableonclickaddoninstall	B	Disable the plugin installation feature and hide it from the server administration user interface.
disablestatsprocessing	B	Prevent stats processing and hide the GUI.
disableupdateautodeploy	B	Disables update deployment. Useful when deployment is done via Git checkouts.
disableupdatenotifications	B	Disables update notifications. Useful when deployment is done via Git checkouts.

Name	Type	Description
disableusercreationonrestore	B	Completely disable user creation when restoring a course. Enabling this setting results in the restore process stopping when a user attempts to restore a course requiring users to be created.
divertallemailsto	S	Divert all outgoing emails to this address to test and debug emailing features.
emailconnectionerrorsto	S	Email database connection errors to someone. If Moodle cannot connect to the database, email this address with a notice.
expectedcronfrequency	N	Moodle checks that the cron is running frequently. If the time between cron runs exceeds this value (in seconds), you get a warning on the admin page. This setting only controls whether or not the warning appears; it has no other effect.
filedir	S	You can specify an alternative to `dataroot`.
filelifetime	N	Seconds for files to remain in caches (default is `86400`, which equals 24 hours). Decrease this if you are worried about students being served outdated versions of uploaded files.
filepermissions		Same as `directorypermissions` in the default parameters, but for created files.
forced_plugin_settings	A	Plugin settings have to be specified as an array of arrays: `array('plugin1' => array('param1' => 'value1', ('param2' => 'value2', …), ('plugin2' => array('param1' => 'value1', ('param2' => 'value2', …), …);`
forcedefaultmymoodle	B	If set, the My Moodle page cannot be customized by users.
forcefirstname forcelastname	S	To anonymize usernames for all students. If set, then all non-teachers will always see this for every person.
gradeoverhundredprocentmax	N	If `unlimitedgrades` is set, you can specify a maximum value (1 = 100%, default = `10`).
handlebounces	B	This is for handling email bounces. Used in conjunction with `minbounces` and `bounceratio`.
httpswwwroot	S	`wwwroot` for SSL pages.

Name	Type	Description
includeuserpasswordsinbackup	B	Allow user passwords to be included in backup files. Use only if you can guarantee that all your backup files remain private, as password hashes can be unencrypted.
keeptempdirectoriesonbackup	B	Keep the temporary directories used by backup and restore without being deleted at the end of the process. See also the *Managing courses in bulk* section in *Chapter 4, Managing Courses and Enrolments*.
langlocalroot	S	Alternative directory to `$CFG->dataroot/lang`.
localcachedir	S	It is possible to specify different cache and temp directories. Use local (fast) filesystem for normal web servers. Server clusters must use a shared filesystem for `cachedir`. `localcachedir` is intended for server clusters; it does not have to be shared by cluster nodes. The directories must not be accessible via the web.
maildomain	S	Your email domain.
mailprefix	S	`mdl+` is the separator for Exim and Postfix, `mdl-` is the separator for qmail.
minbounces	N	The default is `10`. See `$CFG->handlebounces`.
mnetkeylifetime	N	The number of days until the networking key expires. See *Chapter 19, Setting Up Moodle Networking*, for details.
noemailever	B	When working with production data on test servers, no emails or other messages should ever be sent to real users.
opensslcnf	S	Location of the `openssl.cnf` file.
passwordsaltmain	S	Random string added to the md5 password hash. See *Chapter 13, Ensuring Moodle Security*, for details.
pdfexportfont	S	The font used in exported PDF files. When generating a PDF, Moodle embeds a subset of the font in the PDF file so it will be readable on the widest range of devices (the default is `freesans`).
preferlinegraphs	B	This setting will make some graphs (for instance, user logs) use lines instead of bars.
preventscheduledtaskchanges	B	Disable editing of tasks in **Site administration	Server	Scheduled tasks.**
reverseproxy	B	Enable when setting up advanced reverse proxy load balancing configurations and port forwarding.
showcrondebugging	B	Add debug info to cron output.
showcronsql	B	Show executed SQL queries during cron execution.

Name	Type	Description
skiplangupgrade	B	Disables automatic language update and lets translators (lang pack maintainers) keep their `moodledata/lang/*` to update manually.
sslproxy	B	Enable when using an external SSL appliance for performance reasons.
supportuserid	N	Emails to support can be redirected to another user.
tagsort	S	Sort tags in tag cloud by specified field; default = `name`.
themedir	S	Add an extra themes directory outside of `$CFG->dirroot`.
themeorder	A	Priority of themes from highest to lowest. The default is `array('course', 'category', 'session', 'user', 'site')`.
themerev	B	Prevent theme caching.
tracksessionip	B	Moodle will track the current user's IP to ensure it hasn't changed during a session. This will prevent the possibility of sessions being hijacked via XSS, but it may break things for users using proxies that change frequently.
trashdir	S	Alternative location for `$CFG->dirroot/trashdir`.
undeletableblocktypes	A	The blocks in this list are protected from deletion, for example, `navigation`, `settings`.
uninstallclionly	B	This stops admins from uninstalling plugins from the admin user interface and forces plugins to be uninstalled from the command-line tool only, found at `admin/cli/plugin_uninstall.php`.
upgradekey	S	Password protection during the upgrade process. See `docs.moodle.org/en/Upgrade_key` for details.
upgraderunning	B	Pretend Moodle update is running.
upgradeshowsql	B	Show executed SQL queries during upgrades.
usezipbackups	B	Use ZIP compression in backups instead of default TGZ.
wordlist	S	List words used by Moodle's Word censorship filter.

Index

S

Packt.com

Subscribe to our online digital library for full access to over 7,000 books and videos, as well as industry leading tools to help you plan your personal development and advance your career. For more information, please visit our website.

Why subscribe?

- Spend less time learning and more time coding with practical eBooks and Videos from over 4,000 industry professionals

- Improve your learning with Skill Plans built especially for you

- Get a free eBook or video every month

- Fully searchable for easy access to vital information

- Copy and paste, print, and bookmark content

Did you know that Packt offers eBook versions of every book published, with PDF and ePub files available? You can upgrade to the eBook version at packt.com and as a print book customer, you are entitled to a discount on the eBook copy. Get in touch with us at customercare@packtpub.com for more details.

At www.packt.com, you can also read a collection of free technical articles, sign up for a range of free newsletters, and receive exclusive discounts and offers on Packt books and eBooks.

Other Books You May Enjoy

If you enjoyed this book, you may be interested in these other books by Packt:

Moodle 4 E-Learning Course Development – Fifth Edition

Susan Smith Nash, William Rice

ISBN: 978-1-80107-903-7

- Build courses that emphasize the achievement of learning objectives
- Write a variety of effective quizzes that can be taken online and offline
- Make the most of the navigation and user experience improvements made to Moodle 4.0
- Build courses that reflect current interactive teaching practices, including hybrid learning with web conferencing
- Optimize all kinds of content – text, graphics, audio, video, and recorded webcasts
- Encourage student engagement and collaboration
- Incorporate functionality builders for more responsive and adaptive learning

Corporate Learning with Moodle Workplace

Alex Büchner

ISBN: 978-1-80020-534-5

- Understand the Moodle Workplace business model
- Support multiple business entities using multi-tenancy, organizations, positions, job assignments, and teams
- Explore best practices for organizing typical HR processes such as onboarding, compliance, and reporting
- Automate business workflows using dynamic rules and migrations
- Support blended and offline learning via seminar management and the Workplace app
- Incentivize skill development and learning through certificates, competencies, and badges
- Customize Moodle Workplace to reflect an organization's corporate identity
- Familiarize yourself with Moodle Workplace Web services

Packt is searching for authors like you

If you're interested in becoming an author for Packt, please visit `authors.packtpub.com` and apply today. We have worked with thousands of developers and tech professionals, just like you, to help them share their insight with the global tech community. You can make a general application, apply for a specific hot topic that we are recruiting an author for, or submit your own idea.

Hi!

I am Alex Büchner, author of *Moodle 4 Administration*. I really hope you enjoyed reading this book and found it useful for learning how to administer Moodle.

It would really help me (and other potential readers!) if you could leave a review on Amazon sharing your thoughts on *Moodle 4 Administration*.

Go to the link below or scan the QR code to leave your review:

`https://packt.link/r/1801816727`

Your review will help us to understand what's worked well in this book, and what could be improved upon for future editions, so it really is appreciated.

Best Wishes,

Alex

Download a Free PDF copy of this book

Thanks for purchasing this book!

Do you like to read on the go but are unable to carry your print books everywhere? Is your eBook purchase not compatible with the device of your choice?

Don't worry, now with every Packt book you get a DRM-free PDF version of that book at no cost.

Read anywhere, any place, on any device. Search, copy, and paste code from your favorite technical books directly into your application.

The perks don't stop there, you can get exclusive access to discounts, newsletters, and great free content in your inbox daily

Follow these simple steps to get the benefits:

1. Scan the QR code or visit the link below

https://packt.link/free-ebook/9781801816724

2. Submit your proof of purchase
3. That's it! We'll send your free PDF and other benefits to your email directly